Fragmentext Two

From Myth to Mandela

Thank You To:

My parents, Greg Sigl and family, the entire Sigl family, Mark Dyal and family, J.C., Nick Ceglio, Jonathan Lee Riches, Brian Sullivan, Michael Castaneda, V. Vale, Dayal Patterson, Edwin Oslan, Veronica Reyes, Karina Mayorga, Sam, Indy and Esther Z, Brittany and Phil Dreyhaupt, Miguel Aparicio, Brian Godfrey and family, Bret Godfrey (RIP), Mary Ann Godfrey, Margaret Mezey, Tom Suchy (RIP), Michael Shim (the Greatest Living Philosopher), Mohammed Abed, Nathaniely Greely, Lety, Matthew Hart, Ryan and Melissa Blandford, Troy Westover, Chris Ponce, Karla Soto, Cindy Davis, Cody Hudock, Matt Lynch, Daniel Antinora, John and Bridgette Seasons, Daniella, Simon Austin, Denise Duncan, Alex Goldstein, Emily Goldstein, Brenda and Deidre, Kameron Gaxiola, Mike and Hillary Katz, Hamo and Jenny Bahnam, Victor Ferrari, Mike Melika, "Green Eyes" of One Love Tattoo, Greg Freedman (the 704), John Rampey, Will Barfield, Nick DiFonzo, Rob Reider, Ben Margolis, Elaine Layabout, Wes Soderberg and family, Courtney Gibson, Robert Paulson (RIP), Christina Rothschild, the Dewig family, the Home Depot family: the Occasionally Heroic Q, Gundaz, Cris, Whitney, Edwin, the Kevins, Rob Mason, Conner, C.J., Eddie Huckleby, Ryland, Willie, Nyla, Rueben, Cody, Bryan, Luis, Cholita, the O'Reilly family: Jose, Ray, Leo, Wolfboy, Omar, Crash, Aaron, Luis, Jelyna, Ralph, Wayne, Steve Nagy, Leslie and Tony.

Extra Special Thanks to my interviewees for their graciousness and time: Erik Davis, Gary Wayne, Craig Baldwin, Peter Carroll, Derrick Jensen. Please check out their work –it is well worth your time!

This book was edited by Mark Dyal (the, Oxford, commas, are, his, not, mine).

Lastly, this book is dedicated to "past Steve," I hope this is the sort of book you were looking for, bro...

Table of Contents

Part One

Part Two: The Interviews

Part Three

PART ONE: Introduction

The narrative function is losing its functors, its great heroes, its great dangers, its great voyages, its great goal. It is being dispersed in clouds of narrative language elements – narrative, but also denotative, prescriptive, descriptive, and so on. Conveyed within each cloud are pragmatic valencies specific to its kind. Each of us lives at the intersection of many of these. However, we do not necessarily establish stable language combinations, and the properties of the ones we do establish are not necessarily communicable.[1]

"Second, you should look for the irrational, the bizarre, the elements that do not fit: that's what I have come to observe at this meeting tonight. Have you ever felt that you were getting close to something that didn't seem to fit any rational pattern, yet gave you a strong impression that it was significant?"[2]

"This is the West, sir. When the Legend becomes fact, print the Legend."[3]

Conspiracy theories, or more precisely, the threat of conspiracy theories, have plagued western societies since the dawn of modernity. The concern of this book is to address the varied narratives that constitute established conspiracy theories while simultaneously addressing the meta-narrative function that governs those individual and contingent narratives. In doing so, we will not so much deconstruct what is true or false within a particular conspiracy theory as much as analyze a relationship between a universal anthropological structure that promises an epistemological ordering of the unknown, and the instances of

---

[1] Frank, Manfred (1989) *What is Neostructuralism?* University of Minnesota Press, p. 80.

[2] "Major Murphy" as quoted in Vallée, Jacques (2008) *Messengers of Deception: UFO Contacts and Cults.* Daily Grail Publishing. P. 74

[3] From the film, *Who Shot Liberty Valance.*

this structure as it contorts its way through our speech and correspondence – both amongst ourselves and through our media.

While many books on the topic of conspiracy theories take pains to go through the particular narratives themselves; none of them seem especially aware of how these narratives interact with each other, let alone the system that both governs and generates them. In the constructive sense, the generative aspect of the meta-narrative is not merely a factor that sparks curiosity or an ad hoc explanation on the part of the teller or listener; it is also an imperative for the creation of more narratives.

By making the connection between the meta-narrative function and individual narratives, and subsequently exploring it, I am proposing a philosophical examination of conspiracy theories. The relationship I am talking about stems from the work of Immanuel Kant (April 22, 1724 – February 12, 1804) and his theory of the Transcendental Unity of Apperception. Apperception within the discourse of philosophy refers to how our perceptions are posited as being representations within our mind. Simple perceptions, say of a yellow Volkswagen, are ascertained by our senses (in this case, sight) and appear as a representational construct within our consciousness. The concept of apperception adds the dimension of self-awareness to these representations; apperception is essentially a species of self-consciousness. As Henry Allison states:

> Kant appears to have understood apperception in the Duisburg Nachlass as a form of self-consciousness, specifically, a consciousness of oneself qua thinker, that encompasses a consciousness of the act of thinking, of the contents of this act, and of oneself as a subject that thinks, i.e., as a thinking thing or *res cogitans*. The fundamental feature of apperception in these Reflexionen on which Kant focuses and which is involved in each of these aspects is its unity. In his

most explicit account of this topic Kant writes: "The condition of all apperception is the unity of the thinking subject. From this flows the connection of the manifold in accordance with a rule and in a whole, since the unity of function must suffice for subordination as well as coordination" (R 4675 17:651; 163)[4]

This is a succinct encapsulation of what Kant would go on to formulate as the Transcendental Unity of Apperception in his *Critique of Pure Reason*. There is some debate as to whether the unity Kant proposes pertains to the field of epistemology (what is known or knowable) or to the field of ontology (what we can say exists), and this debate in the philosophical discourse leads to the question of whether Kant's conception of apperception merely addresses issues related to simple instances of knowing or if it leads to the idea of the self as a consistent persisting identity. Because we will be examining the question of whether the meta-discourse surrounding conspiracy theories is merely a governing construct or if it also, somehow, engenders or animates the particular theories that fall under its purview, it is important that we retain the essence of Kant's insight, i.e., an insistence of the importance of self-awareness on the part of the subject, throughout our analysis.

Kant will go on to argue that mental representations, insofar as they can be subject to judgment – that is, insofar as they bear conceptual content – are contingent upon the meta-aspect of our consciousness. In contemporary philosophy this has led authors such as Robert Brandom to focus on these phenomena in the context of societal norms and normativity, i.e., the meta-aspect is constituted by the manner in which we think of ourselves as rational beings and it prescribes norms of behavior, which are reflective of this more primordial link between

---

[4]Allison, Henry (2015) *Kant's Transcendental Deduction*. Oxford University Press. P. 121.

rationality (the meta-aspect of consciousness) and our sensory-derived representations.[5]

This rationalist model is what lies at the center of the philosophical discussion of conspiracy theories, as they will be explored in this book. However, since an important component of the conspiracy theory is that it eludes rationality, or at least appears to do so in some forms of discourse, there will be aspects of our analysis that focus on synchronicity, allegory and, especially, myth. The more fully developed these components are within a conspiracy theory, the richer the narratives comprising that theory will be. The second point of focus for this work will be the loss of richness suffered by conspiracy theories in the wake of 9/11.

Hermeneutics and Structuralism: Two Approaches

Although the analysis of representationalism which occurs in this text is largely based on a Kantian sensibility, Kant himself is rarely mentioned. I think that understanding the basic epistemological schema that comprises the Transcendental Unity of Apperception is a necessary step towards the thought of writers who have a more direct impact on the type of textual analysis we will be undertaking; these writers will be largely classified as either Hermeneuticists or Structuralists. Hermeneuticists, such as Heidegger, Schleiermacher, Auerbach and Gadamer follow the line of thought of Giambattista Vico (June 23, 1668 – January 23, 1744), who asserted that to understand a text one needs to

---

[5] In a proper philosophical exegesis on the subject, we would need to discuss the role played by concepts and concept-use in this process, as well as the attitude of the users towards the normative rules granted by concepts. This is far too technical a subject for this book to tackle and could ultimately derail the more general discussion we intend to have. For a further analysis of these specific issues, I recommend John McDowell's *Mind and World*, Robert Brandom's *A Spirit of Trust* and *Making it Explicit*.

inhabit the point of view of the author, assimilating his unique historical and cultural perspective into one's analysis.

This then is the starting point for the Hermeneutical tradition; for a textualist like Erich Auerbach (November 9, 1892 – October 13, 1957) we are looking at the representations as they occur within a close textual reading.[6] For Martin Heidegger

---

[6] See, for instance, the chapter "Miller the Musician" in *Mimesis* in which Auerbach refers to the transference of insights from the past to the present using a sentence so long that it would make Proust blush:

"When people realize that epochs and societies are not to be judged in terms of a pattern concept of what is desirable absolutely speaking but rather in every case in terms of their own premises; when people reckon among such premises not only natural factors like climate and soil but also the intellectual and historical factors; when, in other words, they come to develop a sense of historical dynamics, of the incomparability of historical phenomena and of their constant inner mobility; when they come to appreciate the vital unity of individual epochs, so that each epoch appears as a whole whose character is reflected in each of its manifestations; when, finally, they accept the conviction that the meaning of events cannot be grasped in abstract and general forms of cognition and that the material needed to understand it must not be sought exclusively in the upper strata of society and in major political events but also in art, economy, material and intellectual culture, in the depths of the workaday world and its men and women, because it is only there that one can grasp what is unique, what is animated by inner forces, and what, in both a more concrete and a more profound sense, is universally valid: then it is to be expected that those insights will also be transferred to the present and that, in consequence, the present too will be seen as incomparable and unique, as animated by inner forces and in a constant state of development; in other words, as a piece of history whose everyday depths and total

(September 26, 1889 – May 26, 1976) and especially Hans-Georg Gadamer (February 11, 1900 – March 13, 2002) there is a greater emphasis placed on where we as readers stand in a historical-cultural relation to the authors and their texts. What is key to the Hermeneuticist, then, is the approach of the agents involved; what falls under their contextual purview; the matters that they direct their attention, or their *care* towards; and a view of understanding as a process of mediation.

Structuralism, in contrast, is a bit more focused on the representations themselves and how they are constituted by language. In the introduction to his book, *Structuralism and Semiotics*, Terence Hawkes succinctly summarizes the first principle of Structuralism as the idea that: "[...] the true nature of things may be said to lie not in things themselves, but in the relationships which we construct, and then perceive, *between* them."[7]

Structuralism as it will be employed in this text can overlap with Hermeneutics but starts from the position that the world, as we understand it, is already linguistically constructed. In a divine sense this could mean that it was authored by God (or gods); in a political sense this could be expressed as a plurality of discourses, or even languages, vying for hegemony over each other in determining what laws and norms govern a society. This is not to imply that the structures (discourses and languages) are not in a dynamic state of flux – for they are assumed to be so; however, these changes are occurring within the structures themselves. In contrast to the Hermeneutical position, with Structuralism there is less concern with the intentionality of the

---

inner structure lay claim to our interest both in their origins and in the direction taken by their development."
Excerpted from: Auerbach, Erich (2003) *Mimesis: The Representation of Reality in Western Literature*. Princeton University Press. Pp. 443 - 444
[7] Hawkes, Terence (1977) *Structuralism and Semiotics*. University of California Press. P. 17

subject; the emphasis is placed instead on the system in which the subject finds himself.[8]

Another more dynamic way to think about Structuralism is as the examination of life as a text and of a text as life; people in real life, not books, oftentimes forgoe their own authenticity and merely speak prefabricated languages, e.g., the language of bureaucracy or the language of organized religion. To the layperson, such an individual might just be considered "dogmatic;" but to the Structuralist that isn't the case: the individual is literally animated by the discourse of the governing structure.

I have no strong opinion on any dogmatism that might separate adherents of either of these positions. I will merely present applications of either approach as they occur to me within the specific contexts addressed in this book.

Beginning with the Bible

We will be discussing a great variety of texts, but we will begin with the Bible. As a disclaimer, I will not be treating the Bible as a factual or literal document. At certain points it will be useful to treat the Bible literally, insofar as it helps us establish the mentality of individuals who posit theories from a literalist perspective; but overall, the Bible is merely a text, like any other, in the grand scheme of things.

It is in the Bible that a sense of duality, in which events are both factual and symbolic, was first perfected.[9] In terms of content, Genesis is not the only, let alone the first text to postulate

---

[8] The perception of time is an issue addressed by both approaches, insofar as the passage of time in both a text or the personal experience of a subject can be thought of in arbitrary or unconventional ways.

[9] There is also the textual sense of duality exhibited by the conjoining of the Old and New Testaments, which prescribe radically different moral norms, into one book.

a creation myth, but it is the one that has had the greatest dissemination within Western culture. The Bible has not only perpetrated myths, it has taught people how myths are supposed to work. In this respect, mythic power is created by the ambiguous reciprocity between the factual and the symbolic. This relationship has obviously been cultivated in other religious texts, but it is with the Bible, its genealogies, and textual murkiness (often borne out of centuries of doctrinal squabbling) that we will first direct our attention.

There is also a strongly Structuralist current of thought that goes into and comes out of any examination of the Bible. Western, or Occidental, civilization is constructed just as much out of texts as it is by architecture or individuals; it could even be argued that these objects and subjects are themselves innately textual in some way. Indo-European peoples inhabited Europe for thousands of years in an ahistorical way. They left remnants of their customs but being bereft of writing, generations passed with barely a semblance of permanence. On one hand this can seem like an idyllic existence, since history and societal norms that extend to standards of success that must be lived up to can be perceived as oppressive. On the other hand, writing and the documentation of history gives us a grasp on our lives and the lives of those who preceded us in a way that can be edifying. Either way, our anthropological arrival at writing, and with it the recording of laws, norms, histories, and fables is something that *has* happened and in this sense is an unavoidable aspect of our lives. The Bible is one of those key texts that has not merely instructed or entertained us; it has constructed parts of our societies, often in places where we least expect it.

There is an additional literary quality of textual absence employed in the Bible that differs from epics of a comparable historical pedigree, e.g., *The Odyssey*; something Erich Auerbach terms *background*:

> A consideration of the Elohistic [i.e. Biblical] text
> teaches us that our term is capable of a broader and

deeper application. It shows that even the separate personages can be represented as possessing "background;" God is always so represented in the Bible, for he is not comprehensible in his presence, as is Zeus; it is always only "something" of him that appears, he always extends into depths. But even the human beings in the Biblical stories have greater depths of time, fate, and consciousness than do the human beings in Homer; although they are nearly always caught up in an event engaging all their faculties, they are not so entirely immersed in its present that they do not remain continually conscious of what has happened to them earlier and elsewhere; their thoughts and feelings have more layers, are more entangled.[10]

The subject of "background" here is closely related to the sense of "entanglement," which operates implicitly in literature and storytelling, and only started to gain philosophical traction with Herder and Vico. It would come to the forefront with Friedrich Nietzsche's later thought[11] and what is today called "Continental" philosophy. The issue of entanglement, as it pertains to the

---

[10] Auerbach, Erich (2013). *Mimesis.* Princeton University Press. P. 12

[11] I'm thinking specifically of this passage from *Thus Spoke Zarathustra:*
"Have you ever said Yes to a single joy? O my friends, then you said Yes too to *all* woe. All things are entangled, ensnared, enamored; if ever you wanted one thing twice, if ever you said, 'You please me, happiness! Abide, moment!' then you wanted *all* back. All anew, all eternally, all entangled, ensnared, enamored – oh, then you *loved* the world." Excerpted from Nietzsche, Friedrich (1954) *The Portable Nietzsche.* Edited and translated by Walter Kaufmann. Viking Penguin Inc. P. 435

intertwining of subjects, narratives and events leads us to our next topic.

Significance

In the case of each myth, as of each ritual, it has been possible to question the natives and to learn, at least partially, the significance that they accord to it.[12]

Most of the chapters in this book begin with the words, "The Significance of..." and I would like to clarify why this is so. In *Being and Time* Heidegger defines significance as the relational totality of signification; this signification is a set of relations that *Dasein* makes familiar to itself. It is not really prudent to try to summarize all of Heidegger's theorizing about *Dasein* here; essentially it is a form of being that stipulates a certain degree of awareness on the part of the rational subject. I use it here as a sort of twentieth century promulgation of Kant's Transcendental Unity of Apperception.

   In this respect, the connection between the two concepts is important because we are thinking about and discussing narratives in a way that goes beyond their explanatory, or literal, meanings. We are discussing them as they exist within the world of our, so to speak, meta-consciousness. Because Kant gives us insight into the relationship between the literal and the meta, it was useful to introduce him into our initial discussion. But because Heidegger continues this evolution of thought in a way I find important, it is necessary to incorporate him as well. It is especially necessary in this instance because, as I see it, the concept of *Dasein* and the care and concern that are entailed by it are what make my use of the word "significance" in the text so, how shall we say, significant.[13]

---

[12] Eliade, Mircea (1998) *Myth and Reality*. Waveland Press. P. 5
[13] Heidegger acknowledges this debt in *Being and Time* where he writes: "Self-interpretation belongs to the being of Dasein. In the

For Heidegger we exist in a perpetual state of relatedness to each other and the objects in our shared environment. In contrast to this, the objectivity that scientists project onto their interactions with objects they are studying is something that Heidegger sees as artificial. The scientist who is studying a certain genetic trait, for example, is exercising his attention, or in Heidegger's parlance "care," in the direction of his experiment. This sense of care is, according to Heidegger, something that all humans are directing towards objects and events in their world – the scientific application is just a particular thematization that accords with what we call the "scientific method." This distinction is made clear in Heidegger's thoughts about the mode of "being-with:"

> As being-with, Dasein 'is' essentially for the sake of others. This must be understood as an existential statement as to its essence. But when actual, factical Dasein does *not* turn to others and thinks that it does not need them, or misses them, it *is* in the mode of being-with. In being-with as the existential for-the-sake-of-others, these others are already disclosed in their Dasein. This previously constituted disclosedness of others together with being-with thus helps to constitute significance, that is, worldliness.[14]

By stipulating this, Heidegger is not denigrating the work of scientists, but is instead re-enchanting our own sense of the world and the objects/individuals that disclose themselves to us. In a sense, the things I am interested in as a writer and you are as a reader (Atlantis, UFOs, international banking conspiracies, etc.)

---

circumspect discovery of the "world" taking care of things, taking care of things is sighted too." P. 288
[14] Heidegger, Martin (1996) *Being and Time* translated by Joan Stambaugh, State University Press of New York. P. 116

are disclosed to us at various times in our conversations, readings, and casual thoughts. By using the word "significance" I am directing my *care* towards these topics as things which disclose themselves to me. Though let me stress that I am not merely thematizing them as a scientist might – I will hear out scientism but more importantly I want to preserve the mysterious kernel that lies at the center of these narratives. I want them to disclose themselves to us on their own terms, and this goes beyond the realm of facts and probability. This means we are both directing our attention towards a literary object and noting the "background" inherent to it.

Now, having sketched this out let us briefly turn to the 1996 Introduction to *The Holy Blood and the Holy Grail* wherein Henry Lincoln (I assume it's Lincoln. For more on this inference, see The Significance of the Grail Mythos chapter) writes: "In our book, we had addressed ourselves to matters of historical possibility, historical probability and, whenever facts were available, historical fact."[15] Ostensibly this declaration from a conspiracy theorist seems to fly in the face of my project. I bring this up, though, because I wish to stress that what the theorist who promulgates or advances these theories intends, is to a large extent, negligible.

It is better if the individual who tells these narratives believes that they coincide with fact in the same way that a good novelist creates characters who are real to him. What we are doing is treating these narratives as *literature*, which is not meant to characterize them as inherently lacking truth – literature is a powerful and ordering force in our lives. Oftentimes, the individuals constructing these narratives approach their endeavor with a rigor or intensity that they believe approximates science. However, the texts they create operate as literature and, unlike science, literature makes demands of its audience that work on a variety of psychological and philosophical levels.

---

[15] Baigent, Michael; Leigh, Richard; Lincoln, Henry (2006) Arrow Books. P. 6

Heidegger's aim in *Being and Time* is the analysis of authenticity, and for him this is primarily a moral concern. He is very similar to Kant in that both created a very complex theoretical system that they then used to substantiate a moral theory. Neither's moral theory can be easily summarized without losing critical nuances; fortunately for us we are not reading myths or conspiracy theories in a moral way. To do so would deter from the modicum of objectivity that is already hard enough to maintain when confronted with the myriad texts we are taking on.

Having said this, I think it's relevant to address Heidegger's fundamental point about authenticity and Dasein which suggests that, as we exist in society, we are subsumed into the inauthenticity which comes from thinking in terms of those around us – the "they" that Heidegger makes constant reference to in *Being and Time*. We break out of the inauthenticity of this "they-mentality" by heeding the call of conscience. This call draws us back to an authentic awareness of ourselves as beings that are destined for death. This "being-toward-death" transcends the everyday affairs in which we are embroiled. Jean-Paul Sartre, who followed Heidegger's phenomenological approach, reframed this in a way that put individual freedom in the place of death as the source of authenticity. Both saw human existence as something that is formulating itself as it moves forward in time (which is why the words "potentiality" and "possibility" are so prevalent in *Being and Time*), and therefore cannot situate experiences "concretely" in the past. For this reason, another way we can think of topics that are significant, is that they are worthy of repetition, and possibly, demand repetition.

This approach to the subject of significance is compatible with an understanding that hews more closely to the apprehension of the linguistic properties of objects. On this view, objects emit signs that make a demand on the subject who perceives them only in order to decipher them. In his analysis of Proust's statement: "The mediocre woman one was amazed to find them loving, enriched their universe much more than any intelligent woman could have done." (III, 616). Gilles Deleuze (January 18, 1925 – November 4, 1995) writes:

> The more limited a woman is, the more she compensates by signs, which sometimes betray her and give away a lie, her incapacity to formulate intelligible judgments or to sustain coherent thoughts [...] There exists an intoxication, afforded by rudimentary natures and substances because they are rich in signs. With the beloved mediocre woman, we return to the origins of humanity, that is, to the moment when signs prevailed over explicit content and hieroglyphs over letters: this woman "communicates" nothing to us, but unceasingly produces signs that must be deciphered.[16]

So, for the Structuralist, or post-Structuralist in the case of Deleuze, "significance" arises through an accidental encounter with a sign and the subsequent violence this sign then effects upon us through cognitive disruption and its demand for interpretation. If we accept that this effect is a "demand" for interpretation, then the idea that there is a subsequent "demand" for repetition makes sense, in that the act of interpretation is itself dependent on repetition.

Heidegger also grapples with this issue near the end of *Being and Time* when he gives his famous "Hammer analogy," wherein the instance of a carpenter noticing the weight of his tool prompts a sense of reappraisal:

> Why does what we are talking about, the heavy hammer, show itself differently when our way of talking is modified? Not because we are keeping our distance from handling, nor because we are only

---

[16] Deleuze, Gilles (2000) *Proust and Signs*. Translated by Richard Howard. University of Minnesota Press. Pp. 21 - 22

looking *away* from the useful character of this
being, but because we are looking *at* the thing at
hand encountered in a "new" way, as something
objectively present. *The understanding of being*
guiding the heedful association with innerworldly
beings *has been transformed.*[17]

What Heidegger is describing here is the uncanny moment when
an object familiar to us, which we understand in terms of its
history, purpose, etc., appears in a way that makes us wonder if
we really understood it to begin with. This moment of "newness"
or rediscovery is what I am trying to encapsulate when I use the
word "significance" throughout the text.

Occam's Razor

Now that we have broached some of the philosophical and
literary aspects of our topic it's time we asked ourselves: What is
a conspiracy theory? During the fourteenth century there was a
Franciscan friar named William of Ockham who developed the
theory of parsimony that came to be known as Occam's Razor.
Occam's Razor states that when we need an explanation for
phenomena, the hypothesis with the fewest assumptions is the
strongest.

Pause the book for a moment, and perform a little thought
experiment. Think of conspiracy theories and consider whether
they posit the simplest explanation for the phenomena with
which they are concerned. I think that, with a broad enough view,
conspiracy theories are either very parsimonious or very
convoluted. Most of the theories at the time of my writing this
(2019-2021) fall into the former camp.

This leads to our next question: is Occam's razor, as a
demand for simplicity in explanation, reductive? Does it demand

---

[17] Heidegger, Martin (1996) *Being and Time* translated by Joan
Stambaugh. State University of New York Press, p. 330.

that whatever topic is being addressed be explained in a way that reduces a variety of phenomena to one particular cause? This would be an incorrect reading because all that Occam's Razor demands is *economy*, that one only uses what is needed. However, for conspiracy theorists, necessity is in the eye of the beholder.

In the next chapter we will go through some of the different approaches that conspiracy theorists employ. Much like Structuralists, Hermeneunticists, and any other style of philosopher one can imagine, the people who study and write about conspiracy theories adhere to certain intellectual tenets. But the reason for introducing Occam's Razor here has less to do with the principles and tenets informing the theories themselves than to whom or what the theories point.

Some might read the concept of reductionism (a concept that will occur throughout the text) as being identical to the concept of "confirmation bias." In a case of confirmation bias, the individual who is doing the research cherry-picks data, or narratives, that will confirm his initial hypothesis. Though individuals who engage in reductionism are almost certainly guilty of confirmation bias, the inverse is not nearly as certain. A great many conspiracy theorists begin with the hypothesis that something strange or perfidious is going on around them and at the end of their research boil it down to a confluence of groups and factors, each behaving in a conspiratorial fashion; and then from this, they often arrive at a single group or individual.

It might be easy to take the over-simplification attendant to *some* conspiracy theories as the reason these theories seem too weird to be believed, or even worse *just* unbelievable. However, my contention is that it is a lack of richness, which arises when conspiracy theories are bound less to myths than to a scientific ideal that leads to their not being compelling. In this respect, oversimplification is epiphenomenal – it is merely a by-product of demystification.

Conspiracy theories that are too complex might well be so because the theorist is trying to accommodate every relevant fact or contingency. But on another reading, they are repeating the mythic structure that makes some conspiracy theories great narratives, and in this way are subject to embellishment and exaggeration. However, there is a demand that conspiracy theories be relevant, and in this respect, they must accommodate certain scientific inclinations that have been inculcated over the past few centuries. This can mean everything from causality and gravity to germ theory. The desire to address such issues is largely due to the prevalence of scientific expertise and technology in our societies, but it also refers to a larger issue: that scientism has largely become *the* interpretive technology of modernity.

As I stated earlier, people we encounter in real life often forego their own authenticity and merely speak prefabricated languages like the language of bureaucracy or religion. The reduction of these systems of acculturation to a matter of fluency is a hallmark of modernity. In fact, each of the tools we will use, from the Transcendental Unity of Apperception, Structuralism, to the concept of Dasein, etc. have arisen from philosophers thoughtfully grappling with problems presented by modernity.

Sometimes, in their zeal to analyze or deconstruct phenomena, philosophers, psychoanalysts, etc. will succumb to an unthinking assimilation of experience to their own jargon. It is one thing to speak the language of conspiracy theories but it is another to understand what one is saying. This variance in comprehension relates to my heavy reliance on texts themselves, quoting them, and letting them speak for themselves. Unlike other books which just give facts or "facts" as the case may be, I will fall into over-citation in order to track and document what is being said, by whom and when. This is an addition to the hermeneutical aspect of this work and I will try to keep it from intruding into its overall flow.

Pluralism, Political and Otherwise

Most people who are labeled conspiracy theorists tend to be reductionists: they have found a single entity or group that is behind the phenomena with which they are concerned. I say "most" because there are people who have made a business of conspiracy theorization (Alex Jones comes to mind) who act as if they will reduce everything to a single group but never really come to any conclusive answer at all. In the case of Jones or Allan Watt, this seems analogous to forms of serialized entertainment, such as soap operas, which must keep themselves going indefinitely.

Other theorists are reductionists who definitively blame groups like the Illuminati, Reptilians, Nazi clones, or Satanists, and spend their careers exploring and creating narratives centered on these groups. The focus of this book, on the other hand, is coming at this from the narratives that already exist. The groups that make up the substance of these theories don't necessarily have to exist for us to analyze them, and if they do indubitably exist, like extraterrestrial aliens (just kidding, let's say Freemasons) then they exist as one group within a plurality of groups vying for power and influence.

In a certain respect, my basic political analysis agrees with the conspiratorial mindset which claims that there are "elites" trying to guide the larger population. However, in contrast to a conventional mindset, I see a variety of forces vying with each other for control, hence leaving no teleological mousetrap-like mechanism ensnaring western societies – at least not one that was devised and put in place by purposeful human beings. The formal name for this approach is "Political Pluralism" and its implications were best explored and outlined by the sociologist Robert Michels (January 9, 1876 – May 3, 1936).

Because the underlying assumption of Political Pluralism is that no one group has everything predetermined, assimilating its tenants into our analysis helps avoid some of the pitfalls attendant to conspiracy theorization; unusual alliances can be made and tables can be turned. Political Pluralism tends to come in two forms. The first and most prevalent one – which is exemplified by the work of Isaiah Berlin – is a normative analysis that sees various competing groups agreeing on certain basic societal "goods" and then eschewing extremism in order to achieve compromises that will lead to these good results. Hence, when I say "normative," I'm saying that, according to the Berlinian type of pluralist, this sort of competition and eventual cooperation between groups is how democracies "ought" to operate.

The second form of Political Pluralism, which is less ideological and less common, is an empirical analysis which doesn't maintain that the political ought to operate this way – it just does. This is essentially Michels's view. Michels analyzed how political parties employ a logic of self-interest to exploit the masses and thereby expand their hegemony within the democratic landscape. It is not much of a stretch to interpose this idea of would-be elites into today's political climate where there are not only political parties, but fringe ideologues of every imaginable stripe. On my reading of Michels, each of these groups can vie for political hegemony, or advancement, once they acquire enough financial, political or cultural capital.

For Michels, political parties have arisen in the vacuum left by the demise of monarchy and it is the quest to seize the intrinsic power of this older, more atavistic form of governance that drives contemporary political organization and activity.[18] Michels offers a sophisticated extension of Hobbes's earlier pessimistic view that without a governing state to keep the peace, life would be "nasty, brutish and short." On this pluralistic view, groups and individuals not only seek power, but reproduce class systems that

---

[18] According to Michels this drive towards usurping the power of monarchy results in oligarchy: "The democratic external form which characterizes the life of political parties may readily veil from superficial observers the tendency towards aristocracy, or rather towards oligarchy, which is inherent in all party organization." Michels, Robert (1962) *Political Parties: A Study of the Oligarchical Tendencies of Modern Democracy.* The Free Press. P. 50

mimic older, less tolerant, models. Aristocracy reintroduces itself automatically into those states that initially seek to exclude it:

> The North Americans, democrats, living under a republican regime and knowing nothing of titles of nobility, by no means delivered themselves from aristocracy when they shook off the power of the English crown. [However] the existence of an aristocracy of millionaires, railway kings, cattle kings, etc., is now indisputable. But even at a time when the youthful democracy and the freedom of America had only just been sealed with the blood of its citizens, it was difficult to find a single American who did not plume himself with an idle vanity upon belonging to one of the first families which had colonized American soil.[19]

In this passage we get an idea of the "twofold" way aristocracy reintroduces itself: the first is a society bereft of an aristocratic class-structure, in which certain groups attempt to reproduce that structure. In Michels's time it was millionaires who became the new royal class; in our day and age we can say that it is celebrities (who are only coincidentally very wealthy). The second way is via the citizens' claims to be descended from the "founding stock" of the country. For Michels, the implication of this assertion is a hereditary claim of ownership, which is analogous to the hereditary passing down of ownership in an aristocratic or feudalist state.[20] One more point that needs to be made here is how political pluralism relates to Game Theory.

Game Theory essentially breaks down the strategic interaction among rational decision-makers into mathematical models that are applied to entities competing in the fields of

---

[19] Ibid, p. 53

[20] Obviously claims of being "part Native American" today are a more nuanced and politically correct reiteration of this impulse.

economics and politics. What can be gleaned for our purposes from Game Theory is the concept of a "zero-sum game," which is a competition between various groups in which any advance for one group comes at the expense of another group. A political theorist like Berlin, would say that zero-sum game scenarios do arise in modern democracies, but that they do not have to be the dominant model –groups can come to mutually beneficial agreements. A theorist like Michels, would also contend that zero-sum game scenarios *must not be* the dominant model, but because of human nature they usually are.[21] Based on this elaboration we can classify Berlin's pluralism as being optimistic and Michels's as being pessimistic. Most conspiracy theorists don't talk about issues in terms of pluralities, but it is an inherent aspect of their thinking, insofar as they designate groups as being the causes of society's problems. It could also be said that the inherent pluralism espoused by conspiracy theorists hews closely to the zero-sum game paradigm.

We will return to Michels's pluralistic model whenever there are political implications entailed by conspiracy narratives. Most conspiracy theorists are politically powerless and are rendered increasingly so. Hence their primary method of discourse is not so much in attacking the groups they see as opponents (or the causes of societal ills) in a constructive manner but simply blaming them.

The Blame Game

A large part of what makes conspiracy theories "conspiracy theories" is that they direct blame towards a person or a group, and often a degree of blame that seems absurdly unwarranted. As Robert Anton Wilson puts it in his Introduction to *Everything is Under Control: Conspiracies, Cults, and Cover-ups*:

---

[21] Friedrich Nietzsche's philosophy oftentimes veers into similar territory.

In this "Demonic Dictionary" we deal only with theories that proclaim that *some* persons or groups, whom the theorist can specify, often with front names, hind names, and addresses, deserve all the blame for the horrors that afflict the rest of us – from ecological imbalance to economic hardship, from war to poverty, from drug cartels to the fact that you can't even get a plumber on weekends anymore. Those who want to blame all of us equally do not have a Conspiracy Theory but an Original Sin Theory.[22]

This blame aspect of conspiracy theories seems to be what the public finds most objectionable about them. However, I would like to point out two related facts. Firstly, since my thesis involves analyzing conspiracy theories, and to a large extent considers "reality" itself as a sort of text, can we not say that this textual analysis is therefore literary in nature and that a key component of literature is antagonism? Many myths and conspiracy theories involve Satanism or even Satan himself. Does he not therefore count as one of the greatest adversaries in the history of literature? Naming certain groups as adversaries in one's conspiracy theory might be insensitive or politically incorrect, depending on historical context, but a standard of political correctness ought not to discredit the importance of an adversary in a narrative, or interfere with an examination of who these adversaries are claimed to be by various conspiracy theorists.

Secondly, I stated that conspiracy theories *often* assign an absurdly unwarranted degree of blame to a particular individual or group. Absurd in degree means "a lot" but I intend this to include absurd claims as well.[23] This distinction is emphasized in

---

[22] Wilson, Robert Anton (1998) *Everything is Under Control: Conspiracies, Cults and Cover-ups.* Harper Perennial. P. 5
[23] The "absurd degree" might not be met if there weren't a few absurd claims thrown into the mix.

the first chapter in which we demarcate between what I label "compound conspiracy theorists" and other less reductionist varieties. The Absurd is a vague concept and I am purposely using it here instead of a word like "excessive" because it can apply to a staggering overload of information meant to goad us into acquiescence, but it can also mean fantastical elements. Just as literature needs villains (most of the time – I usually prefer the kind that doesn't) it often needs us to suspend our disbelief as well.

There is a psychological aspect to the concept of blame that needs to be addressed here as well. Blaming someone or something can lead to further action against them or it, but not necessarily so. In geopolitical terms, one nation blaming another for something can lead to sanctions, an embargo, or possibly war. In judicial terms, blame might lead to prosecution, conviction, and sentencing. Individuals who subscribe to conspiracy theories, to the degree that it is a defining factor in their lives, are usually far removed from the realms of political or judicial power. These individuals, it seems, are resigned to a state in which blame is conferred but no decisive action will follow. Blame without any recourse to action, by which I mean decisive mandated action, is impotent. This sense of impotence, if it is perceived by the conspiracy theorist (and it usually is), can lead to greater frustration or possibly abandonment of conspiracy theorization. So, blame is just one component in the tapestry that we are simultaneously unraveling and reassembling. Conspiracy theories are a lot like philosophies: there is no end-all-be-all to them, something that reminds me of a comparison Wittgenstein made between practicing philosophy and organizing a library:

> Imagine we had to arrange the books of a library. When we begin the books lie higgledy-piggledy on the floor. Now there would be many ways of sorting them and putting them in their places. One would be to take the books one by one and put each on the shelf in its right place. On the other hand we might

take up several books from the floor and put them in a row on a shelf, merely in order to indicate that these books ought to go together in this order. In the course of arranging the library this whole row of books will have to change its place. But it would be wrong to say that therefore putting them together on a shelf was no step towards the final result. In this case, in fact, it is pretty obvious that having put together books which belong together was a definite achievement, even though the whole row of them had to be shifted. But some of the greatest achievements in philosophy could only be compared with taking up some books which seemed to belong together, and putting them on different shelves; nothing more final about their positions than that they no longer lie side by side. The onlooker who doesn't know the difficulty of the task might well think in such a case that nothing at all had been achieved. –The difficulty in philosophy is to say no more than we know. E.g., to see that when we have put two books together in their right order we have not thereby put them in their final places.[24]

The Three Tenets of Conspiracy Theorization

In a practical respect, there are three tenets to which conspiracy theorists adhere:

1. There are secretive forces controlling the world, or merely the political institutions of the world.

---

[24] Wittgenstein, Ludwig (1965) *The Blue and Brown Books.* Harper Colophon Books pp. 44 – 45.

2. Given wider exposure, the theory revealing this control will enflame the public consciousness, turning everyone who hears it into a fellow conspiracy theorist.

3. This turn in the public consciousness will create a political revolution (or a revolution in consciousness).

These three factors might seem sinister in certain contexts, but the methodology of how it ideally would play out is about as threatening as a 1960s commercial for laundry detergent in which a housewife convinces her next-door counterpart to change soap brands. Essentially, context is KEY and oftentimes the issue of context is not merely historical, but also pertains to the ideological motivations of the individuals who construct and disseminate these narratives.

For more Left-wing oriented theorists the catastrophic background of a total capitalist-controlled police state was the context in which theories about the assassinations of John Kennedy and Martin Luther King, UFO cover-ups, and sinister CIA machinations were rendered.[25] The catastrophic background for more Right-wing conspiracy theorists is focused on the loss of family values, the decline of Christianity, the sexual revolution, and the proliferation of Communist propaganda in schools.[26] Both sides gave birth to a DIY type of survivalism. Both feared (or craved) some sort of societal collapse: for the left, an ecological collapse; and for the right, an economic one. But over the last few decades these strains have gotten jumbled and we find Right-wing survivalists preparing for an ecological crisis because it ties into certain Biblical end-time prophecies. So, another component

---

[25] The heyday for left-wing conspiratorial theorization was from the early seventies (after the collapse of the hippy counter-culture) to a little after 9/11. It pretty much died after George W. Bush left office in 2008.

[26] Right-wing conspiracy theorization began during the cold war and persists to this day.

to the background for why the conspiracy theorist adheres to the three aforementioned tenets is the inevitability of a societal collapse, or in some cases an all-out apocalypse and a drive to wake up those around you to the ensuing crisis.

Gary Wayne, whose book *The Genesis 6 Conspiracy* plays a substantial role in this book, is a modern-day representative of the conservative Christian conspiracy theorist. His description of antediluvian kings and Nephilim that impose mysticism and idolatry on their subjects using tyrannical force gives us profound insight into the conspiracy theorist's belief that: (2) given greater exposure the theory will enflame public consciousness and that (3) this turn in public consciousness will spark a revolutionary upheaval:

> The people of the antediluvian epoch were so thoroughly terrified through state-sponsored tyranny and intimidation via the Nephilim that they fled from the convictions of the true God because they feared for their lives. Imagine if you lived in a powerful, totalitarian regime like that of Communist Russia or China, Nazi Germany, or the forthcoming world government, universally imposing a ruthlessly evil, state-sponsored religion on all its citizens and responds to opposition with torture and murder.[27]

We can't dwell too heavily on Wayne's particular outlook here, but the sentiment of the above passage is that the "sheeple" are being tyrannized and manipulated either through explicit or covert coercion. Granted, the issue of tyrannical force is complicated, but Wayne definitely sees the present-day United States as being a province of both overt and subliminal control. For Wayne, such a "soft" tyranny could be overturned by the

---

[27] Wayne, Gary (2014) *The Genesis 6 Conspiracy*. Trusted Books, A Division of Deep River Books. P. 84

conversion of atheists, idolators, and non-believers to his own brand of literalist Christianity. The basic kernel of this religious or ideological conviction has arisen countless times before Wayne's book and most likely it will reoccur countless times after ... unless, of course, this Apocalypse thing is for real!

Wayne is not a particularly well-known figure, but he offers a very clear-cut representation of a widespread conservative ideology. I will try to tackle a variety of the big names in the modern conspiracy theory community, but I can't promise to do them all justice. One particularly interesting figure, who had a significant hand in bringing together all walks of conspiracy theorist, was radio host Art Bell. His book, *The Coming Global Superstorm* published in 1999, whether it influenced anyone or not, occurred at the perfect time in history (the late 1990s) and by its very publication granted conspiracy theorists (and weirdos of all stripes) a catastrophic flag behind which they could all assemble.[28] This assembly was short-lived, however, since the destruction of the Twin Towers two years later would, like the mythical Tower of Babel, scatter them into various realms of disillusionment.

The first chapter, "Myth and Narrative," continues some of the themes we have addressed in this introduction and helps lay the philosophical foundation for the information we will be tackling in the rest of the book. After this we will start tackling all the characters, objects and places that made conspiracy theorization so narratively rich and engaging. Throughout the book there will be a rogue's gallery of sorts; not necessarily malevolent figures, but characters who are mysterious and share a certain textual murkiness. Some of these are subjects of their own chapters: Aleister Crowley and Robert Anton Wilson being two examples.

---

[28] It should also be noted that the year 1999 is the year the film *The Matrix* was released and it is featured as the year that the virtual reality construct that is the Matrix itself resets to after every new year's eve.

Most books promoting so-called conspiracy theories have a coherent narrative thread that is heavy with citations but rarely interjects the actual texts cited. This book, since it is not presenting any consistent conspiracy theory, works in the opposite way. Because we are engaging in these texts it is important to cite them explicitly within the narrative. My apologies if this seems disruptive to the flow of the information I am presenting to you.

Chapter Two: Myth and Narrative

As much as I might be inclined to let the innerworkings of this text mimic the mysterious nature of the various narratives I reference, in good faith I must provide a large degree of explication. For lack of a better term, what you now hold in your hands is a post-modern work in the most idealistic sense. The over-arching agenda is not a sterile demystification of conspiracy theories. If anything, it is more akin to what Pierre Klossowski says in *Nietzsche and the Vicious Circle*, "One demystifies only in order to mystify better."[29] In this respect there has been a historical movement in the structure of conspiracy theories insofar as they are cultural narratives. The thoughtful tracking of this structure is in some ways coincidental with, and in other ways identical to, the *Meta* narrative of conspiracy theories. This historical movement can be broken down into a simple dialectical schema:

Thesis: a series, or web of narratives built upon various mythological foundations.

Antithesis: the abolition of the mythical foundations by way of scientism, inaugurated by the UFO fad and culminating in the nuts-and-bolts materialism of 9/11 conspiracy theories.

Synthesis: the reaffirmation of myth in conspiracy discourse, albeit a reaffirmation that is post-modern and permissive of irony. However, in application this new invocation of myth can operate both ironically and unironically because the issue of authenticity has been dislodged from traditional norms.[30]

---

[29] Klossowski, Pierre (2005) *Nietzsche and the Vicious Circle.* Continuum. P. 100

[30] In his exegesis on the "high weirdness" that arose in the seventies following the demise of the counter-cultural movement, Erik Davis describes our encounters with the weird in a modern

This schema is an over-arching survey of the book; I will refer to this as the *Historical Dialectic*. There is another, more immanent, dialectic at work throughout the text and this has to do with the comparing and contrasting of different texts with each other. The synthesis of this process is not a conclusion, or a definitive answer posed to the questions of these differing texts but is instead a more self-aware telling of the phenomena the texts correspond with, I will refer to this as the *Performative Dialectic*. Sometimes, in doing this, I will refer to an author's name as a metonymic catchall for his or her textual output.

We have already thought dialectically about the difference between the Hermeneutical and Structuralist approaches. The primary focus of this chapter is on two topics that lie close to the heart of the Structuralist project: Narrative and Myth. In a definitional sense, narrative is the systematic recitation of an event or series of events while myth is a traditional story which embodies beliefs regarding some fact or phenomenon of experience, and in which often the forces of nature and of the soul are personified; a sacred narrative regarding a god, a hero, the origin of the world or of a people, etc. There is an essential reciprocity that exists between myths and conspiracy theories in a structural sense, in that both are presented as stories that will explain some phenomena. This formal similarity is doxic in nature, insofar as both myths and conspiracy narratives demand the listener to both invest belief and suspend disbelief.

There is also a content-based, or *actual*, reciprocation between certain conspiracy theories and certain myths. However, this relationship is more tenuous than the formal relationship; in fact, for the most part this actual relationship falls apart during

---

context to be "a tension or flip-flop between enthusiastic enchantment and a disenchanted shrug of the shoulders." Davis, Erik (2019) *High Weirdness: Drugs, Esoterica, and Visionary Experience in the Seventies*. Strange Attractor Press & the MIT Press. P. 254

the "Antithesis" part of our conspiracy theory dialectic. At this stage we are almost entirely within the realm of narrative and what Catherine Kohler Reissman says in *Narrative Analysis* is wholly accurate: "Nature and the world do not tell stories, individuals do. Interpretation is inevitable because narratives are representations."[31] As a materialist, Reissman is not interested in myths, she is interested in narratives insofar as narratives are used to establish personal identities. On this view we can extend the power of narrative to certain collective identities. However, these collective identities are ascertainable materially as well. Myth is never really about one individual; it is about a collective and this collective is not ascertainable in any precise scientific or historic sense.

The stories that I will be simultaneously telling and deconstructing, in one way or another, are rife with dualisms. One such dualism pertaining to the reciprocal relationship between myth and narrative is philosophical – the Kantian schema in which consciousness itself is enabled by meta-consciousness – reflects itself onto the relationship between the narrative and the meta-narrative. In my analysis the myth has a certain propriety the conspiracy narrative does not have, yet it develops a dependency on the conspiracy narrative for its continued existence. This duality is also present in my previous assertion that the thoughtful tracking of this formal structure is in some ways coincidental with, and in other ways identical to, the meta narrative of conspiracy theories. The duality of my text, in this respect, is essentially non-conspiratorial in that it abstains from the goal of total reduction. In order for myths to work there has to be a kernel of mystery lurking at their center, and although the majority of conspiracy theories postulate one cause for their narratives, I do not think this is absolutely necessary and find the theories textually stronger, or *richer*, the opaquer they allow their center to be.

---

[31] Riessman, Catherine Kohler (1993) *Narrative Analysis*. Sage Publications. P. 2

It is important to stress that myths are not the same thing as meta-narratives. In one sense they are both necessary for the conspiracy theory as narrative to have any cultural vitality. However, for the vaguely Kantian reasons already mentioned, I assume that all narratives are dependent for their meaning upon governing meta-narratives, thus making the meta-narrative necessary within our understanding of linguistics. Myth, on the other hand does not share this necessary relationship to meaning. For this reason, myth is both generative and supplementary. Myths also, and most importantly, lack self-awareness and self-awareness is the hallmark of anything deemed to be "meta."[32]

By "supplementary" I am referring specifically to how myths inform narratives that are circulating around us at any point in time. In *Myth and Reality* Mircea Eliade argues that myths are alive, and to this extent:

> [...] it is better to begin by studying myth in traditional and archaic societies, reserving for later consideration the mythologies of people who have played an important role in history. The reason is that, despite modifications in the course of time, the myths of "primitives" still reflect a primordial condition. Then, too, in "primitive" societies myths

---

[32] Manfred Frank explains this by saying that myths are a "mode of discourse" and that, as such, they are composed of sentences and phrases with relations to each other but as a whole do not constitute a historical level of discourse. The historical element here is analogous to the "meta" aspect in that it allots for a sense of objective distance in which commentary on the contents of the narrative are possible. In this respect, Frank asserts that it would be "senseless to assert that the succession of the narrative parts [of the myth] had evolved in an actual historical time." Frank, Manfred (1989) *What is Neostructuralism?* The University of Minnesota pp. 41 – 42.

are still living, still establish and justify all human conduct and activity.[33]

By its nature a narrative is contingent upon storytelling, i.e., the act of its creation. There is a certain Platonic schema related to this creative process that I will quickly sketch here: essentially it is a dualistic way of thinking in which there exist permanent forms for all of our concepts and ideas, and that these forms exist in a logical space that we only have access to by way of our intellect. On this model, actions, like constructing narratives for instance, create imperfect/impermanent instantiations of these forms.

In a sense, myths elude the Platonic designation of imperfection because the myth itself is a narrative that has its origins in the eternal, having been initially spoken by a god. This god, we could assume, is either one who has a perfect communion with the forms, or who pre-historically co-existed with the forms in a mythic time before they were raptured (for lack of a better description) into the Platonic realm of abstraction. All narratives demand a certain degree of interpretation, and due to its pedigree, the myth demands the highest degree of interpretation. The dimensions added by conspiracy theories, which draw from and react against myths, is relevancy to the present-day and urgency.

Myth vs. Narrative

To seek the truth is to interpret, decipher, explicate. But this "explication" is identified with the development of the sign in itself. This is why the search is always temporal, and the truth always a

---

[33] Eliade, Mircea (1998) *Myth and Reality*. Waveland Press. Pp. 4 - 5

truth of time. The final systematization reminds us that Time itself is plural.[34]

In the introduction I briefly outlined some of the philosophical concepts we will be using throughout this book, specifically the Hermeneutical and the Structuralist approaches. In a way these approaches can coexist with each other, but they can also be pitted against each other in a way that draws out a new interpretation or reading of the text in question. In certain respects, myth can be seen as an inherently Hermeneutical concept while narrative can be seen as an inherently Structuralist. This interpretation has to do with the space each approach allows for a sacred place where language cannot intrude; what philosophers and writers sometimes refer to as "the ineffable." Eliade claims that myths are intrusions of the sacred into the commonplace and that they add urgency or gravity to our contemporary narratives; but a simpler *raison d'etre* is that they provide societies with norms.[35]

The concept of ineffability generally points people in the direction of God or mysticism. It can also mean that we don't have, or have forgotten, the appropriate words for certain profound or complex experiences. I said that the Hermeneutical approach allots a "space" for the sacred in a way that might imply that the Structuralist position does not also do so; however, that is not correct as Structuralism indeed allots a space for the 'sacred.' But while Hermeneutics is more likely to conceptualize the sacred space somewhere out in the world, the Structuralist, who is reading the world like a text, conceptualizes the "sacred" almost as if it were a space between words in a sentence (it is also for this reason that I put the word sacred in quotation marks when speaking of it from the Structuralist perspective). What is of vital importance is the understanding of the concepts of dialectic,

[34] Deleuze, Gilles (2000) *Proust and Signs*. Translated by Richard Howard. University of Minnesota Press. P. 17
[35] Eliade, Mircea (1998) *Myth and Reality*. Waveland Press. P. 8

discourse, and myth as they relate to the disciplines of Hermeneutics and Structuralism so that we are able to apply them, like tools, to the material presented to us by conspiracy theories.

Philosophically and linguistically, there is a push-pull dynamic between propositions and the context in which they occur. This context has to do with the time and place that these utterances occur, it also involves the intention of the speaker/writer and the background knowledge of the listener. In the Introduction I gave a brief overview of the idea of representationalism as it related to Kant's theory of the Transcendental Unity of Apperception. We can dig a little deeper into this concept here by discussing propositions.

Historically, philosophers have thought highly of propositions because they make true or false statements about the world. One notable philosopher, Gottlob Frege (November 8, 1848 – July 26, 1925), saw propositions as semantic units that, distinct from emotional impressions, could express and transmit timeless, immutable thoughts. These "thoughts" are akin to Platonic forms. In contrast to this view, there are sociologists, psychologists and pragmatic philosophers who saw propositions as being inherently anthropological and intrinsically linked to the here and now contexts of the subjects who utter them. Both approaches have their plusses and minuses; as we move further into modernity, or hyperreality (a subject we will focus more closely on in the latter half of the book), the various scholastic discourses are coalescing into an approach that is context oriented. What's relevant to our discussion is how propositions can either substantiate our mental representations of reality or in fact *are* our representations of reality.

It should be noted that people who study semantics and discourse in general treat propositions as conceptual structures that arise from subjective interaction with a text.[36] To propose

---

[36] *Discourse Analysis* (1983) by Gillian Brown and George Yule. Cambridge University Press. P. 108

that the world itself, or the world of Being (Dasein) is similarly constructed is to take a leap of faith and make an ontological claim about what *actually* exists outside of language. Someone like Catherine Riessman, who I am contrasting with Mircea Eliade in this particular dialectic, makes statements that jive, in a literally interpretive sense with Eliade, e.g., "A teller in a conversation takes a listener into a past time or 'world' and recapitulates what happened then to make a point, often a moral one." Or "Respondents narrativize particular experiences in their lives, often where there has been a breach between ideal and real, self and society."[37] It must be pointed out that Riessman is really focusing on the individual here and the 'world' she references is almost a solipsistic reconstruction.

Because Riessman and Eliade are both ethnographers, studying the traditions, narratives, and differences between cultures, and both employ a wide variety of interpretive tools, there are many points at which their work overlaps. One of these tools, phenomenology, Riessman references in her description of a trip she took to India:

> [...] I went to stay for a few days at a tropical resort in Kerala. Early one morning, I took a walk from my hotel, along a deserted beach. If we adopt the starting point of phenomenology and the lived world of immediate everyday experience, the world of this inhabited beach is "'already there' before reflection begins -as an inalienable presence" (Merleau-Ponty, 1962/1989, p. vii). Walking at dawn, I encounter it at a prelinguistic realm of experience –images, plays of colors and lights, noises, and fleeting sensations –in the stream of consciousness. I am one with the world and make no distinction at this point between my bodily

[37] Riessman, Catherine Kohler (1993) *Narrative Analysis*. Sage Publications. P. 3

perceptions and the objects I am conscious of that
comprise the beach.[38]

This passage is remarkable because it postulates the possibility of prelinguistic experience, which is a very strong claim. Obviously, the structuralist approach (among a few others) would describe our experience of the world to be contingent upon language. A compromise between the two contrasting views might claim that our experiences are mediated by concepts, and such an argument could claim that conceptual content is not necessarily linguistic. Nevertheless, Riessman's characterization of phenomenology here is a strong one and this space she is elucidating is an especially rare and elusive one.

Is it fair to claim that such a state, if attainable, is analogous to what Eliade calls a "sacred space?" There seems to be an experiential affinity between the two, in that there is a sense of ineffability common to both. However, since Eliade claims that the sacred is instantiated because of a re-enactment of myth, he seems to imply that there is a linguistic, or symbolic, inscription of some sort that precedes the sacred activity.[39] This mythological inscription is a writing that precedes the activity that occupies the sacred space, and even if the participants in a ritual (which constitutes a sacred space) are unthinkingly going

------

[38] Ibid pp. 8 - 9

[39] Eliade states: "'Living' a myth, then, implies a genuinely 'religious' experience, since it differs from the ordinary experience of everyday life. The 'religiousness' of this experience is due to the fact that one re-enacts fabulous, exalting, significant events, one again witnesses the creative deeds of the Supernaturals; one ceases to exist in the everyday world and enters a transfigured, auroral world impregnated with the Supernaturals' presence. What is involved is not a commemoration of mythical events but a reiteration of them." Eliade, Mircea (1998) *Myth and Reality*. Waveland Press. P. 19

through the motions, that does not rule out that the myth they are re-enacting is narratively constituted.

There is one other point at which Eliade and Riessman come to loggerheads and that has to do with Riessman's materialism; she states firmly that, as individuals, we do not have access to each other's experience.[40] Eliade takes a more agnostic stance on this: in his work he traces Shamanistic traditions in China, in which the shaman is a mystic who teaches the wisdom of Taoism to members of the village by leaving his body and journeying into a place that is free of time and space.[41] He also documents archaic rites and rituals in which the individual is subsumed into the collective under the governance of myth. One could delineate the two positions by positing that while Riessman begins with a phenomenological foundation and then adds interpretive layers, borrowed from structuralism, on top (we will elaborate on this in the next paragraph), Eliade allows for an almost thoroughly structuralist reading from the outset.

Riessman's materialism leads to a discourse model that begins with pure experiential phenomena (like the walk on the beach) and moves into five subsequent stages: Attending (noting your experiences), Telling (relating your experiences to friends and colleagues), Transcribing (writing down your experience), Analyzing, and Reading (parsing the accounts of yourself and others).[42] The progression attendant to this model articulates one's concept of "self."

Aspects of Riessman's discourse model can be applied to mythic content as well: textual incongruities, such as God's referral to "us" in Genesis, implying that there is a plurality of gods, or that the angels were God's peers, could be a persistent

---

[40] Riessman, Catherine Kohler (1993) *Narrative Analysis*. Sage Publications. P. 8
[41] Eliade, Mircea (1984) *A History of Religious Ideas 2*. Translated by Willard R. Trask. The University of Chicago Press. Pp. 31 - 33
[42] Riessman, Catherine Kohler (1993) *Narrative Analysis*. Sage Publications. Pp. 9 - 15

translation error, or more likely, a failure on the part of the narrator to adequately explain the context. Many of the times I use the word "murky" in this book it will refer to instances like this. However, from a non-materialist and more symbolic point of view, these textual ambiguities are not merely meant to elude interpretation, as their ambiguity exists as an intrusion, in a Deleuzian sense,[43] on the part of the sacred.

Bridging the Gap Between Hermeneutics and Structuralism

Both the Hermeneuticist and the Structuralist approach their subjects with an eye on scientific rigor, drawing us back to our brief assessment of Occam's Razor in the Introduction, not merely as a demand for simplicity of explanation but as an organizational schema for propositions outlining, or actually embodying, a theory.

This is where Stucturalism comes to play a larger role, because, in a way, it views theories as the sum of propositional statements that substantiate the theory. Scientific thinking, insofar as it conforms to the use of hypothetical statements, presupposes that there is a general correspondence between our language and reality. In *The Philosophy of Logical Atomism* Bertrand Russell states that facts are what make propositional statements true or false and that facts are expressed by whole sentences.[44]

Russell's view is quite analytical and therefore removed from the more literary approach we are employing but he lays out certain ideas that we can use to bridge the perceived gap between a conventional or scientific mindset and our hermeneutical/textual approach. Since Russell is addressing the clarity of language and science, he is very interested in fact; and

---

[43] "Deleuzian" in the sense that there is a demand for interpretation.
[44] Russell, Bertrand (1998) *The Philosophy of Logical Atomism.* Open Court Classics. Pp. 40 - 41

for him, as for most philosophers, facts A) pertain to the objective world – they are not psychologically dependent –, and B) they concern certain properties and relations. It is in this respect that Russell is following the outline Frege made of thoughts as vehicles for Platonic forms and that the reference of the thought is a truth-value.

Russell's concerns are circling around what philosophers call the problem of "foundationalism." Foundationalism is essentially the belief that our thoughts and beliefs are based on empirically derived sensations, i.e., from our five senses. There is a wealth of literature devoted to foundationalism, but we will delve into it only briefly enough to justify our textual analysis of myths and conspiracy theories. The most important problem surrounding our discussion as it relates to foundationalism is something I call the *fine grain* problem, which essentially poses the question: how can an experience, which is itself not a belief, justify a belief? The two processes seem qualitatively incommensurate, insofar as beliefs are expressed as propositional attitudes that don't entail a logical relationship to sensation, and which demand an explanation of what their causal interaction would entail; an explanation of which, seems to fall outside the bounds of reasonable philosophical inquiry.[45]

Because of this incongruity, beliefs are propositional and the 'real world' seems not to be a series of propositions; so how do we develop and share our beliefs about this real world? This conundrum drives the reasoning behind Structuralism as well as certain analytic philosophers who propose that scientific or mathematical theories are themselves the set of all possible sentences made true by the theory. Now, this all might seem overwhelmingly obtuse, but what I'm trying to demonstrate is the insurmountability of language in our lives and how this is vital to

---

[45] There is a second, more *coarse grained* you might say, problem with Foundationalism and that has to do with an infinite regress of justification for beliefs. This topic veers too far afield for our purposes and I feel I'm already trying your patience as it is.

any discussion of myths or conspiracy theories. Some people might want to make a distinction between the medium (or text) that delivers a myth or conspiracy theory and what is *actually* happening (or happened) in the "outside" world, or "reality." Instead, I am trying to break down this dualism. Whatever is "happening" in the outside world is already happening in whichever text that is guiding you to the belief in that "happening."

Conversely, the things we see in the outside world that seem to conform to the theories and myths that we've always already imbibed are themselves textual. In the *Pervert's Guide to Cinema* Slavoj Žižek states that when events become too real for us, we tend to fictionalize them. In a certain way an inherent, and unconscious, drive to narration informs the wildly Structuralist things I am telling you, but there is another factor relating back to the idea of a theory (scientific or otherwise) being composed of the statements that it makes true. It is not even necessary for there to be a causal relationship between all the true statements residing within that theory.[46] We see that Occam's Razor is devised with this in mind, in that it posits the hypotheses as propositions that make the theory true.

All Myths are Narratives, But Not All Narratives are Myths

Myths are vital to conspiracy theories because mythic thinking allows the repetition of events by way of rites and rituals. The definitional repetition is also a feature of myth for Eliade when he describes how certain shamanic traditions only allow an entity to be named if its origin is first related.[47] This act of conjoining a name to an appropriate origin narrative, hints at how far back humanity's entanglement with language goes. Expanding on this theme, Giambattista Vico's *The New Science*, published in 1725,

---

[46] I mean "causal" here in the sense of application.
[47] Eliade, Mircea (1998) *Myth and Reality*. Waveland Press. Pp. 26 - 27

laid the foundation for Structuralism by positing the idea that early peoples, when they constructed their myths and legends, were not childishly deluded by these stories but actually understood that they were speaking in metaphor. Vico discovered what he called "the poetic wisdom" of early man:

> They represent, not child-like 'primitive' responses to reality, but responses of quite a different order whose function was ultimately, and seriously, cognitive. That is, they embody, not 'lies' about the facts, but mature and sophisticated ways of knowing, of encoding, of presenting them. They constitute not mere embroidery of reality, but a way of coping with it.[48]

The framework behind Vico's theory in *The New Science* is what we might call "Conceptual Conflation," in which the concepts of poetry and myth are equated in an abstract way. In a concrete way we might say that Vico's claim is that the poetic nature of early man dictated the mythic structures he created and passed onto future generations. Vico, and his Structuralist descendants, claimed that these physically intangible structures were then maintained through repetition because human beings are creatures of habituation.

Vico's theory is a precursor to Neville Goddard's statement that:

> The Bible has no reference at all to any persons who ever existed or to any event that occurred upon earth. The ancient storytellers were not writing history but an allegorical picture lesson of certain basic principles which they clothed in the garb of history, and they adapted these stories to

---

[48] Hawkes, Terence (1977) *Structuralism and Semiotics.* University of California Press. P. 12

the limited capacity of a most uncritical and credulous people. Throughout the centuries we have mistakenly taken personifications for persons, allegory for history, the vehicle that conveyed the instruction for the instruction, and gross first sense for the ultimate sense intended.[49]

Goddard's sentiment is one extreme viewpoint that can't really stand up to a thorough historical analysis, i.e., most likely there are historical characters and events depicted in the Bible (or other myths). I think his viewpoint is worth citing here because, in its reactionary way, it draws our attention back to medium and symbolism, as opposed to an ideal of historical veracity; and because it allows us to understand that the power of myth arises from the fissure existing between a symbolic, or allegorical, understanding of these narratives and the natural inclination we have for historical certainty.[50]

For both Vico and the contemporary Structuralist, primitive man's construction of myths should affect the way we view everyday institutions and norms; however, the emphasis on myth and repetition is also in accord with Mircea Eliade's more esoterically oriented view that mythic thinking allows the repetition of prehistoric events byway of rites.[51] These events, then, are not commonplace but of a significant social or religious nature.

History Vs. Legend

---

[49] Goddard, Neville (2018) *Five Lessons: A Master Class.* Tarcher/Pedigree New York [find p. #)
[50] Note that Goddard's reference to the "limited capacity of a most uncritical and credulous people" that he exhibits a certain historical chauvinism that Vico did not have.
[51] Eliade, Mircea (1998) *Myth and Reality.* Waveland Press. P. 18

Oftentimes people assume that the concepts of "myth" and "legend" are synonymous; this is not an unwarranted assumption. The definitional difference between the two is that legends are supposed to contain some historical facts that are blown out of proportion, but myths need not draw on any historical facts; their significance is explanatory or symbolic. In this short section I will briefly summarize Erich Auerbach's analysis on the relationship between history and legend.

In his essay, "Odysseus' Scar" Auerbach contrasts the work of Homer with the Old Testament. In the Introduction I briefly mentioned that Auerbach sees this distinction in religious terms because he understands the Old Testament as a work that commands its writer and reader to believe in the truth of what is being told. In this section we will address a related aspect in the dialectic Auerbach has set up; this is the dialectic between *Legend* and *History*.

To a certain extent we can say that Auerbach sees legend as being analogous to myth and history being analogous to narrative (within the context of the present chapter). Examples from the text of Auerbach's delineation between the two are as follows:

> Homer remains within the legendary with all his material, whereas the material of the Old Testament comes closer and closer to history as the narrative proceeds [...] Legend arranges its material in a simple and straightforward way; it detaches it from its contemporary historical context [...] it knows only clearly outlined men who act from few and simple motives and the continuity of whose feelings and actions remains uninterrupted.[52]

Whereas:

---

[52] Auerbach, Erich (2003) *Mimesis: The Representation of Reality in Western Literature*. Princeton University Press. Pp. 18 - 19

> The historical comprises a great number of contradictory motives in each individual, a hesitation and ambiguous groping on the part of groups; only seldom (as in the last war [WWI]) does a more or less plain situation, comparatively simple to describe, arise, and even such a situation is subject to division below the surface, is indeed almost constantly in danger of losing its simplicity [...][53]

Auerbach concedes that in many instances the Old Testament is in fact utilizing both legend and history and for this reason he resolves the dialectic between the two concepts by interpreting legend as a "technique."

A post-Structuralist might have a field day with this analysis because it seems as if Auerbach is granting priority or privilege to the historical over the legendary; this argument could be qualified by the fact that he refers to legend as a technique but does not do so with history. I think that such a deconstruction is a little off base because Auerbach is merely explicating history as a richer medium for human communication because it grants its characters a certain degree of development and complexity and therefore gets us closer to a more accurate representation of what the writers and their contemporaries experienced.[54]

---

[53] Ibid, p. 20

[54] For Auerbach the historical process is a representational process that makes the experience of the everyday concrete: "The antique stylistic rule according to which realistic imitation, the description of random everyday life, could only be comic (or at best idyllic), is therefore incompatible with the representation of historical forces as soon as such representation undertakes to render things concretely; for this procedure entails entering into the random everyday depths of popular life, as well as readiness to take seriously whatever is encountered there..." (p. 44)

Ultimately, in Auerbach's analysis the concept "legend" is not equivalent to the concept "myth" and this distinction is contingent upon his conception of history.

The relationship between myth and legend can be developed further, however, if we abandon our conventional attachment to the veracity of history as some sort of science and think of it instead as a technique employed within the study and construction of myth. This might seem outlandish at first, but if we imagine writing a history of some person or event, anyone reading this could go about constructing such a history. And, if we subscribe to Auerbach's theory that history entails a certain attention to psychological detail and character, any one of us could read a book on Napoleon and write a brief historic account of Waterloo.

What we cannot do, however, is consciously construct a myth. Obviously, people have fathered myths, even very recently, but these myths are things that take on lives of their own: they become bigger than their creators. Also, these myths, after they are textually mapped out in books, do not point back to the authors who wrote them or the thinkers who constructed them. No, they point instead out into the world, at the events and objects themselves. Therefore, a historical method can be applied to a cataloguing of myths, but the construction of a history implies the time and place of its construction, as well as some idea as to who the author might be. The myth cannot be constructed in a similar manner, it has to be outside of time and its sense of place must be transferrable, these qualities bestow a sense of anonymity upon its architect(s).

Anonymity in this regard is the closest approximation to objectivity that we can get, and it is considering this that Eliade writes:

> [At] this point it is necessary to emphasize a fact that we consider essential: the myth is regarded as a sacred story, and hence a "true history," because it always deals with *realities*. The cosmogonic myth is

"true" because the existence of the World is there to prove it; the myth of the origin of death is equally true because man's mortality proves it, and so on.[55]

Myths and Repetition

So far, we have discussed narratives, legends, and myths as unique and interrelated concepts. The broader concept of religion has been broached but like the other concepts it has not been exhausted. One of the more salient points we can take from Auerbach's analysis so far has been his definition of religious writing as a writing that *demands* belief from both the author and the reader.

We have already established that myth also demands both a sense of belief and a suspension of disbelief. Now, according to Vico, in his earlier stages man had a similar grasp of symbolism to us contemporaries, in the sense that he could view his myths and legends as largely constructed and therefore could employ, albeit crudely, a certain degree of cynicism within his belief systems. This cynicism, if we can call it that, might be because early man was the one creating these myths out of his 'poetic wisdom.' The opposite view is one in which mankind at some point in history (or prehistory) naively believed his myths (and possibly had no part in creating them). The imperative force that Auerbach places on belief as it pertains to religious writing makes it seem as if the demand for belief is being employed to consciously overcome a developing cynicism. If this is the case then we can say there was a marked difference in mankind's naivete; and what would be significant about this difference is that it would be comparable to an evolutionary leap, as opposed to a gradual development.[56]

---

[55] Eliade, Mircea (1998) *Myth and Reality*. Waveland Press. P. 6
[56] An issue related to this, or possibly identical to it, would be when did we develop the sense of a meta consciousness. Or was this meta-awareness always present and became more fully developed as man became more sapient. According to Julian

The most important takeaway from this preamble should be that we have no definitive answer as to how or when this type of critical thought developed; and therefore it is impossible for me to honestly tell you that myths demand a suspension of disbelief because we can only conjecture as to whether primitive man had either belief or disbelief to suspend. What we do know, however, is a central point for Eliade in both *Myth and Reality* and *The Myth of the Eternal Return*: that myths are tied to rites and rites are necessarily repetitive:

> It may be mentioned in passing that, among primitives, not only do rituals have their mythical model but any human act whatever acquires effectiveness to the extent to which it exactly *repeats* an act performed at the beginning of time by a god, a hero, or an ancestor.[57]

Does this more atavistic demand for repetition mirror the demand for belief in our more secular culture? And can we say that one demand is more sophisticated than the other? And if so, is sophistication even a good thing in this respect? Myth is generally more associated with paganism than with monotheistic religions like Judaism, Islam, and Christianity. This is because paganism conceptualizes life as cyclical and being tied to the seasons (Slavoj Žižek has characterized it as being tyrannically preordained). In contrast to this, both Žižek and Alain Badiou see

---

Jaynes meta-awareness did not develop until roughly 3,000 years ago. See his 1976 book, *The Origin of Consciousness in the Breakdown of the Bicameral Mind* for a full elaboration of Jaynes's theory.

[57] Eliade, Mircea (1991) *The Myth of the Eternal Return*. Princeton University Press. P. 22

Christianity as being a belief system that breaks the fatalistic cycle of paganism.[58]

We can infer a similar type of emancipatory power onto the other monotheistic faiths – they infer it onto themselves. However, what Zizek and Badiou's zeal for Christianity misses is the fact that religions, specifically the monotheistic ones they champion, had to rely on rites. It is this borrowing from myth that makes religion and myth essentially inseparable. And this aspect of myth goes beyond the demand for belief; in fact, it leads back to the cyclical repetition evident in paganism.

Everything we are doing in this chapter is building up to our discussion of myths and the conspiracy theories which are their modern-day progeny. So far, we have established that religion demands belief and when it is coupled with myth, it tends to incorporate rites and rituals, i.e., repetition. The figures we will introduce in the next chapter – Hiram, Melchizedek, and Enoch – are all mythical figures that appear within a religious text. Their nature as bit players in the Biblical narrative might lead one to assume that they would elude the imperative towards belief and repetition, an imperative that would be reserved for explicitly significant figures like Moses or Jesus. Ironically, in the most obscure ways, these figures have led to the greatest degree of belief (conjecture) and repetition.

Types of Conspiracy Theorists

Believers are ensconced within the theories to which they adhere; the theory takes on a heuristic value insofar as it sorts the events of the believer's life into the categories established within the theory itself. The most pronounced instances of this are what I refer to as *Compound Conspiracy Theorists*. Individuals who

---

[58] Žižek has made this point in a variety of works, for a more extensive analysis on the topic see 2000's *The Fragile Absolute: Or Why is the Christian Legacy Worth Fighting For?* and 2001's *Did Somebody Say Totalitarianism?* (Verso).

subscribe to these theories tend to be very literal-minded. There is a great degree of materialist reductionism at play here. Someone like Allan Watt is representative of this model. I call the theories they expound "compound" because they stack facts on top of facts hoping that the similarities and synchronicities between them will inevitably lead the listener into the folds of their theory.

Compound conspiracy theorists can operate at any point on the Historical Dialectic. They can obsess over Atlantis or the Rothschild Family. Most films about conspiracy theories like Oliver Stone's *JFK*, Richard Donner's *Conspiracy Theory* and Franklin Schaffner's *The Boys From Brazil* focus on the obsessive meticulousness which eventually subsumes the main character and everyone associated with him – this is the effect the compound theorist either experiences directly or is trying to induce in his listener. Jordan Maxwell's *Matrix of Power* offers many astounding examples of compound theories, here is one wild example:

> Our founding fathers are probably turning over in their graves as they see what has happened to us, and how we have been deflected from our purpose and our mission in the world, to ultimately become nothing but pawns in the game. Our liberty is threatened. Look at the Liberty Bell, the symbol of liberty. An equal identical bell was found with the same crack, in Moscow. It's a very famous liberty bell, with the same crack. It has become known as a symbol, the symbol of the Brotherhood of the Bell. Bell, being Bel, the ancient God in the Mesopotamian Valley, being the one that we call Beelzebub, or Yahweh.[59]

---

[59] Maxwell, Jordan (2000) *Matrix of Power: Secrets of World Control*. The Book Tree. P. 18

There is a lot to unpack here. Since Maxwell doesn't cite any sources, we can Google the info on his behalf. Wikipedia lists a "Tsar Bell" commissioned by Empress Anna Ivanovna in 1733. I'm not sure if the "Bell" "Beelzebub" connection is the result of sloppy etymology, as all I got from that Google search was Manga, and I don't feel like investigating it further. Perhaps it's an odd shout-out to Art Bell, which is kind of cool if that's the case. A compound conspiracy can be a "gish gallop," i.e., an overwhelming stack of arguments and claims, some of which are dubious, or composed of qualified facts. What makes it a compound theory is that it is a Scooby Doo-style sandwich of claims, facts and coincidences stacked one atop the other.

It is no coincidence, ahem, that compound theorists primarily operate at the point of antithesis on the Historical Dialectic, as the theories they feel consumed by are as real to them as real can get; and they believe that given a scientific level of inquiry, these facts might be laid bare. Think for instance of the end of the documentary *Loose Change*, which asks the audience to share the film with others in order to let the set of revealed facts proliferate.

The next type of conspiracy theory relies more on the symbolism of the theory. I will call these individuals *Symbolic Theorists*. This style is inherently more interpretive and sometimes is not conspiratorial (in the conventional sense of the word) at all. These individuals are more focused on history, myths, and sometimes the occult. The Discordians or the Church of the Sub-Genius are modern incarnations of this *symbolic* brand of theorizing. Symbolic theorists are more prominent on the thesis side of the Historical Dialectic. If they employ compound theorizing it is most often merely a device to break social conditioning or to demonstrate the absurdity of adhering to all the presented facts. These people are the most idiosyncratic and interesting insofar as they think in the language of myth and synchronicity. However, because they neither profess to have, nor demand material answers, they are less popular in the conspiracy theory community than compound theorists.

The third kind, which is the rarest, is the *Dualist* who ascribes both the actualism of the compounded theorist as well as the interpretation of the Symbolic theorist. Dualists like Tracy R. Twyman, when writing about the Grail, countenances the beliefs that the Grail exists as both a bloodline (an interpretive theory) and an actual object that has been passed through history. These individuals circulate throughout the spectrum of the Historical Dialectic while simultaneously eschewing the dogmatic commitment to an actual revealed answer or reveling in the impossibility of there being an answer. The fact that Twyman was investigating Pizzagate conspiracy theories just prior to her death is further proof of her commitment to both the mythic work she published regarding the Grail as well as a quest for real-world answers. Another example of a *Dualist* was Art Bell, who used his radio show as a forum for open discussion on all manner of conspiratorial and occult phenomena.

Twyman herself (at least her early work) is a synthesis between two particular dialectical strands: Ignatius Donnelly's *Atlantis: The Antediluvian World*, which represents the mythic type of narrative[60] on the one hand, and on the other, more materialist-reductionist hand, *The Holy Blood and the Holy Grail* by Michael Baigent, Richard Leigh and Henry Lincoln. Twyman explores the dialectical engagement between these two books in her writing; it entails that the intention of the mythmaker is to construct a narrative that is both fantastical and explanatory while the materialist-reductionist intends to deconstruct a narrative within the construction of a new one –which most likely will be fantastical, though more focused on explanation.

---

[60] See the introduction to the 1976 Dover Edition by E.F. Bleiler: "The men who make the great myths remain nameless, for the most part, unless they happen to be religious leaders. And for the most part mythopoets are fortunate if they create a single viable myth. Ignatius Donnelly, American politician, scholar and author, however, had the remarkable distinction of having created three of the golden myths of our day..."

Obviously, the time that elapsed between the publication of these two books, and the subsequent change in audience is a hermeneutical factor to take into consideration. By this I mean, not so much the scope of historical outlook that the authors had given their respective points in history, but also the level of skepticism presented by their respective audiences. Donnelly's book was written at a time (1882) when members of the Theosophical Society and likeminded groups were circulating throughout various levels of European and American society. The primary resistance to their claims would come from organized religion. Writing one hundred and one years later, the authors of *The Holy Blood and the Holy Grail* knew they would be taking on the religious community but feared the scientific community more, because that was now the vector of society that could effectively discredit their work.

The antithesis in the Historical Dialectic is represented by scientism, which came into its own in the early 2000s and sought, unconsciously, to abolish myth from its structure. This stage is marked by a sense of absolute discomfort with the ineffable and the unknowable. In fact, if there was any crisis presented by the millennium it was this free-fall into scientific fetishism, which has affinities with a tendency to read mythological texts literally, usually with the aim of dismissing them. However, sometimes this ethos of scientism guides fantastically-minded authors in their readings because it is the most socially acceptable way to reconcile the mythology of the text with the scientific reality of our day-to-day lives.

I have found that many conservative Christian writers, who read the Bible in a literalist way, fall into this paradoxical category in which they are essentially trying to present the fantastic "truth" of the Bible while also appealing to an unconscious desire for scientific validation. Oftentimes these writers focus on the idea of an objective truth and thus demonize mysticism, Gnosticism and Hermeticism because of the role they play in relativizing "truth." These same authors will also decry scientism to the extent that it relativizes truth or gives individuals a sense of autonomy apart from God. Interestingly, this ideal of dispelling the mysticism inherent to mythology appears in left-wing, non-Christian thinkers as well. Terrence McKenna, for instance, "did not follow many of the classic mystics in serenely praising the ineffable. The unfamiliar was not an abiding mystery for him; it can be recognized and known."[61]

Timothy Melley couples the subject's sense of autonomy in the postindustrial society with a sense of nostalgia for the "rugged individualism" of America's past and deems both to be essentially liberal in nature. [62] This classification is derived from Enlightenment ideals (and the work of Kant) that privileged a sense of self-derived rationality and agency. The attachment to this ideology-of-the-self, Melley claims, is threatened by ideologies, in the extreme case of post-structuralism, that posit the "individual" as being a total fabrication of governing systems (such as jobs, schooling, and government agencies). Or in the more mitigated parlance of someone like Riessman, in which the inner experiences of the "individual" are "regulated by external communications, which penetrated and inhabited them."[63] These are issues that will reoccur throughout our analysis.

Because Melley's work is focused on the type of individual (both literary manifestations and actual persons in Western society) who might be subsumed within a web of paranoia, he is

---

[61] Davis, Erik (2019) *High Weirdness: Drugs, Esoterica, and Visionary Experience in the Seventies*. Strange Attractor Press & the MIT Press. P. 107. In his chapter on McKenna, Davis makes a point of distinguishing his subject, who employed empiricism and skepticism in his psychedelic experiments, from the prevailing "hippy-dippy" sentiment of the times. Davis states that both Terrence and Dennis McKenna (his brother) "were not seduced by the romance of religion or shamanism so much as the romance of science –albeit a weird science." Ibid, p. 109.

[62] Melley, Timothy (2000) *Empire of Conspiracy: The Culture of Paranoia in Postwar America*. Cornell University Press. Pp. 39 - 43

[63] Ibid p. 50

focusing on the stability of the agents who are doing the investigating. This issue of what constitutes the individual also comes into play in the analysis of myths because we often take for granted a sense of stability as it pertains to legendary and mythic characters. In respects to both analyses, Heidegger grappled with the problem of whether situating a subject within a narrative engendered a sense of staticity, in which the essence of the subject could be definitively grasped. He found this aspiration to be illusory: "With regard to the awkwardness and 'inelegance' of expression in the following analyses, we may remark that it is one thing to report narratively about *beings* and another to grasp beings in their *being.* For the latter task not only most of the words are lacking but above all the 'grammar.'"[64] However, this is not to say that Heidegger is espousing the same kind of externally-constructed subject as the post-structuralist –we will see later that he has certain criteria that authenticate the individual's sense of self. What he is doing is interrogating the ability to question self-hood, or *being*, in a meaningful way.

The grounding of this character development was just one part of a bigger issue that Heidegger approaches from a variety of angles, that is, the noncoincidence of action and recollection, or practice and theory. Essentially, making history and reflection upon history do not, or cannot occur simultaneously. For Heidegger, theorizing about history is different from the practice of living historically, i.e., creating history. Creation of and reflection on do not occur simultaneously –not even for God, who in Genesis creates and then reflects upon his creation.

Likewise, for Heidegger, a cultural-historical heritage is what makes interpretation possible for the individual subject. "The lore of history," he said, "is given only for him who stands in resoluteness; only he can and may know the inevitability of the historical *Dasein*. However, the unknowing ones, and even those

---

[64] Heidegger, Martin (1996) *Being and Time* translated by Joan Stambaugh, State University Press of New York. P. 34

who are drifting around in the unessence of history can, all the same, never release themselves from history and labor."[65]

We will be focusing primarily on narratives and myths in a textual way. The individuals presented in these texts (both ancient and modern) are themselves caught up not merely in the drama of their immediate contexts but also by how they react to, and most importantly categorize, the phenomena. The instinct towards categorization is a primal one: consider the Bible's account of Adam's naming of the animals of Eden. In this capacity he operated as a master-categorizer. It's possible that he might have wanted to bestow a name on a particular animal and that God vetoed this particular appellation; however, the Bible doesn't report this happening. It seems as if Adam was given carte blanche. As we move forward in history, what to call things, or how to classify them becomes a more complicated, and oftentimes a defining, issue.

We must remember that, even if the conspiracy theorist is largely animated by the language of his discourse, the discourse was initiated by a quest for what was lurking beneath the surface of everyday life; and that the instinct towards categorization is a search for a language or schema that makes sense of this hidden world, or substrate. Heidegger defined this underlying substrate of Being as "uncanniness" and wrote that: "Uncanniness is the fundamental kind of being-in-the-world, although it is covered over in everydayness. Dasein itself calls as conscience from the ground of this being."[66]

History and the Apprehension of Time

---

[65] Heidegger, Martin (2009) *Logic as the Question Concerning the Essence of Language.* Published by State University of New York Press. P. 137

[66] Heidegger, Martin (1996) *Being and Time* translated by Joan Stambaugh, State University Press of New York. P. 256

In the Introduction we discussed the Existentialism of Heidegger and Sartre insofar as it is an aspect of Phenomenology proper. The point that I was trying to convey there, and which is evident in my citations of Heidegger, is a basic, ceaseless, always progressing-forward aspect of Dasein. The idea that time is hurtling us forward without any real permanence in this world is disconcerting for most people. Sometimes our apprehension with this has less to do with associating our fleeting nature with the big things in our lives (relationships, careers, houses, cities, etc.), than with the smaller realization of moments passing in a day and then wondering: "Where did the day go?" It is impossible to say this definitively, but a lot of times when philosophers come up with big, earth-shattering, game-changing theories, their inspiration probably came from a small experience, not a grandiose one. I understand that a philosophy of instability and ceaseless change can seem disconcerting when it is the lens through which we view the world at large. However, we should try to reign in our anxieties and focus on the smaller picture.

Because this discussion of myth and narrative revolves around duality, whether represented by the contrast that gives way to dialectical thinking or merely a taxonomic listing of the contents of two different subjects, there is one other topic that is worth a brief exploration: the significance of the types of historical figures who pop up in the course of the narratives we analyze. Mircea Eliade and Oswald Spengler both deal with historical figures that existed within closed temporal systems. By this I mean that when they look at a community or civilization they see linear time as an aspect of the system itself, and any sense of a grand linear time that might transcend these systems is outside of their purview.[67]

---

[67] This point is more accurate in regard to Spengler than it is to Eliade, who addressed transcendent aspects of religious traditions at various times in his work. The Eliade I'm focusing on here is that of *The Myth of the Eternal Return*.

This is more pronounced in Spengler, who essentially sees all the great civilizations – which follow a progression of growth, decline, and death – as existing simultaneously. Eliade, as a spiritual taxonomist, is more agnostic on this subject as he allows for a possibility of exterior metaphysical engagement. Nevertheless, both writers address the topic of historical personage but in a contrasting way. For Eliade the myth as narrative has roles that are akin to placeholders or names, and these names (or titles), are then occupied by individuals. For Spengler, great individuals actually forge these roles through their actions; thus placing Spengler's philosophy more in line with German Idealism. We will have figures like this in our narrative, of course, George Washington, JFK, etc., but, "outside" of these approaches we will have figures like Melchizedek, Enoch, and Hiram who, by appearing in the margins of the text, elude an easy classification. They are obscure figures who generate a murkiness in the textual history that surrounds them. Their presence echoes Auerbach's description of God: he is never fully comprehended, always extending into depths. Before we move onto the topic of individual characters, we need to establish a context, or setting, that existed for ancient man. We will try to accomplish this in the following two chapters.

Chapter Three: The Significance of the Sea

The cosmos and the sea loom large in our mythologies. In a sense, each is the reflection of the other. Both suggest fathomlessness: they are beyond our comprehension insofar as our notion of comprehension is tied to our physical sense of sight. If, however, our sense of sight was taken from us, there would still be a similar feeling of fathomlessness because this is also the feeling of innerspace which marks a limit to our power of cognition – the ability to reason the world into the folds of our individual (or collective) understanding.

The myths and narratives I will focus on in this section situate this limit of cognition within the realm of the sea. Biologically we, and all life on this planet, arose from the Earth's oceanic waters. Perhaps, more primordially, we were seeded by some extraterrestrial entity, but the sea also had a more immediate relationship to our ancestors as a source of food and transportation; it had utilitarian as well as symbolic value. Also, if we adhere to the Freudian structuring of the psyche, the sea can be conceptualized as a metaphor for the Id with its powerful waves of wordless urges and drives.[68] In addition to this, it can also represent the vastness of the unconscious part of our mind.

The Waters of Genesis

Reading through the Bible, we can see that the Book of Genesis, in particular, satisfies Mircea Eliade's definition of myth: "It narrates a sacred history; it relates an event that took place in primordial

---

[68] The contrast between the pre-existing chaos embodied by the waters of Genesis and the more ordered world that God created in their midst occurs in a wide variety of cultures (see Wayne, Gary (2014) *The Genesis 6 Conspiracy*. Trusted Books, A Division of Deep River Books, pp. 582 – 583) and seems to be a theological precursor to Freud's, more theoretical, model of the psyche.

time, the fabled time of the 'beginnings.'"[69] Since our analysis stresses the idea that the conspiracy theory is a natural and modern outgrowth of mythological narrative, to adequately demonstrate this we tie these narrative strands to physically existing settings and objects, such as: earth, sun, sky, sea, etc. Later we can add more abstract things like night or darkness. All of them, as well as their symbolic representations, will reoccur with a Deleuzian sense of repetition in our discussion of the Tarot later in the book.

We need to understand foremost that the sea, as an object of significance, marks two specific places in Genesis that are absolutely vital to our understanding of myths. First, according to the Bible the existence of the sea precedes God's creation of light:

> In the beginning God created the heaven and the earth.
> And the earth was without form, and void; and darkness was upon the face of the deep. And the spirit of God moved upon the face of the waters.
> (Genesis 1,2)

Taking the existence of the sea for granted in this way is possible evidence of an unconscious disposition on the part of the authors; in sketching out the creation of the world this way there is a tacit admission that the possibility of there never having been water was impossible to fathom for early man. Tracy R. Twyman (August 28, 1978 – July 2019), to whose work I will be returning repeatedly throughout this book, gives an excellent summary of this atavistic mentality:

> For people who did not realize that they lived on a spherical rock floating in empty space, but instead saw a flat landscape, with a point on the horizon where the sky met the seas, this was an acceptable

---

[69] Eliade, Mircea (1998) *Myth and Reality*. Waveland Press. P. 5

explanation. It seemed to them that they were surrounded by seas, beyond which was nothing but more water, stretching out to infinity, arching over their heads in what was called "the canopy of Heaven."[70]

The Eden narrative in Genesis, which follows the creation story, depicts the golden age of humanity. It portrays the lost paradise that we are constantly striving to regain. Whether its legend had been written down or not it was by all means passed down orally; nevertheless, it remains an enduring feature of our unconscious. Prior to Adam and Eve's fall there is nothing within Eden that presents a danger; the Tree of Knowledge is foreboding, but that is understood within the hermeneutical horizon of the text, i.e., we, as readers, "know" the narrative is leading the characters towards access of this forbidden thing. The sea, however, like all the animals and plants is not foreboding at this point in the narrative. The lack of danger in Eden is tied to the totality of access to objects, both in their handiness and in their essence; something that was secured by Adam when he named all the animals presented to him by God. In this way he participated directly in the authorship of the world.[71] In a sense, the fall of man marks the point at which aspects of the world became dangerous and mysterious. It is the point at which we lost our definitive, epistemological grasp of the world. The pantomime of disclosure that Heidegger describes when talking about Dasein can be interpreted as having originated from this primordial moment of loss:

---

[70] Taken from the chapter "The Celestial Sea and the Ark of Heaven" published in Twyman, Tracy (2005) *The Arcadian Mystique: The Best of Dagobert's Revenge Magazine*. Dragon Key Press. P. 60

[71] This act of naming, to a certain extent, coincides with Vico's theory of 'poetic wisdom' in that Adam has a hand in the creation of his, and his progeny's, environment.

> With the explication of the existential constitution of the being of the there in the sense of thrown project does not the being of Dasein become still more mysterious? Indeed. We must first let the full mysteriousness of this being emerge, if only to be able to get stranded in a genuine way in its "solution" [...][72]

After Adam's fall nothing is completely present to us or our understanding anymore. Perhaps the potentially menacing or mysterious nature of ambiguous objects, like the sea, comes in part from this lack of totality in our cognitive grasp. The fall instigated a duality into our relationship with the world.[73] For Idealists like Kant and Schopenhauer this was parsed out in a representational way, by which the true nature of objects (or the things-in-themselves) was obscured behind our sensory representations of them. For a more contemporary heir to this tradition, like Heidegger, these objects circulate around us in social settings and we are alerted to their presence or absence by their *handiness*, their availability to our intentions to use them or how they fit within the context of our surroundings.[74] This is not to say that the philosophers just mentioned (or any post-Medieval

---

[72] Heidegger, Martin (1996) *Being and Time* translated by Joan Stambaugh, State University Press of New York. P. 139

[73] It is fair to say that Heidegger saw the historical onset of Dasein as being, in some respects, analogous to the Fall; in Volume Two of *The Black Notebooks* he states: "Mankind believes it must do something with itself –and does not understand that Dasein has already done something with it (beginning of philosophy)- from which mankind fled long ago." Heidegger, Martin (2014) *Ponderings II – VI, The Black Notebooks 1931 – 1938*. Indiana University Press. P. 7

[74] This contextual interpretation of phenomena is closely related to Heidegger's concept of "care."

philosophers) were responding to the fall from Eden or even took it seriously in a historical sense. What I am suggesting is that the Biblical text as well as the works by the above-mentioned authors map out the territory of the same ontological problem: why we lack immediate and total knowledge (or possession) of objects physically present to us.

The same issue was addressed by the early practitioners of psychoanalysis as well; Emma Jung gave this myth-oriented account of her late husband's theory of archetypes as they pertain to the transition from childhood to adulthood:

> The archetypal world exercises an uncanny fascination, indeed it has a numinous effect. It is a world full of wonders; it not only shelters terrible mothers and other monstrosities but is also like the Celtic "Land of the Living" or Paradise, an abode of bliss. The necessity for giving up this world of wonder often excites the most violent resistance, for that which will be received in exchange is mostly far less attractive. The magic of this world is one of the reasons why the state of childhood is greatly loved and worth striving for and why the step into "life" and reality is so difficult. For the same reason so many myths tell the origin of human existence in Paradise, or of a golden age that was lost and replaced by a far less perfect world.[75]

As we will see, this Jungian model of development resonates with the Grail quest, in that the achievement of independent consciousness is comparable to overcoming a series of challenges or defeating an "overwhelming monster."[76] In this way it also coincides with the Hegelian Master/Slave dialectic, which most

---

[75] Jung, Emma & Franz, Marie-Louise (1986) *The Grail Legend*. Sigo Press. P. 42
[76] Ibid, p. 43

contemporary Hegelians regard as an allegory for the struggle towards achieving consciousness.[77]

The consciousness we are talking about in this respect is one that we consider in terms of the sense of subjectivity that accompanies it. It seems safe to say that as our sense of individuality develops, the more isolated we tend feel from the persons and objects in our environment; they essentially lose their sense of immediacy.

The French philosopher, Jacques Derrida (July 15, 1930 – October 9, 2004) formulated the concept of "Deconstruction" as an attempt to outline the impossibility of achieving this sense of possession or immediacy, which he labeled "presence." According to Derrida, presence was: "[An] imagined moment, prior to the arrival of language, when meaning and consciousness are fully present to each other." However, according to Derrida, knowledge of this moment could only be achieved by way of representation. Therefore, "The experience of the moment of presence is *indefinitely postponed, infinitely deferred, perpetually delayed.*"[78] The idealized notion of presence is a principal feature of our Western consciousness. Derrida's approach, which we will return to in a variety of other contexts, approaches this concept in a Universalist manner that presupposes the desire for presence in all rational subjects.

After Derrida, the most prominent contemporary philosopher to address this topic using Biblical terminology is David J. Chalmers. In his essay, "Perception and the Fall from Eden," he defines the Edenic perception of objects as being

---

[77] This can be true for analytic philosophers such as John McDowell or Robert Pippin who debate as to what kind of consciousness is to be achieved and whether the struggle is within oneself or between oneself and others. It can also be true for Hegelians with a Marxist orientation who see class consciousness as the type of consciousness to be achieved.
[78] Boyne, Roy (1990) *Foucault and Derrida: The Other Side of Reason*. Routledge. P. 94

unmediated, one in which we had direct acquaintance with objects and their properties, e.g., "When an apple in Eden looked red to us, the apple was gloriously, perfectly, and primitively *red*. There was no need for a long causal chain from the microphysics of the surface through air and brain to a contingently connected visual experience."[79]

After the fall, Chalmers's story invents two additional experiences that befell humanity: partaking in the Tree of Illusion, which essentially made human sensory experience contingent: "We could no longer accept that visual experience always revealed the world exactly as it is."[80] Next, we partook of the Tree of Science, which revealed to us that there is always a complex causal chain involved in our perception of objects. Chalmers concludes this fictional narrative by saying:

> We no longer live in Eden. Perhaps Eden never existed, and perhaps it could not have existed. But Eden still plays a powerful role in our perceptual experience of the world. At some level, perception represents our world as an Edenic world, populated by perfect colors and shapes, with objects and properties that are revealed to us directly. And even though we have fallen from Eden, Eden still acts as a sort of ideal that regulates the content of our perceptual experience.[81]

Such a reading is an epistemological analysis of our separation from, not so much nature, but from *being in* a state of nature. In a philosophical sense these Edenic properties could be thought of as being analogous to Plato's forms. Plato writes at length on the immateriality, unknowable nature and dependence that the

---

[79] Chalmers, David (2006) "Perception and the Fall from Eden" published in *Perceptual Experience*. Oxford University Press. P. 49
[80] Ibid p. 49
[81] Ibid p. 50

objects we see and experience have on the forms, but he never offers a narrative of humans being separated from them in the distant past. Chalmers posits that a contemporary philosophical approach which views the properties instantiated during our perceptual experiences as *primitive* properties, or simple intrinsic qualities, would be "of the sort that might have been instantiated in Eden." [82] Such a view would take the contents of our experiences to be composed of by objects and properties. In contrast to this view, Chalmers offers a more sophisticated analysis of our consciousness based on "modes of presentation of objects and properties." This view hews more closely to language-oriented approaches to philosophy.[83]

This latter view is more sophisticated because it allows us to judge the epistemic value of sentences. Chalmers's analysis is firmly on the "analytic" side of the philosophical divide (the schools we have been primarily using so far, Structuralism, Phenomenology and Hermeneutics are all on the "continental" side); however, this addressing of phenomena by way of modes-of-presentation illustrates a theoretical divide between us, as subjects, and the world, as mediated through modes of presentation, or more specifically, language. We have already seen, to a certain extent, how the Structuralist and Hermeneutical schools of thought have addressed this issue; the primary thrust of this chapter is assessing it within scriptural and mythic parameters.

The philosophical idea of there being a fissure between us and the world is often pondered religiously in the following terms: we are children of God but through our intelligence, worldliness, and desire for possessions we have moved away from him, and thus the Edenic fall is analogous to our fall from the naivety of childhood into puberty and then adulthood. This reading corresponds with Vico's postulation that mankind's

---

[82] Ibid p. 57. In the essay, Chalmers identifies this view as being indebted to Bertrand Russell's view of phenomenal content.
[83] This view Chalmers links to Gottlob Frege.

transition from the Biblical world into history proper was an essentially developmental process. This can be further substantiated by an additional point that I will address in very simple terms, which pertain to maturity of thought: consider the ages Genesis lists for how long patriarchs such as Adam (930 years) or Noah (950 years) lived. To take these ages as metaphorical is one thing. However, the desire to emulate them is another. One can fairly say that the proclamation, "I want to live nine hundred years!" marks a certain degree of immaturity in the speaker. Maturity not only grants one a sense of modesty in manners but also a certain realism of what life entails; and the understanding that it does not (or would not be desired to) go on indefinitely, or for what we might count as centuries. There is a likelihood that life was more enjoyable in a time that was in closer proximity to the creation (or regeneration, if we are thinking in terms of the Vedic categorizing of Yugas) of the world; and centuries spent appreciating it with very little physical or cognitive decline were the order of the day. Regardless, from our contemporary perspective, a desire for an insanely attenuated existence is a mark of a childlike thought process and is an argument for the theory that the earliest parts of Genesis are an exhibition of a hazy, partially aware, adolescent stage of humanity.[84]

The fall from paradise could then be conceived as being akin to a rite of passage from adolescence to adulthood. However, just because humanity transitioned into a more cognitively aware state of maturity does not entail a greater degree of self-awareness. In fact, the most prominent part of awareness might be directed at what was lost: the separation from God or the separation from nature. For the last few centuries, a literal belief

---

[84] I understand that more practically oriented theologians view these ages as either symbolic or the product of a different method of calculating time. For the sake of this book I am viewing them in a literal way because it resonates with the generally fantastic nature of Genesis.

in this as a separation from God would mark an individual as a "religious thinker," while within the same historical context this distinction would mark said thinker as being of a slighter pedigree than the thinker who discounts the reality of the Bible or the existence of God. Nevertheless, this feeling of separation from nature, or even from our true awareness of ourselves (whatever that might be) is bound to set certain authors and philosophers who seek to quell our sense of the uncanny nature of the world.

Whether it is sparked by religious or secular reasoning, once the idea that there was a primal act of separation between humanity and divinity gains a certain amount of traction in a society's intellectual discourse, the focus of this discourse usually turns inward, towards the self. The idea of the existence of the "self" or how it is constituted has plagued philosophical thought since the Middle Ages. The initial breakthrough came with Descartes' famous "Cogito, ergo sum" ("I think therefore I am.") in 1637. From this assertion it seemed probable that, so long as conscious thought was established, we could ascertain a unified, coherent conception of selfhood. This hope, however, suffered a setback when David Hume asked of the self, "Where is it? Every time I look for it, it vanishes," roughly one hundred years after Descartes.[85]

This topic was broached in the Introduction when we discussed Kant's theory of the Transcendental Unity of Apperception, which entails the notion that the self is present whenever we consciously think in terms of "I."[86] This then opened the door to Structuralism, which in case I didn't mention it before,

---

[85] The Chaos Magician, Peter J. Carroll posits that: "The singular self remains a defining feature of monotheist and post monotheist cultures. It confers a greater sense of personal responsibility than our pagan forefathers would have felt comfortable with." Carroll, Peter J (2008) *The Apophenion: A Chaos Magic Paradigm.* Mandrake. P. 36

[86] Which reiterates Descartes's fundamental insight, albeit in a more contingent, less absolute way.

I'll do so now, is very skeptical about the existence of the "self." And conversely, the Hermeneutical position instigated by Heidegger, with which I am about to regale you.

Heidegger is a notoriously tricky philosopher because the subject he is tackling, Dasein, is tricky. Heidegger's difficulty in many ways can be attributed to a stylistic caution he employs to avoid bluntness. "Being," for Heidegger, is groundless – in the sense that we are "thrown" into the world: "Dasein exists as thrown, brought into its 'there' *not* of its own accord. It exists as a potentiality-of-being which belongs to itself, and yet has *not* given itself to itself."[87] We therefore establish our sense of self by the possibilities that are historically possible for us. We can better understand these "possibilities" if we think of them in concrete terms as objects that were once present-at-hand:

> The historical character of extant antiquities is thus grounded in the "past" of Dasein to whose world that past belongs. According to this, only "past" Dasein would be historical, but not "present" Dasein. However, can Dasein be *past* at all, if we define "past" as "now *no longer objectively present or at hand*"? Evidently Dasein can never be past, not because it is imperishable, but because it can essentially *never* be *objectively present*. Rather, if it is, it *exists*. But a Dasein that no longer exists is not of the past in the ontologically strict sense; it is rather *having-been-there*. The antiquities still objectively present have a "past" and a character of history because they belong to useful things and originate from a world that has-been-the-world of a Dasein that has-been-there. Dasein is what is primarily historical.[88]

---

[87] Heidegger, Martin (1996) *Being and Time*. State University Press of New York. P. 262
[88] Ibid pp. 348 - 349

Designating Dasein in a historical context is not merely emphasizing the transitory, or fleeting, nature of Being, it is granting it both a textual and cultural pedigree. The possibilities that are available to us are possibilities that are available to most people in our community. Generally, contemporary philosophers link this notion to the inauthenticity of group-think and the "they" of which Heidegger is so critical. In one sense this is correct because Heidegger posits that the authentic individual is one who accepts his or her own death as the sole contingency that he or she does not have in common with others:

> The more authentically Dasein resolves itself, that is, understands itself unambiguously in terms of its own most eminent possibility in anticipating death, the more unequivocal and inevitable is the choice in finding the possibility of its existence. Only the anticipation of death drives every chance and "preliminary" possibility out. Only being free *for* death gives Dasein its absolute goal and pushes existence into its finitude.[89]

However, twenty-two years later, in *The Question Concerning Technology*, he writes:

> For man becomes truly free only insofar as he belongs to the realm of destining and so becomes one who listens and hears, and not one who is simply constrained to obey... The essence of freedom is *originally* not connected with the will or even with the causality of willing.[90]

[89] Ibid p. 351
[90] Heidegger, Martin (2013) *The Question Concerning Technology and Other Essays*. Harper Perennial Modern Thought. P. 25

In contrast to authenticity, or the desire for authenticity, the issue of freedom arises as an essential and desired-for aspect of human nature. Just as in the case of authenticity, wherein it is derived from one's own honest apprehension of death, freedom is determined by understanding. Besides arising from our sense of reason, or rationality, Heidegger implies that there is a meditative aspect that requires patience and thoughtfulness on the part of the knowing subject:

> Freedom governs the open in the sense of the cleared and lighted up, i.e., of the revealed. It is to the happening of revealing, i.e., of truth, that freedom stands in the closest and most intimate kinship. All revealing belongs within a harboring and a concealing. But that which frees -the mystery- is concealed and always concealing itself. All revealing comes out of the open, goes into the open, and brings into the open.[91]

The context of Heidegger's remarks is in relation to technology, and the concern is that a preoccupation with technology can divert our attention from "a more original revealing and hence to experience the call of a more primal truth."[92] The primal truth here, we are led to assume, relates to freedom; and the push-pull dynamic between freedom and authenticity within the historical Being of a community is analogous to the push-pull dynamic between concealment and revelation that Heidegger attributes to our faculty of understanding.

The issue of concealment and revelation, in particular, points to Heidegger's critique of what Chalmers deems "Edenic" properties, insofar as the Edenic quality is a full and total apprehension of objects. Heidegger is arguing for an admission of

---

[91] Ibid p. 25
[92] Ibid p. 28

mystery and unknowingness on the part of the subject – that which can be apprehended only does so when it reveals itself to us. As far as what constitutes the subject, Heidegger writes cryptically; we know that he or she is constantly mediating the sinews of freedom and authenticity. However, if we take into account what he says in *Poetry, Language, Thought* we see that a sense of "dwelling" and existing constructively within a community is also of great importance:

> To dwell, to be set at peace, means to remain at peace within the free, the preserve, the free sphere that safeguards each thing in its nature. *The fundamental character of dwelling is this sparing and preserving.* It pervades dwelling in its whole range. That range reveals itself to us as soon as we reflect that being human consists in dwelling and, indeed, dwelling in the sense of the stay of mortals on the earth.[93]

This passage, as well as other parts of Heidegger's oeuvre, indicates an understanding of the subject as arising within the context of a historical community. Intersubjectivity, which was an aspect of Hegel's philosophy as well, can be a double-edged sword, i.e., the outlook is not so rosy when its implications are transplanted into a modern, or post-modern context, in which it is government agencies and social media dictating the subject's sense of self-hood. Just as much as our project is focused on the transition of myths from the past into our modern age we must also be attentive to the ways in which earlier people conceived of themselves and their place in the world. With the first appearance of the sea in Genesis and how this leads to Adam's fall we have fished out a few philosophical ideas on the nature of selfhood;

---

[93] Heidegger, Martin (1975) *Poetry, Language, Thought.* Harper & Row Publishers Inc. P. 149

these will be developed and will reoccur throughout the remainder of the book.

The Antediluvian World

The second important appearance (or indexing) of the sea in Genesis is when God decides to flood the earth to exterminate wickedness and abominations. Here I will give an abbreviated rendering of the text as it pertains to Adam's descendent Noah:

And it came to pass, when men began to multiply on the face of the earth, and daughters were born unto them, that the sons of God saw the daughters of men that they were fair; and they took them wives of all which they chose.
And the Lord said, My Spirit shall not always strive with man, for that he also is flesh: yet his days shall be a hundred and twenty years.
There were giants in the earth in those days; and also after that, when the sons of God came in unto the daughters of men, and they bare children to them, the same became mighty men which were of old, men of renown.
And God saw that the wickedness of man was great in the earth, and that every imagination of the thoughts of his heart was only evil continually. And it repented the Lord that he had made man on earth, and it grieved him at his heart. And the Lord said, I will destroy man whom I have created from the face of the earth; both man, and beast, and the creeping thing, and the fowls of the air; for it repenteth me that I have made them. But Noah found grace in the eyes of the Lord [...] And God said unto Noah, The end of all flesh is come before me; for the earth is filled with violence through them; and behold, I will destroy them with the earth. Make thee an ark of gopher wood; rooms shalt thou make in the ark, and shalt pitch it within and without with pitch. And this is the fashion which thou shalt make of it: the length of the ark shall be three hundred cubits, the breadth of it fifty cubits, the height of it thirty cubits.

The rest of the story is known to virtually everyone: God tells Noah to take his family and two of each animal onto the ark before causing it to rain for seven days. The flood lasts for forty days (forty has numerological significance in scripture: forty days is the same amount of time Jesus fasts in the desert, forty years is how long Moses and the Israelites wander in the desert). This is the first instance of the fear of God's wrath becoming an issue in the Bible and religious feeling in general. The dawn of monotheism is closely accompanied by the feeling of wanting to avoid God's bad side. As Laurent Guyénot describes it:

> "Yahweh's name is the Jealous One" (Exodus 34:14). The Torah emphasizes jealousy as his main personality trait, calling him "the Jealous One" repeatedly (Exodus 20:5, Deuteronomy 4:24, 5:9 and 6:15). What Yahweh demands from his people above anything else is exclusivity of worship. But that is not all. He also demands that all his neighbors' shrines be utterly destroyed: "Tear down their altars, smash their standing-stones, cut down their sacred poles and burn their idols" (Deuteronomy 7:5). Thus spoke Yahweh, otherwise known as *El Shaddai,* "the destroyer god" (Exodus 6:3).[94]

If the opening of Genesis gives the reader the impression that God created the world out of a sense of wonder or a sense of necessity (this more philosophical notion will be discussed in the next chapter in the context of the Gospel According to Saint John), then the flooding of the world personalizes God by way of the emotions of anger and disappointment that motivate his actions. It also indicates that destruction must precede creation and that both are willful acts. This particular aspect of *willfulness* is also

---

[94] Guyénot, Laurent (2018) *From Yahweh to Zion.* Sifting and Winnowing Books. P. 61

duplicated in our understanding of what it means to create a text, as it pertains to the concepts of discipline and determination. One might argue that this sense of willfulness is present at the beginning of Genesis as God, and to a certain extent Adam, write the book of the world; but it is built up in a more mature authorial style in the creation and destruction of the Antediluvian world.

The world prior to this cataclysmic flood is referred to as "Antediluvian" and for the sake of textual analysis we will compare this narrative to some of the narratives surrounding Atlantis, because, you know, Atlantis, to paraphrase Carl from *Aqua Teen Hunger Force*, "is a total classic!" The Antediluvian narrative and the Atlantis narrative are absolutely vital to conspiracy theories for a variety of reasons, one of which is that they provide a point at which a thread can be followed from modern-day phenomena to prehistory. The flood, or the sinking of Atlantis, is a rupture that arose between contemporary human beings and our ancient predecessors, who, due to their historical concealment, are sometimes attributed with vast amounts of technological and occult knowledge. It is a subject discussed by a wide variety of conspiracy theorists, but its particular interest to our narrative/philosophical analysis is that there is nothing inherently conspiratorial about these myths in themselves: they are fantasies which provide a backdrop – much like the backdrop provided by "the waters" in the creation story – for the topical narratives to unfold against.

Talking About Atlantis

There are a lot of books about Atlantis, but we will begin our discussion with Ignatius Donnelly's *Atlantis: The Antediluvian World*. Before getting directly into Donnelly's work, however, I want to focus on E. F. Bleiler's introduction to the 1976 Dover edition of the book. Bleiler, who was the executive vice-president of Dover Publications from 1967 to 1977,[95] presents a specific

---

[95] From Bleiler's Wikipedia page accessed 05/22/19.

type of analysis of the text. Bleiler is scientifically focused, and therefore materialistic, but more importantly, the style he employs in the introduction is one that summarizes the past from the summit of the present. This is an explicitly non-hermeneutical approach because Bleiler indexes Donnelly's work within the milieu of his (Donnelly's) day but is simultaneously oblivious to the fact that he is writing his introduction within the milieu of *his* own day.

For Bleiler, science (at his time of writing) is to a large extent settled, though he makes concessions like: "Even today, however, the question of resemblances between pre-Columbian artifacts, customs, institutions, myths, economic plants, and so on, and those of the Old World is far from being settled."[96] What is settled on Bleiler's view, however, is not the scientific method so much as the air of finality that a reliance on science grants once it has settled into the greater society.

In this schema a theory's validity is isolated from the time period in which it was propounded. Despite these faults, Bleiler provides some useful insight into the thinking of the compound conspiracy theorist:

> Donnelly was essentially an arch-geneticist in the study of cultures. He assumed that similarities between one culture and another indicated common descent or, less important to him, borrowing. If, for example, the North American Indians had occasional copper axes of a certain shape and this same shape was also to be found in Danish axes, Donnelly assumed that there had to be a relationship between the two cultures. A modern archeologist might conclude (from the axes shown)

---

[96] From the Introduction, Donnelly, Ignatius (1976) *Atlantis: The Antediluvian World*. Dover Publications, Inc. P. xvi

that the process of hammering out cold metal tended to create certain shapes.[97]

Bleiler sums up Donnelly's thought as a radical form of material monism that attempts to trace all cultural phenomena back to a single point. For Donnelly, Atlantis was this focal point, anthropologically speaking. This quest for a singular point of emanation is an explicit rendering, by way of the act of searching, for some concept, language, or idea that leads back to the fissure that arose between humanity and nature. By directing the focus of this quest towards Atlantis, Donnelly appears to be placing his faith in the possibility that the answer he's looking for is lurking there among some underwater ruins. "Atlantis," like the great flood in Genesis, is a signifier that points the reader's attention towards the "waters" mentioned in the opening of Genesis.

At the time of Donnelly's writing the "historical" basis for Atlantis was a few references made by Plato in some of his longer dialogues. In this respect, the locating of, and subsequent fidelity to, a feature that was not emphasized as being foundational within the referenced text shows the conspiracy theorist to be a nuanced reader, and it is the translation of an implicit feature into an explicit theory, or discourse, that imparts the grandeur of myth onto the conspiracy theorist. Hence, the pre-existence of the sea within the Creation narrative is the first place within the text that is, as I put it earlier, "vital" to the connection between the myth and the conspiracy theorist. Myth, through its rendering as conspiracy theory, works from an anonymous, collective source to an articulated, personal narrative. The theorizing is an act of responsibility that does not merely distinguish the individual qua individual; it, as Heidegger would say, presupposes the individual as such. Not every theorist will be a monist in the way that Donnelly was, there are individuals who place as much stock in a mythical Atlantis as they do in UFOs or the Nephilim. But the trait that usually draws the most attention to the conspiracy theorist

---

[97]Ibid p. xvi

as being a "conspiracy theorist" is a method of radical reductionism.

Plato

Donnelly gives a list of thirteen propositions he claims can be proven by his treatise. The most important of which were:

3. That Atlantis was the region where man first rose from a state of barbarism to civilization.

5. That it was the true Antediluvian world: the Garden of Eden; the Gardens of Hesperides; the Elysian Fields; the Gardens of Aleinous; the Mesomphalos; the Olympos; the Asgard of the traditions of the ancient nations; representing a universal memory of a great land where early mankind dwelt for ages in peace and happiness.

7. That the mythology of Egypt and Peru represented the original religion of Atlantis, which was sun-worship.

11. That Atlantis was the original seat of the Aryan or Indo-European family of nations, as well as of the Semitic peoples, and possibly also of the Turanian races.

12. That Atlantis perished in a terrible convulsion of nature, in which the whole island sunk into the ocean, with nearly all its inhabitants.

13. That a few persons escaped by ships or rafts, and carried to the nations east and west the tidings of the appalling catastrophe, which has survived to our own time in the Flood and Deluge legends of the different nations of the old and new worlds.[98]

---

[98] Ibid pp. 1 - 2

These are some of his most important points and they coincide quite closely with a lot of contemporary occult/new age views of Atlantis. Any of the items on Donnelly's list that are of lesser importance, which were omitted, I will deal with as they arise. For now, what is important is that Donnelly's theory is textually grounded primarily on the descriptions of Atlantis that Plato gives in *The Timaeus* and *The Critias.* The origin story essentially begins:

> I have before remarked, in speaking of the allotments of the gods, that they distributed the whole earth into portions differing in extent, and made themselves temples and sacrifices. And Poseidon, receiving for his lot the island of Atlantis, begat children by a mortal woman and settled them in a part of the island which I will proceed to describe.[99]

Plato then goes on to explain how Poseidon fell in love with a mortal woman named Cleito, leading him to:

> ... breaking the ground, [which] enclosed the hill in which she dwelt all around, making alternate zones of sea and land, larger and smaller, encircling one another; there were two of land and three of water, which he turned as with a lathe out of the centre of the island, equidistant every way, so that no man could get to the island, for ships and voyages were not yet heard of. He himself, as he was a god, found no difficulty in making special arrangements for the centre island, bringing two streams of water under the earth, which he caused to ascend as springs, one of warm water and the other of cold, and making every variety of food to spring up abundantly in the

---

[99] Ibid p. 13

earth. He also begat and brought up five pairs of male children, dividing the island of Atlantis into ten portions ....[100]

The eldest of these sons was named Atlas who reigned as king of Atlantis and accumulated a great deal of wealth by trading with other lands. Plato describes the land as being especially bountiful, containing all manner of fruits, berries, and beverages. The place was a veritable Garden of Eden, and like Eden it would eventually be lost. The island-dwellers, who had originally been virtuous and noble, began to atrophy morally:

By such reflections, and by the continuance in them of a divine nature, all that which we have described waxed and increased in them; but when this divine portion began to fade away in them, and became diluted too often, and with too much of the mortal admixture, and the human nature got the upper-hand, then, they being unable to bear their fortune, became unseemly, and to him who had an eye to see, they began to appear base and lost the fairest of their precious gifts; but to those who had no eye to see the true happiness, they still appeared glorious and blessed at the very time when they were filled with unrighteous avarice and power. Zeus, the god of gods, who rules with law, and is able to see into such things, perceiving that an honorable race was in a most wretched state, and wanting to inflict punishment on them, that they might be chastened and improved, collected all the gods into his most holy habitation, which, being placed in the centre of the world, sees all things that

---

[100] Ibid p. 13

partake of generation. And when he called them together he spake as follows ....[101]

At this point the narrative abruptly ends, but we are led to assume that Zeus issues the order for Atlantis's destruction. Since the Atlanteans benefited so much from the use of water on their island it is tempting to read a kind of Shakespearean tragedy into its destruction.[102] Most scholarly attempts that overlook the textual reference to the diminishment of the "divine" genetic traits and an increase in the human traits take this path because there doesn't seem to be a clear-cut aporia within the text, a facet which was a hallmark of the Socratic dialogue. Donnelly himself rejects this interpretation stating:

> Neither is there any evidence on the face of this history that Plato sought to convey in it a moral or political lesson in the guise of a fable, as did Bacon in the "New Atlantis," and More in the "Kingdom of Nowhere." There is no ideal republic delineated here. It is a straightforward, reasonable history of a people ruled over by their kings, living and progressing as other nations have lived and progressed in their day."[103]

Another conspiracy theorist, self-described "Christian contrarian" Gary Wayne, who writes extensively about the antediluvian world, takes note of the personage of Poseidon in the minds of early peoples and how his specter would continue into our modern world:

> Central to all the primordial cultures was the famous, mythological sea god Poseidon, who

---

[101] Ibid pp. 20 - 21
[102] Shakespearian tragedy
[103] Ibid p. 23

fathered five sets of scurrilous twins through sexual relations with the daughters of men. Poseidon was brother to the god Zeus, the god who overthrew the rebellious Titans. Poseidon's twins grew up to be giants, Titan/demigods, who reigned over the mythological continent and civilization of Atlantis. Atlantis was, of course, the mythological civilization that most pantheistic cultures of antiquity linked themselves to as the source for their culture. What is most intriguing with the legends of Atlantis is that the Freemasons would like to recreate the Atlantean antediluvian Age of Enlightenment, which had ten kingdoms with ten governments and ten kings, famous for being the helm of antediluvian world government. Freemasons fever to reincarnate world government, rebuilt with the Atlantean model of ten kingdoms, where fallen angels had regular sexual relations with humans. [104]

The result of this sexual union between fallen angels and humans would be the Nephilim, i.e., the giants who walked the earth prior to the flood. Wayne's passage, to a certain extent, dovetails with one of Donnelly's propositions (number 9), which states that: "the gods and goddesses of the ancient Greeks, the Phoenicians, the Hindoos, and the Scandinavians were simply the kings, queens, and heroes of Atlantis; and the acts attributed to them in mythology are a confused recollection of real historical events."[105]

It is crucial to point out that this destruction by the sea is the second "vital" point of connection between the myth and the conspiracy narrative. The development that occurs between these two points works this way: a textual component that precedes, or

---

[104] Wayne, Gary (2014) *The Genesis 6 Conspiracy*. Trusted Books, A Division of Deep River Books. P. 21
[105] Donnelly, Ignatius (1976) *Atlantis: The Antediluvian World*. Dover Publications, Inc. P. 2

at least co-exists with, the Creation narrative is then transformed into a textual component that is significant enough to be used as the end of the text itself. In this case it is not only an ending of the text, but a definitive marking of the end of an epoch, or age (the Antediluvian). Plato's account is so striking, in this respect, because his narration ends right before Zeus utters the proclamation that will destroy Atlantis.

Donnelly, Wayne, and a wide variety of conspiracy theorists, past and present, put a great deal of stock in some version of the Atlantis narrative because "great flood" narratives seem to exist throughout the world's cultures.[106] The most significant one, however, is the flood depicted in Genesis. Donnelly claims that there are five points at which the two narratives converge.

The first is that "the land destroyed by water was the country in which the civilization of the human race originated,"[107] and that this could not have been "Europe, Asia, Africa, America, or Australia, for there has been no universal destruction of the people of those regions [...]."[108] The second is that Zeus destroyed Atlantis for the same reasons that God flooded the earth, i.e., wickedness. The third is that both civilizations were destroyed with water. The fourth is that the Edenic period is depicted in the Bible as being a golden age filled with peace and devoid of sin, and that this description aligns closely with the early ages of Atlantis.

---

[106] Wayne has a whole chapter listing and describing these deluges; Donnelly states that: "the Egyptians, who possessed the memory of many partial deluges, regarded this as "the great deluge of all" which hints at the possibility that Egyptian flood narratives were inspired by the annual flooding of the Nile river. Ibid p. 67

[107] Ibid p. 72. Donnelly argues that these places developed deluge stories after the basic narrative had been imported into them by individuals who had survived the original deluge.

[108] Ibid p. 73

The fifth, and last point, which corresponds with theories about Nephilim is that:

> In both the Bible history and Plato's story the destruction of the people was largely caused by the intermarriage of the superior or divine race, "the sons of God," with an inferior stock, "the children of men," whereby they were degraded and rendered wicked.[109]

For these reasons, Donnelly states conclusively that: "the Antediluvian World was none other than Atlantis."[110]

Gary Wayne, in contrast, is less definitive. He seems to imply that the Atlantis narrative is possibly a secular retelling of the Biblical flood narrative, which conforms to his overall thesis that all religions have myths relating to a great deluge (some have myths of giants as well); hence, somehow, they are all derived from the authentically real story presented by the Bible. However, the level of detail he goes into regarding Atlantis and its goings-on could leave one with the impression that the great flood of the Bible occurred simultaneously with the destruction of Atlantis. One could read Wayne's textual ambiguity in this regard as a technique for preserving the narrative richness that we have identified pertaining to myth.

A significant contrast between Donnelly and Wayne that should also be noted is that Wayne sees the bloodline, which was brought to earth by fallen angels (Poseidon is considered a fallen angel of sorts according to Wayne's theory) as infernal. This bloodline led to the creation of the Nephilim, was preserved by secret societies, and will eventually spawn the Antichrist. Donnelly seems to take Plato at his word and views it as legitimately divine with the increase in human admixture as being the corrupting influence.

---

[109] Ibid p. 73
[110] Ibid p. 74

The question of whether Atlantis actually existed is not merely a topic borne of modernity – it was debated by the ancients as well. After Plato's death, Aristotle dismissed the island's appearance in the dialogues as a fiction. For generations after, there were Platonists who claimed that Plato's account was straight history, while most Aristotelians "took the opposite point of view and maintained that the lost continent was pure myth."[111] Neither view at that time had to countenance the more fantastic aspects of the narrative, which would pop up over the ensuing two thousand years. Donnelly's work does not focus on any of the supernatural claims that have grown up around the Atlantis narrative; most of these theories, which link Atlantis to alien or Tesla-like scientific advances, came about in the Twentieth Century.

The Revival of Atlantis in Popular Culture

You remember Atlantis
Donovan, the guy with the brocade coat,
Used to sing to you about Atlantis
You loved it, you were so involved then[112]

There are many historical figures who had a hand in bringing Atlantis to the forefront of mainstream culture in the mid-Twentieth Century. The first person on this list is Edgar Cayce (March 18, 1877 – January 3, 1945). Growing up as a devout Christian in rural Kentucky, Cayce experienced a variety of physical traumas (being struck by a baseball, being beaten by his father, etc.) that often resulted in him falling into a clairvoyant trance. These trances not only led him to improve scholastically, they also led him to make medical diagnoses of people who either

---

[111] *Mystic Places: By the Editors of Time-Life Books* (1987) Time Life-Books. P . 20
[112] "The Blue Light" by Frank Zappa. From 1981's *Tinsel Town Rebellion*

visited or sent him letters asking for home remedies. Cayce is primarily remembered in conspiracy theory circles for his visions of the ancient world, specifically Atlantis. One of Cayce's biographers, Jess Stearn, ties these visions to the mysteries of reincarnation:

> Atlantis, of course, was born of his flights into reincarnation, since so many had "lived" there once before. In his discourses on Atlantis, describing its progress and collapse, he said the last surviving islands had disappeared in the area of the Caribbean about ten thousand years ago. He predicted that land would rise again one day soon in this area. However, the rise would be gradual, and freshly emerging land might not evidence itself for a while. The Atlantis story was esoteric but fascinating. With the age-old Atlantean breakup, Cayce had seen a dispersal of its superior culture to the Mediterranean, Central and South America, and even parts of the United States.[113]

This paragraph contains pretty much every New Age trope ever conceived regarding Atlantis: superior culture? Check. Survivors of the cataclysm bringing remnants of their culture to other lands? Check. Rising again? Check. It is for these reasons, as well as the fact that Cayce's work dovetailed closely with turn-of-the-century occult mysticism,[114] that he was so important to the revival of Atlantis in popular culture.

Cayce's renown originally stemmed from the diagnoses he proffered to the people who wrote letters describing their ailments. This practice, which took place while he was sleeping, was eventually parlayed into visions of the ancient past and

---

[113] Stearn, Jess (1967) *Edgar Cayce –The Sleeping Prophet*. Bantam Books. P. 11

[114] Despite this, Cayce was by all accounts a devout Christian.

predictions for the future. Cayce did not write out the visions he experienced, this was usually done either by his wife or secretary, Gladys Davis. The texts describing Cayce's visions gained greater notoriety once they were utilized by his biographers: Thomas Sugrue, Sidney Kirkpatrick, Gina Cerminara, and Jess Stearn (among others,) to popularize his persona.

Stearn's biography, written in 1967, seeks to resolve the fabulous nature of many of Cayce's predictions with contemporary scientific developments. The following, which relates to Atlantis, is but one example:

> Cayce often intruded in the areas of science. Once he provocatively spoke of a death ray the Atlanteans had devised to eliminate deadly beasts. In the reading, given in 1933, he predicted a similar ray would be discovered here by 1958 [...] What hogwash this must have seemed at the time, and what hogwash it would still appear, if not for passing press reports such as this, out of Denver in December of 1961: "Scientists are developing a death ray weapon designed to turn anything it is focused on into a wisp of gaseous vapor. Dr. Carl L. Kober of the Martin Company plant disclosed the weapon would be partially nuclear-powered. It would accomplish its destructive work by throwing a fantastically hot beam on the subject ...the disintegration ray, sounding like something from science fiction, would be designed for use in terrestrial warfare."[115]

Such reconciliations were pushed to their breaking-point with Cayce's prediction of a giant cataclysm that would destroy San Francisco, Los Angeles, and New York sometime between 1958

---

[115] Ibid pp. 14 - 15

and 1998.[116] Writing from his vantage point in the mid-nineteen sixties, Stearn notes:

> The Cayce year 1958 has passed, prefacing some earthly fireworks as he suggested, and now 1968, or '69, will soon arrive to test Atlantis rising, though Cayce explained elsewhere that the rise would be gradual, and might not break the surface immediately. After that, who knows? Perhaps the break-ups could be prayed away, as Cayce so often suggested, without such ever materializing. And yet even as a source of destruction was possibly gathering momentum in the crust of the earth, under his very feet, man could still look overhead hopefully for eternal salvation.[117]

The aforementioned "break-ups" are the predicted cataclysms and outside of some large earthquakes, fires, and 9/11, they did not come to pass in the definitive manner predicted by Cayce. On one level, Stearn's recourse to divine intervention might seem like a cop-out and a means to avoiding the failure of Cayce's visions to manifest. However, there is a certain poetic charm to this passage as it seems to implicitly link the power of prayer to change the material realm with the dream-world from which Cayce drew for his visions. The commonality between the two is that both eschew rationality and surrender the subject to an unknown logic, or possibly no logic at all.

Cayce's visions are interesting from a contemporary mystical perspective because they direct our attention to the role played by dreams in our understanding of reality. On a material-scientific level, one could argue that dreams are just a jumbled version of our normal, waking consciousness that occur during various stages of sleep. A more supernatural view could take

---

[116] Ibid pp. 31 - 33
[117] Ibid p. 287

dreaming to be a form of astral-projection, which is essentially what the followers of Cayce claim he was doing; or as a means of perception that uncovers hidden facets of our own unconscious minds, as Freud would claim.

It could be argued that the subjective act of dreaming is so mystifying that one might acknowledge the scientific reality attendant to the act of sleep, but still retain an agnosticism about certain occurrences that take place within dreams, i.e., some appearances might be merely scrambled representations of day-to-day life, while others might act as keys to hidden ideas and moral values that we neglect in waking life. It seems safe to say, that on some level, the act of dreaming can bring us closer to the early "adolescent" state we have associated with man prior to, or immediately following the fall from Eden. Objects, persons, and properties are simultaneously more distinct and apparent, as well as more elusive and mysterious. It is no coincidence that Cayce's visions of Atlantis would gain more ground culturally at the same time that more attention was being paid to dream-states and New Age maxims regarding "the power of dreams."

This "new age" of course occurred in the midst of post-war America and it entailed all manner of science fiction and psychedelic music. Something that Bleiler does not mention in his introduction to *Atlantis* is that Donnelly is fascinated by the notion that a sophisticated, for its day, society existed roughly 11,000 years ago. This trope is often repeated in conspiracy theories and I see it as being hermeneutically dependent upon science fiction and fantasy literature, both of which were by-products of modernity.[118]

Lemuria!

---

[118] *Ratner's Star* (1989) by Don Delillo also addresses the theory that technologically adept societies existed in the distant past. Delillo's treatment, however, mostly eschews science fiction tropes.

In contrast to the case of Atlantis, where we have a literary origin, the case of Lemuria has its origin in scientific hypothesis. In 1864 zoologist Philip Sclater published an article titled, "The Mammals of Madagascar" in *The Quarterly Journal of Science.* In the article Sclater postulated that:

> The anomalies of the mammal fauna of Madagascar can best be explained by supposing that a large continent occupied parts of the Atlantic and Indian Oceans; that this continent was broken up into islands, of which some have become amalgamated with Africa, some with what is now Asia; and that in Madagascar and the Mascarene Islands we have existing relics of this great continent, for which I should propose the name Lemuria![119]

"Lemuria," not to be confused with "Lumania" – the mythological civilization from where the eccentric musical duo of Barnes & Barnes is said to hail – is etymologically derived from "lemur." The attempt to explain the distribution of this species of mammal throughout Madagascar, India, and Africa led Sclater to postulate the existence of Lemuria, which is oftentimes conflated with "Mu," a continent that was purported to have resided within the Pacific Ocean thousands of years ago. [120] In the early-Twentieth Century, Sclater's emphasis on land-bridges fell out of favor in the scientific community, superseded by theories of plate tectonics and continental drift. At this point the torch was immediately picked up by the occult community, specifically, the Theosophical Society. The shift was gradual but began in earnest when the German naturalist Ernst Heinrich Haeckel postulated in

---

[119] https://en.wikipedia.org/wiki/Lemuria_(continent)#Evolution_of_the_idea accessed 01/09/21

[120] According to Sclater's theory Lemuria would have resided in the Indian Ocean, a feature that is neglected in later theories.

the 1876 edition of *The History of Creation* that Lemuria might be the home of the evolutionary missing link.[121] This kind of vague scientific conjecture was all the Theosophists needed to pick up the ball and run with it.

Ideas associated with the lost continent of MU, such as its being the original Eden, were subsequently transposed onto the Lemuria narrative, a trend which persists to this day. The Theosophical Society, which was formed by Madame Helena Blavatsky and Henry Steel Olcott in New York in the 1870s, focused a great deal of their theorization on the mythic prehistory of man. In her writings, Blavatsky addressed both Atlantis and Lemuria, but gave special deference to Lemuria because she believed it to be older.

According to Madame Blavatsky and her followers, the Lemurians were the third of seven "root" races of mankind. Their continent occupied most of the southern atmosphere, and they were originally hermaphrodite people who communicated only by psychic powers conferred upon them by a third eye. The fourth race was the Atlanteans, who evolved from the Lemurians as Lemuria sank beneath the sea millions of years ago; they inhabited a spur of Lemuria in the northern Atlantic that was itself to sink later, finally disappearing about 9,000 years ago. Madame Blavatsky believed refugees from that disaster escaped to Central Asia, where they evolved into modern Hindus and Europeans.[122]

Besides possessing psychic powers, other mystics such as Rudolf Steiner, claimed the inhabitants of Lemuria and Atlantis possessed advanced technology, such as "airships."[123] Needless to say, the idea of these inventions having existed thousands, or

---

[121] https://blogs.scientificamerican.com/history-of-geology/a-geologists-dream-the-lost-continent-of-lemuria/ accessed on 01/10/21
[122] *Mystic Places: By the Editors of Time-Life Books* (1987) Time Life-Books. P. 28
[123] Ibid p. 29

even millions of years ago on earth was a formative influence on the nascent science fiction genre. It would be through these two avenues, occult literature and science fiction, that the idea of a lost, technologically advanced society, that lies deep in the unrecorded past would enter the conspiracy theory culture of the Twentieth Century.

Both occult literature and science fiction operate in the same way. The fascination that people have with Lemuria can be interpreted as an instinct to propose a mythological antecedent to something that is already adequately mythological (Atlantis). It is possible for someone to believe that Lemuria existed and that Atlantis did not. However, this defeats the point because, in a textual sense, someone acquires the belief in Atlantis and then is inducted into the deeper, more esoteric, belief in Lemuria. This process of acquiring more obscure concepts and theories as one advances through the narratives (or descends into the "rabbit-hole") is akin to the Hermetical practices that were utilized by groups like the Theosophical Society and the Golden Dawn, wherein adepts were given more esoteric spiritual studies and spells as they advanced through the ranks of the order.

There aren't a lot of books on Lemuria, the most interesting, and comprehensive, one that I've come across is *The Lost Civilization of Lemuria* by a certain Frank Joseph. Prior to his debut book, *The Destruction of Atlantis*, being published in 1987, Joseph had been known as Frank Collin and had been a member of the American Nazi Party until his Jewish heritage was revealed (his father's surname was Cohn) and he resigned in the late sixties. Undeterred, Collin founded the equally LARPY National Socialist Party of America in 1970.

Throughout the seventies, Collin and his party drew headlines and notoriety with his bombastic and insensitive schemes to hold Nazi rallies in Jewish and minority communities throughout the Midwest. Most of these plans never came to fruition and Collin was ousted from his own party when one of his underlings, Harold Covington, claimed to have found child pornography in Collins's desk and released these images to the police. Collin was arrested and served three years in prison at the Pontiac Correctional Center where he would meet Russell E. Burrows, a prison guard and amateur archaeologist who claimed to have discovered a cave filled with rare artifacts in southern Illinois, which was dubbed "Burrows Cave." Burrows Cave was most likely a hoax, nevertheless, the interaction with a man so enchanted with the hidden mysteries of the distant past most likely gave Collin an indication as to what new avenues he could explore once he was released from prison. Hence, Frank Collin became Frank Joseph.

Despite its infamous pedigree *The Lost Civilization of Lemuria* is a pretty well-written and engaging read. Like Donnelly before him, Joseph specifies a set of propositions that he intends for his book to prove, these are as follows:

1. Lemuria undoubtedly did exist in the ancient past.
2. It was the birthplace of civilized humans.
3. It was the biblical "Garden of Eden."
4. The Lemurians developed and used an incredibly high-level technology, unlike our own and superior to it in some ways.
5. They suffered not one but a series of natural catastrophes over many thousands of years before ultimately vanishing.
6. Their mystical principles survived to fundamentally influence some of the world's major religions.[124]

We have already seen that number two is a repetition of what Ernst Haeckel postulated in the late nineteenth century and number three can be seen as contingent upon this theory (in a metaphorical sense). However, since Joseph speculates that the Lemurians possessed a technology "superior" to our own there is the possibility that besides being the birthplace of civilized humans, this Eden might have been idyllic as well. Joseph's evidence for this technological prowess is the ancient and

---

[124] Joseph, Frank (2006) *The Lost Civilization of Lemuria.* Bear & Company, a division of Inner Traditions International. P. 11

elaborate canal system in Nan Madol[125] as well as petroglyphs, statues, and monuments found on Easter Island. [126] The connection between the two places is then qualified by a "shared script," that was "an inheritance both received from the same Motherland."[127]

Before we move onto points five and six[128] we need to address Joseph's predecessor in this endeavor: James Churchward (February 23, 1851 – January 4, 1936). Churchward was a colonel in the British military and was stationed in India to help with famine relief. During this stay, Churchward was approached by a high priest at a Hindu temple as he was trying to decipher some writing on a bas-relief.[129]This high priest not only aided Churchward in understanding the inscription, but he also took him into his confidence, telling Churchward about a set of tablets that detailed the prehistory of India:

> The tale they told was like nothing found anywhere else. It related that an immense landmass had once existed in the Pacific Ocean from very ancient times. Here, humans built the first organized society, known as Mu, the Motherland of civilization. A theocracy of sun-worshipping priest-kings held sway for thousands of years, during which high levels of spiritual and cultural achievement were reached. Missionaries spread the enlightened tenets of their religion to east and west, while their fellow countrymen enjoyed generation after generation of

---

[125] Ibid pp. 19 - 25
[126] Ibid pp. 75 - 88
[127] Ibid p. 139
[128] There's no need to formally address point number one, since he wouldn't have written the book, or at least given it the title: *The Lost Civilization of Lemuria* if he was skeptical of Lemuria's existence.
[129] Ibid pp. 124 - 125

peace and plenty. About 12,000 years ago, however, the Earth was shaken by violent convulsions, and the kingdom of Mu suffered a natural catastrophe. Its lands were broken up by a series of major earthquakes, then sank almost entirely beneath the sea. Some of the South Pacific islands are the small, scattered remnants of that once might empire. Its people were not annihilated, however. Some survivors sailed as far afield as the Bay of Bengal, where they sparked civilization for the first time in India. Over time, the immigrants were assimilated, but their story still survived in the crumbling tablets gingerly handled by Churchward and the aged priest.[130]

During his lifetime, Churchward travelled to various exotic locales seeking more information about Mu. Oftentimes his ambitions were dashed when interviewees placed this mythical land in the Atlantic Ocean, thus conflating it with Atlantis. Churchward's hopes were rekindled when he befriended Augustus Le Plongeon, an archaeologist who had been deciphering Mayan hieroglyphs.[131] With Le Plongeon's aid, Churchward began work on *The Lost Continent of Mu*, which was published in 1926.[132] Four books followed, while "each book was progressively less credible and more outrageous than the previous one," notes Joseph.[133]

---

[130] Ibid p. 126

[131] Ibid p. 129. A good deal of the obsession with Mayan prophecy, including the 2012 endtimes prediction, can be traced back to Le Plongeon's work and influence.

[132] This is in spite of Le Plongeon's research contradicting Churchward's thesis that Mu was located in the Pacific Ocean; his readings stipulated that it was in the Atlantic.

[133] Ibid p. 133

One of the primary criticisms Churchward faced was that he had no photographic evidence of the tablets he had been shown in India and refused to disclose the location of the temple in which they resided. Despite these problems, Joseph uses some of the basic claims made by Churchward and then conflates the two legendary continents of Mu and Lemuria into one entity. When it comes to explaining the great technologies developed by the Lemurians, Joseph hints at the possibility that they were the result of alien technology. He briefly references explorations undertaken by Erich Von Däniken but seems to be more receptive to the idea that the technology, which was primarily architectural, was contingent upon certain electromagnetic "hotspots" scattered across the continent.[134] This is not to say that Joseph is resistant to purely supernatural theories. "In any case," he says, "the Mu achieved great architectural feats, because they were renowned for their mastery of spiritual forces known as mana, which they received from their god, Ha-Mu-ka."[135]

There is, however, no reason not to reconcile these wondrous phenomena back to a materialistic/scientific explanation, and later in the book we will see that most conspiracy theorists of the last seventy years or so will do so by invoking either alien technology or secret ley lines, which harbor electromagnetic energy that can be tapped beneath the earth's surface. Before we can move on from Lemuria there are two very significant points that need to be addressed. The first has to do with the fifth point of Joseph's thesis: "They suffered not one but a series of natural catastrophes over many thousands of years before ultimately vanishing." For our analysis this entails a dialectical reading of the relationship between Atlantis and Lemuria. The most obvious distinction between the two is that one resided in the Atlantic Ocean and the other in the Pacific; but even though both were destroyed, the narratives surrounding

---

[134] This idea relates to the notion of ley lines and will be discussed more thoroughly when we look at the theories of John Michell.
[135] Ibid p. 168

their respective falls diverge greatly. As we have seen, Atlantis's destruction is linked to the antediluvian flood in the Bible because both were seen to result from mankind's hubris/fall from grace coupled with a divine wrath. In contrast to this, Lemuria's demise is gradual and not divinely directed.

> Missing from most Polynesian traditions is any association with a fall of some kind from heavenly grace. The moralistic version in Genesis seems to be a particularly Hebrew inflection, in which guilt was used by the priests to control their congregations.[136]

Some might see Joseph's comments here as harboring traces of his older ideological persuasion, however, Nietzsche made similar statements about Judeo-Christian morality in *The Genealogy of Morals* and such critiques abound within the occult and new age movements, insofar as they are meant to resonate with paganism ("paganism" conceived as an antithesis of Christianity). The last point of significance that pertains to the Lemuria narrative has to do with point six of Joseph's thesis: "Their mystical principles survived to fundamentally influence some of the world's major religions." The purveyors of these "mystical principles" would have been the "Naacals." Joseph refers to this group as "the Lemurian sacred brotherhood"[137] The Naacals were postulated by Churchward as high priests who journeyed to distant parts of Asia, the Pacific Islands, New Zealand, and both North and South America; they were a "secretive people who preserved what they knew in silence. They were sworn never to reveal any of the rites of the Mu to those who did not belong."[138]

Thoroughly mysterious as they were, we can assume that given the location of their missionary work, the Naacals' belief

---

[136] Ibid p. 138
[137] Ibid p. 125
[138] Ibid p. 175

system was more aligned with Hinduism, Buddhism, and tribal animism. This schema would conform to the dialectic we sketched out wherein the Atlantis/Antediluvian belief system is more in line with a Judeo-Christian idea of divinity. Joseph cites Cayce's brief references to Lemuria as being supplemental to Churchward's basic theory:

> Lemurian spiritual greatness, Cayce observed, was superior even to the high levels or paranormal power developed in Atlantis. Here he is richly validated by an abundance of Asian, Australian, Pacific Islander, and pre-Columbian American traditions that define their versions of Lemuria as the sunken Motherland of sacred wisdom. Australian Aborigines believe that the tenets of their Dream-time cult arrived from the "land of Perfection" before it was engulfed by the sea. Burotu is remembered as the sunken realm of powerful priests who spread the secrets of their high magic from Tonga to the Fiji Islands. The Chumash Indians of southern coastal California believed that the ancestors of their medicine men were missionaries from Lemuria, after which one of their offshore islands was originally named.[139]

The idea of the Naacals as mystical pilgrims who initiated a secret society of sorts in their host communities is a narrative that we will see repeated in a variety of contexts. The Templar narrative, for instance, is for our purposes a reiteration of the Naacal narrative. The initiatic structure, which is a characteristic that some writers attribute to Hermeticism, is also a reiteration of this narrative. Granted, to the true-believing conspiracy theorist, there is a belief in a linear chain of transmission, for example: the secrets possessed by aliens are passed to the Naacal, then to

---

[139] Ibid pp. 262 - 263

Pythagoras, then Plato, then to the proto-freemasonic groups, etc. Blavatsky's Theosophical Society, and its offshoots, would be early-Twentieth Century representatives of this type of ideation.

It is also noteworthy that one of the themes attendant to the Biblical and Atlantis narratives involves a written transmission of lost wisdom, i.e., "the seven sacred sciences" that were passed down after the flood, whereas the Lemurian/Mu tradition implies that the individuals themselves were instantiations of the culture they would or could create; and that they carried the essence of civilization within themselves and had no need of a written set of rules, or theories, to draw upon for this activity. The distinction and divide between word and idea, so to speak, as exemplified here, will go on to play a significant role in the next chapter.

Miscellaneous Spiritual Interpretations of the Sea

This brief section will attempt to tackle some of the mystical traditions borne out of early Christianity and how they relate to an atavistic apprehension of the sea.

I was doubtful about how I could integrate the mythical story of Saint Brendan's voyage into this chapter. My concern was whether the story was applicable to either myths or conspiracy theories. Upon reflection, I realized that it is so, because the supposed trip taken by Saint Brendan is a precursor to the Grail Mythos. So, you might ask: "Why not discuss him in the Grail Chapter?" That's a good question and the answer has to do with my personal connection to the myth, which was enough to make me feel obligated to grapple with this issue at this point in our discussion.

Sometime in the late 1990s, at a place that is itself now somewhat mythical, Tower Records, I encountered a magazine that from its cover promised to indulge all of my interests regarding Aleister Crowley, the Knights Templar, and the history of the occult. This was *Dagobert's Revenge* Volume 4, issue #1. I ended up foolishly lending this out to a co-worker a few years ago and never to get it back.[140] Ironically enough, this particular issue is the most scarce of the entire series. The editor and primary writer for the magazine was Tracy Twyman, whose work is scattered throughout this book because she tapped into a lot of the same things that interest me. The arc of her life also deserves a little bit of examination, in which we will indulge later. But for now it's important to go back in time to that moment when I glanced through this freshly purchased issue of *Dagobert's Revenge*.

The most notable thing about the magazine was that it had the hallmarks of a DIY "Zine" while simultaneously cultivating an antiquated Gothic aesthetic. This aesthetic was achieved through type fonts and illustrations. The most captivating illustration was an engraving, or painting, that looked like the maps made between the thirteenth and seventeenth centuries, that show giant squids, ocean monsters, exotic lands etc.; and which was captioned, "Christ crucified on a giant fish." This engraving however, is fascinating because of its subject matter; contrary to the caption's assertion, it is not the crucifixion of Christ that is occurring on this gigantic fish, but is instead St. Brendan saying mass.

St. Brendan (484 AD – 577 AD) was an Irish monk and explorer who, alongside a group of fellow monks, sailed to the Canary Islands. His story was immortalized in a Romantic novella written around 900 AD. The trip itself, and Brendan's fortitude therein, exemplifies the idea of journeying into the unknown, presaging the Grail quest. More important however is the "island" Brendan supposedly came across in his travels. According to Joseph Campbell, after leaving a green land filled with sheep, where it was summer year long, an extraordinary adventure befell the voyagers:

---

[140] If you take anything away from this book, let it be this: only lend out things you are willing to give away and never possess again.

On what appeared to be an island, level and without trees, they landed and, building a fire, set a cauldron full of fish to boil. However, no sooner was their fire alight than the island began to quake, and when, in terror, they tumbled back into their boat, they saw the island swim away with the cauldron. It was a whale, a great fish, the biggest of the fishes of the world, and it was ever trying to put its tail into its mouth but could not do so, because of its great bulk.[141]

Campbell sees this depiction of the fish trying to bite its own tail as representing the "world-surrounding Cosmic Ocean" – a theme that is common to mythologies all over the world.[142] This is one of a few synchronicities of note, while another is the forty years that Brendan and his shipmates were at sea: a reiteration of the forty years Moses wandered the desert.

After this misadventure with the giant fish, Brendan reversed his course and began sailing westward, whereupon he came across an island full of flowers and trees, "the Paradise of Birds" as Campbell calls it.[143] The textual appearance of this island is a repetition of the Atlantis myth. The island's mystery is shrouded in the sea and the ocean acts as a challenge that must be conquered in a literal sense. Campbell describes this ordeal in both physical and spiritual terms. In the case of the former, he describes how: "Brendan's monks had all but died to themselves in their passage of the terrible sea [...] and now, an undisturbed meditation on the everlasting mystery of being itself, that held

---

[141] Campbell, Joseph (2015) *Romance of the Grail: The Magic and Mystery of Arthurian Myth*. New World Library. Pp. 14 - 15
[142] Note that this also correlates with the Twyman quote regarding the "Canopy of Heaven" cited at the beginning of this chapter.
[143] Ibid, p. 16

them in a state of rapture."[144] In the case of the latter, Campbell says that the voyage showed the monks the radiance of the Kingdom of God as it existed here on earth: "All that is required for the vision is a slight but radical shift in perspective of the eye to bring us to a realization transcendent of the pairs of opposites: *I* and *Thou*, *right* and *wrong*, *this* and *that*."[145]

After these physical and spiritual trials Brendan was said to have travelled back and forth among the islands he had discovered and annually celebrated Easter Mass on the back of the great fish they had initially mistook for an island, and hence the engraving that found its way into the pages of *Dagobert's Revenge*.

Soon after the death of Saint Brendan, St. Maximus the Confessor (580 AD – 662 AD) combined the early Christian focus on the spiritual lineage between Biblical figures – not merely in a genealogical sense but in how they reflect basic spiritual archetypes – with a metaphorical interpretation of the sea:

> The prophet Jonah therefore signifies Adam, or our shared human nature, by bearing in himself mystically a figure of the following. Human nature has slipped from divine benefits, as from *Joppa*, and has descended, as though into a *sea*, into the misery of the present life, and been plunged into the chaotic and roaring waters of attachment to material objects. It has been swallowed whole by the *whale*, that spiritual and insatiable beast the Devil himself. It has been *enveloped with water* all around it, the water of temptations to evil, *up to the soul*, in the sense that human life has been submerged with temptations. [146]

---

[144] Ibid, p. 17
[145] Ibid, p. 20
[146] Maximus the Confessor (2003) *On the Cosmic Mystery of Jesus Christ* (translated by Paul M. Blowers and Robert Louis Wilken).

All of this is important because it represents a dogmatically Christian (Catholic, specifically) counterpoint to a more secular interpretation of the sea that is central not only to Freemasonry but also later critics of Christianity, such as Jordan Maxwell. For Maxwell, who in his book, *That Old Time Religion*, postulates a lineage between Christianity and earlier Egyptian religions (despite his overall emphasis on the role of the sun) makes concessions to aquatic idiosyncrasies:

> It was well understood by ancient man that our weather was caused and controlled by the Sun. It was a simple fact that God's Sun had the power to control storms at will. The ancient Egyptians taught that he did this as he rested in His heavenly boat while crossing the sky. Thus, we read that that God's Sun quieted the tempest, or great storm on the sea, while on his boat.

Unlike the Christian mystical tradition that seeks to reconcile the Gospels of the New Testament with its Jewish antecedents and basically accepts Jesus as a rabbi, or a product of the rabbinical tradition, these secular thinkers are trying to bypass Judaism and tie Jesus to older traditions. Like Maxwell, Christopher Knight and Robert Lomas, whose book *The Hiram Key* will be discussed in greater detail in the next two chapters, see Jesus's role as the Christ as a continuation of the Egyptian god Horus. There is also an emphasis on the "watery" connotations associated with Jesus and his followers, i.e., fishermen, fishes, etc., which, in a literal sense would imply that the men being fished are being brought out of the sea and onto dry land, almost as a sort of

---

St. Vladimer's Seminary Press. P. 148. "Joppa" is where Jonah decided to flee to after disobeying God's command to prophesize in Nineveh. It is en route to Joppa when he is thrown overboard and swallowed by a whale.

awakening. On a less direct, more aesthetic understanding, it is almost as if the historical personage of Jesus contained a multitude of Antediluvian narratives, repackaged for a new epoch.

Chapter Four: The Significance of the Cosmos

Genesis 1 summarizes the creation of the sky and the heavens this way:

> And God said let there be light: and there was light. And God saw the light, that it was good: and God divided the light from the darkness. And God called the light Day, and the darkness he called Night. And the evening and the morning were the first day. And God said, let there be a firmament in the midst of the waters, and let it divide the waters from the waters. And God made the firmament, and divided the waters which were under the firmament from the waters which were above the firmament: and it was so. And God called the firmament Heaven.[147]

This account is perhaps an abbreviated version of an older Jewish legend:

> Several heavens were created, seven in fact, each to serve a purpose of its own. The first, the one visible to man, has no function except that of covering up the light during the nighttime; therefore it disappears every morning. The planets are fastened to the second of the heavens; in the third the manna is made for the pious in the hereafter; the fourth contains the celestial Jerusalem together with the Temple, in which Michael ministers as high priest, and offers the souls of the pious as sacrifices. In the fifth heaven, the angel hosts reside, and sing the praise of God, though only during the night, for by day it is the task of Israel on earth to give glory to

---

[147] *The Holy Bible* (Authorized King James Version). Thomas Nelson & Sons, Genesis 1:3 – 8

God on high. The sixth heaven is an uncanny spot; there originate most of the trials and visitations ordained for the earth and its inhabitants. Snow lies heaped up there and hail [...] Doors of fire separate these celestial chambers, which are under the supervision of the archangel Metatron [...] The seventh heaven, on the other hand, contains naught but what is good and beautiful: right, justice and mercy, the storehouses of life, peace, and blessing, the souls of the pious, the souls and spirits of unborn generations, the dew with which God will revive the dead on the resurrection day, and, above all, the Divine Throne, surrounded by the seraphim, the ofanin, the holy Hayyot, and the ministering angels.[148]

This passage comes from Louis Ginzberg (November 28, 1873 – November 11, 1953), who in the early part of the Twentieth Century transcribed what is commonly referred to as the *Haggadah*, which is essentially a transcription of all the Old Testament stories that existed as oral traditions or appeared in more obscure books related to the *Talmud* or the *Zohar*.

Perhaps the more elaborate legend came about after the shorter version and is the product of embellishment. Regardless as to which story preceded which, the overall mythological reading is made richer by the ambiguity of precedence and acts as further supporting evidence for my claim that the "meta" aspect of mythological narratives entails the demand for the creation of further narratives.

According to Ginzberg, God created seven earths that correspond with these seven heavens. There is most likely an additional numerological correspondence between these two occurrences of the number seven and the "seven spirits of God"

---

[148] Ginzberg, Louis (2008) *The Legends of the Jews, Volumes I & II.* Forgotten Books. P. 12

(Wisdom, Understanding, Counsel, Might, Knowledge, Fear of the Lord, and Delight in the Fear of the Lord) which appear in Revelation 5:6 situated before the Throne of God.[149] The number seven also appears in the esoteric idea of seven "sacred" sciences that were transmitted from Adam to his children.

The story of the Tower of Babel, like the majority of the Book of Genesis, is generally interpreted as a myth whose symbolism is intended to reveal religious truths. Unlike other parts of Genesis, however, the Babel story explicitly imparts an explanation as to how and why different peoples of the world speak different languages. This explicit interpretation clearly marks the story as being mythic; it is also an interpretation that often overshadows any implicit readings that would constitute a strongly religious reading of the text.[150] For this reason, we will analyze this narrative through a variety of lenses: historically, religiously, and in a literary sense, in order to achieve a multifaceted reading that will bring a fuller import of this story into a contemporary context.

The Babel narrative occurs in chapter eleven of Genesis, after the great flood described in chapters six through nine, wherein it states that the city of Babel was located at the beginning of Nimrod's kingdom in the land of Shinar:

> And the whole earth was of one language, and of one speech. And as they migrated from the east, they came upon a plain in the land of Shinar and settled there. And they said to one another, Come let us make bricks and burn them thoroughly. And

---

[149] We can infer that this "Throne of God" is the "Divine Throne" located in the seventh heaven.

[150] A similar example would be the story of Adam naming all the animals in Eden as an explanation for how these names came into being. Keep in mind that both stories are centered around the issue of linguistics: in Adam's case it is names, in the case of Babel it is languages –the medium by which names are articulated.

they had brick for stone, and bitumen for mortar. Then they said, "Come, let us build ourselves a city, and a tower with its top in the heavens, and let us make a name for ourselves; otherwise we shall be scattered abroad upon the face of the whole earth." The LORD came down to see the city and the tower, which the mortals had built. And the LORD said, Behold, the people *is* one, and they have all one language; and this they begin to do: and now nothing will be restrained from them, which they have imagined to do.

Go to, let us go down, and there confound their language, that they might not understand one another's speech. So the Lord scattered them abroad from thence upon the face of all the earth: and they left off to build the city. Therefore is the name of it called Babel; because the Lord did there confound the language of all the earth: and from thence did the Lord scatter them abroad upon the face of all the earth.[151]

The relationship between the explicit secular narrative and the implicit religious narrative is an important element in our discussion of conspiracy theories, insofar as it mimics the distinction between an "official" story and a "conspiracy" theory. The moral of the implicit narrative has to do with modesty in one's relationship with God – work on the tower is halted because it is seen an impious attempt to physically breach Heaven. It also designates characteristics of pride and hubris on the part of the builders. The explicit narrative on the other hand gives us a just-so story about how the different languages came into being. The explicit reading begs for the addition of further contingencies:

---

[151] *The Holy Bible* (Authorized King James Version). Thomas Nelson & Sons. Genesis 11, 1-9

when was this tower built? What real event inspired this myth? Etc.[152]

The city of Babel also represents a man-made attempt to duplicate the paradise of Eden. In this sense it is a retelling of a lost Utopia and within the context of a hermeneutical reading of the Bible (i.e., one that grants the reader the conscious foreshadowing of tragedy) it is, like Eden, doomed. This tragic reading, that the downfall of the protagonists is precipitated by some intrinsic element that had brought them to prominence, initially is formally traced back to the Shakespearian conception of tragedy.[153]

There is a notable distinction between Shinar and Eden in that Eden was not disrupted in the manner depicted in the Babel narrative. Adam and Eve were merely cast from its embrace and forced into the surrounding lands where they would be forced to toil. Shinar and its tower represent a nascent attempt at creating a civilization that, through its societal cohesion, could mitigate the dangers presented by the outside world. In the Bible, God does not literally destroy Shinar, he only destroys the language that gives its society cohesion.

A question arises as to why some people today are under the impression that God physically destroyed the Tower of Babel. One answer is that its destruction was portrayed in films. But

---

[152] This is equally true for Atlantis, wherein it is the idyllic nature and fantastic grandeur of the place that excites the imagination to ask more about the particulars of its existence. This is in contrast to the "moral" reasons given for why it was deemed worthy of destruction –the moral dimension of both stories, to some extent, circumscribe the inquisitiveness of the reader.

[153] There is also a similarity pertaining to the construction of the Tower of Babel and the assembly of the King James Bible. This revision itself mirrors God's decision to destroy and remake the world through the use of a great flood and continues one of the processes we are fleshing out: man's attempt to duplicate God's original work.

what inevitably follows this answer is: why did filmmakers present it this way? Perhaps it was done for dramatic effect. Another possibility is that the event is misremembered because the morality of the implicit reading has seeped into the retelling and, when thinking in Biblical terms, we associate God's wrath as being inherently linked to violence.

However, if we wanted to see this encroachment of the implicit reading in secular terms we might answer that there is an atavistic fear of technology, especially when that technology attenuates man's distance from the soil on which he dwells. This last response is akin to a metaphysical Puritanism that is suspicious of worldly things that promise to alleviate the toil attendant to life itself. A Structuralist interpretation that hews as close to the text as possible might read the Babel narrative as another destructive act of God; however, this time God has turned his wrath towards the text itself in the only way he can do so: by destroying the primordial language of his creation. By doing so, God becomes distinct from the Word of creation. The Gospel of John with its famous opening "In the beginning was the Word, and the Word was with God, and the Word was God." then, can be read as an attempt to rectify this fissure.

It is easy to think of the Babel narrative as like an onion, whereby the outer layers are what is known about the Tower scientifically or archeologically, i.e., that it was based on ancient Babylonian structures known as "ziggurats;"[154] more specifically, it was based on the Temple of Marduk (referred to as Etemenanki); and it stood roughly 300 feet in height[155]. The next

---

[154] Ziggurats were large structures with successively receding stories constructed in ancient Mesopotamia. These buildings were constructed with sun-baked bricks at the core and fire-baked bricks on the exterior. They served a religious purpose in that the tops housed shrines used for religious practices as well as practical purposes to protect people when the region flooded.

[155] From https://www.jewishvirtuallibrary.org/tower-of-babel accessed on 11/08/19

level of inquiry we can imagine as being devoted to the "just-so-story" of the origin of the world's languages. (Note that at this level we are blissfully indifferent to historical accuracy or moral considerations. This is basically analogous to the narrative that unicorns went extinct because they refused to board Noah's Ark).

At the next level, we find a variety of moral interpretations of the narrative. Both the Christian and Jewish traditions acknowledge a sense of hubristic transgression. Professor Ronald Hendel invokes Kafka's analysis that: "If it had been possible to build the Tower of Babel without ascending it, the work would have been permitted."[156] Hendel claims that the achievement of the Tower is itself not an offense to God, but the irresistible desire to ascend it and breach the heavenly realm is so, and it is this irresistible desire that makes us human. Peculiar to both religious and secular Jewish scholars is the textual reading that the desire to remain in one place and make a name for themselves was in direct contradiction with divine purpose as it was expressed to Noah and his sons after the flood: "Be fertile and increase and fill up the earth" (Gen. 9:7). [157] In the religious sense this is interpreted as God commanding the Jewish people to scatter throughout the earth and reject petty tribalism.

On another secular Jewish reading, as given by Jacques Derrida, this is accurate, however:

> In seeking to "make a name for themselves," to found at the same time a universal tongue and a unique genealogy, the Semites want to bring the world to reason, and this reason can signify simultaneously a colonial violence (since they

---

[156] Franz Kafka, *Parables and Paradoxes* (New York: Schocken Books, 1961), 35. Cited from https://www.thetorah.com/article/tower-of-babel-the-hidden-transcript accessed on 11/19/19
[157] https://www.jewishvirtuallibrary.org/tower-of-babel accessed on 11/19/19

would universalize their idiom) and a peaceful transparency of the human community.[158]

Derrida's essay on the Babel narrative is primarily focused on the issue of translation and in this regard it is quite dense. However, the point he makes immediately following the above quotation is that God both ruptures "the rational transparency" and interrupts "the colonial violence or linguistic imperialism."[159] He does this by imposing his name. For Derrida, names are a point at which translation falters because they are not specifically relegated to a particular language. Names can be exchanged for descriptive propositions, and occasionally they are translated in a provincial way, e.g., "Pierre" and "Peter," but primarily they are imported wholesale from the original text into the translation.

Now, Derrida doesn't really believe in the idea of an original text, or I should say more precisely, he does not grant it the higher degree of authenticity (or "stability" if we think in terms of his Existentialist predecessors) that it might be granted on a conventional understanding of translation.[160] For Derrida, the original or "sacred" text is already a translation even if it has a certain mystifying power that engenders a sense of debt on the part of the individual who seeks to translate it. This sense of "debt" is exactly what Derrida is referring to when he speaks of God's name imposing a demand for translation.

---

[158] Derrida, Jacques (1991) *A Derrida Reader* edited by Peggy Kamuf. Columbia University Press. P. 174

[159] Ibid p. 174

[160] For instance, when he writes: "The original requires translation even if no translator is there, fit to respond to this injunction, which is at the same time demand and desire in the very structure of the original." (Ibid p. 182) Derrida is not granting the idea of "the original" a privileged space of objectivity. He is instead talking about our subjective conceptualization of what is deemed "original."

If we look outside Derrida's agenda, which I would roughly describe as destabilizing the foundations of translation, we can see that his thought addresses a few of the themes we will be exploring in this book. One is the relationship between an interpreter of a text and the text itself, which Derrida, following the parlance of Heidegger, characterizes as being analogous to a "debt," or duty to said text. [161] Another is the significance attendant to the act of naming: "Language is determined starting from the word and the privilege of naming." [162] In Derrida's secular interpretation, the religious idea expressed by Hendel as an irresistible action – to climb the Tower (or to bite the forbidden fruit) – is rendered in Structuralist terms as the "desire of translation." And this desire for translation is a desire to get at the authentic meaning lying within the original text. Unlike Hendel's reading, though, this desire for translation is not contingent upon human nature itself, so much upon our innate belief that "the objectivity of translation is guaranteed by God." [163]

Returning to the onion metaphor, at the deepest and final level of inquiry into the Babel narrative we find the occult, and therefore most mythically rich, interpretation. Derrida's essay actually flirts with it on many occasions, for instance:

> The original is the first debtor, the first petitioner; it begins by lacking and by pleading for translation. This demand is not only on the side of the constructors of the tower who want to make a name for themselves and to found a universal tongue translating itself by itself; it also constrains the deconstructor of the tower: in giving his name, God also appealed to translation, not only between the tongues that had suddenly become multiple and confused, but first *of his name,* of the name he had

---

[161] Ibid pp. 182 - 183
[162] Ibid p. 187
[163] Ibid p. 182

proclaimed, given, and which should be translated
as confusion to be understood, hence to let it be
understood that it is difficult to translate and so to
understand.[164]

This quote deals with two issues. First, the completion of the
Tower's construction is analogous to a lack or a limit in what we
are able to think or express linguistically (the realm of the
ineffable, essentially). This ties back to Vico's issue of how man
constructed his symbols out of a mytho-poetic grasping of the
world. Derrida's response seems to be that the incompleteness of
man, exemplified by the inadequacy of language (or drawn to our
attention by the inadequacy of language), is the nexus from which
comes the symbolism that feeds both our myths and our need for
myths. The second issue pertains to names, specifically the name
"Babel" and how it is untranslatable; especially since its very
utterance signifies the confused speech that is "babble." Most
often this mythic level of the Narrative is not so much an
interpretation as it is a genealogy or hidden narrative. The
mystery surrounding the nature of such a reading, the mythic
reading, entails that it not only engenders further narratives but,
like the God depicted in Derrida's essay, it issues an imperative to
create more narratives.

One Final Thought Regarding the Tower of Babel

We won't be able to completely abandon the Tower of Babel
because it is one of the central myths that many of our expositions
will draw upon in one way or another. However, I feel as if I've
laid enough groundwork here about this narrative and its mythic
power, and how that power is largely defined by the self-
inscribed imperative to generate more narratives. The obvious
place the Babel myth leads, in our narrative analysis, is an actual
event: 9/11 and the destruction of the Twin Towers (and we're

---

[164] Ibid p. 184

going to get there, I promise!). But it is repeated in other actual events too, specifically the sinking of the Titanic in 1912. Here we have hubris, famous guests (Molly Brown, Benjamin Guggenheim, Isidor Straus, etc.) and the Sea.

The repetition of names as they are inserted into different translations is one of Derrida's best, and most easy to follow, insights. When Derrida writes that the debt of translation "does not involve living subjects but names at the edge of the language or, more rigorously, the trait which contracts the relation of the aforementioned living subject to his name, insofar as the latter keeps to the edge of the language,"[165] he is following a largely Structuralist tact. However, since Derrida saw his work as being beyond the scope of Phenomenology (what we have been referring to in terms of Hermeneutics) he tends to favor a more Structuralist approach in his writing. I believe that when he talks about the "debt" of translation he is invoking Phenomenology, primarily Heidegger, to a large extent.

Derrida borrows this concept of "debt" directly from Heidegger who describes the "calling" of Dasein as being predicated upon being-guilty. In contrast, a "good" conscience experiences a lack:

> One has interpreted "good" conscience as a privation of the "bad" one, and defined it as an "experienced lack of bad conscience." Accordingly it would be an experience of the fact that the call does not turn up, that is, that I have nothing to reproach myself with. But how is this "lack" *experienced*? The supposed experience is not the experience of a call at all, but a making certain that a deed attributed to Dasein was not committed by it and that Dasein is *therefore* innocent. Becoming certain of not having done something does *not* have the character of a phenomenon of conscience *at all*. On the contrary, it

---

[165] Ibid p. 185

can rather mean a forgetting of conscience, that is,
that one is emerging from the possibility of being
able to be summoned.[166]

Despite the necessity of the sea to the story of the Titanic I place it
here in conjunction with the Tower of Babel because both are
vehicles of hubris. And they are condemned as hubristic with a
sensibility that is closer to our modern sensibility than is Plato's
attribution of hubris to Atlantis, which comes off as a bit of an
after-thought.

There is a connection between the Tower of Babel and the
Titanic (or signifiers like the adjective "Titanic") that relates to
how these narratives are resolved and what this resolution tells
us about myths. In his essay, Derrida occasionally mentions how
the narrative "exhibits an incompletion, the impossibility of
finishing..."[167] These traits are tied to the structure, into which
they are built by way of the text. These are not "positive" traits;
they imply an absence or lack of qualities. However, these traits
are given a moral conclusion insofar as the story ends by
imparting certain implicit and explicit readings. This sense of
resolution sets these texts outside our lives, which as Heidegger
writes:

> Although it always becomes certain in resolution,
> the *indefiniteness* of one's own potentiality-of-being,
> however, always reveals itself *completely* only in
> being-toward-death. Anticipation brings Dasein
> face-to-face with a possibility that is constantly

---

[166] Heidegger, Martin (1996) *Being and Time.* State University
Press of New York. P. 269
[167] Derrida, Jacques (1991) *A Derrida Reader* edited by Peggy
Kamuf. Columbia University Press. P. 165

certain and yet remains indefinite at every moment
as to when this possibility becomes impossibility.[168]

Hence, the power of myth is generated by the visceral invocation of the indefiniteness we associate with authentic Being (being that is oriented towards our uniqueness by virtue of apprehension of our own death or freedom, depending on your interpretation – a lived being) and its juxtaposition with narrative conclusion. In our historical dialectic the drive toward concluding the narrative is generally associated with the fact-based "scientistic" antithesis; but we see here that myths, in their own way, require both sides of the equation, both of which manage to linger in our psyches long after the narrative's conclusion.

Deciphering the Occult

As we have seen with Atlantis, and will see with other events, objects, and places of significance, the ineffable power of myth is usually dissimulated through occultism. Occultism is the name we give to this cultivation of mystery surrounding a myth when it occurs inside of a secular society; mysticism is what we call it when it occurs within a religious society. Conspiracy theories seem to exist only within secular societies and the most interesting one surrounding the Babel narrative is the theory that the men who built the tower were the progenitors of Freemasonry; and that after *their* fall, their descendants would go on to build King Solomon's Temple.

Unlike The Book of Revelations or The Gnostic Gospels, which point outward to the unknowable future and the unknowable cosmos, i.e., objects of thought, the Babel narrative focuses on the agency of men who seek to master the world. For Wayne, the technology used was commingled with a desire for political and social unification:

---

[168] Heidegger, Martin (1996) *Being and Time.* State University Press of New York. P. 285

The people of the plain chose not to be divided –to live as one people, with one language, with one government, with one collective ambition. They bound together with such collective intensity that they rebelled against God, utilizing a clever repository built in antediluvian times by the progeny of Lamech. With this illicit knowledge, nothing was beyond their grasp. The newfound technology and knowledge was sponsored by the spurious religion, which attached itself to the illicit knowledge.[169]

On this reading, the Tower of Babel is not a symbol meant to be deciphered, since the "spurious" intentions that Wayne ascribes to Nimrod and the denizens of Shinar are still at play in our society today. What the Babel narrative represents instead is more like a blueprint rendering of the drives and inclinations (often towards surveillance-security) that would lead to what is called in conspiracy theory literature: "the New World Order." This aspect will be the topic of our next chapter.

Whether or not the builders of the Tower of Babel were proto-Freemasons, these men embodied the spirit of scientific and technological advancement, albeit one that was grounded in the unfathomable depths of a divine will. The tension between these two opposing poles (the mythic and the scientific) will carry us up to the events of September 11, 2001. At which point, the ground that was instantiated by a multitude of occult-inspired narratives was pulled away, much like the Tower of Babel, and the intrigued were left with only scientific facts to guide them in their search for meaning. This transition is the single most important part of this book.

---

[169] Wayne, Gary (2014) *The Genesis 6 Conspiracy*. Trusted Books, A Division of Deep River Books. Pp. 314 - 315

The parts of the Old Testament that we have covered so far – the creation of the Earth, the fall of man, the flooding of the Antediluvian world, and the Tower of Babel – all give explicit origin stories for particular phenomena, such as the names of animals, the wrath of God, and the origin of languages. On a deeper level, though, these stories follow a formal structure of differentiation.

As a text, the Bible maps a progression of myriad peoples and situations from one entity – and one action by said entity – to the next, all of which stems from the creation of Heaven and Earth. The vital work of the subsequent books of the Old Testament is to draw the many (the characters and scenarios described in its books) out of this one entity and this one instance of creation.[170] A question posed by the Bible then is, can this "many" be reconciled with the "One" who had initially discharged it?

The Gospel of John does the most work in trying not only to explicate this problem in theological parlance but also solve it. We can see in the beginning of John the sketching of a dualism that purports a complimentary relation between different parts:

> In the beginning was the Word, and the Word was with God, and the Word was God. The same was in the beginning with God. All things were made by him; and without him was not anything made that was made.[171]

The distinction between God and his creation, as depicted in Genesis, is reframed here after granting a reconciled duality between God and the Word. The reconciliation is achieved by a textual act of identification: "God" identified as "the Word." We

---

[170] I have purposely phrased this progression in this way to reference the philosophical problem of "The One and the Many."
[171] *The Holy Bible* (Authorized King James Version). Thomas Nelson & Sons. John 1, 1-3

cannot say for sure that the authors of John (since John was not historically penned by the Disciple but was written after his death) consciously intended to remedy this rift between God and language. However, the elasticity of the Bible, or more precisely the elasticity of its propensity for mystery and near-infinite interpretation, allows us this nuanced reading. Andrew Weeks sketches the transition from the account in Genesis to the Gospel of John as a move from:

> [T]he origin of the world in terms of the coordinates of the *created world*, in accordance with *space* and *time*, of *above* and *below*, as a *sequence of events*, within an implicit *hierarchy*, in which what is above is higher, and what is below lower, and in which what comes last in order of creation is first in order of importance. If God is transcendent in Genesis, the perspective of his act of creation is nevertheless immanent.[172]

To one in which:

> [T]he perspective of space, time, and nature has shifted to one of timeless immediacy and presence. No longer is there a sequence of distinct events. Here, event has aspect rather than sequence. The beginning is not a first followed by a second and a third. The "beginning" is an eternal present and ground of all that comes into being and lives. The Word or "Logos," according to Kittel's dictionary of the Greek New Testament, is unique in this usage.

---

[172] Weeks, Andrew (1993) *German Mysticism: From Hildegard of Bingen to Ludwig Wittgenstein*. State University of New York Press. P. 19

> Clearly, the Word is Christ. But why this peculiar
> terminology?[173]

From here, Weeks goes on to address the semantics at play in the passage from John. The significance of "the Word" will play a greater role in our discussion of the history of Freemasonry. But for now, I want to focus on the issue of "Logos."

Derrida sees the opening of the Gospel of John as being the founding instance of what he calls *Logocentrism*, which he identified as the philosophical orientation towards reason, and more significantly, the prioritization of speech as the central principle of philosophy and language at the expense of writing. For Derrida, the emphasis on speech is predicated on the immediacy of breath. The voice "hears" itself and allows the speaker to stand in "an absolute proximity to the present [...] My words are 'alive' because they seem not to leave me, seem not to fall outside of me, outside of my breath, into a visible distance; they do not stop belonging to me."[174] This logocentric manner of discussing breath is analogous to the Biblical narrative in which God blew life into Adam; the attachment of language to breath, and the vital nature of breathing, gives us an idea of the universality of logocentrism.

Astrology

Like the sea, the cosmos is a source of mystery. However, the destruction of the Tower of Babel (or the halting of its construction) did not impart the same kind of fear as did the stories of Noah and Atlantis, in which we have the sea being utilized as a divine weapon against mankind. In the story of the Tower of Babel the Lord smites the builders from above. The

---

[173] Ibid, p. 19
[174] Derrida, Jacques (2011) *Voice and Phenomenon*. Northwestern University Studies in Phenomenology and Existentialism. P. 65

cosmos is represented as more of a medium through which God and his angels travel, much like the god Apollo did in Greek mythology.

Even in the UFO mythos that arose in close conjunction with science fiction the cosmos does not evoke the same degree of immediate fear as the sea. An intuitive reading of the sea as a telluric force of movement and destruction analogous to Freud's unconscious (or Plato's passions depicted by the chariot analogy made in the *Phaedrus* dialogue) and conversely the cosmos as a realm of divine reason is an especially apt schematization.

Obviously, the oceans can purvey a great many dangers, but they are dangerous in themselves. Space itself is not dangerous but it can act as an ether through which dangerous or beneficent entities might travel. The belief in astrology corresponds to this idea of the cosmos as medium. Astrology is the arch-argument for recognizing outer space as an embodiment of divine reason insofar as it lays claim to the prediction of human behavior based on constellational patterns. On this view, the stars in the heavens are members of a fixed Platonic realm. Just as Plato saw individuals and objects here on earth as partial instantiations of permanent and immaterial forms, the astrologist draws a similar distinction between our relations on Earth and the movement of the stars and constellations.

The astrological narrative does not demand a great deal of analysis on our part because in its modern iteration it breaks down into either the compound model, in which every aspect of our lives that is astrologically governed is determined by the stars' physical movement, or the less severe interpretive model, in which the movement of the stars allow us to glimpse the future, or the truth of our situation.

In our schema, astrology's significance arises from its implicit devotion to rationalism. I say this despite the often-times irrational behavior of its adherents.

Interestingly enough, Wayne addresses the issue of astrology in dualistic terms: there is one branch that is dignified, practiced by Seth's line, and another practiced by Cain's line from which modern astrology is descended. The delineation between these two lines is central to Wayne's theory and it correlates with a variety of the topics we will be addressing in the next few chapters.

The Emerald Tablet of Hermes

Conjuring up a synthesis between the cosmos and the sea is not an easy task because it doesn't seem like there exists a dialectical relationship between the texts surrounding either entity. As objects, both seem representative of the deep and inexplicable recesses of our consciousness, and so mirror each other. This holds whether you emphasize "consciousness" in an individual or collective sense – they exist in a textual accord with each other.

The Emerald Tablet of Hermes on the other hand, offers a point of synthesis between the Cosmos and Earth. The fact that it was rendered into an actual text should indicate the philosophical dialectic's dependency upon codified language. Richard Cavendish gives the purported genealogy of the Tablet in his book, *The Black Arts*:

> Magicians, who deal in mysteries, are always enthralled by anything which is exceptionally mysterious, and the Emerald Table is impenetrable in the extreme. It is said to have been a tablet of emerald, engraved with a writing in Phoenician characters, which was discovered by Sarah, the wife of Abraham (or alternatively by Alexander the Great), in a cave-tomb where it was clutched in the fingers of the corpse of Hermes Trismegistus. Hermes was the Greek god of wisdom and patron of magic. Hermes Trismegistus –thrice-greatest- was supposedly a grandson of Adam, a sage of

surpassing wisdom and the builder of the pyramids.[175]

Transcribed below is Sir Isaac Newton's translation of the text in its entirety:

1. Tis true without error, certain and most true.

2. That which is below is like that which is above
and that which is above is like that which is below
to do the miracles of one only thing.

3. And as all things have been and arose from one by the
meditation of one: so all things have their birth
from this one thing by adaptation.

4. The Sun is its father, the moon its mother,
the wind hath carried it in its belly, the earth is its
nurse.

5. The father of all perfection in the whole world is here.

6. Its force or power is entire if it be converted into earth.

7. Separate thou the earth from the fire,
the subtle from the gross sweetly with great industry.

8. It ascends from the earth to the heaven
and again it descends to the earth
and receives the force of things superior and inferior.

9. By this means you shall have the glory of the whole world.

---

[175] Cavendish, Richard (1967) *The Black Arts*. Perigee Books, The Putnam Publishing Group. P. 13

10. And thereby all obscurity shall fly from you.

11. Its force is above all force. For it vanquishes every subtle thing and penetrates every solid thing.

12. So was the world created.

13. From this are and do come admirable adaptations whereof the means (or process) is here in this.
Hence I am called Hermes Trismegist,
Having three parts of the philosophy of the whole world.

14. That which I have said of the operation of the Sun is accomplished and ended.[176]

The famous occult/New Age maxim of "As above, so below," stems directly from this fragment and coincides with the strongly deterministic brand of astrology mentioned previously. Historically the text has been interpreted to be about alchemy, and this alchemical process seems to place the alchemist in the role of creator-god, specifically in sections six through thirteen. The fact that Newton took the trouble of deciphering the tablet is evidentiary of the intersection that existed between nascent formal science and the occult prior to the industrial age. It also addresses a question central to Hegel's philosophy, which is sometimes referred to as the "problem of the One and the Many." This problem in Classical philosophy related to how something that is whole and total was constructed from things that were partial and incomplete. Hegel endeavored to answer this paradox by positing the totality of the whole as the result of a temporal process that preserves the moments that comprise it. The Tablet

---

[176] Found online at:
https://www.google.com/amp/s/mythcrafts.com/2017/04/28/isaac-newton-and-the-emerald-tablet/amp/ accessed 09/24/19

of Hermes will reappear in both our discussion of the antediluvian patriarchs and the tradition of Hermeticism.

Oh, You Think Darkness is Your Ally

In contrast to the spirit of cosmic harmony invoked by the astrologer, there exists a mysterious aspect of the Cosmos represented by the darkness of night. This representation can occur in an immediate apprehension of the dark or in a mythical narrative sense. One such narrative that pertains to this is "The Cornish Litany:"

From Ghoulies and Ghosties
And Long Leggety Beasties
And Things That Go Bump In the Night
Good Lord Deliver Us

The litany is of unknown origin. Some date it to the Fifteenth Century and others to the Nineteenth as an Alfred Tennyson (August 6, 1809 – October 6, 1892) composition. Regardless of its origin, which may never be known, this prayer addresses our sense of concern as to what is lurking in the dark, while answering this inherent insolvability with an imperative to quietism; hence its status as a "prayer."

For this section we will translate this sense of uncertainty and inherent indefiniteness in the face of darkness onto three mythical characters. In one sense, the translation, or superimposing if you will, of these characters throughout the rest of this book conforms to the description I gave of Hegel's answer to the problem of the one and the many: they are partial and their movement and reappraisal over time greatly contributes to the whole of conspiracy theorization. By "whole" I don't mean "all" conspiracy theories, but instead those conspiracy narratives that have retained the richness of their mythological antecedents; conspiracy theories that could ideally act as adequate substitutions for older myths.

However, in another way, these three figures do not conform to Hegel's solution to the problem of the one and the many because they are simultaneously mythical *and* marginal. Because the narrative-eye of the myths in which they participate does not focus directly on them, they exhibit no foibles and faults – unlike the main characters of these myths, they suffer no character development. Yet as Auerbach has pointed out regarding the nature of figures in the Bible, we are led to assume that these marginal figures' thoughts and feelings have just as many layers and are just as historically entangled as the main characters of the scriptures in which they appear. In a sense, their obscurity grants them a certain degree of perfection, albeit a small one. They themselves constitute a totality; and the drive to find the narratives that constitute their history, or a total understanding of who they were, is common to most of the authors we will be discussing.

The first of these three characters is Melchizedek, one of the most fascinating and enduring characters from Genesis. In his novel, *The Cathedral*, J.K. Huysmans devotes a brief section to this enigmatic figure:

> Durtal had gone closer to statues, standing by Saint Anne, and was looking at one on the left wearing a pointed cap, a sort of papal tiara with a crown round the edge, robed in an alb girt round the middle with knotted cord, and a large cope with a fringe; the features were grave, almost anxious, and the eye fired with an absorbed gaze into the distance. This figure held a censer in one hand, and in the other a chalice covered with a paten on which there was a loaf; and this image of Melchizedek, the King of Salem, threw Durtal into a deep reverie.
> He was, in fact, one of the most mysterious types of the Holy Scriptures – this monarch mentioned in Genesis as the priest of the Most High God. He consummates the sacrifice of bread and wine,

blesses Abram, receives tithes from him, and then vanishes into the darkness of history. And suddenly his name is found in a psalm of David's, who declares that the Messiah is a priest for ever after the order of Melchizedek, and again he is lost without leaving a trace.

Then quite unexpectedly he reappears in the New Testament, and what Saint Paul says of him in the Epistle to the Hebrews makes him more enigmatical than ever. The apostle speaks of him as "without father, without mother, without descent, having neither beginning of days nor end of life, but made like unto the Son of God, abiding a priest continually." Saint Paul is explicit to show how great a person he was –and the dim light he casts on this figure goes out.

"You must confess that this King of Salem is a puzzle. What do the commentators think of him?" asked Durtal.

"Some have asserted that he was Shem, the son of Noah; others have thought that he was Ham. Simon Logothetes considers him an Egyptian; Suidas believes him to have belonged to the accursed race of Canannites, and that this is why the Bible says nothing of his ancestry.

The Gnostics revered him as an Eon superior to Jesus; and in the third century Theodore le Changeur also asserted that he was not a man, but a virtue transcending Christ, because Christ's priesthood was but a copy of Melchizedek's.[177]

Note the statement: "Vanishes into the darkness of history." We see here, in the explicitly literary form of a novel, a depiction of

[177] Huysmans, Joris-Karl (2015) *The Durtal Trilogy*. Ex Fontibus Company. P. 358

how the Gnostics constructed a proto-conspiracy theory out of the mythic substrate provided by scripture:

> And Melchizedek king of Salem brought forth bread and wine: and he *was* the priest of the Most High God.
> And he blessed him, and said, Blessed *be* Abram of the most high God, possessor of heaven and earth:
> And blessed be the most high God, which hath delivered thine enemies into thy hand. And he gave him tithes of all.[178]

According to Auerbach, Biblical scripture did not seek to narrate the reality of the time in which it was created, in his analysis of the story of Abraham and Isaac he relates:

> Their aim is not to bewitch the senses, and if nevertheless they produce lively sensory effects, it is only because the moral, religious, and psychological phenomena which are their sole concern are made concrete in the sensible matter of life. But their religious intent involves an absolute claim to historical truth. The story of Abraham and Isaac is not better established than the story of Odysseus, Penelope, and Euryclea; both are legendary. But the Biblical narrator, the Elohist, had to believe in the objective truth of the story of Abraham's sacrifice –the existence of the sacred ordinances of life rested upon the truth of this and similar stories. He had to believe in it passionately; or else (as many rationalistic interpreters believed and perhaps still believe) he had to be a conscious liar –no harmless liar like Homer, who lied to give

---

[178] *The Holy Bible* (Authorized King James Version). Thomas Nelson & Sons. Genesis 15, 18-20

pleasure, but a political liar with a definite end in view, lying in the interest of a claim to absolute authority.[179]

Auerbach describes the Biblical stories as incarnating doctrine and promise, and it is this combination that insinuates a background of mystery. However, it can be argued that an analogous evocation of mystery occurs as much for the reader of secular narratives, like *Lord of the Rings* for instance, as it does for the religious believer. As I stated in my brief synopsis of Structuralism and Hermeneutics in the Introduction, the Hermeneuticist is largely concerned with *intentionality*. Philosophically this usually means what is present to the subject's consciousness, but in a broader sense it has to do, as Auerbach suggests, with the motivation and commitment of the author.

For Auerbach, the authors of Genesis have transmitted this sense of commitment to their readership in a way that secular authors cannot. But in addition to this, Auerbach interprets the religious text as being constructed in a way that creates suspense for the reader by not explicating everything that is depicted therein. This conscious cultivation of mystery, by way of what is not revealed, is for Auerbach both a literary device and a legitimate representation of reality as ascertained by the author.

Auerbach's analysis interests me because it gives an account of "mystery" arising from a Biblical text. As we saw from Huysmans's fictional account, there is an aura of mystery surrounding Melchizedek. This is for reasons that Auerbach can explain, as he is referred to as a priest of the Most High God; and in a Hermeneutical sense this can lead to the Gnostic positing of his true identity as of one of Noah's sons. However, Auerbach is looking at his subjects in a direct way, and so his focus is on main characters such as Abraham and Isaac.

---

[179] Auerbach, Erich (2003) *Mimesis: The Representation of Reality in Western Literature.* Princeton University Press. P. 14

I think that the "mysterious" aura and the narrative-generating power of Melchizedek is derived from his *slightness*. As we will see with the figure of Hiram in the next section, what draws our attention to these figures is their existence on the margins of history. According to Auerbach the author's commitment to the historical and religious truth of a central figure like Abraham is imparted to us as a reader; and the reciprocating commitment is essentially a religious feeling, possibly *the* religious feeling to the secularly minded. In my opinion, it is the offhandedness with which the marginal figure is sketched that draws out the mythical feeling that is similarly obligatory; but because it is less explicit it demands a more severe degree of commitment than conventional religious feeling. This would be a similar feeling to the detective or historian who is compelled to search for evidence and clues that will bring this slight character into the light of understanding. The theories that result from this process will have a higher degree of conjecture than ones that discuss primary Biblical figures.

One such theory, put forward by the Gnostics, was that Melchizedek, being the "priest of the Most High God," was a torchbearer of sorts for an ultra-secret religious order whose job was to preserve a undisclosed teaching or truth that is not mentioned explicitly in the Bible. This truth might even elude the creator God, who certain Gnostics called "Jehova" (to distinguish him from the "Most High God" – who was served first by Melchizedek and then later Jesus Christ). This strand of Gnosticism, which is largely informed by Manichaeism, sometimes posits the notion that the serpent from the Garden of Eden was also a representative of this "Most High God," or possibly the God himself. This is one of the obscure tenets of early Gnosticism that informed what might be classified as Medieval sorcery, alchemy, and later, the occult.

For those who are unfamiliar with the term, Gnosticism is not a formal religion like Christianity. The Gnostics were basically early sects of Christians who were trying to formulate a doctrine within their own communities. Because Jesus was Jewish, he has often been interpreted historically as a rabbi, and so his teachings would be formulated as a doctrine that follows from those that are found in the Old Testament. The Apostles and Disciples who had the greatest ease in formatting Jesus's teachings in this way were also devoutly Jewish (Paul, Matthew, etc.) and therefore fluent in this manner of scholasticism. The people *we* refer to as Gnostics (they did not refer to themselves this way) were mostly Gentiles who allowed a lot of their earlier Pagan beliefs to inform their Christian faith. Hence, most of the "heresies" the Church, once it was formalized, accused the Gnostics of committing, were just continuations of Pagan traditions.

Any Gospels written and circulated by these early Christians were ordered to be destroyed by the Bishop of Alexandria in 367 AD; [180] however, a few copies survived. According to Birger A. Pearson, the specific Gnostic Gospel devoted to Melchizedek was originally written in Greek and consisted of 745 lines, of which only 19 were preserved to the extent that they could be translated.[181] The text, as it appears in Robinson's 1990 edition of *The Nag Hammadi Library* has been embellished with a certain amount of "conjectural restoration." The Gospel of Melchizedek has an apocalyptic import:

> They will make [war ...] every one. For [...] whether in the [...] many [...]. And these in the [...] every [one] will [...]. These will [...] with every blow [...] weaknesses. These will be confined in other forms [and will] be punished. [These] the Savior will take them [away and] they will overcome everything, [not with] their mouths and words but by means of the [...] which will be done for [them. He will] destroy Death.[182]

---

[180] The Devil Problem from *The New Yorker* March 26, 1995
[181] Robinson, James (1990) *The Nag Hammadi Library*. Harper San Francisco. P. 438
[182] Ibid, p. 442

This ellipsis-laden excerpt gives us a good idea of the original text's state of disrepair. Regardless, the conjecture employed by the translators is conservative enough to preserve a modest interpretation of the author's intention. There are two very significant aspects of the Melchizedek mythos that are addressed in this Gospel. First, there is this section, which appears early in the text:

> [Furthermore], they will say of him that he is unbegotten though he has been begotten, (that) he does not eat even though he eats, (that) he does not drink even though he drinks, (that) he is uncircumcised though he has been circumcised, (that) he is unfleshly though he has come in flesh, (that) he did not come to suffering <though> he came to suffering, (that) he did not rise from the dead <though> he rose from [the] dead.[183]

This section is vitally important to our analysis because it distinguishes the Gospel of Melchizedek from the modern perception that *all* Gnostics denied the physical resurrection of Jesus Christ. Elaine Pagels, an expert on Gnosticism, states that the belief in the *actual* resurrection of Christ acts as the foundation for the Christian Church and that the belief in such an incredible event is a test of faith. In contrast to this:

> Gnostic Christians interpret resurrection in various ways. Some say that the person who experiences the resurrection does not meet Jesus raised physically back to life, rather he encounters Christ on a spiritual level. This may occur in dreams, in

---

[183] Ibid, p. 440

ecstatic trance, in visions, or in moments of spiritual illumination.[184]

This debate is at the forefront of the conflict between Freemasons who attempt to claim a Gnostic pedigree for their fraternal order and fundamentalist Christians who accuse Freemasons of, among a variety of things, denying the divinity of Christ. We will explore this conflict later, but for now, we should take note that the Gospel of Melchizedek appears, in this respect, to take a decidedly unGnostic stance on the resurrection. It is most likely for this reason that Pearson states that the "Melchizedekians were not Gnostics."[185]

The second significant aspect of the Melchizedek mythos that is addressed in the Gospel is the idea that Melchizedek is actually Christ. Pearson ties this reading to the idea that both Melchizedek and Christ appear in the end times, and because early sects of Coptic Christians referred to Melchizedek as the "Son of God." In corroboration with this assertion the text of the Gospel states:

> And [...] you struck me, [...] you threw me, [...] corpse. And [you crucified me] from the third hour [of the Sabbath-eve] until [the ninth hour]. And [after these things I arose] from the [dead....] came out of [...] into me. [...] my eyes [saw ...they did not] find anyone [...] greeted [me ...]. They said to me, "Be [strong, O Melchizedek], great [High-priest] of God [Most High, for the archons], who [are] your [enemies], made war; you have [prevailed over

[184] Pagels, Elaine (1989) *The Gnostic Gospels*. Vintage Books, A Division of Random House Inc. P. 5
[185] Robinson, James (1990) *The Nag Hammadi Library*. Harper San Francisco. P. 439

> them, and] they did not prevail over you, [and you]
> endured, and [you] destroyed your enemies [...][186]

I find this passage to be a little too fragmented (and filled out with conjecture) to deduce the author's intent to definitively equate Melchizedek with Jesus Christ. However, I have heard contemporary Christians put this theory forward as a valid (though speculative) interpretation of the figure of Melchizedek.[187] It is a fascinating possibility to ponder: the idea that Christ time-travelled back to the time of Abraham in order to anoint him.

For a less science-fictional reading, we can return to a purely textual reading of the Bible and interpret the reoccurrence of Christ as Melchizedek – and Melchizedek as Christ – as a Hermeneutical reinscription of the name of Christ, insofar as the role, as such, is as stated in the Psalm of David: that "the Messiah is a priest for ever after the order of Melchizedek." The hermeneutical aspect is evident in the fact that the identification, if one chooses to make it, of Jesus Christ with Melchizedek comes historically after the depiction of Christ in the New Testament. Gadamer's account of the role played by understanding within the scope of hermeneutical reflection gives us additional insight on the matter:

> The understanding of a text has not begun at all as
> long as the text remains mute. But a text can begin
> to speak. When it does begin to speak, however, it
> does not simply speak its word, always the same, in
> lifeless rigidity, but gives ever new answers to the
> person who questions it and poses ever new
> questions to him who answers it. To understand a
> text is to come to understand oneself in a kind of
> dialogue. This contention is confirmed by the fact

---

[186] Ibid, pp. 443 - 444
[187] From personal correspondence with Don Clasen, 06/04/20.

> that the concrete dealing with a text yields understanding only when what is said in the text begins to find expression in the interpreter's own language.[188]

This reference to the "interpreter's own language" engages the historical-cultural contingencies by which the text in question came under purview. Essentially, on this reading the historical persona of Melchizedek is being conditioned by subsequent readings – it is still evolving. It can be argued that this elasticity of persona could be extended to the figures that were central to the Biblical narratives; and people do this: they constantly redefine figures like Jesus and Moses, etc. But these changes are more controversial because they must contend with the theological commitments and demands that were explicitly articulated by the author.

In contrast, the "minor" figures I am interested in discussing for the rest of this chapter did not seem to take up a great deal of the authors' concentration. They may have even existed as artistic embellishments. These figures were not burdened with what Auerbach deems the propagandizing imperative with which the main characters were burdened. The fact that a Gnostic sect, or an early Christian sect opposed to the Gnostics, set about to construct or disseminate the "Gospel of Melchizedek" is an early example of the conspiracy theorist's instinct to take something from the margin of an established narrative and make it the subject of its own narrative. This phenomenon is demonstrative of one of the central claims of this book: that the meta-narrative aspect of a myth or conspiracy theory entails the imperative to create new narratives.

One final point regarding this fragment is that it references the "Archons." Granted, "Archons" is placed in brackets and was

---

[188] Gadamer, Hans-Georg (2008) *Philosophical Hermeneutics.* Translated and Edited by David E. Linge. University of California Press. P. 57

most likely the result of conjecture on the part of the translators. The Archons were believed by the Gnostics to be "the authorities of the universe and the spirits of wickedness."[189] This belief was integrated into the Gnostic's dualistic theology:

> The central belief of the Gnostic sects, accused of Satanism by orthodox Christians, was dualist. 'For any Gnostic', it has been observed, 'the world is really hell.' Convinced that the world is thoroughly evil, the Gnostics could not believe that it had been created by a good god. They thought that the supreme God, the principle of good, is far away in the distant heaven. The world was made and is governed by lesser deities, called Archons, 'rulers', who are either actively hostile to God or do not know that God exists. For some Gnostics the Archons were the gods of the planets, the guardians who barred the way to the human soul when it tried to ascend through the spheres after death... The chief of the Archons was frequently identified with the God of the Old Testament, who was in Gnostic eyes an evil, savage, vindictive and treacherous deity.[190]

Because Gnosticism is not a formal religious theory there is probably a wide spectrum of opinion on the nature of the Archons among those who consider themselves "Gnostics." The inclusion of the word by the translator might have been a sound inference or it may have been done with the conscious intention to bring the Gospel of Melchizedek more in line with the general tenets of Gnosticism.

---

[189] From "The Hypostasis of the Archons" in Robinson, James (1990) *The Nag Hammadi Library*. Harper San Francisco. P. 162
[190] Cavendish, Richard (1967) *The Black Arts*. Perigee Books, The Putnam Publishing Group. P. 291

Hiram

According to Masonic legend, Hiram Abif (sometimes spelled "Abiff") was the name of the master-builder of King Solomon's Temple. The dynamic between Solomon and Hiram is like the one between Abraham, who was featured as a central figure of the text, and Melchizedek, who was relegated to the margin. There are a lot of books on Freemasonry that I will address in the next chapter. However, for the case of Hiram Abif I will begin by drawing from Christopher Knight and Robert Lomas's *The Hiram Key*, because when one has the opportunity to extensively cite a writer who has postulated that the moon is man-made, as Knight has done (see his 2007 book, *Who Built the Moon?*), then that opportunity must be seized.

Early in *The Hiram Key*, Knight and Lomas focus on the excavations that the Templars conducted on the site of Herod's Temple in Jerusalem early in the Twelfth Century:

> We found further evidence that the Templars had been involved in digging for something under the ruins of Herod's Temple in the writings of Lieutenant Charles Wilson of the Royal Engineers who led an archaeological expedition to Jerusalem at the turn of the century [C. Wilson: *The Excavation of Jerusalem*]. He recovered many old items that can positively be identified as Templar artefacts, from diggings deep below the Temple. As our researches for this book were nearing completion, we had the good fortune to meet Robert Brydon, a scholarly Templar archivist based in Scotland, who now has many of these items in his care.[191]

---

[191] Knight, Christopher & Lomas, Robert (2001) *The Hiram Key*. Fair Winds Press. p. 29

The possibility of such excavations has had an enduring effect on mainstream archaeology: as recently as early 2019 Dr. Albert Lin employed a Light Detection and Ranging Device in the city of Acre in order to detect underground tunnels that most likely were dug by Templars to transport their treasure.[192] This more recent development, which occurred nearly twenty-five years after *The Hiram Key* was first published, is evidence that what might be considered "legitimate" scientific pursuits can be informed or instigated from a type of thought that had been heretofore marginalized. For Paul Feyerabend:

> Progress was often achieved by a 'criticism from the past' [...] After Aristotle and Ptolemy, the idea that the earth moves –that strange, ancient, and 'entirely ridiculous', Pythagorean view- was thrown on the rubbish heap of history, only to be revived by Copernicus and to be forged by him into a weapon for the defeat of its defeaters. The Hermetic writings played an important part in this revival, which is still not sufficiently understood, and they were studied by the great Newton himself. Such developments are not surprising. No idea is ever examined in all its ramifications and no view is ever given all the chances it deserves. Theories are abandoned and superseded by more fashionable accounts long before they have had an opportunity to show their virtues. Besides, ancient doctrines and 'primitive' myths appear strange and nonsensical only because the information they contain is either not known, or is distorted by philologists or anthropologists unfamiliar with the

---

[192] Reported by Alfredo Carpineti for IFLScience! 10/25/19 "Tunnels that may have been used to transport the Knight Templar's Lost Fortune Discovered." Accessed on 1/14/20. Also, see the National Geographic Documentary on the same topic.

simplest physical, medical or astronomical knowledge.[193]

The "Hermetic writings" referenced by Feyerabend here are closely linked to the early Gnostic texts that Knight and Lomas came to use as a cornerstone of their theory.[194] However, it is inaccurate to identify Gnosticism too strongly with the Hermetic Tradition; and we will return to this distinction later. The purpose of discussing Hiram in this section is to properly list him among the trinity of murky historical personages to whom I will be returning, and to give an introductory sketch of his persona. The fuller story must be developed more extensively in the next chapter due to the centrality of Hiram to the mythos of Freemasonry. Knight and Lomas will ultimately tie a narrative line between the figure of Hiram Abif and the Knights Templar and then to modern-day Freemasonry.

When it comes to the Templars themselves, Lomas and Knight are concerned with three questions:

1. What were the Templars looking for in their excavations?

2. What did the Templars find in these excavations?

3. Are the Templars predecessors of modern Freemasonry? And if so, what bearing do questions 1 and 2 have on Masonry?

---

[193] Feyerabend, Paul (1993) *Against Method.* Verso. p. 35.

[194] This is an apt choice of metaphor considering the symbolic connections Knight & Lomas draw between the Biblical passages where Jesus says that the "stone that the builders have rejected shall be the cornerstone" and its interpolation into the Mark Mason's Ritual. Knight, Christopher & Lomas, Robert (2001) *The Hiram Key.* Fair Winds Press. P. 41. We will discuss the Mark Mason Ritual in greater depth in The Significance of JFK chapter.

Before we go deeper into these questions, let's look briefly at the Freudian theory of the unconscious and think about how it might relate to archaeology. By 1925 Freud had formulated that the unconscious was a writing that existed prior to speech. In his essay, "Note on the Mystic Writing Pad," Freud describes the psyche in terms of an Etch-a-Sketch, where the conscious part of the mind is analogous to the wax paper on the top, with the wax base beneath it the unconscious mind. In his theorization of how this model works as an analogue of consciousness, Freud saw an evolutionary build-up of writing that had accumulated on the wax, thus causing our perceptions to be invariably determined (or at least conditioned) by this underlying text.

Freud postulated a Structuralist interpretation of the human understanding that is durational and accumulative, and if we apply these predicates to the field of archaeology, especially early archaeology, then the search by the Templars for long forgotten texts is a kind of performative or literal acting out of a delve into the unconscious. It is also notable because there is a sense of alterity or otherness involved, since the culture being excavated was not the Templars' native culture (they were French) but that of the ancient Hebrews. This mentality indicates a move in the modernist direction insofar as it signifies a temporary abandonment of one's own myths in order to conquer, or acquire, the myths of others.

Anyone who is familiar with the relationship between the Templars and the Grail mythos is most likely aware of the most controversial and "explosive" content supposedly uncovered by the Templars' excavations: that Jesus escaped his death, and his bloodline was carried on for centuries in Europe. Me telling you this is not a spoiler as it is literally a Hollywood movie starring Tom Hanks. I'll treat the subject more seriously when we get to the Grail chapter; for now, let's focus on the two Hirams that appear in the Old Testament. The first is Hiram of Tyre who is mentioned in 2 Samuel 5:11 and 1 Kings 5:1 – 10. This Hiram sent building materials to Jerusalem for the construction of the temple. The second Hiram, who is known as Hiram Abif, was commissioned as one of the master builders of Solomon's Temple and appears in 1 Kings 7:13 – 14.

In respect to narrative analysis, the repetition of Hiram's name is relatively innocent in that it was a common name shared by myriad individuals. This innocence obscures the inevitability of two individuals sharing the same name muddying the interpretative waters farther down the line. Hiram Abif's death is re-enacted in the Master Mason ritual, i.e., the third-degree initiation for Freemasonry, wherein the petitioner for the degree is blindfolded, has a noose placed around his neck, and is told the story of Abif's courage and resilience in the face of death.[195] After this, there is a sort of mock funeral performed[196] followed by a rebirth, with the master of ceremonies declaring:

> "Thus, my dear brother, have all Master Masons been raised from a figurative death, to a reunion with the companions of their former toil. Let me now beg of you to observe, that the light of a Master Mason is but as darkness visible, serving only to express that gloom which hangs over the prospect of futurity. It is that mysterious veil of darkness which the eye of human reason cannot penetrate, unless assisted by that divine light which is from above. Yet even, by this glimmering ray you will perceive that you stand on the very brink of the grave into which you have just figuratively descended, and which, when this transitory life shall have passed away, will again receive its cold bosom."[197]

---

[195] Ibid pp. 8 - 12

[196] "As I touched the ground a funeral shroud was immediately draped around me, so only my upper face was uncovered." Ibid p. 12

[197] Ibid p. 13

Darkness is addressed here as something that can be navigated, and temporarily abated, by the light of reason (which is represented by a lit candle during the ceremony), but will return, inevitably, with the actuality of death. In one sense, this staging of death in order to prepare the petitioner for the actual event is possibly very useful, psychologically speaking. The true meaning in Masonry, though, can be seen in the exaltation of divine reason, the incorporation of pagan rites of rebirth and regeneration into Masonic structure, and the tying of this structure to the initiatic tradition of Hermeticism. In this respect, Freemasonry becomes an institution of Hermeticism. The Hiram mythos will be discussed in the next chapter, but for our purposes in this section I have sought to associate the figure of Hiram with textual murkiness and the sense of darkness, which is generally associated with death.

Enoch

Enoch is the oldest of the three figures discussed in this chapter. There are two Enochs mentioned in the Bible, both occur in the Book of Genesis. The first Enoch is the son of Cain, post-fratricide. Either Cain and Enoch, or just Cain by himself, founds a town in Nablus and names it "Enoch" (Genesis 4:17). This creates an intriguing question, because if Cain killed Abel, then who else but Cain would carry on Adam's lineage? Chapter five of Genesis answers this by telling us that Adam and Eve had a third son, named "Seth," a seldom discussed character in mainstream Christianity, whom we are led to believe carried on Adam's bloodline.

For doctrinal reasons there had to be a blood relative to carry on Adam's legacy, which, in a literal sense is the curse of labor: "By the sweat of your brow you will eat your food until you return to the ground, since from it you were taken; for dust you are and to dust you will return" (Genesis 3:19). In an esoteric sense, however, Adam's legacy entailed the preservation of the "Seven Sciences:" Arithmetic, Geometry, Music, Astronomy,

Rhetoric, Logic, and Grammar. This idea is obviously Biblical in origin because it makes use of the numerologically significant number seven; however, its modern-day promulgation is more relevant to Freemasonry (and those who theorize about the conspiratorial nature and origins of Freemasonry). Wayne describes the genealogical passing down of these sciences this way:

> The sciences bestowed to Adam were of unimaginable worth, for they contained the secrets of the universe [...] The obscure importance of these sciences dictated that they must not be lost. They needed to be preserved among Adam's descendants, provided that Adam's descendants applied this divine knowledge for good. In fact, this was just what Adam did. Adam communicated this knowledge to two of his sons: Cain and Seth. Adam passed the Sacred Sciences onto two very different branches: Seth, whose descendants remained righteous until the seventh generation, and Cain, whose descendants were vile and treacherous from the time God ostracized Cain. The Sacred Sciences were preserved and utilized in two very different manners by the two very different branches of Adam's descendants.[198]

We will delve further into the narratives surrounding Enoch of Cain in later chapters, specifically "The Significance of the Known World."

The more widely known Enoch was a direct descendant of Seth. This Enoch is the seventh son in the lineage and his importance as such plays, yet again, on the numerological significance that the Hebrew people (and later certain sects of

[198] Wayne, Gary (2014) *The Genesis 6 Conspiracy*. Trusted Books, A Division of Deep River Books. Pp. 10 - 11

Christians) placed on the number seven. As an inhabitant of the antediluvian world, Enoch presumably coexisted with the Nephilim who were the offspring of the "the sons of God" (fallen angels or angels that were about to fall) and "the daughters of men" in Genesis 6:1 – 4. As we discussed in the previous chapter, destroying the Nephilim because they were abominations might have been one of God's reasons for flooding the earth.[199]

According to scripture, Enoch lived for 365 years, and for the last of these 300 years we are told that he "walked with God" and then vanished from the earth 669 years before his great-grandson Noah constructed the Ark (Genesis 5:21 – 24). He and Elijah were the only two figures from the Old Testament that absconded to Heaven without dying. There is much speculation as to what happened to Enoch while he "walked with God." The occultist interpretation is that he was either in Heaven or journeying through the cosmos. During this time, he was subject to a variety of visions and revelations, including, but not limited to:

-Seeing the four sides of the Lord of Spirits.[200]

-Seeing all the secrets of the heavens, "and how the kingdom is divided, and how the actions of men are weighed in the balance."[201]

-Seeing all the stars in heaven and God addressing them each by name.[202]

---

[199] *Ken's Guide to the Bible* states as a possible alternative to wiping out the Nephilim that: "God tells Noah that he intends to kill nearly every living creature on earth because the world has become too violent. (Genesis 6:13)" Smith, Ken (1995) *Ken's Guide to the Bible*. Blast Books. P. 23

[200] *The Book of Enoch the Prophet* (2012) Translated by R. H. Charles. Red Wheel/Weiser, LLC. P. 33

[201] Ibid, p. 33

-Encountering the Son of Man who shall "raise up the kings and the mighty from their seats, shall loosen the reins of the strong, and break the teeth of the sinners."[203]

-Seeing the repentance of the Gentiles: "through his name shall they be saved, and the Lord of Spirits will have compassion on them, for his compassion is great."[204]

-Seeing the final judgment of Azazel, the Watchers and their children; a judgment that is actually issued by the "Elect One" who sits on the throne of glory and judges Azazel, and all his associates, and all his hosts in the name of the Lord of Spirits."[205]

-Seeing a "host of wagons, and men riding thereon, and coming on the winds from the east, and from the west to the south. And the noise of their wagons was heard, and when this turmoil took place the holy ones from heaven remarked it, and the pillars of the earth were moved from their place, and the sound thereof was heard from the one end of heaven to the other, in one day."[206]

Most of these claims are prophetic boilerplate. However, the last one sticks out because it describes heaven as having spatial constraints, even though "from one end of heaven to the other" might be a bit of colloquialism.[207] This passage also sticks out because the pillars Enoch describes could be construed mythologically as the pillars created by Lamech to withstand the

---

[202] Ibid, p. 36

[203] Ibid, pp. 38 - 39

[204] Ibid, p. 44

[205] Ibid, p. 48

[206] Ibid, p. 50

[207] Ginzberg describes Enoch as travelling through the "seven heavens," see *The Legends of the Jews, Volumes I & II.* Forgotten Books, pp. 88 - 91

great deluge. On another reading, these pillars might be a reference to the Earth's magnetic poles – the shifting of which is a concern that fits into many contemporary conspiracy theories.

Unlike Melchizedek and Hiram, there is an entire, relatively coherent, Gospel attributed to Enoch; and in this respect, he could be considered a prophet.[208] In its explicit depiction of heaven and the fallen angels in his Gospel, Enoch is ostensibly less shadowy than Hiram or Melchizedek. His motives don't exist as mere inferences but as utterances. All three figures, however, are indexed within Biblical narratives, which subsequently stray beyond their given contexts. This process of straying occupies a large portion of the rest of this book.

For simplicity I will refer to the older Enoch as "Enoch of Cain" and the more well-known Enoch as just plain "Enoch." For people of a more fundamentalist Christian orientation, Enoch of Cain was evil, like his father, so they call him "Enoch the evil." However, since the Bible never really declares him to be evil, I will refer to him by his paternity.

The duality of these two Enochs is not complimentary, as their combined narratives fail to grant a complete image of a mythical figure; nor do they possess distinctive attributes that will be symbolically reconciled by a later mythical reconciliation (such as the theory that the figure of Jesus was in some way a composite of King David's fierceness and Solomon's wisdom).[209] Instead, it is a duality that results in confusion and obscurity, in which speculative theories run amok without possibility of a dialectical synthesis. Wayne claims that, because Enoch of Cain invented writing, he played a role like that of Thoth in ancient

---

[208] Obviously we have just gone through the fragments of the Gnostic Gospel of Melchizedek, what I mean by this statement is that Enoch's Gospel is more formal, not nearly as fragmented as Melchizedek's and "coulda' been a contender" for inclusion in the official Bible -Melchizedek's could not have.
[209] Wayne, Gary (2014) *The Genesis 6 Conspiracy*. Trusted Books, A Division of Deep River Books. P. 268

Egyptian mythology. Likewise, he also flexed his prowess in constructing the Pyramids of Egypt, writing thousands of books that were stored in the foot of the Sphinx, and becoming the father of Freemasonry. Wayne states that:

> Freemasonry believes the Egyptian culture and civilization did not develop instantaneously on its own; rather, according to Legends of the Craft, the Egyptians developed their advanced civilization and achievements from the knowledge obtained from the Pillars of Lamech, likely taken to Egypt with Ham, Hermes, and Mizraim after the Babel dispersion.[210]

Wayne claims that, in their mythological import, the historical figures of Hermes, Thoth, and Enoch of Cain are all closely related (if not the same individual): the creation and dispersion of written language being their commonality. On this view, the link to Egypt is not only qualified as a site of the propagation of this knowledge; it also is presumed to be a storage space for these texts:

> The words of these great, antediluvian, angelic sages were copied down by Thoth/Hermes/Enoch into various books and secured away for safety in temples that stretched along the Nile River. Hermes, as it was generally concluded, later hid his antediluvian secrets somewhere in ancient Egypt. Ancient Egyptian papyrus makes several references to the ancient, hidden chambers, known as the Chambers of Archives and the Hall of Records that contain all antediluvian knowledge. These

---

[210] Ibid p. 63

mysterious chambers were stated to be buried close to the Sphinx.[211]

Ginzberg's work is essential to elaborating upon certain narrative strands within the traditional Biblical narrative. His position holds that there were two Enochs and that Enoch of Cain was most likely "evil" in some way or another but led an otherwise relatively uneventful life. However, Enoch, Seth's descendant, is depicted as a hermit who lived in isolation, occasionally emerging from his spiritual retreat to educate his disciples. Ginzberg notes that:

> The impression made by the teachings of Enoch upon all who heard them was powerful. They prostrated themselves before him, and cried: "Long live the king! Long live the king!" On a certain day, while Enoch was giving audience to his followers, an angel appeared and made known unto him that God had resolved to install as king over the angels in heaven, as until then he had reigned over men. He called together all the inhabitants of the earth, and addressed them thus: "I have been summoned to ascend into heaven, and I know not on what day I shall go thither. Therefore I will teach you wisdom and righteousness before I go hence." A few days yet Enoch spent among men, and all the time left to him he gave instruction in wisdom, knowledge, God-fearing conduct, and piety, and established law and order, for the regulation of the affairs of men.[212]

---

[211] Ibid p. 156. As was previously mentioned, some conspiracy theorists claim that Hermes's library is encased in the foot of the Sphinx.
[212] Ginzberg, Louis (2008) *The Legends of the Jews, Volumes I & II.* Forgotten Books. Pp. 87 - 88

Not long after this revelation Enoch is whisked up into heaven on a fiery chariot; and while there, he experiences the revelations detailed above. Ginzberg adds two more twists to the legend of Enoch, the first of which coincides with Enoch of Cain:

> God called then one of His archangels who was more wise than all the others, and wrote down all the doings of the Lord, and He said to him, "Bring forth the books from My store-place, and give a reed to Enoch, and interpret the books to him." The angel did as he was commanded, and he instructed Enoch thirty days and thirty nights, and his lips never ceased speaking, while Enoch was writing down all the things about heaven and earth, angels and men, and all that is suitable to be instructed in. He also wrote down all about the souls of men, those of them which are not born, and the places prepared for them forever. He copied all accurately, and he wrote three hundred and sixty-six books.[213]

After the angel finishes his dictation, God appears and tells Enoch the "secrets, which even the angels do not know."[214] This includes the creation of the world, the creation and fall of Adam, and knowledge that the duration of the world will be seven millennia, each lasting a thousand years, with an eighth that will be infinite. The transcription of these 366 books might not rival the thousands of books that Enoch of Cain was said to have written, but it is a large literary output, and could be the cause of the conflation of the two figures. It's safe to speculate that *The Book of Enoch* that is known today was either a separate work from these volumes or a mere sliver of them.

It is worth pointing out that the two sources we are utilizing dialectically here, Wayne (on one hand) and Knight &

---

[213] Ibid p. 91
[214] Ibid p. 92

Lomas (on the other), make no mention of Ginzberg's account of this particular heavenly escapade. The second twist that Ginzberg adds to the Enoch legend is that God transforms him into an angel named "Metatron," the most *Voltron*-sounding name bestowed upon any angel:

> When Enoch was transformed into Metatron, his body was turned into celestial fire – his flesh became flame, his veins fire, his bones glimmering coals, the light of his eyes heavenly brightness, his eyeballs torches of fire, his hair a flaring blaze, all his limbs and organs burning sparks, and his frame a consuming fire.[215]

Whether or not Enoch and Metatron are the same individual is open for debate between occultists of varying stripes. The confusion between the two Enochs as it pertains to occultism, however, seems to stem primarily from Freemasonry, which attributes the creation of writing and building to the same being who "walked with God" and was subsumed into heaven.[216] In *Uriel's Machine* Knight and Lomas describe Enoch of Seth's genealogy given in Genesis 5: 21 – 29 as differing from Enoch of Cain's because:

> The originators of this tradition might not have been happy to have this hero be descended from

---

[215] Ibid p. 95

[216] This aspect of Enoch must have been passed down for generations prior to its being written down, since Ginzberg describes an episode in which Metatron whisked Moses up to heaven; during this excursion Moses asks the angel who he is and Metatron replies: "I am Enoch, the son of Jared, thy ancestor, and God has charged me to accompany thee to His throne." Ginzberg, Louis (1992) *Legends of the Bible*. The Jewish Publication Society. P. 312

Cain, the first murderer who killed his brother Abel. He was therefore given a different lineage through Seth, the third son of Adam and Eve, and was said not to have suffered death, but to have walked with God before being taken directly into heaven by Him.[217]

Knight and Lomas claim that the dual lineage given in the Bible was the result of Rabbinical Judaism, and that there was really only one line, descending from Cain.[218] Ginzberg's work, despite its concessions to Kabbalah and mysticism, would be classified solidly within the realm of traditional, Mosaic Judaism. In opposition to Rabbinical Judaism, Knight and Lomas proffer the Qumran Community (or the "Essenes"), who authored the *Dead Sea Scrolls,* as being the more authentic purveyors of the Enoch narrative, and state that their work,

> "Did not survive into Rabbinical Judaism or into Christianity past the first century AD. It seemed to us that there must have once been a great allegiance to the figure of Enoch which died with the Jewish nation during the war that broke out in AD 66."[219]

This emphasis on the authenticity of the Qumran Community, which they associate with Enoch over the more conventional Judaism – itself associated with Moses – fits into a narrative that is critical of monotheism: "Originally, the term 'angel' simply meant a god in the pantheon of heaven, but as the Jews became monotheistic these other inhabitants of heaven had to be

---

[217] Knight, Christopher & Lomas, Robert (2001) *Uriel's Machine.* Fair Winds Press. P. 29. Notice that this passage encapsulates the Masonic conflation of the two Enochs.
[218] Ibid p.43
[219] Ibid p. 92 and also p. 328

relegated to a secondary role that did not compromise Yahweh's unique position."[220]

In one sense, this attack on monotheism is explanatory because it gives a plausible reason as to why God would occasionally refer to himself as "us" in early parts of Genesis. However, it ought to be viewed as an iconoclastic trend in Freemasonry, one that is often coupled with the deconstruction of the Biblical narrative. *Uriel's Machine* claims that the Biblical narrative of Noah was predated by the Babylonian *Epic of Gilgamesh*, and is most likely a repetition of this older narrative.[221] It describes Enoch as a prophet who primarily "saw" the apocalyptic events that he predicted,[222] and claims that the flood was a global catastrophe predicated upon multiple comets and meteorites crashing into the world's oceans around 10,000 years ago.[223] Knight and Lomas even incorporate the "Priesthood of Melchizedek" into their narrative, claiming that it is definitely of Canaanite origin and a purveyor of the Enochian religious tradition.[224]

This speculation leads not only to the Templars and a Grail-related group referred to as "Rex Deus," but also to how this secret information found its way into the rites of Freemasonry. Just as Frank Joseph postulated the Naacals as the original group to have gained untold mastery of the world, and Gary Wayne posits the Nephilim, Knight and Lomas posit a group of proto-Europeans referred to as the "Grooved Ware People," who were, "in principle, as capable of some sort of intellectual development and innovation as we are today, and it is quite likely that then, as

---

[220] Ibid p. 134

[221] Ibid pp. 75 - 78

[222] As opposed to transcribing them into a text that was dictated to him.

[223] Ibid p. 133, this is both hard to believe and a form of scientistic demystification.

[224] Ibid pp. 316 - 328

now, only a small proportion of the population would have understood the science which underpinned their society."[225]

The Grooved Ware People arose at some point in the Megalithic period and they are significant to Knight and Lomas because they removed the supernatural from the Enoch narrative by claiming that Uriel, the "angel" who revealed the disasters that would befall the earth and taught Enoch astronomy, was in actuality a member of this advanced European people, who were mistaken as angels/watchers.[226]

If we take a hermeneutical approach to this issue there are a variety of factors that could lead writers, who were historically removed from the time of the scriptures, to construct narratives that elaborated the properties of these two Enochs into a greater synthesis. For instance, there is a likelihood that the confusion between them arose from the specifically occult practice of "Enochian Magic" developed by John Dee (1527 – 1608) and Edward Kelley (1554 – 1595) from 1582 to 1587. During these magical operations Kelley would enter a trance by way of crystal-gazing and act as a medium to the spirit-world; and Dee would then transcribe the information as it was imparted through Kelley.

The whole project was described in Dee's autobiography, *A True and Faithful Relation of what Passed for Many Years Between Doctor John Dee and Some Spirits*, edited by Meric Casaubon and published in 1659. [227] During these experiments, Kelley encountered a spirit named "Enoch" who communicated a spiritual language consisting of twenty-one letters and nineteen invocations, hence the language came to be called "Enochian." The formalized version of the Enochian alphabet, like the Hebrew alphabet, contains twenty-two letters and is claimed to have been the language spoken between God and Adam. According to

[225] Ibid p. 189
[226] Ibid p. 249
[227] Stewart, Louis (1980) *Life Forces: A Contemporary Guide to the Cult and Occult.* Andrews and McMeel, Inc. Pp. 205 - 206

Ginzberg, Jewish legend stipulates that the Hebrew alphabet coexisted with God prior to his creation of the world:

> When God was about to create the world by His word, the twenty-two letters of the alphabet descended from the terrible and august crown of God whereon they were engraved with a pen of flaming fire.[228]

Each of the letters proceed to come forward, except for one, and give their reason for why God should begin his divine word with them. Each is rejected for harboring a dual meaning that might negate God's intended meaning. God eventually settled on the last letter that approached him, "Bet." The letter that had refrained from petitioning God for this privilege, "Alef" was rewarded for its modesty by being placed at the beginning of the alphabet. It is interesting to speculate as to whether there is an isomorphic correspondence between the Hebrew and the Enochian alphabets. Instead of approaching this question systematically or theoretically though, let's consider it literarily.

In 1949 the Argentinian writer Jorge Luis Borges (August 24, 1899 – June 14, 1986) published a book entitled *The Aleph and Other Stories*. The eponymous story begins with a man grieving the death of a lover who proceeds to become acquaintances with the lover's idiosyncratic cousin, Carlos Argentino. Over time, Argentino reveals himself to be a poet and expresses the fear that his childhood home will be demolished as the cellar of the place contains something he calls an "Aleph," a tool he has been utilizing in the writing of his poetry. Borges describes the Aleph as "one of the points in space that contain all points."[229] Within

---

[228] Ginzberg, Louis (2008) *The Legends of the Jews, Volumes I & II.* Forgotten Books
P. 9
[229] Borges, Jorge Luis (1999) *Collected Fictions.* Translated by Andrew Hurley. Penguin Books. P. 280

the Aleph all the places in the world, seen from every angle coexist. Borges's narrator experiences the Aleph himself and in doing so has a visual experience of the infinite.[230]

There are two ways that we can think of this literary treatment of the Aleph, assuming that it is identical with the Alef that begins the Hebrew alphabet (but not the Enochian, which tellingly has more in common with English). On the one hand we have the notion that the first letter of an alphabet gives the reader access to the alphabet in its entirety. On the other hand, we might see the letter as an isolatable part of the language and in this partiality somehow acts as a key to previously inaccessible levels of metaphysical awareness or insight.

Returning to John Dee's testimony, if it is to be believed, the events he documented occurred roughly one hundred and thirty years before Freemasonry was formalized with the founding of the Grand Lodge in England in 1717, thus making the conflation of the two Enochs a later historical development. However, Dee served in the court of Elizabeth I, so there is a possibility his work influenced the nascent Masonic movement. Angel Millar argues that there is no formal claim made, nor should there be one, about the connection between John Dee and Freemasonry. However, it is in Dee's relationship to Euclid's writings that we find his significance to the tradition of Masonry:

> Yet, while not introducing anything foreign to the stonemasons in terms of additional symbolism, as the author of the preface to the *Elements*, Dee recontextualized Euclid's geometry, placing it in the

---

[230] In an essay twenty years prior, "A History of Angels" Borges claims that the letter "*aleph* corresponds to the brain, the First Commandment, the sky of fire, the divine name "I Am That I Am," and the seraphim known as the Sacred Beasts." Excerpted from Borges, Jorge Luis (1999) *Selected Non-Fictions*. Translated by Esther Allen, Suzanne Jill Levine, and Eliot Weinberger. Penguin Books. Pp. 17 - 18

developing intellectual and esoteric traditions, which saw geometry as exemplifying the Divine. Indeed, Dee clearly sees, and encourages, the reader through further study to see geometry as related to, or expressive of, God, who Dee also refers to as the "Architect."[231]

Millar emphasizes the fact that Dee transitioned from logic and geometry to proto-alchemy and Enochian magic, while maintaining the rigor of his foundational disciplines. Since this transition entails spirits, or angels, the strong implication is that Enochian magic, if it is tied to a Biblical Enoch, must be tied to the Enoch who walked with God and documented the fall of the angels. The work itself, conducted by Dee and Kelley, was a process of dictation and transcription. It conforms to Ginzberg's account of Enoch's experience in heaven, and is, in a certain respect, a repetition of that narrative. However, it also indicates aspects of Enoch of Cain since the "things" that are given to Dee and Kelley are not merely narratives, but an alphabet and a language – the primordial building blocks of communication.

It is important to note that, keeping with the philosophically pertinent aspects I am looking to present, the concept of repetition is of paramount importance. We have seen the idea that Jesus Christ was a repetition of Melchizedek and later we will see this model of partnership, wherein one individual acts as a medium while the other transcribes what is said, will also reoccur later in the book.

One final note I'd like to make regarding the influence John Dee's work might have had on the Masonic tradition has to do with a peculiar comment that Kelley made to Dee regarding the sacred sciences:

---

[231] Millar, Angel (2005) *Freemasonry: A History*. Thunder Bay Press. P. 43

> Our Teachers were deluders, and no good, or sufficient Teachers, who had not in two years space made us able to understand, or do somewhat; and that he could in two years have learned all the seven Liberal sciences, if he had first learned Logick, etc. wherefore he would have no more to do with them in any manner of way, ... and said that ...he took our Teachers to be deceivers, and wicked, and no good Creatures of God.[232]

It seems here that Kelley was condemning the "Teachers" for obscuring the seven sacred sciences, which are supposedly tied to the legacy of Enoch of Cain.

We will continue this discussion about the two Enochs, and any confusion that has arisen between them, in "The Significance of the Known World," but, before we can delve further, we must trace these seven sacred sciences into the historic framework of Freemasonry. In the process we will look at Freemasonry and its offshoots from a wide variety of perspectives, some benign, some ominous.

Conclusion

So far, we have seen three stages in the Genesis mythos:

1. The creation, in which the world is authored by God. The Structuralist aspect of which is further articulated in Adam's naming of the animals and is reinforced, and reinterpreted, in the Gospel According to John.

2. Noah's Ark was a gathering up, cataloging, and sorting of types (flora and fauna).

---

[232] Stewart, Louis (1980) *Life Forces: A Contemporary Guide to the Cult and Occult.* Andrews and McMeel, Inc. P. 206

3. The Tower of Babel was a great dispersion of language-based knowledge – possibly Logos itself.

Out of this succession of Biblical events we have extracted three marginal figures who reoccur in various conspiratorial contexts throughout history. Besides Melchizedek, Hiram, and Enoch there are a whole host of figures that can be described as existing within the murkiness of history. These particular figures were singled out here because they seemed to, or were claimed to, carry the secret of a myth with them. And for the sake of our text, we might look at them as vector points for various mythologies that in turn engendered groups and societies who would themselves become subjects of myths and conspiracy theories.

All three are linked together in this chapter insofar as they represent certain apprehensions of darkness or night. Melchizedek's mythos is tied to the mystery and depth of history, both textual and spoken; Hiram's mythos relates to the darkness associated with death; and Enoch's mythos is twofold. On the one hand, the murkiness is the darkness of heaven or the cosmos, but on the other hand the murkiness surrounding this figure has to do with the content of his narrative. Enoch's story is one of fallen angels who succumb to the temptations of earthly women, and then bring down the wrath of the divine upon mankind. Hence, the temptation of sexuality, which is a reiteration of the "forbidden fruit" in the Eden narrative, albeit more explicitly rendered, is a contrary, telluric, and earthier murkiness that might also be ascribed to the figure of Enoch.

These three characters are not archetypes in the way we traditionally think of the term. They are, instead, slight characters living at the margins of texts and the fact that they draw the eye of the curious reader away from the central focus of the narrative, in a way, gives more of a glimpse into the psychology of the reader than the historical significance of the character. However, outside of this psychological, and hence reductionist reading, these figures all bear repetition. By this I mean that they withstand reiteration throughout myriad texts, as well as demand a certain amount of this reiteration. Both characteristics are points where there is a convergence between mythic imagination, in the sense that mythology communicates symbolically because there is no concrete evidentiary-based narrative, and "meta" in the sense that there exists an imperative to create narratives that either explain or further propagate the myth itself.

Two other literal, textual aspects that warrant the appellation of "murkiness," which Wayne uses, are apt here: an obscure, unrecorded origin, and an obscure vanishing from recorded history.[233] The murkiness of these figures can also be due to the fact that they exist in what Erik Davis calls "a fog of forgetting." Davis uses this expression regarding Dennis McKenna's autobiographical recounting of his psychedelic experiments in South America. Granted, Davis places this sense of forgetting at the center of Dennis's account for what I interpret as Lacanian reasons:

> Things are never quite identical with themselves; there is a weird gap between essence and appearance. This weird gap also means that the basic operation of recursion –of self-reference- paradoxically calls forth the Other that is already within the self.[234]

Whereas I am focusing on this sense of forgetting as emanating from characters who exist at the margins of texts, this detail is coincidental with, or complimentary to, Lacanian analysis which addresses these marginal figures as "partial objects" within the

---

[233] Wayne, Gary (2014) *The Genesis 6 Conspiracy*. Trusted Books, A Division of Deep River Books. P. 175

[234] Davis, Erik (2019) *High Weirdness: Drugs, Esoterica, and Visionary Experience in the Seventies*. Strange Attractor Press & the MIT Press. P. 139. In this particular passage Davis references Latour, however, I believe it coincides with other points he makes regarding Lacan later in the chapter.

narrative parameters of the text. These figures are inherently elusive, and we continuously search for them, or their literary reiterations. However, in an ineffable sense they are inherently forgotten to themselves. The promise of historical or spiritual recovery held out by these individuals may seem like a sinister chimera, but it can also be seen in a manner similar to the Muses: divine, and hence immaterial, figures that spark the creative imagination into action.[235] On a more philosophical note, these individuals are fascinating because they are depersonalized; they are characters that have achieved the circulation begetting a certain degree of "object-hood." In this respect, their textual existence confounds our traditional demarcations between "subject" and "object."

---

[235] The concept of partial objects will be discussed again, and in greater detail, in the Significance of the Grail chapter.

Chapter Five: The Significance of The New World Order

The main purpose of this chapter is to analyze a few of the myriad texts pertaining to Freemasonry and then sketch out the narratives entailed by the concept of a "New World Order." Oftentimes, Freemasonry is summed up in pithy ways that succinctly reference either the spread of Enlightenment ideals, shadowy networks of intrigue, or most often both. Were I to stick with such a brief summarization I might have included the present analysis in the previous chapter. But because Freemasonry has such a rich history it demands an attenuated effort. However, were I to insert an abbreviated analysis on the topic in the last chapter, it would have immediately followed this paragraph:

> Conspiracy theories seem to only exist within secular societies and the most interesting one surrounding the Babel narrative is the theory that the men who built the tower were the progenitors of Freemasonry, and that after *their* fall, their descendants would eventually go on to build King Solomon's Temple. Unlike the "Book of Revelation" or The Gnostic Gospels, which point outward to the unknowable future and the unknowable cosmos. The Babel narrative focuses on the agency of men who seek to master their world.

Such a truncated analysis would then conclude that these men embodied the spirit of scientific and technological advancement, albeit one that was conceptualized as being grounded in the unfathomable depths of a divine will. The tension between these two poles will lead to the events of September 11, 2001, at which point the mythic ground that was constituted by a multitude of narratives was pulled away, leaving men with only scientific facts to guide their search. Hence, for a book devoted to myths and conspiracy theories such brevity would be an affront.

There are many books speculating on the origins and goals of Freemasonry – just flipping through the pages of Arthur Edward Waite's *A New Encyclopedia of Freemasonry* instills the idea that Freemasonry was largely the product of the Enlightenment era, one which was focused on codifying and hermetically passing down information. Regarding this type of project, keep in mind the novelty and vast scope of what the first Encyclopedists or Lexicographers were trying to accomplish when they sought to put down in writing all the known information they could find. Freemasonry presaged this endeavor and did so in an idiosyncratic and ritualized way, one that would lead to accusations of elitism. These accusations can be somewhat tempered with the understanding that literacy was itself a mark of elitism at the time.

Elitism within the context of this fraternal organization is inevitable, to a large extent, because Masonry is organized hierarchically and by degrees – 33 being the highest obtainable degree. [236] From an outsider's perspective, elitism is often conflated with obscurantism and secrecy, both of which were hallmarks of Rosicrucianism, a subject we will turn to shortly. Rosicrucianism adopted elements of Freemasonry (and in turn influenced certain sects of Masonry) that were mysterious and extended this aspect of the tradition into a realm that could best be described as fantastical. As we will see, oftentimes when mysticism and the occult are interjected into a narrative, it is done so in accordance with the idea that there is a historical pedigree that warrants this inclusion. Besides any claims made about the Tower of Babel and Solomon's Temple, there have been claims about a very specific historical-religious group to which many contemporary commentators on Freemasonry have drawn attention. Unsurprisingly, this group is the Gnostics.

Gnostic Progenitors

---

[236] That we know about.

The fourth chapter of *The Hiram Key* is primarily concerned with positing the theory of the Gnostics as a heterogeneous element within Christianity that had to be expelled in order to preserve the hierarchical structure of the Church – a hierarchy that Knight and Lomas insist was preserved by the Church's insistence on the literal resurrection of Christ:

> There are major consequences of a literal belief in the resurrection of Jesus's body which later ascended into heaven. All the authority of the Roman Catholic Church stems from the experiences of Jesus's resurrection by the twelve favoured apostles, an experience which was closed to all newcomers following his ascent into Heaven. This closed, unchallengeable experience had enormous implications for the political structure of the early Church.
> It restricted the leadership to a small circle of persons who held a position of incontestable authority and conferred on this group the right to ordain future leaders as their successors. This resulted in the view of religious authority which has survived to this day: that the apostles alone held definitive religious authority and that their only heirs are priests and bishops, tracing their ordination back to that same apostolic succession. Even today the Pope derives his authority from Peter, first of the apostles, since he was first witness of the resurrection. It was very much in the interests of the rulers of the early Church to accept the resurrection as a literal truth because of the benefits it conferred on them in the form of an uncontested source of authority.[237]

---

[237] Knight, Christopher & Lomas, Robert (2001) *The Hiram Key*. Fair Winds Press. Pp. 38 – 39. This debate is actually still alive

Of course, the Freemasons would go on to duplicate this hierarchical system in their own order, but in a way that emphasized rationality; we have seen this in our discussion of the Master Mason ceremony in the previous chapter. *The Hiram Key* downplays the controlling aspects of this brand of hierarchy in an attempt to link the Masonic rites to Gnosticism, which the authors see as politically liberating, insofar as individuals can achieve knowledge of the Divine without having to appeal to "dogmatic" institutions such as the Catholic Church.

On this note, it goes without saying that Freemasons are not Catholics and Catholics are not allowed to be Freemasons; a fact conclusively evidenced by Pope Leo XIII's Encyclical Letter on the subject. After condemning Freemason oaths to secrecy and the obedience entailed by admission into Freemasonry, the Letter states:

> For, no matter how great may be men's cleverness in concealing and their experience in lying, it is impossible to prevent the effects of any cause from showing, in some way, the intrinsic nature of the cause whence they come. "A good tree cannot produce bad fruit, nor a bad tree produce good fruit." Now, the Masonic sect produces fruits that are pernicious and of the bitterest savor. For, from what We have above most clearly shown, that which is their ultimate purpose forces itself into view –namely, the utter overthrow of that whole religious and political order of the world which the

---

today, within the Catholic Church, if we are to believe Italian journalist Eugenio Scalfari who has claimed that Pope Francis himself denies that Christ was physically resurrected. See: https://www.dailymail.co.uk/news/article-7665347/Pope-Francis-denied-bodily-resurrection-Christ-says-Italian-friend.html

Christian teaching has produced, and the substitution of a new state of things in accordance with their ideas, of which the foundations and laws shall be drawn from mere "Naturalism."[238]

Pope Leo goes on to define "Naturalism" in these terms: it views reason as mankind's guide, over and above duty to God; and it is dismissive of any dogma or teaching that cannot totally fit within the scope of human understanding.[239]

This attitude was bound to create some animosity on both sides. I read Knight & Lomas's praise of Gnosticism at the expense of the Catholic Church to be partly inspired by this sense of antagonism. Knight & Lomas see the Gnostic trend towards disbelief in a literal resurrection of Jesus as being a sign of nascent scientism (or in Pope Leo XIII's terminology "Naturalism") which is laudable, especially by the lights of the ideals of the Enlightenment.

Conspiracy theorists will often link Freemasonry with the Enlightenment, or figures closely associated with it, such as Voltaire or Rousseau, because both seemed to endorse universalistic ideals (liberty, equality, the rule of reason over dogmatism, etc.).[240] A further linking of the Enlightenment to

---

[238] Pope Leo XIII (1978) *Humanum Genus, Encyclical Letter of His Holiness Pope Leo XIII on Freemasonry. April 20, 1884.* Tan Books and Publishers, INC. pp. 6 - 7

[239] Pope Leo seems to be focusing on the more liberal factions of Freemasonry, who he views as engaging in a constant attack to undermine the Catholic Church, Ibid pp. 7- 9. According to Glenn Alexander Magee, prior to this missal, which was issued in 1884, there had been a larger presence of more traditional, less liberal Masons, who have been dwindling in number since the nineteenth century.

[240] Voltaire was initiated into Freemasonry near the end of his life by Benjamin Franklin, who had, while acting as ambassador to France in 1776 had taken the position of Master at the

"Naturalism" occurs in the physicist John Robison's (February 4, 1739 – January 30, 1805) *Proofs of a Conspiracy...* in which he claimed that:

> It is amusing to observe the earnestness with which they recommend the study of natural history. One does not readily see the connection of this with their ostensible object, the happiness of man. A perusal of Voltaire's letters betrays the secret. Many years ago he heard that some observations on the formation of strata, and the fossils found in them, were incompatible with the age which the Mosaic history seems to assign to this globe. He mentions this with great exultation in some of his early letters; and from that time forward, never ceases to enjoin his colleagues to press the study of natural history and cosmogony, and carefully to bring forward every fact which was hostile to the Mosaic accounts.[241]

Voltaire's delight in undermining the "Mosaic accounts" is one key part of a larger, systematic project with which he was engaged, namely the Enlightenment. The aspect of the Enlightenment period that ties it most closely to the lucid Freemasonry presented by Knight & Lomas is what Stephen Mulhall describes as its systematic rejection of "any teleological forms of understanding the natural world" in favor of a rationalistic model

---

prestigious, Paris-based Nine Muses Lodge. Millar, Angel (2005) *Freemasonry: A History.* Thunder Bay Press. P. 204

[241] Robison, John (2014) *Proofs of a Conspiracy Against All the Religions and Governments of Europe, Carried on in the Secret Meetings of Freemasons, Illuminati, and Reading Societies.* CreateSpace Independent Publishing Platform. Pp. 194 - 195

of morality.[242] According to Mulhall, this break from teleology doesn't just remove an idealistic, divinely-guided, end for humanity, it also cuts us off from our primordial points of determination, which in the case of Christianity is original sin. The rationalism espoused by this model within the context of Freemasonry is interesting because it defines the Masons as individuals who are seeking to establish clarity and escape from myth, while simultaneously being ensconced within it by way of their orders and rites.

The project of *The Hiram Key* is then, like scientism, a reductionist project. The underlying substrate to which Knight and Lomas hope to reduce the myths they are tackling down is politics. One of their primary tools in this endeavor is Hermeneutics. The first explicit example of this begins in chapter five when they claim that the second century Christian Church had essentially "looted" the twenty-two Jewish texts that constituted the core of the Old Testament in order to establish Jesus's Messianic pedigree. [243] "Looting" is a harsh term for reinterpretation; Knight and Lomas will later claim that the secrets contained in the Old Testament were purloined from the Egyptians, but let's not get ahead of ourselves.

The paradox presenting itself to us here is that you have two dutiful Freemasons demystifying Masonry while simultaneously claiming that such demystification is essentially the spirit of Masonry. Is this true? It seems more likely that Knight and Lomas are working on the antithetical side of our historical dialectic and that their work is directed at traditional Masonry. The idea that traditional Masonry itself was not a deconstructive force and had very conservative tendencies is a topic we will examine later in the chapter. Regardless, it is ironic that *The Hiram Key* seeks to debunk a myth, but is unaware that the order

---

[242] Mulhall, Stephen (2005) *Philosophical Myths of the Fall.* Princeton University Press pp. 3 - 5
[243] Knight, Christopher & Lomas, Robert (2001) *The Hiram Key.* Fair Winds Press. P. 47

it is defending – while simultaneously demystifying – speaks not the content of that myth but *in the form* of myth. These myths are not confined to the orders' rites, but to its texts as well.

Besides the Gnostics, who appear at the beginning and end of *The Hiram Key*, Knight and Lomas spend the middle part of their narrative deducing that the figure of Hiram in the Solomon narrative was actually a Hebrew appropriation of an earlier Egyptian myth. According to this narrative, an Egyptian King named Seqenenre Tao was murdered by a group of "proto-Hebrews" called Hyksos, who lived in Egypt at the time. The Hyksos assassins were relatives of the Biblical figure Joseph, who essentially organized the "hit:"

> Joseph was given responsibility for the project, and who better to send than two of his estranged brothers, namely Simeon and Levi? If they were found out and killed it would not matter, as they deserved no better for selling Joseph into slavery all those years ago. If they succeeded, all well and good; Joseph would be a hero himself and his brothers would have paid off an old debt.[244]

The motive for the murder was that the Hyksos king wanted to know the secrets necessary to access the Egyptian afterlife. After Seqenenre Tao was murdered in the Temple, without revealing any secrets the assassins were executed, and the Egyptian ruling class enacted a new series of rites to take the place of the authentic rite. According to Knight and Lomas, the story of Seqenenre Tao's murder was rewritten into Jewish legend, much as the creation story from Genesis was a reiteration of Mesopotamian creation stories, or Moses's origin (being found in a raft in the reeds) was a reiteration of Sargon of Akkad's origin

---

[244] Ibid, p. 138

story. From there, this story found its way into Masonic lore and ritual.[245]

Knight and Lomas ground this theory on two things: the idea that the Egyptian concept of "Ma'at," which meant symmetrical order and justice, had been transposed into the Masonic tradition; and that this incorporation must have occurred prior to the discovery of the Rosetta Stone in 1799.[246]

The group that then forms the missing link between the ancient Egyptian rite and modern Freemasonry is the Qumran community, who Knight and Lomas identify as "the Nasoreans" and who they claim authored the Dead Sea Scrolls in the decades after Christ's death.[247] Knight and Lomas's story is not without its problems, though. Firstly, it flies in the face of Masonic tradition, or speaking as an outsider to Masonry, I should say that it *seems* to fly in the face of the more mainstream Masonic works I've surveyed, all of which give a more detailed story of who Hiram Abif might have been.[248] Secondly, it perpetrates the idea, also espoused by Jordan Maxwell, that the Egyptians were tapped into a more authentic form of life or being, and that all our remaining noble institutions today are descendants of Egyptian mysteries.[249] One could chalk this up to the enduring allure of the pyramids, the Sphinx, and hieroglyphics; all of which have been incorporated

---

[245] Ibid, pp. 146 - 151

[246] This claim is made in spite of the fact that "Ma'at" was not a word used by Freemasons at any time in history prior to the publication of *The Hiram Key*.

[247] Ibid, p. 189

[248] The continuation of our discussion on this topic occurs in "The Significance of JFK" chapter.

[249] Sigmund Freud also engaged in this a bit in *Moses and Monotheism* wherein he speculated that certain Jewish rites were borrowed from Egyptian culture, see *The Standard Edition of the Complete Psychological Works of Sigmund Freud Volume XXIII*. Pp. 25 - 28

into many occult systems and are used extensively in Masonic symbolism.

From our perspective as textual analysts, it seems clear that Knight and Lomas adhere to a scientific reductionism that borders on the metaphysical monism we saw in our analysis of Ignatius Donnelly; it seems to be a trait that came to greater prominence in the early-to-mid-stages of modernity. From this starting-point, Knight and Lomas also apply compound theorizing to their thinking. This approach seems to have gained popularity later in modernity; certainly Donnelly employed it, but when he added his extraneous, tangentially related bits of knowledge, it was in service to the historical richness of his narrative about Atlantis.

It is interesting to note that in the eighties and nineties when Knight and Lomas were researching and publishing their work they were contemporaneous with Baigent, Leigh, and Lincoln, as well as Graham Hancock. The totality of these authors, as well as the Ancient Aliens proponents who were gaining steam at the time, indicates that this period represented a collective, or emergent, return to a reductionism that was not metaphysically monistic – because these individuals had substituted scientism for metaphysics – but nonetheless retains the spirit of monism, in that they all sought a single explanatory point from which all the phenomena brought under their purview emanated. Before we continue with Knight and Lomas's endeavor to rehabilitate the Gnostics, we need to address the influence of Rosicrucianism on Freemasonry.

The Rosicrucians

In 1881 the poet Percy Bysshe Shelley published the Gothic horror novel, *St. Irvyne; or the Rosicrucian: A Romance*, in which the protagonist, Wolfstein encounters an alchemist named Ginotti. Ginotti is a member of the Rosicrucians who is trying to find the secret of eternal life. Near the end of the novel, Ginotti offers to tell the secret of eternal life to Wolfstein if he would deny his creator. Wolfstein declines the offer and both are killed by an act of God – as was the style at the time. This story indicates an important facet of what separates Rosicrucianism from mere Freemasonry: the promise of the fantastic. That Ginotti was an alchemist is important to the distinction between Freemasonry and Rosicrucianism. Granted, Freemasonry incorporates many alchemical terms into its rites and degrees, however, these seem to be in the service of allegory for personal and spiritual transformation. Take this excerpt from "The Rite of Unknown Philosophers" in A. E. Waite's *A New Encyclopaedia of Freemasonry* for example:

> (36) Members shall abstain from sophistic operations on metals, holding no commerce with charlatans, as there is nothing more unworthy of a Christian philosopher and seeker of truth. (37) Those who are as yet inexperienced in the Mysteries of Fire may work upon minerals, vegetables and animals, and may even experiment in the depuration of metals, as these things are sometimes needful in the activities of the Order; but it is expressly forbidden to join metals with metals, for this is an evil work. (38) It is permissible to visit the laboratories and conventions of vulgar chemists, provided they are persons of repute, to undeceive them when they are in error, with modesty and in a spirit of charity, but taking care at the same time never to say too much, depending mainly on negative arguments, drawn from the writings of initiated philosophers. (39) It is permissible to promote a desire for integration in the Order in the case of persons who love wisdom

and probity, and who are drawn to Hermetic Science by valid curiosity and not by greed.[250]

According to Glenn Alexander Magee, "the most important event in the history of seventeenth century Hermeticism was the appearance of the Rosicrucian manifestos" in the town of Kassel in Brunswick in 1614.[251] The manifestos were addressed to "all of the learned in Europe," totaled thirty-eight pages, and were signed "the praiseworthy order of the Rose Cross." Despite the importance of Rosicrucianism to the Hermetic tradition, which is a subject that will play a greater role in the next two chapters, we can adequately address the subject here insofar as it is a part of the history of Freemasonry and an inspiration for artists, writers (as evinced by Shelley's *St. Irvyne*), philosophers, and occultists.

The central figure of the Rosicrucian tradition is Christian Rosenkreuz, who was purported to have lived from 1378 to 1484[252] and was instructed in the Hermetic art by Arab mystics in Egypt. The inventor of this mythos was most likely Johann Valentin Andrae (1586 – 1654), a clergyman who studied alchemy, Christian Kabbalah, and Pythagoreanism.[253]

Before we spend an undue amount of time untangling the threads of the Rosicrucian mythos, it is worth noting that you can still find Freemasons out in the world. Regardless of how one feels about it, Freemasonry is an established institution with

---

[250] Waite, Arthur Edward (1970) *A New Encyclopaedia of Freemasonry (Volume Two)*. Weathervane Books. P. 361

[251] Magee, Glenn Alexander (2001) *Hegel and the Hermetic Tradition*. Cornell University Press. P. 51

[252] Daraul tells the legend of Rosenkreuz's age this way: "He died at the age of one hundred and fifty years: not because he had to, it is noted, but because he wanted to –which seems a good enough reason." From Daraul, Arkon (1961) *A History of Secret Societies*. Citadel Press. P. 192

[253] Magee, Glenn Alexander (2001) *Hegel and the Hermetic Tradition*. Cornell University Press. p. 52

chapters, orders, and buildings that have been around for hundreds of years. It is possible that Freemasonry started out as a cargo cult in an order that was believed to have existed in King Solomon's time, or at the earlier Tower of Babel; but at some point in history it became a formal entity, not unlike the Catholic Church or the Rotary Club. Rosicrucianism, wherever you might find it, if you can find it in the world, is still in its cargo cult phase.

The relationship between Freemasonry and Rosicrucianism is in many ways an organizational reiteration of the relationship between Atlantis and Lemuria. Both couplings are viewed with skepticism by mainstream society, but Rosicrucianism and Lemuria are less well-known, more obscure, and demand a greater devotion to research for those who are interested in them.

This statement is not meant to disparage Rosicrucianism, for it is a fascinating topic primarily because it is drawn from and constituted by literature. For the last few centuries there have been numerous artists and writers who happened to be Freemasons, but Rosicrucianism, for those who subscribed to it, used its vague ethos as a guiding force in their work. The French writer, Joséphin Péladan, interpreting art in a Catholic and Universalist way, created the Salon de la Rose+Croix in 1892 to "unite poetry, music, and painting as Wagner had already tried to do."[254]

We've established that in the eighteenth-century Freemasonry was concerned with preserving and passing down knowledge via mythic rites. Rosicrucianism can be said to have served a similar purpose, though its adherents seem to have consistently purported its rites and inventions as having transcended the realm of science. Willy Schrödter (1897 – 1971) catalogued some of these fantastic objects and abilities in his 1954 book *A Rosicrucian Notebook*; these include: the elixir of life, alchemy (specifically the synthetic production of precious metals

---

[254] Jullian, Philippe (1974) *Dreamers of Decadence*. Praeger Publishers, Inc. P. 76

as well as pearls), "ever burning lamps," magical mirrors, and a telescope that operated beyond the range of visible light.[255]

For our purposes, the contrast between the aims of Freemasonry and Rosicrucianism can be framed as a replication of the contemporary philosophical debate on what is "Reason" and what role it plays, or should play, in our discourse and society; the parameters of which were articulated by Jacques Derrida and Michel Foucault in the latter half of the twentieth century. The debate, as detailed in Roy Boyne's *Foucault and Derrida*, began when Foucault postulated that Reason arose as a totalizing and exclusionary force directed at mental illness and idleness:

> His text takes us back in time to uncover the complex history of mental illness. It is a history which begins with the decline of leprosy and which ends with the modern mental hospital [...] The dismissal and concealment of this history can be seen as part of the Enlightenment project, a project which affirms that no part of the social condition is beyond analysis, and thus that the orderly workings of social power can be guaranteed through the development and application of knowledge. This project enshrines a denial of otherness, of difference. It is, effectively, *the* absolutist project, unconsciously designed along lines of complete domination. Foucault felt sure that otherness could not be left behind by the march of time. He thought that it could only be repressed. The desire that formed his words was for the return of the Other,

---

[255] Schrödter, Willy (1992) *A Rosicrucian Notebook*. Samuel Weiser, INC. Pp. 1 -2

> not as a fury, suffering, or a vengeful power out of
> control, but as the right to be different.[256]

Derrida's response to Foucault's project, according to Boyne, was incredulity; he did not believe that madness (which Foucault was equating with "the Other") could be sufficiently investigated using the language of Reason, since madness is the language of unreason. In response to this critique, Foucault reformulated his project to look for another kind of Reason. Derrida rejected this, insisting that Reason was tied to logic and therefore universal and monolithic. Eventually Foucault relinquished this quest for another kind of Reason and began analyzing power relations.

When Derrida defines Reason as being one, unassailable universal condition, he means that: "The condition of reason is not that of a contingent order or a structure of fact. It is not an historically determined structure which could be otherwise. Therefore, any attempt to work against reason will always be contained by reason; reason-in-general cannot be exceeded."[257]

For Foucault, Reason seems to be something that sprang from the Enlightenment and in some way took possession of Western society. Derrida, by contrast, seems to be looking at Reason as that which informs our use of language, and, when it is employed by the sciences, as something that is grounded in logic, specifically the processes of deduction and induction. Boyne does not address this reduction of Reason to either induction or deduction, but we must assume that these very basic logical principles are what Derrida has in mind.

What is missing from this part of the argument is an interpretation of logic that is neither strictly inductive nor deductive, specifically the process of abduction. Drawing on the work of Charles Sanders Peirce, we can take a deductive process as being something like this:

---

[256] Boyne, Roy (1990) *Foucault and Derrida: The Other Side of Reason*. Routledge p.33
[257] Ibid p. 60

If A, then B;
But A:
Therefore B

"A" and "B" are propositions. When Peirce discusses abduction (he calls it "hypothetic inference") in relation to this form of reasoning he does so by talking about how we might substitute other propositions (like "P" or "Q") within the schematic. The fact that Peirce uses the term "hypothesis" indicates that he is thinking in a way that is aligned with science. However, it is in the act of substitution – how and what we come up with as viable substitutes – that we veer away from the cold analytic of science towards the realm of intuition and emotion.[258] For Peirce, our power of reasoning is akin to the moment when we awaken from a dream, wherein this moment of awaking and pondering makes consistent narratives out of jumbled emotions.

Now that we've taken some of the constituents of this debate about Reason into account, we can make some generalizations. For Foucault, Reason is a cultural, totalizing spirit that has animated our culture since the seventeenth century which needs to be countered or undermined in some way. For Derrida such undermining or aversion is not feasible. Reason informs our thought and action almost uniformly, insofar as we are using, and are orientated by, language. In this way, Derrida could be seen as working towards a demystification (or deconstruction) of Reason. And with Peirce we have a sort of

---

[258] One reference to emotion in relation to logic occurs in "Some Consequences of Four Incapacities": "Everything in which we take the least interest creates in us its own particular emotion, however slight this may be. This emotion is a sign and a predicate of the thing. Now, when a thing resembling this thing is presented to us, a similar emotion arises; hence, we immediately infer that the latter is like the former." Excerpted from *Pragmatism, Old & New* edited by Susan Haack.

synthesis of the two positions: he affirms the procedural aspect of Derrida as well as the uncertainty and alterity implied by Foucault.

How does this debate relate to the issue of secret fraternal orders? Can we say that what the Freemasons did or do is in the service of Reason, and if so, which conception of Reason? In a way it does, or has done, all three. First, as it pertains to Foucault's depiction, Freemasonry mirrored and acted reciprocally with the Enlightenment, therefore cultivating a spirit, or *zeitgeist*, of Reason as a cultural phenomenon. It is usually in this regard that it is attacked by its detractors.

Second, as it relates to Derrida's interpretation, Freemasonry made use of Reason in terms of application, but in a very uncanny way. Derrida insisted that Reason exists where language exists and that an archaeology of madness (or the absence of Reason) would either be merely an historical account or silence. By encoding their acquired knowledge within allegory and mythical rites, Freemasons essentially used performances, literature, and symbolism as a way of sidestepping the pretense of total knowledge or mastery evinced by many historians.[259]

If we push this aspect even further, into the supernatural realm purportedly inhabited by the Rosicrucians, we can interpret their fantastic claims (or claims made about them) in one of two ways. The first way involves just a literal belief in these claims; this kind of belief is essentially a duplication of a literalist belief in the miracles depicted in the Bible or the claims made by clairvoyants. The second way is to interpret these inventions and abilities in a metaphorical way; doing so eventually leads back to the artistic and literary avenues from which Rosicrucianism initially sprung. The introduction of Rosicrucianism when it first occurred, and every other time it occurs, represents an attempt at re-enchantment.

---

[259] Recall our discussion of E.F. Bleiler's approach to Donnelly's *Atlantis: The Antediluvian World*.

It still might seem tenuous to conjoin one esoteric pair of fraternal orders with an equally esoteric philosophical argument that occurred in the 1970s, but I think the debate on the nature of Reason sheds light on the inner-workings and philosophical underpinnings of Masonry and Rosicrucianism because both groups worked towards an alignment with the tenets of Reason. However, unlike with conspiracy theorists of today, they did not seek validation from any scientific group that presented itself as the arbiter of Reason –they had an actual role in promulgating what Reason would become, in both the cultural sense (Foucault) and the instrumental sense (Derrida). On this interpretation, Rosicrucianism can be seen as stepping too far outside the bounds of Reason and into the supernatural (and hence, the irrational); however, if we hold to the metaphorical interpretation of Rosicrucianism we can understand it as a force that was directing Reason back towards the arts and literature. In this sense, Rosicrucianism can be interpreted as a radically Structuralist endeavor – an interpretation that, interestingly enough, coincides with Peirce's work. Let's consider this passage from the essay "Some Consequences of Four Incapacities":

> What distinguishes a man from a word? There is a distinction doubtless. The material qualities, the forces which constitute the pure denotative application, and the meaning of the human sign, are all exceedingly complicated in comparison with those of the word. But these differences are only relative. What other is there? It may be said that man is conscious while word is not. But consciousness is a very vague term. It may mean that emotion which accompanies the reflection that we have animal life. This is a consciousness which is dimmed when animal life is at its ebb in old age, or sleep, but which is not dimmed when the spiritual life is at its ebb; which is the more lively the better *animal* a man is, but which is not so, the better *man*

he is. We do not attribute this sensation to words, because we have reason to believe that it is dependent on an animal body. But this consciousness, being a mere sensation, is only a part of the *material quality* of the man-sign. Again, consciousness is sometimes used to signify the *I think,* or unity in thought; but this unity is nothing but consistency, or the recognition of it. Consistency belongs to every sign, so far as it is a sign; and therefore every sign, since it signifies primarily that it is a sign, signifies its own consistency. The man-sign acquires information, and comes to mean more than he did before. But so do words. Does not electricity mean more now than it did in the days of Franklin? Man makes the word, and the word means nothing which the man has not made it mean, and that only to some man. But since man can think only by means of words or other external symbols, these might turn around and say: "You mean nothing which we have not taught you, and then only so far as you address some word as the interpretant of your thought." In fact, therefore, men and words reciprocally educate each other; each increase of a man's information involves and is involved by, a corresponding increase of a word's information.[260]

Previously when we discussed the distinction between the Hermeneutical and Structuralist methods of interpretation, we ascribed to the Structuralist school of thought the idea of individuals being literally animated by the discourses they speak.

---

[260] Peirce, Charles "Some Consequences of Four Incapacities" printed in
Haack, Susan (editor) (2006) *Pragmatism, Old & New*. Prometheus Books. P. 102

Here, Peirce is going even farther, in that he proclaims that the word or sign a man uses is the man himself. For Peirce, the homespun saying of "you are only good as your word" is radically true.

Ensconced as it is in myths and allegories that are repeated and reanimated via rites, Freemasonry exhibits an esoteric form of reciprocation between the word and subject. By acting out the myth within the context of the rite, the Freemason is essentially bringing himself into communion with the realization of his existence as a sign. Now, this is not to say that the development of Freemasonry was in accordance with the conscious recognition of these philosophical implications, for it obviously was not. But it is fascinating that this form of myth and esotericism, when interpreted in this light, coincides so closely with a formal discourse of academic philosophy.

Also note Peirce's statement: "You mean nothing which we have not taught you, and then only so far as you address some word as the interpretant of your thought." This points towards the initiatory aspect of language. Freemasonry and Rosicrucianism – to the extent that it actually exists – are demonstrative of a formal rendering of this concept of initiation, and because they are organized in terms of ascending degrees they mirror the never-ending linguistic project of concept-acquisition and concept-development.

The artistry, or the literary sensibility that has been incorporated and utilized by Freemasons and Rosicrucians for the last few centuries (or however far back one traces it) is what bridges the gap between the academic philosophical debate about Reason and the esoteric fraternal order. Most conspiracy theorists who focus their attention on Masonry are indifferent to this more nuanced approach to the Freemasons' relationship with Reason, or forbidden knowledge, and are far more interested in how this knowledge or influence plays out in a political context. The reduction to politics leads us neatly into the topic of the political implications of A New World Order; an expression that has been used by politicians since the early-twentieth century, it was

George H.W. Bush's speech entitled "Toward a New World Order" delivered to Congress on September 11, 1990, that firmly lodged the concept in the conspiratorial mind.

Before we can address how this statement by the 41st President of the United States is embroiled within the conspiratorial currents surrounding Freemasonry we need to examine its relationship to the first President of the United States. To begin, let's return to Knight and Lomas and discuss their analysis of Barabbas, the rogue who was released instead of Jesus. Knight and Lomas argue that "Barabbas" was not a name but a title. The obvious Structuralist rejoinder to this proposition would be: "What is a name if not a title?" coupled with a demand that the answer not involve circular reasoning. But let's step over that, for now, and return to analyzing the particularities of Knight and Lomas's theory. The claim is deduced from the etymology of the word, "Barabbas," as a conjunction of "Bar" meaning "son of" and "Abba" meaning "father" and the fact that certain versions of the Bible (specifically *The New International Version* and *The Good News Translation*) designate the individual held in Roman custody as "Jesus Barabbas."[261] This semantic confusion will help birth a variety of the theories that will be covered in our discussion of the Grail mythos. It should be apparent that Knight and Lomas are building up to the declaration that the individual we think of as "Jesus" did not die on the cross. The reason I am talking about this here is because the idea of a switcheroo, and an especially grandiose one involving a historical figure of epic proportions, presages the conspiracy theory that the figure of George Washington was merely one of Adam Weishaupt's disguises. The theory that Washington was really Weishaupt is a repetition, or reiteration, of the "Barabbas was Jesus" narrative. From our historical vantage point, it isn't possible to determine which conspiracy confusion (Barabbas = Jesus and Adam Weishaupt = George Washington) historically preceded the other –

---

[261] Knight, Christopher & Lomas, Robert (2001) *The Hiram Key.* Fair Winds Press. P. 50

hermeneutically speaking it is a "chicken or egg" question. All we can say is that both narratives exist, and that there is something about the internal logic of each that makes them, if not interdependent upon each other, at least interwoven with each other.

At this point all we can do is note that the narrative, stated as a proposition, has been repeated and essentially can withstand repetition within the greater historical narrative. In this process the names are essentially titles or placeholders for a subset of subjects. Let's focus on one of these interchangeable titles, "Adam Weishaupt," and see if we can construct an historically plausible narrative of who he was and why his name is so closely tied to the idea of a New World Order.

The Bavarian Illuminati

Throughout the eighteenth century, Freemasonry housed an internal division between progressive and conservative factions. We have already identified the Rosicrucian intrusion into Masonry as having both literary and supernatural trappings, but it should also be noted that Rosicrucianism may have also represented a politically progressive, more Enlightenment-orientated, ethos. Magee points out that Freemasonry in Germany simultaneously embraced the Enlightenment in a nominal way while also seeking a "truer enlightenment" through Hermeticism. [262] This indubitably religious, albeit non-denominational, aspect at play in eighteenth century German lodges led to the creation of the group that would become the almighty grandfather of all conspiracy theories:

> The individuals known as the Illuminati were the reaction to this reaction. The Illuminati were founded in 1776 as a means to advance the ideals of

---

[262] Magee, Glenn Alexander (2001) *Hegel and the Hermetic Tradition.* Cornell University Press. P. 56

the Enlightenment: opposition to traditional religion, superstition, and feudalism, and advocacy of scientific rationalism and the rights of man.[263]

The "Illuminati" referenced here is of course the Bavarian Illuminati, founded by a law professor named Adam Weishaupt (February 6, 1748 – November 18, 1830) who was born in Bavaria and received a Jesuit education until his enrollment at the University of Ingolstadt in 1768. Besides studying and practicing law, Weishaupt dabbled in philosophy; his outlook favored Empiricism and was highly critical of Kant and German Idealism in general. Despite his dislike for Kant, when it came to formulating the doctrines of the Order of the Illuminati, he placed great emphasis on Reason.[264]

We can assume that Weishaupt's conception of Reason was a rarified one intended to be cultivated by the "lovers of wisdom and philanthropy" who were the targets of Johann Valentin Andrae's Rosicrucian pamphlets some one hundred and fifty years prior. Many conspiracy theorists who engage in reductionism will say that the Illuminati was the return of the Rosicrucians, or were Rosicrucianism in new garb. This is a claim that is neither provable nor falsifiable, however, on our reading we can ask if the Bavarian Illuminati narrative is a reiteration of the Rosicrucian narrative. The short answer to this question, is most likely no; because despite the secrecy which was coveted by both groups, the Rosicrucians were essentially created as a fiction that Andrae hoped would come into actuality – they have more of a literary pedigree. Weishaupt's group on the other hand, might have employed fiction in their rites, and were possibly inspired by the Rosicrucians, but their stated goal is intrinsically one that seeks to demystify, whereas the Rosicrucians, whether it was intended it or not, have had a mystifying effect.

---

[263] Ibid, p. 56
[264] See Weishaupt's 1786 book, *Apologie der Illuminaten.*

Perhaps the Illuminati narrative is not a literal reiteration of the Rosicrucian narrative, but was there a political affinity between the two groups? To some extent I would say yes, however, quantitatively speaking, there is scant reliable information available to solidly claim that the groups shared identical political goals. One thing they did share was that both groups added rites to Freemasonry proper, and these Rites coincided with the addition of degrees to the system of Freemasonry. Most everyone is familiar with the fact that Masonry is organized by degrees, and even the average Joe knows that there is something rarified (and possibly spooky) about the 33rd Degree. What is the significance of having this number as the highest achievable rank? On a numerological reading it could have to do with the age scripture records Jesus as being at the time of his crucifixion. It has been claimed that this highest degree was introduced by the Scottish Rite and that this Rite is itself contingent upon the influence of the Bavarian Illuminati. Wayne claims that the degrees of Freemasonry are symbolic of the ascension of the "ziggurat of enlightenment"[265] which we can assume is an abstract, theoretically constructed, version of the Tower of Babel.

It is near the end of *The Genesis 6 Conspiracy* that Wayne lays his cards on the table:

> In this book, I have danced all around the Satan scenario while dropping many hints and subtle conclusions. It is now time to nail down this notion. The Freemasons and all their genitive and associated organizations believe the real god of the universe is Lucifer. Freemasonry and all their associate organizations are ultimately preparing to

---

[265] Wayne, Gary (2014) *The Genesis 6 Conspiracy*. Trusted Books, A Division of Deep River Books. P. 499

bring about the New World Order under the New
Babel that worships Lucifer.[266]

If the 33rd degree was intended in some way to correspond with
Jesus's age *and* if Wayne's declaration of Freemasonry's
Luciferian nature is correct, then we can say that Freemasonry
made this move in the spirit of solidarity with more heretical
strains of Gnosticism. However, if, as I stipulated earlier, there
were more traditionally conservative branches of Freemasonry
that upheld Christian dogma, then the choice of the number "33"
might signify a more traditional sense of reverence.[267]

Before we try deducing what the content or meaning of the
33rd Degree might be, let's try to get a grasp on the Scottish Rite
from which it was derived and its origins. Waite asserts that the
"Ancient and Accepted Scottish Rite" was established in
Charleston, South Carolina in 1801 and that the claim that its
Charter was granted by Frederick the Great is fraudulent.[268]
Waite also goes on to state that the new Rite added degrees to the
existing system of Masonry and that: "The spread of the
SCOTTISH RITE in all countries was rapid and its success almost

---

[266] Ibid, p. 500
[267] One such branch might have been represented by The Swedish
Rite, which employed the "Grades of Saint Andrew." One such
grade, "Hiram and Christ" is intended to show the inductee that in
Hiram's resurrection he is reborn to a new life. "In a word, the
Master-Builder arises as Christ. The Temple of Masonry is
henceforward the House of Christ, at once of earth and of Heaven,
of earth in so far as it is realized here in the heart and life of the
Brotherhood, of Heaven as it is built in Christ, world without end."
Excerpted from Waite, Arthur Edward (1970) *A New
Encyclopaedia of Freemasonry (Combined Edition)*. Weathervane
Books. Volume I. P. 314
[268] Waite, Arthur Edward (1970) *A New Encyclopaedia of
Freemasonry (Combined Edition)*. Weathervane Books. Volume II,
p. 412

phenomenal. It overcame even the ineradicable jealousy and intolerance of the French GRAND ORIENT."[269]

Millar says that the legend of the Scottish Rite extends back to a story of escaped Templars fleeing to Scotland under the guise of stonemasons. Millar acknowledges that the Scottish Rite added degrees to Masonry that related directly to Templar symbolism; fascinatingly, one of the most significant being the death of Hiram, which the candidate to the third degree symbolically re-enacts, and which became a reference to the death of James de Molay.[270] If the Scottish Rite is in some way indicative of the progressive attitudes we associate with the Illuminati, then this reinterpretation (or rewriting) of Hiram's resurrection as de Molay instead of Christ seems to confirm most critics' suspicions about the "atheistic, scientific" nature of Masonry. Or at least Masonry –post Illuminati.

James de Molay was the Grand Master of the Templar Order at the time of the Order's disbandment and arrest on October 13, 1307. One hundred and thirty-nine Templar Knights were arrested and subsequently imprisoned and tortured; any knights that had been warned beforehand, or eluded arrest, fled to parts unknown. De Molay was himself executed on March 11, 1314.[271] It is generally agreed by historians that the Templars were targeted for extermination because they had amassed too much wealth and become too powerful to control. The machinations toward their extermination were set into motion by France's King Philip the Fourth and Pope Clement the Fifth.[272] We will explore the Templars a little more closely later; they are relevant here only insofar as their existence pertains to the

[269] Ibid, p. 413

[270] Millar, Angel (2005) *Freemasonry: A History*. Thunder Bay Press. P. 166

[271] Mackey, Albert (1996) *The History of Freemasonry*. Published by Gramercy Books, a Division of Random House Value Publishing Inc. P. 257

[272] Ibid, p. 256

narrative that escaped Knights of the Order had a direct hand on the formalization of Masonry.

There is no question that narratives about the Templars bore significance for Masonry. The question of whether these escaped knights personally structured the Rites of Masonry is a question for historians, a question that has slipped into the realm of legend. Albert Mackey's approach, which he identifies as being "iconoclastic" seeks a balance between legend and factual history:

> In short, the theory of the iconoclastic school is that truth and authenticity must always, and in the first place, be sought; that nothing must be accepted as historical which has not the internal and external evidences of historical verity, and that in treating the legends of Masonry –of almost every one of which it may be said, "Se non vero, é ben trovato" -*if it is not true, it is well invented* –we are not to reject them as altogether fabulous, but as having some hidden and occult meaning, which, as in the case of all other symbols, we must diligently seek to discover. But if it be found that the legend has no symbolic significance, but is simply the distortion of a historical fact, we must carefully eliminate the fabulous increment, and leave the body of truth to which it had been added, to have its just value.[273]

If we take Freemasonry to be an institution that conjoined a variety of competing Rites and factions, for now let's stick to the Templars, the Rosicrucians, the Bavarian Illuminati, and the founders of the Scottish Rite, and not give-in to the reductionist mindset that sees them as all emanating from the same source. What are the political ramifications of each groups' activity within Masonry? Let's break them down one-by-one.

---

[273] Ibid, p. 8

Historically speaking, there is not enough evidence to prove that the Templars were a heretical sect of knights who introduced Gnosticism, as a form of blasphemy, into Freemasonry; as far as the idea that they were secretly undermining the Church goes, I'm inclined to take the more conventional narrative that they were scapegoated and ultimately routed from achieving a larger degree of hegemony within the medieval world.

As for the Rosicrucians, if we can assume that Freemasonry evolved into a mystically oriented fraternity out of humble guilds,[274] there is no such gradual evolution for the Rosicrucian movement. It just appeared – mysticism, alchemy, and all – out of one person's imagination. There is enough evidence to indicate that the Rosicrucians promoted a certain amount of progressivism in their outlook, but overall, they seem most notable for their supernatural claims and obscurantism.

Now, regarding the Bavarian Illuminati and the founders of the Scottish Rite, these individuals definitely were products of the Enlightenment and sought to bring Enlightenment values into the folds of Freemasonry. If you accept my analysis, this leaves us with one question: was the Freemasonry that got caught up within this revolutionary fervor, really a conservative, god-fearing group prior to this infiltration? Robison argues that they were, and that after a brief spell of corruption at the hands of the Jesuits[275] the Illuminati introduced an anarchic and destructive ethos:

---

[274] This organic development entails the less-spectacular narrative that Freemasonry originated with the workmen who came from Rome to build roads and establish guilds in Britain in the middle ages. See Mackey, Albert (1996) *The History of Freemasonry*. Published by Gramercy Books, a Division of Random House Value Publishing Inc. P. x. This is a claim that Knight and Lomas explicitly reject in *The Hiram Key*.
[275] Robison, John (2014) *Proofs of a Conspiracy Against All the Religions and Governments of Europe, Carried on in the Secret*

It surely needs little argument now to prove, that the Order of Illuminati had for its immediate object the abolishing of Christianity (at least this was the intention of the Founder) with the sole view of overturning the civil government, by introducing universal dissoluteness and profligacy of manners, and then getting the assistance of the corrupted subjects to overset the throne.[276]

Wayne, on the other hand states:

The Illuminati infiltrated Freemasonry in 1782; although some sources backdate this to 1777. Weishaupt is touted as a Masonic reformer. This was a marriage made in spurious heaven, for the goal from Freemasonry's inception was to bring about the New World Order. The Rex Deus-sponsored Freemasonry fraternity welcomed its spurious and mystic cousins of Luciferian devotion while savoring Weishaupt's belief that the Illuminati were created to rule the world.[277]

If it has a Masonic pedigree, the concept of a "New World Order" can be read as a preoccupation of these latter two factions (the Bavarian Illuminati and the Scottish Rite) which would come to hold an undue influence over Freemasonry as a whole. Outside of Masonry, the concept can be viewed as an emergent ideology, one intuited by politicians, artists and writers during the Zeitgeist of

---

Meetings of Freemasons, Illuminati, and Reading Societies. CreateSpace Independent Publishing Platform. Pp. 11 - 12
[276] Ibid p. 82. Interestingly, Robison claims that Weishaupt had turned against his Jesuit handlers prior to establishing the Order.
[277] Wayne, Gary (2014) *The Genesis 6 Conspiracy.* Trusted Books, A Division of Deep River Books. P. 521

the eighteenth century. Before diving directly into the more contemporary political ramifications of this concept, I am going to discuss how it was foreshadowed and engaged by literature. After this we will segue into how this is politically relevant to the United States on both the Left and the Right.

Literature and the Planning of Utopia

Four hundred and six years passed between the publication of Thomas More's novel *Utopia* and Aldous Huxley's *Brave New World;* and in that time a myriad of events occurred that would shape the public's opinion of what a totalized and collective society could be. Among these events were the industrial revolution, the colonization of North America, Marxism, psychoanalysis, a whole host of wars, the development of germ theory and antibiotics, etc. The list can go on and on. Most literature that might be considered modern or post-modern dealt with at least one of these issues.

More wrote *Utopia* in 1516 in Latin, which Paul Turner writes in his Translator's Introduction:

> For hundreds of years Latin served as a universal language through which one could speak directly, not only to people of other nationalities, but to people of other periods as well. *Utopia* is expressed in a timeless medium, which cuts it loose from its own particular age, and saves it from ever seeming linguistically old-fashioned or difficult.[278]

One crucial development that occurred in the time between *Utopia* and *Brave New World* that Turner glosses over in both of his introductions to the 1965 Penguin edition, but which is an implicit factor in the section excerpted above, is the spread of literacy. The dissemination of literacy on the one hand

---

[278] More, Thomas (2003) *Utopia*. Penguin Books. P. xxviii

promises a certain degree of equalitarianism, but on the other, introduces the subject into a new, more bureaucratic, structure of power and dominance.[279] In response to this, Foucault makes use of the concept of "examination" in a transitional sense from observation to testing. Boyne offers this summary of Foucault's analysis:

> If observation was general, the precise calibration of the achievement level of those observed is an even more significant clue to the ways of power in this new order. The examination objectifies even more than the regime of observation. It allows true statements, corroborated by 'evidence', to be made. As if in heed of Plato's theory of metals, or in prefiguration of the functionalist theory of stratification, individuals would thence be justly assigned to their natural places in the order of things. It is also notable that the examination situates the subject within the world of the written and the recorded. The techniques of filing, tabulation and notation were basic to discipline, and to the emergence of the human sciences. The examination begets records; each individual becomes a case; the limit of discernable individuality is lowered. The written record is no longer a privilege of those people of note whose biographical details were preserved for posterity; it has become part and parcel of the operation of power. Individuals are documented, and these writings are *for use*.[280]

---

[279] The fine distinction between these two concepts will be addressed in the "9/11, or Narrative at the Zero Degree" chapter.
[280] Boyne, Roy (1990) *Foucault and Derrida: The Other Side of Reason*. Routledge. P. 114

This passage gives us a very precise insight into how literacy and bureaucracy coalesce into the formal societal and governmental institutions that we see today. The line: "The examination begets records; each individual becomes a case; the limit of discernable individuality is lowered," relates directly to bureaucratic systemization. It should be noted that there is an implication here that as the bureaucratic state establishes itself, writing becomes less of an internal phenomenon for the subject. This is not to say that the subject's internal apprehension of language has been lost, but that the demarcation between the private and the public is irrevocably blurred. Any planning that might occur for a one world government (or New World Order, if that is what that expression signifies) will play upon these same themes of public and private, albeit on a grander scale.

Utopia plays upon the themes of the public and the private on a societal level, if not a governmental one. It is not a book that sets out a plan for an ideal one-world government; it does not have anything to do with establishing harmony between different peoples and nations. Instead, it sets out to describe an island that has eluded cartographers; the name translated from Latin means "No Place." In a sense, More is addressing the issue of the unknown land which might double as the lost paradise. But while More is not concerned with the place's *actual* existence, he is explicitly interested in its literary existence (his choice of Latin qualifies this).

The island of Utopia is constructed as being both communistic and feudalistic:

> At regular intervals all over the countryside there are houses supplied with agricultural equipment, and town dwellers take turns to go and live in them. Each house accommodates at least forty adults, plus two slaves who are permanently attached to it, and is run by a reliable elderly married couple under the supervision of a District Controller, who's responsible for thirty such houses. Each year

twenty people from each house go back to town, having done two years in the country, and are replaced by twenty others. These new recruits are then taught farming by the ones who've had a year on the land already, and so know more about the job. Twelve months later the trainees become the instructors, and so on.[281]

This description of the agriculture of Utopia is prefaced by the declaration that: "No town has the slightest wish to extend its boundaries, for they don't regard their land as property but as soil that they've got to cultivate."[282] There is no private property on the island and the primary job of the town stewards, who are elected democratically, is to see to it that no-one is idle. Everyone goes to bed at 8pm, wakes up at 4am, and works a six-hour shift at whatever their trade may be. The remainder of the day must be spent on congenial activities, most of which involve furthering their education.[283] Being a Christian, More emphasizes a sense of duty (as evinced by the previous excerpts) as well as a sense of piety:

Most Utopians feel they can please God merely by studying the natural world, and praising Him for it. But quite a lot of them are led by their religion to neglect the pursuit of knowledge. They're not interested in science –they simply have no time for that sort of thing, since they believe that the only way to earn happiness after death is to spend one's life doing good works [...] They never find fault with other ways of life, or boast about their own.[284]

---

[281] More, Thomas (2003) *Utopia*. Penguin Books. Pp. 50 - 51
[282] Ibid, p. 50
[283] Ibid, p. 56
[284] Ibid, p. 103

Notice that at this later point in the narrative More's Catholicism clashes with his depiction of the Utopians as seeking to further their education when they are not working. There is much in More's description of an island free of private property that would raise alarm bells for conspiracy theorists who are tracking the antecedents of the New World Order; however, the pious religious aspects of More's work largely offset these attacks.

More's *Utopia* would go on to become a precursor to H.G. Wells's 1940 book *The New World Order*, in which he argues on behalf of a United Nations type of governance in order to prevent further wars. Unlike More, who constructed his work as a sort of religious tract that could be considered, in contemporary literary terms, as "Fantasy," Wells's nonfiction work draws on his background in futuristic science fiction. A more prescient piece of science fiction came from an author who rarely dabbled in the genre. E. M. Forster's 1909 short story, *The Machine Stops* depicted a futuristic society totally governed by technology.

In this story, the inhabitants of Earth no longer live on the planet's surface but reside in a giant machine below the ground. This machine is vast and allows instant communication and total luxury. Two important things happen in the novella that are relevant to our work: the first is that the individuals who dwell within the machine forget that it was man-made and begin worshipping it as a kind of deity. This turn of events presages Jacques Ellul's critique of technology, i.e., that it begins as a servant to man, but eventually man becomes a servant to it. This aspect of the story, the mystification of something that was borne out of human engineering, recalls the adage that "The true sign of falling into a dark age is not merely forgetting how to do something, like mix Roman Concrete for instance, it's forgetting that you had been able to do it in the first place."

The second relevant occurrence in the novel is that the machine stops working. The engineers who built it each had assistants, and those assistants had assistants, and eventually the cohesive understanding of how the machine runs, and how to repair it, became too diffuse. Each assistant becomes a "specialist" lacking the comprehensive know-how to enact practical improvements and repairs. This theory on the breakdown of knowledge would be mirrored in academia with post-modern theorists like Lyotard, who described the breakdown of master-narratives.[285]

Oftentimes, the material that fuels conspiracy theories is treated, in post-modern literature, in a comical or parodic way. This is especially true in the case of Thomas Pynchon, who's *Crying of Lot 49*, Robert Anton Wilson declares to be "the ultimate post-modern novel [...] that deliberately attempts to maneuver the reader into and out of a paranoid framework *several times*, leaving each reader to decide after "the trip" which makes more sense – paranoia or consensus reality."[286]

Taking a more serious tact are authors such as Don Delillo, who packed this exegesis into his 1997 masterpiece, *Underworld*:

> And the man takes a wadded bill out of his pocket and unfolds it like a magic trick and then he waves the money at the group in front of him.
> "You see the eye that hangs over this pyramid here. What's pyramids doing on American money? You see the number they got strung out at the base of this pyramid. This is how they flash their Masonic codes to each other. This is Freemason, the passwords and handshakes. This is Rosicrucian, the beam of light. This is webs and scribbles all over the bill, front and back, that contains a message. This is not just rigamarole and cooked spaghetti. They

---

[285] Two points I neglected to mention here, that are of lesser importance to our analysis are how living in the machine underground is analogous to Plato's Cave metaphor and how living within the comfort of the machine is akin to being consigned to a pod in *The Matrix* films.

[286] Wilson, Robert Anton (1998) *Everything is Under Control: Conspiracies, Cults and Cover-ups.* Harper Perennial. Pp. 136 - 137

predicting the day and the hour. They telling each other when the time is come. You can't find the answer in the Bible or the Bill of Rights. I'm talking to you. I'm saying history is written on the commonest piece of paper in your pocket."

And he holds the bill by its edges and extends his elbows, showing the thing for what it is.

"I've been studying this dollar bill for fifteen years. Take it to the privy when I do my hygiene. And I worked those numbers and those letters all whichway and I hold the bill to the light and I read it underwater and I'm getting closer every day to breaking the code."

And he draws the dollar to his chest and folds it five times and puts it in his pocket, smaller than a postage stamp.

"This is why they're watching me with that eye that floats over the top of the pyramid. They're watching and they're following all the time."

The eye in the pyramid goes back to ancient Egypt where it was referred to as the Eye of Horus. In the myth, Horus, the sky god, loses his eye during a conflict with his father's brother, Set. The father in question was Osiris, "the first god-king of earth." In the ensuing centuries, the eye has been used to symbolize protection, healing, restoration, and sacrifice. The Eye of Horus was known during the Medieval period as "the all-seeing eye" or the "eye of power," and was used by the Knights Templar and later the Freemasons. It was the same image that was added to the U.S. Dollar in 1935 by U.S. President and 32nd degree Freemason, Franklyn Delano Roosevelt.

The modern permutation of the myth of an "all-seeing eye" leapt into the post-modern age with the publication of George Orwell's *Nineteen Eighty-Four*, a dystopian novel published in 1949, wherein the population of Britain is ruled by a shadowy group called "the Party." The theme of authoritarian totalitarianism is explored by way of a KGB-style "Thought Police," two-way surveillance televisions called "Telescreens," the rewriting of history, and a concerted simplification of the language that is imposed on the population. Orwell had written *Nineteen Eighty-Four* in Scotland between 1947 and 1948. The book was perceived to be directed against the Soviet Union by most of its audience. However, as Thomas Pynchon points out in his forward to the 2003 Penguin Edition, Orwell's primary target was the establishment Left, who, in their quest for power inevitably take on the trappings of the authoritarianism that they purported to denounce.[287]

Regardless as to Orwell's immediate intentions, his story has a universal appeal and is often invoked by people on the left, right and middle to denounce their opposition. *Nineteen Eighty-Four* might be prophetic but it wasn't directly prophetic of the way the 1980s played out. It is true that many neighborhoods in the U. S. and Britain became slums that rivaled the gritty, war-torn atmosphere that pervades Orwell's novel, but the intersubjective sterility that the Party tries to inflict upon the masses by way of constant monitoring does not resonate with much of the sleek, neon graphic art of the eighties (Google: *Miami Vice*). In a sense, Orwell was wrong in his predictions, because even if the population was willing to submit to more surveillance and more market interference in their lives, etc., they were also becoming more self-aware, not quite ironic yet, but self-aware enough to be the decade that birthed post-modernism.

Terry Gilliam's 1985 film *Brazil*, which was made during the titular year of Orwell's novel, was intended to project the author's totalitarian vision even further into the future. In the process, Gilliam incorporated a Kafkaesque apprehension of bureaucracy, a portrayal that rendered his dystopia both sinister and incompetent. Gilliam vividly captures *Nineteen Eighty-Four's* sense of confusion, betrayal, and ultimate futility in trying to

---

[287] Orwell, George (2003) *Nineteen Eighty-Four*. Berkeley, an Imprint of Penguin Random House LLC. Pp. ix - xi

locate and collaborate with political dissidents. It is not too much of a stretch to estimate that it is a combination of this sense of futility conjoined with the vicariousness of contemporary forms of media (both social and otherwise) that define our contemporary political climate, a climate that is occurring at the apotheosis of the post-modern age.[288]

Some of the analysis we have employed so far has utilized "post-modern" philosophers, but the larger cultural trend, that we call "post-modernism" developed out of a wide variety of things: film, literature, architecture. The antecedents of which developed in the nineteenth and twentieth centuries but became culturally ascertainable after the counter-culture revolution of the 1960s. This was important, because there was a large degree of irony evident in the absorption of the anti-capitalist hippies into the capitalist system they had previously rebelled against. This assimilation towards the construction of a kinder and gentler form of capitalist exploitation, even though it only existed in televised propaganda, was probably the most prophetic aspect of Orwell's thought as it pertained to the 1980s themselves. The television screen every baby-boomer brought into their home during the decade's heyday was a nascent approximation of the novel's "telescreens."

Expanding on this eighties-centered analysis, Arthur Kroker and David Cook's 1991 book *The Postmodern Scene* addresses the concept of the "all-seeing eye" via modern art:

> Consider, then, the most famous depiction of the disembodied eye, the *rhetorical* eye, presented by René Magritte in his painting *The False Mirror*. Here, Magritte's scandalous image of the eye (i.e., a *simulacrum* of the eye) floats almost innocently as the vast, globular horizon of a translucent, blue sky.

---

[288] One could even argue that the irony of technological complexity married to persistent malfunction, which Gilliam revels in, is another hallmark of our epoch.

Magritte's "eye" is radically severed from its surroundings, magnified in its proportions, and unblinking. We are not in the presence of the eye of the flesh; indeed, we are gazing upon the precise consequence of the closing of the eye of the flesh. Magritte's "eye" is a perfect symbolization, in reverse image, of the nuclear structure of postmodern experience. To gaze upon this disembodied eye is to have a privileged viewpoint on modern experience *turned inside out.* The secret of its scandal is specifically that it reveals no obvious traces of genealogy that would take the viewer beyond the infinite regress of its symbolic effects. The disembodied eye is a powerful visual expression of that rupture in modern experience which was precipitated by the discarding of the myth of the natural (the search for a *representational* founding; at least a *nomos*, if not a *telos*), and the creation of a postmodern, transparently *relational* structure of experience.[289]

The Magritte painting described in the above passage is from 1928. Kroker and Cook view it as an artistic turning point in the movement from the conventional narrativizing that accompanied humanity up to the point of modernity (the post-industrial age) but that somehow was either discarded or lost as we transitioned into our current state of postmodernity. The significance of the eye in this postmodern context is even greater for us when we take into account its use by Freemasons: how they borrowed it from the Egyptians (a hermeneutical borrowing), transformed it into a disembodied object floating atop an incomplete pyramid, and placed it on the U.S. Dollar Bill.

---

[289] Kroker, Arthur and Cook, David (1991) *The Postmodern Scene: Excremental Culture and Hyper-Aesthetics.* St. Martin's Press, p. 79

For Kroker and Cook, there has been a radical change in our societies over the last hundred years, and the disembodied eye portrays this change as the discarding of myth for a "pure sign-system."[290] But the continued hermetic use of this symbol by Masonry, in this context, seems to imply one of two things: either this discarding of myth was the intention of this fraternal order, or that, for one group at least, nothing has changed (i.e., myth has not been discarded) and this eye is actually a sign of permanence. Perhaps the bearers of the "all seeing eye" did not orchestrate the turbulent times of postmodernity, but merely foresaw them.

One conspiracy theorist, Jordan Maxwell, writing just about a year prior to 9/11, framed his approach to Freemasonry, insofar as it exerts a pluralistic leverage on our government and society, this way:

> Our country, like so many before us, and like so many after us, was in fact founded by Freemasons. Freemasonry, in one form or another, has played a role in almost every government that was founded in this world. It is powerful in operation today throughout the world. However, we do want to establish first that what we are *not* talking about is Blue Masonry, or the Masonic Lodges in your hometown. We are *not* talking about the Freemasons that live across the street from you. We're talking about a worldwide fraternal organization that is powerful enough, old enough, and wise enough to operate behind all governments in the world, behind fraternal institutions, and behind international monetary systems in the world. And, yes, they are, in fact, connected.[291]

---

[290] Ibid p. 79
[291] Maxwell, Jordan (2000) *Matrix of Power: Secrets of World Control*. The Book Tree. P. 5

Despite this connection between Freemasonry's use of the Eye of Horus and the all-seeing eye of the surveillance state, there is nothing explicitly said about Freemasonry in *Nineteen Eighty-Four*, nor is there anything explicitly said in its predecessor, *Brave New World*.[292] Written seventeen years before *Nineteen Eighty-Four*, Aldous Huxley's *Brave New World* presented a future in which society's elites had no need to overtly police and monitor their subjects; instead the populace is enslaved by medication (*Soma*) and a spirit of indulgence and gratification. Orwell was not ignorant of this factor, and in his work he detailed the "proles'" devotion to the Lottery, which was their "principle if not the only reason for remaining alive. It was their delight, their folly, their anodyne, their intellectual stimulant."[293]

For Orwell the Lottery is a sham, a "bread and circus," to appease the oppressed, from which nothing substantial resulted. This is not the case for Huxley, whose bread and circuses make up the whole of society. Superficiality has stripped away the meaning of life to the point where people cannot even say for sure that there had been any discernible authentic meaning to life in the first place. There is nothing in *Brave New World* that is symbolic enough to link it to conspiracy theories or myths. In a sense, the premise of the novel entails the eradication of those things in favor of progress and consumption. In a manner similar to *The Machine Stops*, the characters in *Brave New World* deify the signifiers of technological advancement, e.g., the exclamation "Oh Ford!" has replaced "Oh my God!"[294]

---

[292] However, it should be noted that both books attack the hypocrisy of Bourgeois neoliberalism, a political tendency that can be construed as stemming from a literalist reading of Enlightenment Ideals.

[293] Orwell, George (2003) *Nineteen Eighty-Four*. Berkeley, an Imprint of Penguin Random House LLC. P. 88

[294] Huxley, Aldous (2004) *Brave New World and Brave New World Revisited*. HarperCollins Inc. P. 140

Nineteen Eighty-Four and *Brave New World* give two diametrically opposed renderings of how the individual is broken down in a totalitarian society; and in the process, they both proffer new, post-war, definitions of "totalitarianism." These are the two novels that conspiracy theorists oscillate between when they try to find a literary pedigree for current social/political predicaments. They are both well-known and they are distinct enough to create a dialectic. Post-modern literature, which is often more applicable, comes off as excessively esoteric in relation to the issues it addresses, and in its operation expresses a distrust of the over-arching themes of both *Brave New World* and *Nineteen Eighty-Four* – these books, as prophetic as they might be, could just be symptoms of (or reactions against) outdated "Grand Narratives," specifically Freudianism and Marxism.

The concept of Grand Narratives was first critically taken to task by the French philosopher Jean-Francois Lyotard (August 10, 1924 – April 21, 1998) in his 1979 book, *The Postmodern Condition: A Report on Knowledge*. In this work, Lyotard essentially extended the "metanarrative" concept that we have been referring to into the realm of the socio-political. *The Postmodern Condition* is a difficult read and its fame has primarily arisen for two reasons: it attempts to track the decline of modernity insofar as this decline has been sped-up by technological advances; and, more importantly, it argues that concepts like reductionism and teleology have become irrelevant within our postmodern society. Lyotard attacks "metanarratives" such as Marxism and Freudianism based on the claim that they are too totalizing; essentially these theories cannot account for the pluralistic activity of smaller narratives which have been able to seize control of certain elements of the population; replacing the sense of meaning instilled, by Marxism for instance, with a sense of efficiency that has only to do with production and performance.

I prefer not to call these metanarratives because it clashes with how we have been using the term, which is essentially as a function, so I will call them "Grand Narratives." Whether or not

Lyotard was right about the collapse of these Grand Narratives, he was at the right time and right place to make these predictions. What we call post-modern fiction, to a large extent, picks away at the idea of Grand Narratives and takes individuals and objects that exist at the margins of texts and focuses on their idiosyncratic journeys. One helpful way of thinking about the difference between modern and post-modern literature is this: modernist literature often tells grandiose archetypical tales using banal, down-to-earth characters, whereas post-modern literature uses in grandiose archetypal figures to tell banal everyday tales.

The process of plucking characters from the margins and focusing on them relates to what we have done so far, with our identification of Enoch, Hiram and Melchizedek as significant figures. However, we are ourselves not critiquing Grand Narratives, we are talking about myths, and therefore do not use these characters to attack anything; we are merely tracking them. In this process we are not mythbusters – we are merely readers.

The Martyrs of the New World Order

In political terms, the progression we are charting is one in which a variety of groups coalesce around institutions of power within the United States. These groups may be based on ethnicity, a strict sense of duty to one's home country, or a dual allegiance between the United States and a "foreign power;" individuals in these cases are referred to as having a dual loyalty. Sometimes this duality becomes an issue for an individual who is torn between the fraternal organization or religion he belongs to, and his loyalty to the United States. Most of the conspiratorial talking points that were prevalent in the eighties and nineties had to do with Freemasons networking into government jobs and then collectively injecting the American bureaucratic system with Enlightenment ideals that were designed to undermine the social order.

In our day and age this scenario sounds quaint, especially after liberalists (both social and fiscal) have effectively marched through the academic institutions and conjoined this successful conquest with the plutocratic agenda for eliminating borders and opening up the world to global trade and the elimination of unions. Essentially, in the past you had both "Left-wing" and "Right-wing" conspiracy theorists that feared an impending New World Order. Both sides looked at George H.W. Bush's proclamation, and at Bush himself, with suspicion.

To break this down, let's start with the Leftist opposition to the idea of a New World Order. This side was as diverse and multifaceted as the right, with occasional overlaps: there were anarchoprimitivists who were concerned by Jacques Ellul's prediction that as a society becomes more technological, technology becomes less of a tool to the individual and more of a governing force.[295]

Ellul is not brought up often within the Leftist conspiracy theory tradition, as ideologically he was a Catholic Anarchist. However, his 1964 book *The Technological Society* captures the essence of an individualist-based resistance to encroaching technocracy. This sense of individual liberty is summarized as:

> Although the individual existing in the framework of a civilization of a certain type was always confronted with certain techniques, he was nevertheless free to break with that civilization and control his own individual destiny. The constraints to which he was subject did not function decisively because they were of a non-technical nature and could be broken through. In an active civilization, even one with a fairly good technical development, the individual could always break away and lead, say, a mystical and contemplative life. The fact that techniques and man were more or less on the same

---

[295] We can note this concern in Lyotard's depiction of Grand Narratives withering away under the yoke of efficiency and performativity.

level permitted the individual to repudiate techniques and get along without them. Choice was a real possibility for him, not only with regard to his inner life, but with regard to the outer form of his life as well.[296]

Ellul refers to the technocratic aspect that infringes on individual liberty as *automatism,* the technical method that is quantitatively assessed as the most practical and efficient as it assumes a hegemonic place within the society.

A surgical operation that was formerly not feasible but can now be commonly performed is not an object of choice. It simply is. Here we see the prime aspect of technical automatism. Technique itself, *ipso facto* and without indulgence or possible discussion, selects the means to be employed. The human being is no longer in any sense the agent of choice. Let no one say that man is the agent of technical progress and that it is he who chooses among possible techniques. In reality, he neither is, nor does anything of the sort, being merely a device for recording effects and results obtained by various techniques.[297]

This technology-dependent, bureaucratic force which deconstructs the liberty of the individual was echoed by William Burroughs in his piece "No More Stalins No More Hitlers," which was recorded as a spoken word piece for the album *Dead City Radio*:

We have a new type of rule now. Not one-man rule or rule of aristocracy or plutocracy, but of small groups elevated to positions of absolute power by random pressures and subject to political and economic factors that leave little room for decisions. They are representatives of abstract

---

[296] Ellul, Jacques (1964) *The Technological Society*. Vintage Books, A Division of Random House. P. 77
[297] Ibid, p. 80

forces who have reached power through surrender of self. The iron-willed dictator is a thing of the past. There will be no more Stalins, no more Hitlers. The rulers of this most insecure of all worlds are rulers by accident; inept, frightened pilots at the controls of a vast machine that they cannot understand, calling in experts to tell them which button to push.[298]

Left-wing Conspiracy Theorization

Notice that the picture of technological dominance of society painted by Ellul and the diffusion of responsibility described by Burroughs were both presaged in Forster's *The Machine Stops*. The tradition based on resistance to this technological totalitarianism is often referred to as anarchoprimitivism or neo-primitivism; it has a great deal of overlap with the radical environmentalism and eco-terrorism that was more prominent in Left-wing circles in the eighties and nineties. Derrick Jensen is one current-day inheritor of this tradition. In his two-part book *Endgame,* Jensen sets out twenty premises as to why civilization, and in particular industrial civilization, is not sustainable. Much of what Jensen argues pertains to the harms inflicted by civilization on its subjects as well as the environment. The desire for civilization, as Jensen sees it, is akin to the illuminating power of Reason we saw strived for in Freemasonry, however, with the more sinister dimension of consumption and disposal of the resources it utilizes. The fear that abandoning civilization would lead to regression and a new "dark age" is countered, by Jensen, with the assertion that abandoning the drive to civilization is not a process of going "backwards," evolutionarily speaking:

---

[298] Burroughs, Dead City Radio, Island Records 1990

The good news, however, is that we don't need to go "backward" to anything, because humans and their immediate evolutionary predecessors lived sustainably for at least a million years. It is not "human nature" to destroy one's habitat. If it were, we would have done so long before now, and long-since disappeared.[299]

Often Jensen seems to be in step with the older Leftist conspiracy theory trope that sees the idea of The New World Order as a worldwide police state. This was probably the most crucial angle employed by Left-wing conspiracy theorists in the latter part of the 20th century who accused the CIA of distributing crack cocaine in the ghettoes of North America during the 1980s, fomenting civil war in South America, experimenting on U.S. citizens with LSD in the 1950s and 60s, as well as various acts of political assassination (the most prominent of which were Martin Luther King and the Kennedy brothers).

In their day, these conspiracy theorists were activists who often started, or participated in co-ops, and donated to causes like Greenpeace. Their claims against the United States Government were often salient; for instance, the use of LSD on American citizens is documented at length in Martin Lee and Bruce Shlain's 1994 book, *Acid Dreams: The Complete Social History of LSD: The CIA, the Sixties, and Beyond* as well as Stephen Kinzer's *Poisoner in Chief: Sidney Gottlieb and the CIA Search for Mind Control*, published in 2019.

The experiments detailed by Kinzer, Lee and Shlain were part of a program referred to as "Project MK-Ultra," which ran from 1953 to 1973. MK-Ultra was intended as a "brain-washing" program wherein CIA operatives experimented on prisoners, soldiers, college students, etc., with hallucinogens, sensory deprivation, and various forms of physical and sexual abuse. The

---

[299] Jensen, Derrick (2006) *Endgame Volume I.* Seven Stories Press. P. 38

program was instigated by Allen Welsh Dulles in an attempt to compete with the Soviets in the race for "mind control."

Stephen Kinzer speculates that the program was not only inspired by Nazi experiments in the Dachau Concentration camp, but was a "continuation"[300] of them, implying that there were literal Nazis conducting these experiments in the U.S. However, this is a somewhat dubious claim since the head of the operation, Sidney Gottlieb (born Joseph Scheider) was himself Jewish. Similar analysis has led fellow Boomer Alex Jones into the reductionist idea that the U.S. Government is inundated with and controlled by Nazis. Which brings us to the lynchpin of the Nazi-reductionist conspiracy theory: "Operation Paperclip."[301]

It is beyond question that German scientists were brought over to work for the U.S. war effort immediately following Germany's surrender, but prior to Japan's, and that these scientists, most notably Wernher von Braun assisted in the construction of the atomic bomb. The idea that Nazis were brought in wholesale to launch NASA and eventually took over the military industrial complex, and then the United States government in toto is the product of a specific Left-wing conspiratorial narrative that has fluctuated in popularity over the

---

[300] NPR, 09/09/19 "The CIA's Secret Quest for Mind Control: Torture, LSD and A 'Poisoner in Chief." Interview with journalist Stephen Kinzer

[301] It is important to note here that Kinzer does not promote the Nazi reductionist theory. His reference to Dachau has to do with a Dr. Kurt Blome who had conducted a wide variety of bizarre experiments at that camp (and others) in order to develop bio-weapons. Interestingly, Blome's application to participate in Operation Paperclip was rejected because of his war crimes. This, however, did not stop the CIA from employing his services at Camp King in Frankfurt Germany. Kinzer, Stephen (2019) *Poisoner in Chief: Sidney Gottlieb and the CIA Search for Mind Control*. Henry Holt and Company. Pp. 41 - 43

last twenty years. Richard Belzer championed the possibility of this connection from a Left-wing perspective in the late 1990s:

> With more than six hundred titles available on the events in Dealey Plaza and potentially thousands on German history, I knew it would take me years to uncover everything that had been hidden from me. Then it happened! I discovered with perverse awe that there was a connection between my two obsessions. There are researchers who believe that former Nazis who, by the 1960s, had become part of the booming military-industrial complex were among the billionaires opposed to ending the Cold War and therefore conspired to have Kennedy killed.[302]

It was eventually taken up by Right-wing conspiracy theorists like Alex Jones who link the theory of a secret Nazi occupation of the U.S. Government to things like the Bohemian Club.[303] The claim,

---

[302] Belzer, Richard (1999) *UFOs, JFK, and Elvis: Conspiracies You Don't Have to be Crazy to Believe*. The Ballantine Publishing Group. P. 166

[303] Not to be left out of the mix, Maxwell includes a bit about the Bohemian Club in his *Matrix of Power*:
"The last two weeks of July, of every year, a secret meeting is held in our country in northern California, by the world's most powerful people. Bankers, politicians, industrialists, entertainment luminaries, a huge composite of puissant world figures. This group is directly linked with the European ruling elites, and is commonly known as the Bohemian Society. Our now famous Council of Foreign Relations, the government behind the American government, is represented at the Bohemian Grove, along with members of the Bilderberger Group of Europe. A meeting is held, once a year there to decide on a worldwide scale a manipulative agenda concerning your future. A shining example

by both the left and right, that Nazis had overtaken the State Department or the Military-Industrial Complex, and *that's why the government is out to get you* contradicts the stance taken by earlier Leftist academics like Howard Zinn, who proposed that the United States had been rife with inequality and nefarious political machinations from its beginnings. Zinn's model, outlined in *A People's History of the United States*, cleaved closely to the idea of political pluralism, and focuses on the moneyed class, unscrupulous industrialists, and "war mongers" as the groups that have seized hegemonic control in this country.[304]

Earlier Right-wing conspiracy theorists, such as Gary Allen and Larry Abraham argued that the actual Nazis were puppets of the Council on Foreign Relations:

> As World War II approached, the Round Table Group was influential in seeing that Hitler was not stopped in Austria, the Rhineland, or Sudetenland – and thereby was largely responsible for precipitating the Holocaust. A second world war would greatly enhance the opportunity for establishment of World Government. The financing for Adolph Hitler's rise to power was handled

---

of true democracy carried on in the dark. Obviously, here, your votes don't count. Appropriately, the owl was chosen as a symbol for this ilk, for it, too, is at home in the dark. The name *Bohemian* carries a dictionary definition as, "A community of persons who adopt manners and mores, conspicuously different from those expected, or approved of by the majority of society who disregard conventional standards of behavior." From Maxwell, Jordan (2000) *Matrix of Power: Secrets of World Control*. The Book Tree. P. 9

[304] For Zinn these forces are more nuanced and endemic to colonialism. Frank Beard's *An Economic Interpretation of the Constitution of the United States* takes a similarly iconoclastic look at the foundations of American inequality.

through the Warburg-controlled Mendelsohn Bank of Amsterdam and later by the J. Henry Schroeder Bank with branches in Frankfurt, London and New York. Chief legal counsel to the J. Henry Schroeder Bank was the firm of Sullivan and Cromwell, whose senior partners included John Foster and Allen Dulles.[305]

The move in the 1990s towards making the Nazis the total and most hidden source of evil in the country overly mystified whatever National Socialism actually was and dumbed down history into traditional American caricatures of "The good cowboy wears a white hat, the bad cowboy wears the black hat – case closed."[306] The Nazi-focused theories were not wholly bereft of the narrative richness of the conspiracy narratives that had preceded them, but they certainly marked a qualitative drop, and this was a drop in richness that was absolutely necessary for us to move into the scientifically obsessed stage of conspiracy theorization that was the hallmark of the early 2000s, insofar as Nazism was presented as a mid-twentieth century promulgation of the quest for eugenic and scientific perfection, i.e., they became symbolic harbingers for unchecked scientism.[307]

---

[305] Allen, Gary & Abraham, Larry (1971) *None Dare Call it Conspiracy*. Dauphin Publications. P. 67

[306] Countless Hollywood dramatizations, pertaining to nearly every aspect of WWII, played an enormous role in blowing the conflict out of historical proportions.

[307] As has already been stated, the primary reasoning behind the theory that Nazis control our government is derived from Operation Paperclip, as well as the C.I.A.'s employment of former Nazis (such as Kurt Blome) immediately following the war's end. Contrary to the Nazi-reductionist interpretation, much of this involvement was due to laziness and incompetence on the part of the U.S. Government. See Breitman, Richard; Goda, Norman;

In contrast to the simplified narrative of blaming every pernicious and malevolent action taken by the U.S. Government on Nazi infiltration, there was legitimate journalism occurring in the mid-1990s by Gary Webb, and others, which would address the U.S. Government's behavior in concrete terms that did not search for elusively secret motives. Though this is not to say that Webb's fact-finding search did not lead him into labyrinths of intrigue and complexity – it most certainly did!

Gary Webb (August 31, 1955 – December 10, 2004) was born in Corona California. As a young adult he moved frequently before settling in Kentucky to work as a reporter for the Kentucky Post. In 1988 Webb moved back to California to work as an investigative reporter for the San Jose Mercury News. According to Webb's 1998 book, *Dark Alliance*, his groundbreaking story began in July 1995 when he was contacted by a woman who claimed that her boyfriend, Rafael Corñejo, was being railroaded by the FBI for allegedly running a cocaine distribution ring on the West Coast. From here, Webb charted a path that led from Nicaraguan Contras to high profile crack dealers like Freeway Ricky Ross.

On the Nicaraguan side of this conspiracy there was Danilo Blandón, whose family had deep ties to the regime of Nicaraguan dictator General Anastasio Somoza which began in 1937 and ended with the deposition of Somoza's son, Anastasio Somoza Debayle by the Sandinistas in 1979.[308] Debayle would be executed in Paraguay in 1980. Blandon, who had fled Nicaragua to the United States, and somehow, by chance, began operating a cocaine smuggling operation from South America to California; the proceeds of which were funneled to Nicaraguan dissidents, i.e., the "Contras." The Contras, whose name is an abbreviation of "contrarrevolucion" were anti-communist militias composed of

Naftali, Timothy; Wolfe, Robert (2005) *U.S. Intelligence and the Nazis*. Cambridge University Press. Pp. 448 - 451

[308] Webb, Gary (2014) *Dark Alliance: The CIA, the Contras, and the Crack Cocaine Explosion*. Seven Stories Press. Pp. 38 – 43.

Somoza loyalists who were funded by the U.S. Government by way of the CIA.[309]

It's impossible to overstate how significant the CIA's covert funding of the Contras would be to the undermining of national stability and faith in democracy in general. In many ways, this situation *had to* (in an almost fateful sense) correlate historically with the formalization and mainstreaming of post-modernism, because on the one hand we had the benevolent grandfatherly image of Ronald Reagan trying to usher in a revival of 1950s nostalgia, while simultaneously declaring a "war on drugs" with the D.A.R.E. Program. And, on the other hand you had ruthless government agencies not only fomenting revolution in South American countries, with the attendant atrocities, but also callously allowing American cities to be ravaged by unchecked drug distribution.

The paranoia of any conspiracy theorist picking up on this ironic juxtaposition must be amplified by the fact that what seems to be going on here presents the U.S. Government as consisting of layers of intrigue and despotism. At the core layer, if there actually is one, one will find individuals or agencies working beyond the bounds of the law – as well as the awareness of other agencies – in order to pursue agendas, which since they are hidden, must be diametrically opposed to the wishes and interests of the American people. One of the first examples of this duplicity came from certain DEA agents in San Francisco who noticed that: "In this business, if you have people coming in from Nicaragua bringing in cocaine and the rumor was they were taking guns back... that's sort of an interesting combination."[310]

By the mid-eighties, the DEA would become more aware of the CIA's covert operations and would turn a blind eye to Contra-related smuggling, while setting up under-cover stings and raids

---

[309] Ibid, pp. 553 - 554
[310] DEA agent Sandra Smith in a November 1981 affidavit. Ibid, p. 59

on Sandinista officials.[311] The entire debacle, which wreaked havoc in both South and North America, lasted from 1979 to the early 1990s, and was not even mentioned in the Iran-Contra scandal and hearings.

The Iran-Contra affair was essentially another scheme to supply funds to the Contras, this time via an illegal sale of arms to Iran (who was under an embargo at the time). Fourteen administration officials were indicted and eleven convictions were obtained; one of which was Colonel Oliver North, who also had a significant hand in the CIA's drug-trafficking.[312] North was essentially the face of the scandal when it threatened to upset Reagan's second term in office, although his conviction was overturned based on the possibility that his Fifth Amendment Rights may have been violated during the hearings.

Being an old school, John Birch-style Communist alarmist, North found work in the nineties speaking for groups of like-mind conservatives which eventually led to him being elected the president of the NRA. The story of Gary Webb, however, is much more unfortunate. In the final pages of *Dark Alliance* Webb describes how the editors at the *San Jose Mercury News*, where he had been publishing his investigative columns on the subject, killed the story and backed away from the topic by issuing a retraction on May 11, 1997.[313] Webb would leave the paper before the end of the year, finding that much like the "deep state" that had coalesced within the government over the last eighty or so years, an equally mendacious layer had formed inside the country's media apparatus: "[I]t was the smug, snotty, sophomoric crowd that came to dominate the national media from the inside. These characters fell in love with their power to define reality, not their responsibility to uncover the facts. By the 1990s, the media had become the monster."[314]

---

[311] Ibid, pp. 116 – 119, p. 475
[312] Ibid, p. 119
[313] Ibid, pp. 475 - 476
[314] Ibid, p. 480

After leaving *The Mercury* Webb worked as an investigator for the California State Legislature and did freelance journalism on the side. On December 10, 2004 he was found dead in his Charmichael home, having suffered two gunshots to the head – his death was ruled a suicide.[315]

Within the narratives of the Left-wing conspiracy theorist, the FBI is as complicit in the machinations of the U.S. Government as the CIA. Take the case of Karen Silkwood who, in 1972, began work at the Kerr-McGee plutonium plant in Oklahoma. After a series of labor disputes regarding the health and safety of workers were handled in a dismissive fashion by management, Silkwood took a list of plant accidents, safety abuses, and worker grievances to the Atomic Energy Commission in Washington DC.

Unable to formerly file a complaint Silkwood went back to Kerr-McGee and began surreptitiously documenting the plant's abuses. On November 13, 1974, Silkwood was scheduled to meet with a Union Legislative Assistant and hand over the dossier she had assembled; but before the meeting could be held, Silkwood's car was found crashed into a concrete culvert wall and she was dead. [316] In the aftermath, Leftist and environmental groups accused the government of colluding with Kerr-McGee to not only have her silenced but to also cover up any of the information she had discovered. The probability of these accusations having validity was only intensified when the FBI objected thirty times during the Silkwood family's civil case against Kerr-McGee. Threats of gag orders against the family's attorneys by the FBI did not improve their image either.[317]

Along with the mysterious death of Gary Webb, the Silkwood case was an embodiment of how Left-wing conspiracy theorists saw the collusion between shadowy government

---

[315] https://en.wikipedia.org/wiki/Gary_Webb accessed on 9/16/20

[316] Moench, Doug (1995) *The Big Book of Conspiracies*. Paradox Press. pp. 141 - 144

[317] Ibid pp. 144 - 146

agencies and large-scale corporations. Obviously, the strands of these suspicions stem from the political assassinations of the sixties which had their apotheosis with the JFK assassination.

The next phase of Left-wing conspiracy theorization took place between the 90s and early 2000s, when the WTO protests erupted. Essentially, these were Anarchist or Communist actions to protect individual liberty from the threat of global capitalists trying to secure their place atop the world government via economic control.[318] The ideologies of these groups may be contradictory, but in response to financial globalism, each has their valid place: Anarchism as a defense of the individual against the control of a governmental superstructure, and communism as a defense of the proletariat against a world economy dominated by unchecked and rapacious globalism. This movement, which was designated as the "Black Bloc" because the protesters were dressed in all black, was solidly opposed to private property; a statement issued at the time of the protests stated:

> "We contend that property destruction is not a violent activity unless it destroys lives or causes pain in the process. By this definition, private property – especially corporate private property – is itself infinitely more violent than any action taken against it [...] Private property – and capitalism, by extension – is intrinsically violent and repressive and cannot be reformed or mitigated"[319]

From our vantage-point in the post-Trump era it seems novel that twenty years ago the damage done to businesses by the Black

---

[318] Part of the animus against this globalist capitalist agenda was derived from the view that it acted as a new form of colonialism, wherein indigenous people in Asian countries were enslaved to make products for first world countries.

[319] As quoted by Derrick Jensen *Endgame Volume I*. Seven Stories Press. Pp. 81 - 82

Bloc was the intention of the protest and not, as it is today, incidental to the event. It's an interesting corollary that the strongest, and most militant Left-wing resistance to authoritarianism occurred at the time when it cultivated a strong sense of conspiracy theorization. This period lasted from the late-sixties until the mid-aughts and has now, for the most part, been dissimulated into hyperreality.

Right-wing Conspiracy Theorization

Most of the concerns addressed in the previous section were echoed by Right-wing conspiracy theories during the same time period. Both right and left wings were concerned with a centralized consolidation of power. However, in place of environmentalism and workers' rights, Rightists were more concerned with preserving the Second Amendment. I believe the tribalist aspect of each was similar,[320] however, whereas the Leftist viewed the fight in terms of Marxist class struggle and worker solidarity, the Rightist viewed it in terms of religious, specifically Christian, liberty.

The "religious right" concept, which played, and still plays, a significant role in Right-wing conspiracy theorization, can be traced politically to an electoral strategy employed by politicians such as Richard Nixon and Barry Goldwater in order to draw white working class voters into the folds of the Republican Party. The strategy, largely developed by Nixon political strategist Kevin Phillips, was: "An aggressive antiliberal campaign strategy that would hasten the defection of working-class Democrats to the Republican line."[321]

---

[320] The dialectical opposition in the tribal sense would be leftists forming farming co-ops in the sixties and seventies and rightists forming militias in the eighties and nineties.

[321] *Nixon's Southern Strategy*: "It's All in the Charts" by James Boyd. The New York Times (May 17, 1970)

Along the margins of the Southern Strategy there were figures associated with anti-communist groups like The John Birch Society and traditionalist Christian groups who agitated against Communism not so much because of a preference for laisez-faire capitalism but out of fear of Soviet-style religious persecution. Out of this religious side developed abortion clinic bombings and the so-called "Christian Identity" movement – both of which came to prominence in the 1980s.

The richest material produced by this milieu, which is more closely focused on the New World Order proper, comes from the secular anti-Communist cold warrior side of this alliance. Mary M. Davison was a notable early exponent of this brand of conspiracy theorization when she tied the New World Order to the establishment of the U.S. Federal Reserve in 1913. The Federal Reserve would go on to become the perennial bugaboo of Libertarian economists who advocated for a return to the gold standard.

Classic Cold War era conspiracy theory didn't really get a solid historical footing until Gary Allen and Larry Abraham published *None Dare Call it Conspiracy* in 1971. This book conforms to so many conspiratorial tropes (The Council of Foreign Relations, international banking conspiracies, the Rothschilds, etc.) that when it comes to positing something truly radical, and mesmerizingly so, it does so by drawing on the mythic grandeur of conspiracy theory past:

> Karl Marx was hired by a mysterious group who called themselves the League of Just Men to write the *Communist Manifesto* as demagogic boob-bait to appeal to the mob. In actual fact the *Communist Manifesto* was in circulation for many years before Marx's name was widely enough recognized to establish his authorship for this revolutionary handbook. All Karl Marx really did was to update and codify the very same revolutionary plans and principles set down seventy years earlier by Adam

Weishaupt, the founder of the Order of Illuminati in Bavaria. And it is widely acknowledged by serious scholars of this subject that the League of Just Men was simply an extension of the Illuminati which was forced to go deep underground after it was exposed by a raid in 1786 conducted by the Bavarian authorities.[322]

None Dare Call it Conspiracy is focused on Communism, not as a coherent ideology that must be defeated with arguments, statistics and logic, but as a tool that is implemented by the ruling class. The book is very direct on this point:

> "Communism" is not a movement of the down-trodden masses but is a movement created, manipulated, and used by power-seeking billionaires in order to gain control over the world ... First by establishing socialist governments in the various nations and then consolidating them all through a "Great Merger," into an all-powerful world socialist super-state probably under the auspices of the United Nations.[323]

According to Allen and Abraham the end goal of a socialist super-state is being primarily engineered by wealthy bankers. The obvious question that comes to mind is: "Why would the wealthy try to enact a system that is, ideologically-speaking, fundamentally opposed to their own class?" In response to this query, Allen and Abraham lay out the fact that they believe these wealthy elites don't take the tenets of Communism seriously, yet they hope to rule over a society that has been nominally structured around those tenets.

---

[322] Allen, Gary & Abraham, Larry (1971) *None Dare Call it Conspiracy*. Dauphin Publications. P. 20
[323] Ibid, p. 28

The most important take-away from Allen and Abraham's argument begins with what we might call a legitimate counter-argument: how will the wealthy, even super-wealthy, maintain a state of total segregation from the masses they've enslaved with Communism? Allen and Abraham claim that the movement towards Socialism will be fought for by the "downtrodden masses," which are merely pawns of the elites.[324] Simultaneously, these same "elites" will market globalism to American citizens in a way that appeals to their hope for world peace.[325] Once these factors are in place, politically, the security of the "elites" will be based on the literary precedent set by Orwell:

> The real name of the game is 1984. We will have systematic population reduction, forced sterilization or anything else which the planners deem necessary to establish absolute control in their *humanitarian* utopia.[326]

There is a slight problem with the analogy to *1984* here, and it has to do with the discrepancy between Allen and Abraham's insistence that a total world government must be established before an Orwellian dystopia can play itself out, and the fact that part of the dramatic tension of *1984* arose from the conflict between the super-states: Oceania, Eurasia and Eastasia. Perhaps Allen and Abraham assume that external threats can be simulated for the subjects of this global super-state, and then potential dissidents like Winston Smith can be ferreted out by *Stasiesque* agents of the global state.

Ostensibly, this level of sophistication does not lend itself to Allen and Abraham's text because they themselves discern the Soviet Union and China as distinguishable geopolitical entities that are engaged in complex maneuverings against the United

---

[324] Ibid, p. 101
[325] Ibid, p. 97
[326] Ibid, p. 98

States. However, if they read the super-states of *1984* as being purely illusory then we can say that the Orwellian dystopia will be realized by recasting the Soviet Union and China as nations in a virtual conflict with the United States. Nevertheless, the invocation of *1984* here is problematic since Orwell subtly indicates that nuclear war led to the creation of Oceania, Eurasia and Eastasia and this is not a factor that is discussed in *NDCC*.

Returning to the issue of the governing "elites" and the masses, the most interesting thing about what the text creates structurally is the positing of an "other" that exists in a sterile and rarified air. This depiction is not exclusive to the Right; *In First As Tragedy Then As Farce,* Slavoj Žižek (a Marxist) invokes the same environment for the super-wealthy:

> A new global class is thus emerging [...] These global citizens live their lives mostly in pristine nature – whether trekking in Patagonia or swimming in the translucent waters of their private islands. One cannot help but note that one feature basic to the attitude of these gated superrich is *fear*: fear of external social life itself. The highest priorities of the "ultrahigh-net-worth individuals" are thus how to minimize security risks – diseases, exposure to threats of violent crime, and so forth.[327]

The international banking narrative begins with the Rothschild Family because, as Allen and Abraham state, "they were cosmopolitan and international."[328] For this reason, and more, they have engineered every global unrest of the twentieth century, including the rise of Adolf Hitler and WWII.[329] The focal point of *NDCC*'s conspiratorial eye, post-World War Two, is the

---

[327] Žižek, Slavoj (2009) *First as Tragedy, Then as Farce.* Verso p. 4
[328] Allen, Gary & Abraham, Larry (1971) *None Dare Call it Conspiracy*. Dauphin Publications. P. 31
[329] Ibid p. 67

Council of Foreign Relations and the Bilderbergers, both of which hold meetings of politicians and members of the financial community with the "ultimate goal" of establishing a one world government.[330] Part of why *NDCC* became the standard-bearer for the Cold War conspiracy theorist and the militia type Rightists who have followed in their footsteps is that Allen and Abraham make rehabilitating the accusation of "Conspiracy" a part of their project.

> Those who believe that major world events result from planning are laughed at for believing in the "conspiracy theory of history." Of course, no one in this modern day and age really believes in the conspiracy theory of history – except those who have taken the time to study the subject. When you think about it, there are really only two theories of history. Either things happen by accident neither planned nor caused, or they happen because they *are* planned and somebody causes them to happen. In reality, it is the accidental theory of history preached in the unhallowed Halls of Ivy which should be ridiculed.[331]

The final point of contrast between the conspiratorial Left and Right is a truly dialectical one involving the concept of private property. We saw the Black Bloc's statement (circa 1999) condemning private property in the previous section. This attitude, along with environmentalism, pacifism, and equality were the four idealistic pillars of pretty much every potent form of Leftism since the eighteenth century. The prohibition against private property goes back to More's *Utopia*, and like that novel betrays the basic, Christian instinct of liberalism. When Jesus told his followers to abandon their material possessions and follow

---

[330] Ibid p. 74
[331] Ibid p. 6

him, the clear implication was that those possessions would obscure their discipleship.

Ironically, as the left was promulgated in the latter half of the 20th century, an explicit avowal of Christian principles was discarded, and these values fell under the heading of "Secular Humanism."[332] Just as ironically, the right, which is nominally Christian, has been very concerned with private property. It's not just a fear of "them grabbing our guns!" but a fear of losing and living without possessions.

It's possible that this devotion to retaining one's possessions stems from Protestantism more than it does Catholicism, but the more interesting issue here is what ownership says to the individual in contemporary society. For the Leftist, it seems as if the ideal of non-ownership, is an ideal that, if obtained, would be a state of total liberation. In contrast to this, the Right-wing, or conservative, despite nominally adhering to a creed that claims "you can't take it with you," identifies himself by way of the things he owns.[333] These positions, in their pure forms, no longer really exist. The novelty of Cold War conspiracy theorization, both left and right, was that it postulated the tenets of these ideologies in such bold and uncompromising ways.

This concludes the basic historical narrative of how Freemasonry played a significant role in constructing the concept of a New World Order and how this concept has been interpreted through literature and by Left and Right-wingers throughout the latter part of the 20th Century. There is one more important group that we need to discuss before we can wrap up this attenuated chapter.

---

[332] My mother would argue that this moment came into full instantiation when John Lennon released "Imagine."

[333] The additional, conspiratorial wrinkle that can be added to this summary is Right-wingers who believe the radical left is only trying to abolish private property on account of the wealthy elite and the Left-wingers who think that the extreme right is trying to set up a total police state.

The Enduring Mystery of the Jesuits

It was a monument not, as many had it, to the French victory over Prussia, but to the Jesuit victory over France. The birth of Ignatius Loyola was early understood to have erred only in its location: Spain was origin, but none has ever excelled France in vocational guidance for the ideas of others, and it was obvious (in France) that his Society of Jesus could be best advanced through the medium of the French mind.[334]

Founded by Ignatius of Loyola in 1534, the Society of Jesus, or the Jesuit Order, first came under public scrutiny when they were temporarily banned from France in 1594 after a man named Jean Châtel tried to assassinate King Henry IV. Châtel's attempt drew ire upon the Jesuits because he had been their student while attending the Collège de Clermont.[335] Other political intrigues, either directly or tangentially related to the group would follow, including their total suppression by Pope Clement XIV, which lasted from 1773 to 1814.[336]

The Jesuit Order stood out amidst other Catholic Orders because of their rigorous approach to education. Their founder, Ignatius Loyola, insisted that prior to advanced theological studies, the candidate for admission to the Order would endure two to four years of training in philosophy, after which the candidate was encouraged to pursue post-graduate degrees. After

---

[334] Gaddis, William (2012) *The Recognitions.* Dalkey Archive Press, p. 66.
[335] https://en.wikipedia.org/wiki/Jean_Ch%C3%A2tel accessed 08/25/20
[336] Mackey, Albert (1996) *The History of Freemasonry.* Published by Gramercy Books, a Division of Random House Value Publishing Inc. Pp. 286 - 287

this basic training came the stage of Regency, in which the candidate engaged in full-time ministry, usually including teaching. Even then, the candidate faced four years of advanced theological training before ordination.[337]

With such a rigorous training regimen it is no wonder that the Jesuits can appear intimidating. Don Delillo captures this sense of mastery eloquently in *Underworld* when he describes an encounter between one of his protagonists, sixteen-year-old Nick Shay, and a Jesuit Priest named Andrew Paulus. The meeting begins with Shay admitting that any successes that he's had in school have been the result of memorization, not understanding. Paulus responds that memorization is not a means to affecting an authentic education:

> "One of the things we want to do here is to produce serious men. What sort of phenomenon is this? Not easy to say. Someone, in the end, who develops a certain depth, a spacious quality, say, that's a form of respect for other ways of thinking and believing. Let us unnarrow the basic human tubing. And let us help a young man toward an ethical strength that makes him decisive, that shows him precisely who he is, Shay, and how he is meant to address the world."[338]

After stating this, Father Paulus tells Shay that instead of pondering big abstract ideas one is better served by looking at and analyzing the smaller, more mundane aspects of everyday life, such as the parts of a shoe. This leads to one of the most fascinating passages in the novel, where for almost three pages Paulus guides Nick through the names of each unnoticed constituent of the boots he is wearing. From the laces and the heel

---

[337] https://en.wikipedia.org/wiki/Society_of_Jesus accessed on 09/18/20

[338] Delillo, Don (1997) *Underworld*. Simon and Schuster. P. 538

to more esoteric parts like the welt, the counter, the vamp, etc. This exercise builds to Paulus's statement:

> "Everyday things represent the most overlooked knowledge. These names are vital to your progress. Quotidian things. If they weren't important, we wouldn't use such a gorgeous Latinate word [Quotidian] [...] An extraordinary word that suggests the depth and reach of the commonplace."[339]

Philosophically speaking, we might be tempted to tie such a lesson to the Phenomenological tradition of Heidegger's mentor, Edmund Husserl (April 8, 1859 – April 27, 1938). Husserl's approach to Phenomenology was not historical in the way we have described the Hermeneutical school of thought that developed out of his philosophy. In fact, his method was based on the idea of looking at objects as they appear in consciousness, and in doing so, divorcing their appearance from the narratives (both historical and cause and effect) that we might have in relation to them. Essentially Husserl tried to achieve a "pure" conscious apprehension of the object itself.

The theological reading of this lesson is interesting in two ways. First, it seeks out the names of things that are hidden from us by our own ignorance and that within this banality lies a sort of "logocentric" grandeur that has been ordained upon our day-to-day lives. The second aspect is a bit more occultic, in that it seems to imply that a mastery of names grants the knower a certain degree of power over, if not the object, then the reality in which the object resides.[340]

---

[339] Ibid p. 542

[340] Later philosophers, such as Foucault, when dabbling with theological thought, did so in the company of Jesuits. One member of the order even wrote the Introduction to *Religion and Culture* – James Bernauer SJ.

Delillo concludes this short chapter with a hint at the political import associated with the Society of Jesus by having Father Paulus chide Shay for having signed a petition in support of Senator Joseph McCarthy. This portrayal plays to the fears of traditional Catholics who had been drawn into the Right-wing cause during the Cold War because they feared that a Communist regime might persecute their faith into non-existence. Many such individuals formed a contingent that sought to overturn liberal reforms instituted during the Second Vatican Council (1962-65) believing that V2 was instigated by Communist infiltrators. Such suspicions among Catholics, and fundamentalist Christians in general, led many to cast their suspicions on the highly educated and secretive Jesuit Order.

Practically speaking, because the sects within the Catholic Church developed in such a pluralistic way (Dominicans, Franciscans, Carmelites etc.) the threat of Communist infiltration, if it was to occur, would most likely be suspected to have originated from within a rival sect. The fact that the Jesuits saw themselves as an elite Order, beholden only to their own authority (second only to the Pope) added to this suspicion. Alarmist tomes, such as R.M. Whitney's *Reds in America*, originally published in 1924, warned that Communism had already infiltrated the Catholic Church; this book was one of a myriad of voices echoing this concern.

This critique of the Jesuits lives on in more fundamentalist and anti-progressive Christianity, which views the Jesuits as the puppet-masters lurking behind the actions of the Church.[341] Theories that the Pope is secretly the Anti-Christ, which were more prevalent during the reign of Pope Benedict XVI, are also probably an extension of this critique. The author Dan Brown put a lot of work into redirecting this conspiratorial heat away from the Jesuits and onto the Opus Dei order in his 2003 novel *The Da*

---

[341] Another notable proponent of this Christian Fundamentalism was cartoonist and pamphleteer Jack Chick, who attacked both Catholicism and Freemasonry in his work.

Vinci Code. But this was only a temporary reprieve since the focus of that book was the Holy Grail and most true believers became more focused on the hidden history of Jesus Christ's bloodline than contemporary Church activities.

Allen and Abraham are of the Judeo-Christian school, and they often engage in anti-Jesuit conspiracy theorizing; but they are much more focused on the Society of Jesus insofar as it influenced one of their primary enemies, Freemasonry:

> It should be noted that the originator of this type of secret society was Adam Weishaupt, the monster who founded the Order of Illuminati on May 1, 1776, for the purposes of a conspiracy to control the world. The role of Weishaupt's Illuminists in such horrors as the Reign of Terror is unquestioned, and the techniques of the Illuminati have long been recognized as models for Communist methodology. Weishaupt also used the structure of the Society of Jesus (the Jesuits) as his model, and rewrote his Code in Masonic terms.[342]

Allen and Abraham implicate the Jesuits a few other times in *None Dare Call it Conspiracy*, one of the most notable passages of which details their influence on Cecil Rhodes (who is one of the supposed architects of the New World Order named in the book):

> Cecil Rhodes' commitment to a conspiracy to establish World Government was set down in a series of wills described by Frank Aydelotte in his book *American Rhodes Scholarships...* The model for

---

[342] Allen, Gary & Abraham, Larry (1971) *None Dare Call it Conspiracy*. Dauphin Publications. P. 64

this proposed secret society was the Society of Jesus, though he also mentions the Masons.[343]

Jordan Maxwell mines most of the same territory as *None Dare Call it Conspiracy* but with much greater aplomb and variety; his dissertation on Freemasonry, which is very, very, long, contains this paragraph:

In what follows, I shall attempt to show that the modern revolutionary tradition, as it came to be internationalized under Napoleon, during the restoration, grew out of occult Freemasonry. The early organizational revolutionary ideas originated more from Pythagorean mysticism than from practical experience. Moreover, the real innovators were not so much the political activists, as much as literary intellectuals on whom German Romantic thought in general, and the Bavarian Illuminati, in particular, exerted great influence. Here, Billington was specifically talking about the organization of the Bavarian Illuminati. You can't discuss the Illuminati without understanding the Jesuit order of the Catholic Church, because Adam Weishaupt himself, the founder of the Illuminati, was, in fact, a Jesuit priest. He was not *just* an ordinary Jesuit priest, however. In Bavaria he continued to support revolutionary radical thinking against the church, giving to the world what has come to be known, as the revolutionary tradition.[344]

---

[343] Allen, Gary & Abraham, Larry (1971) *None Dare Call it Conspiracy*. Dauphin Publications. P. 63
[344] Maxwell, Jordan (2000) *Matrix of Power: Secrets of World Control*. The Book Tree. P. 11

By specifying the origins of revolutionary tradition in terms of "Pythagorean mysticism" this passage essentially designates the Jesuits as being one of the primary holders and transmitters of the Antediluvian sacred sciences. Such notions, on the surface, must surely run contrary to the work of Knight and Lomas, who we have seen repeatedly attack the Papacy. However, as Knight and Lomas don't mention the Jesuits in their work, it is possible the authors are providing them cover and that the conspiracy theorists are correct: the Jesuits and Freemasons have been working hand-in-hand. This might be an accurate assessment, but it does not line-up with Albert Mackey's history of the Craft.

Mackey begins his argument by stating that the theory of Jesuit and Masonic comingling stems primarily from Robison. His exact reasoning is too complex to go into here, but he concludes that:

> The theory that the Jesuits in the 17th century had invented Freemasonry for the purpose of effecting one of their ambitious projects, or that they had taken it as it then existed, changed it, and added to it for the same purpose, is absolutely untenable.[345]

As for the theory that there was a degree of cooperation between the Bavarian Illuminati and the Society of Jesus that continues in present-day Freemasonry, Mackey agrees with Robison that the Illuminati and the Jesuits were bitter enemies, describing the conflict as a battle of egos.[346] Mackey claims that this confusion arose, in part, from the secrecy surrounding both groups, but also because they both exhibited cunning and unchecked ambition in their attempts at political influence.

---

[345] Mackey, Albert (1996) *The History of Freemasonry*. Published by Gramercy Books, a Division of Random House Value Publishing Inc. P. 288

[346] Ibid pp. 289 - 290

The general trend for contemporary conspiracy theories about Jesuits is more practical than fanciful and does not usually involve any elaborate history or myth-making. This view more or less sees Jesuits as an order within the Catholic Church that is promoting liberalism. There is a certain amount of historical evidence of this, even if the same accusation could be leveled against several organizations operating within the Church.

This is theory is essentially a reiteration of the critique that was brought against the Illuminati for using Freemasonry to spread Enlightenment ideals in the eighteenth century. However, for most conspiracy theorists the mythology of Freemasonry as a whole was too irresistible and eventually blossomed into a tree with roots that would expand into everything from Atlantis and UFO cover-ups to 9/11.

That is, except for one individual named Gail Chord Schuler who began making YouTube videos in 2011. From her videos, Ms. Schuler appears to be a very imaginative schizophrenic woman who, prior to starting her YouTube channel, had obsessively written fan letters to *Star Trek: The Next Generation* actor, Brent Spiner (he played Data on the series). These letters inspired her self-published book *Silver Skies*, which she displays during her first video. Gail, who based on her surname was most likely born Jewish, is a born-again Christian. In her thousand plus videos she details the adventures and struggles of a spaceship named "the Church of Gail" that is in the deep reaches of outer space perpetually battling the Jesuits. So far, the Church of Gail has:

-Been destroyed a number of times, the first instance of this was when crew member, Vladimir Putin gave the order to crash the ship directly into the Jesuit craft it was battling.

-Flown through the center of the sun while being pursued by a giant sentient taco and a giant sentient burrito.

-Been aided by Bill Nye "The Science Guy," who has created weapons and shields for them.

-Seen Lori McBride destroy an entire space fleet while they were on their way to Moonsico for the purposes of imprisoning Sara Avery.

-Been attacked by the Jesuits with photon torpedoes causing the Church of Gail's warp engines and life-support to fail. This disaster was averted through the power of prayer and Gail's removal of her Skype calls from YouTube.

Sometimes when recounting these adventures, Gail herself is wearing aluminum foil on her head. Brent Spiner figures prominently in many of these situations insofar as Gail believes that she is in psychic communication with him and that the two are betrothed. The only thing standing in the way of their matrimony is the Jesuits, who are controlled by a diabolical mastermind named Zack Knight. What is interesting about this situation is not just that the Jesuit conspiracy theory is resurfaced with all the bizarreness of the Freemason theories (and more!) but that it is one person authoring all of this. In this sense, Gail Schuler falls into the tradition of mythmaking. The other interesting facet of this is that many people online theorize that internet trolls are egging Gail on in her delusions. Taken on their own, Gail's tales appear to be a form of absurdist fan fiction incorporating celebrities like Hugh Jackman and Matthew McConaughey within plots that are at times surreal, clever and vulgar.

Gail Schuler's situation prefigures other issues that we will be dealing with later in the book. Right now, I want to address the issue of Gail Schuler within the context of the mythic territory already traversed. We have already discussed Vico's idea of how primitive man created myths to transmit certain societal structures, and the contrary claim by Julian Jaynes that primitive man's cortex was demarcated in a way that made thoughts seem like external voices. Ruling out the intervention of online trolls for the time being, the question about Gail Schuler now is: is she consciously creating the Church of Gail mythology or is she in some way interpreting her thoughts as external communications?

Some people might scoff at the first part of this question and assume that this behavior is so delusional that it cannot be an act. To this I would respond: never underestimate commitment to the bit, just look at Andy Kaufmann. Does anyone really know what his deal was? Though it is highly unlikely, there is a chance that Gail Schuler is pulling off a massive troll on her audience. The second part of the question has to do with why the first part seems so unlikely: Gail seems crazy because her imagination seems inexhaustible. Perhaps the historical analogue that is most appropriate here is the "Sybil," a term which refers to ancient Greek priests who acted as oracles:

> The priests and prophets of the various oracles were the only important religious figures of the early Greeks, and the oracles were the sites of the first Greek temples. The most well-known oracles were at Delphi, Eleusis, Dodona, and Epidaurus, but there were many others as well. Each spoke in a different way. At Delphi, the oracle spoke through a priestess called the Pythia, named after the sacred snake, the python.
> The Pythia would sit above cracks in the ground, from which vapours arose from underground hot springs. She was usually intoxicated. She spoke in a state of psychic frenzy, as if in a trance. The oracle might well have been a remnant of an earlier religion of the Great Mother, who was also associated with snakes and caves.[347]

There is a certain ambiguity as to whether the "oracle" is merely an energy that animates the priestess or whether the

---

[347] Stewart, Louis (1980) *Life Forces: A Contemporary Guide to the Cult and Occult.* Andrews and McMeel Inc. p. 391

energy can only be tapped into at certain sacred places. This is an issue we discussed in reference to conspiracy theorists who postulate the existence of Ley lines or other electromagnetic "hotspots" on the earth's surface. For the time being, we can conclude that if there were such a thing as a "Sybil" in our postmodern age, it is Gail Schuler.

Conclusion

We can think of these disparate groups as being assimilated into Freemasonry proper and then, being not wholly integrated, operating in a pluralistic fashion with each other. Masonry then becomes a sort of political or spiritual state with various factions vying with each other for hegemony. This is compounded if we consider the possibility that nominally internal groups, such as the Bavarian Illuminati and the founders of the Scottish Rite, have possibly rewritten the tenets and ethos of a fairly conventional fraternal organization to seed a hotbed of totalitarianism.

One of the things we should take note of with these different groups (Freemasons, Rosicrucians, Jesuits, etc.) is that conspiracy theorists take them as secretive groups working to gain hegemonic control of our society. The conviction that they have in fact assumed control and now are running everything is a product of reductive, dialectically scientist reasoning. Once the conspiracy theorist adheres to the idea that they can reduce all the world's (or their own) problems to one specific group that has taken power, the notion that this group is taunting the populace with hints as to the extent of its control comes into play. I call this aspect of conspiracy theorizing the "transparency of the elites" theory.

The thinking behind this concept is that the conspiratorial elites are compelled to leave clues to be interpreted in the way that Moriarty left clues for Sherlock Holmes. This concept is prevalent among Compound Conspiracy Theorists; Michael A. Hoffman II is one such proponent of this theory. Hoffman's brand of conspiracy theorization shares similarities with Gary Wayne, in that he is Right-leaning and Christian – he also blames Freemasonry for a lot of things. Unlike Wayne, Hoffman is a Catholic (of some stripe) and does not share Wayne's suspicion of Catholicism. Hoffman and Wayne both criticize scientism, but Hoffman does not share Wayne's Apocalyptic fervor; instead he sees the workings of elites, which he calls the "Cryptocracy," as building a restrictive world order:

> The doctrine of man playing god reaches its nadir in the philosophy of scientism which makes possible the complete mental, spiritual and physical enslavement of mankind through technologies such as satellite and computer surveillance; a state of affairs symbolized by the "All Seeing Eye" above the unfinished pyramid on the U.S. one dollar bill.[348]

Another interesting distinction between Hoffman and Wayne is that while they both trace a similar evolution involving Pythagorus, Plato, the Knights Templar, etc. when it comes to Hermeticism/occultism etc., Hoffman seems to think that the promise of enlightenment offered by such groups is basically a scam,[349] and Wayne sees these promises as real, but spiritually dangerous. The main thrust of Hoffman's *Secret Societies and Psychological Warfare* has to do with something he calls "ceremonial psychodrama," wherein the cryptocracy, which had kept its greatest secrets (described in the text as having been guarded by the "masonic-NeoPlatonic Hermetic Academy") hidden for centuries, have now decided to release them to the public. Hoffman designates Kenneth Grant and Roger K.G. Temple as two purveyors of this esoteric information and connects its release with the "Revelation of the Method" in which crimes,

---

[348] Hoffman II, Michael A. (2009) *Secret Societies and Psychological Warfare* (Sixth Printing) Independent History and Research. P. 50
[349] Ibid, pp. 42 - 43

atrocities, and wars connected to these occult secrets are revealed to the public – whose shock and titillation at the revelation only leads them further down the road of submissiveness and "mental enslavement."[350] Obviously, an event like 9/11 was for Hoffman, and theorists who have followed his line of thought, a tremendous event that might have been the final move made by the cryptocracy before ushering us into our final stages of complacency and submission. We will revisit Hoffman's theories a few more times before book's end. But now we must look further back into the historical narratives that inform much of what we've just laid out.

---

[350] Ibid, pp. 51 -53

Chapter Six: The Significance of the Grail Mythos

The Grail mythos, like the concept of a New World Order, is a nexus around which many of the characters and narratives that are important to this book coalesce. Most readers will be vaguely familiar with the fact that many symbols, traditions, and rites used in Freemasonry trace back to some aspect of the Grail mythos. When discussing the concept, it is important to keep in mind an idea we briefly discussed regarding the fall from Eden, i.e., that an individualized consciousness must be attained through a struggle; because in a significant way the Grail mythos, and the narratives that comprise it, is an allegory for this struggle.

Due to its prevalence in popular culture most everyone is aware that the stories surrounding the quest for the Grail have to do with medieval tropes such as knights, princesses, and castles. Emma Jung summarizes the central narrative of the myth this way:

> The story is known to everyone, at least in its general outlines. A mysterious, life-preserving and sustenance-dispensing object or vessel is guarded by a King in a castle that is difficult to find. The King is either lame or sick and the surrounding country is devastated. The King can only be restored to health if a knight of conspicuous excellence finds the castle and at the first sight of what he sees there asks a certain question. Should he neglect to put this question, then everything will remain as before, the castle will vanish and the knight will have to set out once more upon the search. Should he finally succeed, after much wandering and many adventures, in finding the Grail Castle again, and should he then ask the question, the King will be restored to health, the land will begin to grow

green, and the hero will become the guardian of the Grail from that time on.[351]

Jung is presenting us with the traditional literary account; we will analyze this as well as its modern interpretations in the following two chapters. From the above passage we can straight away see how this archetypal story accommodates three aspects of a Structuralist reading:

1. The mythical kingdom where the castle is located is a sacred space containing the partial object that is the castle itself.

2. The Grail itself as partial object; one that compounds the elusiveness of the whole affair.

3. The key to the kingdom, so to speak, is wholly linguistic in nature: it is asking the correct question.

Like the Bible, the Grail mythos has had an all-pervasive influence in Western society. However, unlike the Bible, from which the Grail narratives draw some of their mythological power – in particular the murkiness of certain figures like Arthur, the Fisher King, and Prester John – the Grail mythos did not *directly* inform a set of formal and dogmatic religions, informing instead occult (the shadow side of religion) belief systems and organizations. The Knights Templar, Freemasonry, and Theosophically oriented groups all draw on the Grail mythos for certain rites or keys to understanding the world.

The Grail mythos had an influence on early anthropology in the form of James George Frazer's (January 1, 1854 – May 7, 1941) repetition of its schematic in his 1890 book *The Golden Bough,* wherein he describes the "priest-king" of the woods who guards the forest until he is supplanted after engaging, and being

---

[351] Jung, Emma & Franz, Marie-Louise (1986) *The Grail Legend.* Sigo Press. P. 9

defeated, in mortal combat with a stronger adversary that has ventured into his territory.

This aspect of the Grail myth, the conquering and replacement of an enemy, is a common theme in literature, and one could argue that its process of conflict and resolution essentially mirrors the Hegelian dialectic. However, it does not mirror it exactly because there is an implication in dialectical reasoning that the antithesis, the figure or narrative that is being combatted, is legible and that its defeat (or sublation) is based on an understanding of it.[352] For Frazer, there is a sense that the hero who battles and defeats the priest-king does not necessarily know what he has gotten himself into once he has entered the sacred realm; and further, that he, like his predecessor, might not even fully grasp the significance of the role he played in his struggle to overcome the priest-king, let alone the significance of assuming his predecessor's role.

This sort of ambiguity is often added to more modern scholarly and literary approaches to the Grail mythos, one of which is *The Waste Land* by T. S. Eliot, published in 1922. Eliot's book-length poem, which takes as its starting point the symbolism of the Fisher King's realm, is an exploration of a single consciousness that is diffracted into a myriad of voices. Since many of the voices Eliot used were conveyed in a contemporaneous British dialect, the "Waste Land" of the title is often interpreted as being a place where everybody is living an inauthentic life.[353]

It is by virtue of these modern approaches to the subject that we get the first inkling of the Structuralist parameters

---

[352] This assessment holds true even if the act of understanding the antithetical narrative or argument is interpreted as being constitutive of the sublation (or dialectical over-coming of the antithesis).

[353] See the interview with Joseph Campbell at https://www.sarahlawrence.edu/magazine/lost-found/features/holy-grail.html accessed on 10/07/20

surrounding the myth of the Grail, and how, on Žižek's analysis, a sign such as the Grail comes to be seen as a symbolic representation that takes the place of some aspect of the "real" that is otherwise incomprehensible to us.

The literary/historical Grail narrative begins in Europe during the eleventh century, possibly prior to the First Crusade, which began in 1096 CE. The Grail mythos is certainly animated by the spirit of medieval chivalry that informed the crusades, and Grail-related tales might have been exchanged between crusaders. However, the literary structure was formalized and made popular by *Perceval or the Story of the Grail* composed by the French poet Chrétian de Troyes sometime in the late-twelfth century.

It is in de Troyes's work that we find the principal features of the myth: the castle, the Grail (as represented by a platter), and the hero's question. De Troyes died in 1191 before he could complete the story which was finished by other unknown poets of the time. The next foundational work in the mythos was Robert de Boron's *Joseph of Arimathea*, (written in the twelfth century) which depicted the Grail as the cup Jesus used at the last supper. The last literary work in the traditional mythos is Thomas Malory's *Le Morte D'Arthur* from 1469, which incorporated the Grail quest into Arthurian mythology. [354] Joseph Campbell identifies two fundamental strains of the narrative, one that stems from a monastic love that is chaste and characterized by the concept of *agapē,* and another more Romantic conception that takes the love between a man and woman to be a religious experience. Campbell focuses the beginning of his study of the Grail mythos on the German poet Wolfram Von Eschenbach's *Parzival*, which appeared in the twelfth century sometime after Chrétian de Troyes's work. He did so because *Parzival* rejects both the pious and Romantic approaches to love, and because Wolfram situates the adventures in a definite historical context

---

[354] From www.ancient.eu/Grail_Legend accessed on 6/25/20

instead of the "never-never land of Arthurian romance."[355] Emma Jung also designates Wolfram's telling of the Grail legend as "distinguished above all others by its compactness, its depth of thought and feeling, and its psychological subtleties, which often sound quite modern."[356]

As the story progressed through these foundational works, numerous characters were developed; one of the most important was the Fisher King who is often identified as the wounded monarch presiding over the Waste Land. There are a variety of possible origin stories for this character, and Campbell identifies him as "Anfortas," giving us this narrative:

> So Anfortas was riding forth, and he encountered a heathen who had ridden from the gates of paradise in quest of the Grail; he had the words *The Grail* written on his spear. And the heathen knight wounded Anfortas, piercing him through the genitals, emasculating him with that spear. Anfortas lost his biological virility, yet he killed the heathen. So here is the pair of opposites, nature and the spirit in collision with each other, as they were in the Middle Ages in Europe, a condition that brought about the Waste Land. The king's whole land was laid waste by this terrific blow. Yet he manages to get back to his castle and is brought to behold the Grail, which keeps people alive.[357]

It is important to note that in Wolfram's poem, the Grail is not a cup but a stone. Emma Jung takes this detail to be an

---

[355] Campbell, Joseph (2015) *Romance of the Grail: The Magic and Mystery of Arthurian Myth*. New World Library. P. 35
[356] Jung, Emma & Franz, Marie-Louise (1986) *The Grail Legend*. Sigo Press. P. 34
[357] Campbell, Joseph (2015) *Romance of the Grail: The Magic and Mystery of Arthurian Myth*. New World Library. P. 50.

incorporation of alchemical symbolism, which she interprets as having psychological relevance; but we can also interpret it as an atavistic precursor to the dialectical thinking we associate with German Idealism. Returning to the possible origins of the Fisher King, Campbell offers a reading of this figure within the archetypal context of Buddhist thought, specifically the *Pancatantra*, in which a Brahmin in search of riches comes to a desert and finds a man with a wheel spinning on his head. The wheel has sharp edges and blood is pouring down the man's body. Upon being asked, "What is that wheel doing on your head?" the Brahmin realizes himself now with the wheel spinning on his head.

Campbell sees this punishment as analogous to the crown of thorns placed on Jesus's head and thereby determines that "our wounded king, Anfortas, is also the wounded Christ."[358] Based on this reading we might extrapolate that the Fisher King narrative is in some way pointing towards the figure of Melchizedek, or an exponent of the tradition instigated by Melchizedek. The reading of the Fisher King as Christ can be compounded by a sloppy reading of scripture, in which Christ is referenced as "a fisher of men." However, according to the Gospels Christ himself is not the "fisher of men" but instead the one who enjoins his disciples to become "fishers of men."[359] In contrast to this interpretation, Julius Evola claims that, according to some traditions the Fisher King is both Joseph of Arimathea and Percival's father.[360]

What seems most significant here is that there is no origin story that can be marked as *the* authentic one. The Fisher King as a name, or title, entails any or all of them. Note that, like the literature that preceded it, the Grail literature played upon pre-existing myths and folktales. As a literary endeavor it was not static but evolving, incorporating and reacting to the folktales and

---

[358] Ibid, pp. 90 - 92

[359] Mark 1: 16 - 20

[360] Evola, Julius (1997) *The Mystery of the Grail.* Inner Traditions International. P. 59

embellishments it engendered – the character of Prester John (who we will discuss later) is one such example of this phenomena.

The Structuralist Reading

I will now go through items 1-3 of the list that constitutes a Structuralist reading of the Grail mythos. Obviously, the Grail myth relies on Christianity, but in hermeneutical terms if we look at the central stories of the Bible – let's say Adam and Eve's fall or Christ's crucifixion – we read these narratives with a sense of inevitability. We, as readers, know what is going to happen going into them. Auerbach identifies this as a formal quality of literature, but it is a particular variety of literature.[361] The more episodic adventures that make up the Grail quest are more open-ended, in a way that is similar to Greek myths or folktales, and are intended to spark an interest in resolution (as any narrative would) but do not harbor the content of said resolution from the outset, as the Biblical narratives do.

This is not to say that there are not endless avenues of speculation that can be pursued in relation to these primary Biblical narratives; as we have seen (and will see again) there most definitely are. However, I would argue – and this relates to the three murky figures of Hiram, Enoch and Melchizedek – that the richest narratives – those that best utilize the tropes of mystery and ambiguity – are the ones that exist at the margins of the text and not in the explicit narrative. The narratives that make up the Grail quest are engaging because they take the margin as their starting point and work towards something that might be considered universally significant. This approach is the guarantor of their narrative richness.

The castle presented in *Perceval or the Story of the Grail* is depicted as having been crafted out of gray-brown stone and

---

[361] Oftentimes, this foreknowledge is hermeneutical in nature, in that it has been cultivated by the societies we were raised in.

ringed around with turrets.[362] In Wolfram's version, Parzival's encounter with the Grail castle is preceded by his encounter with two men who are fishing in a boat. One of them, wearing peacock plumes in his helmet, is the Fisher King. When Parzival asks where he can find lodging for the evening, the king responds that there is a castle up the way and that if Parzival arrives there he will be his host. Campbell refers to this place as an "apparition" which can only appear to an individual who is prepared for it. Once there:

> He is received, and a great procession takes place, with the king lying there wounded. In an immense hall, Parzival, witnesses the ceremonial of the Grail. There are many knights on couches, all about. Anfortas is borne in on a litter.[363]

While this is taking place, Parzival, against his natural inclinations, fails to ask the required question: "What ails thee?" and wakes up the next day to an empty castle. As he rides his horse over the drawbridge, it is raised abruptly and a voice calls out: "Ride on, you goose!" and the castle vanishes. As he is riding through the forest, his aunt approaches and harangues him for not asking the correct question. She says that the castle has disappeared and will not be found again because no-one can visit it a second time. Parzival vows that he will somehow relocate the castle.

His first step in this quest is the renouncing of God.[364] His second step is to venture off into the unknown, along the way encountering a hermit who claims to be the brother of Anfortas,

[362] Chrétian de Troyes (1999) *Perceval: The Story of the Grail*. Translated by Burton Raffel. Yale University Press. P. 97
[363] Campbell, Joseph (2015) *Romance of the Grail: The Magic and Mystery of Arthurian Myth*. New World Library. P. 49
[364] Always a good call when you're enraged, but maybe a little too indicative of immaturity.

the Grail King. This encounter renews Parzival's faith in God. However, the conceptualization of God has matured away from the boyish faith instilled in him by his mother.[365] With this conversion there is a reinforcement of the awareness that Parzival may never re-enter the Grail castle, but he vows to do so again, even if it means breaking the divine mandate.[366]After this, Parzival encounters his long-lost half-brother, Feirefiz, who is also a knight. Not recognizing each other, the two knights do battle until the moment that Parzival's sword breaks in two. Feirefiz throws down his sword and asks Parzifal his name. The two remove their helmets and realize they are brothers. The appearance of Feirefiz is fortuitous because while Parzival has blown his shot at the Grail castle but his half-brother has not. And so the two set out to find the Grail castle, which they do; and upon seeing it the Fisher King asks: "What ails thee?" and becomes the Grail King. Campbell comments:

> Consider what is happening here: he has become the Grail King *without inheriting the wound*. That is to say, it is possible to be in that position intact and entire. This is a very optimistic work about the powers of man.[367]

Running almost concurrently with Parzival's quest in Wolfram's tale is the quest of the knight Gawain, who unlike Parzival is an established member of King Arthur's knights. After setting out on his quest Gawain comes upon a woman tending to a wounded knight. Gawain is able to heal the knight's wound and is warned by the man to not continue further down the road. This only intrigues Gawain, who continues on course until he encounters

---

[365] A significant detail of Parzival's backstory is that he was raised by his mother, while his father was out on Knightly adventures.
[366] Ibid p. 63
[367] Ibid p. 79

Orgeluse, the most beautiful woman Gawain has ever seen.
Campbell writes that:

> This is Woman. Gawain has gone from woman to
> woman, but this one has transfixed him, and he's
> going to remain firmly attached to her, no matter
> what. This is the *anima* image; it's the image of the
> woman by the well that is constantly encountered.
> One thinks of Jacob with Rachael by the well, and
> Moses with Zantipy by the well –and these women
> by the well are something to watch out for. And
> here is Orgeluse, the one he is ready for. This
> encounter catapults him into another sphere of the
> feminine altogether. The other women are simply
> forgotten.[368]

Campbell doesn't discuss the symbolism of "the woman by
the well," but from his description of the transformative power of
this figure we can draw a narrative association between the
feminine and the drawing of water, or water itself. Unlike the case
of the sea, which we associated with mystery and danger, the idea
here seems to be a conjunction of the mystery of the sea with the
nourishment of drinkable, fresh water. Evola writes that
"Orgeluse" is the name designated for the woman who inhabits
the Grail Castle and that devotion to her led to Amfortas receiving
his wound. Orgeluse represents, in some respect a wounding of
"heroic vitality" and the condemnation to a restless and
inextinguishable love. When Gawain overcomes his trials and
tribulations and makes Orgeluse his wife he will have succeeded
where Amfortas failed, as Evola notes:

> Gawain succeeds and makes Orgeluse his bride,
> instead of ending up like Amfortas[...] In relation to
> this, we notice the double aspect that, in conformity

---

[368] Ibid pp. 67 - 68

with what I have already discussed, the theme of the "woman" assumes. On the one hand, here we find the distinction between an earthly knighthood, which is inspired by a woman, and a heavenly knighthood, the object of which is the Grail.[369]

With this analysis we can see that a significant aspect of the Grail mythos has to do with securing conjugal love by overcoming trials and obstacles, it also indicates that the overcoming of these trials is contingent upon maintaining focus on a higher spiritual principle.

Returning to Campbell's telling of the story, after a series of adventures Gawain and Orgeluse arrive at the Château Merveille –the Castle of Marvels. This castle is surrounded by a moat that is as wide as a river, which cannot be crossed until Gawain has defeated a knight. After he does so, a ferryman takes the two of them across the moat and lodges them for the night in his house. The castle is filled with four queens and four hundred princesses. When Gawain wakes up the next morning, he looks out his window and "notices that all the women in the castle are still moving around. [He is] in the fairyland of no sleep, the land of no time. He has passed out of the realm of time into the magical realm of dream."[370]

After arising from bed Gawain asks the ferryman about the Castle of Marvels, who tells him that it is an adventure that can be undertaken, but which no-one can survive. Gawain does not heed this warning and enters the castle. Inside, everything is quiet. The first room he reaches has an ornate bed and the floor is incredibly slippery. This is the adventure of the Perilous Bed, and every time Gawain approaches the bed it leaps away. Campbell theorizes that this scene has a metaphorical dimension, in that it replicates the

---

[369] Evola, Julius (1997) *The Mystery of the Grail.* Inner Traditions International. P. 77

[370] Campbell, Joseph (2015) *Romance of the Grail: The Magic and Mystery of Arthurian Myth.* New World Library. P. 70

scenario in which the newlywed husband pursues his reluctant bride on their wedding night.[371]

Once Gawain makes it onto the bed he is forced to hold on for dear life as it careens around the room. All the while, five hundred crossbow bolts fly at him from all directions, which he is able to deflect by his shield. Finally, a lion enters the room and after Gawain cuts off its paw the two do battle until the beast is slain. After this tenuous victory Gawain is nursed back to health by some of the princesses who reside in the castle. The next day, upon exiting the gate, Gawain runs into Orgeluse who she asks him if he will ride into the forest and do combat with the knight who killed her husband. Before he fights the knight, however, he is to pluck a bough from the tree the knight is guarding. Campbell identifies this particular quest as a reiteration of Frazer's Golden Bough narrative.[372] However, the idea of a tree that is singled out, both for protection by the knight and for siege by Gawain, is a repetition of the narrative of the forbidden tree in the Garden of Eden.

Gawain's adventure mirrors that of Lancelot who also encounters a Castle of Marvels. As characters, Gawain and Lancelot are antithetically drawn, in the sense that Gawain was a notorious womanizer while Lancelot was chaste and religiously devout. Lancelot's experience in the Castle of Marvels is equally surreal:

> Lancelot enters a room where a very old priest is celebrating a Mass; when the priest elevates the host, he almost falls down, because the host becomes, in fact, the body of the young Christ.[373]

Upon seeing this, Lancelot attempts to help the priest but is unable to do so because, as Campbell says, he is "unworthy of

---

[371] Ibid pp. 70 - 71
[372] Ibid p. 73
[373] Ibid p. 138

being present."[374] This "unworthiness" is due to Lancelot's love for Guinevere, the woman who would eventually become Arthur's wife.

In respect to these accounts, the Castle can be read as a partial object in the Lacanian sense because it is elusive in nature, but it also occupies what Eliade calls "sacred space." One might argue that the sacred space of the Fisher King's castle (or the Castle of Marvels) is representative of a certain narrative that must be uncovered, and that the space between the errant knight and this story that he's looking for is analogous to, or a duplication of, the space that exists between the subject and language. On Lacan's view, this space is a fissure that is constitutive of the subject. Therefore, on this reading, the legend of the Grail is a manifestation of not merely finding one's self but finding one's *right* self. This aspect is exemplified in Wolfram's version of the tale, because, in order to save the Fisher King and restore order and prosperity to the land, Parzival must overcome the knight's code of stoic indifference and give into his own truer, inquisitive, and compassionate nature.

In regard to the lost object being a key to the unknown land that might be the lost paradise (spear of destiny, Arc of the covenant, and most significantly, the Holy Grail), there is a lot to say about these objects and before we do so it's necessary to set the stage with a thoughtful preamble:

> To be sensitive to signs, to consider the world as an object to be deciphered, is doubtless a gift. But this gift risks remaining buried in us if we do not make the necessary encounters, and these encounters would remain ineffective if we failed to overcome certain stock notions. The first of these is to attribute to the object the signs it bears. Everything encourages us to do so: perception, passion, intelligence, even self-esteem. We think that the

---

[374] Ibid p. 138

"object" itself has the secret of the signs it emits. We scrutinize the object, we return to it in order to decipher the sign. For the sake of convenience, let us call *objectivism* this tendency that is natural to us or, at least, habitual.[375]

Jay Conway, a contemporary philosopher who has written a great deal about Deleuze, elaborates on this idea of encountering an object that makes us think differently as an important aspect of Deleuze's emphasis on philosophical "apprenticeship." [376] For Deleuze himself, this apprenticeship consisted not only of formal schooling, but the composition of book-length studies devoted to various philosophers and novelists. Conway states, in regard to Deleuze's study of Proust, that:

> In *Proust and Signs*, we also find Deleuze adopting literature as a mediator for the production of a new vision of philosophical apprenticeship. What does Deleuze take to be the classic vision of apprenticeship? This is the idea that through the simple decision to follow a method, individuals begin to think philosophically and continue to do so until they have successfully generated a body of objective representations or necessary truths. The person undergoing a philosophical apprenticeship does so in full awareness they are spending their time doing philosophy.[377]

---

[375] Deleuze, Gilles (2000) *Proust and Signs*. Translated by Richard Howard. University of Minnesota Press. Pp. 26 - 27
[376] Conway, Jay (2010) *Gilles Deleuze: Affirmation in Philosophy.* Palgrave Macmillan. P. 22.
[377] Ibid, pp. 99 - 100

Marcel Proust surely had an inkling of the philosophical gravitas attendant to his work; can we say the same about the authors of the foundational Grail texts? Can we say that the actual crusaders – who were encountering new and esoteric objects in their travails, and whose tales would generate more narrative grist for the Grail myth-mill – had an awareness of their time being spent just as much on philosophy as on crusading?

Deleuze's concept of apprenticeship, as well as its complimentary concept of mastery will play a role in this chapter and the next. This role is normative, in that the knights and crusaders (both the real ones and their literary counterparts) are involved in an ongoing process of learning and engagement with the world that is guided by a variety of internal and external motives: some noble, some base and some banal. Lacan and his concept of partial objects will play a part in the journeying aspect, but in a more empirical sense, i.e., to help us make sense of the phenomena encountered.[378]

Obviously, there is a developmental process to what is going on with Wolfram's Parzival; in one respect he seems fated to fail the test of asking the correct question the first time he sees the Fisher King in pain during the Grail procession at the castle. This failure leads to the consequence of losing access to the castle and being berated for his failure by his aunt. By failing, Parzifal comes to understand what is at stake in his quest: that it is not consequential merely for himself. This awakening to the consequential aspects of success and failure, I would argue, qualifies as a form of philosophical apprenticeship. It especially does so when we take into account Hegel's depiction of failure as leading to correction, and this correction leading to self-consciousness.[379]

---

[378] After that we will be up to our necks in hyperreality, so enjoy the idea of "objects" and the "real" while it lasts!

[379] Brandom's reading of Hegel's Introduction to *The Phenomenology* stipulates that: "any empirical consciousness must have some such "shape." For it must be aware of the

The Grail as a partial object is a trickier subject than the sacred realm in which the castle resides because it is conceptualized as an object and not a place or setting; although, within these early narratives it is tied to its setting. As an object, it can appear as something that can be acquired; the modern-day transition toward adventures that seek to abscond with the Grail and carry it away to a museum *ala' Indiana Jones and the Last Crusade* are indicative of a historical shift in our thinking, in which the object can be dislodged from its space and utilized instrumentally, retaining all of its unique qualities. This, more modern idea of transferability is tied to the object-related feeling of ownership and entails a sense of immediacy that requires more attention than does a setting. To the modern mentality the grail is seen for what it can do, its uniqueness and rarity, and its financial value. These aspects come to the forefront of the modern mind and eclipse the importance of the sacred space in which the Grail is enmeshed.

Regarding this last point, we have a dispositional bias towards settings in that we naturally assume more about how they will behave (or that they merely exist in the first place) than we do about objects. This is one of the primary reasons why losing one's home in a fire is so traumatic, it is not merely the loss of everything, it is the pulling of the rug out from under your feet when you least expect it.

It is no coincidence that Deleuze focused so intensely on the signs emitted by objects in his book on Marcel Proust. Besides being one of the greatest writers of the twentieth century, Proust elaborated upon the various ways that memories and nostalgia

---

distinction between what *to* it things are in themselves and what *to* it they are for consciousness. It is taught that by the experience of error. That aspect of consciousness incorporates a conception of consciousness, and hence constitutes a form of self-consciousness." Excerpted from Brandom, Robert (2019) *A Spirit of Trust: A Reading of Hegel's Phenomenology*. Belknap Press of Harvard University Press. P. 219

are evoked by sensations while exploring the questions surrounding our ownership of these states – within the philosophical context we have set out here this opens up the idea that the partial object was a past possession. So, not only do we have the immediate psychoanalytic/Structuralist diagnosis of the partial object as an elusive object that promises to make the subject whole by filling the gap between him and language, we also have a historical dimension of it having some point of existence, or actuality, somewhere in the subject's past.

What then is the significance of the Grail itself as object? Recall Heidegger's example of the "Hammer":

> In our first characterization of the genesis of the theoretical mode of behavior from circumspection we have made basic a kind of theoretical grasping of innerworldly beings, of physical nature, in which the modification of our understanding of being amounts to a transformation. In the "physical" statement that "the hammer is heavy," we *overlook* not only the tool-character of the being encountered, but thus also that which belongs to every useful thing at hand: its place. The place becomes indifferent. This does not mean that the objectively present thing loses its "location" altogether. Its place becomes a position in space and time, a "world point," which is in no way distinguished from any other. This means that the multiplicity of places of useful things at hand defined in the surrounding world is not just modified to a sheer multiplicity of positions, but the beings of the surrounding world are *released*. The totality of what is objectively present becomes thematic.[380]

---

[380] Heidegger, Martin (1996) *Being and Time* translated by Joan Stambaugh. State University of New York Press, p. 331

Notice the reference to "every useful thing at hand" – is the Grail, or similar objects such as the Spear of Destiny or Ark of the Covenant classifiable as "useful things at hand?" To the modern conception, which assumes that the object can be absconded with, utilized, and sold – essentially detaching it from the Symbolic Order – they are just that. However, in that these objects are mythical and only ascertainable in a meaningful way to the individual who enters into the mythic realm (in a manner analogous to the way Gawain entered the "fairyland of no sleep, of no time,") we can say that such objects, within their narrative contexts, point towards a conception of selfhood that is vague about the concept of possession, whether internal or external. The ambiguity of the Grail, as both an object and a spiritual principle (as Evola views it) is confounding, but because it is a challenge, we ought not to remain subsumed within the murkiness of unknowing; the possibility of "attaining" the object is an imperative to action.

Similarities to Oedipus Rex

Long before the Grail Mythos there was the story of Oedipus Rex, which appeared in a Greek Tragedy penned by Sophocles in the early part of the fifth century B.C.[381] In the play, Oedipus recounts his encounter with the Sphinx who guarded the entrance to the city of Thebes. The Sphinx was a mythical creature possessing the head of a woman, the body of a lioness, and the wings of an eagle. As the guardian of Thebes, the Sphinx would ask a riddle to travelers attempting to gain entrance to the city: "Which creature walks on four legs in the morning, two legs in the afternoon and three legs in the evening?"

---

[381] The version of the Oedipus story found in Sophocles is the most famous, and sophisticated. However, legends surrounding the figure of Oedipus and his father, Laius, date back to the time of Homer (late seventh century B.C.).

The traveller who correctly guessed the answer to this riddle, "man," would be anointed King of Thebes, anyone that guessed incorrectly was devoured by the Sphinx. By guessing the answer to be man – because in his youth he crawls on all fours, in adulthood walks upright on his two legs and in old age uses a cane – Oedipus directs his reasoning away from a literal interpretation of the Sphinx's question to a metaphorical one, in which morning is interpreted as infancy, afternoon as adulthood, and so forth. There is a certain amount of cleverness or "genius" attendant to Oedipus's answer, but there is also a certain degree of deduction (reducing the number of known creatures down to a manageable class, deciding whether the riddle has an answer or not – if it did not, it would not conceptually qualify as a riddle, etc.) and metaphorical interpretation.

Answering the Sphinx's riddle is similar to the question that the knight must address to the Fisher King: "What ails thee?" insofar as it grants the speaker a kind of proprietorship, or stewardship, over the discovered land. The overarching logic between the two is different though because the Sphinx's riddle is intended as a literary device that fits into the overall clockwork trap of Sophocles's tragedy, which is designed to indicate the inescapability of fate.

So far, we have addressed the first two points of the Structuralist reading of the Grail mythos. Regarding the third point, the linguistic nature of the solution to the Grail quest, the question is a sentence that makes the fantastic concrete. This, in a sense, is a repetition of the logic that informs the scriptural narrative of a primal fissure existing between the Word and God. The correct question itself becomes a sort of object that must be located and utilized. Regarding this aspect and how the use of language shapes us, both individually and historically, Heidegger writes:

> But because in the very foundations of our being
> language as resonant signification roots us to our
> earth and transports and ties us to our world,

meditation on language and its historical dominion is always the action that gives shape to Dasein itself. The will to originality, rigor, and measure in words is therefore no mere aesthetic pleasantry; it is the work that goes on in the essential nucleus of our Dasein, which is historical existence.[382]

The Hermetic Tradition

In the previous chapter we discussed certain Masonic organizations and the idea that they were in possession of a secret or hidden knowledge that was passed down through rites and rituals. This drive was seemingly counter-balanced by these organizations' profession of Enlightenment ideals.[383] In this section we will hew more closely to the idea of a secret tradition that is *meant* to be kept secret; there is no outer "public relations" oriented aspect to the Hermetic tradition, and it is, in this respect, that Hermeticism more closely relates to the "murky" figures (Hiram, Enoch, and Melchizedek) who we have been associating with strongly mythological narratives. Hermeticism is also linked with the subject of alchemy and is relevant to our discussion of the Grail insofar as the quest for the Grail has been interpreted in alchemical terms, both literally and metaphorically.

There are a few modern authors who have tackled the subject of this esotericism in a way that has retained its particular sense of exclusivity: Aleister Crowley, George Gurdjief, P.D. Ouspensky and most notably, Julius Evola. It is important to understand that, despite its exclusivity and demand for secrecy, the Hermetic tradition almost always espouses a *Perennial*

---

[382] Heidegger, Martin (1991) *Nietzsche: Volume I: The Will to Power as Art.* Edited by David Farrell Krell. Published by Harper Collins. P. 145

[383] It could be argued, from a fundamentalist Christian perspective, that these esoteric rites led directly to Enlightenment ideals.

Philosophy, meaning that it assumes all the world's forms of spiritual practice are offshoots of a single source of metaphysical truth. This perennial source of validation or illumination is almost like the background radiation scientists believe still persists as a remnant of the Big Bang.

Another thing to keep in mind about the Hermetic tradition is that it views historical personage as secondary to the transmission of this hidden knowledge. If we analyze key sections of works by Mircea Eliade and Oswald Spengler, we can see Eliade as the philosopher who is more attuned to the "timeless" nature of Hermeticism:

> "Myth is the last –not the first- stage in the development of a hero." But this only confirms the conclusion reached by many investigators: the recollection of a historical event or a real personage survives in popular memory for two or three centuries at the utmost. This is because popular memory finds difficulty in retaining individual events and real figures. The structures by means of which it functions are different: categories instead of events, archetypes instead of historical personages. The historical personage is assimilated to his mythical model (hero, etc.), while the event is identified with the category of mythical actions (fight with a monster, enemy brothers, etc.). If certain epic poems preserve what is called "historical truth," this truth almost never has to do with definite persons and events, but with institutions, customs, landscapes.[384]

In contrast to this more Structuralist view, there is Spengler's view of the power of decision that actualizes the hero figure in

---

[384] Eliade, Mircea (1991) *The Myth of the Eternal Return.* Princeton University Press. P. 43

Western history, regardless as to how accurately we might grasp them from our modern perspective:

> Great personalities there must have been to give a mystical-metaphysical form to the new world outlook, but we know nothing of them and it is only the gay, bright, easy side of it that passed into the song of knightly halls.[385]

Note that by distinguishing the Western history as producing a different kind of man – one oriented towards the infinite because of an articulated sense of personality – Spengler is eschewing a perennial conceptualization of history. The Faustian narrative, wherein a learned scientist sells his soul to the Devil in exchange for near-limitless knowledge, is so evocative for Spengler because it embodies the sense of the willful individual both in opposition to, and in reconciliation with, a limitless world; this conception demands a primary sense of "personality":

> [In] the Faustian contrition the *idea of personality* was implicit. It is not true that the Renaissance discovered personality; what it did was to bring personality up to a brilliant surface, whereby it suddenly became visible to everyone [...] Contrition is something that each one accomplishes for himself alone. He alone can search his own conscience. He alone stands rueful in the presence of the Infinite. He alone can and must in confession understand and put into words his own past. And even the

---

[385] Spengler, Oswald (2006) *The Decline of the West: An Abridged Edition.* Translated by Charles Francis Atkinson and prepared by Arthur Helps. Vintage Books, A Division of Random House, INC P. 327

absolution that frees his Ego for new responsible action is personal to himself.[386]

The act of "contrition" here is what I had previously referred to as "reconciliation;" both words imply a conscious sense of self-awareness on the part of the subject, much like the *meta* aspect of consciousness, but possibly more so, in that they entail a traversing of history. Spengler sees this Faustian spirit as a force that grants a sense of subjectivity and therefore as something heterogeneous to other world-historical cultures:

> "The idea of contrition presupposes that the value of every act depends uniquely upon the man who does it. This is what differentiates the Western drama from the Classical, the Chinese, and the Indian."[387]

The distinction between these two outlooks (Eliade and Spengler) is a further unfolding of the dialectical approach we have been employing, in this case it has to do with how we can view the mythic persona (the characters portrayed in myth): from a sense of subjective self-hood, which determines the structure of the mythic narrative (Spengler's view); or, from the mythic narrative itself, in its capacity as a kind of super-structure that determines the character, and possibly the actions, of its constituents (Eliade's view). The contrast between the two perspectives replicates the contrast between Hermeticism, which puts the mythic structure first and the individual second, and the Masonic, which, in practice, has allowed for a more Faustian, personality-driven approach. Spengler will reappear later as we

---

[386] Ibid pp. 335 - 336

[387] Ibid p. 336. This does not, however, mean that the "Faustian" man is not trapped within a civilization that is itself, biologically programmed to go through the stages of birth, growth, decline and death.

get deeper into modernity. For now, we must focus on the idea of a pre-modern tradition that stretches back to the beginning of mankind, and the question of whether or not remnants of this tradition still exist.

Our discussion of Knight and Lomas's argument in the previous chapter focused primarily on their attempt to situate Freemasonry on materialistic, non-supernatural ground. Part of this strategy involved reducing the historical personage of Jesus Christ to that of a political dissident, not a divinely born savior. One part of this strategy that was not really relevant to that chapter, but is to this section, is the idea that Jesus was a member of a Hermetic sect. After claiming that there was no town of Nazareth and that Jesus was actually referred to as "Jesus the Nasorean," Knight and Lomas state:

> We were struck by the phrasing here: it implies that Jesus was a *member* of the Nasorean sect, which strongly suggests that he was not necessarily its original *leader*. It seems that Jesus might not have been the founder of the Church at all.[388]

In this way, Knight and Lomas are tying the early Church, which they associated with the Gnostics, to the Hermetic tradition.[389] Glenn Alexander Magee, however, disagrees with this lineage and posits Gnosticism as being distinctly different in character from Hermeticism:

> All forms of mysticism aim at some kind of knowledge of, experience of, or unity with the divine [...] Hermeticism is often confused with another form of mysticism, Gnosticism. Gnosticism

---

[388] Knight, Christopher & Lomas, Robert (2001) *The Hiram Key*. Fair Winds Press. P. 72

[389] There are a few other instances throughout their oeuvre where Knight and Lomas conflate Gnosticism with Hermeticism.

and Hermeticism both believe that a divine "spark" is implanted in man, and that man can come to know God. However, Gnosticism involves an absolutely negative account of creation. It does not regard creation as a part of God's being, or as "completing" God. Nor does Gnosticism hold that God somehow needs man to know Him.[390]

Magee, I believe is correct in connecting Gnosticism to the older monotheism of the desert-dwelling Semitic peoples and Hermeticism with a pantheistic European tradition. This idea is further qualified by an emphasis many researchers place on the "Essenes," who were a Jewish sect that broke from earlier traditions and promoted asceticism, prayer, and virtue. Writers who connect Gnostic mysticism to them, or who portray Jesus as a purveyor of Gnosticism, such as Knight and Lomas, claim that the Essenes authored the *Dead Sea Scrolls*; however, this position has been heavily contested by some historians.

According to the Biblical account, God is detached from his followers; therefore they are required to make sacrifices to him, heed his commands, and pray to him. The Hermetic Tradition, in contrast, draws God into the realm of the subject; God is interpreted in a Pagan way and becomes omnipresent in nature. This distinction does not relinquish the subject from a struggle to attain unity with God, however; the imperative is essentially just as strong as it is for the monotheist. For this reason, the struggle for attainment, in both ideations of divinity, is presented by way of priesthood, election, and initiation.

Initiation is relevant for study of the Jewish Kabbalah, and is a part of certain Catholic orders, which draw on Gnosticism to some extent. However, it is definitely more of a feature of the Hermetic Tradition than of Gnosticism. This is not to say that Gnostic sects did not use initiatory practices to guard members

---

[390] Magee, Glenn Alexander (2001) *Hegel and the Hermetic Tradition.* Cornell University Press. P. 10

from persecution, as this did happen;[391] but it was not a necessary component of their belief systems in the same way that it was for Hermeticism.

Drawing from the Rosicrucian tradition, specifically the third manifesto titled *The Chemical Wedding of Christian Rosenkreuz*, Julius Evola viewed Hermeticism as best symbolized by the alchemic process:

> Aside from all that has been said, "living the myth" means to arrive by means of symbols at a perception of that metahistorical order in which nature and man himself, so to speak, are found in a state of creation and which, among other things, contains for us the secret of the energies that activate within and behind visible things and human corporeality. We shall see that none other is the premise in all strictly alchemical (i.e., not simply initiatic) operations. [392]

By stipulating that it is "not simply initiatic," Evola is emphasizing that the Hermetic process is truly transformative, which he also claims involves the transmission of silence:

> Concerning all this, we have to realize that the "secret" had nothing to do with any exclusivity of sect or unwillingness to speak, but rather that it was a question of not *being able* to say, in addition to having to prevent the inevitable incomprehension of those who would profane or

---

[391] For Knight and Lomas this happened in the case of Qumran sects who kept the secrets that would go on to make up the rites of Freemasonry. Knight, Christopher & Lomas, Robert (2001) *The Hiram Key*. Fair Winds Press. P. 191

[392] Evola, Julius (1995) *The Hermetic Tradition*. Inner Traditions International. P. 28

distort the teaching. Since the alchemical technique, in its truth, consists of an Art made possible by higher powers set in motion by superior and nonhuman states of consciousness, it is natural to declare that the secret of the Great Work cannot be transmitted, but it is a privilege of the initiates, who by virtue of their own experiences, can alone understand what is hidden behind the jargon and symbolism of the technical texts.[393]

In strictly alchemical terms, the Great Work refers to the creation of "the Philosopher's Stone," which is a mythical substance capable of transforming base metals into gold and silver. We have seen that Emma Jung emphasized the Grail's portrayal as a stone in Wolfram's *Parzival* as an intentional reference to the Philosopher's Stone as an actual object. In the Hermetic sense employed by Evola in the above passage, it refers to a transmutation of the spirit into a state of enlightenment.

There is no doubt that the Hermetical tradition was influenced by Gnosticism, but granted Magee's premise, there exists a fundamental contradiction between the two ontologies. Since Freemasonry clearly *functions* in a Hermetic fashion, and this Hermetic structure is something Knight and Lomas take as a given based on their emphasis on the rites and rituals attendant to masonry, can we say that they are wrong to draw a genealogical line from Freemasonry back to the Gnostics? More precisely, I think this incongruity, which has arisen from their research, is a duplication, at an organizational level, of the fissure, or gap, that we discussed in Structuralist/psychoanalytical terms, i.e., the space that is filled by the partial object. The partial object, in the case presented to us by Knight and Lomas, is the historical personage of Hiram Abiff. This reduction is evident from the number of instances where Knight and Lomas refer to Hiram as

---

[393] Ibid, p. 209

the "key" to unlocking the mysteries of both Freemasonry and Christianity.

A Philosophical Approach to Hermeticism

For a dogmatic Christian like Gary Wayne things are very cut and dry: the divine and righteous way of Biblical scholarship entails reading and interpreting everything in the Bible literally. The converse of this are symbolic or allegorical readings of the Biblical text which allow paganism, under the guise of mysticism, to creep into, and thus contaminate, proper Christianity. [394] Wayne therefore views Gnosticism and Hermeticism to be almost equally blasphemous; he also ties the instinct behind these traditions to the spirit of scientific inquiry.

In the next chapter we will go deeper into Wayne's "historical" account of these movements. It is somewhat ironic that an author who wrote a seven-hundred page book about a brief mentioning of "Nephilim" in Chapter Six of Genesis is hyperbolically opposed to symbolic and allegorical interpretation. But attacking this irony is low-hanging fruit; for the time being it is more appropriate to put Wayne's literalist intentions out there as a point of contrast.

Obviously, the fact that the Gnostic Gospels present an alternative, some might say more materialistic, interpretation of Christ's life is bound to draw a Biblical literalist's ire. However, this ire is mitigated by the fact that Christian literalists who engage in conspiracy theorization must often rely on Apocryphal books such as *Enoch* and *Jubilees* in order to fill in the gaps of their theories. In the case of the Gnostics, you could say that someone like Wayne is, in principle, critical of them for creating a counterfeit version of Christianity.

In the case of Hermeticism Wayne can take a much more directly adversarial stance because, if we take the Platonic

---

[394] Wayne, Gary (2014) *The Genesis 6 Conspiracy*. Trusted Books, A Division of Deep River Books. Pp. 37 - 38

scheme of Forms, i.e., the Good, the Just, etc. we can imagine these things as immaterial suprapersonal concepts that our minds can contemplate. Hermeticism adds a twist to this schema and introduces words, sophisticated words, or words that are more esoteric, which might give a quicker apprehension, or even mastery over, the Forms. The idea of prayers and spells comes from this insight; and Magick, itself derived from Hermeticism, is a tool to bypass a more strenuous route towards spiritual communion. Some, however, might argue that this strenuous route lies at the heart of "genuine" mysticism.

How then does Mysticism, in a more traditional sense, differ from the Hermetic Tradition? Mysticism seems to be a specifically Catholic phenomena that occurred in Spain with authors like St. John of the Cross and Teresa of Avila in the late-16th century; as well as in Germany with clerics like Meister Eckhart, Hildegard of Bingen, and Johannes Tauler in the mid-13th century. According to Andrew Weeks, the mysticism of Meister Eckhart (which is emblematic of Christian mysticism in general) entails a process of abandoning concern for oneself, loving others, and falling completely under the purview of God's will. After this is achieved:

> The true inner asceticism recommended by Eckhart is then translated into knowledge [...] His mysticism, which begins with distance and abandonment in view of the nothingness of all created things, concludes by elevating all words, works, and creatures into the divine light.[395]

Contemporary readers might assume that the mystical state Eckhart explores is akin to the Buddhist state of nirvana, in which the subject is released from the karmic bounds of suffering

[395] Weeks, Andrew (1993) *German Mysticism: From Hildegard of Bingen to Ludwig Wittgenstein*. State University of New York Press. Pp. 85 - 86

that are imposed on all life. Since Christianity and Buddhism are two different systems of religious thought, the types of spiritual activity that go into achieving each state are qualitatively distinct from each other. However, once the state is achieved there is a strong likelihood that the experiences are similar. If this is true, it is an argument for a perennial spiritual philosophy à la what is prescribed by the Hermetic Tradition.

It seems as if, when we study Evola's alchemical allegories enough, we can say that they are aiming at roughly the same thing. There is also the fact that both presuppose a sense of dependence existing between the creator and the subject, which is a concept that Magee attributes to Hermeticism. Weeks lays out the schema, insofar as it applies to the German mystics, in a strongly Structuralist way:

> Though their works are characterized by considerable differences, they nonetheless approach the common theme of the relationship of transcendence and immanence by way of the same canonical texts; and they arrive at a similar solution: *the created world is to its Creator as an utterance is to its speaker*. The world means God, and has been meant by God into being. Created through the Word, the world is wordlike for all who are open to discern its significance.[396]

On this reading, the dependence between God and man is therefore analogous to the relationship between an author and his reader. There is, however, a nuanced difference between the hermeticist and the mystic which has to do with the fact that Hermeticism still appeals to the rational apprehension of causal processes – which relates to the "meta" aspect of consciousness – whereas mysticism seeks to remove, or divert, this awareness and

---

[396] Ibid p. 17

place it in the realm of the unknown, which is conceptualized as God.

Joris-Karl Huysmans (February 5, 1848 – May 12, 1907), who had established himself as a decadent and libertine writer in his earlier works, later in life returned to the Catholicism of his youth. His *Durtal Trilogy*, which was published between 1895 and 1898, was a literary rendering of his conversion; it features myriad injunctions to asceticism, e.g.,

> "Thank him in getting rid of your nature as soon as possible, and leaving the house of your conscience empty for Him. The more you die to yourself the better will He live in you. Prayer is the most powerful ascetic means by which you can renounce yourself..."[397] ... "In fact, the end of Mysticism is to render visible, sensible, almost palpable, the God who remains silent and hidden from all."[398]

Through the course of these three novels, Durtal (Huysmans's fictionalized stand-in) moves from an attraction to Catholic rites grounded on aesthetic appreciation to an intellectual fascination with mysticism and finally subordination to a Trappist monastery.[399] The first mention of mysticism made in the text is in terms of exchange or substitution:

> But there is a task still more arduous and more painful than was desired by these admirable souls.

---

[397] Huysmans, Joris-Karl (2015) *The Durtal Trilogy*. Ex Fontibus Company. P. 99

[398] Ibid p. 55

[399] It is this aspect that led to Michel Houllebecq to make the protagonist of his 2015 novel *Submission* a Huysmans scholar. Albeit Houllebecq portrays his character's conversion to Islam as being a dispassionate and calculated move, in contrast to Durtal's fervent and anachronistic move to a monastery.

> It is not now that of purging the faults of others, but of preventing them, hindering their commission, by taking the place of those who are too weak to bear the shock [...] They draw on themselves the demoniacal fluid, they absorb temptations to vice, preserve by their prayers those who live, like ourselves, in sin; they appease, in fact, the wrath of the Most High that He may not place the earth under an interdict.[400]

This idea correlates with Weeks's analysis of one of the core aspects of Eckhart's claim that in one human being are all human beings, and this intersubjective essence is God:

> Here, unexpectedly, the contours of the Son crystallize out of the interchange of self and others. This thought is then rendered absolute: one should not care more about what happens to one's best friend than about what befalls anyone else.[401]

Because it tends towards a quiet acceptance of the Divine and eschews any "hard" doctrinal positions, the sinews of mystical discourse are rarely addressed in philosophic discourse. In contrast, the Hermetic Tradition can be dissimulated into a more rarified and academic realm via the study of philosophy. As we discussed regarding the Emerald Tablet of Hermes, both science and philosophy were borne of occultic origins. According to Magee, Hegel's earliest project was the reconciliation of

---

[400] Ibid pp. 32 - 33
[401] Weeks, Andrew (1993) *German Mysticism: From Hildegard of Bingen to Ludwig Wittgenstein.* State University of New York Press. P. 84

philosophy and religion. This entailed the acquisition of an antiquated, possibly perennial, wisdom.[402]

Returning to the trinity of marginal, murky, and forgotten figures we've laid out so far; on a surface level it seems like Hiram might be a Hermetical figure since he was a builder (or a priest, on Knight and Lomas's view) and therefore was intended to play a transformative role during his lifetime. However, when we consider the fact that Knight and Lomas, who tie the Masonic lineage to Hiram, are of more of a scientific rationalist perspective, we can understand why they see the origins of Freemasonry to be tied more closely to the ethos of Gnosticism. Then perhaps, the system of rites associated with Hermeticism became a vehicle for Gnostic doctrines; but Magee's distinction between Gnosticism and Hermeticism is compelling and makes it difficult to completely reconcile the figure of Hiram with Hermeticism or Gnosticism – either tradition might claim him, but the inherent textual ambiguity of his character makes him impossible to firmly situate in either camp.

Enoch is tangentially related to the Hermetic tradition because the Kabbalah, with which the narratives surrounding him are associated, informs the aesthetic of Hermeticism. But the dualistic representation of Enoch is in a sense foreign to the nascent paganism of the Hermetic Tradition. The properties entailed by his name are both of a prophet and an educator. The prophet aspect resonates with the Gnostic tradition and the educator aspect resonates with the Hermetic tradition; a duality leaving Enoch not completely reconcilable to either tradition.

Of the three, Mechizedek is the closest thing to being a progenitor of the Hermetic Tradition. He was the priest of the highest god and his priesthood most likely stretched back to time immemorial (and it might extend to the time of Jesus Christ, if we believe the claim that he was a priest in the line of Melchizedek). He seems to be an embodiment of the rites, which he officiates. All

[402] Magee, Glenn Alexander (2001) *Hegel and the Hermetic Tradition.* Cornell University Press. P. 85

three figures are impersonal to some extent, but the idea of the name "Melchizedek" being almost exclusively a title coincides with Eliade's postulation that the mythic narrative creates the roles that different individuals play at various points in time, thus amplifying the sense of an impersonal nature. Furthermore, if we accept the thesis that Eliade's view is more in line with Hermeticism, then Melchizedek becomes the Hermetic figure *par excellence.*

The discussion of officiating over rites, which, by their enactment bestow a title of mythological significance, leads to a final aspect of Hermeticism that we must discuss: the alchemical process as a secularized telling of the Catholic transubstantiation narrative. In describing Philip K. Dick's dabbling in the Episcopalian faith later in his life, Erik Davis describes the "almost alchemical transformation of God into matter" as an important steppingstone towards more in depth grappling with Gnosticism that would preoccupy Dick from *Valis* until his death.[403]

In a way, transubstantiation is a central part of the Grail mythos. The basic narrative is that during the Last Supper, when Jesus consecrated the bread and wine as his body and blood, the bread and wine were *actually* transformed into his body and blood prior to the Disciples partaking of it. The reasoning for doing this at the time seems to be that, knowing his death was imminent, Jesus either a) wanted his Disciples to feel that they had internalized his essence in some material way, or b) wanted to mark the solemnity of the occasion with an act (cannibalism) that was transgressive.

Because the Catholic Church teaches that every time a priest consecrates the host it actually becomes the body of Jesus, I'm inclined to think that Christ's reasoning was the former. Hence, you continuously receive the sacrament to keep him with you throughout your life. Notice, however, that it is possible for

---

[403] Davis, Erik (2019) *High Weirdness: Drugs, Esoterica, and Visionary Experience in the Seventies.* Strange Attractor Press & the MIT Press. P. 276

someone to believe that the act of consecration is symbolic and that nothing supernatural actually occurs – many people take this view. Within this topic we see a reappearance of the debate between people who believe that Jesus's resurrection was a resurrection of his body and those who believe that it was only his spirit.

The lesser-known option for answering the questions posed by the resurrection, which we will dive into deeper in the next section, is that Jesus didn't die on the cross, but instead escaped to France and sired children. Without formally going into the particulars of that narrative here, there is an alchemic aspect of transubstantiation that ought to be addressed as it pertains to the idea of Grail bloodlines and the possibility that the elite class has something mystical encoded in their DNA, which has led to their rulership of the world. Wayne calls this latent potential a "spark:"

> Polytheists believe this spark is encoded in the DNA of a select elite. It can be released through a connection with the universal life force by uniting the world through a vibrating harmonic convergence.[404]

Of course, Wayne adds the prerequisite that for this to happen *in toto* is the establishment of a One World government. In *this* conception there seems to be a reverse transubstantiation.

The Eucharistic metaphor can also be applied to the fruit from the Tree of Knowledge, of which Adam and Eve partook. On a Gnostic interpretation, the eating of this fruit was an initiation into the first stages of gnosis, or knowledge of the Divine. On a Catholic, or generally Christian reading, the partaking of this fruit led to the fall from Eden with the sacrament of Communion a sort

---

[404] Wayne, Gary (2014) *The Genesis 6 Conspiracy*. Trusted Books, A Division of Deep River Books. P. 533

of persistent purification of this fall. On this reading, the Eucharist is not meant to satiate the desire for knowledge (read as "hunger" within the ritual of oral consumption) but a renunciation of it, in the hope of partaking in eternal life (John 6:53 – 54).

The Postmodern Reiteration of the Grail Mythos

The most popular contemporary book on the Grail is the aforementioned *The Holy Blood and the Holy Grail*, which was first published in 1982.[405] The authors approach the subject from the mystery surrounding the Church of Mary Magdalene in the French village of Rennes-le-Château. In 1885 the parish of this small town received a new priest, Father François-Bérenger Saunière. According to Baigent, Leigh, and Lincoln, Saunière made a startling discovery during a renovation of the church:

> In the course of his endeavors he removed the altar-stone, which rested on two archaic Visigoth columns. One of these columns proved to be hollow. Inside the curè were found four parchments preserved in sealed wooden tubes. Two of these parchments are said to have comprised genealogies, one dating from 1244, the other from 1644. The two remaining documents had apparently been composed in the 1780s by one of Saunière's predecessors as curè of Rennes-le-Château, the Abbè Antoine Bigou.[406]

The information contained within these parchments is the central piece of evidence for *The Holy Blood and the Holy Grail*'s argument that Jesus escaped to Europe, got hitched, and that his

---

[405] I say this, not counting Dan Brown's *Da Vinci Code*, which I'm ruling out here because it's a novel.

[406] Baigent, Michael; Leigh, Richard; Lincoln, Henry (2006) *The Holy Blood and the Holy Grail*. Arrow Books. P. 27

bloodline continued into what would be known as the Merovingian Dynasty. On paper, the Merovingians were a family that ruled the Franks from 509 CE to 751, who at the height of their power reigned over some of the largest and most powerful states of Western Europe. However, in conspiracy theory lore, their influence and power, much like the Bavarian Illuminati, is unknowable, widely extensive, and shadowy.

Baigent, Leigh, and Lincoln's elaborate theory claims that there were a variety of messages written in code on these parchments, one of the most telling of which was deciphered as: "To Dagobert II, King, and to Sion belongs this treasure and he is there dead."[407] "Dagobert II," as Tracy Twyman is keen to inform us, was the last in the line of Merovingian Kings. According to Twyman, the Papacy entered into a conspiracy to have Dagobert suffer an "accidental" death while on a hunting expedition. After this was accomplished political power fell into the hands of Charles Martel and thus began the reign of the Carolingian Dynasty.[408]

The next piece of the puzzle, for both Twyman and the authors of *The Holy Blood and the Holy Grail*, is the 1638 painting *The Shepherds Arcadia* by Nicolas Poussin (1594 – 1665), a reproduction of which was purchased by Saunière on a trip to Paris sometime after the discovery of the parchments.[409] This painting, which depicts three shepherds and one shepherdess examining a large gravestone, is significant to this particular version of the Grail mythos because Poussin's name is supposedly located on one of the parchments, and because the grave depicted was said to have actually existed roughly six miles from Rennes-le-Château.

---

[407] Ibid p. 28
[408] Twyman, Tracy (2005) *The Arcadian Mystique: The Best of Dagobert's Revenge Magazine*. Dragon Key Press. P. 2
[409] Baigent, Michael; Leigh, Richard; Lincoln, Henry (2006) *The Holy Blood and the Holy Grail*. Arrow Books. P. 29

The official title of this painting: *Et in Arcadia Ego*, which translates to "Even in Arcadia I am," has itself been subjected to varying degrees of scrutiny with some theories speculating that it refers to Christ's final resting place as being in the French countryside, or a coded message indicating a future cataclysm.[410] Most often, the painting is interpreted as a vehicle for occult symbols, such as pentagrams, as well as a treasure map pointing to secrets lying within Rennes-le-Château.

These secrets, which could be a vast treasure deposited by the Templars, Cathars or Visigoths, or possibly, the revelation of Christ's bloodline as being the "true" meaning of the Grail mythos. Baigent, Leigh and Lincoln ultimately posit the Grail as a metaphor for both the womb of Mary Magdalene and the bloodline of Christ that was carried on by the descendants of the Merovingians after it had been integrated into the genetic line of the nascent French nobility. As I stated in the Myth and Narrative chapter, Twyman is a "dualist" in the sense that she maintains the possibility that the Grail could be interpreted as both the bloodline of Christ as well as the mythical object pursued by Perceval et al, and in so doing, tacitly acknowledging the importance of murkiness in modern mythmaking.

The last ingredient for both Baigent, Leigh, and Lincoln, as well as Twyman, is the Priory of Sion, an organization which they postulate was founded in 1099 in order to preserve the Merovingian bloodline and return it to the throne of France.[411] For the abovementioned authors, this is a tenable summarization of the Priory. However, modern critics have argued that the Priory of Sion was created in 1956 by a man named Pierre Plantard, who hoped to create a neo-chivalric order, and in the process created an elaborate backstory which incorporated such luminaries as Leonardo da Vinci, Isaac Newton, and Jean Cocteau. Mainstream historians dismiss the whole thing as an elaborate

---

[410]Twyman, Tracy (2005) *The Arcadian Mystique: The Best of Dagobert's Revenge Magazine.* Dragon Key Press. Pp. 8 - 9
[411] Ibid p. 3

ruse by Plantard as an attempt to gain entry into high society. Everyone, including Plantard himself, was surprised when his fictional order was revised in the mid-eighties and conjoined with the post-modern reading of the Grail myth.

What is interesting for our purposes is that this narrative is, in one sense, a reiteration of the Rosicrucian narrative – in that its occult pedigree was fabricated by one person who was trying to write such an order into existence. In another sense, it is a reiteration of the Bavarian Illuminati narrative, to the extent that conspiracy theorists insist that it still exists, despite evidence to the contrary.

It is important to note that Baigent, Leigh, and Lincoln were not the first individuals to postulate this post-modern reading of the Grail mythos. Hugh Schonfield's book *The Passover Plot* proposed the esoteric notion that Jesus did not die on the cross in 1963. What *The Holy Blood and the Holy Grail* brings to the table is, on one hand a secular humanist deconstruction of Catholicism, and on the other, a renewed emphasis on an appeal to scientism. Both of these issues are central to *The Hiram Key* and *The Holy Blood and the Holy Grail*, and both entail that Jesus was mortal and most likely indulged in mortal activities, like getting married, before dying a typically mortal death. This is not to say that Knight and Lomas are particularly invested in the theory that Christ escaped to France and engendered a royal dynasty; despite their quibbling about the semantics pertaining to the names "Jesus" and "Barabbas" they are more interested in the idea that Christ was a political revolutionary who maintained the ancient Egyptian secrets that had been preserved by Gnostic sects like the Essenes, and would be carried into Freemasonry. Their idealism in relation to organized religion is tempered with a degree of pragmatism:

> If the whole basis of Christianity can be shown to be a silly mistake, will the Vatican apologize for the inconvenience it has caused, abolish itself and hand over its wealth and power to the Chief Rabbi? No.

Clearly no proof could ever do this, and maybe that is right, because the Church is too large and important to suddenly disappear; but equally it can never be right to hide the truth, because truth must surely be the essence of God. There must be a way for the Church to survive by re-thinking what it knows are mistaken ideas.[412]

Taking an equally circumspect approach to any controversy resulting from their research, Baigent, Leigh, and Lincoln state:

We are well aware, of course, that our research has led us to conclusions that, in many respects, are inimical to certain basic tenets of modern Christianity –conclusions that are heretical, perhaps even blasphemous. From the standpoint of certain established dogma we are no doubt guilty of such transgressions. But we do not believe that we have desecrated, or even diminished, Jesus in the eyes of those who do genuinely revere him. And while we ourselves cannot subscribe to Jesus's divinity, our conclusions do not preclude others from doing so. Quite simply, there is no reason why Jesus could not have married and fathered children, while still retaining his divinity.[413]

This particular nexus of secularism was directed at the Catholic Church and was nevertheless denounced as heretical by the Church and its members. It is interesting that despite being a modern response to the Grail issue – one that removes, or

[412] Knight, Christopher & Lomas, Robert (2001) *The Hiram Key*. Fair Winds Press. P. 192
[413] Baigent, Michael; Leigh, Richard; Lincoln, Henry (2006) *The Holy Blood and the Holy Grail*. Arrow Books. P. 447

remedies, its mythic ambiguities – the authors still attenuated the sense of mythic, textual richness that had traditionally animated the subject.[414] Yet, it is for this reason that this line of theorization about the Grail or the bloodline of Christ is dismissed or ridiculed by actual secular historians. For the real-deal materialist historian the subject itself is not worth saving, let alone worthy of being scrutinized in a pseudo-scientific way.

The adoption of scientific pretense by the conspiracy theorist is, as I have already pointed out, the penultimate move before the mythic significance of the conspiratorial subject collapses or implodes. It is analogous to what Spengler termed Caesarism: a sort of last gasp made by a civilization to restore order and authority before its inevitable decline and collapse.

The Reckoning: The Litigation of the Da Vinci Code

As popular as *The Holy Blood and the Holy Grail* is, it is not the book that brought, what we have been calling the "post-modern" interpretation of the Grail mythos to the public's attention. This dubious honor goes to Dan Brown's *The Da Vinci Code*. In the novel, which draws on the Priory of Sion lore, the protagonists discover secrets pertaining to the Grail myth encoded within the work of Leonardo Da Vinci. *The Holy Blood and the Holy Grail* is even referenced as a source of insight for certain characters, but all of the dry historical analysis is spun into a whirlwind adventure story.

---

[414] For Baigent, Leigh and Lincoln it is an almost equally mythical assertion that Jesus's bloodline was carried on through the Merovingian line and exists in the present day. For Knight and Lomas it is the (slightly) more modest claim that contemporary Freemasonry can trace its lineage back over three thousand years to ancient Egypt, that the Masonic rites were usurped by the ancient Jewish people and then utilized by Jesus Christ, who was, to quote the film *Brain Candy* "just a guy," in a political resistance against the Roman Empire.

Hoping to cash in, Baigent and Leigh filed a lawsuit in London's high court against Random House, the publisher of *The Da Vinci Code*, alleging that Brown had stolen their premise. The case was dismissed in April 2006. To be fair to Brown, his book had drawn a great deal of attention to *The Holy Blood and the Holy Grail* and their litigation seemed a bit greedy. Conspicuously absent from the suit was Henry Lincoln, who, at the time of writing, is ninety years old and looks like an English wizard. In the aftermath of the success of *The Da Vinci Code*, Lincoln appeared on a variety of television programs promoting his theories. Of the three authors, he seems to have invested the most time and interest in the subject and appears to be the heart and soul of the endeavor.

On one of these television appearances, for which I have searched doggedly and been unable to find,[415] Lincoln is sitting down with a scientist of some sort. He explains, in detail, the mathematics, the symmetry, the astronomical and geometrical coincidences that have compelled him to formulate and propagate his theory. The scientist patiently listens to all of this, and then says: "so?" Within the context of the conversation, it was probably the most remarkable comeback, if one could call it that, which one might deliver. It's almost as if you ran into your neighbor as he was on his way to the supermarket, and he informed you that Donald Trump is secretly still president and that the military is planning a governmental coup any day now and you responded: "Ok, but you're still going to the store, right?"

This act of demystification is akin to what is sometimes referred to as a "Zen slap," which is delivered by a Zen master to a pupil in order to awaken them to the moment in which they are residing, as opposed to the abstract and remote thoughts that are preoccupying them. This episode also indicates why conspiracy theories don't significantly alter people's actions: they are bereft of any sense of pragmatism. If we consider the anthropological movement from religion to myth to involve a certain loss of active

---

[415] Which is fitting, given the subject matter of this chapter.

commitment to the narratives presented, then the movement from myth to conspiracy theory has almost totally demolished this sense of active engagement and commitment.

In all of the chapters so far, we have seen the subject matter under discussion being addressed or replicated into a literary medium. The Grail mythos blurs this distinction because it existed first and foremost as literature. In a sense, this literature was a European replication of earlier Greek adventure myths, and like those myths, were purported to take place at a time contemporaneous with the time the tale was being told or written down.

In the nineteenth and twentieth centuries the Grail quest was replicated in adventure novels (some authors who explored this were Talbot Mundy, Edgar Rice Burroughs, Sax Rohmer, etc.). By the 1960s this genre was largely displaced by science fiction, which focused more on technology and the future. At this point in history the Grail legend existed primarily for the sake of historical indexing or occult knowledge.

It is interesting that, as we move forward into the twenty-first century, the science fiction that is being created pulls back from exploring the distant future and tries to realistically focus on the moment that existed between our "present" society and the utopian future that had been presented by science fiction in the 1960s and 70s –this is the "prequel" phenomena that came into vogue in the late nineties.[416] In a sense, the gap that these contemporary shows and films are trying to explore, or fill in, is precisely the space where the Grail narratives resided, in that these narratives explored the distant and remote, but were temporally immediate to their audience. Essentially these narratives might have discussed legends from the past, but they

---

[416] *Star Trek Discovery* for instance takes place a decade before the original *Star Trek* series and is essentially a prequel. Also, when George Lucas decided to tackle his *Star Wars* Franchise again in the late 1990s, he did so byway of a trilogy of prequels. (That were all awful btw)

did so in a way that uniquely filled in, or informed, the reality of the present.

Chapter Seven: The Significance of the Known World

The world is not objectively present in space; however, only within a world can space be discovered.[417]

While we have examined ancient people's ideas of the world in relation to their cosmological beliefs, this chapter will focus more closely on the medieval to modern period. It is important to note that from the ancient era up to the age of exploration (Columbus, etc.) theories of the world's structure would fall in and out of favor. There were ancients who believed the world to be spherical. This theory would fall out of favor in the Middle Ages only to be revived in the 16th and 17th centuries by Copernicus, Kepler, and Galileo. Now, in the 21st century we have seen a revival of the idea that the earth is flat. We will not be discussing the scientific evolution of this theory so much as tracing the dialectic of how these theories have risen and fallen in prominence, and the cultural backgrounds against which they have done so.

Conclusion to the Bloodline Mythos

Like the concept of a New World Order, the quest for the Grail is a huge, multifaceted subject that is bound to spill out onto the characters and themes discussed throughout this book. I pick up the discussion here because I wanted the last chapter to focus more on the actual texts surrounding the Grail itself. In this section we will spend a little more time on what people have conjectured the Grail to be, how this relates to the divergence of the Hermetic and Gnostic traditions, and more specifically, how the Grail might be construed as a metaphor for the secret transmission of knowledge.

---

[417] Heidegger, Martin (1996) *Being and Time.* State University Press of New York. P. 337

We have discussed the intersection of myths and conspiracy theories with literature and art, and, for the most part, these were "highbrow" promulgations of art and literature. In this section I want to focus more on the "lowbrow" means by which some of these myths were disseminated. Many people are aware of Conan the Barbarian as a character in movies; it's doubtful that the novels written about him are as widely read now as they were in the past. Besides being "adventure" novels, these tales, written by Robert E. Howard unveiled a mythological primordial world that had supernatural beings and mythic origin stories. One of the writing-devices Howard used so effectively, as did his contemporary H. P. Lovecraft (who'll we'll get into later), was that he would write dialog that hinted at older, more arcane, histories for his characters and settings, before divulging the fuller narrative later in the story. Adventure novelists like Talbot Mundy or H. Rider Haggard did this as well and the effect was a mystification of places like the Himalayas and Nepal for Western readers in the mid-twentieth century.

The effect these authors were after was dialectically opposite to the effect we discussed in regard to post-modern writers, who primarily sought to demystify "grand narratives." This is not to say that those post-modern authors (Delillo, Pynchon, Rushdie, etc.) did not use and create intrigue, or even mystify their readers – they did, but this effect was part of their craft as novelists; they were very self-aware of what they were writing about and for whom they were writing. Their audience was of the post-Kennedy, post-WWII generations and too jaded to take "tales of oriental intrigue" or fantasy novels set in the primordial past at face-value. At this point in history (the sixties onwards) those types of novels were relegated to specific genres and were no longer considered "literature" in the proper sense.

I did not read Robert E. Howard as a kid, or even see the *Conan* movies; any exposure I had to the things that Talbot Mundy had written about I was by way of Hollywood directors like Steven Spielberg, who basically streamlined these adventure novels into heavily commodified blockbuster films. My first interaction with things that hinted at the work of writers like Howard, Mundy, and H.P. Lovecraft were via cartoons and comic books from the 1970s and 80s.

Take for instance, *G.I. Joe: The Movie* (1987), in which the writers incorporated villains that were intended to give Cobra Commander an origin story, offer him a sort of redemption, and conclude the series. This villainous group was called "Cobra-La" and when it came to providing it a mythic backstory, the writers did not disappoint. Cobra-La was a 40,000-year-old society of serpent people who had been forced into a secluded part of the Himalayas.

The Himalayan area is a significant reference-point since the "Secret Chiefs," who were believed by Aleister Crowley and his mentor Samuel MacGregor Mathers to oversee and influence humanity using telekinesis, were supposedly located in the Tibetan region. The next factor that marks this cartoon as significant is not only that the Cobra-La were severely ancient, but that they retained a linear and unbroken connection to their past. Finally, and most significantly, the narrative of this group of snake people is drawn primarily from Robert E. Howard's "Stygian" people and their sorcerer, "Thoth-Amon." Howard devised these characters, as well as the serpent god, "Set," for the *Conan* and *King Kull* stories he wrote for *Weird Tales* in the early 1930s.

Howard (January 22, 1906 – June 11, 1936) was a contemporary of Howard Phillips Lovecraft (August 20, 1890 – March 15, 1937) who wrote horror tales from what he described as a "Cosmic perspective":

> Now all my tales are based on the fundamental premise that common human laws and interests and emotions have no validity or significance in the vast cosmos-at-large. To me there is nothing but puerility in a tale in which the human form –and the local human passions and conditions and standards- are depicted as native to other worlds or universes. To achieve the essence of real

externality, whether of time or space or dimension one must forget that such things as organic life, good and evil, love and hate, and all such local attributes of a negligible and temporary race called mankind, have any existence at all.[418]

This *Cosmicism*, as it was expressed in Lovecraft's writings, was focused on forces that were incomprehensible to the human mind because they existed in time, space, and dimensions that are not generally accessible to us. The individuals who attempt to access these places, or the individuals that reside in them (most famously, Cthulhu), are acting on atavistic impulses foreign to the western rational mind.

These gods, or "The Great Old Ones" as they are formally referred to by Lovecraft and his fans, can "only ever be fragments of the mysterious, never to be codified or dried out for scholars to pick over."[419] We aren't going to explore the intricacies of Lovecraft's fiction, or his general pessimism regarding mankind; what is of primary interest for us here is his role in the cultural milieu of his time and how he crafted entities and dimensions intended to always be mysterious and incomprehensible.

Unlike parts of the Bible, where characters and situations are murky for a variety of mostly unintentional reasons, Lovecraft intentionally crafted his literary universe to allow vast regions to exist in a state of inexplicability. The impersonal, and often hostile, nature of Lovecraft's literary universe dovetails in many ways with Schopenhauer's theory of all existing things being animated by a ceaseless and striving "will" and Freud's theory of the unconscious. The potential for brutality can be said to

[418] From a letter to Farnsworth Wright, dated July 5, 1927. Excerpted from Ognjanović, Dejan (2017) *Rue Morgue Magazine's The Weird World of H. P. Lovecraft*. Rue Morgue. P. 12
[419] From Phil Hine's essay "The Great Old Ones." Excerpted from Ognjanović, Dejan (2017) *Rue Morgue Magazine's The Weird World of H. P. Lovecraft*. Rue Morgue. P. 32

resonate within the work of Lovecraft's contemporary, Friedrich Nietzsche. However, Nietzsche did personalize the forces said to be at work in his philosophy; his conception of various willful individuals and groups vying for authority and hegemony over each other is very worldly. It is for this reason that Howard's work pertaining to exploration and battle has more in common with Nietzsche's philosophy than does Lovecraft's. Lovecraft will play a role in our discussion of UFO phenomena and the occult, but regarding the known and the unknown world and the men who explore and conquer it, Howard remains the primary literary standard for us here.

The narrative evolution of Robert E. Howard, who died in 1936, to the *G. I. Joe* movie that came out in 1987 would probably not have happened if it wasn't for Roy Thomas. Born in Jackson Missouri in 1940, Thomas began working at DC Comics in 1965 before moving to Marvel later that same year. As a huge fan of the fantasy genre, throughout the 1970s he incorporated many of Howard's ideas into comic book form. Howard had already utilized mythic places like Atlantis and Hyperborea, which he referred to in pseudohistorical terms as the "Hyborian Age": the period of time after the sinking of Atlantis. The organization of his thoughts on this pre-historical time appeared in the short essay, "The Hyborian Age." Utilizing this mytho-historical framework, Thomas expanded on every aspect of Howard's vision and in the process added a greater emphasis on Lemuria than had originally existed in the mythos. Thomas also delved deeper into the character of the god "Set," linking his influence to the sinking of Atlantis and Lemuria (as well as their continued subsistence beneath the ocean) and formulated the idea of a "Serpent Crown" that was used to possess humans who wore it.

Not only was Thomas elaborating on the same myths that had animated Howard's work, but writing from the vantage point of the 1970s, he included references to the conspiracy theories that had descended from them: the idea that Atlantis and Lemuria possessed advanced (and possibly alien) technology, as well as the idea that these places were still in operation. Thomas also alluded to hollow earth conspiracies by incorporating Antarctica into his Serpent Crown mythos.[420]

To conclude my rumination on this cartoon that had inspired my eleven year-old imagination: I find it fascinating that the myth-based narratives of a man born at the beginning of the twentieth century indirectly influenced mainstream pop culture in the 1980s and beyond. The fact that there is not a lot of explicit references back to Howard is telling; it is almost as if these ideas were transmitted through a Hermetic process of initiation, which is the theory most conspiracy theorists would indulge. However, without outright discounting this possibility, or the obvious fact that Roy Thomas was influenced by Howard's work and consciously translated it into the medium of comic books, it seems that perhaps these ideas are a part of our collective unconsciousness; as if snake-worshippers, snake people, and the existence of hidden realms is something human beings experienced in a distant and mythical time but now exist as a fragment of part of our mind that is not rationally accessible to us. The fact that Thomas's expansion on Howard's vision incorporated places like Antarctica (a place of conspiratorial significance) and telepathic communication hints that there is something akin to divination in the artistic process; in a sense, Howard and Thomas might have been on a similar wavelength. This wavelength could be tied to a psychological concept like Jung's Collective Unconscious or, philosophically speaking, to a Platonic realm of Forms or ideas that our minds navigate when we are in a state of creativity.

On an even more occultic reading (which might coincide with the psychological reading) perhaps these characters, and their development, referred in a literal sense to as "the great men of old" were Nephilim and this concept is transferred into the literature of Robert E. Howard as he constructs his Hyborean adventures. Are the snake worshipping cult members derived

---

[420] The recovery of the crown in Antarctica is detailed in *Avengers Annual #18* (1989)

from the line of Cain, or were they fallen "Watchers" who took earth women as wives and sired gigantic offspring?

The bifurcation between Gnosticism and Hermeticism that was sketched out in the Significance of the Grail Mythos is at play to a certain extent here, insofar as Christian conspiracy theorists like Wayne associate the "Serpent People" with the serpent in the Garden of Eden. In contrast with this, Elaine Pagels has pointed out that for certain Gnostic sects, the serpent in the Garden of Eden is a symbol of wisdom[421] which might be tied to earlier mythologies relating to the Female Spiritual Principle. This latter aspect is addressed in a Gnostic gospel entitled "The Hypostasis of the Archons."

The "Archons" in the title are "rulers" who have the bodies of women and heads of animals. These individuals create Adam out of dirt to cultivate the Garden of Eden, and soon after they create Eve out of Adam's side. At this point the Serpent enters the story and rhetorically questions Eve as to which tree in the garden she is forbidden from touching. Eve confirms that it is the tree "of recognizing evil and good."

> The snake, the instructor, said to her, "With death you shall not die; for it was out of jealousy that he said this to you. Rather your eyes shall open and you shall come to be like gods, recognizing evil and good." And the female instructing principle was taken away from the snake, and she left it behind merely as a thing of the earth. And the carnal woman took from the tree and ate; and she gave to her husband as well as herself; and these beings that possessed only a soul, ate. And their imperfection became apparent in their lack of acquaintance; and they recognized that they were

[421] Pagels, Elaine (1989) *The Gnostic Gospels.* Vintage Books, A Division of Random House Inc. P. 30

> naked of the spiritual element, and took fig leaves
> and bound them upon their loins.[422]

It is hinted at here that eating from the tree of knowledge leads Adam and Eve to an awareness of error (if nakedness can be read as error).[423] Pulling back a little, let's look at the symbol of the snake and the naïve interpretation that perhaps primitive ascertainments of animals tell us something that we will eventually discover about them, usually scientific, e.g., that red colored snakes are poisonous. On another Hermeneutical reading, maybe it is the earlier symbolic reading that determines or "colors" our eventual scientific understanding. Or are we just slowly relearning the aspects of our world over and over again?

Recall that Cobra-La was described as having an unbroken connection to their past, a cultural facet that is markedly different from our experience. From a hermetical perspective such as Boehm's, prior to the fall Adam had direct access to divine knowledge, which was consequently annihilated by the fall.[424] Then the great flood would have ended the widespread dissemination of what Wayne refers to as "the spurious sciences" that were a secularized duplication of Adam's knowledge. The idea of a sect of snake people (or any group of people, for that

---

[422] Robinson, James (1990) *The Nag Hammadi Library*. Harper San Francisco. P. 165

[423] If one were to argue that Hegel's thought was an academic interpretation of Hermetic thought, as Magee posits, then it is feasible to interpret the contribution error makes to knowledge in this way: the representational dimension of conceptual content is substantiated by the way in which a misrepresentation is corrected, i.e., the revelation that it is a misrepresentation. This analysis of Hegel's thought occurs in Brandom, Robert (2019) *A Spirit of Trust: A Reading of Hegel's Phenomenology*. Belknap Press of Harvard University Press. P. 98

[424] Magee, Glenn Alexander (2001) *Hegel and the Hermetic Tradition.* Cornell University Press. Pp. 45 - 46

matter) that secretly kept some form of this knowledge alive, either through secret societies or through the inhabitation of faraway places, can lead to the postulation that such a group might have an unbroken sense of its own history. Such ideation can come about in three contexts.

First, in the occult context it is believed that these individuals exist somewhere on the edges of the known world and that their knowledge is telepathically communicated to adepts. Second, in a conspiratorial context, these individuals hide in plain sight as members of elite groups and families that direct secret societies to do their bidding. And third, in an artistic context, which draws primarily from imagination and, knowingly or not, contributes to (and informs) the mythic narratives pertaining to the first two groups. In all three readings it seems as if the invocation of serpents is intended to signify antiquity; possibly the antiquity depicted in scripture or the antiquity of ancient Egypt. As it pertains to the former, we are speaking in terms of the Serpent in the Garden of Eden. Ginzberg details the de-evolution of the serpent after the fall this way:

> The serpent, too, is other than it was at first. Before the fall of man it was the cleverest of all animals created, and in form it resembled man closely. It stood upright, and was of extraordinary size. Afterward, it lost the mental advantages it had possessed as compared with other animals, and it degenerated physically too; it was deprived of its feet, so that it could not pursue other animals and kill them.[425]

In *The Genesis 6 Conspiracy*, Wayne discusses the anthropological archetype of snakes as it relates to certain warrior legends in the ancient settings of Europe, Central

---

[425] Ginzberg, Louis (2008) *The Legends of the Jews, Volumes I & II.* Forgotten Books. P. 31

America, and keeping with the theme of Egyptian reductionism, Egypt. Wayne claims that: "the cobra was unaccountably etched onto the crowns of Egypt from 4000 B.C.E. and before."[426]

The reliance on Egypt for occultists and conspiracy theorists is something that constantly reoccurs. I think that on some level it has to do with how iconic the pyramids, Sphinx, and hieroglyphics are for Western cultures; the fact that ancient people created such monumental works is an inexhaustible source of fascination for us. I think this awe, connected with an apprehension of the sheer antiquity of these objects, is often transferred onto our beliefs about the ancient Egyptians; and it is for this reason that you find Knight and Lomas believing that the secret to life after death was achieved by the Pharaohs and that Freemasonry is a simulacrum, or cargo cult, of this secret knowledge.

Jordan Maxwell's claim that Jesus acquired his unique form of wisdom by travelling to Egypt (which we will discuss in a later section) also draws from this line of thinking. Wayne most likely sees the ancient Egyptian affinity for snakes as essential to his thesis about serpent societies running amok in the distant past, as well as covertly conspiring in our present age; but does not place ancient Egypt at the center of his conspiracy theorization in the ways that these other authors do. Wayne is looking for the universality of this serpent symbolism in a way that conforms to Biblical assertions about the Serpent in the Garden of Eden and its relation to the Watchers and the Nephilim.

The first form of ideation, which is strictly occultic in nature, seems to have a closer connection to the third form of ideation, in that both assume some non-material action is dictating activities in our societies. These views are more synchronistic, in that they acknowledge the unknowable and ineffable forces at play within our regimented, mechanistic apprehension of the world. Concurrent with these views is a sort

---

[426] Wayne, Gary (2014) *The Genesis 6 Conspiracy.* Trusted Books, A Division of Deep River Books. P. 30

of agnostic sense of reverence for these synchronistic forces, regardless of whether they have an occultic efficacy or are merely tied to the powers of imagination and inspiration.

The second type of ideation, which is conspiratorial, fits more within the parameters of a mechanistic world. This view could entail either the transmission of secret knowledge by way of instruction and initiation or by way of "sacred" bloodlines, or both. Regarding the idea of bloodlines, from a cursory glance there appear to be two possible lines of descent: The Merovingian (divine) and Cain/Nephilim (infernal), which might continue to this day. In previous chapters we discussed secret societies that could be controlling the world. If these groups still exist they are operating within a more banal, bureaucratic structure – which might also be of their own making.

Some writers have found the designations of "Divine" and "Infernal," in this regard, to be too dogmatic. Writing for *Dagobert's Revenge*, Boyd Rice gives a more nuanced reading in which he claims that the Merovingians were "sorcerer-kings" who claimed to have the blood of both Christ and Lucifer running through their veins:

> Firstly, let's remember that this bloodline descended from a figure who equates with the Biblical Cain. In certain rabbinic lore, we come across the very interesting notion that Cain was not the son of Adam, but of Samael. It was thought that when Samael appeared to Eve as a serpent, he seduced her. The fruit of that union was Cain. Now Samael was a fallen angel, essentially the Judaic Lucifer. If the Merovingians knew of this version of the story (which they no doubt did), and believed it, it could be the basis of their alleged assertion that

they possessed the blood of both Christ and Lucifer.[427]

Demonologists and occultists sometimes refer to Samael as the serpent in the Garden of Eden, or the fallen angel who put the serpent up to its nefarious task. He is more frequently identified as the angel who stopped Abraham from sacrificing Isaac and later wrestled to a standstill with Jacob. If the latter narratives are correct (as correct as narratives of this nature can be) then Samael was not causing mischief in the Garden of Eden because he had not yet fallen from grace. This reading jives with one esoteric Judaic reading that associates Samael with the Roman Empire; thus his fall coincides with the rise of the Roman Empire to act as an adversary for the Jewish people.

The Gnostics, insofar as they indulged demonology, probably believed Samael to be associated with the Serpent of Eden. Of primary importance for us, in this day and age, is the understanding that Samael was the name of a Swedish death metal band from the mid-eighties. At their inception they showed great promise and were ahead of their time – many consider their early work to be a precursor to Norwegian Black metal. Their first two albums: *Worship Him* and *Blood Ritual* are total classics! After those, the quality of their work took a huge nosedive. On a more serious note, Rice's work traversed all three conceptions of how this secret knowledge might have been transmitted; he is both a knowledgeable scholar of the occult as well as a musician and writer. His work with Tracy Twyman for *Dagobert's Revenge*, however, hewed closely to the second, more mechanistic mode, hence the reliance on a material substrate such as a bloodline. Rice gives us a Nephilim-type of account, wherein a fallen angel impregnates a human. There is another Gnostic account of Cain's

---

[427] Taken from the chapter "Lucifer's Children: The Grail Bloodline and the Descendants of Cain" published in Twyman, Tracy (2005) *The Arcadian Mystique: The Best of Dagobert's Revenge Magazine*. Dragon Key Press. P. 41

origin that reverses the usual Nephilim narrative by claiming that he was the son of Adam's first wife, Lilith, a fallen angel. Lilith might have been a deity from an older Neolithic tradition that has been injected into certain pieces of Biblical Apocrypha. Despite his adherence to the materialistic idea of a bloodline, Rice leaves open the possibility of synchronistic and philosophical avenues of inquiry.

One such philosophical avenue, which can be tied to the Grail question, and the possibility of such a powerful question that it might have transformative powers for the answerer, exists in Pierre Klossowski's discourse on eternal recurrence. [428] Klossowski sees Nietzsche's question of eternal recurrence as something that could delineate the "higher man" from the average person, in that the "higher man" had the courage to accept an infinite repetition of his existence. Klossowski goes a step further and asks how these "higher" individuals might subsist within Western societies, and if in fact, they might constitute a sort of elite class. Klossowski, like Nietzsche, does not see these individuals as necessarily occupying positions of authority. In fact, he reverses the hierarchy:

> The project that foresees a 'class' of *satiated slaves satisfied with their lot* who work to benefit *austere and sober masters*, in accordance with the latter's 'creative tasks', is nothing other than a systematization of what Nietzsche sees in the already existing order: namely, that the false hierarchy of the so-called ruling class, which believes it determines the fate of the rarest individuals, hidden among the masses, in reality frees an inverted and secret hierarchy from its most

---

[428] Essentially the question of eternal recurrence has to do with having the strength of character to accept the infinite repetition of one's life. We will discuss the concept more thoroughly in the Significance of the Tarot chapter.

vile tasks – a hierarchy formed by 'surplus men' who are unassimilable to the general interest. The 'rulers' (industrialists, military men, bankers, businessmen, bureaucrats, etc.), with their various tasks, are merely effective slaves who work *unknowingly* on behalf of these *hidden masters*, and thus for a *contemplative* caste that ceaselessly forms the 'values' and the meaning of life.[429]

In this paradigm, we not only find the "higher men" – the ones who act in a spirit of affirmation in the face of eternal recurrence – blended covertly into our mechanistic society. They are also dictating the norms and values. This concept anticipates some of the themes we will address later, in relation to the Mandela Effect.

The Basic Chronology and One Final Stab at a Redemptive Grail Analysis

It is here that we must temporarily conclude the Grail discussion, which has overlapped with the last two chapters. In principle, we have been discussing two contemporary accounts of a form of knowledge, or tradition. According to most of these narratives, the train of dissemination goes from God to Adam to Adam's sons. This knowledge was then preserved by Enoch of Cain and his son Lamech, who carved the knowledge, in hieroglyphic form, onto two pillars that managed to survive the flood. This knowledge was then acquired by Nimrod by way of Hermes of Trismegistus, who had transcribed it from the pillars after the flood and used it to construct the Tower of Babel. After God smote the builders of the Tower, this information eventually made its way to Pythagoras and his disciples, and from there it was secularly translated into Greek and Hellenic philosophy. According to some occult sources this knowledge may have been bestowed upon

---

[429] Klossowski, Pierre (2005) *Nietzsche and the Vicious Circle.* Continuum. Pp. 121 - 122

Abraham by Melchizedek, which would have preserved it within the Rabbinical tradition.

Wayne attaches particular names to each of these seven sciences and then reiterates a theory of their transmission:

> The chronology will be presented with famous, legendary icons of antiquity recognized as the guardians of the Seven Sciences –Aristotle: dialectics, Cicero: rhetoric, Euclid: geometry, Boethius: arithmetic, Ptolemy: astronomy, Donatus: grammar, and Pythagoras: music. The Seven Liberal Sciences were kept alive in secrecy throughout the millennia by organizations such as the Pythagoras Mystery School that disseminated its obscure knowledge throughout Europe via Rex Deus organizations such as the Knights Templar. They in turn, spawned and passed on the spurious knowledge to organizations such as Freemasonry, Rosicrucianism, and the Royal Society.[430]

In conjunction with this line of transmission, there is an implication that the sensibility of these secret sciences still exists in academia, especially in the study of philosophy. This can be inferred by the fact that both Plato and Aristotle carried on the traditions of the pre-Socratics, while creating new theories such as the concept of Forms and the cave metaphor in which the average person's perceptions are analogous to prisoners watching shadows on the wall of a cave. It is only by escaping the cave and seeing the actual objects by the light of the sun that man has true cognition (these "actual" objects represent the Forms).[431]

---

[430] Wayne, Gary (2014) *The Genesis 6 Conspiracy.* Trusted Books, A Division of Deep River Books. P. 348

[431] With this analogy Plato reveals himself to be the arch-conspiracy theorist. Countless questions spring up from this narrative, such as: who's manipulating the shadows? How are we

Aristotle made advances in logic as well as a proto-scientific system of classification. Both would influence esteemed Catholic theologians, such as St. Thomas Aquinas, who was influenced by Aristotle; and St. Augustine, who was influenced by Plato.

The contemporary sources we have used to discuss the Grail couldn't be in more dialectical opposition to each other: Wayne and Christian fundamentalists view Gnosticism, Hermeticism, and the occult, on their own, or insofar as they inform Freemasonry as evil corruptions of the sacred sciences imparted from God to Adam. Twyman, Evola and other non-Christian theorists see this tradition as, if not good, then potentially beneficial.[432]

Thus we have effectively reached a dialectical aporia, in which it seems like everything we've been discussing sorts the individuals involved into white and black camps, so-to-speak. The "White" camp in this case sees the Grail quest in its earlier literary forms as problematic but somewhat benign (as some mothers in the 1980s saw *Dungeons & Dragons*), with the caveat that any intellectual progression away from it as fantasy literature is tantamount to pure heresy (and possibly puts one in cahoots with Lucifer, Satan and the dreaded Nephilim). The "Black" view then, either revels in the outrage this discourse causes or adopts an air of intellectual aloofness.

To the "White" camp, neutrality on the subject is suspect. However, it is by virtue of neutrality that we are able to discern how these narratives interlock with each other and how they work as narratives and in the world. Speaking to this point, Emma Jung gives this analysis:

---

to know that Plato's Forms are not themselves shadows of some sort? The essence of this analogy provided the basis for Descartes's *Meditations* as well as *The Matrix* films.
[432] Evola considered himself to be "Catholic" –he had an idiosyncratic belief system.

Myths and fairy-tales are also characterized by this
universal validity which differentiates them from
ordinary dreams. There are of course dreams of a
predominantly archetypal character, but these also
contain a subjective element since they usually
occur at moments of real significance for the
dreamer, such as important-turning-points in life,
or in critical situations which require a fresh
orientation or adaptation and for which the present
attitude which dominates consciousness does not
suffice. The appearance of an archetypal image will
draw the individual's attention to its general human
quality or to the idea underlying it. He will become
aware of new, previously unrecognized possibilities
and through them will experience a fresh influx of
energy; for the archetypes possess a numinous
quality and function as a hidden source of energy.
When a myth is enacted in a ritual performance or,
in more general, simpler and profaner fashion,
when a fairy-tale is told, the healing factor within it
acts on whoever has taken an interest in it and
allowed himself to be moved by it in such a way
that through this participation he will be brought
into connection with an archetypal form of the
situation and by this means enabled to put himself
"into order."[433]

Essentially, I'm proposing that perhaps the Grail Quest can be
understood in Hegelian terms of concept acquisition and
articulation. In the above passage, we can see a conceptual affinity
between Jung's "Healing" and Spengler's "Contrition." The healing
that Jung is talking about involves an interaction with a text or
narrative that seems to come from the "outside" of the self and

---

[433] Jung, Emma & Franz, Marie-Louise (1986) *The Grail Legend.*
Sigo Press. P. 37

alters this "self" in an affirming way. In Spengler's concept of contrition, the "self" looks outside of itself at the narratives it has instigated or altered and carries this understanding back into itself as a guarantor of certainty. These concepts are not identical, but they indicate analogous processes. They are also more emotive/reverent terms for processes that occur on a Hegelian conception of understanding.

Very briefly we described the Hegelian process of self-individuation as involving a series of corrections and judgments which occur over time by virtue of a faculty of understanding that discerns what is true and false. In a sense this "understanding" can be reconciled with the concept of an individuated self. This basic understanding then brings us to one of Hegel's most famous philosophical narratives: the "Master and Servant" dialectic.

The basic idea is that two individuals engage in a conflict and the victor does not kill his vanquished opponent, instead, he enslaves him. After this has occurred there is a certain dependency that arises between them, one that is based not only on servitude but also recognition. What has arisen is, "a practical normative conception that understands the Master as a locus of *pure independence,* authority without responsibility, and the Servant as a locus of *pure dependence*, responsibility without authority."[434] Robert Brandom sees the situation of the Master to be defective in both theoretical and practical terms:

> What ties all these dimensions of defectiveness together is the practical conception of Mastery as pure independence, authority without correlative responsibility. We will see that this conception brings with it a more specific commitment to the *immediate constitutiveness* of some of the Master's attitudes   –both   acknowledgments,

[434] Brandom, Robert (2019) *A Spirit of Trust: A Reading of Hegel's Phenomenology*. Belknap Press of Harvard University Press. P. 327

paradigmatically, of authority, and attributions, paradigmatically, of responsibility. This is the capacity of those attitudes to institute statuses all by themselves, regardless of the existence of any complimentary attitudes on the part of others. The responsibilities that the Master's authority abjures are of various kinds, emphasized in different allegorical lessons. He denies responsibility to (dependence of his authority upon) *other subjects*. More particularly, he denies responsibility to (dependence of his authority upon) the *attitudes* of others.[435]

Essentially, the Master is trying to constitute and enforce his sense of selfhood as if it was free from any obligations or responsibilities. Brandom's analysis is unique to contemporary philosophy because it is focused on the illusory foundations of Mastery – since Marx, most writers have focused on the alienation allotted to the existence of the servant.[436] Brandom, however, is

---

[435] Ibid p. 315

[436] For instance, see Julian Pefanis's summary of Baudrillard's critique of Hegel:

"In this context Baudrillard provides a parodic reading of Hegel's genealogy of historical consciousness in an inversion which relies on the slightest inflection to subvert the latter's meaning. "Work," declares Baudrillard, "is slow death." Its origin is to be found in the warrior's refusal to put the captured prisoner to instant, sacrificial, and honorable death. The first political economist was the master who realized the "economic" in the "deferred death" and the "different death" of the slave in servitude. Across the length of history the slaves are domesticated as a form until, in the democratic era they are freed. Free to do what? Free to work. And what is work? "Work is slow death." From Pefanis, Julian (1992) *Heterology and the Postmodern.* Duke University Press. Pp. 131 - 132

utilizing this conceptualization of Mastery to further explore the concept of individuated consciousness. The conflict, which results in the allegory of the Master and Servant, is one in which opposition is given full metaphorical expression. Each combatant enters the conflict willing to fight to the death. We can see an analogous confrontation occurring between the two camps that are battling over the meaning of the Grail mythos: both are battling for an ideological reason outside of their own being, and in Hegelian terms, are fighting on behalf of a commitment. To this extent, Brandom states:

> Being willing to risk one's life for something is adopting a distinctive kind of practical attitude toward it. I have suggested thinking of that attitude as *identifying with* what one is willing to risk and if need be sacrifice one's life for. The claim is that adopting that attitude has a particular effect. It changes one's status, making what one risks or sacrifices *for* an *essential* element of what one really is. That is to say that identification is a kind of *taking* oneself to be something that is also a *making* of oneself to be something. In the case of identification, what one is *for* oneself immediately affects what one is *in* oneself. It is an attitude that is *self-constitutive.*[437]

In the literary terms of the original Grail quest, it is in the willingness to sacrifice one's own life for the cause that grants a degree of nobility to the knights' respective endeavors. With the historical movement of this narrative to the contemporary argument regarding the postmodern interpretation of the Grail mythos, we no longer see individuals risking their lives, but

---

[437] Brandom, Robert (2019) *A Spirit of Trust: A Reading of Hegel's Phenomenology.* Belknap Press of Harvard University Press. P. 328

instead risking professionalism, prestige, and credibility – all of which are aspects of their identities. What the Hegelian model shows us is that the epistemological facets of our understanding are recollective, in that we assemble our knowledge from trial and error as we go. But also, that the larger, often ideological claims that we make do not exist in a vacuum; like the Master's perceived authority, it has to take other narratives into account. It is in this spirit of recognition or acknowledgment that one might attain, in a modern context, what I had said in the previous chapter was central to the Grail quest: not merely the finding of one's self, but of finding one's *right* self.

Terra Incognita

The significance of the principal subjects discussed in the rest of this chapter (the realm of Prester John, Hyperborea, the hollow earth, and the flat earth) differ from the places previously discussed (Atlantis, Lemuria) because these locations are cut off from us, not by some natural (or man-made) disaster but because we left them at some earlier stage in human history (or they exist someplace beyond the scope of our comprehension). The starting point for this type of discourse is the Garden of Eden, which according to the Bible still existed after the expulsion of Adam and Eve but in some remote unknown area guarded by a flaming sword. All the "places" we are going to discuss for the rest of this chapter are in some way haunted by the specter of the Eden narrative.

The cartographic designation of Terra Incognita, or "unknown land," goes back to Ptolemy's *Geography* written in 150 CE. Just as we described the sea and the cosmos as an uncharted territory that is both mysterious and tempting (in terms of exploration), insofar as both are filled with narratives, distant lands have a similar mystique. This was evident in Plato's story of Atlantis, a place that was removed from the telling by both time and place. Even Jesus was apocryphally determined to have gained his wisdom (or powers?) from travelling to a sacred, foreign place:

> For it is written that Christ journeyed to Egypt as a young man and there was taught by Hermetic priests. (And others write that Christ learned the ancient secrets on Atlantis; and still others claim that Christ was taught by priests on Venus.)[438]

Keep in mind the Gnostic connotation here: Venus being the "morning star" is etymologically linked with Lucifer – a connection that has been made by countless occultists and conspiracy theorists.[439] Our investigation into these mythical locales begins with a figure who came into the public consciousness around the time of the crusades.

Prester John

Prester John is a character who played a role in certain Grail legends such as Wolfram's *Parzival*. We are addressing him directly in this chapter because the legends surrounding him tap into something more exploratory than the Grail mythos (however it is conceived). The significance of the Prester John narratives is tied directly to the mythical realm over which he reigns.

The existence of Prester John was first announced to the medieval world via a mid-twelfth century letter sent to both Manuel the Emperor of Constantinople and Frederick the Emperor of the Romans. This letter would go on to be one of the most widely read, circulated, and translated texts of the medieval period. Robert Silverberg states that:

---

[438] Stewart, Louis (1980) *Life Forces.* Andrews and McMeel, Inc., p. 313

[439] Knight & Lomas devote a decent portion of *Uriel's Machine* to the significance of Venus and its relationship to Freemasonry.

It was translated into French, German, English, Russian, Serbian, and many other languages, even Hebrew; it enjoyed a multitude of editions in the centuries prior to the introduction of printing, and then, in the fifteenth and sixteenth centuries, it went through innumerable printed editions in many lands. Beyond all this, the letter was plagiarized on a number of occasions by fantasists and myth-spreaders who borrowed freely from it for their own purposes. Its influence on the imagination of medieval Europe was immense, and ultimately it served as one of the great motivating forces behind the era of exploration and discovery that commenced in the fifteenth century.[440]

The contents of the letter are remarkable. It begins with the announcement of the author's name and general well-wishing, before taking a presumptuous and immodest turn:

"Our Majesty has been informed that you hold our Excellency in esteem, and that knowledge of our greatness has reached you. Furthermore we have heard from our secretary that it was your wish to send us some objects of art and interest, for our pleasure."[441]

This is a bold statement, given that the letter was unsolicited; but it gets better:

"If indeed you wish to know wherein consists our great power, then believe without doubting that I, Prester John, who reign supreme, exceed in riches,

---

[440] Silverberg, Robert (1996) *The Realm of Prester John.* Ohio University Press. P. 41
[441] Ibid p. 41

virtue, and power all creatures who dwell under heaven. Seventy-two kings pay tribute to me.[442] I am a devout Christian and everywhere protect the Christians of our empire, nourishing them with alms."[443]

Given this bit of information, Prester John promises that if the recipients of his letter choose to pay him a visit, they will return home "laden with treasures." So far, so good, but where pray tell might this enchanted land be located?

"Our magnificence dominates the Three Indias, and extends to farther India, where the body of St. Thomas the Apostle rests. It reaches through the desert toward the place of the rising sun, and continues through the valley of deserted Babylon close by the Tower of Babel. Seventy-two provinces obey us, a few of which are Christian provinces; and each has its own king. And all their kings are our tributaries."[444]

At this point in history no one in Europe really knew how far the world extended, so "India" became a catch-all for the east, middle east, far east, etc. After geographically setting the stage, Prester John goes on to enumerate some of the more fantastic aspects of his kingdom:

---

[442] The number "seventy-two" has a certain resonance with conspiracy theorists because it is supposedly the number of members who made up the "Superior College" of the Freemasonic offshoot: "the Initiated Brothers of Asia." Moench, Doug (1995) *The Big Book of Conspiracies.* Paradox Press. P. 81
[443] Silverberg, Robert (1996) *The Realm of Prester John.* Ohio University Press. P. 42
[444] Ibid p. 42

"In our territories are found elephants, dromedaries, and camels, and almost every kind of beast that is under heaven [...] In one of our territories, no poison can do harm and no noisy frog croaks, no scorpions are there, and no serpents creep through the grass. No venomous reptiles can exist there or use their deadly power."[445] Wonders of nature, such as a sandy sea without water, upon the shores, of which wash up a variety of fish, "which are most pleasant and delicious for eating."[446] A river called Physon, "which, emerging from Paradise, winds and wanders through the entire province; and in it are found emeralds, sapphires, carbuncles, topazes, chrysolites, onyxes, beryls, sardonyxes, and many other precious stones."[447]

Resonating with the Grail mythos is the claim that: "In a plain lying between the sandy sea and the mountains is a stone of incredible medical virtue, which cures Christians or would-be Christians of whatever ailments afflict them."[448] The attentive reader will recall that in Wolfram's version of the Grail narrative the Grail was a stone which some identified with the alchemical "philosopher's stone" or the Emerald Tablet of Hermes. In the letter it seems to be more of a natural monument. The final touches are claims regarding the size and might of Prester John's army as well as the just nature of the inhabitants of his kingdom.

The first question asked by historians and the skeptically-minded people of the time, was: Where did this letter come from and who wrote it? Silverberg speculates that it was most likely the work of some anonymous European monk, who conceived

---

[445] Ibid p. 42
[446] Ibid p. 42
[447] Ibid p. 42
[448] Ibid p. 43

and executed the text for literary reasons. [449] Silverberg's reasoning on this count is not merely based on the fantastic descriptions, let alone the literacy, but that the text seems to draw on certain literary sources, such as an obscure biography of Alexander the Great and *The Thousand and One Nights*, which had preceded its appearance. The influence of the latter was especially significant given that the emerald-tipped scepter, which would be associated with the legendary figure of Prester John, had appeared in the "Sixth Voyage of Sinbad" passage, attributed to the King of Sarandib.[450]

Despite its nature as a fabrication, the mythical figure had historical and theological foundations. A variety of sources state that Prester John was purported to be a descendent of one of the three Magi who visited Christ twelve days after his birth. However, according to some versions of the myth, this was not enough to guarantee a Christian pedigree, and this is where the narrative of St. Thomas (the Saint who had doubted Christ's resurrection) comes into play.

According to legend, St. Thomas brought the Christian faith to India. Thomas's endeavors in India are told in an apocryphal work, *The Acts of Thomas,* which apparently dates from the first part of the third century; and which states that after the crucifixion the disciples of Jesus divided the world into missionary regions with it falling to Thomas to carry the faith to India.[451] Like Jonah before him, Thomas was not eager to embark on a journey to a strange land, but he was said to have succeeded in bringing a good number of the royalty over to the Christian faith after a series of miraculous events. As Silverberg states:

---

[449] Ibid p. 46

[450] If this point of reference is correct Silverberg is most likely referring to an early version of *The Thousand and One Nights*, originally written in Farsi and translated into Arabic in the 10th century.

[451] Ibid p. 17

How much of this story can be accepted as a genuine historical record? To the native Christian population of India, virtually all of it must be regarded as an accurate documentary account of the origin of their religious heritage. Several hundred thousand Christians still live along India's Malabar Coast –southwestern India, southwest from Goa –and call themselves "the Christians of St. Thomas." Most of them acknowledge the Syrian Orthodox Patriarch of Antioch as their spiritual leader, though some belong to the Syrian Roman Catholic Church, which acknowledges the supremacy of the Pope. All, however, trace their faith to the missionary work done by St. Thomas.[452]

So, the mythic resonance of St. Thomas's missionary work in India sets the stage for the appearance of the devout Prester John to appear in the public consciousness with the promises contained in his wondrous land. Some scholars read Prester John's letter as "a piece of utopian literature, postulating an ideal commonwealth in order to level moral criticism against twelfth-century Europe."[453] Silverberg details how, as Prester John's letter was translated and copied, wondrous and fantastic elements were added to his kingdom. Among of these was a palace that was inherited from his father wherein the walls and floors are made of crystal, the ceiling is encrusted with jewels, and within which all who drink the wine relinquish their desire for worldly things. St. Thomas himself is reanimated on holidays and preaches to the faithful who gather at said crystal palace. Animals were also added to the kingdom in the form of red, green, black, and blue lions, horned horses, and griffins.[454]

---

[452] Ibid pp. 18 - 19
[453] Ibid p. 55
[454] Ibid pp. 63 - 65

The case of Prester John falls very easily into the context of our general discussion, in that we have assessed three "murky" mythical figures (Enoch, Melchizedek, and Hiram) who scripture purports to have existed at one time or another. Our inquiries about these characters have entailed (and will further entail) the analysis and reconciliation of other historical and mythical characters with these shadowy archetypes. In the case of Prester John the process is slightly different: "Prester John" is given as a title within the narrative of a letter, and this then leads to a quest to find the man who bears this title. In this case we see at work the logic of the "singularity," which as Timothy Melley points out, "signifies nothing so much as nothing, absence."[455]

It is this absence which not only captivated the audience that was entertained by Prester John's letter, but which also prompted the fantastic elaborations that were ascribed to his realm: griffins, roaming gangs of cannibals, dragons, etc. As the location of Prester John's realm was deliberated by both aristocrats and peasants, more stories were fabricated, such as there being a shore where crabs wash up and are turned to stone,[456] and that the fabled Fountain of Youth resided there. This seems reminiscent of Vico's poetic imagination, in that he postulated how early man's fabrications were a symbolic rendering of historical events. However, with Viico there is the distinct possibility that early peoples, since they were not explicitly *writing* history, did not have a full comprehension of what they were doing. In contrast, the men spinning yarns about the realm of Prester John were living during the medieval period and to some extent understood that their story was participating in the creation of a legend. Hermeneutics makes it clear for us that the creation of, or adding to, a legend in medieval times was comprehended in a vastly different way than it is today. Did these

---

[455] Melley, Timothy (2000) *Empire of Conspiracy: The Culture of Paranoia in Postwar America*. Cornell University Press. P. 98
[456] Silverberg, Robert (1996) *The Realm of Prester John*. Ohio University Press. P. 183

men act as "harmless liars," as Auerbach describes this type of mythmaking? Were they trying to gain attention and notoriety for themselves? Was there an artistic impulse to enchant and entertain? Certainly, all these possibilities could be ascribed to the author of the Prester John letter, just as much as they might be ascribed to the jesters, squires, and knights who embellished the tale.

One of the first serious contenders for this esteemed title was a warrior who had been devastating Moslem armies throughout what is present-day Afghanistan and Iran. At the time, some speculated that this man was Prester John, or possibly the grandson of Prester John, and that he would go on to liberate Jerusalem, making pilgrimage safe again. Unfortunately, this warrior-king turned out to be Genghis Khan, who had no intention of saving Christendom.[457] The next notable figure to take up this mantle was Zara Yaqob, the King of Ethiopia who reigned from 1434 to 1468. Part of why an Ethiopian monarch came to be regarded by westerners as Prester John had to do with the aforementioned confusion over where and how big India was. Well-traveled explorers like Marco Polo, who did search for Prester John, believed that the fabled monarch was most likely to be found in modern day Kazakhstan. However, the fact that Ethiopia was the most advanced Christian civilization on the African continent, which was not clearly delineated from the far east at that time, led to this final consignment. Silverberg writes:

> Now that Prester John had been tracked to Ethiopia, one matter was in need of settlement: was this Prester John who ruled there the same man, preserved by the Fountain of Youth, of whom tales had been told for three hundred years, or was "Prester John" merely the title by which all Ethiopian kings were known? That was easy to deal with; obviously the Ethiopian monarchs were

---

[457] Ibid pp. 71 - 73

> mortal men, for in 1428 Yeshak had occupied the throne, and in 1441 envoys from a king named Zara Yaqob had attended the Council of Florence. Therefore "Prester John" must be some sort of generic title, passed along from king to king [...][458]

The Ethiopians however were blissfully unaware of the significance of this appellation – the mythical pedigree that their monarchs claimed was traced back to the lineage of King Solomon, not Saint Thomas or an obscure letter that appeared in the twelfth century.

As we've seen (and will see again), the significance of the names of Enoch, Hiram, and Melchizedek is intertwined with how they have gone on to become titles. As it pertains to the Grail quest, a figure, such as Arthur, would go on to become an indication of a title.[459] And Arthur, being a central figure, does not fit the mold of the three murky figures. However, does the figure of Prester John fit one of their molds, so to speak?

The Book of Enoch was a part of the Ethiopian Bible; hence Prester John as he is misrecognized in the person of the Ethiopian king might imply a reoccurrence of the Enoch character. Also, Prester John is always associated with his royal stature and therefore might be, in some way, aligned with an obscure bloodline or tradition, and in this respect might be evocative of Melchizedek. Evola tells us that:

> The image of Prester John's kingdom historically served as the foundation of the obscure idea of an integration of the forces hidden behind the symbols of chivalry, the Empire, and the Crusades. In a materialistic transposition, this powerful and mysterious Oriental prince, who was not a Christian but a friend of Christians, was invoked to help the

---

[458] Ibid p. 189
[459] We will see this achieved metonymically with JFK.

Christian endeavor in the Holy Land during its most
difficult time, in order to grant a victorious end to
the holy war.[460]

After this intervention failed to materialize, we know that
historically in 1533 the Portuguese nobility and Pope Clement VII
met with Dom Martinho, a Portuguese ambassador, who had
spent several years in the company of Lebna Dengel (the then
King of Ethiopia) and had brought back a letter and a gold cross.
The Pope and nobility received the gift and promised to offer
outreach between the two churches. Throughout this meeting the
idea that Dengel was Prester John was implied. However, the
outreach would never come about because conflicts with Henry
VIII would preoccupy the papacy for the next few decades.[461] But
on a mythical and spiritual level the Prester John enigma lived on.
Evola tells us that in a few traditions "Prester John's kingdom is
identified with Avalon, that is, with the center of the Hyperborean
tradition."[462] This bit of information leads us into our next section.

Hyperborea

Long, long the night, the total night endures.
The Arctic couches an immeasured space.
No mortal eye his stature, length and breadth-
Can compass ever, where he bitter breathes,
But slumbers passive mid the blasting blight,
That fastens all to immobility,

---

[460] Evola, Julius (1997) *The Mystery of the Grail.* Inner Traditions
International. P. 47
[461] Silverberg, Robert (1996) *The Realm of Prester John.* Ohio
University Press. Pp. 274 - 276
[462] Evola, Julius (1997) *The Mystery of the Grail.* Inner Traditions
International. P. 48

And into stillness and to death transmutes.[463]

There isn't a great deal of information available about Hyperborea. The two most salient features of the Hyperborean narrative that pertain to conspiracy theorization are that it appears to be merely a pagan, non-biblical, origin story that was referenced by proto-Nazi occult groups, and that it was explicitly drawn upon by Robert E. Howard for his fictional "Hyborian Age." There are a few books, as well as *History Channel* specials that have discussed the Thule Society, which existed in Germany from 1918 to roughly 1930, and which is largely responsible for a good deal of the conspiracy theorization about Hyperborea. A few sources have speculated on the group's influence on Hitler and other high-ranking Nazis; some of which, like Nicholas Goodrick-Clark's *The Occult Roots of Nazism*, published in 1985, study the group's theories and philosophical antecedents. Goodrick-Clark doesn't explore the possibility that the theories of the group had a strong semblance of coherence, accuracy, or were carried extensively into contemporary occult circles. Peter Moon, however, does.

For this brief analysis I'm going to focus on Moon's *The Black Sun: Montauk's Nazi-Tibetan Connection*; the four volume series on the Montauk Project is a payload of Compound Conspiracy theorization. In the series, Moon begins with the premise that in 1963 a shadowy government agency began experiments in time travel and teleportation at Camp Hero in Montauk, New York. These experiments were purportedly a continuation of the "Philadelphia Experiment" wherein an experiment intended to make a ship, the USS Eldridge, undetectable by radar actually caused the ship to "become

---

[463] Herre, Benjamin Groff (1878) *Hyperborea: Or the Pilgrims of the Pole*. The New Era Steam Book and Job Print. P. 45

invisible to the naked eye and was removed from time and space as we know it."[464]

With this thematic backdrop in place, Moon brings in aspects of MK-Ultra by claiming that young people and the homeless were abducted and experimented upon; a porthole in time, or "time tunnel" was created; extraterrestrials were contacted; the internet was invented; Nazi scientists were employed via Operation Paperclip; and the moon landing hoax was planned and plotted. Some have speculated that, because of the staggering amounts of disbelief that need to be suspended while reading, Moon's work is intended as science fiction or parody. It's obvious that some of these topics have made inroads into mainstream culture, for example, the Netflix program *Stranger Things* borrowed a variety of key themes from Moon's Montauk mythos: teenagers being experimented on, secret scientists doing nefarious experiments, an alien monster that escapes through dimensional wormholes, telekinesis, etc.

This is all good stuff, but what does Moon's feverish imagination have to tell us about Hyperborea and Thule? Interestingly, he begins his narrative by associating Nazi mysticism with Islam:

> The Arabic connection to the Nazis continues to reveal itself when we consider that in the centuries prior to Islam, the magnificent and all compassionate Allah was referred to as "Tualla." This name reveals an undeniable correspondence to Thule, the name from which the Germans crafted the name of their secret brotherhood: the Thule Society. Thule is considered to be the capital city of Hyperborea, the land beyond the poles.[465]

---

[464] The "Philadelphia Experiment" was purported to have occurred in 1943. Moon, Peter (2003) *The Black Sun: Montauk's Nazi-Tibetan Connection*. Sky Books. P. 13

[465] Ibid p. 151

The etymological argument connecting "Allah" with "Tualla" and then "Thule," is one of the most important tools in the conspiracy theorist's toolbox. Many of the authors we've mentioned (Wayne, Frank, Donnelly, and Twyman) engage in this practice to varying degrees. Continental philosophers, specifically Derrida, do so as well. I'm bringing it up here because it indicates an appeal to some of the Structuralist sentiments that we have already outlined: namely words acting as keys to understanding or mastery.[466]

Word games aside, the question we are after is: What does Moon think is the significance of Thule/Hyperborea? He sees it as being vaguely connected with the myth that there is a sun within the center of the earth, this would be the earth's core, but because it is symbolically antithetical to the real sun, it is dubbed the "black sun." He then puts forward:

> Whether an actual description of the universe or simply a colorful metaphor for the truth, the legend of Thule, in its purest form, represented the archetypal powers of the universe. It is the locale where the ancient Elder Race first interacted genetically with the indigenous race of Earth and created the amalgamated human we know today. The Thule Society concerned itself with the Teutonic lore and sacred knowledge of the Elder

---

[466] Here is another example, which points towards linguistic monism: "Thule can be found in several distinct languages and cultures, thus corroborating the idea of a single language as illustrated in the Tower of Babylon story. The Mexicans have a Tule god and sacred city named Tula. The aboriginal Canadians of the northern arctic were known as the Tuule. Genghis Khan, the custodian of the Shensi pyramids in ancient Tibet (now known as Central Asia) named his youngest son Tula or Tule, depending on what version you read." Ibid p. 156

Race. The Norse myths themselves are considered to be coded sacred knowledge of this race's origins. As the first battleground between humans and gods, *Ultima Thule* is identified as the Teutonic Garden of Eden. It also parallels the story of Babylon where mankind lost its connection to the godhead.[467]

"Ultima Thule," was a place that had been depicted in medieval literature as being beyond the borders of the known world. We can see, in this passage, that Moon is setting up the possibility of introducing an "Ancient Aliens" style of argument in relation to the "Elder Gods," as well as implicitly drawing on Lovecraft's "Old Ones."

Moon, at least for a good part of this book, takes on the role of Thule reductionist: "Thule embodies the cosmic order of things and how all religions and myths propagate from this holy seed."[468] In order to claim this in a respectable manner, he maintains that the Nazis who joined the Thule Society corrupted it with racism, brutality, and materialism.[469] Once this stumbling block has been overcome, and the Thule mythos has been sanitized for modern consumption, Moon can get on with the business of reinterpreting the classic narratives of conspiracy theorization. These include an obligatory reference to Pythagoras, i.e., "In Greek mythology, Pythagoras was taught sacred geometry by Apollo, a god who was identified as a resident of Hyperborea;"[470] listing and detailing a wide swath of interconnections between the Theosophical conception of "Vril" (a sort of cosmic lifeforce), the Thule Society, H.P. Lovecraft, and Elder Gods that migrated from Mars to the hollow earth, etc.;[471]

---

[467] Ibid p. 151
[468] Ibid p. 160
[469] Ibid p. 153
[470] Ibid p. 154
[471] Ibid pp. 160 - 168

and, an incredible attempt to bring all of this back to Montauk, New York:

> The ancient German secret societies were interested in Montauk because it was once a part of Thule and resided in the North. This was prior to the continental drift when most geologists believe there was only one main land mass. Geographically, Montauk itself rests atop an undersea volcano which is honeycombed with all sorts of natural lava tunnels. Although you won't easily find this in books, it is a casually disregarded fact. Block Island, viewable from Montauk Point, is a similar mountain top. Whether Thule and Montauk were one and the same is considerably more controversial. Projected maps of ancient geography will show them to be remarkably close.[472]

We will briefly return to Moon's work in our discussion of UFO phenomena. What we've set out so far shows that he engages in a great deal of reductionism, both materialist and metaphysical, and that he definitely engages in Compound Conspiracy theorization, lumping together as many varied signifiers of intrigue as humanly possible. However, the balance that he finds between these two positions makes for engaging, contemporary mythmaking. The diffuse nature of his narratives makes his writing less claustrophobic than conspiracy theorists who are constantly driving at one particular angle.[473]

In contrast to this example of Compound Conspiracy theorization, we have Robert E. Howard's "Hyborian Age," which was essentially a literary undertaking intended to grasp the

---

[472] Ibid p. 154

[473] This could also be due, in part, to the fact that the majority of his work was churned out in the nineties, which was the end of the "golden age" of conspiracy theorization.

mythic history attributed to the "land beyond the poles," and to utilize it within the scope of fantasy literature. Unlike Moon, Howard is not trying to give us an actual "historical" account of Hyperborea. However, to many readers there is the possibility that either a) he is transmitting some esoteric handed-down hermetic knowledge, or b) he is artistically tapped into an imaginative realm that is aligned with certain mytho-poetic "truths." Both possibilities were discussed earlier in this chapter. Howard's approach to the subject, an example of what is sometimes called "world-building," would be utilized extensively in both fantasy and science fiction throughout the rest of the twentieth century. In his preface to the essay, he writes:

> Nothing in this article is to be considered as an attempt to advance any theory in opposition to accepted history. It is simply a fictional background for a series of fiction-stories. When I began writing the Conan stories a few years ago, I prepared this 'history' of his age and the peoples of that age, in order to lend him and his sagas a greater aspect of realness. And I found that by adhering to the 'facts' and spirit of that history, in writing the stories, it was easier to visualize (and therefore to present) him as a real flesh-and-blood character rather than a ready-made product. In writing about him and his adventures in the various kingdoms of his Age, I have never violated the 'facts' or spirit of the 'history' here set down, but have followed the lines of that history as closely as the writer of actual historical-fiction follows the lines of actual history. I have used this 'history' as a guide in all the stories in this series that I have written.[474]

---

[474] Howard, Robert (1936) "The Hyborian Age" found at: http://www.gutenberg.org/files/42182/42182-h/42182-h.htm accessed on 03/02/21

After the cataclysm that sank Atlantis and Lemuria the world devolved into an atavistic and savage place:

> Thick jungles covered the plains, great rivers cut their roads to the sea, wild mountains were heaved up, and lakes covered the ruins of old cities in fertile valleys. To the Continental kingdom of the Atlanteans, from sunken areas, swarmed myriads of beasts and savages—ape-men and apes. Forced to battle continually for their lives, they yet managed to retain vestiges of their former state of highly advanced barbarism.[475]

Just prior to the cataclysm, Howard describes a migration of a Neanderthal type of tribe that had journeyed into the distant north. While there, this group adapted to the harsh climate and became "vigorous and warlike." These people were known as the "Hyborians," and they worshipped "Bori" who was identified as a great ancestor. Much of Howard's description of the Hyborians coincides with what we know of the Vikings and the Eddic Sagas.

It is clear that, when devising his mythos, Howard had studied a good deal of European mythology and possibly some occultism. It's also possible that he was familiar with the work of Friedrich Nietzsche, since he describes the Hyborians as "blond savages of the far north," while Nietzsche referred to the "blond beast" in his *Genealogy of Morality* (first published in 1887). The similarities between the two writers, as noted before, is that they both attach a great significance to physical power, conflict, and domination – whether intersubjectively, or with one's environment. Regardless as to whether there was any thread of influence between the two, what is most significant is that both were tapped into themes that were central to the Zeitgeist. They also invoke the idea of a pagan, or non-monotheistic, rendering of

---

[475] Ibid

the Eden narrative, a fact that may or may not be central to the scientific revolutions taking place during said Zeitgeist. For the next section, we will look at an idea that conspiracy theorists would often tie to both the mythology of Hyperborea as well as the mythos created by Robert E. Howard: the hollow earth narrative.

The Hollow Earth

Everything that we have looked at in this chapter has been concerned with a topographical conception of the limits of human comprehension, as well as a rendering of the mythical past. As we will see, the myths pertaining to Hyperborea and the hollow earth are as rich as those of Prester John and give a clear enough example of how the conspiracy theory acts as a modern retelling of myth.

The hollow earth myth, as we will see, taps into three classic conspiracy theorist tropes: Nazis, UFOs and Hyperborea. We covered some of the more esoteric conspiracy theorization about the Nazis in the last section; how they relate to the hollow earth is tied to the theory that UFOs, as we understand them today, were actually secret Nazi weapons developed near the end of the war. In conjunction with this postulation is the understanding that the Nazis, after being defeated in World War II, escaped to a secret base beneath Antarctica.

In his exegesis on this conspiracy theory, Ian Blake describes a curious incident that supposedly took place in 1942, wherein Hitler held a meeting with his chiefs of staff and reported to them that Germany's top scientists had discovered that, "The earth is concave, not convex" and, essentially, that we are not living on the surface of the earth, but on the inside.[476] According to Blake's telling of the narrative, any Nazi experiments

---

[476] Blake, Ian "The Undying Monster: Hitler & the Nazi UFOs" reprinted in *Rapid Eye* (1995). Edited by Simon Dwyer. Creation Books. P. 118

undertaken to prove this theory failed and the subject was dropped, only to be retrieved and utilized by groups such as the "Aerial Phenomena Enquiry Network" (APEN) during the 1970s. The basic narrative proffered by them, and like-minded groups, was that Hitler, Himmler, and the rest of the Nazis still believed in the hollow earth and conjoined this belief with an interest in "Tibetan esotericism with its persistent references to Agharti and Shamballah."[477] This would then lead to Hitler and his crew (which may have included a "black lodge" of Tibetan monks that had been employed for magical practices during the last years of the Third Reich) to escape with their secret saucer technology to a base beneath either Antarctica or the North Pole. Once established at this underground base, Hitler and Co. contacted the Vril lifeforce and then used their saucer technology to terrorize the world.

If conspiracy theorization was a classic rock radio station, the narrative that UFOs are the work of the Nazis would be analogous to either Deep Purple's "Smoke on the Water" or Blue Oyster Cult's "Don't Fear the Reaper." Using the same scale, the theory that UFOs are, in one way or another, the result of Aleister Crowley's supernatural shenanigans would be "Stairway to Heaven;" UFOs are time-travelers from the distant future (or past) would be "Hotel California;" and the narrative that UFOs are just straight-up extraterrestrials would equate to Journey's "Don't Stop Believing."

We'll deal with these theories in more detail in the UFO chapter. The idea of a subterranean world, that is either mythical or technologically advanced is very old and has played a part in folktales and literature for quite some time; the whole notion of "going down the rabbit hole" is itself derived from Lewis Carroll's 1865 novel, *Alice's Adventures in Wonderland*, in which the titular character escapes to a fantastic underground world. On a darker note, HP Lovecraft also addressed this subject in his short story "The Festival." Published in 1925, "The Festival" describes a

---

[477] Ibid p. 118

young man's trip to New England to participate in an ancient Yule festival:

> It was the Yuletide, that men call Christmas though they know in their hearts it is older than Bethlehem and Babylon, older than Memphis and mankind. It was the Yuletide, and I had come at last to the ancient sea town where my people had dwelt and kept festival in the elder time when festival was forbidden; where also they had commanded their sons to keep festival once every century, that the memory of primal secrets might not be forgotten.[478]

As the narrator journeys through Kingsport, which seems to get older as he progresses, he arrives at his relatives' house. Once inside, a creature that seems to be wearing a mask making him appear human leads him to a reading room to wait for the festival to begin; while waiting he flips through the dreaded, "unmentionable" *Necronomicon*. When he is finally summoned to leave, he follows a group of hooded characters,

> "... out into the moonless and tortuous network of that incredibly ancient town; went out as the lights in the curtained windows disappeared one by one, and the Dog Star leered at the throng of cowled, cloaked figures that poured silently from every doorway and formed monstrous processions up this street and that [...]"[479]

Upon arriving at their destination, an old church, the hooded throng enters and begins descending an incredibly vast stairway.

---

[478] Lovecraft, Howard Phillips (1996) *The Road to Madness*. A Del Rey Book. P. 148

[479] Ibid p. 151. The reference to the "Dog Star" here is significant for reasons that we will address later.

The path downwards is seemingly endless, the destination being a vast body of water, and arising from it, a fiery column:

> Fainting and gasping, I looked at that unhallowed Erebus of titan toadstools, leprous fire and slimy water, and saw the cloaked throngs forming a semicircle around the blazing pillar. It was the Yule-rite, older than man and fated to survive him; the primal rite of the solstice and of spring's promise beyond the snows; the rite of fire and evergreen, light and music. And in the stygian grotto I saw them do the rite, and adore the sick pillar of flame, and throw into the water handfuls gouged out of the viscous vegetation which glittered green in the chlorotic glare.[480]

The story ends with the narrator waking up in a hospital bed and being told that he had been in an accident prior to reaching Kingsport. The Kingsport that he sees from his window, prior to his transfer to Arkham Asylum, is not nearly as ancient as it seemed to him the night before.

This short story touches upon a great deal of the tropes and signifiers that have been seized upon and repeated by mythologically-oriented conspiracy theorists: "The Dog Star" i.e., Sirius; the *Necronomicon*; the hollow earth; the Yule flame, which can be read as a stand-in for Vril; and the idea of an esoteric group operating within the confines of a traditional American society. It's impossible to say that Lovecraft consciously inserted so much convergent esoteric knowledge solely byway of his studies. Sirius-related conspiracies, as well as some of the more off-the-wall Vril theories, wouldn't achieve a solid coherence and dissemination until the 1970s. It seems plausible to leave open the possibility that Lovecraft's literary visions were simply attuned to certain esoteric currents.

---

[480] Ibid p. 153

Returning to Ian Blake's essay, the last anecdote we must discuss in relation to hollow earth theorization has to do with Fred Lee Crisman and events that occurred at Maury Island, Washington in June of 1947. The story begins with an anonymous letter appearing in the June 1946 issue of *Amazing Stories*, the contents of which are as follows:

> "Sirs:
> I flew my last combat mission on May 26, 1945, when I was shot up over Bassein and I ditched my ship in Remaree Roads off Cheduba Island. I was missing five days. I requested leave at Kashmere. I and Captain (name deleted by request) left Srinagar and went to Rudok, then through the Khese pass to the northern foothills of the Karakoram. We found what we were looking for. We knew what we were searching for.
> For Heaven's sake drop the whole thing! You are playing with dynamite. My companion and I fought our way out of a cave with submachine guns. I have two nine-inch scars on my left arm that came from wounds given me in the cave when I was 50 feet from a moving object of any kind, and in perfect silence. The muscles were nearly ripped out. How? I don't know. My friend has a hole the size of a dime in his right bicep. It was seared inside. How we don't know. But we both believe we know more about the Shaver Mystery than any other pair."[481]

The "Shaver Mystery" referenced in this letter pertains to the 1945 novella, "I Remember Lemuria!" published in *Amazing Stories* by Richard Shaver. Shaver, who was a welder in

---

[481] Blake, Ian "The Undying Monster: Hitler & the Nazi UFOs" reprinted in *Rapid Eye* (1995). Edited by Simon Dwyer. Creation Books. P. 120

Pennsylvania at the time, claimed that he began hearing voices that helped him remember a past life in Lemuria. According to Shaver's account, Lemuria, Atlantis, and Mu were visited by beings from another planet and had brought their technology to earth, allowing for the mythical (and Edenic) Golden Age to begin and flourish. At some point, the sun's rays became deadly for the aliens and some of them departed for their home planet, while others built civilizations underground. The technology they brought with them deteriorated over time and the alien race split into two groups: the evil, midget-like "Deros," and the good "Teros." The two factions are locked in battle and the future of the terrestrial world is at stake.[482]

     This anonymous letter, which was published a year after "I Remember Lemuria!" can be read as a modern reiteration of the Prester John letter, in that it instigates wild speculation, elaboration, and sometimes active pursuit. However, unlike the Prester John letter, whose authorship will never be known, we do know that the author of this letter to *Amazing Stories* was a man named Fred Lee Crisman. Crisman is a significant link in the chain that connects these earlier archaic and mythological narratives, which pertain to the hollow earth and Lemuria, with modern-day conspiracy theorization. The two modern points of which I speak are UFOs and "Men in Black."

     The story unfolds this way. On June 23, 1947 Harold Dahl was in a boat moored off of Maury Island with his son and dog when a "doughnut shaped object" appeared in the sky and released a shower of slag onto the boat and nearby area. The slag killed the dog and injured Dahl's son. After taking his son to a nearby hospital, Dahl reported the incident to the owner of the boat, who also happened to be his commanding officer, one Fred Lee Crisman.

     It turns out that Crisman, who had actually been a pilot during WW II, showed up at Maury Island the next day and himself witnessed a doughnut shaped craft in the sky. On this

---

[482] Ibid pp. 119 - 120

same day (June 24, 1947) a salesman named Kenneth Arnold was flying his private plane near Mount Ranier when he witnessed nine UFOs approaching the mountain, which he described as moving "the way a saucer would if you skipped it over water," and thus introducing the appellation of "flying saucers" to the modern lexicon.[483] The third event transpiring on that fateful day, was a visit that Harold Dahl received from a man in a black suit who recounted the previous day's events in great detail and then warned Dahl not to disclose his narrative to anyone, lest he and his family suffer dire consequences.

Many conspiracy theorists have claimed that the individual who visited Dahl was a "Man in Black." Connected with this visit was the disappearance of Dahl's son, who after being gone for a few weeks, returned home in a state of amnesia. Having been the subject of a big budget science fiction film franchise, which some conspiracy theorists have seen as a "psy-op" to normalize them, the Men in Black narratives warrant a good deal of scrutiny. Doug Moench's *Big Book of the Unexplained* devotes a whole chapter to them and describes how these individuals visit people who have recently witnessed UFO phenomena. It is open to speculation whether "MIBs" are a part of a super-secret government agency (as they are portrayed in the films) or if they are themselves aliens. Moench writes that: "MIBs are often baffled by commonplace items such as ballpoint pens, eating utensils, and even food itself."[484] During these visits, MIBs often reveal a great deal of personal information about the people they are interviewing and their presence is intended to induce paranoia,

[483] Ibid p. 121. It should be noted that Blake's retelling of the events diverges in a variety of ways from the Wikipedia account of this incident. I'm referencing Blake's account exclusively because of its coherency and its pedigree as a narrative that was published in an underground magazine.
[484] Moench, Doug (1997) *The Big Book of the Unexplained.* Paradox Press. P. 123

however, they are rarely connected with any actual harm or violence.[485]

All the above information pertaining to the Maury Island Incident was collated and put in a letter by Crisman, which he sent to *Amazing Stories*, whose intrigued editor, Ray Palmer, enlisted the services of Kenneth Arnold to investigate the matter on the magazine's behalf. Upon Arnold's arrival, accompanied by two members of Air Force Intelligence, the story began to fall apart. The first problem was that Dahl was unable to produce a film he claimed to have taken of the UFOs causing the two airmen who had accompanied Arnold to lose interest and board a flight back to Hamilton Air Force Base carrying samples of the slag that had been recovered from Maury Island. Twenty minutes after take-off the plane burst into flames and crashed.

Not long after this, Harold Dahl disappeared, and Fred Lee Crisman was recalled to active duty and stationed in Greenland; fascinating because Greenland is one of the locations that early cartographers and explorers had designated as "Hyperborea" when they still believed such a place existed. As for Kenneth Arnold, the final nail in the coffin of his investigation occurred when the slag samples he had procured from Maury Island were surreptitiously replaced with counterfeits. It was not long after this that Arnold decided to call it a day on his investigation of the Maury Island Incident.[486]

Essentially this story has pretty much everything you could want in a conspiracy narrative: UFOs, Men in Black, mysterious deaths, and disappearances, etc. But that's not all! The story has an epilogue as Crisman's name reappeared in the late-60s in relation to the JFK assassination. According to Blake:

> It happened when District Attorney James Garrison
> of New Orleans subpoenaed one Fred Lee Crisman
> of Tacoma to testify before a Grand Jury

---

[485] Ibid p. 122
[486] Ibid p. 121

Investigation into the assassination of John F. Kennedy. Garrison had apparently become convinced that a man named Clay Shaw was instrumental in the Kennedy affair. Shaw, however, was cleared of all involvement and set free. Garrison's conspiracy theories collapsed in court and today he is largely discredited. Nevertheless, a number of significant events were never explained. Crisman, for instance, never testified at the actual trial. As John Keel has it: "He was hospitalized in 1969 after being shot during an attempt on his life only days before he was due to testify." Crisman eventually recovered and changed his name to Jon Gold. He died in 1978 amid persistent rumours that he had once been either a CIA agent, or an operative in the field of 'industrial warfare'.[487]

The name "Fred Lee Crisman" is not a title that appears in various narratives, wherein the constituents of said narratives seek the originary point, or singularity, to whom the appellation can conform. Crisman himself is the singularity – he is an object that circulates throughout myriad and obscure narratives that are central to modern conspiracy theorization and his appearance in our narrative at the dawn of modern-day UFO phenomena is auspicious. In a way, his appearance represents a shift from the Sacred time" of mythological thinking, in which a name is a title for an individual who will play a role in the mythic narrative, to the modern "Faustian" age, when the individual instigates and alters the narratives in which he finds himself. It is also, in this respect, that we see interconnectedness to be another aspect of "significance" – as a mechanism occurring within the texts that qualifies our assertion, as readers, of "narrative richness." This is

---

[487] Ibid pp. 121 – 122. The possibility of Crisman being a CIA agent and his engagement with Clay in the time leading up to the assassination, were what brought him under Garrison's purview.

a point that was not addressed up until now because it needed to be worked through and discovered before being stated explicitly.

The Moon Landing

Jumping forward now, from the Maury Island Incident to July 16, 1969 when Apollo 11 landed on the moon. This event, which was borne out of the "space race" between the US and the Soviet Union, was a moment of excitement and pride for most Americans. After the glow of the event faded, however, conspiracy theories began to circulate that the whole thing had been faked and that the film presented to the public had been shot and directed by Stanley Kubrick. It is assumed that Kubrick was given the task because of his experience filming 1968's *2001: A Space Odyssey*; there are also said to be hints of his involvement in this conspiracy hidden in his other works – specifically *The Shining*.

Conspiracy theorists who doubt the moon landing return to a few core questions: "How was the event filmed from outside the capsule? And who did the filming?" "How is the American flag waving in space?" "Why do the shadows look like they are the result of multiple light sources?" "Why does the letter C appear to be visible on one of the rocks?" Such questions, and more, have led some to postulate that the whole thing was shot on a movie set.

Some of the clues purported to be in Kubrick's film are:

-*The Shining* is based on a book by Stephen King but Kubrick changed a few of the details when he made the movie, one of which is the appearance of the dead twins. In the book, there was a single child, but it is believed that Kubrick used twins in order to signify the failed Gemini mission by NASA.

-Room 217 was changed to room 237 in the movie because the distance between the earth and moon is roughly 237,000 miles.

-In a shot taken from above, we see Danny playing in the corridor on a patterned carpet. Conspiracy theorists believe that it looks strikingly similar to the Apollo 11 launch pad.

-In a scene where Danny rises up from the carpet, he is wearing a sweater with a rocket with the text "Apollo 11" on it. This is seen as the big clue that Kubrick is indeed hinting at his involvement with the "fake moon landing" project.[488]

The obvious question raised by all of this is: why would Kubrick hide these clues in a film? Some conspiracy theorists would argue that it has to do with Hoffman's "revelation of method" theory. If this is true, then it means that Kubrick, or his handlers, are dangling clues in front of his audience in a cynical and manipulative fashion. Conversely, some have speculated that Kubrick, as an artist, was hell-bent on exposing corruption and the abuse of power and this was a covert attempt on his part to allow the public a chance to catch onto the hoax.[489]

The space race, of which the moon landing was the final component, is analogous to a space age Grail quest, borne out of the literature and optimism of the time. As this literature grew darker and the optimism faded, the urge to demystify this event grew and we can see the conspiracy theorists' attempt to prove the moon landing a hoax as an attempt at demystification. Concurrent with this drive to dispel the optimism of space

---

[488] From an encapsulation of the theory found at https://indianexpress.com/article/entertainment/hollywood/did-stanley-kubrick-confess-his-involvement-in-fake-moon-landing-with-the-shining-5972360/ accessed on 02/27/21

[489] These theories surround Kubrick's work, especially his last film, *Eyes Wide Shut*, which shot its infamous orgy scene at a mansion owned by the Rothschilds. Many conspiracy theorists believe that this film was an attempt by Kubrick to expose the corruption of the elites and that it cost him his life.

exploration was a renewal of millenarianism in the conspiratorial wing of the counter-culture.

2012 Mayan Prediction and the Rise of the Flat-Earthers

Erik Davis traces the interest in the date December 21, 2012 to the research and writings of the McKenna brothers; noting the synchronicity of Dennis McKenna's memoir, *The Brotherhood of the Screaming Abyss: My Life with Terrence McKenna* being published in 2012, the same year that his deceased brother had predicted would be the year of the "apocalyptic culmination."[490]

The date, 12/21/2012, which was supposedly imbued with numerological significance, was said to be the last day of the Mayan calendar. Or at least that was the narrative let loose upon the public, accompanied by a big-budget Hollywood movie, of course. Not everyone predicted doom and gloom, however, as some new agey Burning Man types predicted a "revolution in consciousness, man." Whether or not this revolution occurred is up to the reader. What we do know is that 12/21/2012 was less catastrophic than Y2K. Once the world failed to end, the next move was an epistemological deconstruction of one of its most fundamental qualities: its shape.

To get a grip on flat earth theory, the best place to go is the official Flat Earth Society Website. Unlike any other conspiracy theory, which builds up to the pronouncement that you, the citizen, are being deluded by a hoax of varying proportions, The Flat Earth Society announces immediately: "This website is dedicated to unraveling the true mysteries of the universe and demonstrating that the earth is flat and that Round Earth doctrine is little more than an elaborate hoax."[491] This is exactly the right

---

[490] Davis, Erik (2019) *High Weirdness: Drugs, Esoterica, and Visionary Experience in the Seventies.* Strange Attractor Press & the MIT Press. P. 90

[491] https://wiki.tfes.org/The_Flat_Earth_Wiki accessed on 02/27/21

tact you would take if you were challenging one of the most scientifically well-established theories of the last two thousand years. Some of the reasoning put forward by the Flat Earth Society for why they think the earth is flat has to do with empirical data:

> The evidence for a flat earth is derived from many different facets of science and philosophy. The simplest is by relying on one's own senses to discern the true nature of the world around us. The world looks flat, the bottom of clouds are flat, the movement of the sun; these are all examples of your senses telling you that we do not live on a spherical heliocentric world.[492]

Flat Earthers also place a great deal of emphasis on the "Bedford Level Experiment," which "was an experiment performed many times on a six mile stretch of water that proved the surface of the water to be flat. It did not conform to the curvature of the Earth that Round Earth proponents teach."[493] Any argument presented to Flat Earthers that is contingent upon space exploration is ruled as a hoax that arose during the "space race" and is only maintained today because of greed.

Here we have the rise, and seeming replacement, of an older mythologically-based narrative with a scientistic argument. We know that theories of the earth being spherical existed within various communities in ancient times but had fallen out of favor for a flat model during the early age of exploration. Columbus, Marco Polo, and Magellan are the individuals we associate with reviving the prominence of the spherical model. Conspiracy theorists who promote the flat earth model usually do so by way of scientism à la Baigent, Leigh, and Lincoln. In addition to the promotion of this counter-intuitive theory, which they argue is actually perfectly intuitional, they often indulge in a certain

---

[492]Ibid accessed on 03/08/21
[493] Ibid accessed on 03/08/21

amount of fabrication; not unlike the individuals who embellished the narratives surrounding Prester John and his realm.

Outside of proving the theory to a totally incredulous public, the big question plaguing believers in the flat earth conspiracy theory is: If the earth being round is a lie being sold to the public, who benefits from the propagation of this lie? The answer most likely is the government and big business. For the sake of the narrative analysis which we have undertaken, we can discern flat earth narratives as an act taken by the disenchanted with the promise of further space exploration promised by the moon landing or with the failure of any definitive endpoint for the world to come to pass.

The Curse of Oak Island

Each episode of *The Curse of Oak Island* begins with the narrator saying:

> "There is an island in the north Atlantic, where people have been looking for an incredible treasure for more than two hundred years. So far, they have found a stone slab with strange symbols carved into it, mysterious fragments of human bone and a lead cross whose origin may stretch back to the knights Templar. To date, six men have died trying to solve the mystery and according to legend, one more will have to die before the treasure can be found."

In the show's debut episode we learn about how the two protagonists, brothers Rick and Marty Lagina, were drawn to Oak Island because of an article in *Reader's Digest* they read while teenagers describing the exploits of treasure-hunters who had converged on the island for over two hundred years. This article inspired the brothers to form a pact that they would, when older and financially secure, journey to Oak Island and try their hand at finding the elusive treasure.

The early seasons of the show alternated between the team taking pragmatic stabs at finding the treasure via drilling and excavation, as well as hearing out eccentric guests who speculated on the nature of the treasure and the island's history. Many of these guests postulate that it was the Templars who had come to the island, buried their treasure, and set up elaborate traps such as "flood tunnels" to ensure the treasure would be safe. Some of those who propose the Templar theory incorporate Oak Island into the Grail mythos – with some even speculating that the Grail itself is hidden there. This is an interesting return to the "Grail as object" narrative that had been supplanted by the post-modern "Grail as bloodline" narrative. However, it must be said that this is a rare speculation, as the mythical object most often brought up (on the show) in conjunction with the Templars is the Ark of the Covenant, which some speculate was found by the Templars in Solomon's Temple.

The story of Oak Island begins when three boys named Daniel McGinnis, John Smith and Anthony Vaughn began digging at a depression in the ground at the Island, after seeing strange lights there. They initially believed they would find Captain Kidd's treasure. Every ten feet of digging revealed a platform made of oak logs. At ninety feet there was a stone slab with strange engravings, and after this stone was removed the shaft they were digging was flooded with sea water diverted by a tunnel, causing the initial excavation to be called off. This, however, did not deter other treasure hunters from excavating on the island, most of which came up empty-handed. Later episodes of the show featured McGinnis's descendants who visited the Lagina crew and revealed that the boys had unearthed a few treasure chests. For most skeptics, this treasure was all that was on the island.

Rick and Marty are true believers and as such they get sucked into every tangentially related conspiracy theory, from ancient Hebrews bringing treasure to the island thousands of years ago, to Templars fleeing persecution landing on the island. There has been evidence found by the Lagina crew to indicate the presence of both Spanish and French troops at various points in the island's history. The discussion of the Templars, though, has at times diverted the quest down more esoteric avenues, such as Rosslyn Chapel and the links between the rites of the Templars and Freemasons.

The explicit connection between Freemasons and the Oak Island narrative occurs by way of historian James McQuiston, who argues that the connection between the remnants of the Knights Templar and Freemasonry in Canada began in the early seventeenth century. Founded in 1625 by Sir William Alexander, the Order of the Knights Baronet began settling in Nova Scotia not long after their formation, in order, McQuiston claims, to establish a refuge for Templar descendants and to transport treasure to Oak Island. The riches they guarded were intended to be buried and booby-trapped.

The connection with Masonry goes deeper. Not only was Sir William Alexander a Freemason, but so were some of the most famous explorers of the island: Daniel McGinnis, M.R. Chapel, and Franklin Delano Roosevelt. Hence, the story that three boys, who in 1795 landed on Oak Island after seeing strange lights and began digging what would be the original "Money Pit," might be a cover story for something more esoteric. According to McQuiston, the initial search was directed by Masonic symbols that the three boys saw carved onto nearby trees.[494]

Another theory pertaining to Masonry to which the show has returned a few times is that Francis Bacon (January 22, 1561 – April 9, 1626) might have either planned the elaborate booby-traps on the island, or under the guise of his *nom de plume* "William Shakespeare" hid clues to the location of the Templar treasure on the island in his plays. Tied to this theory is speculation that some of "Shakespeare's" plays might be buried alongside the treasure. The inclusion of Francis Bacon is interesting because it unwittingly invokes the work of Ignatius Donnelly, who played a pivotal role in promoting the theory that Bacon had secretly authored Shakespeare's plays. Let's briefly

[494] Episode "Surely Templar" (Season seven, Episode fifteen)

examine Bacon's relationship with Freemasonry. In his account of the Craft, Millar writes:

> Francis Bacon, whose ideas were the inspiration for the Royal Society, wrote one work that has been considered as having influenced Freemasonry, especially perhaps in regard to its conception of Solomon's Temple, though not specifically its plan. This was his *A New Atlantis*, published posthumously only a year after the author's death in 1627. Not entirely without justification, Francis Yates compares the work to the Rosicrucian manifestos, as she compares the English Baconian movement of learning or science to the Rosicrucianism of Germany. *A New Atlantis* is a story of a ship and its crew that land off the shore of an island called Bensalem. The crew is eventually allowed to land, after some initial skepticism by the islanders as to the character, if not the religious persuasion, of the strangers. The sailors are admitted, however, when they disclose that they are Christians and swear "by the merits of the Savior" that neither are they pirates nor have they spilled blood unlawfully. While the story itself is not especially important, one motif appears that is perhaps relevant. At the heart, or "eye," of the kingdom is a Society of Salomon's (i.e., Solomon's) House, which apparently knows a type of Christian Kabbalah –Christianity being the religion of the island's majority, though we are also told that some Jews live on the island. As it would appear that precious little has not been considered to be the origin of Freemasonry, we might remark in passing that Francis Bacon has been thought its inventor, though this theory has been largely rejected by Masonic scholars. If *A New Atlantis* contributes

anything to our study, it is simply that it illustrates that the Temple had been adopted into Christian intellectualism.[495]

There are a variety of things going on here. First, there is Bacon's reiteration of the Atlantis mythos in his utopian novel. Second, interestingly, the island is called "Bensalem." The root "Salem" is an important reoccurring theme since Melchizedek was "the King of Salem." Third, the native people encountered are linked to the legacy of King Solomon, which was a historical facet of the Ethiopian Prester John narrative. And lastly, because the "Chapel Vault," which is said to lie deep within the original Money Pit, and for which the Oak Island team is in constant search, the place that promises to be the key that will unlock the secrets of the island, is, if not a reiteration of the Masonic Temple, which itself was a reiteration of Solomon's Temple (or a simulacrum, if you will) then an interpolation of the Temple narrative into this particular quest.

The inclusion of the Templar narratives (as a conspiracy trope) and the Francis Bacon narratives into *The Curse of Oak Island* seems to suggest that even modern phenomena, when inspected intensively by our current forms of media, can still (or must) retain a mythic gravity that pulls older more established myths and conspiracy theories into their orbit. It seems as if this "narrative gravity" could wholly, or at least partially, account for the process we have been calling "remystification."

Part of this process of remystification, which *The Curse of Oak Island* reiterates, is the conspiratorial narrative that people in the past were more competent or even capable of fantastic feats that we can neither duplicate nor often comprehend. We saw this in some of the narratives surrounding Atlantis and Lemuria and it comes to the forefront frequently in *The Curse of Oak Island*. Take for example the "Alignment" episode, aired on 12/01/2020,

---

[495] Millar, Angel (2005) *Freemasonry: A History*. Thunder Bay Press. P. 106

which begins its dive into the more arcane aspects of what planning might have been undertaken to create the Oak Island mystery by reviewing Poussin's "The Arcadian Shepherds." The analyses begins by superimposing a pentacle over the painting and conjecturing that this five-pointed star is essentially a treasure map that, when superimposed over the part of Oak Island referred to as "Nolan's Cross," matches up with some of the man-made as well as natural monuments there.[496]

The researchers consulted by the Lagina brothers on this episode are Corjan Mol and Chris Morford. Mol and Morford claim that, using Google Maps, they found that the head of Nolan's Cross forms a straight line leading directly to the Palace of Versailles. They then claim that a perfect line from the Palace of Versailles leads to the site of the original Temple of Solomon, thus connecting all three sites. This speculation resolves itself with Mol claiming that the Templars had conceived of an arch from the Temple of Solomon to Oak Island, and that the artifacts the Templars found beneath the Temple of Solomon were transported to Oak Island and other parts of North America.

There's probably a lot of scientific or conspiratorial analysis a well-educated person could come up with as it pertains to this story. I only have two points, one of which corresponds with the discussion of ley lines that we will discuss in the next chapter. Without getting too deep, the idea behind the concept of ley lines is that there are alignments occurring between various historic structures and prominent landmarks. The twist I see *The Curse of Oak Island* enacting is that the lines upon which Nolan's Cross, the Palace of Versailles, and the Temple of Solomon might lie are, according to this theory, man-made. Obviously some more enlightened soul could come in and say that the Templars used their arcane powers to discover some sort of sacred geometry

---

[496] As the reader will recall, the superimposing of the geometrical shapes in this painting over the landscape of Rennes-le-Château was a key part of the post-modern interpretation of the Grail mythos.

encoded into the earth, but for now, the theorization is at the practical/symbolic stage.

The other point is more of a sociological observation about how the Oak Island team is divided into two groups, one of which is the true believers (who are eager to incorporate any theory into their quest, especially if it makes the whole enterprise more mystifying; Rick Laginas falls into this category). The other group amongst the "Brotherhood of the Dig" is the guys who pay lip-service to the conspiracy theories and hope they might in some way help the discovery process. Unconsciously, however, they most likely suspect that the occult/conspiratorial theorization will derail the whole enterprise. It could do so in one of two ways: 1) failing, like most conspiratorially related endeavors do, or 2) marking the whole adventure as being "weird."

There is a fine line between practical action and mystical mumbo jumbo to maintain in such quests. I know that my general tone is more lenient towards the mumbo jumbo narratives, but this leniency revolves around them as being essentially a kind of literature. One can ascribe to narratives about Noah's Ark, and one can try to locate where such an ark might be in today's world using scripture, but there isn't a practical sensibility available to the literature surrounding mysticism, occultism, etc. that would lead to any discoveries with a real-world, practical sense of significance. That inherent fantastic sensibility is what makes these narratives literature. This seems to fly in the face of what I have been arguing so far, which is that the structure of our worlds has been textually constructed, but we must keep in mind that there is a difference between narratives and texts, slowly and organically forming a society, and seizing upon some text and trying to impose it onto the "existing" world in a way that conclusively vindicates said text's literal import. That's not to say that the latter is impossible, however, there is a far greater chance that the willful individual, or group trying to impose this text, will unwittingly participate in yet another chapter of the myth –but not the *final* chapter on the topic, or possibly a new myth altogether.

In this chapter we have discussed unknown parts of the world in the Heideggerian sense of places toward which we direct our care, our sense of curiosity, and the interconnectedness that pertains to these concepts. The Prester John myth, Hyperborea, and even the flat/hollow earth are all subjects we can track down in a relatively traditional way. By this I mean, we draw on books and websites for information and these sources carry narratives with them. *The Curse of Oak Island* is a little bit different because it is a current, ongoing, episodic series dedicated to unearthing a buried treasure. This particular treatment ratchets up our sense of engagement because it makes it seem like a definitive answer will, or at least can be, achieved any day now.

This is different from the flat earth enthusiast who most likely assumes that even if the "facts" disproving the earth's spherical nature were to be widely disseminated, a public consensus on the issue would still be forcibly suppressed. The fact that *The Curse of Oak Island* is being televised gives the impression that the powers that be (whoever they are) are not working to suppress this information. It's almost as if the forces of hyperreality are now working in concert with conspiracy theorists to uncover the truth, if only for the sake of serialized entertainment.

Does this enabling weaken the narrative strength of this particular conspiracy theory? It seems just as likely that the Oak Island guys will find mythic treasure as scientists will discover that the earth is actually flat. I'm not being dismissive like some bloggers and critics have been, as there's a more nuanced distinction between these two. Maybe a closer connection would be that in some ways, the cynical attitude directed towards the *Curse of Oak Island* audience is a replica of E. F. Bleiler's attitude when writing about Ignatius Donnelly, insofar as it posits the viewers as judging the past from an objective point of scientific certainty. This assumes that the scientific mentality which analyzes events is itself immune to the contingencies of history itself. This was one of Heidegger's complaints about science: that it granted itself an Archimedean point of certainty from which a species of worldly phenomenon could be judged.

This is not the case, since bloggers like Sean Munger (who also claims to be a motivational speaker) are hell-bent on discrediting Rick and Marty's valiant quest to unearth the buried treasure, and professional writers Randall Sullivan and D'Arcy O'Connor vie with each other over who will document this search from its beginnings in the eighteenth century to its modern-day (fingers-crossed) conclusion. With these individuals circling around this story can we really assume that the Oak Island excavators are penetrating some rarified air of the distant past?

The fact that the show is televised is probably the greatest factor in making it seem as if the Lagina brothers are trying to seize upon some text and impose it onto the "existing" world in a self-fulfilling way, and this it seems is an issue that is contingent upon the medium. Very soon we will begin to see how the medium of the media has played a significant role in weakening the power of myth in our society. Outside of this, there is a moral value that I see pertaining to the show, which is that *The Curse of Oak Island* shows a group of men engaging with archaeologists and other scientists. They come from many different walks of life, but they work and speculate together amid a job site. There is a certain classic American charm attendant to seeing these men out of their professional elements and engaging in a collaborative treasure hunt. This is the kind of adventure individuals were offered fifty or a hundred years ago when they went recreationally mining, exploring, hunting, or building something on their property. It doesn't have the Puritanical imperative of "work" that is one of the defining characteristics of American culture. The men on the show are mining an endangered trope and there is a certain wholesome quality to this endeavor that is out of place in our current cultural milieu.

Chapter Eight: The Significance of Monuments

Unlike in the other chapters, the protagonists, if we can call them that, in this one are inanimate objects. There is a certain crossover between the subjects discussed here and sacred objects like the Grail or the Emerald Tablet, secret societies, and the degree to which the world is known. Even though texts pertaining to these artifacts will be discussed, to a larger extent we will have to look beyond those narratives towards the objects themselves and read them as texts. The trajectory of this chapter might not be perfectly linear time-wise, but it does move us from the ancient and obscure to the modern and hyperreal.

The Pyramids

The Egyptian pyramids, along with the Great Sphinx, of Giza don't really need any introduction, as not only are they of great historical and architectural significance, but any conspiracy theory worth its salt incorporates these structures into its narrative. We've already gone over the narrative that Enoch of Cain was not only responsible for the invention of hieroglyphics but masterminded the building of the pyramids. Both Wayne and his nemeses Knight and Lomas indulge in compound theorization by speculating that Enoch had stored a vast library under the Great Pyramid and that the three largest pyramids (Menkaure, Khafre, and Khufu) line up with the three stars in Orion's Belt.

In conjunction with this, Knight and Lomas speculate that ancient people might have considered the "Nephilim" as visitors from the Orion constellation[497] and Wayne further compounds his theory by claiming that one of the Watchers, "Shemyaza" (who may be another name for the head Watcher, Azazel), "somehow repented from his sins but could not face God; he hung himself

---

[497] Knight, Christopher & Lomas, Robert (2001) *Uriel's Machine.* Fair Winds Press. P. 137

between heaven and earth (on Orion)."[498] This would explain why Enoch of Cain, who according to Wayne shrouded his idolatrous and pantheistic rituals in symbolism, set these pyramids to align with his fallen deity.

The theory that the stars in Orion's Belt match up with the pyramids, or the "Orion Correlation Theory" as it is known to conspiracy theorists, was first put forward by Robert Bauval in the *Discussions in Egyptology* Journal Volume 13.[499] This theory was taken up and popularized by Graham Hancock in *Fingerprints of the Gods*, published in 1995. This heavily contested theory is usually promoted by conspiracy theorists in conjunction with speculation that the measurements correspond with ancient, Hermetic axioms; as exemplified by John Michell's declaration that "The side of the base and the height [are in] the ratio of 8:5 [cubits], the harmonious proportion known as the golden mean, providing the first of several examples of this relationship in the Great Pyramid's measurements." These measurements, he claims, can also be achieved through a "cabalistic reduction."[500]

The ancient Egypt narrative, as it is currently understood, begins with Arab explorers, who, in the seventh century came across the pyramids and Sphinx. These explorers marveled at the hieroglyphic inscriptions, many of which dealt with the mummification process, and believed that they either indicated a great treasure hidden inside, or the possibility that the hieroglyphics offered a magical system that allowed for the creation of such treasure.[501]

[498] Wayne, Gary (2014) *The Genesis 6 Conspiracy*. Trusted Books, A Division of Deep River Books. P. 91
[499] https://en.m.wikipedia.org/wiki/Orion_correlation_theory accessed on 04/29/20
[500] Michell, John (1972) *The View Over Atlantis*. Ballantine Books. P. 96
[501] Moench, Doug (1997) *The Big Book of the Unexplained*. Paradox Press. P. 147. It is also speculated that the word "Alchemy" is derived from the old Arab word for "Egypt," which is

Hermeneutically-speaking, we in the West have been inculcated with the belief that the pyramids were built by the Hebrews during their time of captivity in Egypt; a trope that has been reiterated in everything from Cecil B. De Mille's *Ten Commandments* to *The Simpsons*. Historically-speaking, however, most experts on the subject claim that the pyramids were built primarily by Egyptian citizens – many of which were skilled builders and laborers, not slaves. [502] The architectural and geometrical aspects of the pyramids have been obsessed over for centuries, John Michell writes:

> Five thousand years ago, they believed, only God himself could have planned the Pyramid's height exactly equal to a thousand millionth part of the mean distance between the earth and the sun, or contrived its weight to be that of the earth divided by a thousand billion. Piazzi Smyth observed the relationship between the Pyramid's height and the perimeter of its base, the first being equal to the radius of a circle of which the second is the circumference. He plotted the intricate geometry of the inner halls and galleries and the astronomical significance of their sloping angles.[503]

Ascertaining the geometrical complexities of the pyramids can be a daunting task, possibly *too* daunting, as Michell points out that: "Gradually the whole subject of the Pyramid and its measurements fell into the hands of fanatics and consequently,

---

"Keme" because the seventh century Arab explorers' term for this magical Egyptian mode of transmutation was "Al Keme."
[502] https://harvardmagazine.com/2003/07/who-built-the-pyramids-html accessed on 03/13/21
[503] Michell, John (1972) *The View Over Atlantis*. Ballantine Books. P. 91

into general disrepute."[504] You'll recall that in our discussion of
Lemuria and Atlantis I stated that arguments about the wonders
of the ancient world usually fall into one of two camps: "Ancient
Aliens," or the utilization of secret electromagnetic hotspots on
the earth's surface, i.e. Ley Lines; this bifurcation holds here as
well.[505] John Michell was a British writer who initially subscribed
to the idea that Ley Lines were forged into the earth by
extraterrestrials. However, by the time of his most famous work,
The View Over Atlantis, published in 1971, he had largely
abandoned this view and had moved onto the "purer" form of Ley
Line theorization, which is sometimes referred to, in general
terms, as "Earth Mysteries."[506]

In this chapter we have moved from the conjectured
technology and artifacts of explicitly mythic realms, such as
Atlantis or Hyperborea to concrete artifacts of prehistoric
civilization. However, the two (or three, if you count the "religious
argument" which incorporates fallen angels, as being wholly
heterogeneous) options of theorization still stand. The "Ancient
Aliens" argument does not really need any profound explication
here, beyond the supposition, "Aliens did it." Therefore, in this
section we will focus more on the Earth Mysteries' analysis.
Michell's argument, in a strong sense dovetails with one of the
premises presented in *The Curse of Oak Island*, i.e., the brilliance

---

[504] Ibid p. 92

[505] Note that arguments involving the Nephilim, secret societies,
and the "seven sacred sciences" can fall into either camp,
however, from a purely religious standpoint, can also be argued
on their own terms. I would call these arguments, whether they
appear in secular Grail studies, Hermeticism, or Evangelical
Christianity the "religious argument." In such cases, this would
count as a third option.

[506] It should be noted that the "Orion Correlation Theory" can
subsist within either camp: either aliens set the pyramids to
match up with Orion's Belt, or the Ley Lines exist in some sort of
accord with astrological patterns.

and ingenuity of people who existed hundreds (or possibly thousands) of years ago. This brilliance and ingenuity, in one sense is akin to the sense of wonder we might have for the Sistine Chapel; but it also has an uncanny aspect, in that it was a brilliance that lies hidden (either from plain sight or in the distant past) and which defies our imagination in some respect. On Michell's more naturalistic view, earlier peoples might have had greater facility operating within the Ley Lines because they were less enveloped within the facets of civilization, which today we associate with modernity, or technology, and understood nature better. Tacitly implied within this view is the idea that there is something about technology that is a brutal contravening of the natural order.

This sense of transgression is compounded if we consider the idea of a metaphysical punishment that awaits those who violate sacred spaces. *The Curse of Oak Island*, with its foreboding tagline, "To date, six men have died trying to solve the mystery and according to legend, one more will have to die before the treasure can be found," is a reiteration of an important facet of the pyramid narrative: curses.

Everyone is familiar with the Mummy as a horror movie icon and the idea of the "Mummy's curse" but not many people know the historical precedent on which the fiction is based.

On February 17, 1923, archaeologist Howard Carter, his patron, Lord George E.S.M. Herbert, and their crew breached the inner sanctum of Tutankhamun (King Tut). In the process of removing the treasures they found amassed there, a mosquito bit Lord Carnarvon's cheek. Within a few weeks of this momentous day, Carnarvon's bite had become infected, and he would die of pneumonia in his Cairo hotel room on April 5, 1923.[507]

Around the time following the excavation there had been a great deal of speculation in the tabloid press about the possibility that these Egyptian tombs were cursed –the fact that after

---

[507] Moench, Doug (1997) *The Big Book of the Unexplained.* Paradox Press. Pp. 149 - 150

Carnarvan's passing there was found to be a blemish on the cheek of Tutankhamun's mummified body, in the same place where Carnarvan had received his mosquito bite, only fueled this speculation.[508] A variety of deaths would follow: Professors Breasted and LaFleur died after visiting the tomb, as well as the millionaire George Jay Gould and a variety of assistants, nurses, and secretaries who were attached to the initial archeological expedition, a total of **23** people linked to the breach of the tomb died.[509] Out of this madness came the iconic Universal films, wherein the Mummy would go on to join the ranks of Dracula, Frankenstein, and the Wolfman.

Before we move on, let's take a bit of a philosophical look at what the Mummy represents within the Egyptian narrative. Jacques Derrida saw the significance of fictional monsters, such as the Mummy, as figures that pertain to the undecidability of classification; we have no problem classifying the Mummy as a zombie, or a "proto-zombie" in the discourse of film, but for Derrida, such a figure is both fascinating and horrific in that it contaminates our systems of order – it cannot be killed, it has to be resolved categorically, but this resolution might be impermanent and hence undecidability might be a consistent and unavoidable feature of our existence.[510] We can also think of the Mummy in Lacanian terms as a "partial object" occurring in popular culture that metonymically refers to the larger, more complex ancient Egyptian narrative.

But maybe that isn't enough for a book about conspiracy theories. Perhaps we must dig up something even more esoteric and bizarre? In a section that, in some ways, reiterates the

---

[508] Wayne, Gary (2014) *The Genesis 6 Conspiracy*. Trusted Books, A Division of Deep River Books. P. 150
[509] Moench, Doug (1997) *The Big Book of the Unexplained*. Paradox Press. Pp. 150 – 151. The number "23" is a significant number to occultists and conspiracy theorists for myriad reasons.
[510] Collins, Jeff (2011) *Introducing Derrida*. Icon Books. P. 17

transubstantiation narrative, Peter Moon describes the harvesting and consumption of mummies:

> Around the year 1400 AD, the Latin word *mummia* started to appear in English writings. Mummia actually means "mummy powder" which began to find popular use in the early 1200s as a cure-all medicinal powder. Shakespeare wrote about it, and Francis Bacon recommended it "for the staunching of the blood." Most physicians prescribed it as a potent cure for different diseases. As the centuries moved on, there was a major run on mummies. The Egyptians finally cracked down on the practice. They not only wanted to preserve their antiquities but their own use of mummy dust as well.[511]

At least Moon did not conflate Shakespeare and Francis Bacon – which is no small feat! I have not classified Moon as conforming to any of the three explanatory traditions because his writing is a sort of smorgasbord of every different approach and theory you could imagine. The "mummy dust" is significant for him because it relates to one of the two mysterious substances that he incorporates into his narrative. In this case, the substance in question is "occultum" which was utilized by the "Elder Gods" to achieve self-awareness when they first arrived here from Mars.[512]

Returning to earth, the idea of a curse, especially when attached to a tomb, could be seen as a literal explication of a metaphysical fear or terror. The semantic nature attendant to this, as it pertains to Ley Lines and how the geometrical figures incorporated into the measurements of these buildings and monuments are derived from numbers that refer to "mystical

---

[511] Moon, Peter (2003) *The Black Sun: Montauk's Nazi-Tibetan Connection*. Sky Books. P. 262

[512] The other mysterious substance is "Thulium" and we will discuss Moon's analysis of it in the next chapter.

concepts," is addressed by Michell in an uncannily structuralist analysis:

> It is recognized that several near eastern languages, notably those of the Egyptians, Greeks and Hebrews, were adapted for literary use according to the rules of cabalistic geometry. In early times, before the spread of secular literacy had hastened the collapse of the old civilization, the use of letters was reserved for scientific or sacred purposes. The Druids rejected common writing and, according to Caesar, adopted the letters of the Greek alphabet as a medium for divination and philosophical expression.[513]

This seems to add a degree of confirmation to the notion that there is a similarity, or kinship, between Hermeticism and Structuralism. Being a proponent of the Hermetic transmission theory, Gary Wayne, however, does not directly address Ley Lines or the Earth Mysteries school of thought; on the subject of ancient Egypt he cites authors like Hancock and G.I. Gurdjieff in his assertion that denizens of Atlantis were responsible for building the pyramids and the Great Sphinx.[514] Any actuality attendant to this claim is not Wayne's primary concern; his primary argument is that Enoch of Cain is responsible for the building of the pyramids and that they are physical manifestations of the "spurious" seven sciences.

The next part of Wayne's assertion relates to the idea of the pyramids and the Sphinx as being remnants of "an advanced civilization that became mad with knowledge and power."[515] This

---

[513] Michell, John (1972) *The View Over Atlantis*. Ballantine Books. P. 123
[514] Wayne, Gary (2014) *The Genesis 6 Conspiracy*. Trusted Books, A Division of Deep River Books. P. 138
[515] Ibid, p. 138

relates directly to our present discussion of monuments because it is not a conventional, or even intuitive interpretation of these awe-inspiring monuments. It is fair to say that most people look at the pyramids and their imaginations are dazzled by the civilization that crafted these remarkable structures. Just like the rest of the monuments in this chapter, the fact that we don't have an identifiable unbroken historical knowledge back to the time of their creation, and can only recreate the culture piecemeal, is a concrete (pun intended) metaphor for the transition in human consciousness wherein humans became historically aware of their development and place in history.

This phenomenon was the subject of our discussion of the fall from Eden, in which humanity left a timeless golden childhood and entered stages of painful adulthood. All of the monuments in this chapter are remnants of that lost early period of humanity and just as the subject of psychoanalysis, or even nostalgia, spins webs of conjecture as to how past events "really were" or how they arose, the same is true for the archaeologist or conspiracy theorist that incorporates these objects into the web of their theory. Wayne's approach is interesting because, unlike his peers, he has a decidedly more hostile view; to him these monuments are awe-inspiring artifacts of an alien and immoral culture that had rebelled against God. Even though his project is one of demystification, and revolves around seeking a historical thread back to the opening of Genesis, all the objects and narratives he incorporates are mystically charged; and it is his ideology that compels him to denounce them as remnants of a cursed path of deviation from God's will.

The Sphinx

Closely related to the pyramids is the Sphinx, a giant limestone statue on the Giza Plateau. Taken on its own, let alone in conjunction with the pyramids, the Sphinx is a profoundly enigmatic object. We've already discussed the mythical aspect of the Sphinx as a character, as it pertains to the Oedipus narrative, and it's not guaranteed that the famous sculpture was intended to be a representation of that creature. The face of the statue is indeed human, many have argued that the body is that of a lion, Robert Temple argues against this, claiming that the body does not fit other Egyptian depictions of lions, and is more likely that of a hound, specifically the god Anubis.[516]

Robert Temple is basically an "Ancient Aliens" researcher and writer. His breakthrough book, *The Sirius Mystery*, first published in 1976, had a big impact on Robert Anton Wilson's *Cosmic Trigger I* and was designated by Michael Hoffman II as one of the books that the "cryptocracy" allowed to be published:

> Two books by the English writer and *Ordo Templi Orientis* (OTO) initiate Kenneth Grant, the previously cited *Magical Revival* and *Aleister Crowley and the Hidden God* and another by the aforementioned Robert K.G. Temple, *The Sirius Mystery*, revealed secrets of the highest magnitude which have been vigorously protected and hidden at some cost to human life for centuries and in the case of Temple's book, millennia. These books were published with the knowledge and approval of the masonic-Hermetic heirs to this knowledge.[517]

Hoffman's argument, as it appears in *Secret Societies and Psychological Warfare*, is directed more at Temple because he eulogizes the " Hermetic Academy," i.e., the unbroken chain, or Hermetic transmission, of occult knowledge that supposedly traces back as far as Pythagoras (if not farther). Throughout the introduction Temple maintains that, despite his adherence to Ancient Aliens theorization, he is trying to present evidence in an

---

[516] Temple, Robert (1998) *The Sirius Mystery*. Destiny Books. P. 12
[517] Hoffman II, Michael A. (2009) *Secret Societies and Psychological Warfare* (Sixth Printing) Independent History and Research. P. 52

objective (and of course) scientifically respectable manner. His discussion of the Sphinx is primarily focused on the claim that the statue has weathered undue water erosion. Most conspiracy theorists who tackle this subject use it as a springboard to claim, as Temple does, that the Sphinx was built (or instigated) by extraterrestrials. To this extent, he explicitly states:

> In my view, there was ancient extraterrestrial contact with Earth. And I believe that the period of interaction with extraterrestrials and the founding of Egyptian and Sumerian civilization with their help probably fell between 5000 and 3000 BC. We can call the time of this interaction, whenever it was, the Contact Period. I believe that the pyramids and the Sphinx were probably built by the extraterrestrials themselves during the Contact Period [...][518]

Temple claims that the competing arguments, which could be classified as either the result of a manipulation of construction conducted according to Ley Lines or the transmission of a secret and esoteric knowledge transmitted hermetically from Atlantis to Sumeria then Egypt, do not hold the same explanatory value as the Ancient Aliens argument.[519] In his argumentation, Temple is more concerned with addressing a purer interpretation of the

---

[518] Temple, Robert (1998) *The Sirius Mystery*. Destiny Books. P. 14
[519] As I said before, the hermetic transmission theory can be conjoined with either the Ancient Aliens theory or the Earth Mysteries theory. Michells conjoins it with the latter: "The existence of similar and highly developed cosmologies in such widely separated countries as Egypt, China and Mexico implies that all the great civilizations of our era derived from a common source, from some greater tradition, of which each preserved certain relics." Michell, John (1972) *The View Over Atlantis*. Ballantine Books. P. 124

Hermetic argument than the Earth Mysteries argument, and he designates John Anthony West as a key proponent of it.[520]

Temple calls West's argument the "Atlantis Hypothesis" and puts its central argument as being: The amount of water erosion on the Sphinx most likely backdates it to being roughly 12,500 years old because the water erosion would have occurred when the climate was different and there was significant rainfall in the area. Not subscribing to the "Contact Period" theory, West therefore claims the pyramids and the Sphinx were most likely constructed by immigrants who had fled Atlantis after the cataclysm. Though Temple does not name them, this "Atlantis Hypothesis" pretty much lines up with the more anthropocentric theories of Knight and Lomas, as well as Joseph Frank.[521]

Temple counters this line of argumentation by postulating that the pit in which the Sphinx resides was once filled with water. In this regard he extensively cites Herodotus's *Histories*, concluding that:

> From all these passages we can see quite clearly that in the fifth century BC, when Herodotus was an eye-witness, large stretches of water were far more important in Egypt than we assume today. The amazing account of the Great Labyrinth, of the three unidentified pyramids of considerable size adjoining it, and of the artificial lake [all described by Herodotus in passages excerpted by Temple] are

---

[520] Note that there are Ancient Aliens theorists who believe that extraterrestrials built the Sphinx and pyramids 10,000+ years ago.

[521] In some ways it coincides with Gary Wayne's theories, however, since Wayne subscribes to a Biblical timeline he probably would not date the building of the Sphinx and pyramids as far back as 10,000 BC. Also, Wayne would posit the influence of Nephilim, or the Nephilim-worshipping Enoch of Cain as a significant factor in the process.

astonishing in themselves, and have never been satisfactorily explained to my knowledge. Certainly the huge artificial lake sounds like a very good base for visiting amphibians, and is the sort of thing amphibians rather than men would have constructed.[522]

And there you have it: amphibian extraterrestrials from the Sirius system built the Sphinx in the midst of a water park. Most likely they gave the Sphinx a dog's body because Sirius is the "Dog Star" (though Temple doesn't make much hay of this possibility). Michael Hoffman was scandalized, but what can we make of this narrative? Surely the claim that the photographed image of a face taken by NASA's Viking Mars Mission on the red planet's surface bares a strong resemblance to the face of the Sphinx[523] is a more compelling Ancient Aliens argument? Temple is mute on this topic.

We will circle back to Temple's work in our discussion of Robert Anton Wilson. The most interesting development that we have unfolded here is the already established narrative that there has been a Hermetic transmission of secret knowledge – with the added twist that it was imported to earth by explicitly rendered extraterrestrials, as opposed to fallen angels or Nephilim that might be mistaken for extraterrestrials. This development, championed by Temple, is analogous to the post-modern Grail narrative, which arose at the same time as *The Sirius Mystery*, in that both are fantastic, pseudoscientific theories that utilized the air of science available to them at the time to carry-forward essentially mythic narratives. However, in the spirit of Derridian deconstruction, we can suspect that such an invocation of "science" is likely to contaminate, or poison the subject matter. Though, it might not be a deadly poisoning, it is more likely just a

[522] Temple, Robert (1998) *The Sirius Mystery*. Destiny Books. P. 19
[523] Moench, Doug (1995) *The Big Book of Conspiracies*. Paradox Press. Pp. 55- 56

further step down the road of quantification and demystification, leading inevitably to the hyperreal state in which we now dwell.

Stonehenge

In this section we're going to wrap up the topic of ancient monuments with what is probably the most famous prehistoric structure in Europe, Stonehenge. Most researchers date construction on the megalith at around 3000 BC and though there is a degree of Ancient Alien theorization surrounding it, most speculation has occurred in the Earth Mysteries' camp. Michell lays out his conception of the underlying forces at work in the English countryside, and in doing so appeals to scientism:

> We know that the whole surface of the earth is washed by a flow of energy known as the magnetic field. Like all other heavenly bodies, the earth is a great magnet, the strength and direction of its currents influenced by many factors including the proximity and relative positions of the other spheres in the solar system, chiefly the sun and moon. Other influences on the strength and activity of the magnetic current derive from the composition of the ground over which it passes. Over firm, flat country it is placid and regular, while over rocky, broken land it becomes violent and disturbed, reacting with the elements to cause magnetic storms and, in northern regions, auroras and polar lights.[524]

Notice that this reference to Earth acting like a magnet, implicitly contradicts the hollow earth theories we discussed in the last chapter, insofar as the electromagnetic current "bursts up

---

[524] Michell, John (1972) *The View Over Atlantis*. Ballantine Books. P. 70

through the earth's crust,"[525] implying that there is a molten core at the center of the planet – not nothing. Most researchers, conspiracy-oriented or not, believe Stonehenge served an astronomical purpose for the ancients who built and utilized it, Michell states: "That Stonehenge is dedicated above all to the Sun there has never been any doubt."[526] This theory conforms to Wayne's frequent characterization of Enoch of Cain's descendants/adherents being "idolatrous sun-worshippers."

The site as we know it today is not nearly as orderly and precisely constructed as it was in its hey-day – many of the pieces have been knocked over or removed. Nevertheless, it is a remarkable monument:

> Stonehenge is built primarily of bluestone, a type of blue-tinted dolerite, and sarsen, a variety of sandstone harder than granite. The bluestones, of which there were eighty or more slabs originally, have been traced to a Welsh quarry about 130 miles northwest of Salisbury Plain; the sarsen slabs were brought from the Marlborough Downs, about twenty miles north of the site. Since wheeled vehicles were unknown in Britain during the time of Stonehenge's construction, the long-distance transportation involved in moving these massive rocks –some of them weighing as much as fifty tons- is among the more astonishing feats accomplished by Stonehenge's builders and one that has given rise to many conjectures.[527]

Sometime after 1100 BC the site began to fall into disrepair, it would not be until over 2000 years later that native

---

[525] Ibid p. 71
[526] Ibid p. 131
[527] *Mystic Places: By the Editors of Time-Life Books* (1987) Time Life-Books, P. 82

Britons began speculating that the structure may have been the result of giants or that it somehow fit into the Grail mythos, specifically the claim forwarded by Geoffrey of Monmouth in his *History of the Kings of Britain*, wherein he claims that Stonehenge was commissioned by Aurelius Ambrosius and his brother, Uther Pendragon (King Arthur's father). [528] According to this narrative, Ambrosius wanted to build a monument in honor of his soldiers who had fallen in battle against the Saxons. He consulted Merlin, who suggested that he use the stones from the aforementioned quarries. When Ambrosius's men were unable to move the massive stones, Merlin was employed again to use his magic to whisk the stones onto the troops' ships. Some legends claim that Merlin moved them across the countryside himself, without the use of any of Ambrosius's ships.[529] This legend is why Merlin is closely tied to Stonehenge and it is a legend that is a sort of prequel to the Grail mythos.

The authors of *Mystic Places* cite the primary explanatory theories that we have assessed. They seem to be most intrigued by the Earth Mysteries theory, given that the chapter on Stonehenge opens with the story of an unnamed surveyor who, while pointing a divining rod bent into the shape of an Egyptian ankh at the stones, received a startling revelation:

> The result, he reported later, was both startling and painful: A burning jolt of power surged up his arm, hurling him to the ground and knocking him unconscious. When he came to, he found that his arm was paralyzed; it took six months for him to regain its full use. But the experience had proved something to his satisfaction: The earth energy he had come to discover at Stonehenge was real, and it was not to be trifled with.[530]

---

[528] Ibid p. 82
[529] Ibid pp. 82 - 83
[530] Ibid p. 80

Such claims are right up Michell's alley and he dedicates a whole chapter of *The View over Atlantis* to the significance of the megalith. There is a good deal of mathematics involved in his analysis, which can be read as an appeal to scientific validity; one particular section claims that a hexagonal figure can be superimposed within the outer perimeter of the area (the Aubrey hole circle), and that:

> The circle within the hexagon, corresponding to the Aubrey hole circle, has an area of virtually 6660 square yards. The area of the equilateral triangle with side equal to the diameter of the earthwork circle (320 feet) is 44,400 square feet or 6,000 square MY. These numbers are derived from the square of the Sun, the figure of traditional magic for the control of solar energy, and indicate the former use of Stonehenge for this purpose.[531]

Among his diffuse calculations, Michell claims there are geometrical similarities between Stonehenge, the Great Pyramid of Giza, and the Pyramid of the Sun in Mexico.[532] Despite the correlations we have seen arise between Hermeticism, Structuralism and Earth Mysteries theorization, Michell addresses the Hermeneutical horizon (an awareness of the limits of our understanding, and the extent to which historical knowledge allows these limitations to be bypassed) and how it informs his research:

> To understand Stonehenge we have to look at it with the eyes of those who built it, and to them, as to all the ancient philosophers, the ultimate

---

[531] Michell, John (1972) *The View Over Atlantis*. Ballantine Books. P. 133
[532] Ibid p. 134

purpose was the expression of the universal law within one comprehensive system. The proof of the validity of this system depended upon the degree to which it corresponded with the human appreciation of harmony. Because of the amazing perfection of the concept on which Stonehenge is based, its message can be received by all races and generations and interpreted through all media [...] The pervading spirit of faith and confidence which must have inspired the whole vast undertaking could only have been achieved by men who possessed what they believed to be the secrets of cosmic law.[533]

In hermeneutical studies there is a push-pull relationship between the historical context that marks a work, or text, and the idea that the work was created by an anonymous "knowing subject" who somehow stands outside of time. Often, this latter phenomenon is referred to as "genius" and this passage seems to indicate that it is tied to the understanding of "the secrets of cosmic law." Unlike the explicitly Hermetic connotation that we have seen regarding the transmission of this knowledge, Michell is presenting it here in a universalistic light, in that almost anyone can ascertain or access it.

This is in contradistinction to Knight and Lomas, who dabble in Earth Mysteries theorization by citing Alfred Watkins's 1925 book, *The Old Straight Line*, which specifies the techniques used by Freemasonry to align churches along Ley Lines by planting a post in a fixed line of orientation with the rising sun. Knight and Lomas conclude that: "This shows that old Enochian ideas had survived into Freemasonry"[534] and that this extends to the layout of modern cities, such as Washington DC, as well.

---

[533] Ibid p. 135
[534] Knight, Christopher & Lomas, Robert (2001) *Uriel's Machine.* Fair Winds Press. P. 394

These Enochian ideas are to be understood in terms of esoteric transmission. As it pertains to Stonehenge, Knight and Lomas tie the site to the Grooved Ware People, implying that there is some sort of lineage between them and the Druids, who congregated at various megalithic sites throughout the English countryside.[535]

Knight and Lomas also cite Gerald Hawkins's theory that Stonehenge might have acted as a "complicated computer for predicting lunar and solar eclipses" and attempt to rehabilitate it to the best of their abilities.[536] Such modern projections bring us up to the near-present day.

Georgia Guidestones

The Georgia Guidestones originated in Atlanta Georgia and are best known for their 1986 hit single "Keep Your Hands to Yourself." Wait, that's the Georgia Satellites! The Georgia Guidestones were erected in 1980 in Ebert County, Georgia and consist of four standing stone slabs with a pillar in the middle and a capstone on top. The monument was commissioned in 1979 by a man named "Robert C. Christian" and contains a set of ten guidelines written in English, Spanish, Swahili, Hindi, Hebrew, Arabic, Chinese, and Russian. The ten guidelines are as follows:

1. Maintain humanity under 500,000,000 in perpetual balance with nature.

2. Guide reproduction wisely – improving fitness and diversity.

3. Unite humanity with a living new language.

4. Rule passion – faith – tradition – and all things with tempered reason.

---

[535] Ibid p. 331
[536] Ibid p. 155

5. Protect people with nations with fair laws and just courts.

6. Let all nations rule internally resolving external disputes in a world court.

7. Avoid petty laws and useless officials.

8. Balance personal rights with social duties.

9. Prize truth – beauty – love – seeking harmony with the infinite.

10. Be not a cancer on the earth – leave room for nature – Leave room for nature.

Some conspiracy theorists have suggested that the monument and its commandments are an inversion of the Biblical Ten Commandments and are therefore either Satanic, related to the New World Order, or both. On his television show, *Decoded*, Brad Meltzer proposed that these guidelines were birthed of the Cold War mentality and were intended to instruct the surviving members of humanity after a nuclear holocaust.[537]

Meltzer's hypothesis is hermeneutically sound: he is trying to understand the phenomena within the time it originated. What is interesting in relation to our line of analysis is how the Georgia Guidestones are a modern reiteration of Stonehenge. Perhaps Stonehenge contained writing at some point, but when we think of Stonehenge we do not think of writing, we think of the monument itself. The Georgia Guidestones are tied to their legibility in a literal sense. If we consider the Guidestones as a modern Structuralist rendering of Stonehenge, how do the prescriptions on them relate to the ideologies we have discussed so far?

---

[537] *Brad Meltzer's Decoded*, episode 110 (air date: February 3, 2011).

The first guideline, "Maintain humanity under 500,000,000 in perpetual balance with nature," relates to the Rosicrucians' concern regarding over-population and scarcity of resources.[538] The second guideline, which expands on the first one, is a more explicit invocation of eugenics – a topic of concern for most people, especially conspiracy theorists.

The idea of uniting "humanity with a living new language" might be a reference to Esperanto, an artificial language constructed in 1887 that didn't really catch on, and can be read as an indication of a globalist agenda. What's interesting about this guideline, which moves us progressively closer to the modern, is that it adheres to a somewhat Structuralist notion: that language conditions culture.

The fourth guideline, which instructs its adherents to "Rule passion – faith – tradition – and all things with tempered reason" is directly linked to Kantian ethics and Enlightenment ideals. Given the criticism that we've seen writers, such as John Robison, direct at the Illuminati for injecting Enlightenment ideas into Freemasonry, we can connect the ethos of this statement to that conspiratorial narrative. Guidelines five and six can be read as pushing for a "world court" which might entail a world government, or a greater degree of power being granted to the United Nations.

Guideline seven: "Avoid petty laws and useless officials" is the oddball here, in that it is a criticism of bureaucracy; the bureaucratic structure of society has been a consistent bugaboo of people (nationalists, conspiracy theorists, etc.) who would be alarmed by the Georgia Guidestones' proclamations. Number eight is innocuous, while number nine, "Prize truth – beauty – love – seeking harmony with the infinite," seems to point towards the Masonic idea of a great architect who constructed the universe with symmetry and precision. It could also point towards the more impersonal notion of a "cosmic law" as

[538] Schrödter, Willy (1992) *A Rosicrucian Notebook*. Samuel Weiser, INC. P. xi

described by Michell in his analysis of Stonehenge. Guideline number ten seems like just a common-sense plea for environmental conscientiousness.

It's safe to say that if the Georgia Guidestones were not devised by Freemasons, the people who commissioned them were operating on a similar wavelength; and unlike the prehistoric Stonehenge there is a historical self-consciousness at work in the Guidestones. In this regard, we can read this self-consciousness in respect to Heidegger's discourse on the nature of history:

> Among the meanings of the expression "history" that signify neither the science of history nor the latter as an object, but rather this being itself which has not necessarily been objectified, the one in which this being is understood as something *past* claims a preferred use. This significance makes itself known in talk such as "this or that already belongs to history." Here "past" means on the one hand "no longer objectively present," or else "indeed still objectively present, but without 'effect' on the 'present'." However, what is historical as what is past also has the opposite significance when we say that one cannot evade history. Here history means what is past, but is nevertheless still having an effect. However, what is historical as what is past is understood in a positive or privative effective relation to the "present" in the sense of what is real "now" and "today." "The past" has a remarkable ambiguity here. Here "the past" belongs irrevocably to an earlier time; it belonged to former events and can yet still be objectively present "now" –for example, the remains of a Greek temple. A "bit of the past" is still "present" in it.
> Thus history does not so much mean the "past" in the sense of what is past, but the *derivation* from it. Whatever "has a history" is in the context of a

becoming. Here the "development" is sometimes a rise, sometimes a fall. Whatever "has a history" in this way can at the same time "make" history.[539]

In a sense, this awareness of history entails meta-consciousness and the fact that the Georgia Guidestones have to explicitly prescribe their morality makes them an artifact of a very modern conception of history.

The Denver International Airport

Since the focus of this book is on the movement from myth to modernity there is a dialectic at work involving the Denver Airport that is playing out in real time. By this I mean that the narratives are not striving to catch up with the object, they are neck-in-neck. So much so, that the Denver Airport website itself addresses these theories in a direct and humorous way. For this reason, the Denver Airport conspiracy theory is a legitimately post-modern phenomenon, as the airport's existence can accommodate a large degree of irony.

Conspiracy theorist claims about the airport have to do with the idea that there are underground tunnels, that the site will play a significant role when FEMA decides to round up and imprison the population, and that the giant mural inside the airport, "Children of the World Dream of Peace," hints not only at these schemes, but the plans of the New World Order in general.

This whole scenario represents a post-modern conclusion to this chapter because the airport's rebuttal of these accusations goes beyond direct refutation and enters the realm of mockery and irony, e.g., hosting conspiracy theory themed movie nights

[539] Heidegger, Martin (1996) *Being and Time.* State University of New York pp. 346 - 347

and costume parties, etc.[540] Irony then strengthens the cultural significance of the airport and becomes a facet of the institution itself. This is a feature of post-modern phenomena that we will see pop up again in our discussion of the public's cynical apathy in the wake of Jeffrey Epstein's death. But before we turn to that infamous figure, we have to tackle an even more infamous, and older figure, Aleister Crowley.

---

[540] These events, as well as the generally humorous tone taken by the Denver International Airport's official website were more prominent prior to the advent of Covid-19.

Chapter Nine: The Significance of Aleister Crowley

Edward Alexander Crowley was born on October 12th 1875 in Warwickshire England and was raised by his strictly religious father, Edward Crowley in the Plymouth Brethren Church. The Plymouth Brethren were a Protestant sect that had been profoundly influenced by the Dispensationalist theology of John Nelson Darby and espoused a distinctly millenarian theology.[541] Despite their religious severity Crowley's family had come to prominence in the early eighteenth century through their ale houses and brewing company, "Alton Ale," and enjoyed a certain degree of wealth.[542]

Aleister, as he would later dub himself in an attempt to get back to his Celtic roots, enjoyed an idyllic childhood until his father's death in 1887; after which, his mother took him to live with her brother Tom Bond Bishop. Though Aleister had chafed against his father's evangelizing, he had retained a sense of reverence for the man. This was not the case with his Uncle Tom, whom he held in contempt for his religious zealotry. One might say that it was the combination of religious indoctrination, in both the home and at school, as well as his burgeoning philosophical inquisitiveness that drove Crowley away from Christianity. Prior to this relinquishment, Crowley immersed himself in recreational activities like reading, mountaineering, and chess.

As contestable as many of Crowley's accomplishments might be to his detractors or champions, one biographical aspect is certain: in his youth he had been a terrific mountain-climber. This, as well as his great aptitude for chess, indicates that underlying his later philosophical and metaphysical

---

[541] Darby's writings essentially led to the Scofield Reference Bible and the phenomenon of modern day Evangelical Christianity with its attendant beliefs in a period of tribulation and a rapture of all devout Christians.

[542] Kaczynski, Richard (2010) *Perdurabo: The Life of Aleister Crowley*. North Atlantic Books pp. 4 – 5.

pronouncements had been an analytic mind of significant acuity. In Richard Kaczynski's biography, *Perdurabo*, great attention is paid to how Crowley, in his early years of rock climbing, looked at the activity as a way of figuring out puzzles.[543] Chess also gave the young man a medium with which to hone his strategic faculties.

It is probably due to this analytical, and ultimately dialectical, way of thinking that Crowley renounced Christ on December 23, 1897 and immediately sought insight from his opposite, the Devil.[544] This is not to say that Crowley was a Satanist, I don't believe he ever conformed to this title in a meaningful way, so what I mean is that he sought out occult knowledge and this he did so under the auspices of A.E. Waite's *The Book of Black Magic and Pacts* published early the next year. This rebellious move, as well as the myriad contrarian statements and actions that followed it, contributed to the associations that have been made between Crowley and his near contemporary Friedrich Nietzsche, usually by occult-enthusiasts who are trying to seize a bit of philosophical pedigree for their theorizations, or by pedestrian writers seeking to disparage either one of them (in the case of the latter, it's usually Crowley).

The similarities between these two are striking. Besides the partial historical overlap of their lives, both rebelled against the religious upbringing imposed on them by fathers who died early in their respective lives.[545] However, if we consider this passage from *The Confessions*:

---

[543] Ibid pp. 44 - 45

[544] Notice that this is almost a real-life repetition of Parzival's renunciation of God as depicted in Wolfram's telling of the Grail narrative.

[545] In regards to the impact this had on Nietzsche see the second version of his "Premonitory Dream" written in 1861:
"I seemed to hear the sound of a deadened organ coming from the nearby church. Surprised, I open the window that looks over the church and the cemetery. My father's tomb opens, a white form rises from it and disappears into the church. The lugubrious,

The existence of true religion presupposes that of some discarnate intelligence, whether we call him God or anything else. And this is exactly what no religion had ever proved scientifically.[546]

We get a better grasp on the fact that, unlike prior generations, Crowley was compelled to find a place for religion within the modern, scientific age. Both he and Nietzsche valued the idea of a scientific method governing their writing and thought.[547] After this modern notion of rigor is placed in the cockpit of one's sense of judgment both men emphasized an artistic approach, to life (for Nietzsche) and magical ritual (for Crowley). The great distinction is that Nietzsche declared God dead by proxy in *The Gay Science* whereas Crowley couldn't countenance so strong a pronouncement; "Magick" (his more specialized term for magical ritual, thus distinguishing it from parlor tricks) and his writing, specifically *The Book of the Law* were attempts to give religion some semblance of scientific credentials.

---

disturbing sounds continue to bellow; the white form carries something under its arms that I cannot make out. The tumulus is raised, the form descends into it, the organs fall silent. I wake up. The next day, my younger brother, a vivacious and gifted child, is seized with convulsions and dies within half an hour. He was buried beside my father's tomb."
Excerpted from Klossowski, Pierre (2005) *Nietzsche and the Vicious Circle.* Continuum p. 132
[546] Crowley, Aleister (1979) *The Confessions of Aleister Crowley.* Arkana, Penguin Books. P. 397
[547] This is the central theme of Nietzsche's *The Gay Science,* first published in 1882 as well as one of Crowley's maxims: "Magick is the science and art of causing change to occur in conformity with will." Crowley, Aleister (1994) *Magick Liber Aba Book Four Parts I – IV.* Samuel Weiser, INC. P. 128

Around the same time that he was studying Waite's tome, Crowley began reading S. L. MacGregor Mathers's *The Kabbalah Unveiled*. A year later, during an 1898 expedition in the Alps, Crowley encountered a man named Julian Baker who would, along with George Cecil Jones, go on to induct Crowley into the Order of the Golden Dawn. The Golden Dawn was, at that point, the latest and most popular, incarnation of the hermetical secret societies, such as the Theosophical Society, that were in vogue at the time. These organizations appealed to individuals involved in Freemasonry but who were interested in expanding their rites into actual magical rituals. This involved incorporating Tarot cards, astral projection, "skrying" (the practice of looking into an object, such as a black mirror, in order to see remote or future events) and telekinesis. The study of Kabbalah played an important role as well, as the subject had been introduced to the German Idealist tradition by way of Friedrich Christoph Oetinger (May 2, 1702 – February 10, 1782). Oetinger was a theologian who studied the Kabbalah with a circle of Jewish Kabbalists and sought to reconcile these teachings with the early German mysticism in which he was already versed.[548]

After this formal initiation into an occultic secret society, Crowley would go on to join and form a variety of other similar groups, some of which explicitly claimed a Masonic pedigree. To give a complete biography of the man would take us too far afield, but I will bring up a few biographical points when necessary. For our purposes in this chapter, we will try to focus on a few key aspects of his work and legacy. These are Crowley's formulation of "Magick" in a theological and philosophical sense, his transcription (or authorship) of *The Thelemic Book of the Law*, his attempt at founding an Abbey based on the teachings of this book, and his synthesis of a wide variety of schools of philosophy, mysticism, and the occult into his writing.

---

[548] Magee, Glenn Alexander (2001) *Hegel and the Hermetic Tradition.* Cornell University Press. P. 65

Thelema and The Book of the Law

On March 16, 1904, Crowley and his wife Rose Kelly were spending the night in their Cairo apartment. After trying his hand at some magic that was intended to reveal "elemental spirits" in the air, Kelly went into a trance and told Crowley: "They're waiting for you."[549] Two days later, while he was engaging in divination, Kelly told Crowley that the one awaiting him was Horus. After questioning her about the nature of the deity, Crowley accompanied Kelly to the Boulaq Museum and asked her to point out an image of Horus, she went upstairs and identified the god, as he is depicted on the Stele of Ankh-ef-en-Khonsu, which was listed as exhibit number 666.

After this bit of synchronicity, Crowley focused his divination practices on the figure of Horus. On April 7th, Kelly informed Crowley that it was not Horus who was speaking through her, but his messenger Aiwass, and that for the next three days Crowley was to enter the "temple" at twelve noon and transcribe what he heard. This transcription process, which occurred from noon until 1pm on April 8th, 9th and 10th make up the contents of *The Book of the Law*, or *Liber AL vel Legis*. This text was so monumental to Crowley that he later claimed: "My entire previous life was but a preparation for this event, and my entire subsequent life has been not merely determined by it, but wrapped up in it."[550]

During the composition, Crowley claimed that he sat in his study and a man spoke to him over his left shoulder in a voice that

---

[549] Kaczynski, Richard (2010) *Perdurabo: The Life of Aleister Crowley*. North Atlantic Books. P. 124. Some versions of this story place this event in the King's Chamber at the Great Pyramid of Giza, Kaczynski, however lists this invocation as occurring several months after the night Kelly and Crowley spent in the King's Chamber.
[550] Crowley, Aleister (1979) *The Confessions of Aleister Crowley*. Arkana, Penguin Books. P. 393

was "of deep timbre, musical and expressive, its tones solemn, voluptuous, tender, fierce or aught else as suited the moods of the message."[551]

The message began:

1. Had! The manifestation of Nuit.
2. The unveiling of the company of heaven.
3. Every man and every woman is a star.
4. Every number is infinite; there is no difference.
5. Help me, o warrior lord of Thebes, in my unveiling before the children of men!
6. Be thou Hadit, my secret centre, my heart & my tongue.
7. Behold! It is revealed by Aiwass the minister of Hoor-paar-kraat.
8. The Khabs is in the Khu, not the Khu in the Khabs.
9. Worship then the Khabs, and behold my light shed over you!
10. Let my servants be few & secret: they shall rule the many & the known.[552]

This opening salvo contains a few of what would go on to become some of Crowley's classic tropes: "Every man and every woman is a star," and the revelation that Aiwass is the minister of Hoor-paar-kraat. The reference to the "few and secret" who rule over the "many and known" is something that can be interpreted in conspiratorial terms, as in a "secret elite" that might be Masonic, occultic, or tied to bloodlines – it is most likely that Crowley believed that it was a reference to the "Secret Chiefs" hidden away somewhere in the mountains of Tibet. Later in the text, Aiwass imparts a few more declarations that would be significant to the Crowley mythos:

---

[551] Kaczynski, Richard (2010) *Perdurabo: The Life of Aleister Crowley*. North Atlantic Books. P. 127
[552] Crowley, Aleister (1988) *The Holy Books of Thelema*. Samuel Weiser, INC. P. 107

33. Then the priest fell into a deep trance or swoon, & said unto the Queen of Heaven; Write unto us the ordeals; write unto us the rituals; write unto us the law!

34. But she said: the ordeals I write not: the rituals shall be half known and half concealed: the Law is for all.

39. The word of the Law is Θελημα

40. Who calls us Thelimites will do no wrong, if he look but close into the word. For there are therein Three Grades, the Hermit, and the Lover, and the man of Earth. Do what thou wilt shall be the whole of the Law.

41. The word of Sin is Restriction. O man! Refuse not thy wife, if she will! O lover, if thou wilt, depart! There is no bond that can unite the divided but love: all else is a curse. Accursed! Accursed be it to the aeons! Hell. [add the proper accents here]

42. Let it be that state of manyhood bound and loathing. So with thy all; thou hast no right but to do thy will.

43. Do that, and no other shall say nay.

44. For pure will, unassuaged of purpose, delivered from the lust of result, is every way perfect.

57. Invoke me under my stars! Love is the law, love under will [...][553]

Crowley would seize upon "Love is the law, love under will" as his personal motto; "the Law is for all" he would use as the title of a pamphlet which explained the religion of Thelema. The reference to "Sin" as "Restriction" in Section 41 certainly comes close to Nietzschean territory, insofar as it represents a re-evaluation of values, which some would claim amounts to an argument for moral relativism.[554] However, the injunction towards love as a

---

[553] Ibid pp. 109 - 111

[554] Interestingly, there is a stylistic similarity between this passage and the later parts of *Thus Spake Zarathustra* (published twenty years prior to Crowley's dictation), especially the declarations beginning with "O Man!"

guiding principle is: A) not something that Nietzsche would have made and B) a side-stepping, of sorts, as far as the claim of moral relativism is concerned. This is because, for the moral relativist, morality and laws basically evolved out of customs and norms, or they were imposed to maintain peace and order; there is nothing objective, let alone, divinely-mandated about them. The Thelemic position here seems to be promoting a re-evaluation of Sin, and with it, prohibition, in a way that promotes the sort of individualism to which a moral relativist might ascribe. However, the description of "love" here seems to be somewhat divine, if not divinely mandated, because it comes from the mouth of a god (or his messenger).

Initially Crowley had rejected the *Book of the Law*; he left it in an attic and forgot about it. It was only a few years later that he re-discovered it and took it to heart. Some commentators, like Israel Regardie, have speculated that the book had initially rubbed Crowley the wrong way because it went too far in transgressing his latent sense of Christian morality. In some ways this might be true, but there's a very specific action the *Book of the Law* takes that is very similar to Christianity. We have been analyzing the concept of love as it is employed in this text and considering whether the injunction towards love is a license for moral relativism. Remember that the Gospels record Christ at one point claiming that one could replace the Ten Commandments with one maxim: "Love your neighbor as you love yourself" (Mark 12:31). In this proclamation, Christ seems to be invoking the rule of love, so-to-speak, in a way that is uncannily similar to what is done in this chapter of the *Book of the Law*. Both proclamations associate the divine, which is meant to authenticate the law, with the ambiguous concept of love.

Most people would not associate the Christian conception of love, which, to a certain extent, can be conceived in Kantian terms, i.e., that you love other people for who they are, not for what they do for you, with Crowley's conception of love. Regarding this critique, we must first consider that, despite Crowley's reputation as "the Great Beast," and the "Wickedest

Man Alive," there's no reason to think that he didn't harbor a lot of the conventional middle-class British moral values that had been inculcated in him at a young age. Despite his provocations, Crowley's behavior veered closer to casual blasphemy, adultery, holding petty grudges, etc., than with egregious acts like rape and murder. Therefore, I would say that the invocation of love in the text, and later in Crowley's life, was not meant to portray the concept in a lascivious or trivial light, it most likely had a gravitas similar to what we find in Christ's Golden Rule.

However, love being the law, does not make it an unchecked and unlimited force, as love is "under will" and "will," as long as it is "pure," is perfect. Coincidentally, "Thelema" is the Greek word for "will." A perfect will is defined in the text as being one that is "unassuaged of purpose, delivered from the lust of result." Will is tied to purpose, and, in a very Kantian turn, is stoically resistant to the enticement promised by "result." After this, the second chapter of *Liber AL vel Legis*, which we can assume was dictated on April 9th, 1904 takes a stronger turn towards Gnosticism, specifically in regards to the subject of serpents:

1. Nu! The hiding of Hadit.
2. Come! All ye, and learn the secret that hath not yet been revealed. I, Hadit, am the complement of Nu, my bride. I am not extended, and Khabs is the name of my House.
3. In the sphere I am everywhere the centre, as she, the circumference, is nowhere found.
21. We have nothing with the outcast and the unfit: let them die in their misery. For they feel not. Compassion is the vice of kings: stamp down the wretched & the weak: this is the law of the strong: this is our law and the joy of the world. Think not, o king, upon that lie: That Thou Must Die: verily thou shalt not die, but live. Now let it be understood: If the body of the King dissolve, he shall remain in pure ecstasy for ever. Nuit! Hadit! Ra-Hoor-Khuit! The Sun, Strength & Sight, Light; these are the servants of the Star & the Snake.

22. I am the Snake that giveth Knowledge & Delight and bright glory and stir the hearts of men with drunkenness. To worship me take wine and strange drugs whereof I will tell my prophet, & be drunk thereof! They shall not harm ye at all. It is a lie, this folly against self. The exposure of innocence is a lie. Be strong, o man! Lust, enjoy all things of sense and rapture: fear not any God shall deny thee for this.

23. I am alone: there is no God where I am.

26. I am the secret Serpent coiled about to spring: in my coiling there is joy. If I lift up my head, I and Nuit are one. If I droop down mine head, and shoot forth venom, then is rapture of the earth, and I and the earth are one.

72. Strive ever to more! And if thou art truly mine –and doubt it not, an if thou art ever joyous!- death is the crown of all.[555]

This second chapter seems to incarnate a different voice than the first. The tone, urging excess and indifference to suffering, represents a Bacchanalian kind of deity and the indifference to suffering resonates with Nietzsche's later philosophy. Though the Gnostic conception of the serpent as bringer of knowledge is at play here, the serpent imagery seems intended to tie the work to very ancient lunar and matriarchal traditions that had preceded Gnosticism. Granted, Gnosticism, as it was known in Crowley's day (and ours as well), may have been trying to tap into these older forms of religious worship as well; however, Crowley's writing appears to be trying to draw on these older traditions directly.

Much of what is said in this chapter derails from the high-mindedness (both philosophically and morally) of the first. This has led some to claim that it was three different deities who spoke to Crowley. This, if we accept the narrative at face-value, seems plausible. However, *Liber AL vel Legis* is a tripartite work, composed of three chapters, on three consecutive days, so, perhaps there is a bit of a dialectical schema afoot here. Certainly,

---

[555] Ibid pp. 114 - 119

the rational tone of the first chapter characterizes it as the "thesis," the debauchery of the second chapter is pretty unrelenting; enough so, that I would say that it qualifies as an "antithesis." Let's now turn to the final chapter and see if there is a sense of resolution that might be worthy of the term "synthesis."

Chapter Three begins with some straight-up Hocus Pocus:

1. Abrahadabra; the reward of Ra Hoor Khut
2. There is division hither homeward; there is a word not known. Spelling is defunct; all is not aught. Beware! Hold! Raise the spell of Ra-Hoor Khuit!
3. Now let it be first understood that I am a god of War and of vengeance. I shall deal hardly with them.
4. Choose ye an island!
5. Fortify it!
6. Dung it about with enginery of war!
7. I will give you a war-engine.
8. With it ye shall smite the peoples; and none shall stand before you.
12. Sacrifice cattle, little and big: after a child.
18. Mercy let be off: damn them who pity! Kill and torture; spare not; be upon them![556]

If the first day's deity was vaguely philosophical, the second day's deity lascivious and wanton, then this deity sounds almost like the God of the Old Testament, or possibly the Roman god Mars. Crowley distinguished the three respective deities as: Nuit, Hadit and Ra-Hoor-Khuit. To conventional moral sensibility this doesn't seem like a dialectical progression to a higher or more enlightened understanding. One factor that needs to be considered though before proffering this analysis definitively has to do with the fact that Crowley claimed that there was a great deal of Kabbalistic terminology that was encoded into the text, as

---

[556] Ibid pp. 121 - 123

well as sentences composed of words that are meant to be read diagonally through certain pages of the text; hence, a secret or hidden meaning might be ascertained. However, if we cannot directly comprehend these "hidden" messages, how can the text's full import be understood? Perhaps that dilemma is itself a commentary on the inability to completely "possess" a text. Perhaps it indicates a necessity for initiation, or maybe it's just a reward that comes from re-reading and randomly staring at the text.

Crowley, did in fact claim that there was a reconciliation, or harmony, that was achieved by the conjunction of the three chapters. In *Little Essays Toward Truth* he postulates that *The Book of the Law* "makes the unit of existence consist in an Event, an Act of Marriage between Nuit and Hadit; that is, the fulfillment of a certain Point-of-View,"[557] and claims that the transition marked by this "Point-of-View" is from a trance of sorrow (associated with Buddhism) to a trance of wonder. The possibility of a synthesis between the three chapters is also advanced in Chapter 0 of *Magick in Theory and Practice* where Crowley proffers this analysis:

> Infinite space is called the goddess NUIT, while the infinitely small and atomic yet omnipresent point is called HADIT. These are unmanifest. One conjunction of these infinities is called RA-HOOR-KHUIT, a Unity which both includes and heads all things. This profoundly mystical conception is based upon actual spiritual experience, but the trained reason can reach a reflection of this idea by the method of logical contradiction which ends in reason transcending itself.[558]

---

[557] Crowley, Aleister (1991) *Little Essays Toward Truth*. New Falcon Publications. P. 25

[558] Crowley, Aleister (1994) *Magick Liber Aba Book Four Parts I – IV*. Samuel Weiser, INC. P. 139

This is a particularly abstract reading, insofar as the *Book of the Law* pertains to certain historically established deities, i.e., the third chapter is explicitly identified with Horus, who Crowley refers to as "The Crowned and Conquering Child" and is designated as the defining deity for the New Aeon:

> The child is not merely a symbol of growth, but of complete moral independence and innocence. We may then expect the New Aeon to release mankind from its pretense of altruism, its obsession of fear and its consciousness of sin. It will possess no consciousness of the purpose of its own existence.[559]

The last line about "possessing no consciousness of the purpose of its existence" seems to resonate with some of the attacks on the word "because" made in the second and third chapters. "Because" could be a stand-in for the will of God, or a divine mandate. The Aeon of Horus replaces the Aeon of the martyred god and is limited in time. It will be "succeeded by Thmaist, the Double-Wanded-One; she who shall bring the candidates to full initiation, and though we know little of her peculiar characteristics, we know at least that her name is justice."[560]

The war that is so heavily touted in the third chapter may be the wars that would consume humanity for a good part of the twentieth century; hence this chapter may be more descriptive (or predictive) than normative. The denial of self-sacrifice and pity, as Crowley sees it, goes hand-in-hand with the declaration that "Every man and every woman is a star: "each individual must follow their own path and sense of duty. This spiritual libertarianism will be one component of the New Aeon:

---

[559] Crowley, Aleister (1979) *The Confessions of Aleister Crowley.* Arkana, Penguin Books. P. 400
[560] Ibid p. 400

Aiwass, uttering the word Thelema (with all its implications), destroys completely the formula of the Dying God. Thelema implies not merely a new religion, but a new cosmology, a new philosophy, a new ethics. It co-ordinates the disconnected discoveries of science, from physics to psychology, into a coherent and consistent system. Its scope is so vast that it is impossible even to hint at the universality of its application.[561]

Many have debated as to whether Crowley's engagement with Aiwass was an authentic form of divination, i.e., where he literally transcribed the speech of some other-worldly entity, or if it was some deeply subconscious part of his own psyche. Crowley himself felt that Aiwass was external to him, and in fact was his "holy guardian angel," but did feel like his words and presence resonated at a deeply personal level. Kenneth Grant offers us an interpretation that somewhat aligns with the idea propounded in "The Significance of the Known World," in that the artistic act can provide a medium for the transmission of esoteric knowledge.[562]

Being an occultist at the turn of the century, Crowley was well-versed in the legend of John Dee and he seems to have seen his relationship with Rose Kelly to be a reiteration of the Dee/Kelley narrative – Rose's sharing of the same surname reinforces this (though it was Crowley who often claimed himself to be the reincarnation of Edward Kelley). The actual transcription of the Book of the Law can also be read as a reiteration of Ginzberg's narrative of Enoch transcribing the

---

[561] Ibid p. 399

[562] Robert Anton Wilson states that Grant also countenanced the idea that Aiwass might be an entity from Sirius. Wilson, Robert Anton (1998) *Everything is Under Control: Conspiracies, Cults and Cover-ups*. Harper Perennial. P. 35

speech of the angel while in heaven (as was discussed in "The Significance of the Cosmos").

Besides rebelling against Christianity, which is a topic usually brought up in respect to Crowley's work, another aspect of the particular brand of Christianity with which he was raised, and that possibly relates to his postulation of a "New Aeon," is its echoes the tenets of Evangelical dispensationalism. There are a variety of different schools of dispensationalist thought, the underlying theme involves dividing Biblical periods up into schemas, or "dispensations." It is quite possible that Crowley's declaration of a "New Aeon" drew unconsciously, or innately, upon this epochal framework.

The Abbey of Thelema

A serial womanizer, Crowley did not stay with Rose Kelly for long, as the two divorced in 1909. He would go on to have a variety of mistresses, the more mystically inclined of which he would bestow the title of "Scarlet Woman;" this appellation was in keeping with his self-stylization as the Great Beast foretold in The Book of Revelation. In 1920 Crowley decided to set up a monastery where devotees could focus on what he called "the Great Work."

Crowley's Magickal system was pretty eclectic, and in this respect he was a forerunner of the buffet-style spiritualism that was so endemic in the latter half of the twentieth century. Given this tendency, the "Great Work" could refer to achieving nirvana, communicating with one's holy guardian angel, or any number of benchmarks set by the world's religions. Whatever Crowley meant by this expression was contingent upon the uncovering and exercising of one's true will, a subject discussed frequently after the publication of *The Book of the Law*. In his handbook to the **A∴A∴** (the Argenteum Astrum order, formulated by Crowley in 1907) Crowley writes:

The Order of the Star called S.S. is, in respect of its existence upon the Earth, an organized Body of men and women distinguished among their fellows by the qualities here enumerated. They exist in their own Truth, which is both universal and unique. They move in accordance with their own Wills, which are each, yet coherent with the universal Will.[563]

The Abbey of Thelema took its name from François Rabelais's *Gargantua and Pantagruel*, wherein the place was described as an "anti-monastery." Crowley's Scarlet Woman for this "social experiment" was named Leah Hirsig, a Swiss woman he met in Greenwich Village in 1919. The activities that went on at the Abbey ran the gamut from yoga and study to sex magick, some of which may have involved bestiality and blood drinking.[564]

In his handbook for the **A∴A∴** Crowley stipulates that the following of one's "true will" is achieved after an initiate "has destroyed all that He is and all that He has on crossing the Abyss."[565] This concept of an "Abyss" that must be confronted, as well as the closely related concept of the "dweller-on-the-threshold" is a purely occultic reiteration of the Grail quest.

Kaczynski describes the "Ordeal of the Abyss" as a "magical rite of passage designed to obliterate the magician's ego by destroying all he held dear: those physical attachments that Buddha blamed for reincarnation; one's selfishness, or sense of

[563] Crowley, Aleister (1994) *Magick Liber Aba Book Four Parts I – IV*. Samuel Weiser, INC. P. 479
[564] https://en.wikipedia.org/wiki/Abbey_of_Thelema accessed on 04/01/21
[565] Crowley, Aleister (1994) *Magick Liber Aba Book Four Parts I – IV*. Samuel Weiser, INC. P. 481

self."[566] Easily confused with a career spent toiling in retail, the truth of this magical ritual Crowley realized was that:

> Only one who released everything was light enough to cross the desiccated yaw of the Abyss, to surpass the Second Order's highest grade of Exempt Adept and follow the path of the Secret Chiefs and their Great White Brotherhood. By contrast, those who clung to some vestige of their former lives were mired forever in the Abyss, doomed as one of the Black Brothers who elevated their egos to godhead. "I cannot even say that I crossed the Abyss deliberately," Crowley wrote, illustrating that, although few ever advanced this far, the terrible ordeal was an eventuality for all magicians, a consequence of one's earliest oaths.[567]

Essentially, this ordeal of dealing with a bunch of terrible things (which for Crowley may have been merely the consequences of his actions) as well as the relinquishment of one's ego, is the prerequisite for claiming the libertarian ethos of Thelema. Clearly, this ritual is initiatic in nature. It is also problematic, in that, once the ordeal is perceived to be "over" the magician might believe he has "survived" the worst life has to offer; this was clearly not the case for Crowley, who would go on to experience further ups and downs for the rest of his life. However, maybe there is a psychological value to this ritual, in that, once the ego is surrendered, one, as a subject, does become "lighter" and suffers life's iniquities with indifference or even humor.

This was most certainly true for Crowley, who utilized humor and self-effacement in much of his writing and often saw himself as a sort of "Cosmic Jester" who delighted in the

[566] Kaczynski, Richard (2010) *Perdurabo: The Life of Aleister Crowley*. North Atlantic Books. P. 161
[567] Ibid p. 161

paradoxes of existence. This role puts him a little closer to the work of Jacques Derrida, who also devoted himself to a path of rigorous study and discipline but enjoyed playing with the binary conceptions inherent to Western rationality. Both men had an air of mysticism and bemusement about them, though, due to personality traits, Crowley would be more prone to wearing these signifiers on his sleeve, whereas Derrida was certainly more modest.

Crowley, we might say, embodied Salvador Dali's description of himself as both a charlatan and a mystic. Much of Grant's *Outside the Circles of Time* substantiates this characterization, specifically in his portrayal of Crowley as a historical figure in the mold of Rimbaud, Baudelaire, and Lautreamont (and other Dionysian artists who achieved inspiration through intoxication). What is essential for the debauched artist, according to Grant, is that they are able to retain an account of their vision when they return to the world of the everyday.[568] The literary pedigree for this archetype goes back to the scene in Homer's *Odyssey* when Odysseus has himself strapped to the mast of his ship in order to hear the sirens' song without succumbing to the consequences of doing so. The Abbey of Thelema ended up being a disaster and Crowley and his acolytes were chased out of Italy by Mussolini's Fascist regime in 1923 – the great experiment having lasted almost three years.[569]

Crowley's Other Writings and his Connection to Modern-day Conspiracy Theorization

At the risk of repeating myself, like the pyramids and the Sphinx, every modern conspiracy theory "worth its salt," ahem, will incorporate the figure of Aleister Crowley into the innerworkings

---

[568] Grant, Kenneth (1980) *Outside the Circles of Time*. Billing and Sons Limited. Pp. 21 - 22

[569] Kaczynski, Richard (2010) *Perdurabo: The Life of Aleister Crowley*. North Atlantic Books. Pp. 397 - 400

of its narrative. And this is for good reason: "Crowley" is a modern figure who acts as a key to unlocking the connection between myths and conspiracy theories. He himself behaved as an Encyclopedist of myths and ancient religions; so much so, that he inaugurated what we have been referring to as a "compound" mentality about them. Having studied diligently and extensively, Crowley not only referenced modern scientific discoveries and philosophical developments in his writings – he also claimed that their results either had been anticipated by, or dovetailed with, his work.[570]

Crowley, in this sense, embodied the very modern literary concept of creating both an originary work as well as providing a commentary on the context of said work within the text itself. Essentially, this development in modernity represents an attempt to imbue the work of art with its own sense of self-consciousness. Unlike contemporary authors like Don Delillo or Kurt Vonnegut, who achieve this feat solely through their authorial output, Crowley achieved this, in part, from references to his own reputation and infamy.

There are a good deal of stories about Aleister Crowley that might be called "Apocryphal;" these anecdotes are snapshots into the infamy and intrigue cultivated by the magician. The story I'm about to relate might be described as "beyond-Apocryphal." Supposedly, one night Crowley was in his study when he answered a knock on his door. In his doorway stood a man who claimed that, since Crowley had published one of the secrets of

---

[570] One footnote from *Magick in Theory and Practice* states: "The basis of this theology is given in *Liber CCXX, Al vel Legis* which forms part IV of this *Book 4*. Here, I can only outline the matter in a very crude way; it would require a separate treatise to discuss even the true meaning of the terms employed, and to show how *The Book of the Law* anticipates the recent discoveries of Frege, Cantor, Poincare, Russell, Whitehead, Einstein and others." Crowley, Aleister (1994) *Magick Liber Aba Book Four Parts I – IV.* Samuel Weiser, INC. P. 139

the Scottish Rite in one of his books, he had come to informally induct Crowley into the order. Crowley insisted he had done no such thing. The stranger made his way into the study and pulled out *The Book of Lies,* showing Crowley the section in question; to which Crowley, shocked by his own absent-mindedness, acquiesced to membership.[571] For added Oomph tell this story, but then add that the whole incident occurred years *prior* to the publication of *The Book of Lies.*[572] Different versions of this story appear throughout the literature on Crowley, Robert Anton Wilson's version goes like this:

> Aleister Crowley became an initiate of the OTO in 1912 after publishing *The Book of Lies.* The Outer Head at that time, Theodore Reuss, came to Crowley and said that, since he knew the secret of the 9th degree, he had to accept that rank in the OTO and its attendant obligations. Crowley protested that he knew no such secret, but Reuss showed him a copy of *The Book of Lies* and pointed to a chapter that revealed the secret clearly. Crowley looked at his own words, and "It instantly flashed upon me. The entire symbolism not only of Free Masonry but of many other traditions blazed upon my spiritual vision... I understood that I held in my hands the key to the future progress of humanity." Crowley, of course, does not tell us which chapter contains the secret (The present author nominates chapter 69.)[573]

---

[571] Which was most likely not a very big deal. Crowley probably amassed memberships to secret societies the way people today enroll in streaming services.

[572] This was how it was first related to me.

[573] Wilson, Robert Anton (1998) *Everything is Under Control: Conspiracies, Cults and Cover-ups.* Harper Perennial. Pp. 329 - 330

The Ordo Templi Orientis was a masonic organization that claims to be descended from the Knights Templar. Crowley would go on to succeed Reus as the Outer Head of the Order. Curiously titled, *The Book of Lies*, leads us down one more important rabbit-hole in the Crowley mythos: Extraterrestrials. The first interesting point of synchronicity relates to this passage written by Peter Moon:

> My own personal interest in Thule accelerated when I was telling one of my friends how to pronounce the word *Thule*. As we disagreed, I looked it up in the dictionary. Much to my surprise, I discovered a new word to add to my vocabulary: *thulium*. All it said in the definition is that thulium is an element of the rare earth group listed on the periodic table and that it was element number 69. A quick look at chemistry books in various libraries didn't tell me much more, only that it was discovered in Sweden and named after the ancient idea of Thule in the north.[574]

Moon is correct in his description of thulium, but his additional claim that the chemical has psychic properties is more dubious. Moon's numerological analysis is that: "6 plus 9 adds up to 15, the number of the Devil card in the tarot. This, of course, corresponds to Baphomet."[575] However, he is unaware of how the number might be of numerological significance to the Crowley mythos. As indicated by Wilson, Chapter 69 is one of the more notorious chapters in *The Book of Lies* and it goes a little something like this:

THE WAY TO SUCCEED –AND THE WAY TO SUCK EGGS

---

[574] Moon, Peter (2003) *The Black Sun: Montauk's Nazi-Tibetan Connection*. Sky Books. P. 156
[575] *bid p. 157*

This is the Holy Hexagram.
Plunge from the height, O God, and interlock with man!
Plunge from the height, O Man, and interlock with Beast!
The Red Triangle is the descending tongue of grace; the Blue Triangle is the ascending tongue of prayer.
This interchange, the Double Gift of Tongues, the Word of Double power-Abrahadabra!-is the sign of the GREAT WORK, for the GREAT WORK is accomplished in silence. And behold is not that Word equal to Cheth, that is Cancer, whose sigil is 69?
This Work also eats up itself, accomplishes its own end, nourishes the worker, leaves no seed, is perfect in itself.
Little children, love one another![576]

The subtitle "THE WAY TO SUCCEED –AND THE WAY TO SUCK EGGS" was incorporated into the title of the band Ministry's fifth studio album *Psalm 69* and it would seem to appeal to prurient (and juvenile) interests. Yet, there are references to the "Great Work," which for Crowley generally meant the communion with one's guardian angel.

Most likely, the chapter is a reference to sex Magick. However, there is an ambiguity to this reading because it appears in a book titled *The Book of Lies*. Perhaps we might read this chapter in conjunction with Moon's numerological analysis: If 69 is to be read as adding up to fifteen, which is the number of the Devil card in the Major Arcana of the Tarot, what does the symbolism of this card tell us about human sexuality? The image on the card is a depiction of two lovers enchained to Baphomet, whose right hand is raised while his left hand is lowered, indicating the Hermetic motto of "As above, so below." The enchainment of the two individuals indicates falling prey to the seduction offered by the material world: physical pleasure, lust, greed, etc.

---

[576] Crowley, Aleister (1998) *The Book of Lies*. Samuel Weiser, INC. P. 148

Essentially, if this chapter from *The Book of Lies* is significant, it is because a dialectic can be read into it – the synthesis being the injunction to "love one another!" (Love being interpreted here in a selfless, non-avaricious way and possibly the movement out of a "trance of sorrow" brought about by worldly attachments to a "trance of wonder" brought about by the attainment of wisdom and spiritual non-attachment).

Returning to Moon's analysis, thulia is one of the two mysterious substances that he focuses on in his analysis (the other being "occultum") and this leads us to another aspect of Crowley that relates directly to extraterrestrial phenomena. Moon connects Crowley's encounters with a mysterious entity referred to as LAM, with Crowley's stay in Montauk – a confluence of events that Kaczynski confirms in his biography.[577] Kaczynski, however, does not make a great deal of hay out of LAM, who in Crowley's artistic rendering, appears to resemble, what in UFOlogy is referred to as a "grey." Moon picks up the slack in this regard and refers to LAM as a "praeter human intelligence, just as occultum is praeter matter. LAM is actually an archetypal subconscious factor that exists deep within our mental structure [...] LAM links back in time as a representative of the Elder Race."[578]

The similarity of LAM with a "grey" is striking and has led conspiracy theorists to think that an extraterrestrial had engaged Crowley on the physical plane. Whether they met on the physical or astral plane, LAM is an interesting entity in the Crowley mythos because it is uncertain whether he is supposed to be the same entity as Aiwass, who Crowley always indicated was his "holy guardian angel;" and because he represents a shift away from the idea of there being "Secret Chiefs" in Tibet controlling events in the rest of the world. Here we find the shift from the

---

[577] Kaczynski, Richard (2010) *Perdurabo: The Life of Aleister Crowley*. North Atlantic Books. P. 347

[578] Moon, Peter (2003) *The Black Sun: Montauk's Nazi-Tibetan Connection*. Sky Books. Pp. 267 - 268

supernatural existing somewhere on earth to it existing in outer space (or extra-dimensional realms). We have noted this same shift as it occurred on a grand historical scale, e.g., the movement from speculating on mysterious places that might exist on the edges of the Earth in the fifteenth century to speculating on the existence of extraterrestrial life in the twentieth century. What is significant in Crowley's case is that this entire trajectory occurred, and was encapsulated, within the lifetime of just one guy.

The idea of "Secret Chiefs" or a "Great White Brotherhood" is important to occultism as well as conspiracy theorization. The idea originated in Karl von Eckartshausen's *The Cloud Upon the Sanctuary*, published in 1795.[579] The concept of a secluded group of mystics and magicians who used their occult powers to observe and intervene (interfere?) with the affairs of the outside world was utilized by Madame Blavatsky's Theosophical Society and turned up in the fiction of authors associated with the group, most notably Talbot Mundy, whose 1926 novel, *The Devil's Guard* depicts adventurers in Tibet who encounter a diabolical group of wizards who are referred to as "The Black Circle." The mythos made its way into more contemporary literary circles as evidenced by William Burroughs writing this in a letter to Jack Kerouac dated August 18, 1954:

> What am I doing here a broken eccentric? A Bowery Evangelist, reading books on Theosophy in the public library (an old tin trunk full of notes in my cold water East Side Flat), imagining myself a Secret World Controller in Telepathic Contact with Tibetan Adepts...[580]

---

[579] It has been claimed that Karl von Eckartshausen had been admitted to Adam Weishaupt's Bavarian Illuminati, but left shortly thereafter.

[580] Burroughs, William (1993) *The Letters of William Burroughs.* Penguin Books p. 226

It is certain that in his early years, Crowley believed the Secret Chiefs existed; in his autobiography he obliquely links their existence to Thelema: *"The Book of the Law* presumes the existence of a body of initiates pledged to watch over the welfare of mankind and to communicate its own wisdom little by little in the measure of man's capacity to receive it."[581] Some occultists still hold onto this belief, the more scientifically-minded believe that the powers they use are either alien technology beyond our comprehension, linked to the scientific secrets of Nikola Tesla, or both. This, of course, is a reiteration of the Ancient Aliens/Earth Mysteries debate.

In relation to the three murky figures we've been steadily tracking, we can see an affinity between Crowley and Hiram because of the former's involvement in various forms of Freemasonry – both as an inductee and as a creative director. The figure of Melchizedek might, in some ways, be representative of Crowley's role as a Magus and his place in the history of Hermeticism. Melchizedek, in this context, might also signify the studious and devout aspects of Crowley's personality that he kept hidden from all but his closest of associates. The figure of Enoch, perhaps, can be read into the Crowley narrative in terms of the bifurcation of the subject, i.e., as both a public infamous figure with a cultivated image and a private, complex individual, who understood that he was, and must be, "playing" a role. In this very modern context, Crowley represents a philosophical attempt to reconcile the two Enochs, not merely in a moral sense but in an aesthetic way that accommodates for the confusion existing between the two, the space or murkiness that obscures their definite discernment.

In Contrast to Anton LaVey

---

[581] Crowley, Aleister (1979) *The Confessions of Aleister Crowley.* Arkana, Penguin Books. P. 398

It is necessary to compare and contrast Aleister Crowley and another infamous figure with whom he is frequently confused: Anton LaVey. Anton Szandor LaVey (April 11, 1930 – October 29, 1997), who wrote and published *The Satanic Bible* in 1969 while simultaneously promulgating a 'modern' Church of Satan, occupies a place on the antithetical side of the historical dialectic we have seen slowly evolving. Where Crowley sought a scientifically justifiable religion and ultimately devolved into a mishmash of philosophy, Gnosticism, and mythology, LaVey developed a rock solid "might is right" ideology with the emphasis being on engaging the dark side of ourselves in order to achieve a higher degree of honesty.

LaVey did effect a materialist reduction on Crowleyesque spirituality, and the people he attracted to his religion were more pragmatic and less poetic than those attracted to Crowley. To a certain extent this contrast can be understood by comparing the two men's lives. Much less secrecy surrounds LaVey than Crowley, there aren't really any Apocryphal tales (or Ozzy Osbourne songs) about LaVey the way there are about Crowley. However, it is rumored that LaVey is in the background of the inner gatefold photo for the Eagles' 1976 album *Hotel California*. But that doesn't really compete with being personally chased out of Italy by Mussolini or claiming to have the ability to summon the Loch Ness Monster from the depths of his watery lair.[582]

One philosophical concept that is important to the work of both Crowley and LaVey is the definition of "will." Crowley's interpretation of will was similar to Nietzsche's, in that both rejected Schopenhauer's definition of the will being a primordial force that indiscriminately animates all the subjects and objects within one's field of awareness. Both personalized the will, and identified it with the self. Crowley perhaps did not go as far as Nietzsche, and the concept of Magick can be seen as an attempt at mediation with a "cosmic" will. LaVey, being about as atheistic as

---

[582] Moench, Doug (1995) *The Big Book of Conspiracies*. Paradox Press. P. 85

Nietzsche, saw the will in explicitly personal terms. When it came to the "seven deadly sins" – temptations which Schopenhauer might infer arise from the impersonal, universal will – LaVey countered with the idea that they essentially balance each other out; the famous example he gives in *The Satanic Bible* is of one's sense of pride counteracting inclinations towards sloth and gluttony.

Crowley addressed this same subject, albeit in more philosophical terms:

> [T]he opposition of two movements is not always evidence of conflict or error. For two opposite points upon the rim of a wheel move one North, the other South; yet they are harmonious parts of the same system. And the rowlock which resisteth the oar hindereth not but aideth the True Will of that oar. So then self-control is nowise the enemy of Freedom, but that which makes it possible.[583]

Crowley came from an artistic milieu, one that included figures like Aubrey Beardsley, Oscar Wilde, and William Butler Yeats. Like Nietzsche he infused his work with an artistic sensibility. LaVey was more of carnival performer who brought a sense of P.T. Barnum to his work; and as interesting as he might be, neither his output nor his persona possess the same caliber of artistry as that invoked (but not necessarily mastered) by Crowley.

Asbjørn Dyrendal covers a variety of figures and organizations in his essay, "Hidden Knowledge, Hidden Powers, Esotericism and Conspiracy Culture." His over-arching theory has to do with the reciprocal relationship between the individuals who seek to expose conspiracies to a wider audience and the

---

[583] Crowley, Aleister (1997) *The Heart of the Master*. New Falcon Publications. P. 123

esoteric discourses that are purportedly used by members of the conspiracy. Dyrendal's essay on LaVey focuses primarily on the fact that he believed that myths were both anthropologically necessary for the masses and useful for the powerful.

The problem Dyrendal sees arising for LaVey is that the powerful in Western society, e.g., industrialists, politicians, marketing executives, financiers, etc., are themselves embodying a "Satanic" ethos of willfulness, while simultaneously imparting a false consciousness on the public they are dominating and exploiting. LaVey sees this false consciousness, which is tied to consumerism, as being so egregious that it leads to the framing of these behaviors, on the part of the elites, in the conspiratorial terms of an "invisible war" that is:

> Fought 'with technologically advanced chemical and electromagnetic weapons, crowd control, weather control and misdirection to mask the entire operation.' Subliminal messages and other hidden control measures attempt to deprive everyone of that 'wondrous, unique experience' life should be. Satanists should use their insight and 'materialist magic' to make their own subliminals instead, thus avoiding unwanted influences.[584]

Like Crowley, LaVey is both playful and humorous in his attempts to destabilize this power structure. Dyrendal argues that despite the fact that LaVey often argues in academic and scientific terms, his conception of agency is traditional, in that it is undergirded by practical application or experiential authority – "LaVey knows because it works [...] he has *experienced* it."[585]

I agree with Dyrendal's argument, however, I think that the role LaVey plays within the greater narrative of conspiracy

---

[584] Dyrendal ,Asbjørn (2013) Hidden Knowledge, Hidden Powers, Esotericism and Conspiracy Culture."
[585] Ibid

theorization, as we have been tracing it, is an evolution away from Crowley. LaVey's libertarianism is more materialistic, as is his conspiracy theorization – he has a clear idea of individuals with wealth and power manipulating humanity towards desultory ends, whereas Crowley did not. LaVey, therefore represents a decisive move towards the rampant and totalizing scientism we will see dominate conspiracy theorization in the wake of 9/11.

Chapter Ten: The Significance of the Tarot

In the Introduction I stated that the concept of "significance" was important because it demands, or entails, a certain amount of repetition. A little bit later I compared the work of Alex Jones and Allan Watt with a serialized form of entertainment, similar to a soap opera which has to keep itself going indefinitely. On the one hand, the things that bear the signs of significance seem to demand a certain blind, or rote, repetition. On the other, though, sometimes the repetition attendant to significance is akin to a part of a religious liturgy: the congregants are supposed to grasp the overall general meaning of the ceremony and grant that there is a mystery lurking within as well, but be content with not penetrating too deeply into that mystery. The idea of the Tarot deck, and especially Tarot readings, are ceremonial remnants that still hold a degree of popularity within our postmodern, hyperreal society – this is because they still offer the promise of penetrating into the mysteries of existence lurking beneath our day-to-day lives.

The desire, [586] or will, to penetrate and interrogate mysteries has been characterized by Derrick Jensen (and others) as emblematic of a "patriarchal" instinct. An important part of the historical dialectic we have employed has involved a contrast between the reductionism of scientism (which usually advocates for technocracy), and the more mythical, literary interpretation of the world. In this framing it is obvious that I am granting an implicit deference to the latter. However, I want to balance out this account by returning briefly to the subject of Freemasonry.

---

[586] "Desire" is the word that Hegel used in his description of the "primal, demonic drive for complete possession or mastery of the object, for, in effect, the annihilation of otherness. By implication, this drive is simultaneously a will to remove the divide between subject and object, for by cancelling "otherness" it seeks to exalt the self." Magee, Glenn Alexander (2001) *Hegel and the Hermetic Tradition.* Cornell University Press. P. 139

As we've established in previous chapters: Freemasonry was a precursor of modern rational scientific inquiry. It was not the only one nor was it the most lucid. Nevertheless, the spirit of Freemasonry coincided with the ideals of scientific classification and inquiry, and to this end we can perceive an affinity existing between the spirit of Freemasonry and what Oswald Spengler called "The Faustian Spirit." This spirit is analogous to Jensen's concept of patriarchy. Spengler describes the Faustian spirit as a Western movement away from the Classical model of Greece and Rome, which focused on the "sensuously-present individualized body," to a focus on "pure and limitless space."[587] This orientation is borne out of an infinite solitude and gives form to myriad technological and artistic expressions. Spengler sees this spirit in "the colour of Rembrandt and the instrumentation of Beethoven," as well as "the wondrous awakening of the inner life in Wolfram's Parzival."[588] One of the best mediums for the expression of the Faustian spirit is architecture; in particular, the ornamental use of windows, which Spengler claims, "is peculiar to the Faustian soul and the most significant symbol of its depth-experience. In it can be felt the will to emerge from the interior into the boundless."[589]

Spengler refers to this Western zeitgeist as "Faustian" because its ceaseless striving mirrors that of the main character of Goethe's final dramatic work. The legend of Faust, a doctor who sells his soul to the Devil, had been around for at least a few centuries before Goethe tried his hand at the story.[590] For our purposes here, it is worth noting that Goethe was himself a Freemason and may have either consciously or unconsciously

---

[587] Spengler, Oswald (2006) *The Decline of the West: An Abridged Edition.* Translated by Charles Francis Atkinson and prepared by Arthur Helps. Vintage Books, A Division of Random House, INC. P. 97

[588] Ibid pp. 98 - 99

[589] Ibid p. 106

[590] Spengler claims Goethe as a primary influence on his philosophy. Ibid p. 38

incorporated the inquisitive ethos of the fraternal order into his most famous work.

For the sake of this chapter, it is important that we see the development and use of the Tarot as a phenomenon that historically coincides with the Faustian, or patriarchic spirit, in that the cards are a "tool" utilized to inquire into the mysterious innerworkings of the world. This spirit can be interpreted in both positive and negative ways; Spengler, who is often portrayed as celebrating it, frequently stated that he was merely attempting to speak objectively and that the Faustian spirit was something that culturally evolved into prominence. Derrick Jensen views it in exclusively negative terms because he identifies it with the exploitive aspects of modern consumption-based societies. However, one could argue that the insight proffered by the Faustian spirit is what allows us to evaluate and critique contemporary society, and possibly even correct aspects of it. With this said, we must think of the tools of divination, of which the Tarot is the most prominent, as a kind of technology that arose in concurrence with the Faustian spirit of the West.

Myths demand repetition and the Tarot captures myth to facilitate this repetition. You'll recall that Eliade claimed that certain forms of shamanism demanded that if a sacred name was to be spoken, its origin was to be given as well. In a sense, the technology of the Tarot consists of a short-circuiting of this process, in that the demanded origin narrative is symbolically contained within the image depicted on the card. Therefore, like with the written word, you can capture and easily recirculate the myth symbolized by the card.

In a basic sense, the intention here is analogous to the dissemination of written language. In intuitive terms, codifying our ideas and concepts into words would be the first step, while the second is the creation of a written alphabet that captures the phonetics of these words. The third step would be corralling these letters into words, and then sentences, that can communicate our thoughts to others. The line of evolution I have just described assumes that the spoken language comes first. However, it is conceivable that someone could construct a written language in a different order.

In the intuitive schema outlined above, writing and literacy come into play at some point during or after the third stage of development. When Plato describes the creation of writing in *The Phaedrus* he describes a mythical exchange between the Egyptian god, Thoth, who created writing, and Thamus, the god-king of Upper Egypt. In the exchange, Thoth refers to writing as a "Pharmakon" and says that it will improve memory and make the Egyptians wiser. Thamus counters this by saying that the kind of memory enacted by writing is inauthentic and that the wisdom endowed will be the appearance of wisdom, not the real thing.

In his reading of Plato's story, Jacques Derrida seizes upon the word "Pharmakon" and sees it as a key to deconstructing Plato's message, which was that writing is inferior to, or subordinate to speech, in part because it occurred later in the linguistic development process. The most obvious way to argue against Plato's assertion would be to declare that Plato had to write this story down in order to communicate his message to future generations, and therefore Plato's moral is shot through with a certain amount of irony. Derrida, however, focuses on the fact that there is a dual meaning contained in the word "Pharmakon," which can mean remedy or poison, and that its meaning is determined by the ways in which the protagonists interpret it: For Thoth, writing is a cure for bad memory and lack of wisdom; for Thamus it is a poison to those things. Derrida's argument is that writing has characteristics that cannot be interpreted in a binary, e.g., good or evil, black or white, etc. way. Writing is essentially pluralistic.

This pluralism is borne out when we look at the variety of interpretations that can be lent to the designs of the Tarot. As Tarot developed in occult circles, the symbolism of each card was maximized to accommodate as many esoteric references as possible, we have already seen this in the previous chapter, wherein the Devil card incorporates the Hermetic principle, "of above, so below." It also appears in less notable cards, such as the

Ace of Swords card, as it is depicted in Crowley's Thoth Tarot, in which it is intended to symbolically evoke the Excalibur narrative.

The Historical Development of the Tarot

Wayne's references to the Tarot, aside from outright denouncing it, include this Grail-derived genealogy:

> Treasured Grail hallows included the ancient Sword, the Chalice, the Platter, and the Spear, which evolved over time into the four suits of the Tarot Minor Arcana. Tarot cards were devised to pass on secret ideologies banned by the Roman Church; they contained heretical cards like the female pope, an allegory for Mary Magdalene and Isis. Tarot cards are thought to have been created in Milan in the early fifteenth century C.E., but the Legominism codes were lost, until a French occultist decoded the occultist secrets once more in the eighteenth century C.E. Tarot cards survived this period employed as playing cards; the swords, cups, pentacles, and wands of the tarot cards later became the famous spades, hearts, diamonds, and clubs that we know today. Spades/swords were an allegory for the male aspect of gods; hearts/cups were an allegory for the feminine, the Grail/womb; the clubs/scepters/wands represented the Royal San Greal bloodline; and the diamonds/pentacles/pentagrams represented the feminine goddess (Isis)[591]

Ronald Decker and Michael Dummett, who wrote an exhaustively researched trilogy of books on the topic, also trace

---

[591] Wayne, Gary (2014) *The Genesis 6 Conspiracy*. Trusted Books, A Division of Deep River Books. P. 324

their early development to mid-fifteenth century Italy. The archetypical, or standard, format of the deck came about in 1450, consisting of seventy-eight cards in four suits: Cups, Coins, Swords, and Wands. Each suit has ten numeral cards and four court cards. Twenty-one of the seventy-eight cards are "Trump" cards and are numbered. The twenty-second card, which is usually unnumbered (or is given zero or twenty-two), is "the Fool."[592]

Before we go any further into Decker and Dummett's analysis it is worth noting the background of Michael Dummett (June 27, 1925 – December 27, 2011). Dummett was a first-rate analytical philosopher who specialized in philosophy of mind and philosophy of language; his works on Frege and Wittgenstein are of seminal importance, and therefore, it is fascinating that he turned towards an examination of playing cards and the Tarot near the end of his life.

In *A Wicked Pack of Cards*, Decker and Dummett posit a few questions that are pertinent to our analysis, the first motivates the history and origin of the Tarot, which we just examined. The second asks: Was the Tarot deck intended to be the mystically charged magical accouterment we know it to be today, or did it start out as a simple card game that then got out of hand? Decker and Dummett go with the latter explanation:

> It is indisputable that by far the most salient use of Tarot cards, from the first evidence that we have of them, was for playing a particular type of card game. The earliest known documentary reference from Milan occurs in a letter, written in 1450, from Duke Francesco Sforza to his treasurer, asking him to send a Tarot pack, or if he could not find one, an ordinary pack of playing cards. Quite obviously, he

---

[592] Decker, Ronald; Depaulis, Thierry and Dummett, Michael (2002) *A Wicked Pack of Cards: The Origins of the Occult Tarot.* Duckworth Publishers. P. 25

wanted the Tarot cards for play: if he had wanted them for occult purposes, ordinary cards would not have been even an inferior substitute.[593]

One of the primary reasons this confusion arose is because, prior to the early twentieth century, people presumed that playing cards had been derived from the Tarot. Decker and Dummett claim that this was the result of a linguistic error. [594] The confusion was compounded by the fact that the Tarot deck continued to use the suit-signs of Batons, Swords, Cups, and Coins even when they were imported into countries that used the Hearts, Clubs, Diamonds, and Spades suits that were developed in France forty years after the invention of the Tarot.[595]

For Decker and Dummett the development of the two decks was heterogeneous and there isn't a substantial symbolic connection between the two, outside of their usage as recreational past-times. Prior to occultists ascribing esoteric value to the deck, Tarot cards had been used in parlor games in Italy where noble women were given a particular trump card and then a sonnet was composed for them, a practice that dovetails with the troubadour tradition discussed in the Significance of the Grail chapter. Note that in both cases, an artistic, poetic activity historically precedes a more somber and esoteric occult belief system.

The use of the Tarot in parlor games, besides being connected to the generation of sonnets, or for our purposes, "narratives," led to the cards becoming, "an instrument in autopsychotherapy..."[596] wherein the use of the cards aids in a kind of meditative self-awareness. Decker and Dummett deny that this use can be construed as occultic; however, this reading is based on the idea of a formal, text-based system of occultism. If

---

[593] Ibid p. 31
[594] Ibid p. 29
[595] Ibid pp. 30 - 32
[596] Ibid p. 34

we consider the fact that self-help, meditation practices, and yoga had been effectively incorporated into the new age milieu of the 1970s, it isn't tenable to say that this type of "autopsychotherapy" is totally heterogeneous to, or outside the bounds, of occult sensibilities.

Now we come to the subject of how occultists incorporated the Tarot into their system, and in doing so, made it a central part of their mythos:

> The order of the trumps was of critical importance for the occultists' incorporation of the Tarot into the general scheme of occult theory. The principal means for doing so was to correlate the twenty-two trumps (including the Fool) with the twenty-two letters of the Hebrew alphabet, and so to intertwine them with the mystical letter-symbolism that is a salient feature of the Kabbalah.[597]

Decker and Dummett claim that this was a flawed endeavor because occultists failed to take into account that in the original system the Swords and Batons are ranked in descending order: King, Queen, Knight, Jack, 10, 9, 8, 7, 6, 5, 4, 3, 2, 1, Ace. And for the Cups and Coins suits, the order was ascending: King, Queen, Knight, Jack, Ace, 2, 3, 4, 5, 6, 7, 8, 9.[598] This feature was eventually dropped as the Tarot gained popularity in France – one of the hotspots for its occultic interpretation. Decker and Dummett claim that this feature of the original deck was unknown to the occultists who were attempting to conjoin the trump cards to the Hebrew alphabet, and that, furthermore, the connection between the trumps and the twenty-two letters could not have been part of the designer's intentions because "the Cabala was first introduced

---

[597] Ibid p. 37
[598] Ibid p. 37

to the Christian public by Pico della Mirandola more than forty years after Tarot cards had been in existence."[599]

Tying this card game to the Kabalistic tradition was crucial for early occultists because Hebrew mysticism had evolved contemporaneously with Hermetic and Gnostic traditions and therefore resonated with an atavistic Middle-Ages type of mysticism. Also, Hebrew was thought to be the language that was spoken by God in his creation of the world.[600] Therefore, systems such as Cabalism and Hermeticism, which seek spells and rituals that can transform reality, would have an innate affinity for a language that is thought to be the original language.[601]

So far, Decker and Dummett have constructed a narrative that works to demystify the Tarot. The first step in this process of demystification is targeted at origin stories that might date the Tarot back to settings such as ancient Egypt or possibly Atlantis. The second step was the practical analysis of the Tarot cards being used for recreational purposes prior to their adoption as a form of divination. The next step in the process has to do with analyzing the symbolism attendant to the cards themselves; this process revolves around the demarcation between exoteric and esoteric symbolism.

Exoteric essentially means that the symbols being employed can be understood by any educated, or adequately cultured, member of the society: "For them, their symbolic meanings would have been as obvious as it is to us that a woman with a sword and a pair of scales represents Justice; it is these

---

[599] Ibid p. 38

[600] Decker, Ronald and Dummett, Michael (2019) *A History of the Occult Tarot.* Duckworth Publishing. P. 8

[601] As we saw previously, the creation of the Enochian language by John Dee, led to the creation of an originary language, i.e., the language spoken by angels.

meanings that constitute the exoteric symbolism of the cards."[602] The exoteric meaning, however, "in no way rules out that of a deeper level of esoteric symbolism needing specialized knowledge, not possessed by all educated people of the time, to discern; a surface meaning often coexists with another buried under it."[603] In this contrast that we can see how the use and development of the Tarot is analogous to the development of Freemasonry. Freemasonry sought to transmit esoteric, borderline scientific ideas through symbolism and rites; oftentimes the symbolism was exoteric, e.g., a blindfolded man represents an initiate who has not yet understood the mysteries of the seven sciences. The Tarot works in a similar, albeit more impersonal way. There can be an initiatic system of Tarot divination, for instance if one visits a fortune-teller or studies it while participating in an occult organization. However, this is not necessary, as one can simply buy a Tarot deck and an instruction book and do their own divinations. But if one does this, he or she may be accessing the mythic symbolism contained in the paintings on the card but not engaging each myth in a rigorously ritualistic way, as the adept does, and thereby neglecting the esoteric aspects.

Before we delve further into a more detailed analysis of the symbolism of particular Tarot cards, there is a basic philosophical aspect worth pointing out. The Tarot can also be analyzed in a more traditionally philosophically way, i.e., in terms of representationalism. According to Schopenhauer, philosophy ought to address the nature of reality not from the point of the view of the subject or object, but beginning from the representation, or "sense data," that exists between the two.[604]

---

[602] Decker, Ronald; Depaulis, Thierry and Dummett, Michael (2002) *A Wicked Pack of Cards: The Origins of the Occult Tarot.* Duckworth Publishers. P. 43
[603] Ibid p. 43
[604] According to Robert Brandom, this approach was also favored by Hegel: "At the metatheoretical level, Hegel presents his account

These representations obey a causal relationship to each other and therefore a scientific approach never "aims at the inmost nature of the world; it can never get beyond the representation; on the contrary, it really tells us nothing more than the relation of one representation to another."[605] While Schopenhauer's project did involve a certain degree of speculation on the "true" nature of things, what is interesting about this quote is how it lays out representations as if they were cards being turned over on a table. Of course, there is the backdrop of the table, and maybe the lighting we imagine in this scenario, but our focus is on the cards and the story they tell. Both the exoteric and the esoteric symbolism contain narratives, and oftentimes the synthesis of the two gives us a narrative as well.

The Major Arcana

As opposed to jumping directly into a discussion of the historical figures that shaped cartomancy, which is a subject we will briefly address later, in this section we will dig into the relevant aspects of the Tarot deck as it exists today in order to analyze its significance in the manner we have been employing up to this point; within the symbolism we will be looking especially at the imagery insofar as it is related to coincidence and repetition.

We will begin our discussion of the trump cards with the Fool, which as was mentioned above is either unnumbered or is

---

of the relations between phenomena and noumena, things as they are for consciousness and things as they are in themselves, appearance and reality, subjectivity and objectivity, in the form of a *phenomenology*. That is to say that we start with the ways those relations appear to us [...]"Brandom, Robert (2019) *A Spirit of Trust: A Reading of Hegel's Phenomenology*. Belknap Press of Harvard University Press. P. 424

[605] Schopenhauer, Arthur (1969) *The World As Will and Representation* translated by E.F.J. Payne. Dover Publications. P. 28

listed as 0 or 22. According to the system of nineteenth century occultist Eliphas Lévi, the Fool is listed as zero, but the card's placement is between 20 and 21.[606] The Hebrew letter associated with the Fool card when it is placed near the end is "shin." However, if the Fool card is placed at the front of the deck, it is given the letter "aleph." Given its ambiguity, it seems appropriate that the Fool card would accommodate this implacable numbering. The basic image presented on the card is of a young man looking up at the sky just as he's about to walk off a cliff. Some Tarot experts place the card at the beginning of the deck because it represents the transition from naiveté to knowledge:

> The Fool also symbolizes the Spirit of God about to descend into nothing –falling from the cliff- at the beginning of creation. And the Fool is also the perfected spirit of man approaching the One. The Fool nature commences at the moment when a man enters upon the quest for a fuller life and a deeper understanding of life.[607]

There are a few narratives here that resonate with our previous analyses. First, there is the movement from a very basic, immanent, consciousness to the self-awareness attendant to meta-consciousness. Recall that Kant argued that we couldn't have the basic sense of consciousness without the meta, self-aware aspect. Perhaps the Fool symbolizes an unreflective state of consciousness prior to the awakening of this latent meta-consciousness. [608] Second, we discussed this awakening, or transition, in terms of a Biblical allegory: the fall from Eden and in

---

[606] Decker, Ronald and Dummett, Michael (2019) *A History of the Occult Tarot.* Duckworth Publishing. P. 57

[607] Laurence, Theodor (1972) *How the Tarot Speaks to Modern Man.* Stackpole Books. Pp. 26 - 27

[608] Or, an awareness of the distinction between the two forms of consciousness.

terms of anthropology, the transition into puberty. In all these respects, the Fool card appears to presage a sense, or spell, of disenchantment.

A further reading, that has already appeared in our analysis, is that the image is presenting us with two perspectives: God's descent into creation of the world and man's descent into self-awareness and deeper knowledge. Take into consideration what Schopenhauer said about approaching phenomena from the representational perspective. When positing this perspective, he was essentially granting that we can approach phenomena from the point of the subject (this is generally what Hegel and Fichte do), from the object (this is what a great many empiricists and scientifically minded individuals do), or we can approach it from the point of the representation itself. Schopenhauer opted for this route because he believed that the sole function of the faculty of understanding is to "know causality" and that causality, if it exists, exists at the representational level.[609] For our discussion of the Tarot, Schopenhauer's approach can be read as a mediating perspective between two interpretations. All the Tarot cards contain dual readings that are based on a common theme, the Fool, because that card implies a descent from the divine to the earthly, or the movement from the innocence in the Garden of Eden to the worldliness after the fall; it can be subject to some of the more broad and abstract readings allowed by the deck.

In divination, The Fool card means folly, failure, and mistake. It speaks of the follies, failures, and mistakes of the man who has no sense of order either in his immediate surroundings or in the universe at large.[610] This foolishness and naiveté is analogous to Wolfram's depiction of Parzival up until after his first visit to the Grail castle. And as we saw in our chapter on the Grail, what is important here is Hegel's notion of error being

---

[609] It is also, according to Schopenhauer, at the causal level of representations that the principles of logic can be applied. Ibid p. 82

[610] Ibid p. 27

essential to understanding. With a more pagan influenced reading, Crowley posited that the Fool card is associated with the mythical Green Man.[611]

The next trump card is The Magician, which is numbered one and given a Hebrew letter of Bet. In this card's image, a man is holding a wand in his raised right hand while his left hand points downwards. This is the same gesture made by Baphomet in artistic renderings. The one hand up and the other down is meant to signify the Hermetic axiom of: "As above, so below." The choice of hands is telling as well, since magical pursuits for spiritual knowledge and enlightenment are usually referred to as "the right hand path," whereas magical pursuits aimed at worldly and material goals are referred to as "the left hand path." The magician card symbolizes a man with a firm will, faith and conviction:

> The Magician is a type of perfect man represented in the card as standing in an attitude of will which precedes action [...] Upon the table before the Magician lie the four Tarot symbols: the wand, the cup, the sword, and the pentacle. The four alchemical principles of which the world consists, that is the four elements of fire, water, air, and earth, correspond to the four Tarot suits.[612]

These four objects are within the reach of the Magician and are to be used according to his will. Essentially, this card signifies power, or at least mastery, and to a certain extent implies a duty to utilize these tools with temperance and wisdom.

The next trump card is the High Priestess. It is numbered two, and its Hebrew letter is Gimel. This card "symbolizes the union of male and female, of feminine and masculine, of all

---

[611] We will delve more deeply into this figure in the Significance of Robert Anton Wilson Chapter.

[612] Ibid p. 31

opposites, [so] that the two principles may accomplish an equal destiny."[613] This card is straightforward and the association of the number two with duality and the reconciliation of opposing natures would qualify the symbolism attendant to this card as being exoteric.

After the High Priestess is The Empress. It is numbered three, and its Hebrew letter is Dalet. This card continues the theme of uniting opposites at play in the High Priestess card, but it includes the imperative to action. Whereas the exoteric reading of the High Priestess is that card's dominant aspect, this card hints at two possible esoteric readings. The first is philosophical and has to do with the concept of "praxis." Praxis means integrating some piece of theoretical knowledge into one's daily activity. The concept of praxis attained a great deal of traction with Marxist philosophy, but it goes back to the ancients, as most of the early philosophical schools, especially the stoics, stressed the importance of a lived philosophy. The number three is important here, philosophically-speaking, because it relates to the third stage of the dialectical process: synthesis. In a religious context, the number three relates to the Holy Trinity. The other esoteric aspect has to do with the incorporation of the female symbol into the card's design, often placed in the middle of a heart. This seems to evoke the chivalry of Grail quests where the attainment of a princess's hand in marriage must be achieved through the overcoming of trials and feats of heroism.

The next trump card is the Emperor. Its number is five, and its Hebrew letter is Heh. The Emperor represents many of the themes that were present in the Magician but in a context that is wiser and more mature:

> The Emperor's power is the power to differentiate, to choose exactly how his energy is to be used. Realization is first and foremost realization of power. But power is neutral. On the physical plane,

---

[613] Ibid p. 33

it is man who directs power and uses it for good or evil. The work of the Emperor is to direct energy through useful and productive channels.[614]

Many occultists tackle the subject of power attendant to this card in terms of alchemy or Tantric sexual energy. On a philosophical reading, it seems that the Emperor card represents the power of reason, in Kantian terms. With a contemporary rationalist reading, the reference to differentiation can be taken to mean the inferential powers we acquire through acculturation and interpretation of norms. For the rationalist, these powers, albeit miraculous in a certain respect, are not supernatural – the Emperor card represents a shadow-side of this perspective and holds out the promise that there might indeed be something supernatural or divine about the power of reason.

Following the Emperor card is one very important to our overall discussion: the Hierophant, which has a number of five, and a Hebrew letter of Vav. In a philosophical sense the Hierophant card represents an internal awareness on the part of the subject as he comports himself in society:

> The message of the Hierophant card is that man, by exercising and heeding his conscience, will realize that the good of society as a whole should be his constant aim, that as a part of society he benefits or suffers from society exactly what he puts into it. The Hierophant card represents the point in the ascending spiral of the cycle of life where man finds himself in full possession of the power of choice. Heeding his conscience, yielding to higher positive inspiration, he may turn from the pull of his more base nature and devote himself to social welfare.

---

[614] *bid p. 39*

> The obedient man decides to live, not for self alone,
> but for the general good of all people.[615]

This is very much in line with Aristotelian philosophy, not so much the theoretical aspects but with the end goal, which is the concept of Eudaimonia. "Eudaimonia" is a Greek word that is often translated as "happiness;" what it was meant to convey, however, was more multifaceted. It means living a good life, and entails being a well-rounded citizen that engages in intellectual and political discourse.

The esoteric relevance here, however, is very deep, the Hierophant card is astrologically associated with the sign of Taurus, and given Wayne's analysis of Melchizedek's legacy as being related to a Gnostic Bull-cult, we can see that there is a distinct affinity between the Hierophant card and Melchizedek, This is a point that has been borne out in other Tarot studies which adds layers to the Melchizedek mythos. Grail researcher, John Matthews explicitly identifies the Hierophant card with Melchizedek and writes that:

> We first hear of Melchizedek in Biblical tradition as the archpriest and king of Salem. In Genesis 14:18 he is said to have blessed the patriarch Abraham and come forth from the temple to offer bread and wine. This has been taken to prefigure the Eucharistic offering and makes Melchizedek one of the most important Biblical precursors of Christ. This in turn links him with the deeper Christian mysteries of the Grail, which is described as containing the blood of Jesus and being used to celebrate the first Eucharist.[616]

---

[615] Ibid p. 41

[616] Matthews, John (2007) *The Grail Tarot: A Templar Vision*. St. Martin's Press. Pp. 24 - 25

Depicted on the card, the Hierophant sits on a throne between two pillars. On his head is a pope-like crown and in his left hand is a staff, which at the top, is a triple cross. Standing, or possibly kneeling before him, are two priests or monks. It seems as if the Hierophant card is one point from which the ambiguity associated with the figure of Melchizedek stems because, if the entire system of the Tarot is spurious, as some Christians claim, then all the Arcanum figures are false representations, designed to mislead the faithful. This would line-up with the idea of a false, or counterfeit religion and counterfeit pope, being depicted on Arcanum five. However, if we merely take this system and its attendant images at face-value, without applying any background theological suppositions, the Hierophant card merely represents the institution of a formal religion for the betterment of man and society.

The next trump card is the Lovers. It is numbered six and its Hebrew letter is Zain. In an exoteric way, this card represents duality and sexuality. This duality encompasses the concepts of cause and effect as well as vice and virtue. The nude female appears on the left, beside her is the serpent from the Garden of Eden, and on the right is the nude male figure. The Lovers card as a total ensemble indicates the struggle between conscience and the baser nature, between aspiration and the passions, between proper and improper use of sexual energy.[617]

After the Lovers is the Chariot, numbered seven with a Hebrew letter of Chet. The exoteric reading of this card is victory. On a psychological reading, as it might relate to personal betterment, this pertains to overcoming obstacles: both self-generated (drives, impulses, bad habits, etc.) and external. The image depicted on the card shows the chariot being pulled by two sphinxes, one white and one black:

---

[617] Laurence, Theodor (1972) *How the Tarot Speaks to Modern Man*. Stackpole Books. P. 45

The sphinx always symbolizes the passage of time. The white sphinx signifies fortunate periods of time, while the black sphinx, adverse periods of time. Both fortune and adversity serve the man who is victorious over the obstacles and ordeals of life on his journey to success. Both pull his chariot. Both good fortune and bad are harnessed by a dominant will and are subsequently directed by him who exercises such will.[618]

The next trump is Strength. Its number is eight and its Hebrew letter is Tet. This card depicts a woman with an infinity sign as a halo closing the jaws of a lion. It continues the theme of self-confidence and overcoming of adversity we have seen throughout the deck, as the emphasis at play in this card is that the strength is derived from or incorporates love.

Next comes The Hermit, which has the number nine and a Hebrew letter of Yod. This card brings the procession of Arcana that we've seen so far back to a more intellectual theme. In his left hand, the Hermit is holding a staff signifying age, and in his left hand he holds a lantern, which signifies the light of reason. We must wonder if this card, or its exoteric symbolism influenced Nietzsche's narrative of the madman who goes into town with a lantern "looking for God" and only finding bemused onlookers, smashes the lantern on the ground and declares, "I come too early!" In Nietzsche's narrative, assuming that the lantern represents the light of reason as is depicted in the Hermit card, the message is that at that stage of modernity we were still not worthy of the possession of reason – or possibly to the claim of possession. There is some very vague speculation that The Hermit card relates to Prester John. John Matthews, however, makes this connection explicit, and gives his mythical genealogy as being the son of Parzival's half-brother Feirefiz and the Grail Maiden, Repanse de Schoy. The figure of the Hermit card, as Matthews

---

[618] Ibid p. 46

interprets it, is intended to combine the "elements of temporal kingship with spiritual power in much the same way that the Templars were determined to."[619]

Following The Hermit we have The Wheel of Fortune. Its number is ten and its Hebrew letter is Koph. This card marks the point in the precession of Arcana, in which an impersonal object is central – prior to this it has been characters and attributes. The image on the card is overloaded with esoteric symbolism: Hebrew letters, Hermetic and alchemical symbols, and a sphinx. Exoterically the card symbolizes the vicissitudes of chance and the flux of good and bad luck. It also represents the completion of a cycle and the beginning of a new one, which is analogous to the dialectical process, in which the synthesis assumes the position of a new thesis.

The next trump card is Justice, numbered eleven and given the Hebrew letter Lamed. The image on the card depicts a king with a crown sitting on a throne and holding a sword. Its exoteric meaning is justice (obviously), but keeping in mind that:

> Justice is not triumph, however, but a step toward triumph. Any man who thinks success is possible without sacrifice is not seeking success, but an easy way of life. Sacrifice is an essential part of growth.[620]

After Justice is the Hanged Man. Its number is twelve and its Hebrew letter is Mem. This takes the esoteric theme of sacrifice attendant to the Justice card and presents it in an exoteric fashion: a man is hanging upside on the tree of sacrifice. His left leg is crossed under his right leg, which is straight. Despite the Christ-like connotations of this card, sacrifice ending in death

---

[619] Matthews, John (2007) *The Grail Tarot: A Templar Vision*. St. Martin's Press. Pp. 32 - 33
[620] Laurence, Theodor (1972) *How the Tarot Speaks to Modern Man*. Stackpole Books. P. 55

is not the theme here: the face of the figure "expresses deep entrancement, not suffering [...] The figure as a whole, suggests life in suspension, but life and not death."[621]

Nevertheless, the similarity to Christ should be considered here, and possibly St. Peter as well since he was crucified upside down. If these figures are considered in the reading, they should be incorporated in a contemplative and meditative sense. Such a reading would, in many respects, coincide with a pagan reading of the card as being representative of the Norse god Odin, who hanged himself from Yggdrasil, the "Tree of Life," for nine days and nine nights, in order to gain the knowledge of the runes. Decker and Dummett claim that the card was originally titled "The Traitor" and its exoteric significance would have been obvious to most citizens of Renaissance Rome, Florence, or Milan because:

> The bodies of executed traitors were sometimes subjected to this indignity [being hanged upside down from the gallows]. More usually, paintings were made of those deemed traitors to the State, showing them thus hung upside-down; this was a universally understood means of branding them traitors. [622]

This is an interesting bit of demystification, and if we consider Peter's denial of Christ a form of betrayal, then this Biblical narrative would accommodate their reading, insofar as the traitor's hanging might be inspired by Peter's crucifixion. It still doesn't answer how the theme of this card resonates with Odin's hanging, which would explain the serene look on the man's face. There is the possibility that this aspect was slowly worked into

[621] Ibid p. 56
[622] Decker, Ronald; Depaulis, Thierry and Dummett, Michael (2002) *A Wicked Pack of Cards: The Origins of the Occult Tarot.* Duckworth Publishers. Pp. 45 - 46

the card over time. However, it seems viable to posit the theory that the Tarot creators merely intended to create a sense of humble acquiescence in the face of death, regardless as to who the hanging man was prior to death.

The next trump card is Death and is number thirteen with a Hebrew letter of Nun. The card depicts a black knight on a white horse, and its exoteric meaning is pretty obvious. Traditionally, Tarot enthusiasts emphasize the positive "transformative" aspect of this card, most likely to not scare off the newbies. In a philosophical sense, the card does have a beneficent quality if we accept the Hegelian conception of negativity. On a more pragmatic reading, negation in Hegel's system corresponds to error and the correction of understanding that extends from it. On a more metaphysically charged reading, negativity can be loosely associated with the dialectical antithesis, whereby the aspirant, or initiate, passes through a deathlike state of negation in order to achieve a more enlightened state of affirmation (which would correlate with the dialectical synthesis).[623]

After Death comes Temperance. Its number is fourteen and its Hebrew letter is Samekh. The exoteric reading of this card is that it has to do with abstinence, while the esoteric reading, which hews closely to alchemy, involves the blending of two contrasting elements, such as hot and cold or the spiritual and the material. Therefore, the central meaning involves finding a point of balance; the androgynous angel depicted on the card signifies this in-between state.

The next trump card is the Devil, numbered fifteen with a Hebrew letter of Ayin. As with Death, the exoteric reading of the Devil card is obvious. What is interesting about the image

---

[623] This type of reading, which according to Magee is a viable reading of Hegel, pretty much summarizes why it is so very difficult for "serious" analytical philosophers to rehabilitate or incorporate Hegel into their work -his obtuse language and writing style doesn't help either.

depicted on this card is that the figures of the Lovers are repeated, but now they are enchained.

> The Devil card depicts a male and a female chained to the Devil's pedestal. It should be noted that the chains are loose about their necks. The chains can be lifted off, but as the card suggests, the man and woman may have become accustomed to their presence.[624]

In a certain way, the Devil card is antithetical to the Hierophant card, because in that card the figures in the front are facing the Hierophant in a stage of conscious unchained obeisance. The replication of the Lovers in the Devil card portrays the Devil lurking behind the scenes, his actions unbeknownst to the couple. The duality of these two cards may be one key towards understanding the dual nature Wayne attributes to Melchizedek, when his name is used in reference to a Gnostic version of his priesthood.

Next, we have the Tower. Its number is sixteen and its Hebrew letter is Peh. There doesn't appear to be a straight-forward exoteric reading on this card, Laurence writes:

> That The Tower card depicts ruin is obvious on the surface, but the tower, itself, is not a material building. Rather, it is the rending of the House of Life, when evil has reigned supreme therein [...] The Tower card speaks of the ruin of fortunes for those who by virtue of wealth, honor, and position have foolishly become greatly arrogant with pride.[625]

---

[624] Laurence, Theodor (1972) *How the Tarot Speaks to Modern Man*. Stackpole Books. Pp. 65 - 66
[625] Ibid pp. 67 - 68

Obviously, the combination of excessive pride and a tower ought to draw everyone's thoughts toward the mythical Tower of Babel, and just as there is a great deal of ambiguity and "murkiness" around the Tower of Babel narrative, there is around this particular trump card. Decker and Dummett even get a little mystified themselves during their process of demystification:

> The Devil assumes many guises, all of them instantly recognizable. The Tower, on the other hand, is the most obscure card in the entire sequence. It has the most varied nomenclature and the most varied representations: it looks as though confusion set in at an early stage about what it was meant to signify. The names used for it in the early sources do not include 'the Tower'; among them are 'the Fire', 'the Thunderbolt' and 'the Lightning'.[626]

Crowley was especially fascinated by this card for a variety of reasons. First, he saw the destruction implied by the Tower card as a manifestation of a final judgment that would have to take place before the beginning of a new Aeon. We have already seen how Crowley and his followers interpreted the two world wars as pivotal events predicted by *The Book of the Law*, hence the significance of this card plays into the narrative shift from the Aeon of Osiris to the Aeon of Horus. It is most likely for this reason that when Crowley designed his own Tarot deck (the "Thoth Tarot"), he directed the artist, Lady Frieda Harris, to put the eye of Horus in a prominent place above the Tower.

Obviously, placing a disembodied eye above the Tower, to a certain extent, evokes the eye above the pyramid on the Great Seal of the United States. And, if we consider the Tower card to be a pictorial reiteration of the Tower of Babel, then the placement of

---

[626] Decker, Ronald; Depaulis, Thierry and Dummett, Michael (2002) *A Wicked Pack of Cards: The Origins of the Occult Tarot.* Duckworth Publishers. P. 46

the eye also suggests the conspiracy theory that there was an intergalactic portal, or "stargate," at the top of the Tower of Babel. Crowley claims that this portion of *The Book of the Law* is a reference to the Tower card:

> Invoke me under my stars! Love is the law, love under will. Nor let the fools mistake love; for there are love and love. There is the dove, and there is the serpent. Choose ye well! He, my prophet, hath chosen, knowing the law of fortress, and the great mystery of the House of God.[627]

In the Thoth Deck, the dove is depicted on the top left side of the eye and a serpent is depicted on the top right. The choice between the two ostensibly appears to be a choice between God and the Devil, or possibly between the paths of white and black magick. The Tower card also pops up in Thomas Pynchon's seminal postmodern novel, *Gravity's Rainbow*. Published in 1973 and set in post-war Europe, the novel incorporates a wide variety of pop cultural and scientific references but focuses especially on the production and launching of V-2 rockets. On the scientific side of the over-arching narrative there are references to physics, a deterministic universe, and the statistical impact patterns of rockets. On the more metaphysical side, there are references to occult groups, conspiracy theories, and the Tarot.

The Tower card comes into play in a section near the very end of the book titled "Weissmann's Tarot:"

> Of 77 cards that could have come up, Weissmann is "covered," that is his present condition is set forth, by The Tower. It is a puzzling card, and everybody has a different story on it. It shows a bolt of lightning striking a tall phallic structure, and two

---

[627] Crowley, Aleister (1988) *The Holy Books of Thelema*. Samuel Weiser, INC. Pp. 110 - 111

figures, one wearing a crown, falling from it. Some read ejaculation, and leave it at that. Others see a Gnostic or Cathar symbol for the Church of Rome, and this is generalized to mean any System which cannot tolerate heresy: a system which, by its nature, must sooner or later fall. We know by now that it is also the Rocket.[628]

This modern reiteration of the Tower as a rocket, and not just any rocket, but the space-age ideal of a rocket, one which, as an avenging force "represents victory over splendor" and, on the Kabbalist Tree of Life "connects the sephira Netzach, victory, with Hod, glory or splendor"[629] leads to the exclamation: "What? A dialectical Tarot? Yes indeedyfoax! A-and if you don't think there are Marxist-Leninist magicians around, well *you* better think *again!*" [630] Technically the dialectical process to which this statement refers is between the demons that accompany the seraphim and a new kind of demon that arises on the bridge between them, which is itself created by the Tower. The significance evoked here is not merely "rockets," but is the atomic bomb and atomic peril in general, of which William Burroughs speculated:

Can any soul survive the searing fireball of an atomic blast? If human and animal souls are seen as electromagnetic force fields, such fields could be totally disrupted by a nuclear explosion [...] and this is precisely the ultrasecret and supersensitive function of the atom bomb: a Soul Killer...[631]

[628] Pynchon, Thomas (2006) *Gravity's Rainbow*. Penguin Classics. P. 762
[629] Ibid p. 762
[630] Ibid p. 763.
[631] Burroughs, William (1987) *The Western Lands*. Penguin Books. P. 7

If this is the most salient modern, or postmodern, reading of the Tower arcana then the significance of the card relates not only to the move into scientism that was prompted by the end of World War II and culminated in 9/11, but its significance also resonates with the conspiracy theories that postulated a correlation between our nuclear activity and UFO phenomena; whether it be us triggering the concern of extraterrestrials with our destructive activity, or by actually tearing a hole in the space-time continuum, and hence, unknowingly replicating the eye of Horus/stargate phenomenon.[632]

The next trump card is The Star. Its number is seventeen and its Hebrew letter is Tzaddi. The image on the card portrays a nude woman kneeling on her left knee as she pours liquid from two containers, one in each hand. One is being poured into the lake before her and the other onto the land in the foreground. The symbolism here is esoteric, of the land and sea being united by a feminine energy. The simplicity of the scene contrasts strongly with the chaos and destruction of the preceding Tower card:

> Herein is truth symbolized, nude, as truth can be perceived only when stripped of dogmatism and preconceived ideas, when it is not wrapped in illusions which The Tower card destroys.[633]

After The Star we have The Moon, whose number is eighteen and Hebrew letter is Qof. The card depicts an anthropomorphic moon serenely looking down at two dogs standing before a gate, and a crawfish crawling out of the water. Laden with symbolism though it may be, this card seems to exude the old-school Italian charm that Decker and Dummett would see

---

[632] These subjects will be formally addressed and explored in greater depth in the Significance of UFO Phenomena chapter.
[633] Laurence, Theodor (1972) *How the Tarot Speaks to Modern Man*. Stackpole Books. P. 71

as hallmarks of the Tarot's origin. In terms of esoteric meaning, Laurence writes that:

> In divination, The Moon card symbolizes deception, secret enemies, and false friends. Those who respond negatively to The Tower card phases of life see enemies all around them.[634]

Next is The Sun. Its number is nineteen and its Hebrew letter is Resh. The image on the card shows a naked child riding a horse while the stoic sun looks outward to the bearer of the card. There is a Eudomonic and rationalistic quality to the narratives emanating from this card:

> The Sun card ensemble personifies the sexes truly wed, the laws of harmony obeyed, and happiness in the midst of privations and adversities. The figured sun represents self-consciousness, self-awareness – the direct light as antithesis of the reflected light (Moon). The characteristic type of progressing man is symbolized by the naked child, for such a man has become as a little child; a child in the sense of innocence and simplicity, which is true wisdom.[635]

The next trump card is Judgment, with a number of twenty and a Hebrew letter of Shin. Crowley deemed this card The Aeon. Michael Tsarion claims that one of Crowley's highpoints was his reinterpretation of the Tarot, specifically in his alignment of the Judgment card with the Aeon of Horus:

> The imagery of Arcanum 20 (in the Thoth Tarot) is based on the essence of what Crowley received from his guide [Aiwass]. Following in the footsteps

---

[634] Ibid p. 74
[635] Ibid p. 78

of Christian mystic Joachim of Fiore, he wrote of how history had a trinitarian structure. Specifically, there are three great epochs corresponding to three periods of the so-called "Platonic Cycle" of 25, 920 years. (This cycle is traditionally divided into *twelve* divisions making the famous signs of the zodiac.) The first epoch, which Crowley named the *Aeon of Isis*, was a period of Matriarchies which allegedly terminated around 255 BC. During this age societies were predominantly eccentric, egalitarian and pantheistic. The superseding period was the *Aeon of Osiris*; an age of Patriarchal communities which maintained dominion until approximately 1900 AD. The present *Aeon of Horus* is, therefore, the period of the sovereign individual, the Son or Child of Creation; and as with any period of birth, the age has seen several traumatic events.[636]

Tsarion sees this current Aeon in purely liberatory terms. The traditional Tarot representation shows an angel blowing its horn over a crowd of rejoicing nude figures; exoterically it denotes emancipation, or at least collective rejoicing. The individuals are standing within tombs, which implies the theme of resurrection, leading us to see the Judgment in question as the "Great Judgment" at the end of time.

The final trump card is The World. Its number is twenty-one and its Hebrew letter is Taw. The card depicts a young female nude surrounded by a garland. In each of the four corners are the four living creatures of Revelation 4:6 – 8: a lion, an ox, an eagle, and a man. There is an exoteric narrative of attainment or "success" attendant to the symbolism of this card:

[636] http://www.michaeltsarion.com/aleister-crowley.html accessed 12/02/20

> Success has come to him who understands evolution in its deepest sense: the evolution of inner man as symbolized by the four creatures in The World card. The head of the Man indicates that both intelligence and intuition (male and female) are necessary guides to ultimate success in life. The eagle signifies sex energy, but sex energy which is used to lift one to lofty goals and heights. The bull represents the fructifying agent of will and points out the necessity for positive action. The lion denotes that moral courage which is necessary to true success and which comes from the proper use of sexual energy.[637]

Laurence states that even though this card gives a narrative of attainment and fulfillment, the adept might still find a void within himself. This void, which according to Lacan is an unavoidable, or defining, aspect of being human, leads back to The Fool, and a repetition of the cycle. This return to the beginning then brings us to our next section.

Repetition and Significance; or the Significance of Repetition

Regardless as to whether the reader has ever used a pack of Tarot cards or not, it should be evident from the above summary that they are chock full of symbolism, so much so that one can see in them a very early model of compound conspiratorial thinking at work. Since we are only devoting one chapter to the subject it is imperative that we locate the aspects of the Tarot that are the most salient to our discussion and therefore, the most significant.

One way to tackle the question of what is "significant" in the mythic sense is to ask: what warrants repetition, and how much repetition? Eliade has claimed that ancient rituals are

---

[637] Laurence, Theodor (1972) *How the Tarot Speaks to Modern Man*. Stackpole Books. P. 83

intended to recreate the sacred narratives attributed to the gods, which amounts to an anthropological or theological analysis. How can we address the phenomena of repetition from a more modern and philosophical perspective though? Heidegger attacked this question in his interrogation of Friedrich Nietzsche's idea of "Eternal Recurrence." This concept, sometimes referred to as "The Eternal Return" was first addressed by Nietzsche in this famous passage from *The Gay Science*:

> *The greatest weight.* –What, if some day or night a demon were to steal after you into your loneliest loneliness and say to you: "This life as you now live it and have lived it, you will have to live once more and innumerable times more; and there will be nothing new in it, but every pain and every joy and every thought and sigh and everything unutterably small or great in your life will have to return to you, all in the same succession and sequence – even this spider and this moonlight between the trees, and even this moment and I myself. The eternal hourglass of existence is turned upside down again and again, and you with it, speck of dust!"
>
> Would you not throw yourself down and gnash your teeth and curse the demon who spoke thus? Or have you once experienced a tremendous moment when you would have answered him: "You are a god and never have I heard anything more divine." If this thought gained possession of you, it would change you as you are or perhaps crush you. The question in each and every thing, "Do you desire this once more and innumerable times more?" would lie upon your actions as the greatest weight. Or how well disposed would you have to become to yourself and to life *to crave nothing more*

fervently than this ultimate confirmation and seal?[638]

One of the decisive points that Heidegger makes in his massive and daunting analysis of Nietzsche is that the thought of the Eternal Return has to be "thought in the true thinking of being as a whole, namely, that such thinking is a cry of distress, arising from calamity."[639] The "cry of calamity" is a reference to actions depicted within *Thus Spake Zarathustra*. However, we can discern that this "cry" also resonates with Heidegger's own moral philosophy, in that the existential moment of angst is the moment when the thought of Eternal Recurrence carries the most weight for the thinking subject.

For Heidegger, this thought demands integration into our deepest sense of being, and in doing so, is a sort of secular reiteration of the Eucharist narrative. Keeping with the pseudo-religious reading, however, it is a thought that demands a sense of reverence on the part of the thinker. This sense of reverence is contrasted with characters in *Thus Spake Zarathustra* who reduce the thought to "a mere ditty, into empty talk [...]"[640]

This empty talk is sometimes referred to as a "barrelhouse song" and its deleterious effect is constituted by the trivialization of the thought of eternal recurrence. At the risk of sounding like Slavoj Žižek, does not this interpretation resonate with the repetition of the hermetic "As above so below" gesture as it appears in the Devil card? When it was utilized by the magician it seemed to be serving the purpose of understanding the descent of

[638] Nietzsche, Friedrich (1974) *The Gay Science: With a Prelude in Rhymes and an Appendix of Songs* by Friedrich Nietzsche; translated, with commentary, by Walter Kaufmann Vintage Books. Section 341 (pp. 273 – 274)
[639] Heidegger, Martin (1991) *Nietzsche: Volumes One and Two* translated by David Farrell Krell. Harper San Francisco, a Division of Harper Collins Publishers (Volume Two) p. 55
[640] Ibid p. 55

the Fool and the arising of an awareness of meta-consciousness. Now, in the hands, pun intended, of the Devil it evinces a kind of mockery.[641] This is a mockery of human progress. However, in a Hegelian sense, it can be interpreted as a state of negation that must be passed through in order to retain and advance one's sense of understanding.

The repetition of the hermetic principle is not the only repetition that occurs within the imagery of the Devil card – remember that the Lovers are also reiterated here, also within a derogatory context. This too can be read in terms of a negation that must be overcome, but what is the meaning of such repetitions within a medium given over to repetition? The answer will most likely entail an acknowledgement that it is not merely a homogenous repetition at play here, but a repetition punctuated by *difference*.

This leads us to one of the other perspectives in contemporary philosophy that draws heavily on the work of Friedrich Nietzsche, that of Gilles Deleuze and specifically his book, *Difference and Repetition*. Published in 1968, *Difference and Repetition* seeks to clarify our thinking on a variety of topics, one of which is representationalism. Both Heidegger and Deleuze are considered "postmodern" philosophers in some respect because they proffered critiques of representational thinking.[642] We're not going to wade into all the details of the debate for the simple reason that anything that officially becomes a "debate" in philosophy is a subject with a series of arguments for and against a theory; and proving or disproving representationalism is not the aim of this book – I've referenced writers so far who have

---

[641] Also, note that in the Magician card the right hand is holding a wand symbolizing spiritual vitality, whereas in the Devil card the lowered left hand holds a club, symbolizing brute material forces.
[642] Richard Rorty, who was not a post-modern philosopher also attacked representationalism from an analytic perspective in 1979's *Philosophy and the Mirror of Nature*. Essentially, such attacks on the theory were part of the zeitgeist.

representationalist preconceptions and others who have fought to dispute them, hopefully in a way that is *useful* for us. The only reason the issue is being addressed here is because the Tarot is a medium that is literally representational.

Early in *Difference and Repetition* Deleuze states that:

> If repetition is possible, it is due to miracle rather than to law. It is against the law: against the similar form and the equivalent content of law. If repetition can be found, even in nature, it is in the name of a power which affirms itself against the law, which works underneath laws, perhaps superior to laws. If repetition exists, it expresses at once a singularity opposed to the general, a universality opposed to the particular, a distinctive opposed to the ordinary, an instaneity opposed to variation and eternity opposed to permanence. In every respect, repetition is a transgression. It puts law into question, it denounces its nominal or general character in favour of a more profound and more artistic reality.[643]

The predicates of "distinctive," "artistic," and "singularity" for Deleuze indicate a Nietzschean conception of the will. "A will willing itself through all change, a power opposed to law, an interior of the earth opposed to the laws of its surface," is how Deleuze characterizes it.[644] It is important to keep in mind that while Deleuze is addressing both repetition in a psychological sense as well as in a physical, or scientific, sense, the thrust of his work is situated at the fissure between these two realms. Making sense of this fissure, or gap, is a priority for the two modern philosophical approaches we have utilized so far: Hermeneutics

---

[643] Deleuze, Gilles (1994) *Difference and Repetition*. Translated by Paul Patton. Columbia University Press. Pp. 2 - 3
[644] Ibid p. 6

and Structuralism. As was mentioned earlier, Deleuze is often referred to as a "poststructuralist" and he gives us insight into how the subject of repetition plays a role in his system of thought; specifically how it does away with the issue of representationalism:

> The mask, the costume, the covered is everywhere the truth of the uncovered. The mask is the true subject of repetition. Because repetition differs in kind from representation, the repeated cannot be represented: rather, it must always be signified, masked by what signifies it, itself masking what it signifies [...] Repetition is truly that which disguises itself in constituting itself, that which constitutes itself only by disguising itself. It is not underneath the masks, but is formed from one mask to another, as though from one distinctive point to another, from one privileged instant to another, with and within the variations. The masks do not hide anything except other masks.[645]

The theoretical narrative he is spinning here is dizzying and offers a sense of foundation within a will that is capable of affirming repetition. Such a will is exemplified by the individual, who when confronted with the possibility of eternal recurrence in Nietzsche's narrative, exclaims: "You are a god and never have I heard anything more divine." Attendant to this sense of affirmation in Deleuze's narrative is artistry, which we saw was a key component in both Nietzsche's and Crowley's discourses. Deleuze was a "legitimate" philosopher so he didn't mention Crowley in his writings, but we can see how the work of both falls within the parameters of his philosophical narrative.

With this said, how do we apply these ideas to cards which traffic in both representations and repetition? The first thing that

---

[645] Ibid pp. 17 - 18

we can point out is that the design and creation of the cards marks a certain degree of artistry in that the creator is trying to load the imagery of each card with as many signifiers as is relevant, while maintaining the subtlety necessary for interpretation; keeping in mind that each interpretation is suspended within the context of the cards by which it is surrounded, as well as by the query of the petitioner.

Historically, both Deleuze and Heidegger saw themselves as pushing philosophy into the twentieth century, and while Heidegger insisted on the somber integration of eternal recurrence into one's thoughts, Deleuze argues that Heidegger's thinking about being is still subordinated to the "identity of representation." Deleuze insists on something more radical:

> In reality, the distinction between the same and the identical bears fruit only if one subjects the Same to a conversion which relates it to the different, while at the same time the things and beings which are distinguished in the in the different suffer a corresponding radical destruction of their *identity*. Only on this condition is difference thought in itself, neither represented nor mediated.[646]

Therefore, it is not enough to merely think the thought of eternal recurrence, one must think "difference in itself;" and in a sense this is a demarcation between the world of myth – which is dominated by repetition – and the thinking of difference – which is an interrogation of, or active participation within, the mythic realm. This breaks down the distinction between the "real" and its simulacra: "Taken in its strict sense, eternal return means that each thing exists only in returning, copy of an infinity of copies which allows neither original nor origin to subsist."[647] This is the

---

[646] Deleuze, Gilles (1994) *Difference and Repetition*. Translated by Paul Patton. Columbia University Press. P. 66
[647] Ibid p. 67

thinking that informs the mask metaphor quoted above and it demonstrates how Deleuze's poststructuralism radically does away with an originary grounding for myth.

The difference between these two approaches to recurrence and repetition, as it relates to the idea of Eternal Return, is that while Deleuze seems to take it as a primitive facet of his ontology, Heidegger interprets it in a more voluntaristic way –a thought, almost like a Fregean idea, that can be accepted and integrated. Both warn against the danger of trivializing this thought and advocate a reverence for it. However, Deleuze argues that there is nothing behind the mask, so-to-speak, besides the infinite repletion of simulacrum, whereas Heidegger grants us the possibility of attaining some sense of authenticity.

Let us keep in mind that the fundamental function of the cards is to make all this symbolism, condensed into representations, into a form that can be held, shuffled, and dealt. This handling gives us a sense of control over the cards. The sense of total control is shaken by the introduction of chaos by way of shuffling, cutting, and dealing them out. And it is not only within the Tarot, but within playing cards as well, that this randomness is interpreted as the intervention of divinity. This process then is repeated *ad infinitum* during the life of the card owner.

The Numerological Significance of the Tarot

It's important to point out that besides their repetition of themes, during a reading, the position of a card as either right-side up (dignified) or upside-down (ill dignified) is a factor in the interpretation of the card's meaning within the context of the reading. The symbolism when the card is "ill dignified" is obviously the same but the shadow-side, or more base and materialistic aspect of the symbols, is meant to be incorporated into the narrative that constitutes the reading.

In "The Significance of the Cosmos" we discussed the idea that there might be a correspondence between the twenty-one letters of the Enochian alphabet and the twenty-two letters of the

Hebrew alphabet. The number twenty-two plays a prominent role in the construction of the Tarot system, as well as occultism in general:

> The occultists associate the twenty-two letters of the Hebrew alphabet with the twenty-two works of creation in the Book of Genesis and the twenty-two books in the Old Testament. (The occultists always cheerfully assert that there are twenty-two books in the Old Testament, although the Christian version gives many more and the Jewish version lists twenty-four.) In these works of creation, therefore, is the key to all wisdom, all truth, all knowledge of God and the universe. The cabalists associate them with the Twenty-two Paths, which are the roads that lead from one sephira (level of human perfection) to another. For them, the numbers and the Paths account for all that is in the universe, and they are the soul's way to God and the magician's way to power...[648]

The numerological import read into each card can be interpreted as a process that is akin to compound theorization – in fact, any time numerological significance is invoked in conspiracy theorization it should be read as a mechanism of compound theorization. Some of the more notable numerological aspects attendant to the Tarot have to do with the numbers attached to particular cards, such as the number thirteen being attached to Death and the number twelve (as in twelve disciples) being attached to the Hanged Man. Sometimes the numerological significance is ascertained by the process of division, as in the Moon, which is number eighteen being the sum of three sixes.

---

[648] Laurence, Theodor (1972) *How the Tarot Speaks to Modern Man*. Stackpole Books. P. 15

The drive to conjoin Hebrew letters with the Tarot, as well as the integration of the Kabbalah into European occultism, was largely influenced by Eliphas Lévi (February 08, 1810 – May 31, 1875). Born into a Roman Catholic household in Paris, Alphonse Louis Constant took the pen name Eliphas Lévi after leaving the seminary in an attempt to transliterate his name into Hebrew – because, as we've noted, during this period people believed Hebrew to be the language spoken to Adam by God. Decker and Dummett characterize Lévi's activities as an attempt to "amalgamate all occult traditions."[649]

Lévi's work influenced a wide swath of occultists: the Theosophical Society, the Golden Dawn, dissident groups of Freemasons that identified as Rosicrucians, etc. As was mentioned in the last chapter, Aleister Crowley studied the Tarot extensively and essentially brought Eliphas Lévi's project into the modern era. Decker and Dummett discuss Crowley's conception of the Tarot and how it informed his pupil Kenneth Grant's teaching that the trumps do not correspond to the sephiroth on the Kabbalah's "tree of life" but instead refer to the pathways between them:

> Crowley's *Liber CCXXXII, Liber Arcanorum (Book 231, Book of Secrets)* was an important source for Grant's alternative Tree. Crowley shows 22 sigils for 'the houses of Mercury [Thoth] and their genii' and 22 sigils for 'the cells of the *qliphoth* and their genii'. It will be recalled that the *qliphoth* are the shadowy remnants of that cosmos which existed prior to the present one and which still exists outside it, according to Cabalists. Both sets of sigils correspond to the Hebrew letters, and therefore can be arranged on the pathways of two distinct Trees, one for the 'lights' and one for the 'shadows'. The

---

[649] Decker, Ronald and Dummett, Michael (2019) *A History of the Occult Tarot.* Duckworth Publishing. P. 41

Tarot trumps are involved in the design of the sigils and in 22 verses of scripture by Crowley. He then lists the shadow-demons by their names, each commencing with the associated letter (Amprodias for *Aleph*, Baratchial for *Beth*, and so on through the alphabet). Grant gave special significance to the sphere of Daath as the gateway through which adepts can enter the infernal pathways. He came to see these as 'tunnels', belonging to Set, i.e., the Egyptian god of darkness and chaos.[650]

We can also see how this reading resonates with the excerpt from *Gravity's Rainbow* that we analyzed in relation to the Tower card, as well as the chaotic and praeternatural forces that appear on the pathways between the sephiroth. This passage, as well as Grant's linking of the *qliphoth* back to "Typhon," the mother of Set, gives us deeper insight into the snakelike, feminine, and lunar aspects that were prominent in the second chapter of Crowley's *Book of the Law*. Grant's vision of the occult, according to Decker and Dummett, "becomes an ambitious synthesis of Cabalism, visionary states, UFOs, interplanetary visitors, sex magic and a new aeon."[651] All of these traits – and more – are ingredients in the postmodern stew in which we are about to indulge.

---

[650] Ibid p. 310
[651] Ibid p. 310

Chapter Eleven: The Significance of UFO Phenomena

"You know how everybody's into weirdness right now? Books in all the supermarkets about the Bermuda Triangle, UFOs and how the Mayans invented television... well the way I see it it's exactly the same: there ain't no difference between a flying saucer and a time machine."[652]

UFO sightings and the JFK assassination mark the beginning of modern-day conspiracy theories proper. UFO phenomena is interesting because its roots are tied to a kind of mythology that is analogous to the previous stories we've discussed, e.g., Atlantis, the Tower of Babel, etc., indicating that there are strands of UFOlogy which *are* textually rich; but within this same framework, we will begin to trace this textually rich narrative as it moves from the mysterious and mythic to the explicitly materialistic. In this capacity, UFOs will be tied to New World Order conspiracies, ideas of man-made UFOs, fairy phenomena appearing as UFOs, and, of course, the so-called "Ancient Alien" theory.

Explicitly Mythic Origins

Our town, our town
Do love a stampede
Stampede by my old jacket in the park
Someday I'll pick it up, look for the label and whisper:
Tilt, it ain't got none
Tilt, got none at all[653]

British occultist, Kenneth Grant (May 23, 1924 – January 15, 2011), who had served as Aleister Crowley's personal secretary in 1945, is the port of entry for our discussion of the mythic roots of

---

[652] The character Miller, from the 1984 film *Repo Man*
[653] From the song "Tilt" by Scott Walker, 1995.

extraterrestrials. Both Grant and Robert Anton Wilson interpreted Crowley's portrait of "LAM" as an extraterrestrial alien; their interpretations, however, were not identical: Wilson, who much like Crowley himself, was a trickster who enjoyed playing with life's ambiguities, could have put forward his speculation in either jest or seriousness (or, most likely both). Grant, being more of a "serious" occultist, took the LAM drawing as undeniable proof that Crowley had been in contact with aliens of some sort.

Having successfully persuaded himself, and a few other Crowleyites, of the validity of his theory, Grant postulated that certain magicians, mystics, artists, and writers throughout time had also been in contact with extraterrestrial aliens. Around the work of these writers, Grant would construct his magickal system. The most notable members of this pantheon were Madame Blavatsky, John Dee, Aleister Crowley and science fiction author H.P. Lovecraft.[654]

In some respects, the life of Kenneth Grant deserves a fuller treatment than the one allotted to him here. Along with Israel Regardie he was an intellectual heir (and promoter) of the work and legacy of Aleister Crowley. Much like Crowley and Robert Anton Wilson, Grant developed an idiosyncratic and hyper-literate system, wherein complex supernatural phenomena are interpreted in relation to mystical and literary texts. In this section we will analyze his focus on extraterrestrials and interdimensionality in relation to the work of the more scientifically oriented computer scientist Jacques Vallée

---

[654] "Certain fugitive elements appear occasionally in the works of poets, painters, mystics, and occultists which may be regarded as genuine magical manifestations in that they demonstrate the power and ability of the artist to evoke elements of an extra-dimensional and alien universe that may be captured only by the most sensitive and delicately adjusted antennae of human consciousness." Grant, Kenneth (1980) *Outside the Circles of Time.* Billing and Sons Limited. p. 14

(September 24, 1939 – present). This is not to say that Grant does not make appeals to scientific validation; in the following passage he does so by presenting the magician in a light similar to a psychologist; as one who perceives unconscious forces at work within his patient's psyche:

> Contemporary science agrees with the sacramentalist's attitude to matter. The world is seen as a play of forces which sometimes burst into manifestation, and, at other times remain veiled behind the apparently innocuous forms of everyday objects [...] The work of the magician lies in reifying these powers by bringing them into alignment with the subconscious energies that form the basic substance of manifestation.[655]

Note that, as an occultist, Grant is assuming the existence of "forces" at work within matter and saying that these correspond to, or can be brought into "alignment with, the subconscious." Before we pursue this line of thought any further let's use the above description as a guide to interpreting this account from Jacques Vallée's *Passport to Magonia*:

> The mind of Private First Class Gerry Irwin was blank when he woke up on March 2, 1959, in Cedar City Hospital. He had been unconscious for twenty-three hours, at times mumbling incoherently something about a "jacket on the bush." When he became conscious his first question was: "Were there any survivors?"
> The story of Private Irwin is a mysterious one, and very little has been done to clarify it. It has been mentioned only once in UFO literature, by James

[655] Grant, Kenneth (1980) *Outside the Circles of Time*. Billing and Sons Limited. P. 32

Lorenzen, director of the APRO group, and has not, to the best of my knowledge, been the subject of subsequent investigation. Such an investigation, however, would throw light on some aspects of the UFO problem now gaining considerable publicity and causing some concern to those who follow the development of the sociological context of UFO reports. Perhaps, as Lorenzen suggests, there was a military investigation that has been kept secret. If so, secrecy on the part of the authorities, if they are really concerned with the nation's peace of mind, is not the best course, as the following review of the few well-established facts of the Irwin case, which serves as an introduction to a discussion of the problem of "contact," makes clear.

Late on February 28, 1959, Gerry Irwin, a Nike missile technician, was driving from Nampa, Idaho, back to his barracks at Fort Bliss, El Paso, Texas. He was returning from military leave. He had reached Cedar City, Utah, and turned southeast on Route 14 when he observed an unusual phenomenon, six miles after the turnoff. The landscape brightened, and a glowing object crossed the sky from right to left. Irwin stopped the car and got out. He had time to watch the object as it continued in an easterly direction until hidden from view by a ridge.

The witness decided that he might have seen an airliner on fire attempting a forced landing, in which case there was no time to lose. Consequently, instead of resuming his journey, Irwin wrote a note ("Have gone to investigate possible plane crash. Please call law enforcement officers.") and placed it on the steering wheel of his car. Using shoe polish, he wrote STOP on the side of his car, in order to make sure people would find his note, and then started out on foot.

Approximately thirty minutes later, a fish and game inspector did stop. He took the note to the Cedar City Sheriff, Otto Pfief, who gathered a party of volunteers and returned to the site. Ninety minutes after he had sighted the strange "object," Gerry Irwin was discovered unconscious and taken to the hospital. No trace of an airplane crash was found.

At the hospital, Dr. Broadbent observed that Irwin's temperature and respiration were normal. He seemed merely to be asleep, but he could not be awakened. Dr. Broadbent diagnosed hysteria. Then, when Irwin did wake up, he felt "fine" although he was still puzzled by the object he had seen. He was also puzzled by the disappearance of his jacket: he was assured that he was not wearing it when he was found by the search party. Irwin was flown back to Fort Bliss and placed under observation at William Beaumont Army Hospital for four days, after which period he returned to duty. His security clearance, however, was revoked.

Several days later, Irwin fainted while walking in the camp, but he recovered rapidly. Several days afterward, on Sunday, March 15, he fainted again in an El Paso street and was taken to Southwest General Hospital. There his physical condition was found similar to that observed in Cedar City. He woke up at about 2:00 AM on Monday and asked: "Were there any survivors?" He was told that the date was not February 28 but March 16. Once more he was taken to William Beaumont Hospital and placed under observation by psychiatrists. He remained there over one month. Lorenzen reports that, according to a Captain Valentine, the results of the tests indicated that he was normal. He was discharged on April 17.

The next day, following an unidentifiable but very powerful urge, he left the fort without leave, caught a bus to El Paso, arrived in Cedar City Sunday afternoon (April 19), walked to the spot where he had seen the object, left the road, and went back through the hills –right to a bush where his jacket lay. There was a pencil in a buttonhole with a piece of paper wound tightly around it. He took the paper and burned it. Then he seemed to come out of a trance. He had to look for the road. Not understanding why he had come there, he turned himself in and thus met Sherriff Otto Pfief, who gave him the details of the first incident.

The Lorenzens contacted Irwin after he returned to Fort Bliss and undergone a new psychological examination, as futile as the previous one. His case came to the attention of the Inspector General, who ordered a new examination. On July 10, Irwin reentered William Beaumont Army Hospital. On August 1, he failed to report for duty. One month later he was listed as a deserter. He was never seen again.[656]

On Grant's theory, the story of Private Irwin would constitute a magical narrative and the action moves from the subject of the story outwards to the phenomena he encounters. Grant's theory is subject-centered while Vallée's is object-centered, as he focuses on the effects enacted upon the subject (insofar as the object of consciousness has efficacy upon the subject).

However, within the heart of both approaches there is a shared ambiguity as to where the subject ends and the object begins. Private Irwin's jacket is an example of what Lacan called

---

[656] Vallée, Jacques (2014) *Passport to Magonia*. Daily Grail Publishing. Pp. 95 - 97

objet petit a, existing in the phenomenal world for the purpose of masking Private Irwin's eventual disappearance. Irwin himself can only disappear once this contingent partial object is recovered. On Grant's view, absence is a condition of Being in general; and paradoxically this absence is generative: it generates the UFO encounter as well as the jacket which acts as a key that Irwin has reified out of his experience.[657] For Vallée, the subject may or may not be a coherent entity. This is significant to his reading of the scenario as an ambush by forces outside of his control (or will). These "forces" seemingly elude perception because they elude rationality. It is in this sense that the jacket becomes a symbolic object that masks, or is emblematic of, these forces.

Let's examine the features of this story from a strictly Structuralist standpoint; Slavoj Žižek gives us this succinct analysis of objects:

> This is also a fundamental feature of the logic of the Lacanian object: *the place logically precedes objects which occupy it:* what the objects, in their given positivity, are masking is not some other, more substantial order of objects but simply the emptiness, the void they are filling out. We must remember that there is nothing intrinsically sublime in a sublime object -according to Lacan, a sublime object is an ordinary, everyday object which, quite by chance, finds itself occupying the place of what he calls *das Ding*, the impossible object of desire. The sublime object is an object elevated to the level of *das Ding*. It is its structural place -the fact that it occupies the sacred/forbidden

---

[657] On page 38 of *Outside the Circles of Time* Grant refers to Man as "a supreme absence". I want to specify here that Grant does not refer to the story of Private Irwin in his work; I am merely extrapolating his theory within the context of Vallée's case study.

place of jouissance -and not its intrinsic qualities that confers on it its sublimity.[658]

As both a structuralist and a psychoanalyst, Lacan sought to explain the idea of the "self" or the "individual" in terms of the linguistic structures by which it is governed. This is why the space within the structure being occupied by the sublime object is seen to mark a void or absence. Both Grant and Vallée are giving us readings that jive with Lacan's (and Žižek's) analysis, but they are, despite their difference in perspective, agnostic about the nature of this void. For them it is not merely a point of negation, or nothingness, so much as it is a point of irrationality.[659]

The attentive reader will notice that the concept entailed by the *objet petit a* is analogous to the concept of the partial object that we discussed in the Significance of the Grail chapter. In the earlier discussion we focused on the object as objectively existing (most likely in a timeless or eternal sense) and acting like a key to kingship, wealth, eternal youth, or another world. In our modern retelling of this story the object is more personalized, more idiosyncratic. As Lacan says: "The subject is, as it were, internally excluded from its object."[660]

The McKenna brothers offer us an even more explicitly symbolic story pertaining to the relationship of the partial object to the narrative-like structure of reality. In *High Weirdness* Erik Davis relates an incident that occurred in La Chorrera during a

---

[658] Žižek, Slavoj (1989) *The Sublime Object of Ideology.* Verso. P. 221

[659] It is in keeping with Lacan's attitude of rationalism and scientism (which he inherited from Freud) that he offers us the concept of "jouissance" in relation to the subject. Jouissance is what we call a feeling that is both pleasant and unnerving. This peculiar feeling on the part of the subject is the key for the psychoanalyst in his reading of the patient's narrative.

[660] Taken from the essay "Science and Truth" printed in Lacan, Jacques (2006) *Ecrits.* Norton and Company. P. 731

battery of psychedelic experiments, wherein Terrence and Dennis McKenna recalled a long-lost object from their childhood: a silver key that opened a wooden cabinet owned by their grandfather. At some point during their reminiscence Terrence asked Dennis if he could produce the missing key. In response, Dennis asked Terrence to open his hand, and if this narrative is to be believed, placed in Terrence's palm a silver key.

Though Davis does not directly address the issue of partial objects in his text, we can clearly see that this narrative is navigating an identical terrain. Davis uses the apt designation of "impossible object:"

> The liminal twist introduced by the physical presence of the key also changes the character of Terrence's tale and our position as readers. The key represents a tipping point between fantastic appearances and impossible objects, a point where most of us, already bending over backwards to make sense of this tale, simply "draw the line." What we had been reading as memoir –even a drug-distorted memoir from a less than reliable witness splashing in the deep end of *folie a deux*- suddenly becomes something else. The tale of the key becomes an invading anomaly or, on the flipside, a sneaky, even underhanded fiction. Either way it is the sort of "in-between" threshold story we can most easily manage by invoking the literature of the paranormal.[661]

Davis expresses an understandable distress at the fact that this story is now pressing upon issues pertaining to the paranormal: psychic phenomena, action at a distance, etc. And this is a

[661] Davis, Erik (2019) *High Weirdness: Drugs, Esoterica, and Visionary Experience in the Seventies*. Strange Attractor Press & the MIT Press. P. 146

dimension the McKennas' story possesses that Private Irwin's does not.[662] It's almost as if the three types of partial object stories we have tracked so far follow an evolution: in the case of the Grail, the object is hidden and lost, forever the object of pursuit, its attainment only achieved within a literary context. With the transition into the space-age and the story of Private Irwin's jacket we have the object recovered seemingly by accident or chance, and the recovery being historically documented.[663] In the final reiteration, epitomized by the McKenna brothers and the silver key, it is almost as if the object is now willed into existence and that the recovery narrative is intended to be mythic or apocryphal. Once this Rubicon is crossed the satisfactory result is inevitably tarnished by the mark of the supernatural; and not an innocent, supernatural coincidence but a supernatural beholden to the will, an almost Faustian "Deal with the Devil" type of scenario.[664]

The connotation of malevolence tied to the will echoes Grant's statement about the world being seen as "a play of forces which sometimes burst into manifestation, and, at other times remain veiled behind the apparently innocuous forms of everyday objects." It's important to not be lured into a dismissal of Grant

---

[662] It is important to note that Davis does offer a Structuralist interpretation of the silver key story by saying that "Synchronicities in particular forge signs and stories out of phenomenal events [...] at such moments space-time looks very much like a text and physical objects begin to function more like words or symbols than like the lifeless objects we assume them to be." Ibid, p. 146

[663] Whether or not the documentation has solid historical veracity is beside the point here, what is important is the *intent* to historically document it.

[664] One can of course schematize this evolution in dialectical terms wherein the thesis is the partial object as forever elusive, the antithesis is the partial object regained by chance and the synthesis is the partial object regained by act of will.

based on his pedigree as a magician; his claims about the nature of reality may be a stretch, but they are not what is controversial in his thought, what is controversial is the notion that these forces can be subject to manipulation.

Grant retains the mythic import in his analysis of UFO phenomena by presenting the interaction with the phenomena as like a key fitting into a lock; and were he to tell us the story of Private Irwin, he would presuppose this notion in the telling. Vallée's version affects the sense of mystery that gives it its power because he is agnostic in his understanding of how the subject interacts with such phenomena. The text is not merely a remnant of the experience it depicts, like a ghost story, it is in service to its effect. In this respect, Lovecraft's name returns as a signifier that conjoins these various narrative strands:

> And what returns to us from this sounding is, as Terrence himself ironically reports, the dream tales of H.P. Lovecraft. At the beginning of "The Silver Key" (1926), first published in *Weird Tales*, we meet the dream adventurer Randolph Carter. Lovecraft introduced this character in an earlier story that concerned a demon-haunted passageway between everyday reality and the underworld –a passageway that Lovecraft had himself dreamed about before writing it down. In "The Silver Key," Carter is an older, duller man, whose diminished capacity for wonder is due precisely to his inability to occupy the shared threshold between reality and fantasy [...] Carter does still dream on occasion. One night he encounters the shade of his dead grandfather, who tells him about a key hidden in the attic. Upon waking, Carter digs around and discovers an actual silver key, encrusted with symbols. With the key in hand, Carter sets off on a journey to his childhood home, where he rediscovers a portal into the magical dreamworlds

of his youth. Eventually he disappears without a trace. [665]

The ending of Lovecraft's fictional tale and the factual story of Private Irwin are identical in that both main characters vanish. I want to point out a fundamental difference regarding the objects featured in these stories as it pertains to the evolution, or dialectic, previously sketched out. In the thesis (the Grail) and the synthesis (the silver key) we have objects that are strongly intentional: they are at the forefront of our narrators' conscious thought. With the antithesis, represented by Private Irwin's jacket, the object only presents itself at the forefront of the narrative near the story's end. This is notwithstanding the fact that it had been at the forefront of Irwin's thought upon regaining consciousness (along with the altruistic concern for the presumed passengers on the nonexistent aircraft). This object, which sits on the side of the antithesis and which I am using in a metonymic relationship to the modernity of the mid-twentieth century, is largely incidental. Hence, its seemingly incidental recovery is keeping with its nature.

In everything we have discussed pertaining to UFO phenomena so far, especially the theory that Jack Parsons and L. Ron Hubbard ushered in the UFO age, which will be discussed in the next section, there is at play a dynamic, will-oriented aspect to the thesis, or aeon governing the later stages of modernity.

The Babalon Working

In *Outside the Circles of Time*, Grant traces the beginnings of modern UFO appearances to the "Babalon Working" performed by L. Ron Hubbard and JPL scientist John Parsons:

> The Working began in 1945-6, a few months before Crowley's death in 1947, and just prior to the wave

---

[665] Ibid, p. 147

of unexplained aerial phenomena now recalled as the 'Great Flying Saucer Flap'. Parsons opened a door and something flew in; he supposed it was Babalon and the fourth chapter of AL; others have supposed other things but all are agreed that something unusual, something inexplicable by mundane laws, occurred around that time.[666]

This particular ritual had been preceded by the previously detailed, "Amalantrah Workings," undertaken by Crowley between January and March of 1918;[667] and Grant connects both events to Thelemic scripture:

"I am the Lord of the Forties: the Eighties cower before me and are abased. I will bring you to victory and joy: I will be at your arms in battle and ye shall delight to slay. Success is your proof; courage is your armour; go on, go on, in my strength; and ye shall not turn back for any!" (III:46)

This section is often read as a prediction of WWII as well as the nuclear explosion of Hiroshima, which Grant cites as a possible factor in the opening of an extra-dimensional portal through which UFOs began entering our plain of existence (a theme that was picked up by David Lynch in his 2016 series *Twin Peaks: The Return*).

Part of what informed our analysis of Aleister Crowley was the ambiguity, and playful attitude towards binary opposition, that he shared with French poststructuralist Jacques Derrida. It's important to note here in our discussion of Kenneth Grant that, even if he doesn't ostensibly arrive at definite conclusions, and to

---

[666] Grant, Kenneth (1980) *Outside the Circles of Time*. Billing and Sons Limited. P. 50

[667] http://www.boudillion.com/lam/lam.htm accessed on 08/19/19

a certain extent, plays with a similar ambiguity his writing style is nevertheless marked by a sense of conclusiveness. Grant writes with an intent to define, although, in this crucial section of his book, he cannot definitively pinpoint what it was in the 1940s (The Babalon Working itself, Hiroshima, nuclear testing in New Mexico, etc.) that *The Book of the Law* predicts.[668] He also floats two distinct theories about the intentions of the UFOs: did they merely travel through the portal opened through a magickal ritual or were they enlightened beings who had become more interested in our planet because we had finally discovered nuclear power, and who were now directing their activities towards undermining our self-destruction? Grant was not the originator of this latter interpretation of events – Frank Herbert had described an intergalactic ban on nuclear weapons in his 1965 science-fiction novel *Dune.*

Whether or not you find the idea legitimate that extraterrestrial aliens have a benevolent interest in protecting us from ourselves or preventing us from destroying the cosmos, there is a facet to this theory that plays into one of the textual threads we have been following since the beginning: namely, the repetition of the Edenic narrative wherein Man discovers a forbidden piece of knowledge which leads to divine intervention – an intervention that is prohibitive. On this reading it also references another event in Genesis: The Tower of Babel narrative, wherein God prevents man from ascending to his heavenly realm (which we can assume metaphorically entails knowledge or wisdom but in terms of nuclear power might mean weaponry).

For our purposes, this development within the mythical or occultic text is one of the definitive movements of our shift into

---

[668] Also consider: The Gospel of Thomas, a Gnostic text that had been lost sometime around 400 AD, was discovered in a jar in the Egyptian desert in December 1945. See the interview with Elaine Pagels in the February 2004 (Volume 2, Number 10) of *The Believer* for more information on this.

modernity: the replacement of the divine as a truly religious, ineffable, and enigmatic force with a materialistic, scientific entity, or group of entities. As a shift towards scientism by an explicit occultist that runs contrary to the work of a scientist, Vallée interprets the modern UFO phenomena as a manifestation of older, mystical phenomena. Grant allows for this reading to some extent but ties it to subjective magical or artistic processes.

The substance of what actually occurred during Parsons and Hubbard's "Babalon Working" will most likely never be recovered as the narratives surrounding it have already been pored over from a variety of different perspectives. John Whiteside Parsons (October 2, 1914 – June 17, 1952) was a rocket scientist who helped found the Pasadena-based Jet Propulsion Laboratory in 1936, and "converted" to the Thelemic religion in 1939 shortly after reading Crowley's *Konx Om Pax*.

According to Kaczynski, despite his scientific pedigree Crowley was always skeptical and slightly wary of Parsons' declarations of magickal prowess. These began in earnest in 1945 after his first wife Helen left him and Parsons transferred his affections to her sister, Betty.[669] Not long after moving in together the two began engaging in sex magick and made the acquaintance of Naval Lieutenant and science-fiction writer L. Ron Hubbard (March 13, 1911 – January 24, 1986). Now, if Crowley was cautious in his dealings with the overly enthusiastic Jack Parsons, he was downright suspicious of Hubbard's intentions and influence on Parsons. This attitude turned out to be one of Crowley's more prescient intuitions. Not long after involving himself in Parsons and Betty's magickal workings, Hubbard began an affair with Betty, which distressed Parsons, but apparently did not amount to a deal-breaker.[670]This prompted Parsons towards intensifying his bond with Hubbard by a) getting into a scheme to

---

[669] Kaczynski, Richard (2010) *Perdurabo: The Life of Aleister Crowley*. North Atlantic Books. P. 537
[670] Ibid p. 537

buy and sell yachts with him, and b) trying to "summon an air elemental and thereby cause Babalon to be born in this world."[671]

From January 4th to January 18th Parsons and Hubbard conducted rituals in the Mojave Desert. When he returned to the Thelemite-sponsored Agape Lodge in Pasadena, Parsons encountered a new member, Marjorie Cameron, and concluded that her appearance was the result of his workings. The two began a conjugal relationship. In February he returned to Mojave with Hubbard to complete the Babalon working, it was during this time that the two "received" *The Book of Babalon*, "ostensibly the fourth chapter to *The Book of the Law.* When Cameron became pregnant, Parsons concluded she would give birth to Babalon."[672]

I know what you're thinking: "That's really great, bro... but what about buying and selling used yachts, that's a promising endeavor too, right?" Well, actually, no, it isn't. Allied Enterprises, the yacht-flipping company created by Parsons and Hubbard, was rocked by betrayal from the outset:

> Jack agreed that Ron and Betty would take $10,000 of his money to the East Coast, buy the boat, and sail it back to California. Unbeknownst to Parsons, Hubbard had asked the Chief of Naval Personnel for permission to sail to South America and China; he had no intention of returning. After a couple of weeks passed with no words from his partners, Parsons deduced this for himself. Not to be taken in, Jack took a train to Miami and discovered that Allied Enterprises had purchased three boats in all: a yacht plus two schooners that they bought on mortgages exceeding $12,000. He tracked down the schooners but could find no trace of Ron or Betty.[673]

---

[671] Ibid p. 538
[672] Ibid p. 538
[673] Ibid p. 539

After this misadventure was settled via litigation, Ron and Betty kept one of the schooners and split the legal costs with Parsons, minus a promissory note of $2,900 signed by Ron and Betty. The whole thing was a disaster and Parsons severed his ties with Hubbard and escalated his magickal practice, taking the "oath of the abyss" in 1949. This is the same ego-destroying process Crowley had claimed was the prerequisite for achieving contact with one's Holy Guardian Angel. Unfortunately, whether or not Parsons succeeded in this challenge, he would not have long to enjoy his success. He died three years later on June 20, 1952 while handling explosives in his home, [674] adding a surreal ending to a surreal life of, as the famous book deemed it, "Sex and Rockets."[675]

However, if we grant the Babalon Working to be merely a timestamp for the beginning of UFO phenomena in the modern age, we can still move forward into the realm of speculation as to what UFOs are. Vallée sees them as being the modern iteration of what in the past had been called "fairy folk:"

> For the time being, let me simply state again my basic contention: the modern, global belief in flying saucers and their occupants is identical to an earlier belief in the fairy-faith. The entities described as the pilots of the craft are indistinguishable from the elves, sylphs, and *lutins* of the Middle Ages. Through the observations of unidentified flying objects, we are concerned with an agency our ancestors knew well and regarded with terror: we are prying into the Secret Commonwealth.[676]

---

[674] Ibid p. 555

[675] The full name of this Jack Parsons' biography published by Feral House in 1999 is *Sex and Rockets: The Occult World of Jack Parsons.*

[676] Vallée, Jacques (2014) *Passport to Magonia.* Daily Grail Publishing. P. 67

"The Secret Commonwealth" refers to a book by the seventeenth century Scottish clergyman Robert Kirk, which details interactions between country folk and supernatural entities. *Passport to Magonia* is essentially a modern-day *Secret Commonwealth* in that it catalogs a wide variety of UFO phenomena and compares them with archaic stories of interactions with fairy-folk. Some of the encounters are sinister, some benevolent, and some, like the case of Private Irwin, profoundly mysterious. In all respects, Vallée characterizes the phenomena as lying somewhere beyond the grasp of conventional scientific thinking:

> For a scientist, the only valid question, in this context, is to decide whether the phenomenon can be studied by itself, or whether it is an instance of a deeper problem. This book has attempted to illustrate, and only to illustrate, the latter approach. And the conclusion is that, through the UFO phenomenon, we have the unique opportunity to observe folklore in the making, and to gather scientific material at the deepest source of human imagination. We will be the object of much contempt by future students of our civilization if we allow this material to be lost, for *"tradition is a meteor which, once it falls, cannot be rekindled."*[677]

Vallée's project is a cataloguing of phenomena that seeks to connect phenomena, much in the way that the compound conspiracy theorist does; however, he sees a value in the preservation of the narratives themselves, thus preserving their mythic richness. Grant and Crowley certainly grant this mythological aspect a great deal of importance, but channel it into

---

[677] Ibid p. 159

a conception of individual will that uses it for magickal or artistic purposes. To this extent, Grant notes that:

> Our minds may not understand, but in the deeper layers of the subconsciousness where humanity shares a common bed, there is an instant recognition. Similarly, a magician devises his ceremony in harmony with the forces he wills to invoke, so an author must pay considerable attention to the creation of an atmosphere that is suitable for his operations. Words are his magical instruments, and their vibrations must not produce a merely arbitrary noise but an elaborate symphony of tonal reverberations that trigger a series of increasingly profound echoes in the consciousness of his readers.[678]

This is as clear of a reiteration of the narrative of the "magician-searching-for-the-linguistic-key to the cosmos" as one can get, and, in doing so, it presupposes a magickal vision of the world that is essentially Structuralist. This contrasts with Vallée's attempts to redefine the horizons of scientific inquiry and understanding –which we might read as being Hermeneutical in nature. Vallée and Grant agree that these entities or forces have been interpreted in the past as demons, dwarves, or fairies etc.[679] Both suggest that these entities are interdimensional – Grant draws his arguments from literature, the occult, and art, while Vallée drew from recorded case studies.

---

[678] Grant, Kenneth (1980) *Outside the Circles of Time*. Billing and Sons Limited. P. 13

[679] A similar theory was put forward by Carl Jung in his 1959 essay, "Flying Saucers: A Modern Myth of Things Seen in the Sky" wherein he points out similarities between perceived UFO phenomena and primitive beliefs about heroes and gods.

Grant tackles the subject of the fairy-folk from within a Structuralist paradigm:

> During many years of research in mythology and folklore, this writer has been repeatedly surprised by the disproportionately large amount of material containing allusions to doors, gateways and other means of ingress and egrees to alien worlds, faery worlds, demon worlds, shadowy worlds peopled with the denizens of other dimensions. Entrance or outrance depended upon a knowledge of particular words or phrases intoned in a special way, or of gestures similarly esoteric.[680]

He then goes on to argue that all the magical grimoires, alchemical, and mystical texts that the world has known served as both commentaries on these enchanted realms as well as invocative keys to accessing them. This claim brings us to the question of whether H.P. Lovecraft's fabrication, *The Necronomicon*, can be classified as one of these texts.[681] Grant understood that Lovecraft did not believe the supernatural things he wrote about had any bearing on reality; but he sees the act of dreaming, which was central to Lovecraft's creative process, as an unconscious process that brought the author into contact with "the vast voids beyond," which are consciously sought by the magician.[682] Therefore, Grant would claim *The Necronomicon* as one of these mythic grimoires and that the fictional "Great Old Ones" can accommodate associative readings with the Biblical Nephilim as well as the snake-worshipping cults associated with ancient lunar religions.

---

[680] Ibid p. 41
[681] The logic encapsulated within this question will become more and more prominent in our general discussion from here on out.
[682] Ibid pp. 42 - 43

In contrast to Grant, Dejan Ognjanović acknowledges Lovecraft's use of dreams but argues that his work's imaginative potency, like that of Jorge Luis Borges, was contingent upon skillful world-building, which weaved fictional personages through both authentic and invented book titles, geographies, and events;[683] and he saw Grant's interpretation as bordering on misuse.

In conclusion to this discussion of the mythic/occultic narratives surrounding UFO phenomena we can discern that despite their differences there is more agreement between Vallée and Grant than there is disagreement. Even though Vallée's approach is more emblematic of Hermeneutics and Grant's hews more closely to Structuralism,[684] the two approaches represent a complimentary accord between a mystical outlook and a scientific one. The dialectical interaction between these two positions gives the observer a fuller perspective on the narratives surrounding the subject. Now, if we have created the need for a more robust dialectical antagonism between mythological theories and scientism as it pertains to the topic of UFOs, there is a whole host of narratives into which we can dive ...

However, we got here, we're here now.

Whatever sparked the modern-day UFO craze is ultimately unknown. We do know that its beginnings coincide with the end of World War II (September 1945), the Maury Island Incident (June 1947), and Jack Parsons' Babalon Working (late 1945 to early 1946). However, in the minds of most Americans, the UFO phenomenon was formally kicked-off in July of 1947 with the alleged UFO crash in Roswell, New Mexico. This event, coupled

---

[683] Ognjanović, Dejan (2017) *Rue Morgue Magazine's The Weird World of H. P. Lovecraft*. Rue Morgue. Pp. 29 - 30
[684] These are labels that I am applying, neither has, to my knowledge identified themselves with a particular philosophical movement.

with the existence of the Area 51 military base in Nevada, which is purported to conduct experiments using alien technology recovered from crashed spaceships, has been a persistent touchstone for both conspiracy theorists and the general public for over seventy years.

Countless books have been written about these subjects. In 2011's *Area 51: An Uncensored History of America's Top Secret Military Base,* Annie Jacobsen (b. June 28, 1967) traces the incident back to black operations ("black ops") conducted by the US Government that had begun with the Manhattan Project, which had run from 1939 until 1946. Jacobsen credits the scientists and government agents behind this project, which resulted in the invention of the atomic bomb, as writing the rulebook for how black operations would be conducted from this point on.[685] For Jacobsen, the events of Roswell, the operation of Area 51, and the UFO craze in general are connected to government black ops, the Nazi defeat in WWII, and the development and use of atomic power:

> It is from the Atomic Energy Act of 1946 that the concept "born classified" came to be, and it was the Atomic Energy Commission [the entity that the Manhattan Project morphed into post WWII] that would oversee the building of seventy thousand nuclear bombs in sixty-five different sizes and styles. Atomic Energy was the first entity to control Area 51 –a fact previously undisclosed- and it did so with terrifying and unprecedented power. One simply cannot consider Area 51's uncensored history without addressing this cold, hard, and ultimately devastating truth.[686]

---

[685] Jacobsen, Annie (2011) *Area 51: An Uncensored History of America's Top Secret Military Base.* Back Bay Books. P. *xvi*
[686] Ibid p. *xviii*

From this point, which we have already seen play an explanatory role in Kenneth Grant's UFO theorization, Jacobsen weaves a tale of post-war deep state intrigue. Her narrative asserts that the crash at Roswell involved a disc and not a weather balloon, as the US Military initially reported (and claimed again in 1994), and that bodies were recovered from the crash site:

> These were not aliens. Nor were they consenting airmen. They were human guinea pigs. Unusually petite for pilots, they appeared to be children. Each was under five feet tall. Physically, the bodies of the aviators revealed anatomical conundrums. They were grotesquely deformed, but each in the same manner as the others. They had unusually large heads and abnormally shaped oversize eyes. One fact was clear: these children, if that's what they were, were not healthy humans. A second fact was shocking. Two of the child-size aviators were comatose but still alive.[687]

So, where did these pint-size pilots come from? Jacobsen's theory is pretty succinct: near the end of WWII, as the US and the Soviet Union were dividing up the Nazi rocket scientists, Stalin picked the Horten brothers (Walter and Reimar) in an early round of the draft. In a later round he made a pick that was really outside the box, a man who wasn't a rocket scientist at all: the infamous Josef Mengele. Stalin would then enlist the Horten brothers to create a flying saucer – just like the ones they were designing for the Nazis – and Mengele would "create" the pilots:

> When Joseph Stalin sent the biologically and/or surgically reengineered children in the craft over New Mexico hoping it would land there, the engineers were told, Stalin's plan was for the

---

[687] Ibid p. 368

children to climb out and be mistaken for visitors from Mars. Panic would ensue, just like it did after the radio broadcast of *The War of the Worlds*. America's early-warning radar system would be overwhelmed with sightings of other "UFOs." Truman would see how easily a totalitarian dictator could control the masses using black propaganda.[688]

There you have it. Essentially Nazis were responsible for the event that formalized the UFO phenomenon that enchanted the American psyche. Jacobsen's novel twist is in arguing that it was under the auspices of the Soviet Union that this nefarious deed was done. For her book, Jacobsen interviewed over 73 government officials that had worked at or been briefed about the goings-on at Area 51. On her appearance on *The Daily Show with Jon Stewart* she says that she kept anonymous the engineer who had given her the most revealing information about this event, so we will never be able to check the veracity of this narrative.

The role played by Nazi scientists during the Cold War will be an ongoing theme for the next two chapters of our book. For Jacobsen, the subject pertains primarily to the larger issue of a clandestine government agency withholding, and utilizing, technology on its unwitting citizenry. Both left and right-wing conspiracy theorists who incorporate UFO narratives into their writings share this suspicion of the government. Left-wing conspiracy theorists placed blame on more inscrutable agencies like the CIA, while right-wing conspiracy theorists looked more at concretely defined groups like the ATF and FBI. But both, insofar as they subscribed to theories about government cover-ups of UFO phenomena, imagined the issue to be related to super-secretive, possibly unknowable, agencies.[689]

---

[688] Ibid pp. 371 - 372

[689] "Project Blue Book" which was begun by the United States Air Force in 1952 would be one such agency. The project's purpose

Most left-wing conspiracy theorists, who were more preponderant in the 1980s, began their journey "down the rabbit-hole" with the JFK assassination (the suspicious murder of an iconic progressive politician) then, if they had the tenacity, moved onto UFOs. A favorite strand of this brand of theory posits that UFOs were developed by Nazi scientists near the war's end – à la Jacobsen, which is contingent upon the infamous "Operation Paperclip:"

> In 1945, German scientists had already been experimenting with flying-disc theory for many years. So when, a few years later, it seemed that World War II might take a nasty turn, Adolf Hitler began planning a last-ditch scenario in which he would dazzle the Allies with the "Wunderwaffen" his scientists had devised, including working flying saucers. Although the Germans couldn't get their "spacecraft" off the ground in time to win the war, their advances did save them. American intelligence was so intrigued by what the Nazi scientists had discovered about saucer design and propulsion that a secret deal between the United States and Nazi Germany was struck. Immediately after the war, a think tank of over four hundred top Nazi scientists in the field of saucer research and development and up to fifteen thousand scientific and technical personnel were quietly folded into the American

---

was to investigate UFO claims; the Air Force terminated their involvement in 1969 and transferred any ongoing research to the University of Colorado. *Project Blue Book* (2019). Edited by Brad Steiger. MUFON Books an imprint of Red Wheel/Weiser, LLC. P. 16

aerospace industry in an action known as "Operation Paperclip."[690]

Right-wing theorists might also draw on this theory as well for varying reasons: contempt of the Nazis for ruining their "brand," or reverence for their scientific rapacity. However, there are conspiracy theorists of all ideological stripes that don't believe flying saucers were the invention of Nazi scientists. For these people, aliens really are from outer space, and the purpose of Area 51 is to cover up this disconcerting information. In fact, to these theorists, writers like Jacobsen are part of a conspiracy to cover up the "fact" that we have been visited by, and that our government is possibly in contact with, extraterrestrials.

The theorists we're going to address for the rest of this section, Steven M. Greer, David Icke, William Cooper, and Nick Redfern are all basically antithetical (in a dialectical sense) to Kenneth Grant and Jacques Vallée, in that they ascertain aliens and UFOs in what could be deemed a conventional way. This is not to say that there isn't any nuance to their interpretations, it's just that these theories fit more concisely into a particular scientific outlook that perceives these phenomena as occurring objectively. Meaning that, phenomena, once properly experienced, can be understood and folded into some sort of established scientific or historical narrative. This would run contrary to Vallée's insistence that the scientific method of inquiry itself must evolve as it tests the parameters of "whether the phenomenon can be studied by itself, or whether it is an instance of a deeper problem." The authors in question here presuppose that UFO phenomena **can** be studied by itself. Also, on

---

[690] Belzer, Richard (1999) *UFOs, JFK, and Elvis: Conspiracies You Don't Have to be Crazy to Believe.* The Ballantine Publishing Group. P. 167. It should be noted that Belzer addresses the theory that UFOs might be tools of the United States government, in this particular book he also addresses alternate hypotheses for the phenomenon as well.

a literary note: if the narratives of Grant and Vallée seem to be drawing more from mythic and occult narratives, the thinkers in this section draw more from science fiction in constructing their theories.

We will begin with Steven Macon Greer (b. June 28, 1955), who is a traumatologist with a B.S. degree in biology from Appalachian State University and an M.D. from James H. Quillen College of Medicine of East Tennessee State University. In 1990 Greer founded the Center for the Study of Extra-Terrestrial Intelligence. He is the closest thing we have to a real deal, "the truth is out there, aliens are real" conspiracy theorist. Because of this, his ideas are easy to summarize: the United States Government is covering up the existence of UFOs because they a) are trying to avoid mass panic, and b) they are hoarding alien technology all for themselves because they are not-so-secret Fascists who adore secrecy and malevolence for the sake of secrecy and malevolence. Apropos of this, Richard Belzer states that Greer told him that there are "165 former government and military employees who, if they knew they would not be prosecuted, would be willing to come forward right now and tell us just how we have come to engineer these UFOs."[691] The UFOs in question would be alien spacecraft that top-secret military officials have recovered and re-engineered.

I bring up Greer first because his angle is very blunt; he's also gained a certain degree of notoriety from the 2017 Netflix documentary *Unacknowledged*. His theory is easily summarized and offers three big takeaways:

1. There's a "shadow government." Don't even look for it because it'll never be found.

2. Aliens are legitimately "real" in any kind of *Star Wars/Star Trek* sense one can imagine.

---

[691] Ibid P. 141

3. Most importantly, anti-gravity technology exists! Our shadow government stole it from the aliens when they crashed here on Earth, and we've mastered it. If only this technology could be turned over to the *people,* we could solve the world's problems. Greer is also of the opinion that our use of nuclear weapons alerted aliens to our presence and that they are trying to prevent our self-destruction.[692]

Prior to *Unacknowledged* Greer had co-produced the film *Sirius* in 2013. *Sirius* followed Greer's exploits as a UFOlogist and in it he first put forward the theory that UFO technology, specifically, propulsion, has been seized by the U.S. Government. The most interesting aspect of this film, however, is its title, and the synchronicity it has, as a signifier, with the work of Robert Temple and Robert Anton Wilson.

In many ways Greer's story mirrors that of Robert Lazar (b. January 26, 1959) who claimed to have been hired as a physicist for a company called "EG & G" sometime during the 1980s. Once employed and granted security clearance, Lazar claims that he worked at Area 51 with the task of reverse engineering the propulsion systems of alien spacecraft. After personally inspecting nine different saucers and having been harassed on countless occasions to ensure his silence, Lazar came forward in 1989 and told the media what he had witnessed. This, of course led to more harassment.[693]

Lazar and Greer both insist that the Government's use of alien engineering revolves around anti-gravity technology; both claim to have been employed in the upper echelons of US security classification; and both rock the 1980s style computer programmer glasses. But, while Lazar would go on to be arrested

[692] These claims were made by Dr. Steven Greer during his appearance on the *Jonesy's Jukebox* radio program. Originally aired on 95.5 KLOS, July 24, 2019.
[693] Moench, Doug (1995) *The Big Book of Conspiracies*. Paradox Press. Pp. 93 - 95

and prosecuted for his involvement in a prostitution ring in 1990, which his proponents say was set up to discredit him, and again in 2006 for violating the Federal Hazardous Substances Act by shipping restricted chemicals across state lines, Greer, however, has not run afoul of the law and is instead gaining notoriety.[694]

Both Greer and Lazar see the possibility of aliens through a scientistic lens and if they import the kind of mythological thinking that has been the focus of our work, they probably do so in an ancient aliens manner, which takes our religious narratives and myths as having been caused by extraterrestrials who visited Earth in the distant past.

Another, more well-known character in this line of theorization is William Cooper (May 6, 1943 – November 5, 2001) who was, like his contemporary Art Bell, truly an emblematic figure for the conspiracy theory zeitgeist of his time. Cooper's narrative could have been crammed into the Significance of the New World Order chapter, however, in order to contemporize him with Bell, Greer, et al, he is featured here.

Cooper's 1991 book, *Behold a Pale Horse* is interesting because it is essentially a postmodern reiteration of Gary Allen and Larry Abraham's *None Dare Call it Conspiracy*, as it postulates a network of shadowy groups controlling the government, but updated with claims pertaining to extraterrestrials. The three most notable contributions that Cooper made to contemporary conspiracy theory discourse, after the inclusion of extraterrestrials into a relatively conventional New World Order schema, was his reprinting of executive orders and internal memos, theorization regarding the cause and spread of HIV/AIDS, and his demise.

Cooper's reprinting of "official documents" has been the subject of much speculation and criticism. True believers see

---

[694] This 2006 charge is most likely less serious than it seems, as it is most likely related to Lazar's participation in the annual Desert Blast Festival, in which participants detonate explosives or experiment with homemade jet-powered vehicles.

these photocopies as undeniable proof of a conspiracy, whereas critics see them as inconclusive and unnecessary. Both skeptics and UFOologists have questioned whether Cooper, who had only achieved the rank of petty officer second class during his time in the Navy, could have accessed the "top secret" documents he claimed to have seen and reported. For our purposes none of this matters – all that matters is that Cooper felt compelled to appeal to a legalistic sense of veracity to legitimize his theories by including facsimiles of government memos in his opus.

Cooper's theorizing about the origin and spread of AIDS in *Behold a Pale Horse*[695] is another advancement towards scientism in the culture of conspiracy theorization. If *None Dare Call it Conspiracy* was content to treat socialism, communism, and globalism as ideologies that metaphorically spread like diseases, Cooper is here referring to a concrete viral reality. And this is a definitive point in the progression away from myth within conspiracy theorization; it is a move within the content of the text towards an accumulation and proliferation of signifiers that are intended to refer to the mundane, the day-to-day, and the newsworthy.

The last aspect, Cooper's demise, is just as crucial for the significance of his narrative as the other two. On November 5, 2001, Apache County sheriff deputies attempted to arrest Cooper at his home in Eager, Arizona. He was charged with aggravated assault with a deadly weapon and endangerment; however, Cooper had also been wanted by federal authorities for tax evasion since 1998.[696] Following a shootout with the deputies, Cooper was fatally shot. His death at the hands of the state, along with the shootout at Ruby Ridge in August 1992 and the Waco siege in April 1993, bolstered the militia movement in the United

---

[695] He claimed that it was a manufactured disease designed to exterminate blacks, Latinos and homosexuals.

[696] https://en.m.wikipedia.org/wiki/Milton_William_Cooper accessed on 04/20/2021

States and led to the conceptualization of Cooper as a martyr murdered by the New World Order.

Adding to the intrigue of Cooper's death, for most conspiracy theorists, is that it occurred on the heels of the 9/11 World Trade Center attack. This coincidence is especially notable for our purposes because 9/11 is the moment when a more "traditional" form of conspiracy theorization died, and a more scientifically orientated and quantitative form took its place.

In this context Cooper's death is especially significant as his work was a bridge between the established tropes of the old school (the Illuminati, Bilderbergs, etc.) and the new school obsession with deeply intricate government machinations such as false flag attacks and interpreting UFO phenomena in explicitly scientific terms.

Understanding UFOs in scientific terms in contemporary discourse is usually going to take one of two routes: a) that it is essentially a man-made phenomenon (this is Annie Jacobsen's view), b) that extraterrestrials have been involved with human development in one way or another since our beginning. This latter type of theorization is usually related to the subject of "Ancient Aliens," however, there are a few writers, David Icke (b. April 29, 1952) and Nick Redfern (b. 1964) being prime examples, who fall into this category but bring the topic into much more sensationalistic, and mythic, territory.

Essentially, Icke and Redfern assert that aliens interbred with early humans and the resulting bloodlines have been cultivated by the ruling classes. The scientistic aspirations of these theories stem primarily from alien abduction narratives. Many abductee narratives fall into one of two camps. One is the description of a sterile and scientifically oriented group of three-to-four-foot-tall humanoids with large heads, large almond-size eyes, a slit for a mouth, and no nose. These are usually referred to as "grays" and have been the predominant alien-type described in abduction narratives since the 1960s. The other notable group describe aliens that are, while humanoid, covered in scales and sport reptile-like features; hence they are referred to as "reptilians."

The intentions of the grays in the overall narrative of UFO abductions are ambiguous, and their physical countenance seems almost to be a manifestation of the technological aspects of modernity. The reptilians, however, seem to be a manifestation of ancient snake and lunar-oriented cults. They seem more menacing, and according to Icke, can shape-shift at will. Not only is this reptilian conspiracy theorization an attempt to accentuate the alterity of the ruling elites, who according to Icke are secretly reptilians, it is analogous to the reiteration we saw with the Grail mythos, wherein a mythic narrative is translated into a materialistic theory that makes explicit pleas for scientific validity.

Both Icke and Redfern incorporate the mythic "snake-brotherhood" narratives associated with the Nephilim, the fiction of Robert E. Howard, Kenneth Grant, and Aleister Crowley into their reptilian theories. In this respect, the reptilian theories that exist in today's conspiracy culture contain a significant remnant of the mythically rich narratives that had proliferated throughout the 70s, 80s, and 90s.

To this end, Redfern refers to the Anunnaki, an ancient Sumerian equivalent of the Nephilim. According to this theory, the Anunnaki's reasons for visiting our planet (from their home-world of Nibiru) had more to do with acquiring Earth's gold deposits than any interest in human evolution:

> [The] grand scheme of the Anunnaki was to secure our gold, turn it into small flakes, and then disperse the absolutely massive amount of flakes into the atmosphere of Nibiru. Effectively, and in theory, this action would create a planet-wide blanket of gold that would span the entire skies of Nibiru.[697]

---

[697] Redfern, Nick (2015) *Bloodline of the Gods*. The Career Press, Inc. Pp. 56 - 57

And why would the Anunnaki want to coat their sky with gold dust? To patch a hole in their ozone layer, of course. From this conjecture, Redfern moves on to postulate that the reptilians might actually be the Anunnaki themselves.[698] Redfern is more interested in tracing the reptilian phenomena with its mythic antecedents, and part of his work entails speculating about individuals whose blood types are "Rh negative" being partially descended from the Anunnaki. Icke is not nearly as interested in the mythic antecedents, focusing instead on grafting the reptilian theory onto established conspiracy theories involving the Merovingian Dynasty, the Rothschilds, and the Bush family (among others). This speculation goes on to incorporate blood-drinking rituals, human sacrifice, and shape-shifting, etc. Both writers espouse a semblance of a scientistic model but are compelled to incorporate (and reiterate) mythic narratives of some kind or another into their schemas and both set the stage for the ancient aliens narrative.

Space Age Reincarnation: the Return of Melchizedek

As we have seen, the names of the three murky figures presented in The Significance of the Cosmos have been reinscribed into a variety of modern conspiracy narratives: Enoch has been a reoccurring theme pertaining to the Nephilim, the Gnostic gospels, and Freemasonry; Hiram regarding Freemasonry and political assassination (discussed in the next chapter); and now we return to the figure of Melchizedek as he pertains to UFOs and extraterrestrials.

This section deals not so much with UFOs themselves as it does with individuals who claim to be in contact with them, and/or working on their behalf. Unlike theories in which aliens are actually angels (or fallen angels) or "fairy folk," the subjects corralled into this section are coming at the topic from a position

---

[698] Ibid pp. 176 - 177

that is conditioned almost exclusively by science fiction literature. However, this does not mean that they are indifferent to the occultic or Gnostic aspects, as these characters, and the individuals who document them, are making a conscious effort to synthesize the occultic with science fiction.

The narrative in question, as it was conceived within the parameters of science fiction, begins with Philip K. Dick's novel *VALIS*, first published in 1981. This book is one of Dick's most personal and, in my opinion, one of his best. (If you haven't already read it and you don't want to have the story spoiled you should jump ahead to the next section.) The story begins when the narrator, Horselover Fat, begins experiencing visions of a pink beam of light he believes is revealing hidden secrets of the universe. Fat lets some of his friends in on the visions and they collectively begin to speculate as to what might be causing them. One of the theories they propose is that the beam is originating from an alien satellite orbiting Earth. Not long after this, the group discovers a film called *Valis* that contains obvious references to the revelations experienced by Horselover Fat.

After viewing the film, the group devise a plan to locate and visit the film's makers, Eric and Linda Lampton. Eric Lampton is a rock star modeled on David Bowie. Upon reaching the musician's estate they encounter the couple's two-year-old daughter, Sophia Lampton. Sophia is a personalized incarnation of the Gnostic conception of Holy Wisdom and she cures Horselover Fat's schizophrenia, revealing his true identity, "Philip K. Dick" to himself. It is then revealed that Eric and Linda are aliens from a constellation called Albemuth and that VALIS was built on their home world to help them withstand the pathology caused by the toxicity of Earth's atmosphere.[699]

VALIS, and the two novels that followed it, *The Divine Invasion* and *The Transmigration of Timothy Archer*, were primarily informed by an experience that Dick refers to by its date as "2-3-74." As the story goes, during recovery from having his

---

[699] Dick, Philip (2011) *Valis*. First Mariner Books. P. 204

wisdom teeth removed, Dick went out onto his porch in Fullerton California to accept a delivery from the local pharmacy. Upon greeting the delivery woman, he was struck by the golden fish medallion that hung on a necklace around her neck. Dick asked the woman about the significance of the fish and was told that it was a symbol used by early Christians to identify each other as members of the faith. This moment was a catalyst for Dick, who claimed that afterwards he began having visions of ancient Rome lurking behind the façade that was the surrounding Orange County. The realization that Dick claims to have had was that he and the delivery woman were both secret Christians, living in fear of immanent persecution by the Roman Empire. After this initial revelatory experience Dick experienced a pink beam of light like the one described in the novel.[700]

The connection between the symbol of the fish and the early Christian community, who if they were not Essenes themselves were influenced by them, firmly situates *VALIS* within the milieu of post-sixties' mysticism and Gnostic revivalism that were beginning to saturate the New Age culture of the day.

The power of the novel primarily stems from the disorienting shifting of self-awareness between the personas of Horselover Fat and Philip K. Dick. Deftly incorporated into this playing with notions of personal identity, in terms of a narrating authorial force, is the novel's function as a *Roman à clef* of sorts, translating real-life friends and celebrities into his fictional realm. The third, and most explicitly philosophical component is the revival of Gnostic ideas within a science fiction-oriented context. Dick explicitly incorporates Gnosticism into several parts of his narrative, specifically the idea that Jehova, or the creator God, has trapped humanity in an illusory prison: "We are in a living maze and not in a world at all,"[701] and the accompanying New Age idea

---

[700] Davis, Erik (2019) *High Weirdness: Drugs, Esoterica, and Visionary Experience in the Seventies*. Strange Attractor Press & the MIT Press. P. 299

[701] Dick, Philip (2011) *Valis*. First Mariner Books. P. 207

that the "third eye" must be opened by VALIS if we are to escape this maze.[702]

VALIS is both the satellite orbiting the Earth and the animating force of Holy Wisdom, which inhabits Sophia Lampton's body. This force is purported to have animated pretty much all the great religious figures: the Buddha, Krishna, Jesus Christ, John Coltrane, etc. "There is only one, over and over again, at different times, in different places, with different names. The Savior is VALIS incarnated as a human being."[703]The power of *VALIS* is also tied to the Promethean promise/danger posed by nuclear energy with the character, Brent Mini (who was modeled after Brian Eno), suffering from multiple myeloma, which was caused by a "proximity to VALIS." Mini says: "The levels of radiation can sometimes be enormous. Too much for us."[704]

There is a potent synchronicity between Dick's novel and the UFO related cult activity of the time. In *Messengers of Deception: UFO Contacts and Cults*, Jacques Vallée describes how he accidently stumbled across graffiti on a Parisian subway wall that stated: "The Lord is an Extraterrestrial" which allegedly emanated from the "Order of Melchizedek."[705] Seeing this graffiti leads Vallée to track down and join "The Order of Melchizedek."

Other fringe groups encountered along the way include the excessively complex *Urantia Foundation* and the ominous *Human Individual Metamorphosis* group (H.I.M.), which had been founded

---

[702] Ibid p. 207

[703] Ibid p. 204. In an interesting bit of sci-fi synchronicity, in February 1981, the same year that *VALIS* was published, an episode of the television show *Buck Rogers in the 25th Century* aired an episode titled "The Golden Man" in which the crew of the Searcher spacecraft encounters a golden-skinned boy named "Vellus." Vellus has the alchemical ability to alter the molecular structure of metals

[704] Ibid p. 203

[705] Vallée, Jacques (2008) *Messengers of Deception: UFO Contacts and Cults*. Daily Grail Publishing. P. 71

and led by M.H. Applewhite.[706] H.I.M. is especially notable because it would eventually morph into the "Heaven's Gate" cult that gained international attention when thirty-nine of its members committed suicide on the night of March 19, 1997 in the hopes that their souls would hitch a ride on a spacecraft that the group believed was trailing the Hale-Bopp Comet.[707]

The Order of Melchizedek was a little trickier to pin down than these other groups. Vallée found that they peddled a lot of the same New Age type propaganda as other UFO contact cults. All of the groups evinced an "us vs. them" mentality that had been a prominent feature of the militia groups that had drawn upon *None Dare Call it Conspiracy*. But instead of a Christian belief in a rapture or apocalypse, the alien contact cults placed their faith in extraterrestrial intervention or, as in the case of Heaven's Gate, a cosmic reincarnation. *VALIS* demonstrated a concern directed primarily at the human condition, and the quasi-Gnosticism that Dick offers us is intended to mitigate the problems that arise from being human. The ostensive conflict of the persecuted Christians in the Roman Empire that Dick sees erupting behind the façade of Orange County is intended as a metaphor for the persecuted hippies and the imperial US Government, headed by a Richard Nixon figure ("Ferris F. Fremont"). Vallée's account reiterates this conflict but situates it between the UFO contact groups and the scientists and government officials who are keeping the truth from them.[708] One of the leaders of the Order of Melchizedek, Dr. Grace Pettipher, homed in on this aspect in one of her interviews:

[706] Ibid pp. 86 - 87

[707]

https://en.m.wikipedia.org/wiki/Heaven%27s_Gate_(religious_gr oup) accessed on 04/22/21. P.S. We have no proof that this plan didn't work.

[708] Vallée, Jacques (2008) *Messengers of Deception: UFO Contacts and Cults*. Daily Grail Publishing. P. 83

Dr. Pettipher recalled her first visit to San Francisco, at the height of the hippie movement. She couldn't believe that so many souls from the ancient world had reincarnated at the same time, but that only confirmed her theories, she felt. The hippies came from Greek times, and she found proof of this in their later disappearance from America: hundreds of them now live in caves in Greece; she has seen them.[709]

The twist in this account is that Dr. Pettipher identifies the reincarnated hippies with a pagan people, the ancient Greeks, whereas Dick identified them with the early Christians and Gnostics. In her lectures, Dr. Pettipher also veers into Julian Jaynes's territory by claiming that prior to Abraham, "there was no question of psychic powers such as clairvoyance. There was cosmo-voyance, the vision and hearing of God."[710] Dr. Pettipher is one part of the Order of Melchizedek puzzle, the other is a man named Ivan who runs the Parisian branch of the Order.[711] Both groups trace their lineage back to a Pennsylvanian man named Hiram Butler who, after having lived fourteen years as a Hermit, emerged in the late 1880s with a new ascetic religion which preached sexual abstinence and agricultural self-sustainability. After gaining enough of a following, Hiram Butler moved his congregation to a farm in Placer County, California. [712] His successor was a man named Enoch Penn, who proselytized the

---

[709] Ibid p. 107

[710] Ibid p. 105. The reader will recall Jaynes's argument in *The Origin of Consciousness in the Breakdown of the Bicameral Mind* that individual consciousness arose in the second millennium B.C., and that prior to this development, people took their personal thoughts to be externally derived.

[711] Ibid pp. 100 - 101

[712] Ibid pp. 142 - 143

teachings throughout what is now known as "Silicon Valley."[713] As the religion developed, UFO phenomena and lore was incorporated, with many of these groups interpreting the Biblical interaction between Melchizedek and Abraham as being the most significant, and possibly the first, intrusion of an extraterrestrial entity into the earth's historical narrative.

So, let's turn back to the mythological origins of Melchizedek. In The Significance of the Cosmos we discussed Melchizedek in a generally positive light; and if not totally positive, he was less ambiguously drawn than either Enoch or Hiram. If there was a duality inherent to either of those two characters, there was a plausibility that it could be reduced to the fact that there were near-contemporaneous individuals with the same name. This is not the case with Melchizedek, as any duality in his character would have to be internal.

Ginzberg gives us the first indication of problematic aspects of Melchizedek's character:

> In spite of his great success, Abraham nevertheless was concerned about the issue of the war. He feared that the prohibition against shedding the blood of man had been transgressed, and he also dreaded the resentment of Shem, whose descendants had perished in the encounter. But God reassured him, and said: "Be not afraid! Though hast but extirpated the thorns, and as to Shem, he will bless thee rather than curse thee." So it was. When Abraham returned from the war Shem, or, as he is sometimes called, Melchizedek, the king of righteousness, priest of God Most High, and king of Jerusalem, came forth to meet him with bread and wine. And this high priest instructed Abraham in the laws of

---

[713] Notice the repetition of the names of all three murky figures: Hiram, Enoch and Melchizedek within this one turn-of-the-century religious cult.

the priesthood and in the Torah, and to prove his friendship for him he blessed him, and called him the partner of God in the possession of the world, seeing that through him the Name of God had first been made known among men. But Melchizedek arranged the words of his blessing in an unseemly way. He named Abraham first and then God As a punishment, he was deposed by God from the priestly dignity, and instead it was passed over to Abraham, with whose descendants it remained forever.[714]

There's a lot to discuss in relation to this narrative. Wayne has a short chapter entitled "The Bull Cult of Melchizedek" near the end of *The Genesis 6 Conspiracy* where he etymologically ties the name "Melchizedek" to the Baal cult:

Molech, son of Baal, also haunted the Israelites. Molech, as in "Melchi" of Melchizedek and its genitive Enochian Essene sun cult, was a Semetic deity who demanded the sacrifice of children, a custom robustly forbidden by Moses and Israelite Law.[715]

Early depictions of Baal show a man with a Bull's head, which Wayne ties to features of classical mythology such as the Minotaur; the "golden calf" made by the Israelites in a moment of disobedience as they wandered the desert for forty years under the stewardship of Moses; and the bull-cult reigned over by Poseidon in the heady days of Atlantis. After Atlantis sank, the bull cult might have been incorporated into the Canaanite mythos

---

[714] Ginzberg, Louis (1992) *Legends of the Bible*. The Jewish Publication Society Pp. 106 - 107
[715] Wayne, Gary (2014) *The Genesis 6 Conspiracy*. Trusted Books, A Division of Deep River Books. P. 586

adopted by the Philistines.[716] The narrative, then, is that the Canaanite Order of Melchizedek is a divergent mythos from the Hebrew tradition that went on to inform various Gnostic sects, as well as the Essenes:

> The contemporaneous Masonic Order of Melchizedek consequently follows the (perverted) Canaanite Order, claiming it to be the true Order, and further reclaiming Melchizedek, Abraham, David, Solomon, and Jesus as its descending patriarchs. The Gnostics possess a gospel of Melchizedek, which not surprisingly, denotes its spurious followers as Children of Seth, the Gnostic Nephilim Seth, who maintain the spark of the divine required for the harmonic convergence and ascension into godhood when the world unites under one world government and religion.[717]

There is a reference at the beginning of "The Gospel of Melchizedek" to someone being sent to "the congregation of [the children] of Seth,"[718] but it is unclear whether this individual is Melchizedek or someone named "Gamaliel." It is also open to speculation whether these children of Seth are of the Biblical line descended from Adam or some Nephilim imposter. Given our previous discussion of this Gospel and how it differs from Gnostic beliefs at the time, I think we should be skeptical of any attempts to incorporate this text into the narrative of a Canaanite Order that is seeking to create a counterfeit Order of Melchizedek.[719]

---

[716] Ibid pp. 588 - 589

[717] Ibid p. 589

[718] Robinson, James (1990) *The Nag Hammadi Library*. Harper. P. 440

[719] Such a counterfeit order could be represented not only by the Order of Melchizedek documented by Vallée, but also within the teachings of the *Urantia Foundation*, which claims that: "In the

Regardless as to whether these more negative interpretations ought to be integrated into the canonical myth of Melchizedek, they do imbue his personage with a greater sense of ambiguity. One could argue that it is the synthesis created from these two interpretations: on one hand Melchizedek is a divine figure, possibly Christ himself, who appears and disappears with no record of his mortality. Or possibly, he is a more materialistic, yet mystically-packaged, recycling of an older, slightly more obscure figure, which then conditions his name to become a signifier for an obscure UFO contact cult.

In terms of Philip K. Dick's narrative: given the Gnosticism informing his life and work, can we speculate that the entity of VALIS can be read as a reiteration of "Melchizedek"? If the answer to this question is "yes," then are we to interpret it as an occurrence of the authentic or the counterfeit Melchizedek? Possibly, it is a combination of both, partaking in both the beneficial (the revealing beam of pink life) and the deadly (the radiation that, over time, causes Brent Mini's cancer). What is most salient, however, is that the figure of Melchizedek has been reborn within the later stages of modernity, and as Vallée says, a number of real people in our day and age "truly believed in Melchizedek and his cosmic role..."[720] and in this respect, his name has become a mythically derived signifier that is emblematic of resistance to the governing scientific materialism of the last two centuries.[721]

Ancient Aliens

---

universe of Nebadon the Father Melchizedek acts as the first executive associate of the Bright and Morning Star." Thus linking his identity to Lucifer, "the lightbearer." Vallée, Jacques (2008) *Messengers of Deception: UFO Contacts and Cults.* Daily Grail Publishing. P. 134

[720] Ibid p. 137

[721] Ibid p. 138

At the point of synthesis in our UFO dialectic sits the so-called "Ancient Aliens" narrative. Historically, this theory, which was formally kicked-off with the publication of Erich Von Däniken's *Chariots of the Gods?* in 1968, was concurrent with the heyday of textually rich UFO literature.[722] However, the theory only came into its own, in a historic-dialectical sense, once it entered (and saturated) popular culture under the aegis of a television program produced by Prometheus Entertainment for the History Channel.

First aired on April 20, 2010[723] *Ancient Aliens* seeks to carry the fundamental insight of *Chariots of the Gods?* to all spheres of life. Most likely everyone reading this is very familiar with the program and its basic premise, but I will still present a brief overview. The three primary protagonists are Giorgio Tsoukalos, David Hatcher Childress, and Philip Coppens. This is not to exclude the importance of narrator Robert Clotworthy, who eggs the proceedings on with his running commentary.

Essentially, each episode takes some facet of history, religion, or mythology and interprets it through a lens in which the cause of the phenomenon is extraterrestrial intervention, or "ancient astronauts." This heuristic begins with architectural feats like the pyramids and Stonehenge and ends with George Washington consulting with UFOs about how to win the Revolutionary War. Obviously, the whole enterprise reeks of compound conspiracy theorization as well as explanatory monism, as a wide variety of synchronistic phenomena is supposed to be derived from one originary source: aliens.

The attentive reader will recall that I stated in The Significance of the Sea that most contemporary conspiracy theorists will attempt to adhere to the tenets of scientific

---

[722] 1968 is also the year that Stanley Kubrick's film *2001: A Space Odyssey* was released. Based on a sort story by Arthur C. Clarke, the film ambiguously touches on the idea of ancient alien intervention in early human development.
[723] "4/20" –need I really say anything more?

materialism when explaining the wonders of the ancient world by one of two paths: either alien intervention, or an esoteric capacity to manipulate certain Ley lines on the Earth's surface. The ancient aliens narrative adheres to the former, obviously.

For a theorist who favors the Ley lines argument, or is aloof to the issue of ancient alien intervention, like Frank Joseph, there is a clear-cut claim that the individuals who brought the seeds of civilization to foreign lands were gifted with an aptitude for manipulating electro-magnetic forces. Joseph identifies these culture-bearers as the "Naacals." Knight and Lomas also posit that culture had to be the result of colonization, and the group they posit as filling this role is the Grooved Ware People. Despite having palled around with Robert Temple in their spare time, Knight and Lomas seem hell-bent on identifying prehistoric "supernatural" activities with proto-Europeans, and not with aliens.[724]

In this respect, Knight and Lomas are keeping with Vico's theory of "poetic wisdom," in that the fabulous and mythic nature of the narrative is a facet of its reiteration. Ancient alien theorization is seemingly antithetical to Vico's theory, as it posits that early man was forced into mythological thinking because he couldn't make sense of the fantastic events he was seeing. Conspiracy theorists such as Joseph, Michell, Knight and Lomas, etc., believe mythological thinking is a symbolic language, or structure, that preserved the "true" knowledge in a manner that was intended to be esoteric. It is essentially the fidelity to this knowledge originating within human reason, which Knight and Lomas, in particular, see as being the primary animating force of Freemasonry, driving them to an unwillingness to pass this off as anything that is either divine or extraterrestrial.

It might seem like ancient aliens theories are anachronistic insofar as they are contingent on actual texts like *Chariots of the*

---

[724] It goes without saying that Gary Wayne is strongly resistant to the ancient aliens hypothesis, in that he argues that aliens are actually angels or demons.

Gods?, Fingerprints of the Gods, and references to myths and legends. However, the theory is, for better or worse, forever bound to the eponymous television show. Since everyone born after 1995 has moved onto mostly internet-related conspiracy theories such as the Mandela Effect, child-trafficking on the darkweb, and "deep-fake" videos. The challenge, in this respect, is for the more narratively rich ancient aliens theory is to make itself intriguing to clickbait culture. There are two challenges to this endeavor:

1. The allure of ancient aliens theories was basically a scholarly one, as it forced the reader into a systematic re-evaluation of history and historic texts. So, at some point ancient aliens inductees will have to wade through some dry or not immediately entertaining material; and this flies in the face of the hedonist spirit that informs clickbait culture.

2. Two mediums vie for hegemony online: memes and videos. Videos interest us here because this is the medium that will purport definitive evidence of flying saucers. These videos, unless they are too long and tedious, are on the side of scientific reductionism as they are displayed as documentary evidence.

With this point I am drawing an equivocation between scientism and clickbait culture, but I am only doing so because both are heavily reliant upon sensory input and immediacy. There is also an aspect of confirmation-bias lurking beneath the surface of both. Take for example, UFO footage shot in New York City in late September 2019. As the cameraman, Mauricio Lopez, focuses in on the shape in the sky he states: "I believe in UFOs, and I think I've got one right now."[725]

Confirmation-bias is, or should be, anathema to the scientifically minded and should therefore prevent us from

---

[725] https://dailystar.co.uk/news/weird-news/mystery-object-likened-death-star-20377926 accessed on 10/03/19

completely conflating the two mindsets. However, the desire for immediate factual confirmation of phenomena is powerful and can lead to individuals who zealously consume video content believing that they are seeing something that could constitute scientific fact.

In contrast, the ancient alien theorist might just as enthusiastically believe the videos depicting UFOs, however, he views them with the ideological baggage of why the aliens are here, what they have accomplished in the past, and what their future plans might be. The ancient aliens theorist is bringing significantly more narrative content into the viewing and discussion of the video than the mainstream UFO enthusiast. The cultural phenomenon is circular: it is the sensationalistic aspect of ancient aliens as a pseudoscientific theory that made it popular enough to warrant a television show, which then, ultimately went on to undermine its own sense of credibility.

In this cultural context, it is interesting to note that in the tug-of-war between memes and video for internet hegemony, it is memes that are on the side of the ancient aliens theorist. It doesn't matter if the memes are mocking Giorgio Tsoukalos's hair and spray-tan; all that matters at this stage of postmodernity is that they exist, they are funny, and they lead to the generation of more memes.

For modern-day conspiracy theorists the prospect of extraterrestrial intervention took the place previously occupied by earthly entities like the Rothschilds, Freemasons, and the Trilateralist Commission, etc., by claiming that all these groups, as well as historical figures, were in contact with, and controlled by, aliens. The most postmodern aspect of ancient aliens theorization is that, unlike the theorists we've gone through – Grant and Vallée (who based their examination of the topic on myth), Greer, Icke and Redfern (who set out to eschew myth, but ultimately defer to it in some explanatory capacity) – the ancient aliens theory seeks an erasure of myth; seeking instead to rewrite the story of prehistory in a way that eliminates any mystery – and then falls victim to the very same nihilism in which it traffics.

In a pseudo-scientific sense, Ancient aliens theorists reproduce Stephen Mulhall's question of "What justifies the choice of the capacity to choose as the basis of one's life? What confers meaning on it?" Such a question suggests that Man's existence cannot determine its own significance on its own terms, that "Meaning can only be given to one's life as a whole by relating it to something outside it; for it is only to something outside it that my life can be related *as a whole*."[726] The ancient aliens theorist sees this "something outside" in the most ulterior of terms.

I Hate to Rain on Your Parade, but...

This is the end of the line for this topic. We're going to conclude with two scientific theories that argue against the existence of extraterrestrials. The first is the "rare earth hypothesis," which postulates that a planet that can sustain life would have to lie in a so-called "Goldilocks Zone;" some of the ideal factors for such a zone would be: a range of distance from the star that it orbits that would accommodate temperatures allowing water to remain in liquid form, a moon that can stabilize the climate, being located in a galaxy that is structured like ours and is not "irregular," (e.g., has too much radiation or too many interstellar collisions that might upset the general equilibrium). The list goes on. Essentially, adherents of the Goldilocks Zone theory argue that even if there are planets in our galaxy, or nearby galaxies, that have some similarities to Earth, the odds of finding one that fits the bill are infinitesimally long.

Loosely related to this theory is the possibility that the rare planets capable of sustaining life have not advanced beyond us in terms of technology but are actually far behind us. If this is the case, then it could give credence to the conspiracy theory that extraterrestrials are, in actuality, future denizens of Earth

---

[726] Mulhall, Stephen (2005) *Philosophical Myths of the Fall.* Princeton University Press. P. 58

returning to its past. This is a theory that Art Bell and Brad Steiger explore in their 1999 book, *The Source: Journey Through the Unexplained*, speculating that archaeological artifacts could have been built and left behind by time-travelers;[727] and that UFO abductions might be "our descendants from the distant future returning to study certain negative genetic traits that they now have the capability to refine or eliminate."[728]

The second argument against the possibility of extraterrestrial life that we will examine was forwarded by Nick Bostrom in his paper, "Where Are They?" published in the May/June 2008 issue of The MIT *Technology Review*. Bostrom builds on the rare earth hypothesis but adds the concept of a "Great Filter," which he borrowed from economist Robin Hanson. In his paper, Bostrom is careful to stipulate that he is talking about the observable universe and that, were life to exist beyond this horizon, it would be of no consequence because there would be no way for us to ever have any contact with these entities.

The Great Filter as Hanson and Bostrom conceive it is an improbable, possibly vastly complicated, hindrance that only life on earth could have overcome in order to have come into being. The Great Filter is an event that would make improbable one of the necessary evolutionary steps towards attaining intelligent life as we know it. These steps begin with biogenesis (the creation of life), the first proper replication of DNA that allowed for mutation, tool utilization, etc., and conclude with interstellar colonization.[729] Essentially, there is a possibility that we passed the Great Filter at some distant point in the past. However, Bostrom, as well as others, postulates that the Great Filter might actually lie ahead of us, hence his fear that discovering life, or remnants of life, on

---

[727] Bell, Art & Steiger, Brad (1999) *The Source: Journey Through the Unexplained*. Paper Chase Press. P. 32
[728] Ibid p. 97
[729] We will revisit Bostrom's work in our chapter on the Mandela Effect and see that interstellar space colonization might not be the final phase of evolution that he has in mind.

other planets would indicate that such an interspecies ending catastrophe still awaits us.

Funnily enough, after these two arguments are taken into consideration, it is Vallée and Grant who are still left standing because they do not insist on an extraterrestrial origin for UFO phenomena. Bostrom's concern with a Great Filter that lies in our future sees it as an extermination point that will essentially set human life back to zero. In terms of the textual analysis in which we have engaged, I don't think the possibility of a Great Filter is something we should be overly awed by. As far as its narrative is concerned, it is essentially a reiteration of the Big Bang/Big Crunch narrative that some physicists have projected onto the cosmology of the universe.[730]

UFOs are an essential part of modern-day conspiracy theories and in this chapter we have seen how the craze began as an extension of the occult (or folk religious movements, as in the case of Hiram Butler's Order of Melchizedek), moved into what we might call a proto-scientistic, materialist phase, and then finally with the popularity of *Ancient Aliens*, as a concept and TV show, achieved a kind of post-modern synthesis of the two.

Everything we've discussed gives us a portion of the history of this area or study as well as glimpses into why it is interesting for conspiracy theorists. One point I'd like to stress here though, and this operates in conjunction with UFOlogy's attempt at scientism, is how this facet of conspiracy theorization acted not only to excite interest in casual observers but also to stigmatize the people who believe its tenets. This is a stigma that had not been a serious issue for conspiracy theorists prior to the UFO era insofar as they saw themselves as conducting a sort of political/historical analysis. This stigma, however, would

---

[730] The theory of Sir Roger Penrose regarding the Big Bang is that it was not a singular event but one that reoccurs repeatedly for aeons -as one universe distends into nothingness a singular point emerges to begin the cycle again. This has been dubbed the "Conformal Cyclic Cosmology" theory.

eventually spread to all other branches of conspiracy theorization, beginning with the assassination of John Fitzgerald Kennedy.

.

Chapter Twelve: The Significance of JFK and Political Assassination in General)

On August 10, 2019 financier Jeffrey Epstein was found dead in his jail cell at the New York Metropolitan Correctional Center. This event, like many of the mass-shootings and celebrity deaths that had occurred prior to it, generated a large amount of skepticism in conspiracy-oriented circles. However, this reaction was not limited to the conspiracy theory community, as the death of this high-profile individual also elicited a great deal of skepticism from the public at large.

Epstein's case is significant in that it is tangentially tied to political intrigue, espionage (intelligence agencies such as the CIA and the Mossad), as well as conspiracy theories like Pizzagate; but those aren't the primary reasons why it will be addressed later in this chapter. The reason for its inclusion is that Epstein's death, as well as other notable deaths at this point in modernity, represents a third stage in the dialectic of political assassination and the movement of Western society into an even more advanced state of hyperreality.

Thesis: The Assassination of John F. Kennedy

John Fitzgerald Kennedy was born on May 29, 1917 in Brookline Massachusetts to Joseph and Rose Kennedy. After a distinguished career in the U.S. Navy from 1941 to 1945[731], Kennedy (often referred to as "Jack" by friends and family) served in the U.S. House of Representatives from 1947 to 1953 and in the U.S. Senate from 1953 to 1960.

He was elected to the Presidency in 1960, an event that not only marked the end of the 1950s, a decade marked by a

---

[731] Notable awards during John Kennedy's service were the Navy and Marine Corps Medal, the American Defense Service Medal, as well as a Purple Heart for an injury to his back that occurred in August 1943 while commanding the PT-109 Torpedo Boat.

particularly naïve brand of prosperity that came in the wake of America's victory in World War II, but also instantiated the Kennedy family's ambitions to become an American political dynasty. Seymour Hersh details the lengths to which the Kennedy patriarch went to advance his son's political aspirations:

> Joseph P. Kennedy did more than invest his time and money in his unrelenting drive in 1960 to elect his oldest surviving son president. He risked the family's reputation – and the political future of his sons Bobby and Teddy – by making a bargain with Sam Giancana and the powerful organized crime syndicate in Chicago. Joe Kennedy's goal was to ensure victory in Illinois and in other states where the syndicate had influence, and he achieved it, after arranging a dramatic and until now unrevealed summit meeting with Sam Giancana in the chambers of one of Chicago's most respected judges. The deal included an assurance that Giancana's men would get out the Kennedy vote among the rank and file in the mob-controlled unions in Chicago and elsewhere, and a commitment for campaign contributions from the corrupt Teamsters Union pension fund.[732]

Even though it was Joseph Kennedy's plan to enlist Giancana and the Chicago syndicate in his endeavor to get his son elected, this instance of criminal interference in the election was fully understood by Jack and Bobby and would weigh on them during Kennedy's brief time in office. There is a strong likelihood that this bout of ballot fraud was not new to Joseph Kennedy, who had worked extensively on his stepfather John F. Fitzgerald's 1918 campaign for a seat in the US House of Representatives.

---

[732] Hersh, Seymour (1997) *The Dark Side of Camelot.* Little, Brown and Company. P. 131

Kennedy's term (January 20, 1961 – November 22, 1963) was marked by a wide array of events that would condition the country's burgeoning culture. These included: the creation of the Peace Corps, the Bay of Pigs, John Glenn's orbit around the Earth, the Cuban Missile Crisis, as well as a whole host of steps toward the dismantling of racial segregation.[733] This combination of space age innovation with sweeping justice reform at a time when the average voter tended to identify the government as being an emanation of its figurehead, forged the JFK persona into the beloved icon that we know today.[734]

Just over halfway through his term in the White House, JFK was riding in the backseat of a Lincoln Continental in a motorcade through Dealey Plaza in downtown Dallas, Texas on November 22, 1963, when tragedy struck. At 12:30 in the afternoon shots rang out and Kennedy was rushed to the nearby Parkland Memorial Hospital with a massive head wound. Within a few hours, after being pronounced dead, Lyndon B. Johnson was sworn into office.[735] Lee Harvey Oswald would be arrested in the Texas Theatre for the murder, as well as the murder of Dallas Patrolman J.D. Tippit later that afternoon, and then subsequently shot to death by nightclub owner Jack Ruby on Sunday November 24th in the basement of the Dallas Police Headquarters.

Countless books, novels, television programs, and films have addressed what happened on that fateful day and its aftermath. There is not enough space to pick through each one individually, but fortunately there are enough commonalities and discernable themes that we can piece together a narrative analysis of JFK's death, as well as the events leading up to it, which may have played a part in its occurrence.

---

[733] https://millercenter.org/president/john-f-kennedy/key-events accessed on 04/30/2021

[734] This is a trait that still exists today, albeit in a more cynical and convenient form.

[735] Ibid

Investigative journalist Seymour M. Hersh argues in *The Dark Side of Camelot* that there is a great deal of proof that the Italian Mafia helped Kennedy win the 1960 Presidential election. According to Hersh, Kennedy's father, Joseph Kennedy Sr. was the mastermind behind employing gangsters to help his son win Illinois through voting fraud. John Kennedy's friendship with Frank Sinatra, who was known to have mafia connections, specifically with Sam Giancana, also played a part in the Mafia's alleged involvement in the election.[736] This liability was not only a topic of speculation among Washington insiders of the day but would also become grist for the conspiracy theorist's mill in the ensuing decades.

The involvement of the Mafia in JFK's bid for the presidency (and his subsequent downfall) is only one piece of the nefarious puzzle that is the JFK assassination. Before we can dive into the conspiracy theories circulating around this remarkable event, we must address the significance of some of the figures that pop up in them. I use the term "significance" here in the philosophical sense that has been emphasized so far, but would like to add that: these figures are significant within the context of modernity because they intersect with other popular conspiracy theories (The New World Order, UFOs, Men in Black, etc.) and because, as characters, their roles within these narratives are reiterations of individuals found in older theories and myths. Hence, their appearance in relation to the murder of JFK warrants both attention and repetition.

Despite their assistance in helping Kennedy win the election, the Mafia soon found themselves under a great deal of scrutiny by Attorney General Robert Kennedy's Justice Department. Because of this about-face, some have alleged that high-ranking members of the criminal organization were responsible for planning JFK's assassination. However, despite considering possible Mafia involvement, most conspiracy

---

[736] Hersh, Seymour (1998) *The Dark Side of Camelot.* Back Bay Books. Pp. 214 - 215

theorists focus on a few other notable characters they believe may have been involved in conspiring to assassinate the president; specifically, members of the US Government plotting an overthrow on behalf of the "deep state." According to David Talbot's *The Devil's Chessboard*, the CIA's founder, Allen Welsh Dulles, was one such key figure because of a harbored resentment towards JFK for the Bay of Pigs fiasco.[737] In his earlier book, *Brothers: The Hidden History of the Kennedy Years*, Talbot summarizes JFK's focus on dealing with Latin America using charisma and ideology instead of direct military intervention:

> With his youth, Catholicism, movie-star looks, and progressive appeal, JFK thought he could out-market even the dashing Fidel and Che in the war of ideas, selling democratic reform as an alternative to armed revolution. Kennedy did, in fact, succeed in electrifying Latin America during his brief presidency, during which he made three trips to the region. Huge crowds inevitably greeted his appearances with a frantic adoration that threatened not just Castro, but his beribboned generals and wealthy despots who greeted the American president. [738]

Dulles was also painted in an ominous light by Oliver Stone's highly publicized 1991 film *JFK*; however, in a more nuanced and less conclusive manner than the one utilized by Talbot. The founder of the website *Salon* and frequent contributor to *Mother Jones*, Talbot is essentially a remnant of the old school, Nazi reductionist left-wing conspiracy theory tradition. Given that Talbot's focus in *The Devil's Chessboard* is the CIA he emphasizes

---

[737] In which the CIA tried to instigate an overthrow of the Fidel Castro led government using Cuban exiles.

[738] Talbot, David (2007) *Brothers: The Hidden History of the Kennedy Years.* Free Press. P. 62

the degree of Nazi subversion to which the agency succumbed from its inception in 1947 to the present – thereby presenting the "deep state" as almost a kind of neo-Nazi organization.[739]

In Talbot's hands, Dulles, who had been dismissed from the CIA following the Bay of Pigs fiasco, becomes a caricature of a "might is right," Commie bashing, American imperialist. The three ideological motivations given for Dulles's behavior are: 1) dedication to preserving the WASP elites' (who, for Talbot are identical with the nation's financial elites) place at the top of the American economic food chain. 2) antagonism towards anticolonial liberation movements taking place outside of the United States.[740] 3) a desire to defeat international Communism. For Talbot, all three of these motivations are indications of latent Nazism, therefore a historical genealogy is needed to make this connection, to which the majority of *The Devil's Chessboard* is devoted.

It is doubtful, however, that Dulles was ideologically sympathetic with the tenets of German National Socialism. Most likely, he subscribed to the elitist ideas of older American-bred eugenicists like Madison Grant, Dr. Albert Priddy, and Lothrop Stoddard. Talbot writes that while Dulles was employed in the U.S. embassy in Turkey the following events occurred:

> One day the young American diplomat was given a copy of *The Protocols of the Learned Elders of Zion* by a British reporter who had fished the scurrilous document out of a secondhand bookstore in Istanbul's old European quarter. *The Protocols* purported to offer a secret plan for Jewish world

---

[739] The concept of a subversive "deep state" operating by its own nefarious rules has been employed by conspiracy theorists of every political stripe.

[740] One specific instance of this is the 1954 Guatemalan coup orchestrated by the CIA to overthrow the country's democratically elected president.

domination, and included tales about Christian children being sacrificed for Passover feast rituals and other lurid fantasies. By the time Dulles got his hands on the book, which was the creation of the Russian czar's anti-Semitic secret police, the document had been widely denounced and discredited. But Dulles took it seriously enough to send a coded report about the secret Jewish "plot" back to his superiors in Washington.[741]

It's an interesting piece of character assassination; unfortunately it's contradicted by Richard Breitman's documented claim that Dulles's correspondence with Washington regarding *The Protocols* was to encourage the State Department to denounce the book as a forgery:

> He [Dulles] held some negative stereotypes of Jews, but in 1921 he was directly involved in efforts to expose the now infamous *Protocols of the Elders of Zion* as a forgery. He was unable to persuade the State Department to denounce the document publicly. [742]

There is a modicum of passable information to be gleaned from *The Devil's Chessboard*, so long as one keeps in mind that David Talbot is a baby boomer, and as such, believes in his heart of hearts that John Fitzgerald Kennedy was a Christlike figure who died, in one way or another, at the hands of the ultimate evil, i.e., Adolf Hitler.[743] This is not to say that Talbot is parochial, or so

[741] Talbot, David (2015) *The Devil's Chessboard*. Harper. P. 46
[742] Breitman, Richard; Goda, Norman; Naftali, Timothy; Wolfe, Robert (2005) *U.S. Intelligence and the Nazis*. Cambridge University Press. P. 25
[743] A more interesting boomer eschatology, in my own opinion, is the one that keeps JFK as the savior but inserts Charles Manson as

blinded by his admiration of Kennedy to not see him as a complex human being, intellectually he is tempered in his treatment of JFK's strengths and weaknesses. His admiration seems to be more of a generationally derived instinct or gut reaction.

Before we move forward we should note that there is a hermeneutical element at play in this boomer worship of the Kennedys. One of the entailments seems to be the projection of metaphysical absolutes onto historical figures. This makes sense if we look at the baby boomer generation as wholly subsumed within a culture that had transitioned from a reliance on the theological abstractions of organized religion, which for our purposes can be viewed as sets of dogmatic narratives with mythic antecedents, to the more simplified culture of political demagoguery exemplified by film and television. In the latter mediums, good and evil had to be addressed in explicit terms that lacked nuance. The boomer psyche is one that internalized the moral caricatures with which it was bombarded on film and television and extrapolated them onto the primal ideas of good and evil that religion (and literature) had hitherto wrestled with in more complex and sophisticated ways.

As a further point regarding this hermeneutical analysis, neither John nor Robert Kennedy were themselves boomers; they were a little older, so the boomers looked up to them as benevolent older brothers as they transitioned from aspiring prep school attendees in the fifties to free love espousing hippies in the sixties. However, this should not obscure the reality that the stable and saintly older brothers were still politicians, and they used the cultural turbulence as a weapon in their struggle for political power, as well as for American global hegemony; a fact that slowly emerged as the nation became the pre-eminent global super-power following the end of World War II. Talbot's description of JFK moving to marketing ideas and drawing

---

the diabolical figure that, in one way or another, brings about the magical era of the sixties that had been inaugurated by the election of Kennedy.

common people in with charisma is synchronistic with the boomers' new simplified conceptualization of good vs. evil.

Another aspect fueling this type of analysis (not just from Talbot, but many of his younger colleagues) is the air of mystique surrounding the declassification of documents – whether they pertain to MK Ultra, JFK, Roswell, or the Nazis. We've already established the simplistic "good" and "evil" binary that the baby boomers (and certain members of generation X) impose upon the political narratives they encounter every day. The promise of declassified documents, which might radically redefine an established issue, is almost like a contemporary (and decidedly secular) form of divine revelation; because at this stage of modernity, we can't countenance the belief in a god who will reveal the unknown narrative. God's role is now played, or subsumed, by the government. The declassified documents then, in turn, become a kind of postmodern scripture.[744]

Unlike the Roswell incident, Kennedy's assassination undoubtedly occurred, to be followed by the assassinations of Martin Luther King Jr. and Robert Kennedy. These are historical events that are largely undeniable. I'm sure someone might come up with a theory that they were body doubles or clones or something similar, but I haven't come across it ... yet. Whether you argue the traditional conspiracy theorist's view that it was *not* Lee Harvey Oswald who killed JFK, or you take the more nuanced view that it *was* Oswald who carried out the assassination, there will be a variety of conspiratorial alleyways you can be led down.

In his first book, *UFOs, JFK, and Elvis: Conspiracies You Don't Have to be Crazy to Believe*, Richard Belzer seems to be struggling to balance his ideas with a perceived demand to

---

[744] This sense of validity obtaining from official documents was something that we saw inform William Cooper's conspiracy theorization.

entertain his audience.[745] By 2012's *Dead Wrong: Straight Facts on the Country's Most Controversial Cover-ups* he had adopted a more serious and thoughtful analysis of his topics. In the introduction he firmly stakes his place on the "Oswald did not do it" side of the equation and, interestingly enough, approaches the issue in a textual way, i.e., in the form of an argument against Vincent Bugliosi's claim that Oswald did do it.[746] It isn't really necessary to pit these two viewpoints against each other dialectically, because once we've reached the point of events occurring in the modern era the argumentative aspect of the dialectic loses a great deal of its effectiveness. In part, this is because, properly executed, the dialectical method draws on abstraction and theoretical thinking – not so much on the mere comparison of data.

On a more immediate, sociological level, the dialectical method of analysis still has gravity insofar as it abides "Symbolic Exchange," which is a concept we will delve into a little later. For now, we'll say that symbolic exchange is a type of object transference, or action, that harkens back to older sociological models based on concepts of honor, duty, and sacrifice. In other words, an action conforms to the tenets of symbolic exchange if it involves the giving or acceptance of something that is unique and irreplaceable, the action of the giver is marked by a sense of sacrifice, or at the very least, uniqueness.

It might sound risible to claim that the assassination of JFK eludes this form of analysis – what greater symbolic exchange is there than the death of a great statesman? So, yes, we sacrificed our saintly president but what did we get in return? Why, deception and a Kafkaesque deferment of responsibility that

[745] There is also the possibility that he was unduly influenced by the gonzo nature of *The Big Book of Conspiracies*, which he lists in *UFOs, JFK, and Elvis*'s bibliography.
[746] Bugliosi gave his analysis of the JFK assassination in his 2007 book, *Reclaiming History: The Assassination of President John F. Kennedy.*

eventually faded off into the morass of hyperreality in which we currently reside. To paraphrase Baudrillard's critique of modernity: "the Dialectic has stopped."[747]

This is not to say that a certain kind of dialectical thinking cannot be retained and injected into the narratives surrounding JFK's assassination. It's just that, at the level of factual analysis, it is more a game of tabulating data. I will, in fact, track a dialectical flow of certain assassination narratives, but it will, by necessity, consider assassinations that did not result in death (as in the case of Nixon) or assassinations that are completely shrouded in mystery (Jeffrey Epstein). It is significant to our discussion that this transitioning from a reliance on the *symbolic* to a reliance on the *actual* coincides with the historical progression through the twentieth century.

The issue of symbolic exchange gives us the opportunity to add an additional detail about the historical development of the dialectical method, or dialectical thinking, which is that, historically, it has been informed by a kind of Christian (or Trinitarian) logic.[748] By this I mean it duplicates the pattern of life (thesis), confrontation with death, or negation (antithesis), and

---

[747] To a certain extent this pronouncement was the postmodern equivalent of Nietzsche's Madman declaring that "God is dead" in *The Gay Science.*

[748] What I am about to outline here is not the only reading of the Hegelian schema. Brandom's pragmatic reading of what constitutes "Hegel's final idealist view" is constituted by three commitments: "The first commitment is to what I have called 'conceptual realism.' The second commitment is to what I call 'objective idealism.' The third is to what I call 'conceptual idealism.' I offer these claims as a tripartite analysis of Hegel's idealism, claiming that his view is what you get if you endorse all of them. I take it they form a hierarchy, with each commitment presupposing those that come before it." From Brandom, Robert (2019) *A Spirit of Trust: A Reading of Hegel's Phenomenology.* Belknap Press of Harvard University Press. Pp. 204 - 205

resurrection or rebirth (synthesis). One might look at this philosophical process as a secular rendering of a divine way of reasoning about phenomena, specifically historical phenomena. This is particularly relevant here, because some of the assassinated figures, such as JFK and Martin Luther King Jr., assume Christ-like proportions in their death. Oftentimes the tragedy of the death projects a sheen of "holiness" back onto their life.[749] This sheen of holiness is then contingent upon the concept of sacrifice, specifically the sacrificing of one's own life.

"Holiness", though, is not what most people (who are under sixty) today would project onto JFK, as more often he is remembered for his charisma and serial adultery. Belzer and co-author David Wayne list some of Kennedy's most notable sexual conquests: "Marilyn Monroe, Jody Campbell, Ellen Rometsch, and Mary Pinchot Meyer."[750] All of which were kept out of the press for decorum's sake and possibly at the behest of FBI Director J. Edgar Hoover, who was possibly holding the information back for his own purposes, should Kennedy's actions veer too far from the FBI director's agenda.[751]

---

[749] The idea that the dialectical process is derived from Christian theology is made by Glenn Alexander Magee, who cites Hegel's interpretation of his own work as following in the Hermetical tradition that perceives the Holy Trinity in everything; "that all things have this divine Trinity in themselves, not as a Trinity pertaining to the ordinary conception, but as the real Trinity of the Absolute Idea." Magee, Glenn Alexander (2001) *Hegel and the Hermetic Tradition.* Cornell University Press. P. 49 The Trinitarian view of divinity also exists in Hinduism with the trinity of Brahma, Vishnu and Shiva.

[750] Belzer, Richard & Wayne, David (2012) *Dead Wrong: Straight Facts on the Country's Most Controversial Cover-ups.* Skyhorse Publishing. P. 79

[751] It has been claimed that Harry Truman, John Kennedy and Richard Nixon all had entertained the notion of firing Hoover but abstained out of fear that he would leak personal information on

Seymour Hersh ties the issue of blackmail to JFK's choice of Lyndon Johnson (August 27, 1908 – January 22, 1973) as his running-mate in the 1960 US Presidential election. Apparently Johnson and Hoover were close friends and the two conspired to utilize Hoover's information pertaining to Kennedy's extramarital affairs as well as his father, Joseph Kennedy's shady business dealings, to pressure JFK into naming Johnson as his running mate. Hersh summarizes the imbroglio thusly:

> The principles are long dead, and the world may never know what threats Lyndon Johnson made to gain the vice presidency. Kennedy knew how much Hoover knew, and he knew that the information was more than enough to give Johnson whatever he needed as leverage. Kennedy's womanizing came at great cost: he could be subjected to blackmail not only by any number of his former lovers but also by anyone else who could accumulate enough specifics about his affairs – even an ambitious fellow senator. [752]

Once the shock of Kennedy's death had sunk in, the nation began grasping at reasons for its occurrence. The official explanation for Oswald's killing of Kennedy is that Oswald was a Castro-sympathizer and Communist who acted alone in retaliation for the US Government's meddling in Cuba. Other dubious forces in the background, such as the Mafia and the C.I.A., who had worked together on Operation Mongoose in 1961 to assassinate Castro, complicate the story. So does the possibility of Lyndon Johnson having dubious and/or sinister motives. For

---

them that he kept in his secret files. See https://en.m.wikipedia.org/wiki/J._Edgar_Hoover accessed on 05/04/2021

[752] Hersh, Seymour (1997) *The Dark Side of Camelot.* Little, Brown and Company. Pp. 129 - 130

Belzer, these motives are closely tied to Johnson, who had "a long and sordid political career that was littered with murdered adversaries and corruption involving mobsters."[753]

Contrary to what I said about applying the dialectical method to the particulars of the narratives surrounding the event itself, Kennedy's assassination, and the theories that rose up around it, are vital to the overall dialectical structure of this book because it had a fundamental transformative effect on conspiracy theorization. This is because, not only was it an *actual* documented event but because the conspiratorial narrative now offered two points of entry. In one, people could ask the questions they'd always asked of myths, which is the question of "why." Why was this done? Who could have done it? What were the motives? These questions grapple with the situation in a way that prioritizes the meaning of the event over the technicalities of the event itself.[754] The second point of entry that gained a heightened validity post-JFK was the question of "how." In the grander scheme of things, "how?" is a more trivial question. However, for some, more empirically minded philosophers, it is the only real question because it is the only answerable one. This second, more quantitative, aspect is what we will see gaining steam as the twentieth century comes to a close.

We've already gone over some of the "whos" and "whys" so now we ought to countenance the "hows." Conspiracy theorists who attack the official JFK assassination narrative usually focus on both "whos" and "hows" but they anchor their cases to the "hows" because the allure of scientific plausibility seems to hold the promise of total validity (and hence, widespread acceptance) for their theory. These theories focus on the "impossibility" that three rifle shots fired from Lee Harvey Oswald on the sixth floor

---

[753] Ibid, p. 149. Conspiracy theorists who suspect Johnson's involvement also hone in on the fact that the assassination occurred in his home state.

[754] For religion, myths and the occult this can be broadly described as a "metaphysical" meaning.

of the Dallas Book Depository could have killed Kennedy and wounded Texas Governor John Connally and James Tague.

In 2010, former Minnesota Governor (and professional wrestler) Jesse Ventura attempted to recreate Oswald's supposed feat of firing off three shots within six seconds with the same kind of rifle Oswald was alleged to have used. Based on the results of this experiment Ventura concluded that such a feat was impossible.[755] Further exploration in the realm of "how" leads inevitably to the "Zapruder film," which Belzer claims reveals that prior to the frontal head shot, "The president had already been shot through the throat and Governor Connally, seated in front of JFK in the presidential limousine, has also reacted to at least one bullet that has passed through his own body."[756]

Digging into the details of the JFK assassination you will find lots of coincidences and idiosyncratic narratives. One such narrative is that G. Gordon Liddy and E. Howard Hunt, who play greater roles in the next section, were present in Dallas at the time of the shooting, supposedly disguised as derelicts.[757] Hunt, who has been described as the very archetype of a CIA agent, had been involved with the Bay of Pigs fiasco. According to his oldest son, Howard St. John Hunt, near the end of his father's life the spymaster drew up a diagram linking Lyndon Johnson with the names of CIA agents David Morales, Bill Harvey, and Cord Meyer – Meyer's inclusion was especially interesting since it was alleged

[755] Belzer, Richard & Wayne, David (2012) *Dead Wrong: Straight Facts on the Country's Most Controversial Cover-ups.* Skyhorse Publishing. P. 105
[756] Ibid, p. 89
[757] These two, and a third man, supposedly Frank Sturgis, have been referred to in JFK conspiracy theory circles as the "three tramps." Some have even speculated that one of the tramps may have been Fred Lee Crisman.

that his wife had had an affair with JFK – who he accused of being the primary architects of the assassination.[758]

St. John Hunt made these claims in the April 5, 2007 issue of *Rolling Stone*. Although he was uncertain if his father had actually been in Dallas that day, he claims that his father had knowledge of the conspiracy but swore to the end that he had no role in its execution. The additional piece of the puzzle that this narrative adds is the idea of a second shooter being located on the infamous "grassy knoll." The shooter in this narrative is presumed to be Corsican Mafia assassin Lucien Sarti.[759]

The grassy knoll, which is a sloping hill inside the plaza, has become an important part of the Kennedy mythos, as has the film of the assassination shot from the knoll by Abraham Zapruder; both "grassy knoll" and "Zapruder film" have entered the American lexicon as they metonymically refer to conspiracy theorization in general. Besides showing the president's motorcade before and after the shooting, the Zapruder film captures an overdressed man carrying an umbrella, who performed a dance routine prior to the shooting. There has been some speculation that "Umbrella Man" as he is referred to in conspiracy circles, acted on behalf of the assassins to coordinate the affair, or was himself the shooter.[760]

In his 1975 book *Appointment in Dallas: The Final Solution to the Assassination of JFK*, Hugh C. McDonald claims that Oswald, Ruby, and a third man, whom he refers to as "Saul" were recruited by a coalition of powerful multinational organizations.[761] On

---

[758] https://www.rollingstone.com/feature/the-last-confession-of-e-howard-hunt-76611/amp/ accessed on 05/03/2021

[759] Ibid accessed on 05/03/2021

[760] Belzer, Richard (1999) *UFOs, JFK, and Elvis: Conspiracies You Don't Have to be Crazy to Believe*. The Ballantine Publishing Group. P. 22

[761] McDonald, Hugh (1975) *Appointment in Dallas: The Final Solution to the Assassination of JFK*. The Hugh McDonald Publishing Corp. P. 195

McDonald's theory, Oswald was set up in the book repository to fire shots near the president's motorcade, while the man he dubbed "Saul" (supposedly derived from a Bible passage in which "Saul caused Uriah, the Hittite, to be placed at the forefront of the battle") delivered the fatal shots.[762] Ruby's role, then, was to eliminate the patsy, Oswald. Who was this Saul and from where did he fire his shots?

McDonald claims to have interviewed this mystery man and states that he is a jet-setting professional assassin.[763] Prior to his alleged encounter with Saul he had seen photographs of him near Dealey Plaza. Other investigators have claimed this man to be "Georgi Visko." According to McDonald, Saul/Visko fired shots from a building that was across the street from the building Oswald was in.[764] According to McDonald's narrative, Saul believed that he was supposed to execute Oswald immediately after the assassination, disguising his shots in the hail of gunfire Oswald would have expected to come from the Secret Service; however, the Secret Service did not return fire and Oswald was temporarily spared.[765] Whether McDonald's theory is to be taken seriously is open to speculation, but what he is presenting here is yet another version of the archetypical "second gunman" narrative. What is especially interesting is that a name from the Bible was inserted into this most modern of political intrigue narratives. McDonald's appellation was a misnomer because there was no "Saul" that placed Uriah at the forefront of the battle – it was King David who did that. However, the impetus to incorporate a name from the Bible, specifically one that indicates a dual nature ("Saul" became Saint Paul on the road to Damascus) indicates not merely a need to narrativize the event but to narrativize it in a way that draws upon the mythic.

---

[762] Ibid p. 58
[763] Ibid pp. 203 - 204
[764] Ibid p. 170
[765] Ibid pp. 175 - 177

Regardless of any interest in conspiracy theories, many people have cast JFK as a modern-day Abraham Lincoln. Both played an emancipatory role for African-Americans during their terms in office, both governed during pivotal times in the nation's history, and both were assassinated. There are other, more arcane, synchronicities: both were succeeded by a vice-president surnamed Johnson, and both had assassins who died soon after the assassination.[766] However, given the narrative repetition we have seen so far, is it not too far afield to say that had Lyndon Johnson really been responsible for Kennedy's death, might not the narrative being reiterated be the story of Cain and Abel? Cain was older than Abel, much as Johnson was older than Kennedy. Also, if we believe the narratives that claim that Cain was a bloodthirsty warmonger [767] then there is a moral similarity between him and Johnson, insofar as Johnson navigated the United States into the disastrous Vietnam War.

The Warren Commission

The Warren Commission, set up by Lyndon Johnson to investigate JFK's assassination on November 29, 1963, was intended to quell the nation's sense of unease in the aftermath of the tragedy. According to Belzer, Chief Justice Earl Warren, who led the commission, initially declined the newly sworn-in president's request to head the inquiry, but was browbeaten into it by Johnson, who feared that allegations of conspiracy might undermine his presidency.[768] In this sense, it is highly ironic that the Warren Commission and the report it issued would not only

---

[766] There is a sixteen item list of coincidences between the two, most are true, however "facts" such as: Lincoln had a secretary named Kennedy and Kennedy had a secretary named Lincoln are unverified.

[767] A theory propounded by Gary Wayne and various other fundamentalist Christians.

[768] Ibid, pp. 29 - 30

become a key resource for conspiracy theorists,[769] but also that the investigation it conducted would, in itself, generate a great deal of conspiratorial lore.

Mysterious deaths and disappearances surrounding the creation of the Warren Report are discussed in the opening chapter of *The Big Book of Conspiracies*. Some of the more mysterious ones are: Warren Commission member Hale Boggs died in a plane crash after expressing doubt about Oswald's marksmanship; George Demohrenschildt committed suicide with a .20 gauge shotgun hours before he was scheduled to testify before the Commission; Lt. William Pitzer, who had taken the original autopsy photos of JFK, was found dead of a self-inflicted gunshot wound on October 29, 1966 – despite being left-handed, he was found with a pistol in his right hand; Gary Underhill, who had reportedly told friends that the CIA was involved in the assassination, was found dead of a self-inflicted gunshot wound as well.[770] The list goes on, author Jim Marrs claims that 103 people related to the investigation died in mysterious circumstances between 1963 and 1976.[771]

The Warren Commission Report was completed on September 27, 1964, and reached the conclusion that Oswald had acted alone and had fired three shots from the sixth floor of the Texas School Book Depository. The three primary witnesses on which the document relied were Marina Oswald (Lee Harvey Oswald's widow), Howard Brennan (who claimed to have been

---

[769] Belzer begins his attack on Bugliosi's defense of the official narrative in *Dead Wrong* by saying that even if Bugliosi had read every page of the twenty-six volume Warren Report, he nevertheless, willfully ignores the contradictions and omissions contained in the report.

[770] Moench, Doug (1995) *The Big Book of Conspiracies*. Paradox Press. Pp. 13 - 19

[771] https://spartacus-educational.com/JFKdeaths.htm accessed on 05/05/2021

eating lunch across the street from the Book Depository and saw Oswald fire from the sixth-floor window), and Helen Markham.

Markham testified that she had witnessed Oswald murder of Officer J.D. Tippit forty-five minutes after Kennedy's assassination at Dealey Plaza. According to Belzer, neither Markham nor Brennan were able to immediately pick Oswald out of a police line-up, but were allowed to testify because they succinctly corroborated the Commission's foregone conclusions.[772] The Warren Report has gone down in history as a document that no one was, or is, satisfied with. For this reason it acts as a port of entry into JFK conspiracy theorization, but then, maybe that was the goal along …

Timothy Melley, who refers to the assassination as "the postwar source of conspiracy theory par excellence"[773] claims that the "lone gunman" theory espoused by the Warren Report represents one side of a simulated rivalry between two complementary notions of persons in the social order.[774] The first notion is "the epitome of capitalist individualism: the antisocial, "lone gunman" in the tradition of the American Western – not only in the figure of Lee Oswald but also in that of Jack Ruby."[775] The other notion is an inability, or reluctance, on the part of the public to accept individualist explanations for such an incredible event and to suspect a conspiracy involving an embodiment of collective power. Melley resolves this dialectic by claiming that:

> There is thus an uncanny similarity between the dominant approaches to this notorious postwar event. If the Warren Commission's lone-gunman

---

[772] Belzer, Richard (1999) *UFOs, JFK, and Elvis: Conspiracies You Don't Have to be Crazy to Believe.* The Ballantine Publishing Group. P. 39

[773] Melley, Timothy (2000) *Empire of Conspiracy: The Culture of Paranoia in Postwar America.* Cornell University Press. P. 134

[774] Ibid p. 135

[775] Ibid p. 133

theory triggers guilt about the lone gunman being a patsy for the social, then grand conspiracy theories such as Stone's tend to conserve –albeit in a collective "body"- the classic attributes of the individual agent. While disagreeing over who (or what) counts as an agent, both assassination theories agree about the qualities an agent must possess. To be more specific, both accounts register a *desire for* but a *difficulty with* the notion of agency articulated by liberal individualism. While lone-gunmen accounts tend to conserve this model at the level of the individual, conspiracy theory conserves it, paradoxically, at the level of the social.[776]

Melley is talking about the "social" anthropologically, where the society that produces an individual, like Lee Harvey Oswald or Jack Ruby, possesses a certain responsibility for their actions. Robert Brandom argues that a fundamental aspect of Hegel's apprehension with modernity is based on a similar sense of collective responsibility:

It is possible only when we understand ourselves in such a way that we *all* take responsibility for what *each* of us does, and we *each* take responsibility for what *all* of us do. Although the individual is still understood to play an essential role –without which nothing would be done- the recognitive community is understood to play an equally essential role in the individual's capacity to do anything. In a real sense, to be the doing of an individual agent, each action must be the doing of all.[777]

---

[776] Ibid p. 136
[777] Brandom, Robert (2019) *A Spirit of Trust: A Reading of Hegel's Phenomenology*. Belknap Press of Harvard University Press. P. 465

There are aspects of the social, however, that are tied to the zeitgeist of the times and therefore embody a literary, or mythic quality; this aspect of the sixties is our next point of focus.

Camelot of the Real

Before we move on to other notable assassinations and deaths we need to look at how, despite the fact that the Kennedys' assassinations fall later on our timeline and hence hew closely to the scientific-reductionist viewpoint, there is still a significant insertion of the mythic in the overall JFK narrative. This insertion relates primarily to the sacred space evoked by the appellation of the name of "Camelot" to the Kennedy Administration. From a historical perspective, Leslie Alcock is dismissive of an actual Camelot having ever existed:

> The truth is, however, that attempts to identify Camelot are pointless. The name, and the very concept of Camelot, are inventions of the French medieval poets. 'Camelot' first appears in the variant manuscripts of the *Lancelot* of Chrétien de Troyes, suggesting that it was invented around the end of the twelfth century. Before that, Geoffrey of Monmouth had established one of Arthur's chief courts at Caerleon, others being at London and Winchester. There is no archaeological or historical justification for any of these suggestions.[778]

When referring to JFK's presidency as "Camelot," most people assume that it was a mythical place, and that they are invoking the name as a reference to something from a fairy-tale. However, as we've seen before, the mythic elements of the past are dissimulated into our cultural narratives in a way that can

---

[778] Alcock, Leslie (2001) *Arthur's Britain*. Classic Penguin. P. 163

retain very deep and rich associations. By designating Kennedy's presidency as "Camelot" we are unconsciously and metonymically implying that JFK himself is a sort of reoccurrence of King Arthur.[779] Regarding the etymology of that particular kingly name, Julius Evola notes that:

> The name Arthur is susceptible to various interpretations, the most reliable of which attributes to it the Celtic words *arthos* (bear) and *viros* (man). Nennis had already explained: *Arthur latine sonat ursum horribilem.* This meaning of a dreadful virile force is connected with a symbolism of Hyperborean origin and at the same time points to the idea of a central or "polar" function. In fact, the bear is one of the sacred symbols of the ancient Nordic cult and simultaneously, in astronomic symbolism, corresponds to the "polar" constellation Ursa Major. Moreover, in the corpus of traditional texts, symbols and names eventually establish a relation between this constellation (with the symbolism of the pole or of the center referred to it) and Thule, a name designating the Hyperborean "White Island," the traditional center. Thus the polar, the Hyperborean, and the regal elements converge in the figure of Arthur. The unilaterally virile and warrior aspect that could be supposed in Arthur as an ursus horribilis is also modified in the legend by Arthur's being always accompanied, as some kind of complement or counterpart, by Myrddhin or Merlin, who holds a spiritual knowledge and power. This Merlin seems less a

---

[779] Or, more precisely, that his name is a signifier designating a (modern) reiteration of the Arthurian narratives.

distinct person and more the personification of the transcendent and spiritual side of Arthur himself.[780]

Evola also points out that Arthur has a significant association with being a warrior who evinces a strict sense of chivalry and who commands the admiration of his fellow knights; he is a natural leader. This corresponds with Kennedy's military service, which, while not unique to his presidency (Washington, Grant and Eisenhower had all been generals), the combination of this service with his charisma, so effectively conveyed by the televisual medium, essentially instantiated him as a new Arthur of the post-war age. With this role came the idea that America was being reborn: the civil rights movement was throwing off the shackles of systemic racism, there was a post-war economic boom, and thanks to Eisenhower's highway system, the country was interconnected and more accessible. The only black spot in the collective American mind would be the Cold War and the threat of Communism. All these factors played into the mythologizing of the Kennedy Administration.

There is another even more symbolic and nuanced component to the JFK mythos as it pertains to his embodiment of "Arthur" that corresponds with the way in which Arthur assumed the throne:

> According to the legend, Arthur demonstrated his innate right to be the legitimate king of all of England by passing the so-called test of the sword, namely, by successfully taking a sword out of a great quadrangular stone on the altar of the temple, obviously a variation of the "stone of kings" that belonged to the ancient tradition of the Tuatha de' Danaan. Here we find a double, convergent symbolism. On the one hand, we have the general

---

[780] Evola, Julius (1997) *The Mystery of the Grail.* Inner Traditions International. Pp. 31 - 32

symbolism of the "foundation stone," which hints at the polar idea; thus the allegory and the myth allegedly refer to a virile power (i.e., the sword) that needs to be drawn from that principle. On the other hand, to take the sword out of the stone may also signify the freeing of a certain power from matter, since the stone often represents this meaning.[781]

This sword-in-the-stone narrative brings us back to the subject of Freemasonry. In *The Hiram Key* Knight and Lomas claim that Jesus's citation of an older scripture, which states that, "The stone which the builders have rejected. That one is the cornerstone,"[782] informs the Mark Mason's ritual, which commemorates the initiate's ascension to the fourth degree of Freemasonry. There are two significant references to stones in Waite's entry on "Mark Masonry:"

I carry no brief for maintaining that any Masonic Ritual is altogether perfect in its parts or unreservedly honourable to its builders, but those who have followed the story of the mystic stone which is now *Lapis reprobatus*, now *caput anguli*, now set in its place to complete the Arch of Doctrine, now torn therefrom in quest of the Lost Word, will know that the CEREMONY OF ADVANCEMENT in the MARK DEGREE deserves to be set in its proper place with due pomp and worship.[783]

---

[781] Ibid, p. 33

[782] Some version of this statement occurs in three out of four of the Gospels: Matthew 21:4, Mark 12:10 and Luke 20:17.

[783] Waite, Arthur Edward (1970) *A New Encyclopaedia of Freemasonry (Combined Edition)*. Volume 2, p. 35

The "Lost Word" most likely refers to the part of the Hiram legend where, prior to his death, Hiram threw his necklace, which contained a jewel inscribed with "the word," down a well to prevent his assassins from obtaining it; and with it, the key to the Egyptian afterlife. Prior to his death, though, it was recorded that Hiram had accidentally killed a kinsman of Solomon named Cavelum by dislodging a stone that fell and struck Cavelum dead. Waite makes reference to this later in the "Mark Masonry" entry:

> **The Stone of Destiny**. –At the same time there is a memorable story attaching to the stone which brought about the destruction of Cavelum, though it has been dragged in from other sources and is wrested in its present application. (1) On this stone there stood the angel with the flaming sword to keep the way of Paradise when Adam and Eve were expelled. (2) It formed the top of the altar raised by Abraham for the sacrifice of his son Isaac. (3) It was the pillow of Jacob when he saw in his vision the mystical ladder on which angels went up and came down. (4) Innumerable attempts were made to place it in one position and another during the building of the First Temple, but it found no rest anywhere till it became the capstone. (5) It was saved from destruction with the Temple, was cherished as a palladium by the Jews, and after the death of Zedekiah was carried by a migrating colony, with "Scota, the King's daughter," under the leadership of the prophet Jeremiah. (6) It was taken to the "Isles of the Sea" and preserved as a Stone of Destiny "by the people of Scota." (7) Finally, it was "stolen" by Edward, King of England, and placed in the Coronation Chair at Westminster Abbey, "where it still is." The point about this traditional history is

its very curious admixture of materials.[784] I should add that the MARK DEGREE is recognized in Scotland, and so also in Ireland, as an Integral part of pure and Ancient Masonry.[785]

If you can make it through that passage without humming the Stonecutter's "We do!" song you'll have noticed that not only does it give insight into the Masonic approach to symbolism and the genealogy attendant to the rituals intended to preserve it, but it also directly pertains to the "JFK as reoccurrence of Arthur" theme. If we think of JFK as a digression from the established policy of American imperialism and oppression, we can frame the metaphor of the sword being pulled from the stone as Kennedy, the Irish Catholic upstart idealist, seizing the presidency from the "foundational stone" of Masonic, Protestant political power, or hegemony.

Also, we have seen how the story of Hiram has inspired Masonic rites pertaining to resurrection; Kennedy, indirectly related to this as well as the Arthur narrative, intimates that his "Camelot" entailed a story of resurrection. This narrative of restorative justice via an idealistic young politician was nurtured in the hearts of baby boomers up until the late-90s.

However, some conspiracy theorists posit a seemingly anti-resurrection narrative, in that Kennedy's assassination resembled the Masonic "killing of the king," which, according to

---

[784] That is an understatement.
[785] Waite, Arthur Edward (1970) *A New Encyclopaedia of Freemasonry (Combined Edition)*. Volume 2 pp. 37 – 38. In relation to this, recall that in Wolfram's iteration of the Grail narrative, the Grail is a stone, not a cup. This stone has an almost equally rich origin narrative connected to it, in that it was supposedly removed from Heaven by angels that remained neutral in the conflict between the good and the fallen angels. Once safely on earth, it took on the significance of the fabled "Philosopher's stone."

The Big Book of Conspiracies, was the second step towards the creation of the New World Order; the first being the creation and destruction of primordial matter (achieved by the atomic testing in New Mexico on July 16, 1945); and the third being the bringing of *Prima Materia* to *Prima Terra* (accomplished by carrying moon rocks back to earth by Masonic astronauts such as Buzz Aldrin).[786] If there is a resurrection narrative here, it is a metaphysical one that pertains to a vast political transformation.

Though it is drawing on Hoffman's *Secret Societies and Psychological Warfare*, *The Big Book of Conspiracies* pushes Hoffman's theorization towards the idea of a literal Armageddon disguised as a New World Order, while Hoffman is more focused on how the Kennedy assassination inaugurated a confrontation between the American public and the hidden power that rules the world. [787] For both texts, the three steps are defined as "alchemical," a hermetic feature that Hoffman draws on when he writes: "the alchemical intention of the killing of the 'King of Camelot'..."[788] For Hoffman, the alchemical process is constituted by the use of televisual trauma that works to sink the collective-mind into a simulacrum:

> There is a sense of existing in a palace of marvels manipulated by beautiful but Satanic princes possessed of so much knowledge, power and experience as to be vastly superior to the rest of humanity. They have been everywhere. They have done everything. They run the show which mesmerizes us. We are determined to watch it. We are transfixed and desperate to see their newest

---

[786] Moench, Doug (1995) *The Big Book of Conspiracies*. Paradox Press. Pp. 196 - 197

[787] Hoffman II, Michael A. (2009) *Secret Societies and Psychological Warfare* (Sixth Printing) Independent History and Research. P. 85

[788] Ibid, p. 84

production, their latest thrilling revelation, even when the thrills are solely based upon the further confirmation of our dehumanization.[789]

Regardless of how Hoffman views JFK as a political figure, he sees the Camelot myth that was attached to his administration as the emanation of a certain American idealism that had to be destroyed – in a violent and graphic way – in order to achieve a very modern reiteration of an alchemical transformation: that of the antiquated rustic America of old into a futuristic state of hyperreality.[790]

It should also be noted that the idea of an "alchemical" transformation can imply sorcery, a practice some decry as evil in nature – Hoffman and Gary Wayne would agree with this characterization. On this reading, the sorcerous act would be a mystification, an act of bringing the audience under the sway of an illusion. However, on a more neutral reading, like the one that Magee attributes to Hegel, the alchemical process metaphorically refers to a process of purification and an overcoming of evil.[791] If we wanted to extend this more gregarious reading onto the destruction of JFK's "Camelot" we could say that the assassination itself was inexcusable but the result, which was a forced confrontation between the public and the sinister machinations of the government, constituted the dispelling of a harmful illusion. The kernel of this confrontation existed, and was maintained, in the outrage of the sixties and the media was quick to redirect the energy of this moment into all manner of digressions. Hence, one

---

[789] Ibid, pp. 86 - 87

[790] It is debatable as to whether Hoffman would sign off on all the philosophical aspects of Baudrillard's concept of hyperreality, nevertheless, his use of the term "simulacrum" as well as the pessimism of his predictions resonates with the French post-modernist.

[791] Magee, Glenn Alexander (2001) *Hegel and the Hermetic Tradition.* Cornell University Press. Pp. 144 - 145

could argue that it is the media itself, not only as an entity within a political plurality looking out for its own interests, but as a medium that needs to constantly announce and affirm its own validity, which has ushered the public into the age of hyperreality.

As a closing thought on Arthurian symbolism and its relation to Hermeticism I would like to draw the reader's attention to the fundamental discrepancy between Knight and Lomas's project and mainstream Freemasonry. We have seen that Knight and Lomas try to incorporate scientific reasoning into their theorization and, in a vein similar to Ignatius Donnelly, seek to reduce divergent phenomena to a single causal point. In this quest they have enlisted the early Gnostics as forebearers, or guardians, of proto-masonic rites and histories. I want to be very clear here: Knight and Lomas's theory that Hiram was actually Seqenenre Tao, and the related idea that the Biblical stories tied to Freemasonry had been usurped by the Hebrews who wrote the bulk of the Old Testament **is** contradictory to mainstream Freemasonry.

I see the distinction between Knight and Lomas on the one hand and mainstream Freemasonry on the other as being emblematic of the tensions in the late-eighteenth century that led to certain Masonic groups like the Bavarian Illuminati adopting anti-traditional scientific rationalism and other Masonic lodges embracing Hermeticism.[792] It is in this respect that the dialectic between Gnosticism and Hermeticism is repeated in the twentieth century.

This is significant and very interesting because we have the Gnostic/reductionist application of the mythic narrative followed by a deconstruction that reveals that Hiram **is** Seqenenre Tao, which is itself a claim about identity. The subject that was implacable in myth is reified or made a concrete substitutional object, by virtue of his name within the new historical narrative. In contrast, the mainstream view (as exemplified by someone like Waite) that is more accommodating

---

[792] Ibid, pp. 56 - 57

to a traditionally Hermetic approach takes the view that Hiram is just Hiram but allots that the symbolic objects circulating around him in the mythical narrative, such as the "Stone of Destiny," are themselves substitutional with other mythic objects.

The upshot of this fidelity to Hermeticism is that objects in myths (even if these objects are characters) themselves contain a multitude of narratives, and they must remain objects to traverse a variety of myths. The irony of the reductionist viewpoint, by contrast, is that it has to utilize the path initially laid out by the Hermetic, or non-reductionist, narrative in order to affect its reductive project. [793] Since we have only been analyzing conspiracy theories and myths, not subjecting them to reductionism ourselves, we can say that "JFK" was a reinscription of "King Arthur" within the twentieth century narrative and that this claim is not as strong, or outlandish, as saying that "JFK was King Arthur;" a proposition which Knight and Lomas would most assuredly decry as ludicrous in this day and age, but might be presented as a conspiracy theory two thousand years from now, in a manner similar to the claim that Melchizedek was actually Jesus.

What the Hermetic tradition seems to be granting us is the almost magical ability to narrativize. The objects appearing within these narratives are points of entry because they are symbolically charged. I know that this digression is only tangentially related to JFK but it wraps up the distinctions between Hermeticism and Gnosticism insofar as they relate to the dialectic between mythological and reductionist thinking. It also gives us a more fine-tuned means of apprehending some of the more hidden

---

[793] This is explicitly acknowledged on page 26 of *Uriel's Machine*: "Many oral traditions contain symbolic elements that may themselves be clues to real events, so it might be wrong to dismiss such stories as tribal myths." Note the pejorative use of "myth." Taken from Knight, Christopher & Lomas, Robert (2001) *Uriel's Machine*. Fair Winds Press.

entailments of the scientistic and reductionist arguments that came to the fore, historically, following the assassination of JFK.

Antithesis: The Symbolic Assassination of Richard Nixon

On June 17, 1972 Washington D.C. police arrested five men who had broken into the Democratic National Committee headquarters inside the Watergate Office Building. Who, within the Nixon administration, had conceived the plan to break into the office and plant wiretapping devices, is debatable. What we can say with certainty is that the most reliable narratives focus on former FBI agent G. Gordon Liddy and active CIA agent E. Howard Hunt.[794]

The disgrace following the scandal forced Nixon to resign from office on August 9, 1974, interesting for our analysis because his resignation signaled to the American populace both justice and resolution. Nixon's resignation, more than Altamont or the Manson Family murders, was the bookend on the sixties' counter-culture because it was presented as a just resolution to the reign of a corrupt administration, onto which all the governmental misdeeds of the sixties had been projected. It is interesting that this cultural denouement, and the media situating itself coterminously as the official generator and moderator of narratives, both revolved around the same thing: recorded information. The Watergate affair was settled decisively, unlike the Kennedy assassinations, not because Nixon was widely

---

[794] Stephen Kinzer states that Sidney Gottlieb's Technical Services Division had prepared false identity paperwork for Liddy and Hunt prior to the break-in, and had supplied Hunt, in particular, with espionage devices such as hidden cameras and disguises. Kinzer, Stephen (2019) *Poisoner in Chief: Sidney Gottlieb and the CIA Search for Mind Control.* Henry Holt and Company. P. 208

hated [795] but because the medium by which his crime was committed was essentially information-based.

The Kennedy assassinations might have been concluded in a decisive manner at another time or place in history, but not at the time and place they occurred. The shift into modernity that was marked by the beginnings of the UFO craze was essentially in full effect by 1963. The public just didn't know it yet. There would be no satisfactory answers or justice; for them, Nixon's resignation eleven years later would have to do. It is for these reasons that Watergate has sometimes been referred to as "the inflection point" at which the media turned the tables on the executive branch of the government. From this point forward politicians would be beholden to the power of the media.

In *Simulacra and Simulation* Baudrillard characterizes the end of Nixon's Presidency as a "simulated murder," i.e., a simulation of death that was staged to escape an actual death. For this reason, Baudrillard argues that Watergate was not so much a scandal as it was a simulation of a scandal, one which was "a lure held out by the system to catch its adversaries – a simulation of scandal for regenerative ends" [796] This regenerative aspect designates a procession of simulacra in which information systems, like the media or the internet as a whole, reiterate narratives that have no necessary correspondence with what the average person would consider "Real."

I want to clarify two points here; first, the word "simulacra" designates a copy, usually an artistic rendering, of something that is, by virtue of its representational nature, inferior to the object that is being copied. For Baudrillard, the concept of simulacra takes on an additional, social, meaning, in that the object that is represented often does not exist, or has ceased to exist, therefore the copy has a truth-value that is not based on its

---

[795] Though this might have been a contributing factor to the media making a concerted effort to bring about his downfall.
[796] Baudrillard, Jean (1994) *Simulacra and Simulation*. The University of Michigan. p. 16

relationship with the thing it was intended to represent, but within the context of a system (often a "hyperreal" system) in which it subsists.[797]

The second point that Baudrillard discusses is how a cultural phenomenon, like the film *Apocalypse Now* which acts as a simulacrum of the Vietnam War, gives a clear-cut demonstration of an artistic representation taking the place of an event. His use of Watergate as an example, however, hews closer to our project because it is not an artistic or representational rendering, but merely a narrative that becomes iconic and then subject to reiteration. This is evidenced by the fact that scandals following Watergate, such as "Russiagate," "Chinagate," "Climategate," and "Travelgate," are designated as newsworthy scandals by the application of the "gate" suffix. The idea that the need for them to be "newsworthy," i.e., that they need to generate reporting, controversy, and outrage, is an indication that the phenomenon being "documented" has now taken a backseat to its use in the media, hence we can say there is a disparity between the media coverage and the "real" – or at least the "real" that most people assume exists in their day-to-day lives.

The symbolic assassination of Richard Nixon was crucial in the dialectical movement from the assassination of JFK to the death of someone like Jeffrey Epstein. For JFK, the powers that be (whoever they may be) withheld information that could lead to a public understanding of what actually happened in Dallas on November 22, 1963. In the case of Jeffrey Epstein, the public already knows that it will never know what happened, it knows enough that it could never imagine being able to legitimately demand an answer.

The fact that the FBI had declared conspiracy theories to be a threat to democracy a week before Epstein's death was an

---

[797] The subject of hyperreality will be tackled directly in the next section.

unnecessary gesture.[798] The American public did not need to be particularly primed for this sort of complacency. From a conspiratorial mindset, the FBI press release was either an act of Kafkaesque or cosmic irony; Kafkaesque in the sense that there are secret agencies who indomitably control the world; cosmic in a sense that is bound to the ineffable logic of coincidence.

As with all the other subjects presented in this book, the phenomenon does not occur in a vacuum. There is a network of contingencies surrounding phenomena. What this means is that Americans are not innately indifferent to discovering the truth at the heart of conspiracy theories, in this case assassinations, solely because they have been numbed by mass media and video games, or because they have less integrity than they did fifty years ago. No, there are a variety of factors that contribute to this indifference, one of which is a sense of powerlessness.

This powerlessness can be viewed as an integral part of the later stages of modernity (as was predicted by E.M. Forster in his novella *The Machine Stops*), and it is concurrent with our high level of media/internet saturation. Conspiracy theories in this context seem empowering because they take the fact that the truth of a suspicious event can never be conclusively (or satisfactorily) proven as license for any manner of theorization.

Synthesis: The Argument From Hyperreality

If we accept the theory of political pluralism as having the greatest explanatory value, we must address the role of the media, as it has become a social power, vying for hegemony. Before I begin, I want to stress that, yes, in a certain respect the "media" is a homogenous group vying for hegemony within our society. Most people who complain about the "media" will identify it as a monolithic entity – hence the Donald Trump-derived

---

[798] This occurred on August 1, 2019. Reported in https://new.yahoo.com/fbi-documents-conspiracy-theories-terrorism-160000507.html accessed 09/23/20

epithet of "fake news." For the most part, I will refer to the media in a similarly combinatory way. However, this is not meant to obscure the fact that within the media itself there are a variety of pluralities vying with each other for dominance and narrative-control. I am only using the former reference for simplicity's sake, and because it draws more attention to the fact that these divergent narratives are dependent on the medium by which they are conveyed.

More and more these days we hear people who are ostensibly opposed to the media talk about how the public in general is becoming progressively more distrustful of what they hear and see on the news.[799] People who believe such things are potentially more deluded than even the most dyed-in-the-wool conspiracy theorist because they are approaching the topic from the outside and haven't spent enough time trying to understand how the media, or even entertainment, works within our culture. To say that "people are losing faith in the media" is akin to claiming that people are losing faith in *The Simpsons* or *The Big Bang Theory*. 24-hour news channels or news websites don't provide information in the same way as a traffic report on the radio or the five o'clock news. Instead, they provide news-related entertainment, and entertainment is an inherently richer form of narrative; it doesn't give us immediately pragmatic information, it *informs* our worldview.

Politics essentially works for the media now and the media is a multifaceted commodity that people use for social identification, much the way they used religion sixty years ago. In its entertainment function the media simulates myth, but because it is a copy further removed from the mythic process it is necessarily less *rich* in content and character; and this lack, if you

---

[799] This claim is not the same as the more statistically valid claim that younger people get their news-related information more from social media accessed from their phones than they do from established networks like CNN and Fox.

agree on calling it that, is fine with most people in the United States.

I've peppered a lot of the preceding material with references to Baudrillard and hyperreality, but the point of this section is to give a more systematic account of how Baudrillard came up with his theory, how he justified it, and how it works in the role of a synthesis for the dialectic of this chapter. Once this role as synthesis has been established, we can then use the theory (or thesis, dialectically speaking) as an almost authoritative guide to the narratives we will tackle for the remainder of this book. Baudrillard grounds his analysis on the claim that:

> History is a strong myth, perhaps, along with the unconscious, the last great myth. It is a myth that at once subtended the possibility of an "objective" enchainment of events and causes and the possibility of a narrative enchainment of discourse. The age of history, if one can call it that, is also the age of the novel. It is this *fabulous* character, the mythical energy of an event or of a narrative, that today seems to be increasingly lost.[800]

Working from this hypothesis, Baudrillard seeks to focus on a variety of issues that were of great significance during the reign of modernity: Capital, Ideology, and most importantly, Communication; which follows the lead of Marshall McLuhan (July 21, 1911 – December 31, 1980), who focused on how societies were structured less by the content of what was communicated (the message) than by the nature of the media that was used to convey the communications. We can see by the above quote that Baudrillard apprehends the power of myth because it seems to elude strict categorization as either "message" or "medium." The myth in question, "history," was conveyed in a

---

[800] Baudrillard, Jean (1994) *Simulacra and Simulation*. The University of Michigan. P. 47

variety of mediums: books, articles, spoken word, art, etc., and the content of said history varied from telling to telling.

On this reading, Baudrillard tackles the JFK assassination within the context of his discussion of Watergate, and what he writes is telling:

> All previous presidents pay for and continue to pay for Kennedy's murder as if they were the ones who had suppressed it – which is true phantasmatically, if not in fact. They must efface this defect and this complicity with their simulated murder. Because, now it can only be simulated. Presidents Johnson and Ford were both the object of failed assassination attempts, which, if they were not staged, were at least perpetrated by simulation. The .Kennedy's died because they incarnated something: the political, political substance, whereas the new presidents are nothing but caricatures and fake film...[801]

This section is important because it opens up a dichotomy of sorts between the "authenticity" represented by the Kennedys and the proliferation of "simulation." If McLuhan's basic schema can be simplified as a dichotomy between medium and message, Baudrillard's schema, simplified, can be expressed as a dichotomy between hyperreality and simulation – simulation is the "messaging," so-to-speak, which occurs within the medium of hyperreality.[802] So what does Baudrillard mean by simulation within the context of hyperreality? To answer this question, we

---

[801] Ibid, pp. 23 - 24

[802] It is important to note that the "authenticity" being ascribed to the Kennedy's in this passage is inscribed within the parameters of modernity, and therefore, is not meant to convey a tremendous sense of authenticity; it is more likely that they were appropriate and effective avatars for the concept of political power.

must first address how we moved collectively from the modernity of the early-to-mid-twentieth century to the hyperreality of today. Part of this has to do with the slow disappearance of symbolic exchange. Prior to the industrial revolution, the objects that circulated in a society had a certain uniqueness about them. For instance, the carpenter's hammer (as per Heidegger's example) had intrinsic qualities that related to the carpenter's status in society, his class, how he had been educated, and what he did for a living. Perhaps we could say that the object had a metonymic relationship with its owner.[803] Likewise the objects that belonged to a king, baron, or whatever, designated his royal class and could only be circulated among others within his class.

Once the industrial revolution came into its own, objects could be manufactured and circulated on demand. At this point in history, the bourgeois class began manufacturing and buying reproductions of furniture, clothing, and accessories, which had hitherto only been owned by nobility. This was damaging to the symbolic order because it replaced whatever vaguer metaphysical notions that had played a role in inheritance and royal lineage with a value based upon financial exchange.[804] This not only devalued the royal caste, but also played a role in devaluing the knightly caste, as their codes of chivalry based on honor and duty were replaced by a mercenary interest. Granted, mercenaries, or soldiers who joined an army solely for financial considerations had always been an issue, but with the disappearance of the symbolic order, these materialistic considerations moved from the margins to the foreground.

Converging with this disappearance of the symbolic order is what Baudrillard defined as the *three orders of simulacra*. In the first order, which corresponds to the pre-modern period, the

---

[803] Hence the hammer and sickle on the flag of the Soviet Union.
[804] Note also, the idea of inheritance and how it played a role in Michels's theory of political pluralism, i.e., being descended from the founding stock gives one a greater administrative say within the political discourse.

image (usually a work of art) is a counterfeit of the real. There is a clear understanding on the part of the observer that the image is just an illusion – a place-marker for the real thing. In the second order, which historically corresponds with the industrial revolution and to a certain extent, the beginning of modernity, the distinctions between the image and its representation begin to break down because of mass production and the proliferation of copies. Such production misrepresents and masks an underlying reality by imitating it so well, and thus threatening to replace it (e.g. in photography or film); however, there is still a belief in the possibility that, through critique or effective political action, one can still access the hidden facets of the real. This stage coincides strongly with the movement away from the symbolic order described above. [805] In the third order of simulacra, which corresponds with late-stage modernity (or the postmodern age, depending on your interpretation), the subject is confronted with a "precession" of simulacra; that is, the representation *precedes* and *determines* the real. There is no longer any distinction between reality and its representation; there is only the simulacrum.

The primary force dominating subjects residing within the third order of simulacrum is simulation, which Baudrillard claims is "beyond true and false, beyond equivalences, beyond rational distinctions;" conventions upon which our notions of power and the social are dependent. [806] Baudrillard's conception of simulation within this third order of simulacra overlaps with Ellul's theory of technique, specifically in terms of its omnipresence:

> [In] fact, from the moment a function becomes hyperspecialized to the point of being capable of being projected from every element on the terrain

---

[805] In respect to these issues see also the work of Frederic Jameson and Walter Benjamin.
[806] Ibid, p. 21

"keys in hand," it loses the finality proper to it and becomes something else altogether: a polyfunctional nucleus, an ensemble of "black boxes" with multiple input-outputs, the locus of convection and of destructuration. These factories and these universities are no longer factories nor universities, and the hypermarkets no longer have the quality of a market [...] These new objects are the poles of simulation around which is elaborated, in contrast to old train stations, factories, or traditional transportation networks, something other than a "modernity": a hyperreality, a simultaneity of all the functions, without a past, without a future, an operationality on every level.[807]

Notice how this passage relates to one of the themes that we encountered in the Grail mythos: the appearance of, or quest for, the central point or pole of the known world. In a world dominated, or defined, by hyperreality, not only are objects valued primarily for their commodity or fetish-value over their use value, but they also take on the central quality of nuclei, around which subjects orbit and circulate. Since it is now an object-oriented, or in Ellul's parlance, a technologically oriented space that we inhabit, innately human-centric concepts like "past" and "future" are relinquished.

All of this entails the concept of "hyperreality" and the "Argument from Hyperreality" is thus an appeal to this model's explanatory power. To a certain extent, whether or not the average person understands this argument in the theoretical language we have just explored is negligible; on an intuitive level he or she does. To qualify this statement, let's directly address the case of Jeffrey Epstein. With the death of JFK the public believed it was owed answers which it would eventually get. In contrast, with Epstein everyone knew from the announcement of his death

---

[807] Ibid, p. 78

that there would never be any answers. The meme: "Jeffrey Epstein didn't kill himself," was just that, a meme. To some extent, memes might have the ability to change the fabric of hyperreality (a theme we will address in our chapter on the Mandela Effect), however, they are primarily a snarky and sarcastic nod of acquiescence to the status quo. It sounds incredibly cynical (and incredibly postmodern) to say this, but Epstein's death served the hashtag (#epsteindidntkillhimself) more than it served any nefarious cabal that might have ordered it.

Has the script changed in the time that has passed between these two heavily publicized deaths (Kennedy's and Epstein's)? No, because the script is essentially the same myth, with the same ambiguities and mysteries, only now it is writ large on the screen of the omnipresent media.

So, now with this posited as a hueristic, does this mean we will be compelled to dive head-first into total and abject skepticism? No, but it does undermine our faith in the media and inculcate a sense of skepticism towards everything we see and read, insofar as we understand that the messages being conveyed exist primarily as grist for the mill of the medium that is conveying them. However, if we step back and regain a modicum of objectivity, in one sense it reaffirms the Structuralist reading of narratives as texts meant to be parsed and interpreted. It also reaffirms the hermeneutical need to situate the narratives we encounter, not only within the media field in which they arise, but in context with ourselves, our experiences, and the world we inhabit outside of the myriad of screens that populate our day-to-day existence.

Cultural Assassination: John Lennon

On December 8th 1980, John Lennon (October 9, 1940 – December 8, 1980) was walking back to his New York apartment from a recording session when he was shot and killed by Mark David Chapman, a man, who had approached him a few hours earlier asking for an autograph. Lennon's death sparked an outpouring of grief that would cement the sixties icon as a counter-culture messiah.

One particularly obscure conspiracy theory that arose after John Lennon's death and was formalized by Miles Mathis into a fifty-four-page PDF document, is that after faking his death, Lennon re-emerged as a John Lennon impersonator named Mark Staycer. Staycer is a Canadian actor who had portrayed Lennon in the 2009 movie *Let Him Be*, which itself toyed with the theory that John Lennon was still alive. It is not only because of hyperreality that this movie could, or would, be made, but it is also because of hyperreality that conspiracy theorists seized upon the movie for confirmation of their theory that Lennon was still alive. It could be argued that there is a certain consistency pertaining to this situation that relates to our understanding of the world today, one that is tied to the counter-intuitive idea expressed by Kant: the notion that our basic, or simple, consciousness exists only by virtue of the super-structure of our meta-consciousness. Likewise, within the context of hyperreality, we have the counter-intuitive notion that the movie "confirming" the conspiracy theory could only have been made because it will inevitably be latched onto as a source of confirmation for said theory.

Another aspect of hyperreality opened up here pertains to the subject of doubling. We have seen how in the earlier, mythological, model there was a duality attendant to the figures of Hiram and Enoch, which lent their names a largesse of narrative richness.[808] This feature, combined with their marginal status within the text, led to them being "murky" figures who inspired myriad attempts to unravel the essence of their natures. The doubling that is occurring here, as well as other notable places, such as the theory that postmortem photographs of Jeffrey Epstein were of a body double and not the actual Epstein, is the

---

[808] If there was a sense of doubling regarding Melchizedek it is either in the form of his secret identity being one of Noah's sons, or, the more metaphysically charged theory that he was actually Jesus Christ.

embodiment of a dialectical engagement between the thesis-stage of mythology and the antithesis-stage of scientism; in that the myth of a character's miraculous escape is explained in scientifically identifiable terms. The "double" proposed by the conspiracy narrative is one that has, in some way, whether by cloning or make-up, been scientifically engineered to duplicate the missing individual; and the need for this doubling is dictated by political (practical) reasons on behalf of a group or agency, not mystification on behalf of God or some obscure occult entities.

Beyond this corporeal duplication, the "Lennon faked his own death" theory is a reiteration of the much older "Paul is dead" narrative. The two theories (Paul is dead, Lennon faked his own death) also work in contradistinction to each other, given that the theory that Paul died claims that he was replaced by a clone-like imposter sometime in the Beatles' early years, while the Lennon theory argues that the musician became his own imposter.[809] It is almost as if the collective instinct towards myth is dissimulated into a scientistic medium and that this medium makes certain evidentiary demands that had not existed in earlier, more mythologically grounded eras. The fact that Mathis spends so much of his essay analyzing the physical traits and characteristics of Lennon's face and voice in defense of his theory is proof of this.

Mathis's theory is, however, an outlier; not many conspiracy theorists deny that Chapman killed Lennon, but as in the case of the Kennedys they question whether he acted alone, was ordered at the behest of some department in the U.S. Government, or was possibly a brainwashed MK Ultra type of assassin.[810]

---

[809] This conspiracy theory about John Lennon is also a reiteration of the "Elvis is still alive!" narrative that gained a lot of traction in supermarket tabloids during the eighties and nineties.
[810] Most conspiracy theorists would accept Lennon's assassination to have actually occurred because it fits within a web of synchronicity: his shooting taking place in front of the

In this latter respect, it is worth noting that theories postulating that Lennon faked his death are usually linked to MK Ultra-related conspiracy theories, such as the ones surrounding Laurel Canyon, as they assume he was some kind of secret agent who retired after his agenda spreading secular globalism was finished. [811] This begs the question, though: why would the government that these people believe assassinated the Kennedys and Martin Luther King Jr., and blew up the Twin Towers, allow an agent to just "retire" and assume he would keep his mouth shut? Perhaps Lennon faked his own death to get away from his deep state controllers and appeared in *Let Him Be* as a way of turning the tables on his former masters, who, within the context of this type of theorization, are constantly taunting us with bits and pieces of information pertaining to their own nefarious doings.

Ultimately, the death of John Lennon is a repetition of the Christ-like sacrifice narrative we have seen play out with JFK, RFK, and MLK. The untimely death of these figures, however,

---

apartment building where Roman Polanski shot 1968's *Rosemary's Baby* and the possible MK-Ultra style influence of J.D. Salinger's *Catcher in the Rye*, which had been pivotal for Chapman as well as Robert John Bardo and John Hinckley Jr.

[811] Mathis makes this connection on page 31 of his essay, "Proof that John Lennon Faked his Death" saying that the "propagandists" behind the Beatles had been pushing for the destruction of Christianity, hence Lennon's "bigger than Jesus" quote. Later in their career (around 1967) "Intelligence imported the manufactured drug culture into the Beatles' regimen, including pushing LSD and other drugs. The Beatles denied that "Lucy in the Sky with Diamonds" was written to push LSD, but that denial falls flat. Do you really think it is just an accident the song title includes the initials LSD? No. Many of the 60s bands were turned into drug pushers on purpose. These drugs were one of the top weapons of Intelligence against the hippies and the anti-war movement."

runs contrary to the sense of completion that is read into the Christ narrative, which was exemplified by his statement, "It is finished," just before expiring on the cross. Hence, the narrative that these characters inhabit seems unfinished and out of control, with boundless suspicion being cast on the purveyors of the crimes, both real and imagined.

A Trinity of Political Assassinations for the Postmodern Age

Let's look now at three individuals who are not politicians or celebrities, but who nevertheless met a suspicious and violent demise. Each of the three share a common characteristic: none of them were politicians themselves, though they were close to politics. The first individual is Vincent Foster (January 15, 1945 – July 20, 1993) who had been a friend of Bill Clinton and served as Deputy White House Counsel during the first six months of the Clinton Administration. Foster's body was found dead from a gunshot wound in a secluded part of Fort Marcy Park in Fairfax County, Virginia.

Vincent Foster is significant to today's conspiracy theory landscape because, to a certain sect of conspiracy theorists, his death is the first in the so-called "Clinton Body Count" index. The idea that Bill and Hillary Clinton assassinated political liabilities was first suggested by Larry Nichols's film *The Clinton Chronicles* in 1994 and was promoted by the televangelist Jerry Falwell.[812]

Though he is more inclined to promote left-leaning conspiracy theories, Belzer claims that, despite the official ruling of suicide, Foster was most likely murdered, and that this murder was probably instigated, and covered up, by the Clinton Administration.[813] He reasons that Foster, being more scrupulous

[812] https://en.m.wikipedia.org/wiki/Clinton_Body_Count accessed on 09/17/20
[813] Belzer, Richard & Wayne, David (2012) *Dead Wrong: Straight Facts on the Country's Most Controversial Cover-ups.* Skyhorse Publishing. Pp. 223 - 225

than his superiors, was planning to resign from the administration before he was forced into an ethical compromise, or worse yet, perjury, by the immanent "Whitewater" scandal.[814] Though he doesn't make very strong claims regarding Foster's involvement in Whitewater, Belzer offers a variety of arguments for why Foster's death should not be read as a suicide. Some of these are as follows:

-People around Foster prior to his death claim that he was generally in a good mood and showed no signs of depression.

-Confusion as to whether or not the gun used actually belonged Foster. There has also been some debate as to whether the gun identified by witnesses at the scene was the same as the one identified in police reports.

-Blood pooling evidence that suggests that the body was moved postmortem; suggesting that his body had been dumped at Marcy Park.

-Foster's keys were missing from the scene of the crime.

-The claims of certain homicide experts that there had been "foul play."[815]

-Foster's car was apparently moved after his death.[816]

---

[814] Ibid, pp. 250 – 251. The immanence of the implications of this scandal is evidenced by the fact that the same day that Foster died the FBI raided the office of former Arkansas Judge David Hale. Hale would be one of fifteen people convicted in the course of the Whitewater Scandal.
[815] Specifically Detective Mark Fuhrman, ibid, p. 235
[816] Ibid, pp. 227 - 234

Belzer utilizes a variety of other forensic-related details for his argument. However, since our project is not to prove or disprove any conspiracy theories, we will take Foster's death as the first victim in the "Clinton Body Count" narrative. The next notable member of this club was only four years old at the time of Foster's death, with his mysterious demise occurring twenty-three years after Foster's. His name was Seth Conrad Rich.

Seth Rich (January 3, 1989 – July 13, 2016) was born in Omaha Nebraska. At the age of twenty-five he began working for the Democratic National Committee as the voter expansion data director. At four in the morning on Sunday, July 10, 2016, Rich was shot a block from his apartment and died almost two hours later at a nearby hospital. A few weeks after Rich's death, which appeared to have been a botched robbery, conspiracy theories appeared on the subreddit /r/TheDonald claiming that Rich had been assassinated because of his supposed involvement with DNC emails that had been released by WikiLeaks on July 22, 2016. These theories had been repeated by a variety of people on the Right; Julian Assange, the founder of WikiLeaks, however, has refused to disclose the identity of the individual who provided the emails.

Given the little information we have on Seth Rich, it appears evident that he was a ride-or-die DNC/Clinton operative who most likely would not have turned against his employers for any reason. However, anything is possible, I guess. Left-wing media outlets, such as NPR, generally blame Russia for spreading the "Seth Rich was the DNC leaker narrative"[817] because, of course

...

The third, and most infamous, person on this list is Jeffrey Epstein. Epstein was born in Brooklyn, New York in 1953. Despite leaving the Courant Institute of Mathematical Sciences at New York University without receiving a degree, in 1974 he was given

817

https://www.npr.org/2019/08/08/749450421/disinformation-the-murder-of-seth-rich accessed on 12/02/20 a job teaching mathematics at the prestigious Dalton School in Manhattan, run by headmaster, Donald Barr. Donald Barr is notable in this narrative for a few reasons. First, he is the father of President Donald Trump's Attorney General William Barr. Second, he was a member of the Office of Strategic Services (the OSS, which was the precursor to the CIA) during World War II. And third, in 1973 he wrote and published a science fiction novel titled *Space Relations*, which involves a planet where the overlords engage in intergalactic child-sex-trafficking.

After being dismissed from the Dalton School in 1976, Epstein became an assistant to a floor-trader on the stock market before moving up to the position of options trader at Bear Stearns Companies, Inc. After leaving Bear Stearns, Epstein founded his own financial consulting firm, Intercontinental Assets Group, which focused on helping clients recover money that had been embezzled by lawyers and brokers. It was during this period, in which Epstein helped rich socialites as well as government agencies, that Epstein's activities most likely came under the purview of either U.S. or foreign intelligence agencies. During the eighties, nineties, and early oughts, Epstein made a variety of connections: MIT, Harvard, Towers Financial Corporation, Liquid Funding Ltd., a company called "Carbyne," which is connected to Israel's defense industry, as well as his own financial management firm (J. Epstein & Company). His activities during these three decades were incredibly diffuse and going into all of them would take us too far afield.[818]

Important for our analysis was his connections to powerful people, his trafficking of underage girls, and his possible ties to intelligence agencies. Regarding the last point, we know that one of Epstein's clients was Adnan Khashoggi, a Saudi Arabian businessman who had some involvement in the Iran-Contra Affair.[819] There have also been articles claiming that Epstein told

---

[818] You can just Wikipedia the guy for yourself.
[819] https://en.m.wikipedia.org/wiki/Jeffrey_Epstein accessed 10/28/20

people he was an intelligence agent and possessed an Austrian passport that listed his place of residence as Saudi Arabia.[820] Possibly, most damning of all is the fact that Alexander Acosta, who was the U.S. Attorney for South Florida in 2007 when Epstein was given an eighteen month prison sentence in exchange for pleading guilty to the charge of procuring for prostitution a girl below the age of eighteen, stated that he'd agreed to a non-prosecution deal with Epstein because he had been told to "back off," and that "Epstein belonged to intelligence and leave it alone."[821] Acosta made these remarks in 2017. Prior to this there had been some speculation that Epstein's relative immunity to prosecution might have been based on some sort of secret information he was giving to the FBI regarding insider trading.

There has been a great deal of speculation as to which government intelligence agency Epstein might have been working for. John Schindler speculates that the strongest possibilities are Mossad, the KGB, or the Saudi General Intelligence Presidency. He rules out the CIA because:

> The U.S. Intelligence Community is lenient about the private habits of high-value agents or informants, but they won't countenance running sex trafficking rings for minors on American soil, for years. While it's plausible that Epstein was sharing some information with the FBI –many criminals do so to buy themselves some insurance-

---

[820] Ibid, accessed 10/28/20
[821] "It Sure Looks Like Jeffrey Epstein Was a Spy –But Whose?" By John R. Schindler at https://www.observer.com/2019/07/jeffrey-epstein-spy-intelligence-work/amp/ accessed 10/28/20. It is also worth noting that some of Epstein's attorneys were Alan Dershowitz, Ken Starr and Steven Pinker.

it's implausible that he was mainly working for the Americans.[822]

I would say that given what is known about MK Ultra, let alone the CIA's involvement in Iran-Contra, that the U.S. Government has the propensity to show a great deal of leniency for criminal activities. However, the fact that his longtime girlfriend, Ghislaine Maxwell, was the daughter of Robert Maxwell, one of the founders of the Mossad, as well as Epstein's early involvement with Carbyne, make the Mossad a prime candidate. Schindler states that Maxwell had been accused of working for the KGB by British counterintelligence, and this, along with Epstein's ties to Saudi Arabia, muddies the waters significantly.

Outside of espionage, which is a topic that is open for debate, Epstein's criminal activities, as exposed by investigative journalist Julie Brown, involved at least 80 victims who alleged that they had been part of a sex ring run by the financier.[823]

The sex ring, which involved individuals from all over the world, took place primarily in New York and on Epstein's personal island in the Virgin Islands. Little Saint James, or "Epstein Island," as it is more commonly called, has been of particular interest to conspiracy theorists because of a strange building painted with blue and white stripes with a gold dome on top. Some have claimed that the structure is a temple, and Christian conspiracy theorists who are especially interested in tracing secret societies back to Atlantis, most likely interpret the statue of Poseidon standing at the entrance as damning evidence of Epstein's behavior being aligned with devil-worship.[824]

---

[822] Ibid, accessed 10/28/20

[823] https://www.nytimes.com/2019/07/09/business/media/miami-herald-epstein.amp.html accessed on 05/12/2021

[824] https://www.insider.com/jeffrey-epstein-private-island-temple-2019-7%3famp accessed on 05/12/2021

Epstein's second arrest on July 6th, 2019 in New Jersey prompted a search of his 21,000 square-foot Manhattan mansion, which uncovered hundreds of photos of nude girls as well as CDs that may have footage recorded by CCTV of guests partaking in illicit sexual activities. What was the point of this activity? If we look at it through the lens of political intrigue and espionage it seems as if the goal was blackmail. Some of the people caught up in the intrigue were Prince Andrew, Matt Groening, Alan Dershowitz, and of course Bill Clinton, who logged 26 flights on Epstein's private jet, nicknamed "The Lolita Express."[825]

As a bookend to the Epstein affair, on November 3rd, 2019 Trevor Noah had Hillary Clinton on the *Daily Show* and asked her how she had Jeffrey Epstein killed, and went on to joke with her about being a boogeyman for Right-Wing conspiracy theorists. I'm not claiming that the Clintons had anything to do with Epstein's death, but I am saying, however, that this moment is emblematic of the hyperreality in which we are immersed, and that the hyperreality not only prevents us from "getting to the bottom of things," but makes us question if there is even a "bottom of things" that can be gotten to.

This trope had existed in literature and film for decades, but its synchronization with the disappearance of the real from our culture was probably best manifested in the 1995 film *The Usual Suspects*, in which the entire story told by the main character unravels into a tall tale at the film's end. This film was a product of the early-to-mid-nineties quest for authenticity, a quest which led to a boom in music, film, and literature, and is a kind of counter-point to something like Oliver Stone's *JFK*, wherein a reverse process happens: all the information previously shown is pieced together at the end into an arguable

---

[825] Lolita is a reference to the titular character from a Nabokov novel about a man who falls in love with a teenage girl.

theory.[826] For this, and a few other reasons, *JFK* is a work of baby boomer nostalgia for the idealism of the sixties, one seeking to demarcate the evil people working within the government and organized crime from the perceived goodness of the Kennedy administration. The famous line: "We are through the looking glass here" represents the moment in which the dichotomy between these forces is realized, and in an ironic way re-establishes the contrast between the forces of good and evil.[827]

By the end of the nineties, we would encounter a group of younger filmmakers that would seize upon the essence of this quote and put it to un-ironic use; I'm referring specifically to the *Matrix Trilogy,* which explicitly posited the moment of being through the looking glass as the apprehension of a totally simulated reality that is radically different from the one we live. Of course, there was a conventional sense of moral conflict on the other side of this glass as well, but as the films wore on, the threat posed by simulation and the hyperreal was itself renewed, in different degrees and forms. Therefore, the viewer *did in fact* experience a radical departure from the real; one that was conceptual and theoretical and not centered around particular events, such as the assassination of JFK.[828]

---

[826] The theory Stone puts forward is that the military-industrial complex had Kennedy killed in order to prevent downsizing of the military as well as to maneuver the U.S. into the Vietnam War.

[827] I say "ironic" because the statement of being through the looking glass implies that a more traditional outlook on life has been sublated by a newer and stranger one; for Stone, it seems as if the statement refers to a sense in which a more conventional, and traditional, sense of morality has been reclaimed.

[828] Timothy Melley sees this movement, as it exists in film and literature, as being one that projects the interior machinations of a secret, coherent cabal onto the exterior i.e., society as a whole. Melley, Timothy (2000) *Empire of Conspiracy: The Culture of Paranoia in Postwar America.* Cornell University Press. Pp. 144 - 145

These films bring us up to the point in our analysis where the millennium, which promised almost cosmic levels of change and disaster, would occur with very little incident. The year after is a different story; Arthur C. Clark had held out the promise of technological advancement that could lead to space exploration. The events of 9/11/2001 dashed these aspirations and tied humanity, both physically and psychologically, closer to earth. This is interesting because the three murky figures we have been tracking were terrestrially bound (outside of Enoch's trip to Heaven). It almost seems as if the three individuals we have examined in this section, who all play significant roles within the so-called "Clinton Body Count" narrative are a telluric and less mythologized reiteration of the three ancient and murky figures.

All six of these figures are of the earth, and each hide mysteries. The first three are presented as holding metaphysical, or even mystical, secrets. The latter three, who appear a good two to three thousand years later, carried secrets that were contingent upon their roles in politics. Once these latter three died, their sense of mysteriousness lived on, almost as if their ghosts were guarding knowledge that, if released, could lead to massive social upheaval. There is no one-to-one correspondence of traits and attributes between these two sets of figure. The first set is mythic and the second is factual. Are the conspiracy theories that arise from the deaths of Foster, Rich, and Epstein mythic? Are these theories narratively rich enough to substitute for myths? We will encounter this same question on a much larger scale when we analyze 9/11.

Postscript: Who are the "Assassins"?

The last question we will focus on in this chapter is who is committing the assassinations. Obviously we have already discussed the individuals that have been singled out as being responsible for the deaths of these public figures, but what mythology informs these actions and the cultural role that these individuals inhabit?

The word "assassin" indirectly comes from the legacy of an 11th century Shiite Imam named Hassan-i Sabbah who commanded a region in Nizari (present day Iran). At his castle in Alamut, he ran an elite military academy that came to be known by outsiders as the "Order of Assassins." The power of Hassan-i Sabbah, and his cultic dominance over his followers, grew from a division between orthodox followers of Islam who believed Mohammed to be the "bringer of divine inspiration" and the smaller, more secretive, Shiah sect, who believed Ali the fourth Imam to be a more important religious figure.[829] The conflict between the two teachings can be interpreted in terms of a debate between the authority of a law that is bound to a foundational text versus an authority that is bound to the organizational power represented by a priest-class (the Imams).

The educational system initiated by the Shiahs (also referred to as Ismailis) blended strict discipline with the promise of hidden knowledge in a stew of timeless brainwashing:

> Students had to pass through nine degrees of initiation. In the first, the teachers threw their pupils into a state of doubt about all conventional ideas, religious and political. They used false analogy and every other device of argument to make the aspirant believe that what he had been taught by his previous mentors was prejudiced and capable of being challenged. The effect of this, according to the Arab historian, Makrizi, was to cause him to lean upon the personality of the teachers, as the only possible source of the proper interpretation of facts. At the same time, the teachers hinted continually that formal knowledge was merely the cloak for hidden, inner and powerful truth, whose secret would be imparted

[829] Daraul, Arkon (1961) *A History of Secret Societies*. Citadel Press. P. 14

when the youth was ready to receive it. This 'confusion technique' was carried out until the student reached the stage where he was prepared to swear a vow of blind allegiance to one or other of his teachers.[830]

The imparting of secret knowledge, an essentially Structuralist endeavor, entailed the revealing of secret names and words that were to be repeated by the adepts. This act took the mythic thinking Mircea Eliade ascribed to archaic communities and duplicated it within a cloistered, secretive environment. This, as we have seen, is akin to the idea of a secret or esoteric narrative being hermetically passed down to a hierarchically arranged group of adherents. In this case, the Hermetic process is decidedly militaristic and oriented towards securing ideological ends.

It was around 1088 that Hassan-i Sabbah, after a series of misadventures, retreated into the Rudbar mountains of Iran and began his project of single-handedly reviving the faltering Ismaili revolution. His primary conquest in this region was the Castle of Alamut. In 1271, Marco Polo described the realm established by Hassan-i Sabbah in terms that resonate with the Prester John mythos: A luxurious garden stocked with every delicious fruit and vegetable; gold ornamentation, and silk furniture adorning the palace; streams of wine, milk, and honey, beautiful women, etc.[831] Hassan-i Sabbah created and maintained this artificial paradise because he wanted to give the young men he was training to become political assassins a taste of the after-life they would enjoy once they were killed performing their nefarious deeds. How extravagant Sabbah's realm actually was can be debated, but most scholars on the subject agree that whatever indoctrination the trainees experienced was coupled with the use of hashish,

---

[830] Ibid, p. 15
[831] Ibid p. 21

hence the word "assassin" being derived from the Arabic word "Hashishin," which means "users of hashish."[832]

In one of his last novels, *The Western Lands*, William Burroughs explored the ancient Egyptian conception of the afterlife. In this narrative, Hassan-i Sabbah plays a significant role:

> What did Hassan-i Sabbah find out in Egypt? He found out that the Western Lands exist, and how to find them. This was the Garden he showed his followers. And he found out how to act as Ka for his disciples.[833]

"The Western Lands" is the expression designating the Egyptian afterlife after the dead subject has passed through the Land of the Dead. The Ka is the soul that remains with you after death and acts as guide through the spirit-world.[834] In regard to Alamut, Burroughs writes that Hassan-i Sabbah "wasn't attempting old-style territorial politics. Alamut was never intended to be permanent. It was intended to gain time to train a few operatives for the future struggle..."[835]

This novel, published in 1987, was the culmination of over forty years of fascination with the legacy of Hassan-i Sabbah.[836] In the sixties, Burroughs had been taken with the philosophical import of Hassan-i Sabbah's famed motto: "Nothing is true,

---

[832] Moench, Doug (1995) *The Big Book of Conspiracies*. Paradox Press. P. 156

[833] Burroughs, William (1987) *The Western Lands*. Penguin Books. P. 193

[834] This theme appears in European literature, specifically in *The Divine Comedy*, wherein Dante Alighieri is guided through the afterlife by the ancient Roman poet Virgil.

[835] Ibid p. 215

[836] The "Old Man of the Mountain" and his apocryphal slogan: "Nothing is true. Everything is permitted" was one of the primary subjects of 1964's *Nova Express*.

everything is permitted," which he coupled with the theory that Hassan-i Sabbah used hashish and young men dressed as women to create hallucinations of an Islamic heaven. Now, near the end of his life, we see him moving towards a complete metaphysical overhauling of his previous conception by resettling Hassan-i Sabbah's persona within the parameters of literature, and specifically a literature that embodies the author's grappling with his own mortality.

When Sabbah died at the age of ninety, his organization suffered from a lack of leadership due to the execution of his two sons. [837] Various Imams assumed nominal leadership of the Assassins, but the organization had largely gone underground and was diffused throughout the region by the time the Mongols overran Alamut in the early thirteenth century. When the region was restored to the Assassins in 1260, it was at the behest of the Sultan of Egypt, who would utilize the organization for his own political ambitions.[838]

The personage of Hassan-i Sabbah can be read in a variety of ways; William Burroughs is probably the most prominent proponent of a complex literary reading that looks at the Imam's teachings and actions in a detached, abstract way. Other conspiracy theorists have seen the Manson Family murders in August of 1969 as being of a similar drug-induced ilk.[839]

In some ways, we can read the jet-setting, politically connected and unflappable Jeffrey Epstein as a postmodern reiteration of the Hassan-i Sabbah narrative. What Daraul says of Sabbah and the Order of Assassins, "They had perfected their method of securing the loyalty of human beings to an extent and

---

[837] Daraul, Arkon (1961) *A History of Secret Societies*. Citadel Press. P. 28
[838] Ibid p. 36
[839] Moench, Doug (1995) *The Big Book of Conspiracies*. Paradox Press. Pp. 157 - 158

on a scale which has seldom been paralleled,"[840] might be equally applied to Epstein. Both possessed enchanted realms where worldly desires were fulfilled, for Sabbah it was Alamut and for Epstein it was Little Saint James. Whether or not Epstein's intrigues were tied to explicit acts of political violence we may never know. However, there was a distinction between the men who fell victim to the lures of each. Sabbah's adherents were poor and uneducated dupes, whereas Epstein took in cynical, wealthy, and careless men of an elite pedigree. In this respect both figures represent a Faustian deal-with-the-devil scenario for individuals who could not overcome their most worldly and base desires.

On other, more conspiratorial readings, Sabbah's techniques for brainwashing in the cause of political assassination can be read as the blueprint for lone gunmen style assassinations orchestrated by the deep state. It is in this respect that the subject of Operation MK Ultra again comes to the fore. Stephen Kinzer's depiction of the program's mastermind, Sidney Gottlieb, is a portrait in contradiction. On the one hand he conducted experiments wherein large doses of LSD were given to unwitting subjects from all walks of life, leading to seizures and states of psychosis,[841] and on the other, he spent his later years gardening, praying, and volunteering at a local preschool.[842] A number of notable people were caught up in the CIA's psychedelic experiments: Allen Ginsberg, Ken Kesey, Robert Hunter (lyricist for the Grateful Dead), mobster James "Whitey" Bulger, as well as hundreds of unknown individuals. The total number is unknown due to CIA Director Richard Helms' ordering of the destruction of all files relating to the project in 1973.[843] Undoubtedly villainous during his career with the CIA, Kinzer believes singling Gottlieb

---

[840] Daraul, Arkon (1961) *A History of Secret Societies*. Citadel Press. p. 27
[841] Kinzer, Stephen (2019) *Poisoner in Chief: Sidney Gottlieb and the CIA Search for Mind Control*. Henry Holt and Company. P. 97
[842] Ibid pp. 256 - 258
[843] Ibid p. 209

out as single-handedly responsible for the abuses and fallout of MK Ultra is misguided:

> Portraying Gottlieb as having been unsupervised and out of control was a sensible strategy. It obscured the fact that senior CIA officers like Dulles and Helms approved and encouraged his work. Just as important, it deflected attention away from the institutional responsibility of the CIA, White House, and Congress.[844]

Are we to assume the worst about the MK Ultra Project? I don't mean if the abuse and drug experiments aren't true – the government has already admitted to those. I mean, if the people subjected to such brainwashing might have become assassins. If this is the case then it seems as if it is indeed a reoccurrence of the Hassan-i Sabbah narrative.

This brings us back to JFK, because his assassin, or the man officially purported to be his assassin, has not merely been historically dissected and terminally psychoanalyzed, he has also appeared as an enigmatic figure in the works of some of the twentieth century's most prominent authors. Don Delillo's *Libra*, published in 1988, explores Lee Harvey Oswald's life with the author's customarily detached style. Using Oswald's astrological star sign as the port of entry to a fictional analysis of his life – a technique that would not have been possible prior to the postmodern age – indicates how art within the postmodern milieu works dualistically: it destabilizes prior grand narratives (such as astrology) while paradoxically adding a degree of legitimacy to narratives previously discarded by scientism. This is not to say that someone could completely and unironically rehabilitate something like astrology, but that archaic approaches to interpreting the world (phrenology, homeopathy, astrology, etc.) can be textually revived because of their symbolic import.

---

[844] Ibid p. 261

What is most important is that the application is done not within a spirit of belief but within a spirit of novelty or irony. It is the novel, or new, application of the anachronistic technique that informs the subject at hand with an older, more mythologically endowed, sensibility.

Libra's narrator is Nicholas Branch, a former CIA agent commissioned to write the agency's secret history of the assassination. It is an overwhelming task, Branch soon realizes as the evidence he accumulates infinitely proliferates: "The ceaseless collection of historical "evidence" has begun to simulate the event which it is supposed to document – thus unsettling the relation between evidence and event, representation and referent."[845] Hence, in the form of a postmodern novel we obtain a Byzantine vision of the Argument from Hyperreality: not only is the demarcation between past and present blurred but it is object-centered, the object here being the evidence related to the crime.

In his analysis of *Libra*, Timothy Melley describes the narrator's quest to have "a thing be what it is."[846] "Evidence," like the Grail, the Philosopher's Stone, the McKenna Brothers' silver key, etc., itself becomes an object that signifies a "hidden truth."[847] In the case of our analyses, we can speculate the role of evidence to be a postmodern reiteration of these *kinds* of objects, and like these objects, it signifies one (or possibly many) hidden narratives. The narrative Delillo settles on posits JFK's assassin to be Lee Harvey Oswald. The twist, however, is that Oswald himself is the last piece of the conspiratorial puzzle, as his role has been scripted in advance:

> Before the conspirators know anything about Oswald, they build their plot upon an *imaginary* assassin, creating masses of fake documents –

---

[845] Melley, Timothy (2000) *Empire of Conspiracy: The Culture of Paranoia in Postwar America*. Cornell University Press. P. 139
[846] Ibid p. 140
[847] Ibid p. 140

newspaper clippings, purchase orders, telephone calls – all in order to "put someone together, build an identity, a skein of persuasion and habit, ever so subtle... a man with believable quirks" (78). The rich interior of this handmade assassin, according to his creator, Win Everett, is to be revealed in a slew of false documents that will "show the secret symmetries in a nondescript life" (78) and convey a sense of "lingering mystery ... a purpose and a destiny" (147). When the conspirators discover Oswald, he is more like their imaginary character than they can believe.[848]

This notion is similar to McDonald's claim that Oswald, Ruby, and Saul were chosen by the conspiracy to play their roles beforehand. In contrast to Saul, who is a suave jet-setting assassin, Oswald is a regular blue-collar guy. We also get the sense that public figures who will have gravity and world-changing transformative powers must have their "purpose" and "destiny" written out beforehand ... Faith in the ineffable, or God, that was a facet of mythology, has been abandoned for the security of the written word.

Norman Mailer's *Oswald's Tale: An American Mystery*, published in 1995, is a straight-forward biography that only occasionally veers into the postmodern literary speculation employed by Delillo, albeit in a more introspective way. This is because Mailer had met JFK prior to his election and was deeply shocked by his assassination. In Mailer's hands, and following his strict research regiment, which included travelling to Russia, countless interviews, and access to official KGB documents pertaining to Oswald, the portrait is the inverse of Delillo's: the

---

[848] Ibid p. 146

assassin became "a character who's worthy, to some little degree, of the size that history has given him."[849]

Both Mailer and Delillo assert that Oswald did in fact assassinate Kennedy. However, despite their differences, they both view Oswald as a culturally transitional figure existing at a nexus-point of political ideology, social unrest, and alienation. It is as the anonymous American man who is condemned to obscurity while trying to achieve notoriety via violence, that we are allowed, via these two narratives, to enter the mind of Oswald. Once inside, the old philosophical questions of "what is the self" re-emerge, and we find these two literary giants wrestling with the fissure at the heart of Being, the "primordial gap" that Žižek declares to be within immanence itself:

> The primordial gap is thus not the polar opposition of two principles (masculine and feminine, light and dark, opening and closure...) but the minimal gap between an element and itself, the Void and its own place of inscription [...] The tension between immanence and transcendence is thus also secondary with regard to the gap within immanence itself: "transcendence" is a kind of perspective illusion, the way we (mis)perceive the gap/discord that inheres to immanence itself. In the same way, the tension between the Same and Other is secondary with regard to the noncoincidence of the Same with itself.[850]

Essentially Oswald became the historical figure in which this perplexing state of "noncoincidence" could be both embodied and explored in a relatively neutral and dispassionate way. If, for

[849] Lennon, Michael (2013) *Norman Mailer: A Double Life*. Simon & Schuster. P. 672
[850] Žižek, Slavoj (2006) *The Parallax View*. Massachusetts Institute of Technology. P. 36

instance, someone tried to write a postmodern novel regarding Stalin or Hitler, they would first have to grapple with the evil these men did, and this grappling would inevitably pervade the entire work and disrupt the purity of the exercise. In the case of Oswald, it is the conspiracy theory, the possibility that he *may not have done it*, which gives the author the license for detachment, and essentially the license for literature. It is in a literary sense that Oswald's remark that he was "just a patsy"[851] becomes emblematic, not just for the conspiracy theorist who believes unseen forces are working all around him, but also for any individual caught within the barrage of information that constitutes modern society.

What is most fascinating about Oswald (or Sirhan Sirhan or James Earl Ray) is that he stepped into the mythological role of "assassin" in a way that conforms to Eliade's theory that the historical personage is assimilated to his mythical model. In this sense, Oswald as an actual person becomes voided, he becomes a reinscription of the anonymous political assassin and his name endures only in that capacity.

---

[851] It is purported that Oswald made this famous remark to journalist Seth Kantor while in custody.

Chapter Thirteen: The Significance of Robert Anton Wilson

The figure of Lee Harvey Oswald has become something of a post-modern Rorschach test, his anonymity having made him a nexus-point wherein a variety of conspiracy theory tropes converge. The subject of this chapter, Robert Anton Wilson, presented himself as a writer who was carrying the work of a variety of intellectual and artistic misfits (Aleister Crowley, Wilhelm Reich, James Joyce, Alfred Korzybski, Buckminster Fuller, etc.) into the twenty-first century, but outside of this his significance is tied to traversing between various points of political and philosophical intrigue and the synthesizing of these experiences into a subversive and surreal worldview.

Robert Anton Wilson, sometimes referred to as "RAW," was born in Brooklyn, New York on January 18th, 1932. Though he was roughly ten years older than most of the baby boomers who would make up the sixties' counter-culture movement, he would end up in that milieu. At first, Wilson's interests lay more in the political sphere than the cultural – he attended the 1968 Democratic National Convention, not Woodstock. His importance to our analysis begins in the late sixties when he began editing the forum section for *Playboy Magazine*. This is where Wilson would meet future collaborator, Robert Shea. After leaving *Playboy,* the two would go on to co-author the three books (*The Eye in the Triangle*, *The Golden Apple* and *Leviathan*) that would make up the epic *Illuminatus!* Trilogy published in 1975.

Illuminatus! was an attempt to tackle all the existing conspiracy theories of the time from a humorous counter-cultural perspective. The story begins with detectives Saul Goodman and Barney Muldoon decoding a series of memos belonging to the editor of a radical Leftist magazine who has gone missing. As their investigation unfolds, the memos reveal a secret connection between the Bavarian Illuminati and Hassan-i Sabbah's Order of Assassins. This trilogy, along with the work of William Burroughs, was critical in bringing the obscure "Old Man of the Mountain" into the fringe corners of the seventies' counterculture.

As the story progresses the characters encounter almost every conspiratorial trope imaginable: the Bavarian Illuminati; Atlantis; Gnosticism; the assassinations of JFK, RFK, and MLK; aliens; and a group we will discuss later in this chapter, the Discordians. The work is intended to index these theories, and hence, like most postmodern fiction, exhibits a large degree of self-awareness. As Erik Davis notes: "The twists of self-reference they unleash propagate up the authorial chain until they spill outside the frame, and make a stab at transcendence."[852]

Unlike the postmodern novels we've briefly discussed, *Libra, Underworld, Gravity's Rainbow* and *Valis*, there is a madcap energy about *Illuminatus!* that seems to push its narrative over the literary edge. In contrast to the work of Delillo, Dick, and Pynchon, who exercise a strong sense of control over how much their text is intended to intersect with the reader's immediate comprehension of the world, Wilson and Shea bombard the reader in an almost cartoonish fashion. It is for this reason that, though many enjoy the *Illuminatus!* Trilogy, they see it primarily as an important jumping off point for Wilson, who would come to grasp these issues from within a more intimate and personal framework. This is exactly the tact he would take in his next work, *Cosmic Trigger I: Final Secret of the Illuminati*, which many claim is his defining work.

Cosmic Trigger

Wilson begins *Cosmic Trigger: Final Secret of the Illuminati* by detailing his authorial predicament after researching and writing on the Illuminati to the point of obsession. His description of the Bavarian Illuminati, in a historical sense, which he maintained for most of his life, was as a group of Enlightenment-oriented, democratic idealists that were "suppressed by the Bavarian

---

[852] Davis, Erik (2019) *High Weirdness: Drugs, Esoterica, and Visionary Experience in the Seventies.* Strange Attractor Press & the MIT Press. P. 255

government for allegedly plotting to overthrow all the kings in Europe and the Pope to boot;"[853] a claim which, we have seen, echoes the criticisms made by John Robison, two centuries prior.[854]

The transition to a more personal, and hence, compelling, framework for *Cosmic Trigger* comes from Wilson writing from the perspective of his own lived experience. *Cosmic Trigger* is not a strict autobiography, but it utilizes autobiography extensively to explain how the concepts and coincidences that dominate the book came into the author's life. The themes of this single work will be the focal point for this chapter. In this section we will tackle two key aspects of *Cosmic Trigger* that relate to the personal nature of the work: drug use and perceptions of authority. The more metaphysical and abstract components of the text will be addressed in the next two sections.

Wilson has consistently identified himself, or at least his persona, as a plurality of entities: the semanticist, the reporter, the husband, the numerologist, the shaman, the skeptic, etc.[855] For the majority of *Cosmic Trigger* he uses the term "we" over "I" to indicate this personal plurality. Politically speaking, and this relates to his sense of "I," Wilson is a Libertarian, and he is careful to track his drug experimentation in terms that transgress the boundaries between conservatism and liberalism. On the one hand, we have his first writing about LSD use in an objectively reported piece for *The National Review*[856] and on the other, his

---

[853] Wilson, Robert Anton (2016) *Cosmic Trigger I: Final Secret of the Illuminati* (Second Edition). Hilaritas Press, LLC. P. 2

[854] Wilson identifies this particular complaint with Robison in his entry on "The Illuminoids" in *Everything is Under Control*. Wilson, Robert Anton (1998) *Everything is Under Control: Conspiracies, Cults and Cover-ups.* Harper Perennial. P. 249

[855] He lists 24 "selves" who live within his person Wilson, Robert Anton (2016) *Cosmic Trigger I: Final Secret of the Illuminati* (Second Edition). Hilaritas Press, LLC. P. 1

[856] Ibid p. 19

contempt for the ACLU and liberal intellectuals for not coming to the defense of Wilhelm Reich and Timothy Leary.[857]

Libertarianism was the key that allowed Wilson to shake off the shackles of the Catholicism of his youth and begin his studies of the occult, sex magick, and drug use. The use of mescaline and peyote led to Wilson's encounters with the mythical "Green Man," who we will analyze in the next section, as well as a deeper engagement with UFO phenomena and cosmic consciousness. Drug use essentially brought Wilson into a psychic realm that he refers to as "Chapel Perilous."[858] Well, technically, it was a combination of psychedelic drug use and reading Aleister Crowley's *Book of Lies* that inaugurated this chapter of his life, but we will tackle Wilson's appropriation of Crowley in a later section.

The drug use we are talking about here is political, as it put Wilson at odds with the US Government, and sociological, in that it put him in contact with countercultural figures like William Burroughs and Timothy Leary. The oppositional aspect of this use of mind-altering substances careened Wilson's work in the direction of baby boomer Nazi reductionist theories; although, being a pluralist at heart he always refrained from whole-heartedly endorsing such clear-cut identifications. However, there is an aspect to his thought in this period, much like Philip K. Dick during the *VALIS* period, that paranoically sees a new Inquisition lurking behind every government mandated corner.[859]

The binary opposition between the concepts of "freedom" and "oppression" is not very complex when it is utilized for political sloganeering; however, it informs the more nuanced sociological bonds that Wilson formed in the counterculture during the sixties and seventies. We will see in the next section how the use of organic psychedelics brought Wilson into a state where he felt to be attuned, or even communicating, with the

---

[857] Ibid pp. 52 - 55
[858] Ibid pp. 4 -5
[859] Ibid p. 54

plant world. According to Deleuze, this idea of vegetative communication plays a key role in Proust's literary treatment of homosexuality:

> The entire theme of the accursed or guilty race is intertwined, moreover, with a theme of innocence, the theme of the sexuality of plants. The Proustian theory is extremely complex because it functions on several levels. *On a first level* is the entity of heterosexual loves in their contrasts and repetitions. *On a second level*, this entity splits into two series or directions, that of Gomorrah, which conceals the (invariably revealed) secret of the loved woman, and that of Sodom, which carries the still more deeply buried secret of the lover. It is on this level that the idea of sin or guilt prevails.[860]

The symbolic power of the drug user being an individual that, by its very nature, resists incorporation into the mechanistic designs of a "stable" and "governed" society is analogous to the figure of the homosexual in this reading.[861] Both statuses, within modernity, represent heterogeneity and resistance to the religious mores that inform the laws and norms of society. It was during the sixties that both positions were championed by the counterculture as designations that signified resistance to control.

There is another aspect that applies to the style of communication employed by both figures which has to do with the world created by their respective narratives:

> "This is no longer the world of speeches and of their vertical communications expressing a hierarchy of rules and positions, but the world of anarchic

---

[860] Deleuze, Gilles (2000) *Proust and Signs.* Translated by Richard Howard. University of Minnesota Press. P. 134
[861] William Burroughs exhibited both of these traits.

encounters, of violent accidents, and with their aberrant transverse communications."[862]

This deeper truth, which pertains to the code of the outlaw (something that Burroughs instinctively understood, but took Wilson and Leary decades to discover), is the ironic kernel at the center of Wilson's thought, insofar as he espoused Libertarian ideals. On the one hand, Wilson demanded establishment support for Leary and the utopia promised by LSD studies, coupled with the desire that such research be regulated and essentially approved of by the state, or authority, or whatever. On the other hand, he instinctively understood that the communication provided by such drugs would inevitably lead to subversion or was itself inherently subversive.[863]

It is in this respect that we can see the entrance to Chapel Perilous, or the Chapel Perilous narrative as an outsider, or "outlaw" discourse – one that, by its nature, will expose the synchronicities hidden by the controlled society. Chapel Perilous is akin to Crowley's crossing of the Abyss, and what other occultists have described as an encounter with the "Dweller on the Threshold." We have seen how, for Crowley, it entailed a relinquishment of one's ego. Wilson claims that you come out the other side of the experience "either a stone paranoid or an agnostic; there is no third way."[864]

This then brings us back to the implicit comparison made between Lee Harvey Oswald and Robert Anton Wilson at the very beginning of this chapter. Both individuals found themselves at an

---

[862] Ibid p. 174

[863] Wilson attaches a new age connotation to this communication when he describes, what seems to him, to be a telepathic communication with Leary while the latter was imprisoned in Folsom Prison. Wilson, Robert Anton (2016) *Cosmic Trigger I: Final Secret of the Illuminati* (Second Edition). Hilaritas Press, LLC. P. 94

[864] Ibid p. 4

indefinable point existing somewhere between the stages of modernity and postmodernity, both unwittingly felt a sense of ambiguity as subjects within the milieu they inhabited, and both, in a sense, entered Chapel Perilous. Granted, the two men were very different in nature, Wilson being more innately scholarly and less prone to violence than Oswald. Both attempted to make sense of their respective predicament by reading and writing their way out of their perplexing conditions, but it was Oswald who left Chapel Perilous with a dogmatic notion that he **must** do something. Even if he didn't actually shoot Kennedy, he was drawn into the conspiracy, and willingly entered it. Wilson, by contrast, emerged from Chapel Perilous as an agnostic. So agnostic, that he would spend the rest of his life cataloguing bizarre, fringe, conspiratorial narratives, free from any concern that this activity could jeopardize his agnosticism, or sanity.

The Green Man

One day while coming down from peyote, Wilson was in his garden doing some weeding when in the corner of his eye he saw a "man with warty green skin and pointy ears, dancing."[865] The figure quickly disappeared, and after researching the phenomenon in the works of Carlos Castaneda, deduced that the entity was named Mescalito, and was "one of the spirits of vegetation."[866]

The characterization of a "vegetative" discourse or form of communication we touched upon in the previous section gives the impression that, at the very least, it is a discourse that is shrouded in silence and possibly guided by telekinesis or unknown and unseen affinities. This description holds true not only in regard to Wilson's glimpses of the Green Man but also his counterculture associates (e.g., by the time Leary was arrested on January 18, 1973 in Afghanistan, Wilson grieved over the situation, while

---

[865] Ibid p. 22
[866] Ibid p. 22

acknowledging that the two had only seen each other about a dozen times in the last decade.)[867] It seems as if the bond between the two men had more to do with an innate affinity than with lived companionship.

The mythical figure of the Green Man, however, goes beyond the work of Carlos Castaneda and is a subject that, historically, entails a wide variety of European narratives, one of which explicitly harkens back to the Grail mythos. As the knight Gawain was described as having green armor and green skin, some have even seen Gawain as an avatar, or reiteration, of the archetype of a primordial forest-spirit. This appellation might be due to the narrative that Gawain drank the "water of life" after overcoming a series of knightly challenges. Green can also be seen as representing nature, and therefore, the enchanted forest world existing outside the realm of civilization. In this respect, Gawain shares this trait with other medieval figures. Carolyne Larrington writes:

> The Green Man is originally a decorative motif: typically an image of a man's face peering out from a cluster of stylised oak-leaves, leaves which, in turn, grow out of his cheeks and forehead. This 'foliate head', as the image is technically called, is very widespread in English church architecture. Occasionally the club-wielding Green Man, the type who can be described as the 'combative Green Man' is to be found emerging out of the vegetation surrounding just such a head. In a classic article in the journal *Folklore*, published in 1939, Lady Julia Raglan identified the foliate head with a whole clutch of folkloric characters: 'the Green Man, Jack-in-the-Green, Robin Hood, the King of May and the Garland'. Quite a number of disparate figures find themselves bundled together here, as she seeks to

---

[867] Ibid p. 88

argue that the foliate head is a representation of some ancient vegetation god, the spirit of spring regrowth and natural fertility.[868]

The mythical Green Man, when worked into contemporary literature, repeats some of the alterity we have seen occur within the Enoch narratives. Larrington describes how Tolkien used the myth to inform the "Ents," his benevolent, giant tree creatures in *The Lord of the Rings* novels. Kingsley Amis, Tolkien's student at Oxford, wrote a ghost story in 1969 titled *The Green Man* wherein the titular character represents a frightening and dangerous forest deity.[869] It's possible that Wilson's interpretation is almost neo-pagan, in that he would agree with Larrington's statement that despite our conventional morality, the Green Man ...

> "... has become representative of all that the modern world undervalues, excludes, or lacks. He doesn't *do* anything; he has no story, no legend, except those invented for him by modern writers, but his appearance, as a hybrid of man and plant, insists that humans are inextricably part of that natural world which we in the West are so keen to subjugate."[870]

And it is within this pagan reasoning that the figure of the Green Man is both wondrous and frightening – eluding a definitive orientation towards good or evil.

In this naturalistic context, the Green Man represents a return to the soil.[871] But in the context of the trinity of murky

---

[868] Larrington, Carolyne (2017) *The Land of the Green Man*. I.B. Tauris & Co. Ltd. P. 226
[869] Ibid pp. 228 - 229
[870] Ibid p. 232
[871] Which, for Wilson, would be predictive given his moving to Ireland later in life.

figures we have been tracking, and this is the postmodern detail that Wilson contributes to our analysis, he is an elliptical character that appears in the corner of your eye (just as Enoch, Melchizedek and Hiram appear in the corner, or margins of a Biblical text) and then disappears.

The Hermeneutics of Crowley Studies

Robert Anton Wilson, like UFOlogists Steven Greer and Robert Temple, had a fixation with Sirius. Temple's work is explicitly referenced in *Cosmic Trigger* and Wilson entertains all the UFO theories we have set on the table so far: legitimate extraterrestrial entities, interdimensional beings that have appeared in various guises throughout history, entities summoned through magick etc. Because he consciously resists the western tradition of logic, he only grants each one a passing deference, not giving any a primacy of explanation.

It is within the Sirius mystery that Aleister Crowley comes to play a key role in Wilson's analysis. Prior to reading *The Book of Lies*, which helped prompt him into his vision quest, Wilson's only knowledge of the occultist was that he had been a decadent drug addict and supposed Satanist.[872] After he came to reconsider Crowley, Wilson would go on to incorporate most of the mythologies surrounding the man into the text of *Cosmic Trigger*.

This interpretation begins with Wilson's insistence that Crowley was constantly injecting surreptitious references to Tantric Yoga throughout his many works – a claim that persuaded Wilson himself to practice yoga, both sober and stoned on marijuana. After this came the conviction that Crowley was the scion of a secret illuminated teaching "possibly going back through Renaissance magick societies, medieval witchcraft, the Knights Templar, European Sufis, etc., to Gnosticism, and thence

---

[872] Wilson, Robert Anton (2016) *Cosmic Trigger I: Final Secret of the Illuminati* (Second Edition). Hilaritas Press, LLC. P. 65

back possibly to the Eleusian Mysteries and Egyptian cults."[873] The only thing missing from the chronology is Atlantis. It's interesting to note that this hermetical genealogy put forward by RAW coincides to the T with the one put forward by Gary Wayne – the key difference is that Wayne condemns it, while Wilson sees it as cause for celebration.

After establishing this pedigree, Wilson tries "Crossing the Abyss" himself. The technique that he uses to eliminate his ego is to refrain from saying the word "I" for an entire week. While Crowley's behavioristic technique involved cutting himself on the arm with a razor every time he said "I," Wilson's less severe method involved biting his thumb each time he uttered the word.[874]

As this personal experimentation was going on, Wilson was noticing a wide variety of synchronization going on around him. These instances involved the consistent reappearance of the number 23, which Burroughs also saw as a significant number; as well as conspiracy theories surrounding Watergate, which coincided with events depicted in the then-unpublished *Illuminatus!* manuscript. Sirius would be an important signifier in this unfolding web of synchronicity. Taking inspiration from the work of Kenneth Grant, Wilson came to believe that the "Dog Star" was the originating source for Crowley's 1904 transcription of *The Book of the Law*. Grant writes that:

> Crowley identified the heart of (his magical) current with one particular Star. In Occult Tradition, this is "the Sun behind the Sun," the Hidden God, the vast star Sirius, or Sothis...[875]

---

[873] Ibid p. 70

[874] Ibid p. 71. It should be noted here that the reliance on paying attention to language shows a strong affinity for Structuralism.

[875] Grant, Kenneth (1973) *The Magical Revival*. Weiser. P. 50

Tied in with this revelation is Grant's claim that the name of one of the sects founded by Crowley, the Order of the Silver Star, is itself a reference to Sirius.[876] The color silver would become relevant to an experience wherein Wilson's son, Graham, claimed to have encountered a woman with silver skin who told the boy he should become a physicist when he grows up.[877] The meeting happened soon after the family believed to have witnessed a UFO land on a hilltop not far from their house. Of this mysterious silver lady, who Wilson believed to be the female counterpart of the Green Man, he writes:

> She is, of course, another archetype from Jung's collective unconscious, and was around long before Christianity. The Egyptians called her Nuit and connected her specifically with the star Sirius. But statues of her go back at least to cave statues dated c. 30,000 B.C.[878]

Nuit, as we have seen, appears in the opening of Crowley's *Book of the Law* and Wilson goes on to make myriad claims about Crowley and Sirius. These involve Robert Temple's claims that intergalactic travellers from Sirius visited the Dogon people of Western Africa thousands of years ago; the novel idea that intergalactic travel might not have been physical, but was instead achieved by a kind of cosmic telekinesis; as well as Timothy Leary's claims of being a sort of reincarnation of Aleister Crowley.[879] We're going to come back to this last claim at the end of the next section, but before we do, we need to tackle Wilson's appropriation of quantum physics, which is a project he began

---

[876] Wilson, Robert Anton (2016) *Cosmic Trigger I: Final Secret of the Illuminati* (Second Edition). Hilaritas Press, LLC. P. 97
[877] Ibid p. 39
[878] Ibid p. 40
[879] Ibid p. 116

during *The Cosmic Trigger* period and would continue until the end of his life.

Pop Physics

All the subjects discussed in this chapter fall into the category of what Erik Davis calls "marginal media." Davis's *High Weirdness* tracks the cultural evolution of the postmodern mysticism that culminated with Philip K. Dick's *VALIS* Trilogy and extends to fringe culture-jammers like the Discordians and the Church of the SubGenius. Coming to the topic from a philosophical angle, Davis formulates the experiences and writings of his subjects in strongly hermeneutical terms:

> I want to track how features of their environment –
> building blocks like texts, technologies, metabolic
> and sonic forces- loop around to become mobilized
> within experience itself: seeding it beforehand,
> shaping it on the fly, and identifying it in reflective
> and literary hindsight.[880]

The legacy of Robert Anton Wilson ultimately revolves around three tropes of activity: the injecting of occult esoterica into the counterculture of the early seventies, the refashioning of conspiracy theory narratives into surreal fiction, and the incorporation of quantum mechanics into both the occult and philosophy. Quantum mechanics would increasingly preoccupy Wilson throughout the eighties and nineties[881] and it is this scientific theory that coincides with what Davis refers to when speaking of features of the environment looping around and mobilizing experience itself.

---

[880] Davis, Erik (2019) *High Weirdness: Drugs, Esoterica, and Visionary Experience in the Seventies.* Strange Attractor Press & the MIT Press. P. 31

[881] For example, see 1990's *Quantum Psychology.*

According to Davis's account, a philosophical approach to quantum physics had been a significant part of the work of scientists like Heisenberg, Einstein, and Bohr, but had disappeared by the early seventies until its revival by the Fundamental Fysiks Group in Berkeley California in 1975.[882] The Fundamental Fysiks Group was initially intrigued by the issue of quantum entanglement, wherein quantum particles are seemingly capable of instantaneous "communication" while separated by a large swath of space-time. Theoretically this would entail that communication occurs faster than the speed of light. This obviously relates to Wilson's speculation that interstellar contact, albeit physically impossible, could be possible via telekinesis. However, is this application of quantum theory valid? Allow me a brief tangent.

It's debatable whether the correlation that occurs between these two sub-atomic particles can be deemed "communication." The problem with this appellation has to do with the larger issue of whether a bit of technical knowledge can be taken out of its own specific jargon and put into more colloquial usage. Critics of so-called "narrativization" feel that the "untranslated" information loses some of its conceptual richness, or worse, may acquire incorrect conceptual facets, when it is metaphorically translated to reach a wider audience.

Probably one of the best demonstrations of the distinction between purely theoretical (or technical) knowledge and the attempt to narrativize said knowledge is in the relatively recent McGinn/Kurzweil debate that began in 2013, in the March 21 issue of *The New York Review of Books*. The gist of the argument was that Ray Kurzweil, in his capacity as a director of engineering at Google, decided to write a book called *How to Create a Mind: The Secret of Human Thought Revealed*. When reviewing the book, the philosopher Colin McGinn attacked a problem he considered endemic in modern pop-science literature: Homunculism, which is the description of complex scientific discourse in terms of

---

[882] Ibid, pp. 70 - 71

ordinary human interaction; in this case it was Kurzweil's description of firing-axons "recognizing" and "predicting" signals. McGinn writes:

> Presumably (I am not entirely sure) Kurzweil would agree that such descriptions cannot be taken literally: individual neurons don't say things or predict things or see things—though it is perhaps as if they do. People say and predict and see, not little bunches of neurons, still less bits of machines. Such anthropomorphic descriptions of cortical activity must ultimately be replaced by literal descriptions of electric charge and chemical transmission (though they may be harmless for expository purposes). Still, they are not scientifically acceptable as they stand.[883]

We can interpret McGinn's resistance to what seems like the dumbing down of science as a defense of a discipline that can only be approached through a principled and systematically educated rigor, one which, from the outset, has abandoned an appeal to ordinary language. The humanity, and hence frailty, of "ordinary" language is what stands in the way of truly grasping that which does not speak i.e., the profound secrets of the universe, which can only be approximated via mathematical equations and axioms. In this regard, it is possible to interpret formal scientific jargon (regardless of the discipline) as an attempt to bypass conventional language and introduce a sense of obscurity that effectively mirrors the ineffable nature it is attempting to document.

---

[883] Originally found in *The New York Review of Books* Website (March 21, 2013) a site that used to be free, but has since changed its policy. You can now find the review reprinted at http://integral-options.blogspot.com/2013/03/ray-kurzweils-how-to-create-mind.html?m=1 accessed 10/29/20

The McGinn/Kurzweil exchange represents a debate that has existed at least since Plato. The mysteriousness associated with quantum entanglement led to the publication of pop-physics books like Fritjof Capra's *The Tao of Physics* (1975) and Gary Zukav's *The Dancing Wu-Li Masters* (1979). Wilson's oeuvre differs from these mainstream works because of its persistent incorporation of all three of the above-mentioned tropes. And though he often veers towards the path of simplification, there is evidence of a certain reverence for the inherent complexity and ineffability of many of the topics he tackles, be they scientific or mystical, which evades the stereotypes associated with "pop physics."

However, there are some problems with Wilson's approach. Davis hones in on Wilson's frequent claims of skepticism – which Wilson says was shared by Crowley – and questions its consistency. [884] Davis describes both men as indulging in an "as if-ism" that treats synchronicities and flights of fancy as if they were true, because doing so "produces richer effects, both in terms of experience, and in the subsequent blossoming of possibilities." [885] However, indulging in this mindset, and I agree with Davis on this point, endangers the security of the skepticism one presumes one is returning to after the indulgence.

Davis summarizes Wilson's exit from Chapel Perilous as resulting from an encounter with Jacques Vallée at a "Crowleymass" that the former helped organize in October 1974. According to Davis's account, the level-headed computer scientist injected a renewed sense of skepticism into Wilson's increasingly untethered psyche. The primary source of unmooring from reality, as it occurs within the text of *Cosmic Trigger*, appears to

---

[884] Davis, Erik (2019) *High Weirdness: Drugs, Esoterica, and Visionary Experience in the Seventies*. Strange Attractor Press & the MIT Press. P. 234
[885] Ibid p. 239

stem primarily from the influence of Timothy Leary, beginning with Leary's book *Terra II...A Way Out,* published in 1974.

In *Terra II*, Leary claims that he (and fellow prisoners at Vacaville Prison) had been receiving telepathic transmissions, referred to as the "Starseed Transmissions," from a galactic higher intelligence. The higher intelligence informed Leary of a variety of things, some of which were:

-"It is time for life on Earth to leave the planetary womb and learn to walk through the stars."

-Life was seeded on Earth billions of years ago.

-Human beings must abolish "larval identities of race, culture, and nationality."

-The secret to immortality will be discovered within the structure of DNA.

-Mutate!

-Humanity's voyage back to its rightful home in outer space will be made possible by the Japanese.[886]

Wilson appears to have bought all of this hook, line, and sinker and goes on to some concerted speculation as to when the secret of immortality will be uncovered (the year 2000 is batted around a bit ... as was the style at the time). Clearly this utopianism spoke to an unchecked hippy idealism that was fundamental to Wilson.[887]

---

[886] Wilson, Robert Anton (2016) *Cosmic Trigger I: Final Secret of the Illuminati* (Second Edition). Hilaritas Press, LLC. Pp. 105 - 106
[887] I wonder if one of his twenty-four unique personas was labeled "sixties utopian idealist"?

This is important to our narrative analysis because, if we look at Wilson as a microcosm of modern conspiracy theorization, we can track an evolution from intellectual and scholarly interest in phenomena, to a process of tracking and tabulation that embeds the subject (who is doing the tracking) within the network of the phenomena, which then led to paranoia. Wilson's example is a little more extreme, since he dabbled explicitly in drugs and magick, however these are contingencies attendant to modernity. This second stage, which would be referred to as the "Chapel Perilous narrative" or the "Sirius transmissions," was really just a period of time in which Wilson noticed a lot of synchronicities; so much so, that they began to build up steam. Davis notes that:

> *Cosmic Trigger* is an attempt both to communicate the pathological extremes of extraordinary experience and to rescue its author from mysteries whose infectious charisma is nonetheless sustained, and even broadcast, through the act of writing.[888]

For our purposes, this is a man who has transformed himself into a compound conspiracy theorist, capable of reconciling Aleister Crowley, telekinetic communication with a higher intelligence, the God of Genesis, and the irrational number **pi** all within a single paragraph![889] It's also worth noting that the obsession with immortality that takes up over fifteen pages of *Cosmic Trigger* is a postmodern reiteration of the naivety we discussed in "The Significance of the Sea," wherein I argued that from a contemporary perspective, a desire for an insanely attenuated existence is the mark of a childlike thought process. It's

---

[888] Davis, Erik (2019) *High Weirdness: Drugs, Esoterica, and Visionary Experience in the Seventies.* Strange Attractor Press & the MIT Press. P. 257

[889] Wilson, Robert Anton (2016) *Cosmic Trigger I: Final Secret of the Illuminati* (Second Edition). Hilaritas Press, LLC. P. 111

interesting that the tribulations of the Chapel Perilous narrative would entail this sort of regress. However, perhaps it is not a regression and merely the result of a process of re-enchantment, one which duplicates the hazy, partially aware adolescent stage of humanity depicted in humanity's most ancient religious texts – and perhaps this is a necessary component of a religious text, regardless of time and place. The theme of religious texts engendered within the throes of postmodernism will be the subject of the next two sections.

The Discordian Society

Despite having appeared in the pages of *Illuminatus!* the Discordians were an actual group that developed separately from Robert Anton Wilson's imagination. Founded by Kerry Thornley and Gregory Hill in Southern California in 1959 during a visit to an all-night bowling alley.[890] The subject of conversation for the evening was why there was so much chaos and discord in the world; conjuring a unique blend of offbeat humor and intellectual hipsterism, the two decided that chaos was itself an all-permeating and fundamental feature of the universe.

What began as a parody religion, with Hill taking on the moniker of "Malaclypse the Younger" and Thornley adopting "Omar Khayyam Ravenhurst," soon acquired some distinctly

Though the two would incorporate a variety of highbrow and lowbrow intellectual currents into their collective writing and mythos, their primary source of inspiration came from antiquity, namely a Greek myth regarding Eris, the goddess of chaos, throwing a golden apple with the inscription **ΤΗ ΚΑΛΛΙΣΤΗΙ,** which translates as "to the most beautiful" into the midst of a wedding feast the gods were attending. The ensuing chaos, and resentment erupting between Hera, Athena, and Aphrodite would inevitably lead to the Trojan War.

---

[890] Gorightly, Adam (2014) *Historia Discordia: The Origins of the Discordian Society*. RVP Publishers. P. 235

gnostic narratives. One secret gnostic teaching that especially resonated with the Discordian mythos is the idea that the god who created this world, Jehova, is kind of evil and therefore all material things in the world tempt and ensnare us in a thoughtless engagement with them (sometimes Jehova is referred to as "the demiurge"). Hence all the spiritual practices and beliefs that move us away from the "material" world direct us to a higher entity (who for the Discordians is Eris) intends to help us escape our enslavement to this world.

This, basically Manichaeistic conception of reality, resonates with what Kerry Thornley writes in one of the introductions to the *Principia Discordia*:

> Jesus was not the Son of God at all but – as He says again and again in the Bible – He was the Son of Man. Actually, His mission was to warn us against God – a laser-armed computer-robot space station sent to regulate or destroy humanity.[891]

The *Principia Discordia* was first published in 1965, and is a mixture of clip art, collage, and typed memos. Some of the memos have a faux official letterhead, thus mocking the appeal to authenticity made by conspiracy theorists such as William Cooper's *Behold a Pale Horse*.[892] Within this mélange there are elements of humor, such as the claim that planning a pilgrimage is just as good as actually making one.[893] Conspiratorial intrigue, such as a letter from The Bavarian Illuminati (whose letterhead announces: "The World's Oldest And Most Successful Conspiracy") that claims:

---

[891] Malaclypse the Younger (2014) *Principia Discordia*. Lunatic Pope Press. P. 17

[892] Though the *Principia Discordia* predated *Behold a Pale Horse* by about twenty six years.

[893] Ibid p. 52

Our teachings are not, need I remind you, available for publication. No harm, though, in admitting that some of them can be found disguised in Joyce's *Finnegan's Wake*, Burroughs's *Nova Express*, the King James translation of *The Holy Bible* (though not the Latin or Hebrew), and *The Blue Book*. Not to speak of Ben Franklin's private papers (!), but we are still suppressing those.[894]

And Zen-like koans such as "If you can master nonsense as well as you have already learned to master sense, then each will expose the other for what it is: absurdity."[895]

Ironically enough, the initial run of the *Principia* was reproduced on a mimeograph machine belonging to New Orleans District Attorney Jim Garrison.[896] Garrison had been interested in talking with Thornley since the latter's testimony before the Warren Commission on May 18, 1964.[897] Thornley had known Lee Harvey Oswald personally, having served in the Marines with him. Garrison and Thornley would not get along, however, and Garrison would go on to make statements alleging that the Discordians were somehow involved in JFK's assassination.[898] This coincidence was enough to intrigue Wilson and include the Discordians as protagonists in the *Illuminatus!* Trilogy. Many people at the time believed Wilson invented the names "Malaclypse the Younger" and "Omar Khayyam Ravenhurst" in a

---

[894] Ibid p. 72. The inclusion of *Finnegan's Wake* here is significant because it is the literary text from which quantum physicists derived the word "quark" -quarks being sub-atomic particles.
[895] Ibid p. 74
[896] Gorightly, Adam (2014) *Historia Discordia: The Origins of the Discordian Society*. RVP Publishers. P. 23
[897] Ibid p. 23
[898] This included the allegation that the Discordians were a CIA front. Ibid p. 23

manner similar to Lovecraft's invention of "the mad Arab Abdul Alhazred" who had supposedly authored *The Necronomicon.*

In its capacity as a parody religion, Thornley initially saw the Discordian Society as a means for providing "mystical reasons for the disorder around us; to promote unworkable principles of discord – in short, to provide the world with a workshop for the insane..."[899] This statement was from a letter dated April 11, 1964 and indicates an affinity with the proto-Surrealist theory of "Pataphysics" formulated by Alfred Jarry roughly seventy years prior. Pataphysics was intended to be a parody of science, i.e., it is "the science of imaginary solutions."[900] Julian Pefanis states: "To the pataphysician the play of aesthetic values has replaced religious and divine prestige..."[901] For Jarry this aesthetic was absurdist and entailed an idiosyncratic sense of humor. This was equally true for Thornley and Hill, who blended their absurdism with the conspiratorial tropes of the day, essentially taking books like *Proofs of a* Conspiracy and *None Dare Call it Conspiracy* and flipping them on their heads.

It is in this respect, that the Discordians introduced Wilson to the idea of weaponizing conspiracy theorization, thus placing the Illuminati on the side of the counterculture. Part of this project involved adopting institutions, symbols, and even physical structures, such as the Pentagon building, as supposed evidence of their participation on (the winning) side of a rumored conspiracy. The Pentagon was an especially notable inclusion because it is a symbol consummately antithetical to the spirit of Eris:

> The Pentagon represents the Aneristic Principle of Order[...] The Pentagon has several references; for one, it can be taken to represent geometry, one of

---

[899] Ibid p. 75
[900] Pefanis, Julian (1992) *Heterology and the Postmodern.* Duke University Press. P. 10
[901] Ibid p. 10

the earliest studies of formal order to reach elaborate development; for another, it specifically accords with THE LAW OF FIVES. It also is the shape of the United States Military Headquarters, the Pentagon Building, a most pregnant manifestation of straightjacket order resting on a firm foundation of chaos and constantly erupting into dazzling disorder; and this building is one of our more cherished Erisian shrines.[902]

The "Law of Fives," which was devised by Thornley, holds that "all incidents and events are directly connected to the number five, or to some multiple of five, or to some number related to five in one way or another, *given enough ingenuity on the part of the interpreter.*"[903] In this passage, we see here that the Pentagon is religiously esteemed for its synthetic value as a physical emanation of the seemingly antithetical forces of order and chaos. This synthesis entails a certain amount of nihilism since Wilson concludes that with the Law of Fives, "You have achieved Discordian enlightenment when you realize that, while the goddess Eris and the Law of Fives are not literally true, *neither is anything else.*"[904] Outside of a postmodern sense of emptiness, in Discordianism we can detect an almost Zen-like demand that the adept (if that word is applicable here) has to build up, via intellectual exercise, a deconditioned attitude towards the norms and conventions of a materialistic, and hence uninteresting, orderly society. The next group we will address takes this attitude to new and cartoonish (literally) heights.

The Church of the SubGenius

Malaclypse the Younger (2014) *Principia Discordia.* Lunatic Pope Press. P. 51
[903] Wilson, Robert Anton (2016) *Cosmic Trigger I: Final Secret of the Illuminati* (Second Edition). Hilaritas Press, LLC. P. 57
[904] Ibid p. 57

Unlike the Discordian Society, in which two guys from Whittier claim authorship, the Church of the SubGenius, which ostensibly was also founded by two guys – Reverend Ivan Stang (real name Douglass St Clair Smith) and Philo Drummond (real name Steve Wilcox) – in 1979, purports itself to be the religious handiwork of a mythical 1950s salesman/prophet named "J.R. Bob Dobbs." Bob Dobbs would go on to become the focal point of the SubGenius faith. His smiling, all-American, pipe-smoking visage is a postmodern encapsulation of the SubGenius narrative and belief system. The following is a brief overview.

J.R. "Bob" Dobbs was contacted by a divine entity, named Jehovah 1, through a television set he built in 1953. Jehovah 1 is representative of both the Abrahamic deity of the Bible, as well as pagan deities like Odin and Ra. Jehovah 1, whose wife is the goddess Eris, intended for Bob to play a leading role in a "conspiracy" against mankind. This conspiracy was to deprive humanity of "Slack." Bob, however, defected from this mission and began teaching his followers how to use their imagination and see through the cultural manipulations dominating Western society.

One of the secrets revealed to the chosen few who accept Bob's teachings is that they (the SubGenii) are descended from Yetis (mythical snow creatures in the Tibetan mountains, similar to Bigfoot).[905] Another is that humanity is surrounded by UFOs at all times, "brooding, impatient, waiting for the right moment to suddenly make themselves visible to us like a plague of metallic insects." [906] And lastly, that Bob is "protected by the very randomness of the Universe, for he himself is the *most* uncertain, random principle."[907] Bob Dobbs telepathically communicated the

---

[905] Referred to as "Yeti resurrected" in some texts. Dobbs, J.R. "Bob" (1994) *Revelation X* translated by The SubGenius Foundation, Inc. Fireside. P. vi

[906] Ibid p. viii

[907] Ibid p. 5

above information, and much more, to Philo Drummond in 1972, who would go on to convert Stang. Later that year the two began churning out the SubGenius propaganda, I mean teachings, in pamphlet form.

In contrast to the Discordians, SubGenius literature is heavily influenced by both comic book art, as well as advertisements found in comic books from the sixties and seventies. It often aims for humor for humor's sake and therefore evinces a much stronger sense of cynicism than the Discordians. Slogans such as "Give a man a fish, and you feed him for a day. Give a man a GUN, and OTHERS will feed him for a lifetime,"[908] and chapters like, "Outsmarted by UFOs? Now –Get Even!!" abound in SubGenius texts. Where the Discordians maintained a semblance of Zen transcendence and political dissidence in their utilization of pastiche and comedy, the Church of the SubGenius pushes past this and mocks even those counterculture ideals.

The goal of SubGenii's satire and mockery is the achievement of "Slack." Slack, as the name suggests, is not merely "laziness, but a kind of *active sloth*. It is what 'Bob' calls 'surfing the Luck Plane' – floating down the Path of Least Resistance – 'greasing the skids' and EXPLOITING your MISTAKES."[909] No mere Homer Simpson campaign slogan *à la* "Can't someone else do it?" to the SubGenii, Slack is infinite and indefinable. The primary motivation of the "Conspiracy" is to steal Slack from us by forcing us into work and tricking us into spending our money on marketed trinkets that offer only the illusion of True Slack.

Within the context of our analysis, we can see an interesting symmetry between the Rosicrucian mythos, which claimed to have been based on the writings of the mythical Christian Rosenkreuz, and the Church of the SubGenius, which claims *its* foundational documents to have been written by the inter-dimensional, time-travelling Bob Dobbs. A key aspect of our discussion regarding the Masonic and Rosicrucian groups in The

---

[908] Ibid p. 33
[909] Ibid p. xvi

Significance of the New World Order chapter pertained to the faculty of reason and how these groups essentially utilized literature and art as a means of preserving their esoteric knowledge; and how conspiracy theorists generally tend to overlook this aspect and focus instead on political influence and power. In a sense, groups like the Discordians and the Church of the SubGenius are adhering to the same path set out by the Masonic groups, the only difference being that their literature and art is explicitly humorous and iconoclastic. If Goethe or Voltaire was representative of the Masonic ethos of literature in their day, Philip K. Dick, the now defunct *World Weekly News*, Robert Anton Wilson, and film-maker Craig Baldwin would be the exemplars for this more recent, and more ironic, batch of esoteric orders.

It is no coincidence that these groups are indebted to postmodernism and the collapse of authoritative master-narratives. Whereas Freemasons and Rosicrucians might celebrate the air of mystery surrounding their rites and practices, they often denied the accusation that they were nefariously subverting society or crafting a New World Order. Groups like the Discordians, the Church of the SubGenius, and the San Francisco-based Cacophony Society simultaneously demystified their practices while over-aggrandizing the influence and control they have over politics and society at large.

In a historical sense, the strategy of these groups is reminiscent of an attitude towards reason that goes back to Diogenes, a Greek philosopher who lived in Athens in the mid-third century BC. During his lifetime, Diogenes preached a contrarian philosophy of poverty and lived virtue over theoretical scholasticism, which came to be identified with the philosophy of cynicism. He lived and ate unconventionally and would occasionally troll Plato during his lectures. A life well lived! The spirit of cynicism introduced by Diogenes was so iconoclastic and self-effacing that it eludes even radical philosophers of the modern era, such as Derrida, Foucault, and Peirce, largely because they were too serious, or at least took themselves too seriously. The philosophers who would become the true inheritors of

Diogenes's brand of cynicism are few and far between, and it is not unreasonable to suggest that the founders of these explicitly pseudo-religions should be included on such a short-list.

Conclusion

To finish up this chapter I wanted to home in a bit more closely on Davis's *High Weirdness* and a similarity it shares with one of the central themes of our work so far. Davis has a philosophical approach that, for the most part, combines pragmatism with empiricism, and from this position tackles the psychedelic legends of Terrence and Dennis McKenna, Robert Anton Wilson, and Phillip K. Dick. The theme that unifies the three sections of Davis's book is the seemingly external intrusion of an "alien" consciousness into the life of each respective case study.
In summation, Davis writes:

> The links between our psychonauts bring up the inevitable matter of comparison. On the one hand, Dick's experiences clearly resonated with the bouts of high weirdness suffered by both the McKennas and Robert Anton Wilson. We have a similar mix of sacred and profane, of extraterrestrial possibilities and paranoid conspiracies, of mystical databases, redemptive psychoses, and turbulent time loops – all of which suggested that the world as we know it is not at all what it seems. Like these men, Dick also availed himself of the postwar intellectual's bag of tricks: existentialism, psychoanalysis, experimental psychology, sociology, and comparative religion. Finally, he worked out the consequences of his experiences in reflexive and abidingly fascinating texts –novels and essays that themselves helped constitute the pulp canon of American weirdo

culture, even as they seeded that trash stratum with elusive memes of the sacred.[910]

The similarity, focusing on three characters,[911] resonates with one major aspect of our project, which is the singling out, and tracking of, Enoch, Melchizedek, and Hiram – one might even say that Davis's "elusive memes of the sacred" relates to the kind of murkiness and mystery that I have ascribed to these characters. The dichotomy between the three figures upon which Davis has chosen to base his work, and the three figures we have picked out of the periphery and tracked in their repetition, is analogous to the primary dichotomy of this book, i.e., between the Tower of Babel and the Twin Towers.

There are a variety of factors that constitute this dichotomy; one of them is the movement from myth-based narratives to ones that are science-based. The other factor, which is tied to the former but has less socio-historical significance, is that, in both cases, the earlier grouping deals with individuals and objects (Babel, Hiram, etc.) that are purely mythic. There is no way to conclusively prove they had an actual or concrete existence. Whereas the items in the later grouping (the Twin Towers, Philip K. Dick, etc.) are historically verifiable, for the time being – for we cannot say with certainty that they too will not fall into the realm of mythology at some point in the distant future.

Before we move on to the Twin Towers and confront the issue of scientism as the prevailing ethos of conspiracy theorization, I want to point out one final aspect of the dichotomy between the three modern figures Davis focused on and the three mythological figures that have reoccurred in our book. The three figures I drew attention to either created or participated in the

---

[910] Davis, Erik (2019) *High Weirdness: Drugs, Esoterica, and Visionary Experience in the Seventies*. Strange Attractor Press & the MIT Press. P. 270

[911] I'm essentially conflating the McKenna brothers into one character here for the sake of symmetry.

creation of myths. Because they were marginal, and not central, figures, their names circulated throughout history, in occult circles, up until the UFO age. The modern figures that Davis focuses on may well circulate into the indefinite future, but their primary significance is that they catalogued and repackaged the mythology and esotericism that had preceded them. In this respect, Davis's book is a biography of occult encyclopedists. If they foretold the future, they did so by reinterpretation and reiteration of the past. And now, without further ado, I present to you more of the past ...

Chapter Fourteen: 9/11, or Narrative at the Zero Degree

In the schema outlined in The Significance of the Cosmos chapter, we roughly outlined three narratives pertaining to the mythos of Genesis, which mark different stages of development:

1. The creation, wherein the world was authored by God. The Structuralist aspect of this reading is reinforced by Adam's naming of the animals.

2. Noah's Ark was a gathering up, cataloging and sorting of types (flora and fauna).

3. The Tower of Babel was a great dispersion of languages and language-based knowledge.

This essentially outlines a narrative of creation, followed by a cataloging and gathering together, then finally, dispersion. Noticeable in this schema is that the substance of what is under consideration moves from the concrete (or what we assume is concrete and externally existing to individual consciousness, i.e., the earth, animals, and plants) to a state of possession; in that all necessary animals and objects are resigned to a state of *belonging to*, or being under the guardianship of, Noah. And finally, we reach a state in which the signifiers of what had previously been taken for granted, as referring to physical substance, were not only dispersed but turned against their representational content, to the extent that they became unrecognizable to their users.

Rectifying this heterogeneity as it had occurred within the abstract space of language ought to be the central preoccupation of the more symbolic Biblical narratives that followed. The issuing of the Ten Commandments, for instance, can be interpreted in an explicit way as the codification of moral commands in the form of divinely inscribed laws. Conversely, on the reading I am offering here, the morality of the laws is merely a way of more firmly securing the act of linguistic coding; this act of reconciliation is then a repetition of the Noah's Ark narrative. Only the substance of the commands points to actions related to objects, not the objects themselves.

The Catholic doctrine of Christ's death as a representation of the rapprochement between God and Man, that the original sin which led to man's downfall was absolved by this execution, should also be interpreted in terms of linguistic coding. This is evident because the story of Christ is a tragic narrative that is consciously constructed to encompass pathos, irony (the "King of the Jews" placard), betrayal, and redemption. It represents Christ as a man who, through his sacrifice, repays humanity's debt to God.

This concept of repayment dovetails with Heidegger's discussion of the word, "outstanding":

> In Dasein there is inevitably a constant "fragmentariness" which finds its end in death. But may we interpret the phenomenal fact that this not-yet "belongs" to Dasein as long as it is to mean that it is something *outstanding*? With regard to what kind of beings do we speak of something outstanding? The expression means indeed what "belongs" to a being, but is still lacking. Outstanding, as lacking, is based on a belongingness. For example, the remainder of a debt still to be paid is outstanding. What is outstanding is not yet available. Liquidating the "debt" as paying off what is outstanding means that the money "comes in," that is, the remainder is paid in sequence, whereby the not-yet is, so to speak, filled out until the sum owed is "all together." Thus, to be outstanding means that what belongs together is not yet together.[912]

---

[912] Heidegger, Martin (1996) *Being and Time* translated by Joan Stambaugh, State University Press of New York. P. 225

The "fragmentariness" referred to in this passage is meant in an ontological sense of what is present-at-hand, which is Heidegger's contextual approach to discussing the absence of an absolute, objective, and linear experience of existence itself. In this respect, it resonates with the work of Lacan and Žižek, who following Freud, postulate a fissure or gap at the center of our being. For Lacan and Žižek this fissure exists insofar as we can distinguish ourselves from each other and from our environment. [913] However, since the existence of this fissure is traumatic in nature, we fill it in with narratives. So, how does all this relate to 9/11?

From "Technique" to Simulation

The three-part schema is a linear way of delineating how knowledge is generated, differentiates itself, and suffers dispersion. Myths and mythmaking, which are vital to the narratives in which we are interested, are primarily related to the first two categories. Obviously, myths can encapsulate all three stages within the stories they tell, but what they *do* is: generate, name, and codify via an oral tradition. Because their subject matter is pre-historical and opaque, effective myths replicate their subjects' sense of mystery when they are retold and dispersed. Myths, and the conspiracy theories generated from them, cultivate the kind of inquisitiveness usually evoked by ghost stories and detective novels. The more closely a conspiracy theory tries to hew to "facts," the more it sacrifices its narrative richness.

9/11 is the point at which conspiracy narratives evidently discarded all semblance of the mythical and attempted to lay

---

[913] This is a bit of an oversimplification on my part, Žižek discusses the nuanced web of incompatibilities between the Heideggerian and Lacanian schools of thought extensively in 1999's *The Ticklish Subject: The Absent Centre of Political Ontology.*

claim to that which is factual and scientifically verifiable. On the one hand, this signaled a closure of the era of conspiracy theorization that had proliferated prior to 9/11. On the other hand, in a performative sense, it conformed to the third stage of the schema: dispersion insofar as grounding the conspiracy theories on an appeal to science made them, ostensibly, more accessible to the uninitiated.

There is an additional, meta-aspect attendant to this repetition: the Tower of Babel, which for the sake of our over-arching narrative was the mythic and pre-historic antecedent of the 9/11 narrative, and was, in substance immaterial – it was a fiction that occurred in an imaginative space. In contrast, the Twin Towers in substance were a material part of the everyday modern world; they existed in a concrete space.

Now, what's to say that the Twin Towers will not go on to become mythic in their own right after a significant passage of time? That is certainly possible. However, I can only write from my own vantage point in history, therefore they seem real enough to me, though I never saw them in person.

In our discussion of political assassination, we briefly compared two sets of murky figures: the mythic trinity of Enoch, Hiram, and Melchizedek and the contemporary trinity of Foster, Rich, and Epstein. We noted that the latter trio were in possession of secrets and had been the subject of conspiracy theories. The question which we did not posit is: Are the conspiracy theories attached to these three modern figures able to acquire enough richness that will make them, over time, achieve mythic status? The answer to this question is "no." Their secrets relate to specific points of time in the ever-shifting sands of political intrigue. Also, the point of modernity at which these individuals perished was dominated by a scientistic, not mythic, sensibility.

However, for a few reasons, the same analysis does not hold for the Twin Towers. First, they were inanimate objects that served a variety of functions, some pragmatic and some symbolic. Second, despite being engineering triumphs (read: scientifically significant) the Twin Towers are associated with such a massive catastrophe that there is a very good chance that after a certain passage of time (perhaps a hundred years, maybe less, maybe more) they might accumulate a degree of mythological import that is on par with the Tower of Babel.

To better understand how modern society has transitioned away from myth we turn again to Jacques Ellul's theory of technique as it pertains to economics; which is fitting because the practical significance of the World Trade Center was essentially an economic one. Describing schools of economic theory and interpretation, Ellul claims that an air of secrecy and elitism has been created by the "technicians" who inhabit this pecuniary realm:

> The authority in which they clothe themselves takes the form of a secret vocabulary which is incomprehensible to the outsider even when it is employed, as often happens, to enunciate the most obvious facts. Technique always creates a kind of secret society, a closed fraternity of its practitioners. It is a new thing in the milieu of economics to note a kind of studied incommunicability. Up to now, every man with a little education was able to follow the works and theories of the economists. To be able to follow them today, one would have to be both a specialist and a technician.[914]

We see in this analysis how the participants in the stock market, great and small, achieve their position in concurrence with a degree of linguistic and conceptual acquisition. Possession of the specialized vocabulary qualifies one's position among the financial elite, and utilization of it grants the user a hand in the shaping of reality, e.g., the market. In this sense, the situation Ellul

---

[914] Ellul, Jacques (1964) *The Technological Society*. Vintage Books, A Division of Random House. P. 162

is describing is a postmodern reiteration of the Hermetic narrative, which we will address in a moment.

In a more philosophical sense, Robert Brandom argues that the norms we adopt, whether as a society or as a smaller group, are conceptually articulated via language.[915] In the context of modernity, language becomes the primary medium of recognition and mediation. When we carry this reading into the context of "State Power" (which is the topic Brandom is focusing his analysis on here) or an elite class (such as the financial insiders Ellul is focusing on), language creates the governing norms and the norms in turn demand sacrifice:

> Those individuals actualize State Power by relinquishing the pursuit of their private interests, sacrificing their subjective attitudes for the sake of, and so identifying with, the norms that State Power thereby embodies and actualizes.[916]

Market mastery does encompass (or simulate) sacrificial and initiatory aspects associated with the Hermetic tradition, as films like Oliver Stone's *Wall Street* (1987) emphasize the sacrificing of ethics for entrance to the world of high finance. But, in contrast to the more ritualistic instantiations of Hermeticism, it is a world that is bereft of artistry. There might be innovation at play, but it operates in a rote and prescribed manner. It is for this reason, as well as the rarified economic jargon intended to isolate the lay person from a comprehensive understanding of the workings of the market, that many have claimed the economy has more to do with appearances than actuality.

It is only with the almost scripted demise of the towers that we get an uncanny sense of artistry at play – perhaps this is

---

[915] Brandom, Robert (2019) *A Spirit of Trust: A Reading of Hegel's Phenomenology*. Belknap Press of Harvard University Press. P. 506
[916] Ibid p. 506

why the composer Karlheinz Stockhausen compared the attacks to a symphony? The base desire to impose a narrative on the event, since merely the presence of narrative provides a modicum of reassurance, is where 9/11 conspiracy theories originate. We have reached a stage in modernity where people cannot deal with major catastrophes that erupt from randomness, so there must be some agency planning and executing such events. We have, to borrow an expression from David Foster Wallace, grown accustomed to our cage of simulation. So, what are some of the trinkets decorating said cage? They are either Hallmark Channel style platitudes or conspiracy theories... and I'm all out of platitudes, so here's some conspiracy theories.

The Nuts and Bolts of 9/11

When 9/11 conspiracy theories first started to circulate it is reasonable to assume that normal people grasped the gist of them without needing to hear all of the details. I say this because eleven months prior to the attack, George W. Bush had been elected president after a bitterly contested election. Bush was thus reviled by half of the country, as well as the majority of the media; and therefore a national emergency in which his primary duty was to console/avenge a grieving nation could be seen by even the most casual of cynics as a callous attempt to cast his administration in a better light. This is an accessible enough starting-point to the slightly curious down a rabbit-hole of conspiratorial thinking.

David Ray Griffin argues that there are two basic theories arising from 9/11. The first, he calls the "official conspiracy theory," which claims, "The attacks of 9/11 were planned and executed solely by al-Qaeda terrorists under the guidance of Osama bin Laden."[917] This is the "official" narrative of the event and was promulgated by the Bush Administration. The second

---

[917] Griffin, David Ray (2005) *The 9/11 Commission Report: Omissions and Distortions*. Olive Branch Press. P. 5

conspiracy theory, which Griffin calls the "alternative theory" comes in "weak" and "strong" versions. The weak version is that the Bush Administration, or members of the intelligence community, knew about the attacks but either did nothing, or didn't do enough, to prevent them. The strong version of the alternative theory is that "the Bush Administration was actively involved in the planning and execution of the attacks."[918]

Being a trained philosopher, Griffin is most compelling when he focuses on the texts surrounding the event, specifically the 9/11 Commission Report. Griffin found the background of the 9/11 Commission to be highly questionable, as it was headed by Philip Zelikow, who had been an advisor to then-Secretary of State Condoleezza Rice.[919] According to Griffin, his job as the executive director of the 9/11 Commission was to formulate a narrative that "presupposed the truth of the official conspiracy theory from the outset."[920] Hence, in the eyes of conspiracy theorists everywhere, the 9/11 Commission Report would be just a reiteration of the Warren Commission Report.

When it comes to digging into the materialistic aspirations of the 9/11 "truther" movement, Griffin does not disappoint. What he states in the following paragraph encapsulates the entirety of the scientistic kind of reasoning that permeates nearly every 9/11 conspiracy theory:

> One problem is that fire had never before caused steel-frame high-rise buildings to collapse, even when the fire was a very energetic, all-consuming one, such as the 1991 fire at One Meridian Plaza in Philadelphia. Indeed, tests had been performed to see if very hot fires could cause steel-frame buildings to collapse, as the report on Building 7 of the WTC by FEMA (the Federal Emergency

---

[918] Ibid p. 5
[919] Ibid pp. 8 - 9
[920] Ibid p. 11

Management Agency) pointed out. The Commission says that to its knowledge, "none of the [fire] chiefs present believed that a total collapse of either tower was possible." This might be regarded as an implicit acknowledgement on the Commission's part that no such collapse had ever occurred before.[921]

The 9/11 Commission Report itself reiterates the two most salient components of contemporary conspiracy theorization, both of which eschew mythological thinking in favor of scientific-materialism; these are the questions of "who?" – which actors were involved – and "how?" – what are the technical means attendant to this tragedy? The quote by Griffin is one of countless scientifically oriented analyses propagated on the internet, most of which point to the theory that the planes crashing into the towers were a cover for a controlled demolition by explosives placed in the basements of the buildings. Some conspiracy theorists have gone so far as to speculate that planes never hit the towers and what was televised was in fact a series of holograms – Griffin does not endorse this theory, but it is an example of what he refers to as the "alternative" conspiracy theory narrative.

In researching the "who" of 911, Griffin meticulously tracks the questionable trajectories of all the known hijackers, suspicious flights that were allowed out of the US for Saudi nationals after the attacks,[922] payments made by Pakistan's Inter-Services Intelligence agency to suspected hijackers,[923] prior US financial support for al-Qaeda, and most importantly the Bush Administration, which framed the events of the day as "a new Pearl Harbor."[924]

---

[921] Ibid p. 25
[922] Ibid pp. 71 - 74
[923] Ibid p. 104
[924] Ibid p. 118

The obvious implication of this last assertion, which was a fundamental component of JFK conspiracy theorization, is that the deep state engineered a tragic event to drastically increase military spending – with the corresponding possibility of military escalations. The fact that this spending did increase, as well as the wars that were started following 9/11, it is understandable that one of the components of Griffin's theory is that even if the 9/11 Commission Report evinced a sense of bipartisanship, its thesis had been largely corralled by Republicans, specifically Republicans in thrall to the power of the Bush Administration. Many 9/11 conspiracy theorists, due to their overwhelming contempt for George W. Bush, would incorporate an implicit favorable bias towards the Democratic Party into their narratives.

This contrasted with the conspiracy theories that reached their golden age in the 80s and 90s and were relatively apolitical because theorists were disenchanted with the whole Western democratic process and believed life itself was doomed to be controlled by unknown forces outside the theorist's control. Politicians, in this schema, were at best seen as actors controlled by shadowy figures. The comedian Bill Hicks summarized this sentiment with a routine in which he speculated that whichever candidate winning the presidential election was brought into a secret room and shown a film of the Kennedy assassination from a never-before-seen angle and then asked, "Any questions?" To wit, said candidate would respond: "Just one: what's my agenda?"

From a philosophical point of view, we can understand coherent political discourse as an endeavor that presupposes a dialectical process of reconciliation, or dialogue, that would ideally lead to some form of resolution. The golden age conspiracy theorist, however, was a heterogeneous element suspicious of the possibility of such a reconciliation (as would any skeptic) that also doubted the integrity of the system itself, as well as the players. To the conspiracy theorist (prior to 9/11) these individuals ought to be thought of as merely actors. In this way, the conspiracy theorist formulated a new set of norms that was his group's proxy within the pluralistic battle for political hegemony. When 9/11 brought politics to the foreground it neutralized this radically subjective discursive component of conspiracy theorization, which was the only component that conspiracy theorists could advance within the struggle for political dominance. Resigned political affiliation and a semblance of faith in the political process would then signal the death of the Golden Age of conspiracy theories.

An additional problem 9/11 brought to the forefront was that it reinvented the conspiracy theorist's agenda as wholly reactionary in nature; it did not posit anything that could adequately replace the ruling ideology. What became most ascertainable from 9/11 – which was only hinted at from UFO, Illuminati, and JFK obsessives – is that now there was a definitive point: subscription to the idea that 9/11 was "an inside job," which demarcated a group of people as legitimately crazy. This reinforced what Žižek called the "cliché about conspiracy theories [being] the poor man's ideology":

> "When individuals lack the elementary cognitive mapping capabilities and resources that would enable them to locate their place within a social totality, they invent conspiracy theories which provide an ersatz mapping, explaining all the complexities of social life as the result of a hidden conspiracy." [925]

This move towards explicitly delegitimizing movements that questioned the official narrative is unfortunate, insofar as the anti-war movements that sprang up in the wake of the attacks were the last unironic (and unsimulated) countercultural

---

[925] Žižek, Slavoj (2006) *The Parallax View*. Massachusetts Institute of Technology. P. 375

movement that would stake a legitimate and defined place within the national conversation.[926]

The Reduction Point

The Reduction Point is the fundamental element to which each reductionist conspiracy theory boils down. Oftentimes, the conspiracy theorist boiled things down to a group or individual, but the conspiracy still contained an opacity or "murkiness" that prevented it from total exposure. 9/11 changed this, as it was explicitly tied to an object; and as Deleuze pointed out, our natural inclinations, which he calls "objectivism," tempt us into attributing to the object the signs it emits. 9/11, like the fruit in the Garden of Eden, tempts us into the clutches of scientism and entices us with the promise of transparency, or the end of "murkiness."

Likewise, the groups caught up in the 9/11 narrative become objectivized, more so than the groups and individuals caught up in the JFK narrative who still exhibited some trace of myth. The myth is now gone with 9/11, but it is not completely dead. It will reawaken, but before it does it must replicate the panic and hysteria wrought by the destruction of the Twin Towers. In Baudrillard's final book, *The Agony of Power*, he states that:

> The West, having destroyed its own values, finds itself back at the zero degree of symbolic power, and in a turnabout, it wants to impose the zero degree on everyone. It challenges the rest of the world to annihilate itself symbolically as well. It demands that the rest of the world enter into its

---

[926] I will grant that the "Occupy Wall St." movement might be a contender for this last gasp of a legitimate leftist protest, however it was not as big or as clearly articulated as the anti-war movement of the early aughts.

game, participate in the generalized, planetary exchange and fall into its trap [...] There is a moral and philosophical confrontation, almost a metaphysical one, beyond Good and Evil. Islam? The United States? It doesn't matter! There is a confrontation between two powers. It is an asymmetrical potlatch between terrorism and global power, and each side fights with its own weapons. Terrorism wagers the death of terrorists, which is a gesture with tremendous symbolic power and the West responds with its complete powerlessness. But this powerlessness is also a challenge.[927]

This relates directly to the Argument from Hyperreality and is a claim whose validity relies on the idea that parody and masquerade are means by which power operates in our society.[928] Notice that the power referenced in this passage is "symbolic power," which is linked to the idea of Symbolic Exchange, and, for our purposes here, can defined explicitly in terms of sacrifice.

When Baudrillard talks about how "power" has replaced "dominance" does he mean these terms in a metaphysical or discursive sense, e.g., "the discourse of power" or the "discourse of dominance"? He is cagey on this point, and I think his point in

[927] Baudrillard, Jean (2010) *The Agony of Power*. Semiotext(e), p. 114

[928] "When people make fun of the carnival, the masquerade of the elections in America every four years, they are being too hasty. In the name of critical thought, of very European, very French thought, we do a contemptuous analysis of this kind of parody and self-denial. But we are wrong, because the empire of simulation, of simulacra, of parody, but also of networks, constitutes the true global power. It is more founded on this than on economic control." Ibid, pp. 114 - 115

The Agony of Power is that the dialectic between a discursive and metaphysical model (which is essentially what the Structuralist vs. Hermeneutical debate amounts to for many) has been superseded by the current stage of hyperreality in which we find ourselves. It seems as if the destruction of the World Trade Center not only inaugurated a full immersion into hyperreality, but also, in doing so, indicated that this state of immersion was itself an endpoint of sorts.

It is in the sense of an endpoint that we can bring up a feature of Biblical prophecy that is explicitly tied to the "end times:" namely, the appearance of the "Antichrist." This subject, as you can intuit, is a product of Right-wing, Christian conspiracy theorization. The appearance of the Antichrist in the Bible occurs in the Gospel of John but is presaged by Matthew 24 and Mark 13. (There is also some debate as to whether the Book of Daniel prophesied such a figure in its depictions of conflicts between a northern and southern king that would occur at the end of time.) At the time of 9/11 and the ensuing Operation Desert Storm, many conspiracy theorists speculated that the Antichrist might be Osama bin Laden or possibly Saddam Hussein, thus replacing the more mythologically-charged idea that it might have been someone like Aleister Crowley (who hyperbolically referred to himself as the "Beast 666") or a much less intriguing figure that will eventually oversee the finalization of globalism and usher in the "New World Order."

This last characterization of the Antichrist fits into the present analysis, specifically in relation to Wayne's insistence that the Antichrist be the reoccurrence of Nimrod, the King of Shinar. This is a narratively astute move on Wayne's part as it obliquely draws attention to the reverberations made by the mythical Tower of Babel that have reached our present day. Wayne asserts that within our modern and sci-fi obsessed culture, "Babel" will refer to "a future that is prophesying humankind will be united, speaking with one voice, living under one government and one religion, centered in a universal life force, all in the tradition of *Star Wars* and the Tower of Babel, which will ultimately be replaced with the Luciferian religion once the Antichrist takes power."

It doesn't stop there, however. Wayne ties man's technological hubris to these dire words of prophesy, and it is not too much at this point to imagine the "ziggurat of technology" as a proxy that has been repeated, and will continue to be repeated:

> All this will be an opportunistic venue for the modern Nimrod to wave his fist at God in complete rebellion, to climb the ziggurat of technology and knowledge to wage battle with the oppressive Adonai, just as Nimrod of Babel had threatened to do. Scripture says, It [the Antichrist] grew until it reached the host of the heavens and it threw some of the starry host down to the earth and trampled on them" (Dan 8:10) The world will be led into a galactic war through this alien deception.[929]

This reoccurrence of Nimrod, not only as the Antichrist, but as a steward for the technology of which the ancient Tower of Babel was merely a precursor, is fascinating in light of its contrast with the theory that Melchizedek was an incarnation of Christ who blessed Abraham. It's almost as if the Biblical text allows these definite figures (or their signifiers) to bounce around from one context to another. In this respect, the character of Nimrod takes on some of the murky characteristics we ascribed to Hiram, Enoch, and Melchizedek in our narrative analysis. The fact that Wayne is looking forward to the future and whatever problems we might have with aliens therein, means he is neglecting the elephant in the room: the twin ziggurats of technology and capital that were destroyed on September 11, 2001, and how they might have served as a modern reiteration of the Babel narrative.

---

[929] Wayne, Gary (2014) *The Genesis 6 Conspiracy*. Trusted Books, A Division of Deep River Books. Pp. 351 - 352

The Pain of Confirmation

In his analysis of 9/11, Baudrillard makes a variety of interesting comments. One of the less novel ones, which had occurred to mainstream pundits of the time, was that once the second tower was struck, a sense of confirmation that what was happening was a concerted attack and not merely an "accident" became a stark realization.[930] Morris Berman, who designates 9/11 as an epoch-defining moment for America, uses a definitional tone in his assessment:

> What the United States did in the rest of the world, it did with a vengeance in the Middle East. The same overzealous policy of military containment, which created so much havoc at home and abroad, proved to be especially destructive in its application to countries such as Iran and Iraq. Once one knows the history of all this, it is no great stretch of the imagination to conclude that the events of September 11 were the tragic but inevitable outcome of our foreign policy in that part of the world.[931]

The history Berman is referring to amounts to a cultural clash that existed between Islam and the globalization marshaled by the West, a dialectical tension that 9/11 made explicit. Berman characterizes these antithetical attitudes as "tribalism" and "secularism," respectively. Tribal societies are heavily dominated by culture and tradition, don't separate church and state, and tend to place the community above the liberties of the individual.

---

[930] Baudrillard, Jean (2003) *The Spirit of Terrorism* translated by Chris Turner. Verso. P. 42

[931] Berman, Morris (2006) *Dark Ages America: The Final Phase of Empire.* W.W. Norton & Company. P. 159

Secular societies, in contrast, separate church and state, and prioritize the freedom of the individual to be "left alone."[932] Berman sees the positives and negatives of both attitudes and goes at great length to describe the alienation, indifference, and technological dependence of a secular society like the U.S., as well as the fundamentalism and sometimes brutal treatment of some Islamic regimes. The issue of technology is where the two perspectives get blurred:

> On the one side, then, faith over reason, and the community over the individual; on the other, the notion that the whole world is and should be little more than one big supermarket. However, it is no longer quite so stark as this; there are a lot of crossovers. The *souks* of Aleppo are now probably selling jeans from the Gap; evangelical Christians in the Midwest hold bible study meetings in Starbucks [...][933]

And it was, of course, technology that facilitated the carnage of 9/11. Baudrillard's analysis of the globalization symbolized by the World Trade Center and its inevitable clash with the more traditional Islamic culture adds degrees of metaphysical symbolism to Berman's historical-political analysis: the Twin Towers were "perfect embodiments" of definitive order. [934] "Definitive order" here refers to a situation in which global power has monopolized the constituents of reality to such an extent that alternatives to global capitalism cannot be imagined without a violence of thought:

---

[932] Ibid pp. 82 - 84
[933] Ibid p. 94
[934] Baudrillard, Jean (2003) *The Spirit of Terrorism* translated by Chris Turner. Verso. P. 6

It was the system itself which created the objective conditions for this brutal retaliation. By seizing all the cards for itself, it forced the Other to change the rules. And the new rules are fierce ones, because the stakes are fierce. To a system whose very excess of power poses an insoluble challenge, the terrorists respond with a definitive act which is also not susceptible of exchange. Terrorism is the act that restores an irreducible singularity to the heart of a system of generalized exchange.[935]

Baudrillard sees this singularity, encapsulated in the events of 9/11, as the opening shots of a war in which triumphant globalization begins battling itself.[936] The fall of the Twin Towers allegorically refers back to their long-lost, and possibly imaginary, predecessor, the Tower of Babel. However, within the context of this reading, the Tower of Babel was thwarted by the intervention of God, whereas the spirit of global capitalism, which informs and qualifies the World Trade Center, ends up being an inherently self-defeating strategy that turns around and destroys the structures embodying it. This inherent alterity to something taken to be coherent repeats the Structuralist idea of there being a fissure located within the center of being (discussed in the beginning of the chapter). One might even argue that the towers, being duplicates of each other, were a concrete realization of this fundamental sense of division or incongruity. According to the "official" theory promoted by the Bush Administration, the sense of confirmation – that this was indeed an attack – disenchanted many Americans with the realization that other countries hate them and are willing to go to unbelievable ends to displace them from the perch of global dominance. Therefore, the conspiracy theorist's attempt to situate this malevolence within the government itself is both an attempt to deny this international

935 Ibid p. 9
936 Ibid p. 11

enmity as well as an attempt to reconcile the sense of subjective incongruity that has manifested in almost every sphere of our society.

The ascertainment of this incongruity at a global level, which was architecturally instantiated by the Twin Towers, inevitably births a singularity:

> In the case of the Twin Towers, something particular is added: precisely their symmetry and their twin-ness. There is, admittedly, in this cloning and perfect symmetry an aesthetic quality, a kind of perfect crime against form, a tautology of form which can give rise, in a violent reaction, to the temptation to break that symmetry, to restore an asymmetry, and hence a singularity.[937]

Baudrillard views this attempt by the terrorists to restore asymmetry as illusory, pointing out that terrorism is ultimately a working part of the global network that brought it into the world. However, there is another duplication at play here: the symbolic confirmation of existence each tower offered the other was repeated, traumatically, by the confirmation instantiated by the second tower being struck. In emotional terms, confirmation allows for grief to be fully experienced. Paradoxically, grief then demands answers to questions surrounding the concluding event, but because of its somberness tends to push the explanations away from the materialistic plain of explanation and into a more metaphysical realm. Our society has tried to insulate us from this emotion primarily by way of simulation ever since that fateful day; and the media has played a tremendous role in this, as Baudrillard states: "There is no 'good' use of the media; the media are part of the event, they are part of the terror, and they work in both directions."[938]

---

[937] Ibid p. 42
[938] Ibid p. 31

One Final Post-Structuralist Reading of 9/11

In this book we have evaluated the "significance" of events and figures primarily in terms of synchronicity, allegory, and myth. All three aspects have demanded a certain amount of factual, or for the skeptically minded, textual material. We have seen that, in relation to subjects such as the Grail, the Templars, and the similarities between Atlantis and the Antediluvian world, there has been an extraordinary amount of synchronicity – so much so that exhaustively pointing out each one would have derailed the accounts themselves. When it comes to 9/11 there doesn't seem to be any profound sense of synchronicity. There was the possibility that the event was predicted by Steve Jackson's *Illuminati* card game, but if that was truly prophetic, it is a separate issue. The essence of synchronicity as it pertains to 9/11 is contained totally and superficially within the material details pertaining to the event itself. 9/11 is bereft of meaningful synchronicity. Now, there is one numerological caveat to my claim which has to do with the fact that this disastrous attack occurred on the date of "9-11," which is the number that, we here in America, dial for emergency services.[939] So, there is a degree of ominous synchronicity at play here, however, the reference point is not ancient in any respect, but contemporaneous with the buildings that were destroyed.

In terms of narrative richness, 9/11 as a source-point for conspiracy theories is not merely bereft – it is a black hole. At first glance, it is not grounded in any readily ascertainable mythos, and the conspiracy theories that had presaged it were swallowed up in its wake and replaced by scientific analysis. However, in a way loosely analogous to Roger Penrose's theory that the universe is not merely instigated by one big bang followed by collapse but is a series of big bangs and collapses that goes on infinitely, 9/11 is like a black hole that absorbs and destroys mythical meaning, but

---

[939] In the UK they dial "119."

which will eventually collapse, spawning a new "big bang" of conspiratorial mythos.[940]

There is a new category of conspiracy theorization that avails itself to us at this stage of modernity that involves the replacement of synchronicity with prophecy. A case in point is an episode of an *X Files* spinoff show, called *The Lone Gunmen*, which aired an episode in March of 2001 showing a false flag attack being planned on the World Trade Center.[941] As with the Titanic narrative, there is a literary antecedent to the events that followed the tragedy as well, in the form of the character Emmanuel Goldstein, who was a villain presented to the population of Oceania in *1984* – in the novel he is declared to be a traitor and only appears on television screens to incite the population. Some conspiracy theorists described the media's dissemination of Osama bin Laden's image (but never in the flesh so to speak) as a realization of Orwell's "prediction." [942] Technically speaking, the individuals who initially put forward this idea (William L. Anderson, Cass Sunstein, etc.) were not conspiracy theorists; the point they were making was a sociological. In this respect, the discussion revolves around how literary devices are incorporated into political and social narratives. On a more conspiratorial note, the question is less about whether an act of literature has predictive powers than if

---

[940] Obviously the analogy is not perfect since Penrose is describing cosmology and we are describing an anthropological/sociological phenomena -nevertheless, both come to us in narrative structure.

[941] I will pursue this more in our discussion of the Mandela Effect: questions such as "how far in advance are these things planned?" "Are they planned at all?" "Do people that predict these things in artistic mediums write on the behalf of the secret groups who orchestrate events or are they tapped into a primal source of information, such as the universe itself?"

[942] https://en.m.wikipedia.org/wiki/Emmanuel_Goldstein accessed on 04/20/20.

the author possesses a certain acuity about human nature that leads to a type of intuition, which, when put in writing, might be mistaken for predictive powers.

This return to older narratives, in which the reading of how pop-cultural artifacts (books, games, TV shows, etc.) prefigured disastrous events, has been a reoccurring theme in our discussion. So far, we have noted how conspiracy theorists speculated that Jules Verne's 1865 novel, *From the Earth to the Moon* predicted the moon landing, Crowley's *Book of the Law* predicted World War II, and Morgan Robertson's 1898 novel, *The Wreck of the Titan: Or Futility* predicted the sinking of the Titanic.

This type of recontextualization is attendant to the readings people have made of John's reiteration of the Genesis narrative in the opening of his Gospel. You'll recall that, following Andrew Weeks's analysis, the perspective of a proper historical rendering of sequential events depicted in the Gospels, is replaced by a perspective of timeless immediacy and presence:

> In the Prolog of John, the Word is paradoxically immanent and transcendent. The Word acts in creation, yet remains unto itself, remains *with* God, and *is* God. The self-identity of the eternal Word is therefore dynamic: an identity that gives rise changelessly, which resides in eternity while entering into time. This duality is matched by the light that shines in the darkness, but cannot be comprehended by the darkness. Where the creation account in Genesis represented God through his actions, and his actions in terms of our world of time, space, matter, and number, John instead places transcendence and immanence abruptly vis-à-vis one another. The becoming of the world is refracted through the eye of eternity. If we regard

the created world as a riddle, implicit in Genesis, this riddle now moves into the forefront in John.[943]

This redoubling, and the space that it allots for the passage of time – we might say that it has a "reverence" for the passage of time, acknowledges that the future is not fully accessible to the artist in the time of his writing, painting, or whatever. But that this artistic act, because of its reverential nature, will eventually sync up at a future modally relevant date[944] and that it is *significant* not only because of this inevitability but also because, as a text, it can be revisited countless times.

The potential for countless revisitations that can yield new readings is part of what we have called "narrative richness" and it is endemic to mythology. Both accounts of the creation of the world in the Bible are rich in this sense. However, the perspectival shift in John adds an additional layer of richness that has informed philosophy and theology more than the Genesis account. It is a narrative that has made greater headway into the modern world, so-to-speak.[945] This predictive type of writing does not occupy the bulk of mythical transposition. The majority of the narratives we have analyzed prefigure future events in a more symbolic way: Melchizedek prefigures Jesus, Atlantis is a prefiguration of the Biblical Flood, Seqenenre Tao prefigures

---

[943] Weeks, Andrew (1993) *German Mysticism: From Hildegard of Bingen to Ludwig Wittgenstein*. State University of New York Press. Pp. 20 - 21

[944] I insert the concept of modality here to cover the bases of contingency. Obviously alternate realities discussed by conspiracy theorists are analogous to "possible worlds" as discussed by philosophers. We will briefly address modality and possible worlds in the next chapter insofar as they relate to the flexibility of what we take to be "the real world." However, a full scholarly exegesis on the topic is beyond me and I would direct the interested reader to John Divers's (2002) *Possible Worlds.*

[945] Specifically with the concept of "Logocentrism."

Hiram Abif, Arthur prefigures JFK, etc. These figures, as they arise historically, are reinscriptions of the older names, and as we move forward in time they lose a degree of their narrative richness.

This is also the case with the Twin Towers narrative being a reiteration of the Tower of Babel, but there is an interesting bit of mythological significance in relation to 9/11 and one of the three murky figures who have reoccurred throughout our narrative. I'll grant that, if the Illuminati or Freemasons, had anything to do with the event, then, possibly there is a very tenuous connection to Hiram Abif. Possibly, if the building was demolished from the ground level with explosives there could be an architectural motif that connects everything in a thematic way. And while there is no discernable connection with Melchizedek, with Enoch there might be something significant. As we've seen, Enoch is an inherently dualistic figure and the confusion between the stories of the two characters bearing that name exhibits a dependency that existed between the two towers themselves, as well between the World Trade Center as a unit and their prehistorical predecessor. The Tower of Babel had no double at its time of creation; however, in a hermeneutical sense it does now.

Enoch of Cain performs the function of doubling the more well-known descendent of Seth. We can interpret this role as merely literary, metaphysical, or somewhere in-between. Just as the Tower of Babel had to reach its completion once it was researched, analyzed, and mythologized hundreds and thousands of years after its supposed completion, the codependency of the two Enochs had to be revealed in hindsight. The co-dependency I am stressing here rests upon the concept of the soul and its alterity from the body it inhabits. In relation to this, Baudrillard posits that the idea of a soul arose in accord with the principle of unification, which was an inchoate concept stemming from a more primitive spirituality ascertaining "Shadow, spectre, reflection, image" as instantiations of the "Double." This duplicate self could be a chimera borne out of a misapprehension of the fundamental fissure, or break, residing at the center of the subject. Baudrillard states that the concept of the soul represents a reconciliation of sorts that the concept of a "double" only exacerbated:

> On the contrary, the historical advent of the 'soul' puts an end to a proliferating exchange with spirits and doubles which, as an indirect consequence, gives rise to another figure of the double, wending its diabolical way just beneath the surface of Western reason. Once again, this figure has everything to do with the Western figure of alienation, and nothing to do with the primitive double.[946]

In this final poststructuralist (and super dense) analysis, the doubling inherent to a modern structure like the World Trade Center physically and textually embodied the alienation of late-stage capitalism and total globalization. With that said, now we turn to the issue of "false flags" of which many conspiracy theorists have claimed 9/11 was a prime example.

Sandy Hook and the Rise of the False Flags

The concept of a "false flag" attack is derived from a tactic wherein pirates would fly a national flag to deceive a ship they were planning to attack. This move was translated into land battles and used during WWI and WWII. 9/11, being an event of such political and cultural magnitude, prompted individuals in conspiracy theory circles to wonder if it had been staged by the government, or rogue agencies within the government under the guise of foreign nationals, thereby ushering in the era of false flag hysteria. This theory would then be extended to various domestic incidents that occurred throughout the 'aughts.

---

[946] Baudrillard, Jean (2007) *Symbolic Exchange and Death*. Sage Publications Ltd. P. 161

The mass shooting phenomena, which began in the late-1990s, ought to be seen as a follow-up to the serial-killer hysteria that had gripped the 1970s and 1980s. Outside of Charles Manson, who wasn't himself a serial killer but is kind of godfather to them all, there aren't really any conspiracy theories around these guys; and they're pretty much all guys: John Wayne Gacy, Jeffrey Dahmer, Richard Ramirez, Ted Bundy etc. There's a certain mythos to some of them, Ed Gein for instance, but it's impossible to tell how much of the mythology around him was the result of *Psycho* and *The Texas Chainsaw Massacre* – two movies that claim to be loosely based on his actions. The shift from this more macabre and ghoulish form of death and terror to a more random and impersonal model occurred during the cultural changes of the 1990s, beginning with the capture and beating of Richard Ramirez by gang members in the streets of Los Angeles and reaching the point at which it deserved a name with the murder of Gianni Versace by Andrew Cunanan in April 1997. Dubbed a "spree killing" by the media at the time, a whole host of mass-shootings would follow, some notable ones being the Thurston High School shooting on May 21, 1998, the North Hollywood shootout on February 28, 1997, and the Columbine High School massacre on April 20, 1999.

If we read the serial killer phenomena of the 70s and 80s as a repetition of the disenchantment that occurred after the fall from Eden, wherein the "free love hippy" age gives way to a dangerous and incomprehensible reality that is embodied by sinister figures lurking in the shadows, the hysteria surrounding those figures was directed, and intensified, by the media and horror films. The mass-shootings, though, can be read as a more scientifically oriented codification of violent outbursts, one which interprets them almost as if they were analogous to natural disasters.

To be clear, this is not an "either-or" distinction: there were mass-shootings during the age of serial killers and serial killers in the age of mass-shootings; however, here we are looking at the phenomena that defines the era. Also, it is important to stipulate that TV news, programs, and movies are not wholly dictating the significance of these events at this point in history; to some extent they are, but for the most part, they are along for the ride. The move from the intentional terror of the serial killer phenomenon to the mass-shooting phenomenon is more of an emergent cultural shift that we should be hesitant to designate as being totally dictated by one personage or group.[947]

Mass-shootings continue to be the dominant means of violent intrusion into the social order, and since 9/11 the media has characterized several of these shootings as political violence; it is in this regard that the issue of them being staged events, or false flags, gained greater circulation. The false flag accusation can be construed as either the attacker was a federal agent, or had been primed by federal agents, or the entire thing was staged, and no event took place – conspiracy theorists, such as Alex Jones, have fixated on Sandy Hook as a prime example of this. With the claim that these mass shootings are false flag attacks orchestrated by the federal government to limit, and then eventually abolish, the Second Amendment, also comes the conspiratorial notion of "crisis actors." Crisis actors are individuals who portray nearby bystanders or victims of these tragedies.

The accusation of a false flag attack has explicit political connotations, even if the person making the accusation cannot clearly delineate who they believe is behind the event. For instance, for a few years after 9/11 *Rolling Stone* magazine would occasionally make a casual reference to one of their interviewees "questioning the official 9/11 narrative." This was not done to ridicule or marginalize the celebrity being profiled but instead to portray them as questioning the establishment, because that's what's cool, right? However, once George W. Bush was out of office and Barack Obama took his place, questioning 9/11, unless you were specifically attacking the Bush Administration, was not acceptable.

---

[947] Though there have been conspiracy theorists who speculated that Jack the Ripper was committing "Masonic murders."

Sandy Hook was an event where (some) Right-wing conspiracy theorists denied the event outright, whereas an event like the Las Vegas Route 91 Harvest Music Festival shooting in 2017 was too big to be denied. Interestingly, there was no mention in Right-wing media of crisis actors in Las Vegas, but instead a more concerted attack on the "liberal mainstream media" for not pursuing information surrounding shooter Stephen Paddock more thoroughly. This can't be due solely to the size of the Las Vegas shooting, as the additional factor for attacking the media and not positing the presence of crisis actors had to do with the fact that the people killed at the festival primarily matched the demographic of Trump supporters. There are a variety of conspiracy theories that sprang up around Stephen Paddock – that he had been contracted by the CIA, etc. – but whatever the circumstances of the event or his motivations, he has been subsumed into the black hole of mysterious anonymity that consumed other notorious figures like Jeffrey Epstein and Lee Harvey Oswald.

With 9/11 and all the conspiracies that followed it, scientism is the rule, and this rule demands culprits who could conceivably be held guilty in a court of law. Just as recently as October 2019 we have seen some victims of the 9/11 terror attack seek compensation from Saudi Arabia for the role it played in the hijackings. Federal officials will not declassify a 2012 report that detailed the ties between Saudi Arabia and the hijackers because it might endanger national security. Living in the hyperreal context of postmodernity and confronted with these enigmatic and impersonal figures, whether Osama bin Laden or Jeffrey Epstein, who cannot be "called" to account for their purported actions in a meaningful way, the whole affair has to suffer dissimulation through litigation and pecuniary compensation, thus reinforcing the sense of indirectness attendant to our mythologically bereft state-of-affairs.

The Rise of the Surveillance State

Orwell's *1984* plays one more, crucial, role in our tracking of narratives in the aftermath of 9/11 which is its depiction of the state monitoring its citizens. The average American today, even if they are not conspiratorially minded, probably assumes that the US Government is monitoring a great deal of their cell phone communications. If pressed, most of the people who assume so can pinpoint the agency that is doing this monitoring as the NSA. But what is the NSA and from where did it come?

The National Security Agency was founded on November 4, 1952, which was coincidentally around the same time that an encryption coding firm named Crypto AG was founded by Boris Hagelin (also in 1952). Hagelin came to the fore of the enterprise because he had been the primary investor in AB Cryptoteknik, a company founded in 1920 by Swedish engineer Arvid Gerhard Damm, who had patented the C-36 mechanical cryptograph machine in the early 1920s. Hagelin, who was also an inventor, took over the company after Damm's death in 1927 and later sought to sell encryption machines to the United States Army during World War II.[948] After the war, and around the time that the NSA was founded, Hagelin befriended William F. Friedman, the chief cryptologist for the NSA, and began supplying encryption systems to the nascent agency. The scandal starts to really pick up steam in June of 1970 when Crypto AG was sold to the CIA and the West-German Intelligence Service, BND, for 5.75 million dollars.[949]

Prior to this buyout the company had been selling encryption machines of dubious quality to governments all over the world; it was only after the CIA came into play that these machines were utilized as spying devices for the United States Government. The operation, which involved the CIA and BND rigging the devices Crypto AG sold to other countries, was first known by the code name "Thesaurus" and later "Rubicon."

---

[948] https://en.wikipedia.org/wiki/Crypto_AG accessed on 05/09/20
[949] Ibid accessed on 05/09/20

According to Greg Miller's article for the Washington Post this rigging of encryption machines exposed the foreign governments who were clients of Crypto AG to "the privilege of having their most secret communications read by at least two (and possibly as many as five or six) foreign countries."[950] The cache of purloined communications is truly astounding:

> They monitored Iran's mullahs during the 1979 hostage crisis, fed intelligence about Argentina's military to Britain during the Falklands War, tracked the assassination campaigns of South American dictators, and caught Libyan officials congratulating themselves on the 1986 bombing of a Berlin disco.[951]

Contrary to the Nazi reductionist conspiracy theories of someone like David Talbot, the CIA.'s actions here were not the result of an intention to fight international communism on behalf of a beleaguered fascist ideology secretly adored by unseen elites within the agency. No, the CIA was acting on behalf of the United States Government's international hegemonic interests, and in so doing partnered with the governments of West Germany and Israel to spy on nations like Saudi Arabia, Libya, India, Pakistan, and Iran, which they perceived as threats to the geopolitical status quo. To push this point even further: the two biggest communist countries in the world, Russia and China, were never Crypto AG clients.

Crypto AG, which exploited poorer countries on a variety of political and financial fronts, was, as Miller says, one of the most "audacious" undertakings ever carried out by the CIA.

950

https://www.washingtonpost.com/graphics/2020/world/national-security/cia-crypto-encryption-machines-espionage/accessed on 05/11/20

[951] Ibid accessed on 05/11/20

However, its proximity to the NSA, both in development and operation, makes one wonder how intensely the US Government has, and still is, monitoring its citizens. The revelation that the NSA had, in fact, been spying on US citizens was brought to the public's attention in June of 2013 when Edward Snowden, a former NSA contractor, supplied agency documents to a variety of major media outlets. [952] For historical context, Snowden's revelation of these documents came three years after WikiLeaks released classified State Department cables, and five years before the CIA would pull out of Crypto AG after collapsing the company's infrastructure.[953]

By the end of June 2013, the U.S. Department of Justice charged Snowden with two counts of violating the Espionage Act of 1917 as well as the theft of government property. Within three days Snowden flew to Moscow and has been residing there ever since. Scott Horton's *Lords of Secrecy*, which was crafted to address the issue of secret agencies like the NSA and CIA that threaten to undermine democracy, often falls into the anachronistic trap of believing that there might be a judicial or political process capable of reversing this "empire of secrecy." Any misgivings he might have regarding the efficacy of these official, and rather idealistic, redresses tend to fall into the domain of the Argument from Hyperreality, and with this the realization that these injustices are not tried in courts but in the media; and this trial gives everyone watching the notion that they are somehow democratically involved in the process and that a just conclusion will be reached. But as we have already speculated, the process leads to no "real" conclusion.

On a more practical level, Horton gives a pragmatic analysis of how the simultaneous rise and compromising of the NSA (or, more specifically the so-called "Deep State") was the result of a confluence between a dependency on new technology,

---

[952] Horton, Scott (2015) *Lords of Secrecy*. Nation Books. P. 129
[953] According to Miller the company was finally liquidated in 2018.

miscommunication/adversarial relations between competing agencies, and the inflation of security clearance:

> In the American empire of secrecy 854,000 Americans hold top secret security clearance, and roughly 5.1 million have secret clearance. Is it reasonable to assume that such an enormous community of persons with access to highly classified materials can keep secrets?[954]

This point is significant because it leads us away from the traditional Left-Right dichotomy that had dominated politics until the early 2000s and into a reoccurring context we have addressed since "The Significance of Political Assassination" chapter: the issue of hyperreality; and not merely hyperreality but a certain political apathy, or incompetence, that has accompanied this envelopment into hyperreality. This aspect coincides with a point that Miller makes in his article about Crypto AG, namely that while the U.S. Government did not respond to requests for comment made by the press, nor did they dispute the authenticity of the documents detailing the espionage conducted by the CIA, NSA, and other involved agencies. It is reasonable to argue that on the one hand, they don't have the competence to muster a sophisticated lie in their defense, while on the other hand, they know full well that even if everything they are accused of is provable it will be met with a shrug of indifference by the passive American public.

Given all the evidence we have regarding domestic espionage and deep state intrigue, let's consider Chuck Klosterman's statement:

> "Suppose we had indisputable proof [the US Government] paid the Saudis to blow up the World Trade Center, and members from both political

---

[954] Ibid, p. 150

parties had signed off on it. And the day after this proof emerged, George W. Bush announced that he would give a speech at ground zero explaining why this decision was made."[955]

If this were to occur, Klosterman speculates there would be some sort of protest rally at Bush's speech, there might too be some violence, but nothing significant would happen because there is just too much apathy and political inertia to affect an actual revolution: "We have reached a point where the reinvention of America is impossible, even if that were what we wanted. Even if that were what *everybody* wanted." [956]

Klosterman's essay about political revolution is short but very insightful. He posits that given the size of the country and the complexity of its bureaucracy and media apparatus, there is no cause that could incite the American populace to try to overthrow its government, and that even if there were, no one would know what to do if it somehow was overthrown. He concludes that: "Modernity has created a cosmic difference between intellect and action, even when both are driven by the same motives; as such, the only people qualified to lead a present-day revolution would never actually do so."[957]

Skeptical Reactions to Conspiracy Theories

This final section could have bookended The Significance of UFO Phenomena chapter, but it is more fitting to place it here. There are a few reasons I have for this decision. The first is that events like Roswell and Maury Island might have drawn incredulous reactions from intellectuals but these reactions were, for the most part, shared by the public in general. Also, the idea that there was

---

[955] https://www.esquire.com/news-politics/news/a2301/esq0107revolution/ accessed 11/14/20
[956] Ibid
[957] Ibid

a conspiracy on the part of the government to cover-up UFO phenomena didn't really gain traction until the sixties and seventies. The idea that the U.S. Government, or any other nefarious group, might have plotted to have the Kennedys, as well as MLK, assassinated was something that resonated with a large enough section of the public that not only was the Warren Commission formed to head off such rumors, but public intellectuals and politicians actively sought to discredit this idea in a pejorative way, i.e., labeling proponents of said theories to be "conspiracy theorists." The so-called "9/11 Truther" movement expanded the realm of influence occupied by conspiracy theorists to the point where it had to be addressed, and combatted, by the mainstream media.

Skepticism as an intellectual movement, much like atheism. Is important to our narrative because it turned the screws on conspiracy theorists and made them adjust their theories towards a more scientistic orientation. On another level, it shifted the title of "skeptic" from the individual who "does not believe the official narrative" to the individual who would prefer the official narrative to "the kooky alternative theory." The shift from qualitative, myth-oriented, conspiracy theories to quantitative scientific renderings of events that reached its zenith (and endpoint) with 9/11 would not have been possible without this societal pressure. To be frank, since I am not addressing myths or conspiracy theories in a way that emphasizes their truthfulness, I don't really need to consult the experts who have sought to debunk them. However, I want to address a specific conspiracy theory debunker, Dr. Michael Shermer. I had picked up a copy of *Skeptic Magazine* (Volume 25 Number 1, 2020) in late March 2020 hoping that its cover story: "Conspiracies!" would grant me a different, more scientific perspective on this torturous subject. Unfortunately, the cover story was pretty much an advertisement for Shermer's Audible lecture series on the topic. I found it interesting that Shermer described his lectures as "myth-shattering" – a turn-of-phrase that aligns with the scientistic reductionist mentality I had anticipated.

Shermer takes the New Zealand Mosque shooting as his starting-point and claims that "Individuals act on their beliefs, and when those beliefs contain conspiracy theories about nefarious goings-on, those acts can turn deadly."[958] While kind of a typical sentiment in our current political climate, it's also arguably inaccurate if you consider that the proposition: "Actions based on beliefs that contain conspiracy theories *can* turn deadly," is contingent on the proposition: "People act on their beliefs." Such a pronouncement begs the question: how often do people act on beliefs? And, furthermore, what beliefs warrant "action?" I believe that *The Third Policeman* by Flann O'Brien is a fantastic novel; what actions does this belief command of me? Maybe I'll recommend it or buy it as a gift for friends; but my overarching point here is that most beliefs don't result in actions and the great majority of actions that result from beliefs are innocuous.

Shermer tries to add a bit of nuance to his essay by saying that some conspiracy theories are legitimate; and he lists a few that would be deemed legitimate by his perceived audience of affluent, scientifically oriented, neoliberals: Watergate, the Pentagon Papers, and the "Southern cabal" that attempted to secede from the United States. Strangely, he tramples across the legacy of JFK for attempting to assassinate Castro and Lyndon Johnson for keeping the Vietnam War going. He is also dismissive of, or at least evinces a tone of dismissiveness towards, the idea that the CIA distributed crack cocaine to aid the Contras. There's no way that I'm going to buy his audio book to find out the intricacies of his views.

Nearing the end of the essay I was only interested in whether Shermer was going to endorse the hot-button issue of the day: tech censorship. I assume from his tone that he does, but he was canny enough to only hint at his suggestions for remedying the problem of conspiracy theories – if you want the answer to this question you will have to shell out more money.

---

[958] From "Why People Believe Conspiracy Theories" by Dr. Michael Shermer. *Skeptic Magazine* (Vol. 25 No. 1, 2020) P. 17

This is probably all the ink I'm going to spill on people that go out of their way to debunk conspiracy theories in today's political climate. I think it synopsizes the fact that: A) they are ideologically driven in their own way. Granted, past skeptics were most likely not promoting censorship the way they seem to be today, but their motivation in shutting down particular conspiracy theories was in service of a certain ideological status quo. And B) they, like the conspiracy theorists they condemn, have a product to sell – they just have a more "high-brow" marketing strategy. So, maybe I'm more of a cynic than a skeptic.

Chapter Fifteen: The Significance of "This Is It" by Kenny Loggins

There've been times in my life,
I've been wondering why.
Still, somehow I believed we'd always survive.
Now, I'm not so sure.
You're waiting here, one good reason to try.
But, what more can I say?
What's left to provide?
(You think that maybe it's over, only if you want it to be.)
Are you going to wait for a sign, your miracle?
Stand up and fight.
(This is it)
Make no mistake where you are
(This is it)
Your back's to the corner
(This is it)
Don't be a fool anymore
(This is it.)
The waiting is over. No, don't you run.
No way to hide.
No time for wondering why.
It's here, the moment is now, about to decide.
Let them believe.
Leave them behind.
But keep me near in your heart.
Know that, whatever you do, I'm here by your side.
(You say that maybe it's over, not if you don't want it to be.)
For once in your life, here's your miracle.
Stand up and fight.
(This is it)
Make no mistake where you are
(This is it)
You're going no further
(This is it)

Until it's over and done
(No one can tell what the future holds)
Etc.

Ask most people what song, or music, they think should be the official soundtrack to conspiracy theorization they will probably draw a blank.[959] If they are thinking in terms of UFOs and alien abductions, maybe they will think of the theme from *The X-Files*, which is pretty iconic. Nevertheless, it is "This Is It" by Kenny Loggins that MUST be the conspiracy theorist's anthem.

My reasoning is straight-forward: the chorus, THIS IS IT, points to the moment of total revelation that is so essential for the reductionist conspiracy theorist. THIS is the revelation of *who* is at the root of our problems. THIS is the moment of realization that will change the way you, the wide-eyed novice (up until this very moment), see the world for the rest of your life.

In most of the topics we have poured over there have been a variety of texts vying for the title of Greatest Explanatory Value. Sometimes these are actual texts, for instance Kenneth Grant and David Icke, which offer opposing interpretations of the same phenomena. At other times these texts are objects or events so large or mythic that they, by mere virtue of being referenced, encapsulate a whole textual world, e.g., Atlantis. What is vital to this method is that it is in some way dialectical: oppositions are posited to invoke a resolution. In the case of our analysis, that resolution is a meta-text of conspiracy theories.

When the conspiratorial reductionist of today posits the "who," be they the government, the Illuminati, the Nazis,

---

[959] Upon writing this sentence, "Hotel California" by the Eagles popped into my head. There is a vague sense of mystery and menace in this song (as well as rock n' roll Apocrypha regarding the album cover and whether or not Church of Satan founder, Anton LaVey is lurking in the background), just as there is in "Sympathy for the Devil" by the Rolling Stones. But these are just passing impressions, which are relegated to footnotes.

Reptilians, the Communists, or extraterrestrial aliens, it is done within the absence of a dialectical movement in the narrative. Instead of a discussion, or sublation, of the thesis, there is further tinkering to make the scope of the theory's explanatory power ever wider.

Any reductionist scheme, even Alan Watt's ambiguous "them" might take into account pluralism – politically and discursively – but ultimately grants a hegemonic totality to one of these groups. And this hegemony becomes "conspiratorial" in a conventional sense when whichever group is picked as the "who" is granted either omnipotence or omniscience. It is one thing to posit that states-of-affairs move teleologically, but another to claim that the group you believe is oppressing you sees, or has orchestrated, the teleological endpoint, or has the ability to manipulate it in some way.

These movements are ultimately textual, and they are grist for our mill, but the point of this brief chapter is to point out how the reductionist of today points to a material, or sometimes immaterial *who*, and how this tendency has increased as history progresses.[960] This leads one to believe that all the groups that are mongering these theories are blindly grasping different parts of an elephant in the room. This elephant is modernity.

---

[960] This reason for the chapter is actually second to my desire to have a chapter entitled "The Significance of 'This is It' by Kenny Loggins."

Chapter Sixteen: The Mandela Effect

"Everybody has that feeling when they look at a work of art and it's right, that sudden familiarity, a sort of ... recognition, as though they were creating it themselves, as though it were being created through them while they look at it or listen to it and it shouldn't be sinful to want to have created beauty?"[961]

On June 25th, 2019 Christopher Anatra, the president of NECS Inc. posted a video to YouTube titled *Quantum Physics, the Mandela Effect and perceived changes to your NECS Entrée data.*[962] In the video, Anatra says that over the past few months his tech support people have been receiving calls and emails from clients who use his company's software, claiming that the numbers on their reports don't "appear to be accurate." Anatra says that once these claims are manually audited, the information initially reported by the NECS software is confirmed to have been correct. He then goes through a pretty standard list of products that have been misremembered by consumers – McIntosh apples, Stove Top Stuffing etc. – before telling his viewers that: "Quantum physics states that there are an infinite amount of parallel universes and that the nature of our universe, and all others in the multiverse, is that they are holographic." The Mandela Effect is a mass confabulation that is presumably linked to the holographic and permeable nature of these parallel universes... hence, the inconsistencies in data being reported by NECS software is subject to any incongruities that might arise from this dimensional permeation.

    This video was by no means the defining moment in the burgeoning Mandela Effect narrative, but it attracted people's attention because Mr. Anatra, who appears to be a legitimate executive, was seen publicly espousing a fringe conspiracy theory.

---

[961] Gaddis, William (2012) *The Recognitions.* Dalkey Archive Press. P. 535
[962] Or did he?

Outside of enthusiastic conspiracy theorists, the reaction was one of either bemusement or cynicism, with the cynics claiming that Anatra was using the Mandela Effect as an excuse for peddling shoddy software.

The term Mandela Effect was coined in 2010 by paranormal researcher Fiona Broome when she realized she had a false memory of Nelson Mandela having passed away sometime in the 1980s. In actuality, Mandela did not die until 2013, but Broome was shocked by how vividly she seemed to remember his passing and that others shared this false memory. Not long after detailing this incident, conspiracy theorists online began cataloguing similar false memories. Some of these are remembering "Looney Tunes" cartoons as "Looney Toons," the "Berenstain Bears" as the "Berenstein Bears," and "Oscar Mayer" as "Oscar Meyer." Some of these misrememberings are visual and not semantic, such as misremembering how many rows of seats there were in the car that John Kennedy was riding in when he was shot (there were three, not two) and the *Star Wars* droid C-3PO being completely gold (he had a silver right leg). Besides these there are a host of other examples.[963]

On its own merits, the Mandela Effect is an appropriate conspiracy theory for our particular stage in postmodernity. It is very much a product of the reductionist mindset (or, if not a product, then an aftereffect of a prolonged exposure to a reductionist mentality), because it presents a problem that demands a proof – like a math problem. However, since we've been discussing conspiracy theories in their most ideal form as texts derived from myths (which are something more than mere texts), I would like to posit one postmodern solution to the Mandela Effect problem: that the instantiations of the phenomena arise from contradictions implied within the text itself.

---

[963] https://www.esquire.com/lifestyle/g29077060/mandela-effect-examples/ accessed on 06/20/21

Let's look at the book that I am currently writing, which you are currently reading, for an example. In The Significance of the Cosmos I stated:

> A question arises as to why people think that God physically destroyed the Tower of Babel. One answer is that its destruction was portrayed in films. But what inevitably follows this answer is: why did filmmakers present it this way? Possibly it was done for dramatic effect. Another answer is that the event is misremembered because the morality of the implicit reading has seeped into the retelling and, when thinking in Biblical terms, we associate God's punishments as being inherently violent.

I wrote this because I had distinct memories from my childhood of seeing the Tower of Babel destroyed in a particular film, but I cannot remember its name, and I left it there because of Giordano Bruno's concept "Ben trovato," which we briefly discussed before, which means that even if something is not literally true it is "well founded." There was also a more personal reason: I didn't want my memory to be wrong, not so much because of nostalgia but because that memory had played a role in codifying my understanding of the Old Testament.

The narrative richness we associate with literature and mythically-derived texts is qualitative – intense scrutiny of details can play a part in this, but not to the point where such scrutiny overtakes the overall meaning of the text itself. For literature, there are a variety of large and small features of the text that a reader can conceptualize in a general way, and we can say that the text has "done its job," so to speak, once these are ascertained by the reader. In a hyperreal society, which consistently defers to the quantitative over the qualitative, an attention to detail – as if details are of primary importance – will become a much more prominent feature of comprehension.

So, when I claim that collective misrememberings are essentially built-into the text itself, what I am saying is that the culturally engendered narratives we are subjecting to quantitative scrutiny were never intended to be subjected to such a reading. Interestingly enough, each of the Mandela Effects, except for the primary one involving Mandela himself, are incredibly trivial. Analyzing the Nelson Mandela narrative, we can see *why* people might believe he died in prison in the 1980s, essentially because it's a more romantic narrative. These sorts of misrememberings are unconscious attempts to re-enchant the more mundane moments from our past, and the fact that they are collective in nature, implies a general tendency in human nature towards embellishment and narrative richness.[964] This dramatic form of confabulation is evident in my (possibly false) memory of seeing the Tower of Babel destroyed in a film as a child.

This explains some of the more interesting Mandela Effects, though most of them aren't really that profound and indicate an emergent trend of language evolving. Sometimes, it is the evolution of technology that is at play. For instance, an interesting recent occurrence relating directly to my writing is the shift from double-spacing after a period to a single space. In school (a long time ago) the rule was "two spaces after a period, one space after all other punctuation." Now the rule has changed because of changes in technology, i.e., fonts on PCs, are proportional, whereas on typewriters this was not an issue. But there still seems to be a qualitative difference at play here. Did someone or some group of people "meme" this cultural shift away from two spaces? It seems that even without the advance in technology we would have lost the additional space inevitably because we are consuming information so fast that any rule slowing down consumption would be weeded out.

---

[964] Even the misremembering of "Kraft Stove Top Stuffing" as "Stouffers Stove Top Stuffing" indicates a poetic inclination towards alliteration.

This returns us to the question of how much of this phenomenon is "memed" (socially engineered and transmitted), how much is a "natural" evolution towards efficiency, and how this encapsulates the conspiracy theorists' question of: "Are we being consciously misled or are we collectively going astray?" So far in this chapter we have given examples of the Mandela Effect, we are about to go into some philosophical reasoning for making sense of it as well as other developments, such as "Pizzagate," that vaguely overlap with it in a historical context. At the end we will tackle the possible scientific explanations for the Mandela Effect.

How Does the Mandela Effect Relate to Hyperreality?

Throughout the last few chapters we've discussed the work of Jean Baudrillard. Many people who are interested in postmodern philosophy were very interested in what someone like Baudrillard might say about a catastrophic event of the magnitude of 9/11, because if you assume that looking at events as texts (the Structuralist perspective) removes us from the conventionally understood realm of direct experience, then Baudrillard's theories of hyperreality and simulation are even further removed, as events are not even "read" in themselves so much as they are experienced only as part of exposure to a medium, e.g., as a program on television.

This interpretation presents events as exceptionally thin and superficial, so much so that it casts doubt on the existence of an external world. Anyone interested in this theory in the aftermath of 9/11 had to think: "Surely Baudrillard must concede that **this** happened." However, Baudrillard has always given a certain amount of leeway to "the real;" in his book *The Gulf War Did Not Take Place* he admits that the atrocities of the war occurred to the extent that we can morally condemn the military action itself; however, the traditional sense in which we can cognitively grasp war has disappeared and the war itself became a simulation. The thesis of hyperreality has an atavistic aspect to it, insofar as it seems to reproduce Plato's cave analogy. But unlike Plato's story in which humanity is born into an illusory state which it then has an opportunity to escape, in the case of hyperreality humanity has slowly succumbed to an omnipresent illusory state. This is a collective issue because even if one or more individuals "unplugs" from the matrix of near-instant communication, news, and social media, they will most likely still inhabit a society that is saturated with these things. It is almost as if the condition of hyperreality offers the option of an unsimulated reality as if it was a good to be consumed, when in actuality it is, arguably, just another shadow.

Another factor entailed by the Mandela Effect, in this context, is the promise that "You too, can become one of the people manipulating the shadows on the wall." Originally, this promise was held out only for people entering the media or entertainment industry, but now it has extended to anyone operating a phone and posting to social media; we are all just internet content creators. In effect the symptom of simulation in our contemporary society mandates that everything (all cultural signifiers) must be repeated until they are null and void (another Avengers movie???). The Mandela Effect works on the margins of this process, asking if certain bits even occurred in the first place. In this way it is deconstructive, working on the margins of our society. It is a symptom; its condition of possibility is hyperreality.

It is almost as if the immediacy of information and the immediacy of its availability, which has facilitated the development and dissemination of conspiracy theories, has an innate tendency to blur the line between the scientific and the occult. Derrida notes that Thoth (Hermes), being the father of both strands of knowledge, is inherently ambiguous:

> Every act of his is marked by this unstable ambivalence. This god of calculation, arithmetic, and rational science also presides over the occult sciences, astrology and alchemy. He is the god of magic formulas that calm the sea, of secret accounts, of hidden texts: an archetype of Hermes,

god of cryptography no less than of every other – graphy.[965]

Given this mythological pedigree, Derrida claims writing, which was Thoth's contribution to man, to be an ambiguous tool that is utilized by both science and the occult.[966] At a very basic semantic level, Derrida is addressing the gap between a word and its meaning; this can then be attenuated to sentences and whole texts. If we take the Platonic scheme of forms – the Good, The Just, etc. – and imagine these things as representations able to be contemplated in our minds, Hermeticism, as an occult practice, adds a twist to this schema and introduces words, sophisticated words, or words that are more esoteric, which might give a quicker apprehension of the forms. The idea of prayers and spells comes from this insight; and magick itself becomes a tool used to bypass a more strenuous route towards spiritual communion. The hyperreal landscape in which we find ourselves now adds to this the instant access of information found on the internet.

In the Significance of the Grail chapter, I quoted Mircea Eliade's statement that,

> "Popular memory finds difficulty in retaining individual events and real figures. The structures by means of which it functions are different: categories instead of events, archetypes instead of historical personages. The historical personage is assimilated to his mythical model (hero, etc.), while the event is identified with the category of mythical actions (fight with a monster, enemy brothers, etc.)."

---

[965] Derrida, Jacques (1981) *Dissemination*. The University of Chicago Press. P. 93
[966] Ibid p. 94

The Mandela effect, insofar as it relies on our tendency towards generalization, is not a postmodern return of myth so much as it is the return of myth *within* the postmodern age.

Free-Fall into the Rabbit-Hole: Postmodernism Re-evaluated

What is appealing about the "classic" postmodern theorists like Baudrillard, Deleuze, Lyotard, Derrida etc. (regardless of whether they accepted or rejected the label) is that they foretold multiplicity in a radical way. Roland Barthes once proclaimed: "Let a thousand flowers bloom." And, in a sense, they have, in the form of blogs, podcasts, and social media. The postmodernists predicted the quest for authenticity, the hyperreality of our media-saturated landscape, and radical and unchecked multiplicity. In such a landscape it is the most wild and outlandish narratives that generate the most "clicks."

Take the book *Nephilim Crown 5G Apocalypse* by Dean Henderson published independently (like the book you are now reading) in July of 2019. Ostensibly this work tackles the latest conspiracy theory craze: 5G. But unlike authors who tackled 9/11 as a technological spectacle by dissecting the nuts and bolts of the event, Henderson must animate the technology of this imminent threat with heavy doses of the mythic building blocks over which we've been pouring. We don't even have to crack open the book – the chapter titles tell us everything we need to know. Here's a sampling of them:

1. Facebook: The New Tower of Babel

4. Crown Castle and the 5G Beast

6. Why Trump is a Rothschild Tool

9. Minions Feeding Vampires

10. Illuminati Usurpation of the Yang

13. Nephilim Demons Surfacing

21. Rockefeller War on Venezuela Continues

26. Illuminati, Nazis, & the Illegal State of Israel

31. Silicon Valley Cyborg Disruptors

I'm pretty sure that a good deal of the friends and acquaintances who knew that I was writing a book about conspiracy theories thought my table of contents would look similar to what I've just transcribed. I'm only curious as to whether Chapter Ten: "Illuminati Usurpation of the Yang" is about former Democratic Presidential hopeful Andrew Yang. Maybe the whole book is a colossal joke meant to lampoon conspiracy theorists by corralling every imaginable topic in which they might be interested into an ALL CAPS journey into over-referential paranoia. Since the theme I've been exploring is that conspiracy theories, at their best, are acts of literature, I can't be overly dismissive, because satire, if this is the case, is a laudable literary device.

On Amazon.com Henderson sums the work up as: "My 6th book is a free fall to the depths of the rabbit hole. Though I haven't found the bottom yet, I can see clearly that our entire "reality" has been fabricated by our long-time feudal lords. And they don't appear to be human." This last sentence is a reference to the Nephilim, who are most likely the reduction-point of Henderson's theory. Whether *Nephilim Crown 5G Apocalypse* is intended to be taken seriously or not, its over-the-top nature is dispiriting primarily because it seems to betray a lack of substance. This lack of substance more than anything else threatens the book's literary potential. However, I think there is a novel way we might be able to apprehend this work (and other over-the-top works of this nature): if we imagine each chapter not as the summation of whatever sentences are contained therein but instead as being akin to the elaborate and lavish paintings that adorned sci-fi novels of the fifties and sixties.

In the Significance of the New World Order we examined how literature helped pave the way for the society of today and how postmodern literature grappled with the intersubjectivity and lack of stability resulting from the tumultuous cultural events of the post-WWII period. The Mandela Effect is a kind of interactive version of this. Some conspiracy theorists might say that lesser instances of the effect, like The Berenstain Bears, were used to test the waters for greater *1984esque* historical rewritings. When it comes to this type of theorization, many of the usual culprits still exist – international banking cabals, Illuminati, aliens, etc. – but more and more the medium (the mainstream media) is called out not only for active participation but as a possible source of control. In contrast to this controlling force, the internet briefly appeared to represent a space that was devoid of this control, and in which emergent trends and memes could arise and circulate. As of the time of writing, the autonomy (or "dereliction" in Deleuzian terms) of the internet has been greatly eroded by corporate interests; the likelihood that the medium will return to its atavistic and unregulated form is slim.

The Prophetic Powers of Steve Jackson's "Illuminati"

I first encountered Steve Jackson's game *Illuminati* in the mid-1990s, just as it was being re-released as *Illuminati: New World Order* (INWO). The original game was a conventional board game in which players adopt the role, and idiosyncratic goals, of a traditional conspiracy theory bugaboo. The options are the Bavarian Illuminati, the Gnomes of Zurich, the Discordian Society, the Adepts of Hermes, The Society of Assassins, Shangri-La, UFOs, the Servants of Cthulhu, the Network, and the Bermuda Triangle.

The original game, inspired by Robert Anton Wilson and Robert Shea's *Illuminatus!* Trilogy, was released in 1983.[967] On a meta-level interpretation the game did three important things: it catalogued and schematized a wide variety of groups and individuals who play roles within conspiracy theories; it portrayed these groups as pluralities, each battling for control of the world; and, lastly, it satirized all parties involved, making the game more enjoyable and the esoteric information more accessible to people who are not naturally curious about such matters. These three facets correspond, respectively, with three topics we have already discussed: the cataloging and organizing of information mirrors the same endeavor undertaken by Freemasonry during the Enlightenment; conceiving the groups as vying for hegemony over one another in the quest for world domination mirrors political pluralism; and the humor and satire employed is closely related to that employed by Robert Anton Wilson, the Discordians, and the Church of the SubGenius.

It is arguable that the more playful, Left-wing side of conspiracy theories on display in such nineties cultural artifacts as Richard Linklater's 1990 film *Slacker*, Craig Baldwin's 1992 film *Tribulation 99*, the 1992 episode of *Seinfeld*, "The Boyfriend," which featured a parody of the JFK assassination, and Doug Moench's 1995, *The Big Book of Conspiracies*, were all presaged by Steve Jackson's *Illuminati*.

One reason for this is Jackson's prescient and sardonic analysis of pop culture insofar as it relates to conspiracy theories. The other has to do with the aspect of transparency, i.e., the old expression, "laying all your cards on the table." Steve Jackson's game, in a literal sense, did exactly this. In a sense, the replication of these theories, entities, and individuals into a physical board

---

[967] Shea supported the game and wrote an introduction to the game's first expansion set; Wilson did not and planned to sue Jackson, but was talked out of it by his agent. Walker, Jesse (2014) *The United States of Paranoia: A Conspiracy Theory.* Harper Perennial. P. 249

game was analogous to the invention of Tarot in the mid-fifteenth century.[968] As was stipulated in the Significance of the Tarot chapter, capturing concepts as paintings on cards that could be physically handled was a way of mitigating, or even controlling, forces that seemed beyond our comprehension. *Illuminati* not only did that, but also added humor as an additional tool with which we can assert control over the mysterious.

The follow-up to *Illuminati*, released in 1995, was the afore-mentioned *Illuminati: New World Order* which followed the format of the highly successful *Magic: The Gathering* (released in 1993). This new format was based on players buying and collecting packs of cards, which offered a greater diversity of topics (most of which were hilarious) but also made the game more consumption-based. Even though *Illuminati: New World Order* was not as groundbreaking as its predecessor, it is this version of the game that became a nexus for later conspiracy theorists. The original 1983 version of the game tracked and codified existing conspiracy theories, whereas the 1995 version generated them. In the evolution of this one game, we clearly see the meta-aspect of narrative as it becomes both a commentary and a source of instigation for further theorization. What eventually transpired was that conspiracy theorists saw events depicted on trading cards that they believed predicted the future. Some of these events were: 9/11, the election of Donald Trump, and the Covid-19 Pandemic. Once these similarities or coincidences began circulating, conspiracy theorists were torn between the possibility that the cards had the power to predict, or

---

[968] An ad for the game that ran in 1995 states: "*Illuminati* is a tarot for our times. Who controls whom, who does what to whom... The combinations that appear on your table may mean something, or nothing. What do *you* see there?" Reprinted in Jackson, Steve (1995) *The INWO Book*. Steve Jackson Games. P. 41

even dictate, the future, and the possibility that Steve Jackson somehow knew these events would come to pass back in 1995.[969]

The opposition between these two camps mirrors the dialectical movement we have been tracking so far: on one side is the mythically derived occultic view, and on the other is the idea that representatives of some clandestine group visited Jackson and revealed to him their twenty-year plan of machinations. It should be noted that, even though Jackson was inspired by Robert Anton Wilson's *Illuminatus!* Trilogy, his work supersedes Wilson's insofar as the humor he employs is less scatterbrained and more culturally attuned – he addresses more issues in a more comprehensive manner, giving most everyone a port of entry to conspiratorial thought. Jackson's mindset epitomized the zenith of 1990s-era conspiracy theorization in all its satiric and iconoclastic glory. Part of his mission statement for the mid-nineties re-launch addresses the then nascent issue of political correctness:

> One of the first things we decided about **INWO** was that it would be politically *incorrect*. The cards are not designed to offend ...but they're designed to be funny, and if someone happens to take offense, that's just too damn bad. So nothing is sacred. Stereotypes are not to be shunned; they're grist for the satirist's mill. A lot of groups are drawn as their

---

[969] Aiding theorists who lean towards this angle is the fact that the office of Steve Jackson Games was raided on March 1, 1990 by the Secret Service. During the search a manuscript pertaining to Jackson's game *GURPS Cyberpunk* was seized on suspicion that it was a handbook for computer crime. Jackson later sued the Secret Service in 1993 and was awarded $300,000. https://en.m.wikipedia.org/wiki/Steve_Jackson_Games accessed on 06/20/21

foes would like to see them. It's the tabloid view of the world: Everyone is corruptible.[970]

This sensibility makes for some entertaining cards, whether it be "Trekkies" who are described as "Peaceful, Weird, Fanatic," "Daycare Centers" which depict a woman in full occult regalia performing magical rituals before a group of children (the caption reads: "Drop your kids off, and we'll take care of them. So to speak...") or "Conspiracy Theorists," who are described as a "powerless and much-mocked group [that] is prized by the Illuminati, because their wild ravings often contain useful ideas"[971] – flipping through an INWO deck of cards may not reveal the future but is sure to elicit a guffaw or two from even the most world-weary skeptic.

Pizzagate

As we saw with the death of Jeffrey Epstein, whether assassination, suicide or a body-double was involved, we can cynically say that it was done for the sake of the media. The media cannot really be harmed within this realm in which it has created and thrives. Individual companies and reporters could be hurt or destroyed but the media, and I mean this in the sense of all media, Left, Right, whatever, as perpetual-motion machine, will go on for as long as there is electricity.

On November 5, 2019, Project Veritas released footage of ABC News co-anchor Amy Robach candidly discussing her attempts to get an exposé on Jeffrey Epstein aired on the network. According to Robach, who appears to be unaware of the fact that she is being filmed, the material she had also implicated Alan Dershowitz, Bill Clinton, and Prince Andrew. Because of the volatile nature of this story ABC refused to air it, but it eventually

---

[970] Jackson, Steve (1995) *The INWO Book*. Steve Jackson Games. P. 3
[971] Ibid p. 65

got out, and when it did, it was referred to as a "bombshell." This is just one instance of the media's duplicity, but we have to ask ourselves: has this revelation actually changed anything? Your average American might express a distrust of the media, or complain about its political slant, but he or she most likely still uses it; and this use is unconscious because it is ingrained in us.

The only change that might have occurred is that members of the media feel threatened by impotent cries of "fake news" and then concertedly point the media apparatus towards the people or trends around which the individuals attacking them circulate. Inevitably, this just produces more grist for the media mill and nothing more.

One of the stranger trends, or memes, the media pursued during and after the election of Donald Trump in 2016 is "Pizzagate;" and there were a lot of constituents at play in this narrative. If we Google the term now you will only find pieces debunking the theory – such is the nature of Google these days. Here is a concise recount of the theory: In June and July of 2016, Wikileaks released almost 20,000 emails that had been hacked from the Democratic National Committee. Later, in October of that year, Wikileaks released 20,000 emails belonging to Hillary Clinton's campaign chairman, John Podesta. These emails were scoured by members of online message-board groups such as 4chan and 8chan for salacious or incriminating content. Now, if what these groups found in the emails is salacious or incriminating is highly debatable. Clearly, there is nothing blatantly salacious in any of the leaked material, however it being incriminating or not is contingent upon the strangeness of the content and wording of the emails in question.

Before I straight-up post the most questionable ones here, I want to resume my encapsulation of the theory. So, after the leaks were scoured for clues, online conspiracy theorists believed they were seeing a coded dialog in the emails, and that the coded words were being used to refer to either child pornography or actual children who were being trafficked for the intent of molestation and abuse. The key words the theorists picked up on were: "pizza," "pasta," "hot dogs," "dominoes," and "ice cream." "Pizza," or more specifically "cheese pizza" was considered code for "child pornography." "Dominoes" was code for "domination play." "Pasta" was code for "prostitutes." Theorists weren't quite able to make up their minds about "ice cream."

After this groundwork was set into place, Pizzagate theorists immediately connected Podesta with Comet Ping Pong, a pizza parlor and venue run by a man named James Alefantis, who had communicated with Podesta via email in 2008.[972] James Alefantis was a somewhat prominent figure in Democratic Party circles; he had enjoyed a handful of meetings with President Obama, used Comet Ping Pong as a location for fundraisers, and had previously been in a long-term relationship with Media Matters CEO, David Brock.

Once this connection was made, Pizzagate theorists (who were primarily Right-wing) began speculating about whether there were underground tunnels beneath Comet Ping Pong where abducted children were being transported. Nearby Besta Pizza was also implicated in the conspiracy theory when a triangular symbol found on their menu was publicized as being a coded sign for "boy-lover." Compounding all of this were the photos that Alefantis shared via his Instagram page, one of which featured a child with her hands taped to a table. Pretty much none of the images on Comet Ping Pong's Instagram that were circulated in connection with Pizzagate looked like the work of a business that was trying to whet your appetite. Another aspect related to both John Podesta and Comet Ping Pong that was brought into play was their respective choice of art. Both John Podesta and his brother, Tony, were interested in the avant-garde and had participated in "Spirit-cooking" installations with a performance artist named Marina Abramović. These performances, as well as

[972] "John Podesta is Ready to Talk About Pizzagate" by Andy Kroll. Published in *Rolling Stone*. December 9, 2018. https://www.rollingstone.com/politics/politics-features/john-podesta-pizzagate-766489/ accessed on 05/20/19

the art that the Podestas were known to collect, would be strange from a conventionally middle-American perspective, but from a broader, more sophisticated one, could be analyzed away as appealing to a darker aesthetic. One thing that Pizzagate theorists clearly got wrong about the Podestas' art collection was in claiming that a headless sculpture ("Arch of Hysteria") by Louise Bourgeois owned by Tony Podesta was inspired by the positions in which serial killer Jeffrey Dahmer would put his victims after killing them. This was patently false, since Bourgeois had explicitly detailed that the work was related to Freudian psychoanalysis and its historical treatment of women.[973] The art inside Comet Ping Pong might also have been very strange, but it seemed to change quite frequently; having never seen it first-hand I'll never know. What the controversial art hanging inside Comet Ping Pong was we'll never know either because we only have access to the internet for this, and unlike the weird Instagram posts who's to say what art actually hung on the walls of Comet Ping Pong except those who went there and saw it firsthand?

There were also rumors about the Podestas using the Clinton Foundation to traffic Haitian children which were incorporated into Pizzagate. Essentially all of this fevered speculation came to a head on December 4, 2016, when a 28 year-old man named Edgar Welch entered Comet Ping Pong armed with a rifle in order to see if any children were being held captive. At this point the mainstream media denounced Pizzagate *en masse*, and the whole theory fell apart. Even Right-wingers who had previously promoted the theory, such as Alex Jones, now disowned it as nonsense.

Pizzagate essentially died because it was a "gish gallop," a term coined by Eugenie Scott, which is a technique of overwhelming an opponent with arguments, some of which might be dubious. The "gish gallop" is a hallmark of certain conspiracy

---

[973] In this respect, Bourgeois was participating in the post-modern deconstruction of "grand-narratives."

theorists we've already discussed, like Allan Watt, or 9/11 theories in general. Most of the conspiracy theories that we've defined as reductive (dialectically scientist) will resort to stacking multiple arguments on top of each other. What was interesting about Pizzagate in this context was that the theory really took aim at actual people and was very explicit about what was suspected. I think there are only a few salient questions that Pizzagate theorists could have asked, and had they stuck to these points, they might still be somewhat relevant. The remnants of the theory that I don't think the media can ever really dispel are:

1. The bizarre and suggestive content of Alefantis's Instagram account

2. The content of some of Podesta's email exchanges. The most notable ones are as follows:

```
On Sep 2, 2014 2:54 PM, "Sandler, Susan"
<ses@sandlerfoundation.org<mailto:ses@sandlerf
oundation.org>> wrote:
```

Hi John, The realtor found a handkerchief (I think it has a map that seems pizza-related. Is it yorus? They can send it if you want. I know you're busy, so feel free not to respond if it's not yours or you don't want it.

Susaner

```
From:                John              Podesta
[mailto:john.podesta@gmail.com]           Sent:
Wednesday, September 03, 2014 9:29 PM To:
Sandler, Susan Subject: Re: Did you leave a
handkerchief
```

It's mine, but not worth worrying about.

This is kind of a strange exchange, but the fact that there are other people cc'd in the email mitigates the sinister implications a bit because, if there was child-abuse blackmail afoot, including other people in the (coded) discussion of it increases the chances that it will be leaked. However, the inclusion of these other individuals might have been meant to emphasize, or compound, the blackmail. Initially I found the references to "ice cream" in the following email to be suspicious. Not in a sexual way, but in a "coded reference to illegal drugs" way:

```
Laura, I consider ice cream, its purchase, and
its consumption a rather serious business. We
can't just willy-nilly toss it out and about
in casual references, especially linked with
the word "free".

Regards, Kris Cleary
```

And it is presented in this way by Pizzagate theorists. But if you read the email to which it was responding:

```
From: Laura B. Macrorie Sent: Friday, June 12,
2015 11:38 AM To: Announcements Subject: Ice
cream for FREE (time) today!

Please consider taking this 10-minute survey
about frozen desserts created by Georgetown
MBA candidates for our capstone project. We
have a quick turnaround to analyze the data,
so we're trying to get as many people to take
it as possible over the next few days (read:
feel free to pass it along to family, friends,
and even people you don't even like that
much). I offer lifelong friendship and a more
relaxed        demeanor     in      exchange.      ;-)
```

http://mcdonough.az1.qualtrics.com/SE/?SID=SV_
aXBa8MifXAjivad Thank you!!

P.S. Sorry about the misleading subject
line...but hey, it got you to read this,
right??

So, that clears that up.

On Thu, Oct 8, 2015 at 9:26 AM, Tamera
Luzzatto
<tluzzatto@pewtrusts.org<mailto:tluzzatto@pewt
rusts.org>> wrote:

With enormous gratitude to Advance Man
Extraordinaire Haber, I am popping up again to
share our excitement about the Reprise of Our
Gang's visit to the farm in Lovettsville. And
I thought I'd share a couple more notes: We
plan to heat the pool, so a swim is a
possibility. Bonnie will be Uber Service to
transport Ruby, Emerson, and Maeve Luzzatto
(11, 9, and almost 7) so you'll have some
further entertainment, and they will be in
that pool for sure. And with the forecast
showing prospects of some sun, and a cooler
temp of lower 60s, I suggest you bring
sweaters of whatever attire will enable us to
use our outdoor table with a pergola overhead
so we dine al fresco (and ideally not al-
CHILLo). I am ccing Trudy to repeat the
invite, and sending pining wishes-you-could-
come to Rima, John P, and Laurie & Chris.

Con amore, Mrs. Farmer L

There are other people cc'd in this one, but the listing of the
children's ages is just plain weird and it's understandable why it

would raise some eyebrows. In my opinion, this is possibly the most potentially damning email of the lot.

There are a lot of references to pizza and food in general, but Podesta is Italian, he probably really likes pizza. The majority of food references are very precise menu rundowns like this:

```
If we are still on for dinner on Saturday,
June 06 Possible menu _ Indian: suggestions
welcome.


1. Mixed grill of Tandoori chicken, lamb, and
Lahori fish: Pizza oven. Garnished with ribbon
onions in lemon mint chutney.
2. Garlic Naan ( freshly baked, pizza oven @
550 degrees) 3. Greek Yoghurt with shredded
cucumber and fresh corriander garnish.
4. Basmati rice Pilaff with fresh green peas,
Saffron and roasted pine nuts garnish.
5. A lentil dish. Dessert: A block of Vanilla
Ice cream heaped with mixed seasonal berries
and Roasted Almond praline spikes, drizzled
with Amaretto. or with fresh sweet mango.
```

You can make whatever you want from all of this. When it comes to Pizzagate we must ask what version of Pizzagate a believer in the theory subscribes to: tunnels under a pizza parlor in Washington D.C., or emails from a political insider that allude to child-trafficking? There does seem to be a tenable connection between politics and pedophile rings, or outright sexual abuse if we include Operation MK Ultra in the equation.[974] Ironically, given that Pizzagate was a theory leveled at the upper echelons of

---

[974] Stephen Kinzer describes an MK Ultra subproject called "Operation Midnight Climax" wherein unsuspecting "johns" were slipped LSD while visiting a CIA-controlled bordello. Kinzer, Stephen (2019) *Poisoner in Chief: Sidney Gottlieb and the CIA Search for Mind Control.* Henry Holt and Company. Pp. 141 - 144

the Democratic Party, the figures and scandals that have been more well-documented, in respect to such allegations, have been tied to "conservative" institutions like the Catholic Church and the Republican Party.

The woes of the Church, in regards to this issue, are legion and I will get to a few instances of abuse and cover-up that are relevant to our topic of political intrigue in a bit. Let's start with a figure who had ties to both the Catholic Church and the Republican Party, Roy Cohn (February 20, 1927 – August 2, 1986). Cohn was a lawyer from New York City who first came to national attention by assisting in the prosecution and conviction of Julius and Ethel Rosenberg, a couple who had been charged with espionage. The couple were convicted in 1951 and subsequently executed in 1953. Not long after the Rosenbergs' execution, Cohn became Senator Joseph McCartney's chief council and assisted in McCarthy's attempt to blacklist and purge suspected Communists from the government. [975] McCarthy's efforts are often confused (or conflated) with hearings made by the House of Un-American Activities in 1947 regarding allegations of Communist agents working in Hollywood, which led to the infamous "blacklisting" of numerous writers, producers, and directors.

Cohn, however, had a life outside the straight-laced, button-down world of the red-hunting Republican Party. Prior to, and after, his rise to notoriety, Cohn involved himself in muckraking through his close connections to gossip journalists such as Walter Winchell and George Sokolsky. Oftentimes the gossip and blackmail in which Cohn indulged involved the threat of exposing homosexual affairs. Together with his forays into bribing and blackmail, Cohn also enjoyed an extravagant social life, often partying at Studio 54, a nightclub that he legally represented, as well as attending sex parties at the ranch of

---

[975] On a somewhat ironic note, Cohn, who was gay, seemed to be indifferent to McCarthy's antipathy towards homosexuals and his stated aim to prevent them from holding office.

multimillionaire Shearn Moody, who provided young male prostitutes to his guests.[976]

Roy Cohn died of AIDS in 1986, but his shadow is cast wide on today's political landscape. Not only was he a mentor to Donald Trump and Roger Stone, he also associated with known predators like Cardinal Spellman (May 4, 1889 – December 2, 1967). Spellman, who had been the Archbishop of New York from 1939 until his death in 1967, was also the Apostolic Vicar for the United States Armed Forces. It was while in this capacity that Lucian K. Truscott IV claims Spellman tried to fondle him when the latter was a West Point cadet conducting an interview with Spellman for the West Point student newspaper.[977]

Spellman, who was sometimes referred to as "Mary" within Catholic circles, along with Roy Cohn and J. Edgar Hoover, formed a sort of post-war trinity hell bent on hunting down communists: Roy Cohn through his work with Joseph McCarthy; Hoover through Cointelpro, an operation that ran from 1956 – 1979 and was used to infiltrate, disrupt, and discredit dissident political organizations; and Spellman, who not only supported McCarthy's efforts but would characterize adversaries as Communists to discredit them. Besides their contempt for communism and their hypocritical blackmail of political adversaries who engaged in the same sort of sexual behavior as themselves, Cohn, Hoover, and Spellman all had a strong antipathy to John F. Kennedy.

It is for all these reasons, and more, that conspiracy theorists have traced these three individuals' political involvement to a variety of assassinations, the co-opting or disruption of political movements, and the covering up of sexual

---

[976] From the article "King Cohn" by Robert Sherrill published by The Nation. https://www.thenation.com/article/archive/king-cohn/tnamp/ accessed 08/04/20

[977] https://salon.com/2019/02/09/i-was-groped-by-a-man-called-mary-the-world-changes-but-not-the-catholic-church/ accessed on 11/12/20

abuse scandals, in both the Catholic Church and in the Republican Party. The last point converges in the Franklin Scandal, which gets its name from the Franklin Savings and Loan of Omaha, Nebraska. The allegations that make up the Franklin Scandal are almost a complete summary of the-picture-on-a-milk-box-horror stories you could associate with the 1980s. According to investigative journalist Nick Bryant, who has researched and written extensively on the subject, the Franklin Scandal:

> Is about an interstate pedophile network that flew kids from coast to coast. What we are seeing with Jeffrey Epstein, we saw in the Franklin scandal, although I think the Franklin pandering network was much, much bigger than Jeffrey Epstein's network. There were two primary pimps. There was a pimp in Nebraska, Larry King. He was getting children that had fallen through the cracks, from foster-care homes, from Boy's Town Orphanage and from some other institutions. There was another pimp living in Washington, DC, who was involved in this, Craig Spence, who had his home wired for audio-visual blackmail. Anybody who took part in any of those parties at Craig Spence's home was definitely blackmailed.[978]

Lawrence King had come to the nation's attention by singing the National Anthem at the 1984 Republican Convention and was someone who was developing a significant amount of clout within the party. According to Bryant, King had embezzled forty million dollars from Franklin Savings in Loan while managing the institution. [979] Had this embezzlement not occurred, claims Bryant, there is a strong likelihood that King's trafficking

---

[978] https://news.isst-d.org/an-interview-with-nick-bryant-part-i-the-franklin-scandal/ accessed on 11/12/20
[979] Ibid

operation would have continued to evade the attention of law enforcement.

The activities in which King and Spence were involved revolved around molestation, child-trafficking, and child pornography. Prior to Bryant's investigation, another researcher named Gary Caradori, who had collected photographic and document evidence related to the case, died mysteriously in a plane crash. When everything was said and done, the only people sentenced to jail time was one of the accusers, Alisha Owen, who served four and a half years for perjury.

The salaciousness of the Franklin Scandal dovetailed with the so-called "Satanic Panic" that surrounded the McMartin preschool trial, which went from 1987 to 1990. Unlike the McMartin case, which was most certainly a modern-day witch trial spurred on by rumors and false testimony, the Franklin Scandal is justifiably open to speculation. Bryant claims that victims of King and Spence's trafficking operation often fell into lives of crime, drug use, and prostitution. But unlike the McMartins, who had no political connections, King and Spence were very well connected politically and had easy access to the levers of power. Bryant claims that, when looking at the Franklin Scandal, special attention needs to be paid to the political process:

> Americans think it is special interest money that is co-opting the political system. Which is true, but political blackmail is also co-opting the political system [...] The thing about it is that there are people who come up in my interviews that I couldn't mention in my book –just because they are so powerful. It would be like one victim who has a very damaged, shattered life testifying against some august powerbroker. That would be the first round knockout as far as credibility goes.[980]

---

[980] Ibid

Bryant sees it as a cyclical process, in which drugs are used to entice, or coerce, disaffected young people into these trafficking networks, and then, effected by abuse and drug addiction, are unable to be credible witnesses.

One such individual who might have been involved in the Franklin Scandal, and subsequently slipped through the cracks, was a boy named Johnny Gosch. Gosch was a newspaper boy in West Des Moines, who, at the age of twelve, disappeared during his paper route in the early hours of September 5, 1982. During the initial investigation, a neighbor reported that he had seen Gosch talking with a man in a blue Ford Fairmont with Nebraska license plates. After receiving calls from neighbors complaining that they had not received their newspaper, Johnny's father searched the neighborhood and around 7am found Johnny's wagon full of newspapers two blocks from their home.

Johnny Gosch was one of the first children to appear on the side of a milk carton and over the years a variety of private investigators and research journalists have tried to get to the bottom of his mysterious disappearance. Johnny's mother, Noreen Gosch, who has been very vocal about law enforcement's mishandling of the case, claims that Johnny briefly visited her in 1997. According to Noreen, her son appeared at her door at two in the morning in the company of another man. She then claims that the visitor identified himself as her son and proved this by showing her a birthmark on her chest. After this visit, Noreen visited the FBI office in Iowa and had them do an updated sketch of Johnny's appearance.[981]

At one level, most of the people who are aware of the Gosch case wonder if it points to a child-trafficking ring; some might further speculate that such a ring might be tied to certain

[981] John Gosch Senior, who was divorced from Noreen at the time of the supposed visit has said that he cannot verify whether or not it actually took place.
https://n.m.wikipedia.org/wiki/Disappearance_of_Johnny_Gosch accessed on 11/16/20.

political or financial elites. At another level, there are conspiracy theorists that try to tie this disappearance to Lawrence King, the Franklin Scandal, and Pizzagate. And at the deepest level of intrigue we have conspiracy theorists pondering the question: how closely does this updated police sketch resemble a man named Jeff Gannon? Gannon is a journalist who appeared at four George W. Bush press conferences and regularly at White House press briefings.

Gannon came under scrutiny from fellow journalists because he lacked any background in the field, and because he wrote for "Talon News," a conservative online publication that some speculated was a bogus enterprise run by PACs. Gannon, whose real name is James Dale Guckert, brought this attention upon himself and his "employer" by consistently asking softball questions. However, it is most likely the notoriety that was stirred up when his background in the male escort industry[982] was brought to light, that drew conspiracy theorists to begin positing the question: "Is Jeff Gannon actually Johnny Gosch?"

One such conspiracy theorist, Tim Schmitt, published a piece entitled "Johnny Gosch, Jeff Gannon, Hunter Thompson, and the Unraveling of a Troubling Tale" on April 6, 2005. In this piece, Schmitt relies primarily on four sources: private investigator Sherman H. Skolnick, who penned a piece for his website in February of 2005 claiming that Gannon is Gosch; "retired FBI agent" Ted Gunderson; retired New York detective Jim Rothstein; and Paul Bonacci. Bonacci claims that he was a member of the same sex-slavery ring into which Gosch was forced and had been made to participate in Gosch's kidnapping.[983]

---

[982] According to Gannon's Wikipedia page, he was listed on various escort sites under the name "Bulldog." https://en.wikipedia.org/wiki/Jeff_Gannon accessed 11/16/20

[983] https://educate-yourself.org/cn/goschgannohuntertrublingtale05.shtml accessed on 11/17/20

The link that has, let's say, a degree of objective value in the connection between the triangle of Gosch, Gannon, and the Franklin scandal has to do with Craig Spence's involvement with a homosexual escort service that was being investigated by the Secret Service; this investigation was reported on in a *Washington Times* article in June of 1989.[984] Yes, this is the same Craig Spence who Nick Bryant alleges participated in child-trafficking with Lawrence King. It was also alleged that Spence was given late night access to the White House and that he and his companions occasionally toured the place after hours. Six months after the story had been made public, Spence committed suicide. At the time of his death Spence was working as a lobbyist for the Japanese government; in a passage that presages the scandals surrounding Jeffrey Epstein, Eleanor Randolph notes that:

> On July 18, *The Post* published a long profile in the Style section of Spence, the mystery man who concocted an elaborate lifestyle that included salon-style parties where people sat around with his clients and discussed trade policy. It also told how Spence suggested mysteriously that he bugged his friends and worked for an intelligence agency.[985]

We can speculate that the persona of "Jeffrey Epstein" is a sort of reiteration of the "Craig Spence" narrative, in that both were deeply involved in finance, prostitution, and political intrigue. Both claimed to be working for intelligence agencies and were purported to have secretly recorded clients and guests. And both "committed suicide."

---

[984]

www.washingtonpost.com/archive/lifestyle/1989/08/01/the-bombshell-that-didn't-explode/ff09cbd0-7d64-428b-8415-a6998b9f0c65/ accessed on 11/17/20

[985] Ibid

The connection between Spence and George H.W. Bush's Administration was cemented by *The Washington Times'* sensationalistic headline: "Homosexual prostitution inquiry ensnares VIPs with Reagan, Bush." By Randolph's estimation, the Times' reporting tended a little too strongly towards conjecture and over-reach, but the events still warranted investigation.

Spence's involvement with this scandal, which occurred during Bush Senior's Administration, led some conspiracy theorists to speculate that Gannon's presence in the press pool at the White House during Bush Junior's Administration was the continuation of a Republican orchestrated trafficking operation. So, with that reasoning in place, we can conjecture that Gosch was one of the boys trafficked by Spence. However, if one is (unintentionally) aiming to create, or codify, a compound conspiracy theory, we get some claims like these:

-Jeff Gannon's supposedly real name is "Jeff Guckert." The use of two names with the initials J.G., which are also Johnny Gosch's initials, is one of Gannon's clues as to his true identity.

-"Gannon" was the name of a newspaper editor who published a letter Noreen Gosch wrote upon Johnny's disappearance and Gosch's use of it is an oblique reference back to the aftermath of his disappearance.

-Jeff Gannon supposedly has a birthmark on his chest similar to Gosch's.

-That Gosch took on the persona of Gannon/Guckert in order to infiltrate and then expose his kidnappers. However, Gannon/Gosch cannot reveal his true identity yet because it would endanger himself and his family.

-Gannon posted an article on his website titled: "Hiding in Plain Sight."

These theories are all conjectured, with varying degrees of credulity, by Schmitt in his essay. They are standard coincidence-oriented propositions that purport to have a materialistic sensibility. This sensibility is compounded when he claims that certain individuals are trying to secure a DNA sample from Gannon (which would be a fool's errand if we don't have Gosch's DNA on file somewhere). All this conforms to the quantitative standards set by 9/11 conspiracy theorization. However, we are living in the post-9/11 world of simulation, and therefore, other, more mysterious propositions using more ambiguous, yet genre-established, signifiers must be incorporated, i.e., two references to the MK Ultra and Monarch programs.

These references are signifiers of older, more established conspiracy theory tropes. However, I think they reveal an attempt not so much to refer to those programs themselves as to access the mythological import, and attendant narrative richness, conveyed by them. The only problem with invoking these conspiratorial tropes is that one must do so in a skillful manner, like a great novelist indulging in a genre exercise. Going overboard with them is tantalizing, making for some wild reading, but also risks demolishing the credibility of one's thesis, as well as the credibility of one's sources. Schmitt accomplishes all this in one paragraph. After claiming that famed "Gonzo" journalist Hunter S. Thompson had a side-gig directing snuff films in the eighties, Schmitt ties this activity to Paul Bonnaci, writing:

> The snuff film that Thompson allegedly made with Paul Bonnaci is believed to have been filmed at Bohemian Grove, a summer camp of sorts for the rich and powerful. Bohemian Grove is a secluded area outside of Sacramento, California, where world leaders and dignitaries meet annually for a retreat that involves neo-pagan activities, including mock human sacrifices made before a large owl statue referred to as "Moloch." While conducting this ritual, which they call "The Cremation of Care,"

participants are dressed in Druid robes and chant and sing before Moloch.[986]

Schmitt's evidence for Thompson's involvement in all of this is primarily based on the coincidence of the famed writer's suicide occurring on February 20, 2005, supposedly the same day that the Gannon/Gosch connection was first made public. Schmitt, and his sources, speculate that Thompson was either murdered to silence him, or he committed suicide to evade prosecution.

The problem with this conjectural leap, besides its tenuous nature, is that it betrays the author's eagerness to be accepted within the parameters of the conspiratorial genre. For our textual/narrative analysis the most significant aspect is that it involves the re-emergence of a historical personage under a new name and title. "Johnny Gosch, kidnapped paperboy" is re-identified as "Jeff Gannon, reporter by day, male escort by night." It's a postmodern reiteration of the phenomenon that we've seen occur with the names "Melchizedek" and "Prester John" and, in this respect, demonstrates an innate myth-oriented sensibility that pushes towards repetition, lurking beneath the surface.

Another such reoccurrence, which none of the Pizzagaters brought up, is: "John Podesta, campaign manager by day, human trafficker by night" and "John Podesta, campaign manager by day, UFO researcher by night." The Wikileaks emails revealed that John Podesta had looked into and discussed UFO phenomena with a wide range of individuals, from NASA astronaut Edgar Mitchell to Blink-182 guitarist Tom Delonge. Delonge was so impressed with Podesta's knowledge on the subject that he had him

---

[986] https://educate-yourself.org/cn/goschgannohuntertrublingtale05.shtml accessed on 11/19/20

interviewed for a documentary the guitarist was producing on UFOs.[987]

Conspiracy theorists can now speculate on whether this bit of information was placed in the mainstream media as a way of muddying the waters around the topic of Pizzagate, or if Pizzagate was itself a diversion from the "real" issue of UFOs. My guess is that most will go with the former.

The Rise of QAnon

The Pizzagate conspiracy theory brings us back to a theory that we addressed in The Significance of the New World Order, the transparency of the elites, which postulated that the individuals controlling society communicate their dastardly plans to the public, either to desensitize them (Hoffman's theory) or because they are psychologically compelled (like Moriarty intentionally leaving clues for Sherlock Holmes). This interpretation of events, i.e., that the elites are somehow covertly broadcasting their illicit activities to the masses, is a form of conspiratorial theorization that has crossed over into slightly more mainstream forms of media. The so-called "QAnon" conspiracy theory is a movement that has extended from Pizzagate theories and conjoined them with the idea that there was a secret agent (or agents) operating within the Trump Administration, in order to bring the pedophile elites to justice.

QAnon theorizing, since being banned from most social media platforms like Twitter and Facebook, takes place on anonymous message boards like 4Chan. One narrative posted in the /pol/ section of the site gives this backstory for the secret agent that is Q as being a person with an official position in the Trump Administration, who is in his mid-thirties and is close friends with former National Security Advisor Michael Flynn. This

---

[987] https://www.nbcnews.com/news/us-news/clinton-campaign-chief-john-podesta-s-interest-ufos-out-world-n674711 accessed 11/11/20a

is just one theory; some believers have posited Q to be a network of people working throughout the Trump Administration and the Pentagon. The "deep state" or corruption that QAnon adherents insist exists usually involves pedophilia, child-trafficking, human sacrifice, cannibalism, worship of Satan (or Moloch), and possibly the ingestion of "Adrenochrome." More skeptical observers have conjectured that some faction of the Trump Administration itself surreptitiously encouraged the QAnon movement in order to stir up his base.

The QAnon theory is interesting in two respects. First, it counters the sinister transparent activities of the "elite" with the actions of a super-secret covert agent that has infiltrated their ranks. In this regard, it is combatting a dualistic system that traffics in transparency with a theory that peddles in monistic and shrouded secrecy. Second, whereas political partisans hijacked the 9/11 truther movement, here we have conspiracy theorists hijacking, to varying degrees of success, the political machine itself, as evidenced by Trump and other officials unknowingly retweeting QAnon memes during his presidency.

As it pertains to hyperreality, this phenomenon can be interpreted using Baudrillard's idea of reversibility. The concept of "seduction," which Baudrillard connects to the concept of simulation, is something that eludes the quantifying, interrogative, and scientistic mentality that has come to the forefront of modernity. Here we find two reversals in Baudrillard's thought. The first relates to the meta level of philosophy and the analysis of systems of thought as they occur within society. In this regard, Baudrillard is changing the emphasis from the instrumental or power-focused approach to an approach that favors the invisible, and possibly ineffable. The second way that seduction and simulation come into play, and which relates to the rise of QAnon, is that the orientation towards the invisible and ineffable invokes imaginative spaces. This is not meant to be read as the "imagination" as if it was a Kantian faculty, like the "understanding." No, this is the positing of a "no-place" (like a "utopia") that eludes and undermines the sense of reason that is purported to be the governing ethos of western societies. In his essay, "Our Theatre of Cruelty" Baudrillard elaborates on how this can be strategically employed:

> The secret is to oppose to the order of the real an absolutely imaginary realm, completely ineffectual at the level of reality, but whose implosive energy absorbs everything real and all the violence of real power which founders there. Such a model is no longer of the order of transgression: repression and transgression are of the old order of the law, of the order of a real *system* of expansion. In such a system, all that comes into contradiction with it, including the violence of its opposite, only makes its expansion accelerate. Here, the virulence comes from the implosion [...] At bottom, the profound tactic of simulation is to provoke an excess of reality, *and to make the system collapse under an excess of reality.*[988]

In this light, the QAnon phenomenon succeeds as a societal destabilizing force where the terrorism of 9/11 failed. However, I believe that its influence, as perceived by those that are hostile to it, is more akin to a virus than an implosion. This imaginary space, which exists primarily on the internet, can be read as a reiteration of the sacred space that people in the Middle Ages projected onto the realms governed by figures such as the Fisher King and Prester John. However, unlike a land that is "over there," at the edge of the world somewhere, it is an invisible landscape lurking behind the everyday world. Given that this hidden "landscape" came into prominence after 9/11 and is postmodern in nature, it accentuates aspects of life that are sinister and threatening, not enchanting or wondrous. The prominent figures are an inversion

---

[988] Baudrillard, Jean (2001) "Our Theatre of Cruelty" published in *Hatred of Capitalism: A Semiotext(e) Reader.* P. 54

of those featured in the Grail mythos; they are wealthy and famous; they appear on magazine covers and television shows. All the mystery surrounding these figures circulates beneath the thin veneer of their photographed image, and though secretly no one rationally expects for these mysteries to be brought to light, QAnon exists as a kind of faith, if not in revelation, at least in justice.

Tracy Twyman: A Mysterious Conclusion to an Enigmatic Life

There is not a lot of information available about the life of Tracy Twyman. Most of what's on the internet is in conspiracy themed chatrooms, and the individuals claiming to have known Twyman are, let's just say, not the most credible. What we do know with some verifiability is that she was born on August 28, 1978, in Kansas City, Missouri, and died of an apparent suicide on July 9, 2019.[989] Twyman's heyday was in the early nineties when she met and formed a friendship with musician Boyd Rice. Together the two would collaborate on *Dagobert's Revenge,* as well as appear on evangelical radio shows to scandalize and troll the hosts.

We've gone over a good deal of the substantive material that Twyman and Rice produced in the nineties, as it pertains to the Merovingian mythos, the Grail, and Aleister Crowley. But in her final years it seems she parlayed her notoriety into a variety of subjects: the relationship between alchemy and modern-day economics (*Money Grows on the Tree of Knowledge*), the Ouija Board and conjurations (*Clock Shavings),* and most notably, child-trafficking and mind control (*Mind-Controlled Sex Slaves and the CIA*). Her later research seemed to involve connecting the dots between occult practices and human-trafficking, and this is the link that her mourners and champions insist led to her death.

989

https://obits.columbian.com/obituraies/columbian/obituary.aspx?n=tracy-renee-twyman&pid=194790052 accessed 11/24/20

Near the end of her life, Twyman did a few interviews and monologue videos in which she detailed events she experienced, and what she believed was going on behind-the-scenes. One video published on June 30, 2018, titled "Twyman Trip #8: The Internet is Compromised," begins by talking about how her website had gone down a month prior and she had been locked out of her Google account. She then describes the hacking of her wifi and communication devices. This surveillance, she believed, involves mind-reading: "The techniques used by these companies allow them to monitor both an image of what you are thinking about, and an audio stream of your own voice inside of your head."[990] From here she seems to spiral into every manner of topical paranoia: AI, computer chip "Mark of the Beast" implants, and QAnon. Throughout, she describes individuals who are contacting her and egging on her ordeal. The situation seems to be uncannily similar to the trolls who egg on Gail Schuler; however, Schuler, being of a more optimistic bent, seemingly keeps rolling with the flow. Twyman, who probably took things a bit more light-heartedly in her youth, apparently got totally sucked into her paranoia and suspicions as she researched these topics, and it led to a truly unfortunate fate.

In her life's trajectory we can discern the movement that is central to our narrative: the shift from a qualitative mythic orientation to a quantitative scientistic one. We can see how the more scientifically based paradigm makes severe and nearly impossible demands on the subject to "fight the system" and mobilize others to do so as well. This new paradigm is bereft of levity or playfulness and demands action on the part of the subject, an action that is Sisyphean and therefore conducive of cracking under the pressure (if that is what happened).

The Ironic Return of Literature

---

[990] https://tracytwyman.com/plusultra/twyman-trip-8-the-internet-is-compromised/ accessed 11/24/20

I didn't want to address this topic in the literature section of The Significance of the New World Order because it would have taken us too far afield of the primary themes of that chapter; I will address it here because it coincides with the idea that there is a collective construction of "reality." The issue I want to briefly address doesn't have to do with the question of what is possible, but what is morally acceptable; namely, is it morally permissible to enact something in "the real world" that has already occurred in a dystopian novel or film?

Let's begin with Rosa Foods, a company that in 2014 created the "Soylent" brand of meal replacement drinks, bars, and powders. Everyone is probably aware of the 1973 film *Soylent Green* by virtue of its famous line: "Soylent Green is people!" How then, can this product exist? Answer: hyperreality. The inspiration for *Soylent Green* was the 1966 novel *Make Room! Make Room!* by Harry Harrison, which focused on overpopulation (a theme near and dear to some conspiracy theorists). In the book, "Soylent" refers to steaks made of soy and lentils and there is no mention of cannibalism – putting the brand more in line with contemporary products like "The Impossible Burger." *Make Room! Make Room!* is cited as an influence on the mastermind behind the real-life Soylent, Rob Rhinehart, who said that the name was chosen to "pique interest" and cause potential customers to investigate the product more thoroughly.[991]

In a sense, here we have a consumer product that is trying to rewrite, or rebrand, the essential ingredient of a dystopian work of art and while the invocation is to some extent ironic or cynical, it can also be viewed as an attempt to re-examine, and rehabilitate, the foundational text upon which the "Soylent Green" meme is built. Hence, such current events demand we discuss the role of literature in the Mandela Effect. However, the Mandela Effect has to do with the emergent phenomenon of misremembering some usually trivial fact, not about consciously

---

[991] https://en.m.wikipedia.org/wiki/Soylent_(meal_replacement) accessed on 06/22/21

"meming" or re-engineering an existing cultural artifact. It seems as if the cultural artifact – the shock of the ending of *Soylent Green* in this case – is a kind of sacred object in our hyperreal world. It is coveted, like the Grail, not for the act of possession, but as an intellectual property that can be rebranded and repurposed – utilized within a new context. This new contextualization then frees the object from the "good" and "evil" connotations with which it had been saddled in its original literary or filmic medium. It is this freedom from an inherent sense of good and evil that can lead to claims of nihilism from those with a moral investment in Western culture; for us, it merely signifies that any facet of culture can be detached and repurposed for new, simulated, ends.

The mark of a great science fiction writer is not merely the creation of believable and interesting characters and engaging plots but the integration of these into a setting that is equally interesting and engaging. A further demand often made on the science fiction author is that they import a sense of prescience into their works. This sense of prescience can be thought of as an ability to foretell the future; more often it is the ability to identify existing sociological trends and extrapolate them into the future. The ironic naming of a product, such as Soylent, in today's cultural climate, can be further interpreted as an attempt to tap into this anachronistic literary sense of prescience and narrative richness.

What if we push a little further past this example, and, instead of a corporation using a provocative name to market their product – which can be read as alternatively cynical or clever – we look at an individual who takes the ideological elements of a dystopian work of fiction and lauds them? Such is the case of Klaus Schwab, who with co-author Thierry Malleret, penned *Covid-19: The Great Reset* in 2020. Schwab, who is the founder and chairman of the World Economic Forum (WEF), holds a doctorate in engineering and hosts meetings in Davos that are attended by some of the world's most notable investors, politicians, and celebrities.

Much like The Council on Foreign Relations, the World Economic Forum has come under fire from conspiracy theorists because they are supposedly trying to either: a) spread communism, or b) implement Naziesque programs. Most of these conspiracy theorists are rebuffed with the claim that the WEF has no real power to implement policies – it merely suggests them. However, non-conspiracy theorists such as Naomi Klein, have criticized the elitist nature of the group and the dangerous effects its proposals might have on ordinary people. What then, are the dystopian ideas that Schwab and his ilk are putting forward? To set the stage, let's put one of Schwab's previous proposals, from 2016's *The Fourth Industrial Revolution*, on the table: the implanting of microchips that act as cell phones. One of the themes of *The Fourth Industrial Revolution* which is developed further in *Covid-19: The Great Reset*, is that some form of technocracy will reign in the near future, so we might as well embrace it. The WEF also famously promoted the idea that by the year 2030 people in cities will have no possessions:

> Welcome to the year 2030. Welcome to my city –or should I say, "our city." I don't own anything. I don't own a car. I don't own a house. I don't own any appliances or any clothes. It might seem odd to you, but it makes perfect sense for us in this city. Everything you considered a product has now become a service. We have access to transportation, accommodation, food, and all the things we need in our daily lives. One by one all these things became free, so it ended up not making sense for us to own much.[992]

The essay from which this is taken was written by an individual named Ida Auken and was published on the WEF's website on November 11, 2016. Also described in the essay are clean energy and flying cars. *The Great Reset* is basically an extension of this

---

[992] https://www.weforum.org/agenda/2016/11/how-life-could-change-2030/ accessed on 1/21/21

theme and its tone is managerial, in that it asks how we will manage and engineer the lives of the world's populations in the wake of Covid-19. The panic, and subsequent lockdowns, which resulted from the Covid 19 outbreak of 2020 is almost a perfect example of the implementation, by the state and mainstream media, of *1984esque* modifications to the societies they govern. But this dystopian future has a Baudrillardian twist as the citizens affected by these restrictions, curfews, and closures are incredulous towards the situation but never directly challenge the fact that the emperor is not wearing any clothes. This contrasts with the *1984* scenario, wherein most everyone partakes of a frightened silence and the hero must fight through layers of bureaucracy and political intrigue to discover the truth. Instead, everyone knows the disease, despite its lethality, is the means for a media spectacle. It is to be paid lip-service and nothing will be revealed – just as nothing will be revealed about the death of Jeffrey Epstein.

This is truly a postmodern situation. To the conspiracy theorist, the elaborate staging of the lockdown and safety measures is the system's conditioning of its subjects for a "real" epidemic. Tied to this are theories that Corona virus tests are a ruse to collect DNA. From a more anthropological view, one that allows for the argument from hyperreality, one might say that the lockdown and accompanying measures indicate a superstitious staging of the epidemic in an irrational attempt to ward off the real thing when it comes (much like the function of totem poles in earlier societies). Finally, to a theorist who is fully in thrall to the explanatory power of the argument from hyperreality, the lockdown and accompanying measures mask the absence of the real in a manner similar to Baudrillard's summarizing that: "nature reserves are erected as memorials, or tombstones, to nature."

There is a certain validity to all three viewpoints, however, given the pluralistic model we have been following, it is only feasible to say that *some* parties within the conspiratorial model are pushing for these things. Unlike the conspiracy theorist, I would say that the drive for increased lockdowns was intended to collapse smaller businesses to benefit large corporations.[993] The other models touch upon the irrational and superstitious nature we have dealt with throughout this book. What the pandemic has reinforced is that, in a modern context, when the superstitious and irrational is tethered to myths and legends, it is less pervasive. But once it moves unchecked into the realm of scientific and political discourse it can be more diffuse, and possibly more pernicious.[994]

So, to briefly return to Davos and the WEF's celebration of a technocratic state that eliminates private property and established norms, there are a few things upon which we can speculate. The first is that Schwab and his cohorts seem to be promoting an almost *Star Trek* kind of utopia where people are not only conditioned out of owning or wanting possessions, they are also conditioned out of finding a certain degree of self-identification from ownership. In Schwab's own writings he doesn't really discuss concepts like "happiness" or "freedom" with the same emphasis that he gives to "security" and "sustainability." Most likely this is because he is addressing the concerns of his fellow elites. He allows writers who post their articles on the WEF website, such as Ida Auken, to talk about "fun" and "excitement" but it comes off about as compelling as an infomercial. The duality of these two tones brings us to a Žižek inspired critique that this is an example of totalitarianism with "a smiling face." Drastic and brutal changes are enforced under the guise of liberation and helpfulness.

With a literary analysis that likely coincides with more of a pessimistic conspiratorial worldview, we might speculate that the

---

[993] Like the one that is printing and distributing this book for me.
[994] As of the date of my writing this (11/24/20) the damage has been primarily economic, e.g., the closing of small businesses, bars and restaurants and the rapacious profiteering of huge corporations and academic, with record numbers of students failing in their studies.

nihilism and despair attendant to dystopian literature are essentially inescapable. In a sense, the prophetic power of a text overrides the will of the individual, or even the structure in which he or she exists. This is akin to the idea that an individual can be literally animated by a text. However, unlike the individual who is animated by a narrative, which is procedural in nature, these individuals seem to be in thrall to a narrative that is abstract and literary. Compounding this is the self-conscious awareness that these literary constituents portend negative consequences.

This situation goes beyond the usual scenario of a celebrity doing charity work for the poor while also treating his or her personal assistants horribly, which can be described as mere hypocrisy. In this case, the individual is consciously acknowledging the truthful import of something like *1984*, lauding it, and simultaneously saying: "history must be re-written." In the same vein as this critique, which combines dystopian literature with postmodern analysis, when the WEF and other like-minded groups make these contrarian proposals, they still utilize signifiers like "freedom" and "well-being;" thus indicating a lack of conviction to actually embody the role of super-villains. This lack of conviction is what makes the entire scenario which they envision dystopian. Even Schwab's references to "inclusion," "sustainability," and "progress" are more tempered, respectable words, attempting to elicit similar idealistic responses – just from a more high-minded audience.

"The Great Reset" wherein humanity is thrust into the brave new world of no possessions, instant communication, complete surveillance, and a totally homogenous global community is the world the WEF wants, and says **must** be created, and that the response to Covid-19 is the perfect opportunity to bring it about. It is only frightening because the individuals promoting this agenda don't have the courage or aplomb to play the role of "super villain" – when Burroughs said "no more Stalins and no more Hitlers" part of what he feared, it appears, was not just an indifferent bureaucratic superstructure but an innate shirking of moral responsibility towards either good or evil. The lack of conviction on the part of Schwab and his cohorts is, to a certain extent poetic a la the aphorism that the "road to hell is paved with good intentions," but it also indicates an unremarkable sense of homogeneous inauthenticity that merely bleeds into the backdrop of simulation in which we are already immersed.

As to the question of whether these dystopian schemes can come to fruition, conspiracy theorists can at least take solace in the fact that a society without possessions flies directly in the face of the hyper-consumerist reality of the West. Also, it is one thing to inculcate the repetition of ideological slogans in the general populace, but quite another to change behavior. The American public is imbued with a great deal of inertia and incompetence. We have proven ourselves to be incapable of creating a utopia; perhaps we are too incompetent to achieve a dystopia as well? This then raises the question: is a failed dystopia itself a kind of dystopia? Is it worse or better off than an achieved dystopia?

Are We Living in a Simulation?

Contrary to the argument from hyperreality, which posits the possibility that we once had but lost a "real" or "actual" world, the theory that we will be discussing here assumes that our entire world, and possibly universe, has been devoid of "reality" from the beginning. The "Simulation Argument," posits that all human beings are virtual entities living in a computer simulation. It came to prominence when the Swedish philosopher Nick Bostrom wrote a paper on the topic for the April 2003 issue of *The Philosophical Quarterly*.[995] In Bostrom's paper he presented a three-part dilemma, or "trilemma," in which one of the three following propositions must be true: One, humans always go

---

[995] https://www.scientificamerican.com/article/do-we-live-in-a-simulation-chances-are-about-50-50/?fbclid=lwAR3Z48buarFAmC3qqNEJuZ14LKtLQmqW6xLZmhJQ144FKhGUxjCjpGxF7og accessed on 10/29/20

extinct before they can reach the stage where they can create simulations; two, that even if humans make it to that stage, they are unlikely to be interested in simulating their ancestral past; and three, the chances that we are living in a simulation ourselves are about 50-50.

A Columbia University professor named David Kipping took these three propositions and reduced them by one, based on the reasoning that the first two would yield the same results. In a certain respect Kipping was working dialectically, as on one side we have a physical hypothesis (there are no simulations) and on the other we have the simulation hypothesis (there is a "base," or non-simulated, reality – and there are simulations too.)[996] Kipping then granted each hypothesis a fifty percent probability using Bayesian reasoning. To further calculate the probabilities of these models he looked at which could generate simulated realities, and which could not. To this end he postulated that if the physical hypothesis was true, then there was zero percent chance that we were living in a simulation. Conversely, if the simulation hypothesis is correct, most of the simulated realities would not be capable of replicating their own simulations, while the ones that were would exhaust the computational resources to do so.

Some philosophers enjoy dabbling with this type of thinking. During an informal speech from a few years back, Slavoj Žižek gleefully described the subatomic world as analogous to a part of a video game's scenery which the creators did not thoroughly program. There are a lot of interesting questions the simulation scenario raises. One has to do with the issue of free will – but let's set that aside for the moment and focus instead on the fact that the *Scientific American* article from which I am taking this information takes for granted that we ourselves are autonomous subjects living within a simulation (if the theory is true). The writer even makes the obligatory *Matrix* reference, and I think this conveys an idea of innate self-hood that had been put into question philosophically since the time of Hume.

---

[996] Ibid

The simulation argument is most convincing when it is most terrifying, i.e., that we ourselves are simulations being played almost like a video game within a simulated world. This thesis would annihilate any lingering questions involving free will. However, it still would allow for the idea of a continuous and identifiable "self," as one would have to possess enough continuity and distinction to be a playable character. But with a less theoretical reading, we can ask why the word "simulation" needs to entail a technological model. I have already argued, in accord with Baudrillard, that simulation is real, or at least real enough, and in our society is contingent on technology. But can we imagine a less technologically advanced society that subsists primarily in a simulated state? Yes, and these simulations usually stem from ideologies. Ideologies do entail a sense of progress, but it is not necessarily a technological progress; though it is difficult to clearly distinguish the two in conceptual terms. One way, however, would be through an explicitly occult reading.

Among the many theories put forward by Peter Moon in his Montauk conspiracy theory is that we are living in a simulation. Moon describes an almost Platonic realm where the physical universe was drafted; he calls it the "blueprint room," and says it "represents the creation zone at its highest level. It is also linked to zero time in that this creation zone is outside of three-dimensional space and time."[997] Moon sees the "blueprint room" as a mythical realm, or possibly a "golden age" humanity inhabited at some distant point in the past:

> In the example of the blueprint room above, the physical universe could be said to have been set in motion when Adam decided to leave his job as a draftsman and explore what was outside. Somewhere along the line, the ability to trace one's way back to the blueprint room was lost. In other

---

[997] Moon, Peter (2003) *The Black Sun: Montauk's Nazi-Tibetan Connection.* Sky Books. P. 251

words, he went into a virtual reality hologram arcade and could not come back to his original reality. Intelligent observation will demonstrate that there have been plenty of operations from the blueprint room, or a rival one, ever since.[998]

So, perhaps the simulation we are living is not being controlled by extraterrestrial aliens but was engineered by humanity itself aeons ago. If this theory is broadly entertained it opens possibilities that factions of people, either consciously or unconsciously, are accessing the "blueprint room" via linguistic transmission, and hence, altering the fabric of reality. This certainly puts us back in the realm of Antara's appeal to Quantum mechanics with which we began this chapter, but it also intersects with the idea that memes are tied to a Hermetical apprehension of the world.

Some people see the simulation argument in sociological terms: essentially that proponents of the theory are falling prey to the type of representational thinking that has been borne out of video games. There is the additional problem of infinite regress, as in, where does the simulation end? How are we to say that we are living in a simulation but that the aliens controlling us are not? Perhaps computer simulations, or virtual reality, which we are using to understand this thesis is conceptually inaccurate, or bereft, and that the universe cannot be explained in these terms? There is one last bit of trivia on this subject on which I will elaborate regarding simulation.

Physicist S. James Gates gained a certain amount of notoriety when he claimed that equations arising from his research in "string theory," wherein some of the mathematical structures that underlie our physical understanding of the world, bore an uncanny similarity to "error-correcting" code used by computer programmers. This revelation led to simulation theorists claiming it as further evidence for their claim. However,

---

[998] Ibid p. 252

Gates has argued against simulation theory and stated that his research only indicates that the universe is constructed with an elegance that we associate with mathematics. Gates too, it appears, believes that the concept of a computer simulation is inadequate to explain our experience of the world.

The Man Who Shot Liberty Valance, Or One Final Shot at the Mandela Effect

Certain lines from films have been caught up in the web of the Mandela Effect, most notably, "Play it again, Sam" from *Casablanca* and "Mirror, mirror on the wall, who's the fairest of them all?" from *Snow White*. Though, it is much less famous, the line, "This is the West, sir. When the legend becomes fact, print the legend," from *The Man Who Shot Liberty Valance* has been consistently misquoted as well. Some variations are: "When the truth becomes legend, print the legend," "When you have to choose between history and legend, print the legend," and the simple injunction to just "print the legend."[999] The plot of the film involves a journalist named Maxwell Scott who is writing a piece on US Senator Ransom Stoddard (played by Jimmy Stewart) who rose to prominence after killing an infamous outlaw in his youth.

During Scott's research, he uncovers the truth that Stoddard did not kill Valance, as the fatal shot was actually fired by his friend Tom Doniphon (played by John Wayne). When Scott uncovers this, he decides not to reveal it to his readers and states the famous line. It's a fitting end to our book because it involves a famous, sometimes misremembered, line delivered by a character whose role is that of a scribe – a collector and transmitter of narratives.

The line itself is often attributed to the film's director, John Ford, or Dorothy M. Johnson, who penned the short story on

---

[999] https://sevencircumstances.com/2018/06/15/the-mystery-of-the-misquoted-quote-from-the-man-who-shot-liberty-valance/ accessed on 06/24/21

which the film is based, but it was actually crafted by screenwriters James Warner Bellah and Willis Goldbeck. The line, like other misremembered quotes from movies, does not really change very much in its various misquotations. However, the gist of it is essentially ambiguous: is it a scientistic indictment penned by twenty-first century screen writers of the "yellow journalism" that was rampant in the Old West, or is it a reverential allowance for poetic license? In a sense, both positions are preserved when a more thorough historical analysis is undertaken. After all, the screenwriters themselves are simultaneously constructing and deconstructing a myth within the process of writing the film. It can be construed as an anthropological analysis of mankind's gravitation towards legendary and mythic narratives, but it is also meditative and allows a dramatic space for myth within the historical narratives that we create; if only for the fact that it is this elusive element that draws us towards these narratives in the first place.

This is the last question we will pose in relation to the Mandela Effect, and it relates to pretty much everything we have discussed so far in this book: What happens when the legend is, as U2 would put it, "Better than the Real Thing"? What happens, for instance, when the real-life character of Doc Holliday is replaced in the public consciousness by Val Kilmer's portrayal of him in 1993's *Tombstone*? It seems as if we need to find a space within our simulated reality – which is always catering to the most fleeting of distractions, a space, or brief interstation – to allow for a sense of re-enchantment.

Such a space would have to maintain a balance between the historical facts informing our understanding of the events that dictated the actions and lives of characters, while allowing myth to hint at the question of why these narratives have captured our attention and *why* we repeat them – even if we can't verbally express it, these narratives have been, and deserve to be, repeated.

PART TWO: THE INTERVIEWS

Legendary filmmaker, Craig Baldwin has been active in the cinematic underground since the mid-seventies. This interview was conducted over the phone in 2020.

How're you doing?

Thanks for asking, I'm not going to pour out my problems to you right now because you would be overwhelmed. I lease a storefront in a pretty competitive area and the landlord has seized upon this time during the pandemic to do a seismic retrofit on the building. So I have to literally evacuate my whole studio, and that's what I do every day: tear apart my studio. In case you don't know, I'm not just a filmmaker, I'm also a curator, so I'm not making any films and I'm not doing any curating – I've turned into a mover. It's a real drag and one of the most trying times of my life.

I'm sorry to hear that. Can you tell me a little bit about your involvement with Negativland and the culture-jamming that they engaged in in their heyday?

I like those guys, it's really unfortunate that three of them have died. I identified with them, Don Joyce was older than me, Mark Hosler was younger than me, but basically they were my tribe here in NorCal. Negativland represents Contra Costa County, if you know what that means.

I don't know what that means, I know it's a place that's referenced on the first few albums, especially on *A Big 10-8 Place*.

It's kind of like Orange County for you, like the loser suburbs. They weren't from the city and they didn't pretend to be. They worked with their authentic environment, which was commercials and hideous billboards and things like that. So, that's what they meant by "Negativland": no culture. And then they did their best with it by flipping it and turning it around and that's what culture jamming is. They certainly were culture jammers, They may or may not have used the term.

They would talk about "jamming," like there was *Jamfest '84*...

Yeah they did use the term. That was in my movie *Sonic Outlaws*, that concept doesn't come from the art world, it actually comes from CB radio scanners. Younger people that were into CB culture at the time would radio jam the frequencies and make fun of the older guys who were more serious about it. They didn't have to go to school or read a book to learn how to do it -they just screwed around with it. They're totally my heroes. Of course Don Joyce was a master craftsman, who had already been on KPFA. I just loved their music and when I saw that they were in trouble with the U2 case, I made my move and that's how *Sonic Outlaws* came about.

In the book that I'm writing I have a chapter on Aleister Crowley, who I want to talk with you about, and I have a chapter on Robert Anton Wilson that also discusses the Discordians, the Church of the SubGenius and this obscure group that was around LA in the nineties called the Cacophony Society ...

Of course I know the Cacophony Society! You could even say that I was part of the San Francisco branch of that. The San Francisco Cacophony Society preceded the LA Cacophony Society. Oh, and there's a Portland Cacophony Society, that's what "Santacon" is all about. The story goes like this: there were groups in San Francisco that were interested in activities that were interventions in the urban milieu, like climbing over the bridge, or breaking into abandoned buildings and having parties, or going on the cable-car naked – stuff like that. That was the Suicide Club and that preceded the Cacophony Society. This is just a little before punk rock.

This was before punk rock?

I'd say it was about the mid-seventies; there was a kind of cultural vacuum there after the hippie era, but in San Francisco there were still a lot of free thinkers, and people who were interested in claiming the land – it wasn't all taken over by corporations yet. The cacophony society eventually led to Burning Man, before it went corporate.

One of the people I reference a lot in the book is Jean Baudrillard and he's got a pretty pessimistic outlook about things in our culture. You've said some things so far, about Contra Costa County and corporate advertising, corporations usurping spaces that belonged to an undefined counter-culture, etc. Do you see the eventual corporate overtaking of every counter-culture to be inevitable?

That's a good question, but it kinda puts me in a corner. I'm not going to say "yes" or "no." I think it's a struggle, that's what the Cacophony Society was, the Suicide Club was and Burning Man was. Rock n' roll and punk rock, all those were efforts to fight back and I'm part of the struggle. My whole life has revolved around fighting back, so I'm not going to say that corporations are going to take over. It's not over yet.

You've evaded the threat pretty well. I remember in 2001 or 2002 I wanted to get a copy of *Tribulation 99* and I went to Vidiots here in Santa Monica and they said it was going to be eighty bucks or something, and I somehow got ahold of your address and I sent you like fifteen bucks and you sent me a VHS copy with a note.

I do that all the time, but you can't necessarily construct a theory based on little ol' Craig Baldwin, there's a lot of people who do that, but we're overwhelmed. We need structures of course, to fight back. It's not just a bunch of optimists and idealists –which I am. There's places where that kind of idea of utopia still thrives. It's not the majority, but the majority isn't necessarily evil people either.

Your film *Tribulation 99* seems like something that could've been made at any time after 1966, you were so enigmatic on that. The same goes for *Mock Up on Mu* –I see it as you saying: "yeah, this has to exist because there's something intrinsically entertaining about it to me, and I know it would be that way for other people."

I don't deny that, but it's more than that. My films are actually documentaries in a way and they are reports about history, and they are critical. Anyone could enjoy them for the wrong reasons, of course, entertainment, quote unquote, but that's not really my goal. Making art, which has a formal elegance, is important combining that aesthetic with a critique exists within a discussion within culture. A discourse or an argument; another culture could understand it as an autonomous work of art, as you're arguing for, but that's not really where they're coming from. It would be hard to make such a film without having an engagement with a real struggle, in the case of Nicaragua and Cuba as they relate to *Tribulation 99* and also in the case of *Mock-up on Mu*, which involves the idea of Scientology being an oppressive cult. An artist's intentions are a huge discussion, but since you're talking to the artist, now you know what my intentions were.

That's good. I like getting that feedback. As regards to *Mock-up on Mu*, and I want to dive into this in more detail because that's a really important movie, I interpreted the character of L. Ron Hubbard in that film as being an indictment of Scientology to some extent. But I also saw him as being this

plutocratic, technocratic American figure who you pitted against Crowley, and Crowley was a sort of liberating figure. They seemed more archetypical.

You are younger and living in Southern California, you accept something like Scientology as normal. But it's not normal. When you treat it as if it's an everyday thing, you see it every day and you say: "well that's part of my life," then you become subject to it or passive to it.

I guess I kind of am passive to it. Obviously, I'm totally dismissive of it as a cult or whatever ...

It's a big business in it's own way but in this case it's not just selling more widgets or whatever, it's selling personal salvation. *Mock-up on Mu* is like the film before it, *Spectres of the Spectrum*, it has a critique of consolidation, centralization and moving away from the autonomy that I'm arguing for –these sites of resistance. My whole argument was not to attack the structure of corporate consolidation of wealth –I'd had to have gone to economics school to do that- I made my argument on the ground that I'm more familiar with, which is popular and sub-culture. I do know about Kenneth Anger and I do know about poets and science fiction writers and that's where I felt I had some leverage. The Jack Parsons story is a part of the New Age movement and the point centers around that movement's separation into the O.T.O., on one hand and Scientology on the other. There's been books and movies about it, and I picked up on that history and the issues of loss of autonomy and surrender to corporations, in terms of spiritual development, that were involved in it.

Has Crowley's writing had any impact on you?

I see him as a counter-cultural character who did generate this critique very early-on. I'm not saying that he didn't try to take advantage of people or wasn't a power-monger himself; of course he was a complicated man. If you look at history, he's someone who's been a little bit marginalized, and that's what I was referring to as the "sub-culture" and my job as a non-fiction filmmaker is to kind of retrieve these people. Crowley understood that Christianity was bankrupt and he offered a different thing. My thing is not to offer another religion as an alternative to Christianity, in a way Scientology tries to do that. If you look at their logo, it's a cross! They just appropriated the Christian Cross, they didn't break out of it, but Crowley tried to. My feelings on him are very complicated and I didn't try to make a movie about him, I tried to create a world in which these people brought up and generated ideas that had an impact on California subcultures. It wouldn't happen today because rocket scientists aren't going to talk to poets, but in the post-war period it did happen and Jack Parsons embodied that inquisitiveness and blending of a wide range of ideas.

In the book, when I paint the portrait of the heyday of the leftist movement that might have had an innovative take on conspiracy theories, I'm drawing on guys like William Burroughs, Derrick Jensen, and Jacques Ellul – people that might be characterized as "archeo-primitivists" …

I think I've heard of that last guy, did you say: "Ellul"? What did he write?

He wrote a book called *The Technological Society*.

I'm sure there's a trillion books called that. Was this guy a nihilist?

He was a French Catholic Anarchist in the sixties. In the book he talks about how technology arises as something that arises as a tool that a society uses, but at some point the tables are turned and technology uses us.

I haven't read him, but I think there's a lot of truth to that. I think technology, and its dominance in our society, is a part of this huge argument about an autonomous sense of self and freeing yourself from ideologies. All these ideas are products of struggle and discussion.

When you're talking about these autonomous spaces, do you see them as being inherently free of ideological influence?

That's not wrong, but I don't think anything is really free of ideology. I think that we are embedded in an ideological emulsion – we're floating in it, and there are better and worse ideologies. You wouldn't even be talking to me if you didn't have an ideology and vice versa ...

That's true.

So, language is a carrier of that. We have to be aware that words and phrases are laden with ideology. You said that your book was trying to get back to the larger myths and I go for that. In that respect, there's some value to the Christ myth, or Islam, or even Scientology. There's reasons why these things work, but the people who sign up for these things should ask: "why am I paying these guys to do this for me, when I could do it myself?" Ideology is in place, we're born into it, we're created by it. So, the idea is to break that Oedipal bond, not only with our parents but our community and think a little more freely. You'll never completely break out of it, but enough to where we can have a critical discussion, like what we're having now or your book, where you can raise these ideas.

Are you familiar with Steve Jackson's game *Illuminati*?

No. What did he do?

He created a board game about conspiracy theories and it involves parody, pop-culture, satire and a humorous sense of intrigue. To me it really resonates with your work, especially on *Tribulation 99*.

Well I admire him without even knowing him. I like the idea of a board game. Making a fun, spectacular movie, filled with special effects is a little bit like a board game: it's taking the argument to a pop-cultural form. It he's critiquing the Illuminati –good for him! I'm not the guy to go to for this other world of the Trilateral Commission, or whatever ... I just took them as clay to make a sculpture out of them.

Your sculpture in *Tribulation 99* is amazing though; the way that you match up the narration with some of those scenes is priceless...

It's just filmmaking. It's craft and it's the only craft I've really mastered. Films are in the service of ideas, which do not have form. Film is kind of a language and the language is in service to the argument. I'm not trying to be an enigmatic, Dennis Hopper kind of guy, I'm trying to present ideas.

Peter J. Carroll has written extensively on the subjects of magick, philosophy and science. This interview was conducted via email in 2020

What was your early life like? What were some of the things that you experienced in your youth that sparked your imagination and possibly led to your interest in the occult?

I found a great contradiction between the religion and the science they tried to teach me at school. I made frequent anthropological reports by telepathy to imagined aliens in orbit about the strangeness of life on earth. I found that some things I really wanted came to pass against all reasonable probability.

Was there any literature or philosophy that inspired you early on and that you still engage with today?

Early books on DIY witchcraft like Paul Huson's *Mastering Witchcraft* from the public library.

In regards to literature, I would imagine that people associate you with writers like J. G. Ballard, Jorge Luis Borges, Philip K. Dick and William Burroughs; do you see any connections between your work and these writers? Are there any literary influences you have that might surprise us?

My early serious reading about magic came from Eliphas Levi, Aleister Crowley, and MacGregor Mathers (The Golden Dawn material) and Austin Spare.

Was Kenneth Grant's work an influence on you? Do you have any thoughts on his incorporation of H.P. Lovecraft into magical theory?

I think the value of Kenneth Grant's work lies in what he brought to attention in the work of others, Crowley, Lovecraft, and Austin Spare in particular. Grant seemed to have an obsession with murk and obscurity and gothic darkness which the reader can profitably ignore.

I came across your work in the mid-nineties and at that time I was getting into industrial music, Robert Anton Wilson, Aleister Crowley, etc. The nineties was sort of a revival of that particular counter-culture. What was that time period like for you? I know you were published in Christopher Hyatt's *Rebels and Devils,* did you feel a sense of affinity with the other authors featured in that book?

My formative years occurred in the 1970s (Born 1953) I loved the flavour and style and omnivorous intellectual appetite of Robert Anton Wilson. I like artrock.

What artrock bands do you like (past and present)? In general, what are some of your favorite albums?

I like early Pink Floyd, Emerson Lake and Palmer, Deep Purple.

Very early in *Liber Null* you introduce the flow chart that shows the survival of the magical tradition. Included are Gnosticism, the Templars, the Bavarian Illuminati, etc. These are all subjects that I am addressing in my book. One of the dialectics that I explore is this: on one hand you have the idea that the sciences that existed in the antediluvian period had to be transmitted in a somewhat linear (or Hermetic) way, i.e., from Enoch to Hermes to Pythagoras to Plato etc. And on the other hand, the idea that there doesn't need to be a literal transmission and that the essence of these sciences can just appear, or be accessed, within meditative or magical states that aren't necessarily tied with any tradition. It seems like Chaos Magic would be more aligned with the latter

interpretation. What are your general thoughts on this
subject and how have they evolved over the years?

That chart represents ideas that fed into Chaos Magic, the
historical connections remain speculative. My
Psychohistoric Mechanism of the Aeons, or 'Aeonics' (Liber Kaos)
tidies it up methinks.

**In relation to the last question, people talk about the
Illuminati in a wide variety of ways –you yourself have used
the term- what does it mean to you and how have your
thoughts on the subject changed over the years?**

Illuminati just means those with some real or pretended
knowledge in a field, I reckon that Chaos Magic represents a more
advanced take on magic than any of its predecessors and thus
Chaos Magicians represent the Illuminati of Magic at present.

**You were one of the first people to blend a rigorous approach
to physics into your magical theories. I was re-reading the
"Bootstrapping the Serpent" section of *Liber Kaos* and it, at
least to my mind, seemed to have foreshadowed Julian
Barbour's attempt to fix the problems in the theory of
relativity by removing the concept of time (the book in which
he explored this, *The End of Time*, was published seven years
after *Liber Kaos*) Are you familiar with Barbour's work and, if
so, did you also see a similarity?**

Barbour's work does not convince me, there seems little point in
denying that time as a concept has a high explanatory value in our
understanding of the universe, and we can only understand the
universe by making concepts about it.

**I found the physics material on your website to be daunting.
Have you always had an aptitude for mathematical equations**

or has your mastery developed in accordance with the magical and philosophical topics you wanted to pursue?

No, I did Chemistry at Uni. I had to study the physics and maths from books, and with collaborators, and lately the net,

What are your thoughts on the "Mandela Effect"? It seems like the idea that history can be rewritten evolved out of, or is at least linked to Chaos Magic. However, the fact that it seems to be an emergent phenomenon (speaking sociologically) might contradict the Panpsychist premises you put forward in *The Apophenion*. In this respect, is the Mandela Effect an anthropological outgrowth of a more primal metaphysic, i.e., the quantum physics attendant to panpsychism?

I suspect that quantum physics underlies a universal network of communication of sorts, I currently research this more deeply for my forthcoming book The Occultaris.

In regards to the idea that "quantum physics underlies a universal network of communication of sorts." Do you see the pursuit of a unified field theory to be misguided because quantum physics ought to be seen as the primary lens through which phenomena ought to be understood?

The attempt to quantise gravity will probably fail, I see more promise in trying to geometricate the quanta and express everything in terms of spacetime geometry. I think that this could lead to a unification of sorts in which everything remains weakly entangled with everything else as in the Pusey Barrat Randolph theorem and in most magical and mystical philosophies.

This a very topical question and it has to do with the Corona Virus. I live in Los Angeles and people here seem to be in an interesting situation: on one hand, many of them believe that the virus is incredibly deadly and liable to kill them and their loved ones. On the other hand, they see the face coverings or masks that they wear as having an almost Talismanic value. It's almost as if they think that were it not for the mask they would be isolated at home, but as long as they have it they have a key that allows them access to the life they led before the pandemic. I'm very curious as to what your thoughts on this subject are.

If humanity did nothing about Coronavirus about one person in a thousand would die worldwide eventually. This may well happen anyway unless an effective and cheap vaccine appears. The seriousness of an infection does seem to partly depend on the number of attacking virus particles, so social distancing and mask wearing does make sense, on the other hand some people do overestimate the effectiveness of a mask, although masks do remind people to keep their distance. I have a fancy one that I quite enjoy wearing with my black pointy wizards hat as I imagine it makes me look like some occult bandit or rebel physicist. I have very much enjoyed the time to think and write that lockdown has provided.

Erik Davis has written extensively on the subjects of esotericism, philosophy and the convergence of these themes in the 1970s subculture of California. This interview was conducted over the phone in late 2020.

I actually had a whole list of questions that I was going to ask you, but it disappeared this moment, which I guess is appropriate, given what we're going to talk about ... What is it that got your mind working towards writing *High Weirdness*?

There's different ways that I can answer that question, depending on what you're looking for in regards to your project.

I'm not looking for anything, I just want it to be a vérité sort of thing...

That's cool. *High Weirdness* started out as a project only about Philip K. Dick and about his religious experience and how it manifested in, or related to his writing and some of the questions that I asked there and even some of the material that's in the Philip K. Dick section of the book goes back to college –to the 1980s. When, I would say that I had intellectual, psychedelic and imaginative kinds of inspirations all sort of comingling. I had discovered Philip K. Dick, Robert Anton Wilson and the occult –all this stuff that was interesting in a world-building sort of way. And at the same time I was studying critical theory, particularly ideas about simulation and propaganda, you know, Jean Baudrillard and other post-Structuralists. Particularly, people who were looking at new technologies, who were changing what reality was and if we could even point towards reality and the political/ideological implications of that. There's something about that "false world" scenario that is exciting. Both kind of terrifying and fascinating, like a quality of both liberation and doom, and there's something about the mixture of those flavors that I was really drawn to. Neither the full light, nor the full darkness, but some kind of trickster realm in-between; there's a trickster thread running through all this stuff. I had always wanted to do a serious academic project on Philip K. Dick, I had worked on the *Exegesis* and I was involved in the publication of the abridgment that came out. So, for whatever reason, just before I started writing the dissertation, I froze; I didn't want to do it entirely on Philip K. Dick. Part of it was that I just didn't want to have my mind living in his universe 24/7 for two or three years, and another part of it was because, at the end of the day he's just a singular guy, whereas if I pull back it's no accident that his story happened in the early 1970s in California. It wasn't a one-shot, because there were these other people who had these extraordinary mystical experiences in the seventies and also in California, so I realized that there was something bigger there. Initially I thought the project would meditate more than it does on what was shared between these guys, there's some discussion of it and there's some obvious resonances that are both implicit and explicit. But once I got started writing about these individual guys, there was so much to say that I just told Terrance's story and told Robert Wilson's story. But I'm much happier that it came out that way because I had to build a picture of that time and set up some shared resonances, and it made it more of an expansive project.

Yeah, I had already started working on this book when I saw *High Weirdness* at Book Soup in West Hollywood and I thought: "Wow this is what I need right now!" I think the tripartite structure of the book, focusing on three figures, makes it better than if it had just been on Philip K Dick himself, because I think the commonalities are there.

Yeah

So, one of the notes I remember making has to do with some of the early parts of the book where you're talking about Empiricism and Pragmatism, and it seems like you have an innate skepticism towards, let's say the "supernatural." Did you find the philosophy of Empiricism or Pragmatism to be a

good grounding force for you personally, or in your writing as you approach these figures?

I would say that there's an aspect of that that has always been part of me byway of an inherent skepticism. When I was young and first exploring psychedelics and spiritual practices, I was always much more of a freak than a hippy. I was more interested in just the weirdness or the unusualness of it, than the idea that it was going to lead to enlightenment or peace on earth. I always loved Frank Zappa.

I love Zappa too.

The Grateful Dead and Frank Zappa are at the same level of influence for me, but I tend more towards the sardonic. Philosophically, because I was very influenced by post-structuralism, I have an anti-metaphysical base. I'm very interested in Phenomenology, I do, in a Derridean way or whatever, don't think language can do what it says it's going to do. I don't think the language of God can do what it says it's going to do. It doesn't mean that I don't think there are large mysteries, or that we're not imbedded in mysteries –in fact I do think that. But I don't try to ground that in some kind of system or some kind of revelation or some kind of confidence in language's ability to articulate that. So, there's an inherent skepticism around the discourse of spirituality or supernaturalism.

I'm also influenced enough by anthropology and sociology to appreciate the way that nuanced, secular accounts of religious experience or the supernatural, can actually explain a lot of what's going on, without having to invoke supernatural entities or metaphysical principles. In that way, I'm a pragmatist, in that I don't think that any one perspective is going to be adequate for handling the problem. My pragmatism follows the lines of William James more than it does "rational" pragmatism. For James, religion is part of the picture: religious ideas, metaphysical ideas, visionary ideas –they happen to people, and as concepts they can be useful. It can be useful to believe that you have an eternal soul because you live your life differently. He didn't care whether the eternal soul actually existed but he was giving room for religious and spiritual concepts because of the way that they function in life. Some pragmatists, rationalists, reject that – they think it's dishonest. But I don't. I'm fascinated with supernatural and New Age ideas, not so much in what they claim, but how they work.

Would you say that you're agnostic about these things?

Yeah, but I don't use that word because it has a lazy, disinterested quality to it, whereas I'm kind of interested in actively not knowing the core of whatever it is that I'm interested in exploring. Where I differ from secular and rational scholars is that I think we are embedded in a mystery -a vast, overwhelming, bizarre mystery that we will never get to the end of. I think that you honor the mystery by being skeptical, because then it strips away all of your fantasy, projection and desire. I think that reality is plural, and it's probably plural all the way through and that means that multiple perspectives and multiple personalities within the self have multiple ontologies; there are different ways that things are, and most people disagree with that, they say: "no, there is being and there is non-being." Robert Anton Wilson said, and this relates to the concept of pluralism, that: "yeah, there's a lot of people in me: there's the shaman, the poet, the guy who works and the skeptic –and the skeptic gets veto rights most of the time" and that to me is a beautiful way of thinking about it. We have multiple modes of experiencing the world, poetic, religious, etc., but the skeptic deserves more deference. For me it's a pragmatic way of responding to the complexity of reality. Most people when they're writing tend to boil things down and they either fall into one position or the other, either skepticism or belief and the skeptic usually doesn't like the religious believer and the religious believer doesn't like the skeptic, but I like everybody! I really try to like everybody, and I fail, it's hard to like MAGA Q-Anon conspiracy theorists, although I try to understand where they're coming from, and that's part of my commitment to a pluralism and a pragmatic understanding of how different world-views function, and not be so judgmental about things all the time.

There's like three questions that popped into my head while you were talking, and the first one you could probably answer pretty quickly. You were saying that you see things as being a constantly evolving mystery, do you see a teleological understanding of reality to be attendant to the "rationalistic" philosophical model?

Not necessarily because you can be a rationalist and reject any sort of larger teleology. You can still run into contradictions, but in a way that's a generic scientific attitude, like: "we're just in a meaningless universe and atoms were jumping around and they formed larger entities and evolutionary processes selected for these larger complexities, and we're just these meat-robots, etc." So, you can talk about local teleologies, like DNA wants to replicate – is that a teleology? Is DNA driving towards replication? Sure, but that's not the same thing as saying that there's an overall meaning to the universe, or a great pattern that is drawing us forward. You can be a rationalist and not be invested in teleology, just like you can be open to the mystery and not be invested in teleology because you just don't know.

One of the other things that popped into my head while you were talking earlier was this quote I read on my break at work last night. It's from Michael Lennon's biography of Norman Mailer, let me read it to you really quick. It's a quote from Flaubert: "The artist should be in his work like God's creation; invisible and all-powerful, he should be felt everywhere and seen nowhere." So, when you were talking about the different aspects of you as a writer, how does that quote resonate with you as far as your persona? Do you feel that there are certain times that you reveal too much of yourself, or do you have a feeling that you want to instantiate

a sensc of mystery about how the book they are reading came into being?

I'm not sure if I follow your question entirely, but I see what you mean. I would say that that's in process. It was always in process, but it's more true now because my project now, Burning Shore, involves more personal stories. So, I'm actually actively playing with the degree of revelation and concealment that go on in the writing, it's a very significant topic for me right now and it is difficult …

I think it's really significant because theirs times when I'm writing my own book, and I realize that it's getting really dry, and when I interject a certain kind of humor, that's not properly academic, it gives me a certain spark. That relates to the Norman Mailer biography because after *The Naked and the Dead* he wrote a lot of mediocre stuff and he had to come to grips with himself as being the persona who was creating the works and that made him become a better writer and that happened, like you said, within the text itself. That sort of self-realization and the sense of yourself as an artist coming-to-the-fore can be kind of uncomfortable as well, because you don't know how far you can push it.

I want to make a comment about humor. I've always been invested in having my writing be entertaining. Even the more dry things that I've written, the more scholarly things, I've always wanted it to be entertaining. Part of the entertainment is humor and part of it is writing well, richly or with a strong sense of rhythm, etc. So, that's a certain part of the persona: that I might be saying very profound things or offering really critical perspectives but that there's also sort of a showman persona at work there too. People who like my work often tune into the sense that I have this kind of sprightly persona that could be funny. When people recognize my writing it's because I have those characteristics along with saying things that are interesting to them. Now, I have more of a sense that there's a persona in the picture, partly because now I'm more aware of writing for people who like "Erik Davis" – people who are more interested in just me. And at the same time I'm also realizing how much of my own attitudes, opinions, whatever are the result of my own experiences. I am the way I am because of where I grew up, what my temperament is, the people I met, the drugs I took, etc. So, in a way, the mystery of who I am is more and more like the history of who I am. Not all of it, not the animating awareness maybe, but the character that I have. I've always been resistant to that kind of self-focus and that has to do with authorial revelation and concealment. What are the reasons to conceal? There are a number of reasons: one, it's weak writing, most of the time, journalistically, critically and philosophically, to play on yourself – your anecdotes, your experiences, etc. There's another reason for concealment and that has to do with not wanting people to know where you're coming from, because I don't even know where I'm coming from. If I overly explain where I'm coming from, in the text, I'm lying, because I don't totally know where I'm coming from and I give the reader a false sense of stability. I don't want to convince people of anything, at most, I want to seduce them into the conundrum that I'm in. There are a lot of concrete arguments that can be made, but you have to be careful when you overly identify the avatar in the writing because it lets people off the hook.

One of the parts where I first interjected myself into the book was regarding a copy of this obscure magazine called *Dagobert's Revenge*. I came across a copy of it at Tower Records when I was in my early twenties and it blew my mind. I ended up lending it to a co-worker like nine years ago, and now, that issue, is, like, totally unavailable. In some ways it's analogous to this story that Jacques Vallée tells in *Passport to Magonia* about this Private Irwin who goes to investigate what he thinks is a plane crash and winds up in, like, a coma, and his jacket goes missing. After he comes out of the coma there are months of strange behavior before he

goes back to where the plane crash, or UFO phenomena occurred and he disappears, leaving only the missing jacket behind. In my book I compare it to your story of the McKenna brothers and the magical appearance of the key. There's something about these dream-like objects that appear elliptically in your life, they're partial objects, but I see them as being a particular and personal object that acts as a key to the big and abstract unfolding of mystery that you were talking about.

It carries on this idea of revelation and concealment. I mean, it's not much of a revelation if it's an abstract idea – the more concrete the revelation or symbol is the more magic is happening. But if it's just revealed and then that's it and nothing else happens to it and it's just sitting on your shelf then it becomes utterly mundane. So, the disappearance of the object becomes another way of referring to this deeper logic of revelation and concealment.

Tied to that, is there the fact that you took it for granted and now have to search for it again – like, the activity of searching?

I think that's true, or the recognition of the absence. If you take Lacan's idea, which I don't t totally agree with, but that's fine: you can never access the real, you can only access the symbolic structure that is placed over it. When the symbolic structure breaks down, or when there are cracks and gaps in the symbolic structure, then arguably you are closer to this terrifying and delectable confrontation with the real. So, when concrete objects, which are loaded with value, play disappearing games, it feels like you're getting to one of those cracks in the symbolic. And of course it's more intense when it's a real object, as opposed to a line in a book that you keep looking for over and over...

Yeah, but that's kind of an object too ...

I'm trying to think of some of the more concrete things in my experience that have had that function but nothing comes to mind. I just keep coming up with thoughts about synchronicity and that seems to be related to revelation and concealment as well. Because in a good synchronicity what is being revealed is there's an almost undeniable sense that there is some larger implication, or plot happening right now and you can't put it back in the box.

Does it also mean that the object is something more than it appears to be?

In the sense that it becomes a hieroglyph, yeah I would say so.

I had a similar experience with a part of your book. As a kid I used to watch *That's Incredible!* And there was this episode where they were talking about these guys who did paranormal research and they created a history for a fictional character from like the 1700s, then after writing this character into existence they held séances just to see if they could elicit some paranormal activity. Now that was a thing that I saw when I was a kid and it stuck with me my whole life because there was something about the narrative that they were relating that was going to riddle me for the rest of my life. And it's a TV show from the seventies, so it's really obscure and seemed like something I would never come across again. Then I see on page 254 of your book, you talk about the Toronto Society for Psychical Research and you tell the story of that experiment, with the character Phillip and that was like what you described: it kind of blew my mind. Because it was like "here's this thing that had this big impact on me and I'm finding it again randomly." It's like Freud's conception of the uncanny –I'm finding this thing that's familiar to me because it played a part in forming my psyche, in this place where I did not expect to find it.

It's a wonderful feeling, I think it's one of the reasons that we read, or at least I read, is to stumble across those moments. There's a way that books and other media sort of talk to each other that becomes an entrée into the mystery.

Returning to the issue of pluralism, in the book and in general, I tend to favor a politically pluralistic model based on Robert Michels and Isaiah Berlin, in that I see all these different groups vying for hegemony within the system. And none of the groups has everything teleologically locked-in, where everything is going to fall into place. And the conspiracy theorist might subscribe to a pluralistic model might think that whoever is orchestrating the "New World Order" had everything locked-in, and everything we see is a part of that plan somehow. I understand the pluralism of the self, that you are talking about, but I also like the idea of a pluralism of groups that are vying for hegemony, and each one has a set of narratives that inform them and that they embody. So, essentially you have a bunch of narratives competing for dominance.

Oh yeah, I basically agree with that because I recognize that the dominant narrative, quote, un-quote, is actually a fractured product of multitude accounts that are coming from multiple groups with multiple agendas –and that's just the nature of things. Now that's obviously something that comes to the fore in democracy and that's where you get into the territory of Karl Popper's *Open Society*: you don't get the divine king, you don't get the totalitarian vanguard party running everything, well, what do you get? You get a fucking mess. I remain a big fan of democracy in that broader sense. I would like to believe that things like compromise, tolerance and multiplicity are still real viable options in a situation where there are no perfect answers. In terms of understanding what's going on, particularly now. Looking at it in terms of multiple actors with multiple agendas and multiple narratives, struggling for power, I think is a good way of viewing it. Conspiracy theorists will always resist that perspective as deeply threatening and the reason it is deeply threatening is not just because you're pushing back against the idea that there is one cabal that's in control of everything. But it's also threatening because if you acknowledge the pluralism of the multiple conspiratorial agendas and agents, and that could be the fluoride one, the chemtrail one, the Hollywood pedo one, the moon landing, etc., undermines the very attractive quality of conspiracy thinking: that it's all one plot. Once I say that it's not just one plot, then I'm actually back in the Open Society, whether I want to be or not! The logic of pluralism, which I think is more true to actual political reality, as well as ontological, psychological and metaphysical realities, is that that pluralism is true even in the conspiratorial world-view. And conspiracy theorists, particularly the unsophisticated ones, have to repress that because if they acknowledge it they undermine their essentially monotheistic program.

I think the reason why the high-water mark for me was the stuff involving Robert Anton Wilson, the Discordians and Steve Jackson is because there was a sense of reverence on their part to allow the mysteriousness at the heart of these theories to be. Even if you're having a lot of fun with it, like the Discordians did, there's a reverence that allows the mysteriousness at the heart of the theories alone, to be mysterious. And that high-water mark was annihilated by 9/11, which is so symbolically rich because you have these two towers which actually existed, in contrast to the Tower of Babel which existed mythologically. And everything resonating from the Tower of Babel is very mythologically powerful and rich, and once the Twin Towers are destroyed then there's no mythological richness and everything is just trying to ape scientism.

I'm getting a better sense of your approach ... it's very rich.

Yeah, that's what I'm going for. It's been really great talking to you, man. Thanks again!

Derrick Jensen is a writer and activist who has written and lectured extensively on the subjects of ecology and the effects of civilization on the environment. I spoke with Derrick Jensen over the phone on November 4th, 2020, the day after the presidential election.

How are you doing today?

I'm ok, how are you?

The book that I'm interviewing you for is, in part, about how myths inform our societies. What are some of your general thoughts about that subject?

I'll start to say something, but if that goes in a direction that's not helpful, let me know and I'll go in a different direction.

No, you go whatever direction you want.

Fundamentally, humans are storytelling creatures. That's how we learn to be human, and the stories that we tell ourselves and each other – I guess, the weak word would be "influence" and the strong word would be "determine" – how we perceive and experience the world. And then that influences our behavior and that, in a reinforcing cycle, influences the stories we tell. We can give a bazillion examples of that: if one of the stories is that you are God's chosen people, then it might be okay for you to take other people's land. Or, if one of the stories you tell is that you are the apex of evolution –assuming evolution has an apex- then it will affect your behavior in that you might consider it okay to conquer the entire planet. This is how advertising works. The stories that they tell in advertising are "if I buy a Happy Meal I'm going to be happy." This works on every level from the linguistic to the social. One of the things I think about a lot, is if I type into my word processing system: "the tree who grows over there" it will tell me that it's grammatically incorrect. That is an example of how we tell the stories, and then the stories we tell, affect our behavior because if you perceive the tree as a "that" than if you perceive it as a "who."

You mentioned the idea of people perceiving themselves as being at the pinnacle of evolution. There was this guy, Ignatius Donnelly who wrote a book about Atlantis, and the guy who wrote the introduction when it was republished by Dover, in like 1976, basically writes with this authoritative tone, as if the science is settled on everything that was written about in the book. I don't know if people walk around thinking that they're at an evolutionary apex but I think that throughout modernity we've had points where we thought that the science was settled and we could go back and critique all these random writers from the past. Do you think that that is something that's endemic to modernity or humanity in general, this assumption that we've reached the pinnacle of intelligence?

I think in terms of reaching a pinnacle of intelligence, we have the great chain of being, *scala naturae*, which is 2500 years old. It was proposed by Aristotle in his history of animals, and in it he arranged life with minerals at the bottom of the hierarchy and then plants, and then various animals -near the top were humans, and above that angels and gods. So, this idea that humans are near the top is pretty old. The Greeks also considered the barbarians to be inferior, and on one hand that's supremacist, but on the other hand, I think that inherent to us, there's a kind of in-group/out-group mentality, where our family is closer to us than others. A lot of indigenous peoples, their name would literally mean "the people" and everybody else is basically, well, everybody else. So, on one hand I think that the great chain of being is very clearly hierarchical, and ripe for exploitation because if I perceive myself as superior to everybody else then it's a very small step to being able to exploit anybody else. But at the same time I think it's very natural to perceive oneself and one's group as a special group. The thing I don't think is inevitable is to perceive oneself and one's group as superior. An example of this is, my mom died two years ago and her death meant more to me than the death of a random eighty-six year-old woman –and that's really all I mean by saying that perceiving one's own group as special is inherent.

Would you describe the great chain of being as a myth or was it more of a pragmatic thing that kind of worked for a while?

Could you define what you mean by myth, in the context that you're working with in the book?

I didn't expect to have to define it right now. For me myths are sort of malleable, and they kind of fix characters and objects within narratives, but they don't fix things definitively. And in a more post-modern sense, they kind of elude an easy characterization between medium and message. In my work I'm giving myth a sort of privileged space, if you want to use that terminology, in that I think that it's kind of an ineffable narrative space that's elusive to most of the discourses prevalent in our society today.

When you're talking about conspiracy theories moving from qualitative to quantitative, it reminds me of Joseph Campbell talking about myth being more important than history... and this is a direct quote from him "history is just journalism" and that myths speak to qualities like beauty, love, community, or whatever. I guess histories can too. Are you arguing that conspiracy theories changed from mythology to history?

I would say that they changed from being oriented towards mythology towards making an appeal to history, and also an appeal to science, which I think is an even more pernicious discourse than history.

There's something that I really want to recommend, if I may?

Oh yeah...

That you read Frederick Turner's *Beyond Geography*. I interviewed him back in the nineties and the basic point of *Beyond Geography* is that a lot of indigenous religions are cyclical and one of the differences with Christianity is that Christianity posited itself as a historical, as opposed to cyclical religion. And what he meant by that is that it posited that Jesus was a real guy and that he literally lived and he literally died, and literally rose again. Turner goes on, for the entire book, about the implications of switching from, what we might call a mythological religion to a historical religion and what that means for spirituality in general and its relation to other religions, etc. I think that it's really fascinating, this notion of switching from more mythological tendencies to more historical or scientific tendencies.

I appreciate the recommendation and will definitely check that out. What you said reminds me of something that Žižek said, I think in his book on totalitarianism, about how Christianity broke the circular movement that was prevalent in paganism and that at a certain point God interjects himself in the role of Jesus, breaking the circle and giving you a radical moment of autonomy. And he really likes that...

I hear what you're saying, but it's completely horrifying. Nature is cyclical, there's birth, growth, death –trees grow in the forest, then they fall over and decompose. I was raised a Seventh Day Adventist, really religious, and I remember being about seven and having this realization that: "wow, it's really interesting that nature follow the story of Jesus with the death and rebirth." But I got it backwards, the real story is that Jesus was a mythological story about death and rebirth.

I was raised in a pretty strict Catholic family and I think I had the same intuition as you did. Our society gives us this idea that you mythbust, you occupy a rational space that wants to

hone things down into more coherent, easily summarizable narratives. I think it's that scientistic model that insists that the Jesus narrative be grafted onto the more naturalistic narrative, but I also think that there's something ineffable, and inherently indefinable, about the changing of the seasons and the cyclical aspects of nature.

I have a couple of semi-random thoughts on this topic. First, I think that this is longer-term progression that goes back beyond Christianity being perceived as a historical religion. I'm also thinking about the written word and how that has changed things. There have been some cultures that have intentionally made it so that their laws have not been written down because they believe it's important that their laws remain living – I'm not valorizing this, I'm just saying that there's different perspectives. And this belief entails the idea that if something gets written down it has an authority that extends beyond just the words; it sort of becomes frozen in place. Which also can be really really important, because if you have a nation like the United States, where the population is like 300 million or whatever, that's more people then you can have relationships with and so we need to have strict definitions of what is and what is not murder, what is and what is not theft. What was that theory, was it called "Duncan's Number"?

Oh yeah, it's like something like fifty or a hundred people are the maximum that you can fit into your personal social set...

Right. And my point is that, if you have a smaller number than that, then this whole thing of not writing down the laws makes sense. Think of family situations: you negotiate stuff. Your parents say that the bedtime is ten o'clock but that's not written in stone because there's special occasions like birthdays and things like that. You can't do that with a million people. My point is that having stuff written down is in itself a form of changing even a myth to history, because if it's oral it's alive and can evolve, whereas the *Iliad* and *The Odyssey* remain the same as they did, in many ways, which I'm not saying is better or worse, but it switches it to history. The other thought that I had was that this conversation reminds me of my book *Dreams*, is that one of the things that happened in the scientific revolution was that it removed meaning from the world, and using your language, I would say that it changed our perspective of the world from a mythological one to a quantitative one. One of the things that happened with the scientific revolution was that, before it occurred, the world before then was living and filled with wonderful adventures and wonderful beings, etc. – and we don't even have to stick with physical nature: how much poorer is the world when it doesn't have fairies and leprechauns in it? And that's the whole point of *Dreams*, when I talk about my muse, I'm actually talking about a real being and she's non-corporeal, but she isn't some part of my sub-conscious. There's a huge difference between living in a world that is already full of meaning and living in a world where you have to project meaning onto it. Another point that I make in *Dreams* that relates to this is how the scientific revolution really was an inevitable end result of the Abrahamic religions, in that, you have a sky god and you remove meaning from the earth, and you put meaning onto this distant god, a long ways away, who you will never see until you're dead. As opposed to having meaning being immanent. So, that's a huge transformation: to remove meaning from the earth and put it out there and then all the scientists did was come in and turn out that light, extinguish that meaning that comes from so far away. I think it was Isak Dinesen, who said that: "any suffering can be survived as long as it's part of a story, as long as there's meaning in it." I'm perceiving this as a long movement of demythologizing and demystification. However, I want to be really clear on one point: I've been offering critiques of science for twenty-five years now and I'm really irritated with this post-modern, "two plus two equals five" bullshit. My problem with science is not that it's wrong, which is what a lot of these people seem to be claiming, my problem is that science is only one way of perceiving the world...

That's postmodern, though.

What?

That's kind of a postmodern position.

No, see I hate fucking postmodernism. I hate it so much. Ok, I agree that there are multiple stories and multiple ways of perceiving reality, hell, there are bears sitting outside my house right now, they perceive the world differently than we do because their vision is poor and their sense of smell is so incredibly strong and that's a different way of perceiving the world. Yes, I agree that there are competing different narratives, which I agree with then extend that to the claim that therefore there are only narratives and no reality?! We can tell whatever stories we want but they don't trump reality. My point is that I don't have a problem with science, I have a problem with science pretending it knows everything.

I just want to say, for the record, because I use postmodern writers for my analysis, I think that someone like Baudrillard, even though he was really critical of the idea of the "real" but he was kind of a contrarian who was using his discourse to point out the hypocrisies, not just in science but in the media. And coming from academia myself, I'd say there's just as much denial of reality on the so-called "analytic" side of philosophy where they kind of deny reality with all these thought experiments, which are just less-imaginative digressions from reality. So, I would say that philosophy in general is sort of rife with this indifference to the real that you pointed out.

I completely agree and that's a huge problem.

Gary Wayne is a contrarian Christian scholar who writes and lectures on the topics of Biblical prophecy and scriptural interpretation. I interviewed him over the phone in early 2020.

How're you doing today?

Not too bad. I've been busy trying to meet some deadlines and preparing for a two-hour show that I'm going to do tomorrow.

You primarily go on other podcasts and talk about your work – you don't have your own podcast, do you?

I do, but it's just a thirty-minute spot I do on the Daily Renegade. I do something called "The Christian Contrarian" on there twice a month. I might do a podcast down the road, but I'm so darn busy with doing other interviews that I don't really have time, and the second thing is that I don't want to compete with the people who have me on their shows.

Also, you wouldn't just be competing with them – you'd be competing with everybody and his brother who does a podcast.

It's not like the world needs another podcast, but maybe I'll change my mind when I'm not as busy.

It's gotta be one of the worst things when people get encouraged by their friends, who are telling them that they're funny and witty, then, with all these high expectations they start a podcast and it bombs.

It's not so easy to do. It's one thing if you're going to be interviewing other people, right? If you're good at asking questions and having a dialog, but if you're just doing something on your own it might be easy to do a few shows, but once you get to thirty shows or fifty shows it's hard to keep coming up with ideas.

The first question I wanted to ask you about was your background, but what you said kind of made me think of something that is relevant to my book. There is this part where I talk about personalities like Alex Jones and Allan Watt, and how, because their career is based on them getting to the heart of this secret thing or whatever, they can't have the secret thing be revealed because they won't have a career anymore.

That's a bit of a conundrum. I wouldn't say that I'm in that sort of situation though because I actually want people to know whatever I'm researching or whatever I'm talking about, and how that relates to whatever kind of conspiracy I would suggest that there is evidence for. There are some legitimate things that you can put together that literally says to anybody with some common sense that there's something there and then there's other stuff that just goes off on unsupported evidence, allegations, speculation, imagination, you name it. Some people are into conspiracy theories because that's just what they like to do. If you can't verify sources then it becomes more fiction than conspiracy.

In the reading that I've done I've noticed a trend in conspiracy theorization, and I would say that you are part of this trend, it's sort of a phenomenological monism or reductionism, where people try to explain a lot of different phenomena, maybe not using the same physical source, but a closely-related set of narratives. So, for your stuff you basically trace it all to the Nephillum and Caine and we can follow the narrative line back to that source. I think that someone like Alex Jones doesn't really believe that there is a central narrative, they just want to have a constellation of narratives that they can float between just to keep their thing moving forward.

On my approach, one wants to be very careful as to whether you're doing self-promotion or whether you're actually trying to figure things out and trying to explain things that have happened, and are happening, in a way that makes sense to other people. When I went to write the book I wasn't intending to write a conspiracy book, my main passion was prophecy, so I thought about tackling the funny creatures called "giants" that appear in Genesis 6, and connect that to endtimes prophecy. So I thought: "let's just write a short book on that."

It's not so short.

Well, that's what sort of happens on the way to the Colosseum. I'm a history buff and a mythology buff and I knew there was significant parallels between these giants and those in myths from all over the world, and I thought: "well maybe I'll put a little of that into the book." If you understand prehistory and endtime prophecy in the Bible, you'll understand that there is a conspiracy of the rebellious ones against God that is continuing right through to the endtimes, but that's not what I wanted to write about –I just wanted to connect these entities to the endtimes. But when I started on the topic of mythology that led me into the question of "what was the mythology of a culture based on?" It's usually based on the religion that dominated the culture and dominated the organizational structure and the ruling class, which worked hand-in-hand. When I understood that, and that the learning, which was an offshoot of the religion in the elite class, was the mystery schools and that was the beginning of secret societies – then I thought: "Well, I have to research secret societies." I start to research secret societies, thinking that it's a loose end, but lo and behold, they take their creation back to the same events in Genesis, with the descendants of Caine, the fallen angels, the Nephillum, the creation of the seven sacred sciences by Enoch that leads to the development of mysticism and then development of the mystery schools, and their patriarchs are those descendants of Cain. I went down the rabbit-hole for twelve or thirteen years -just researching secret societies. The more I dug, the more connections I found and that's what turned it into a conspiracy book. When I did my outline I had not envisioned it that way. I wrote the first ten chapters pretty easily and it ended up being a hundred chapters and I left three hundred and fifty pages out, for editing purposes, before I sent it in to be published because there's just so much information out there; it's just endless.

I was around fifty pages into my book and I was writing about Enoch; I always knew there was a lot of stuff about Enoch and I saw that there was another Enoch, who was Cain's son but no one really talks about him. In my draft I foolhardily wrote: "no one seems to be very interested in this other Enoch, they're interested in this one that walked with God." But then someone tipped me off to your book and I bought it and was like "uh oh." Returning to the issue of the transmission of knowledge through the ages, I got my Master's degree in philosophy and when you see how that discipline plays out at the academic level, how I sort of did, it doesn't come off as very secret or arcane. Pythagoras and Plato are kind of mysterious characters, but when you see how it ends up in philosophical conversations today, it doesn't seem like it could inform anything nefarious; it's just academic.

And that gets to the issue of how that whole understanding branches out into a religious aspect, even though sciences were governed by the religion aspect and the ruling class, at that time, but there was a separate arm of the development of understanding the world and teaching it. They didn't just teach it to the poor, they only taught it to the elite, there was that continual communication with the past and the development of that knowledge was connected to the doctrines of polytheism.

Obviously Plato and those people were polytheists to some extent. Plato seems to me, to be someone who was secretly arguing for some form of proto-secular humanism. I think that polytheism was a cultural trapping for them.

You have to understand that Plato wrote the *Critias* and the *Timaeus* and that's the story of Solon in Egypt who transcribed the writings off of the pillars. He also tells the Atlantean story of their ancient world and he passing it on as though it was history. And that's about fallen angels, Poseidon being one of them, marrying a human female and producing ten hero Nephilum gods to rule the Atlantean Empire. So, he's not really elevating his understanding to a secular level, he's elevating everything back to an honor of the gods and there maybe something even above that but we're not able to define that. As we get some of these polytheist religions developing towards the idea of a "universal lifeforce" that lots of them have today, they keep trying to reassemble that original religion.

For them, that "original" religion is some sort of polytheistic, pagan, sun-worshipping kind of thing?

It is. They wouldn't frame it quite that bluntly, it's that dualistic religion, in which good and evil are in perpetual conflict.

Like a Manichean sort of thing?

It's all the same core belief system, yes.

I have some prewritten questions I wanted to ask you, and of all the people I'm going to interview, you're the one I have the most questions for. One of the questions has to do with the "Day Six People" – I'm not Jewish, I don't think you are, I don't know, but am I descended from the day six people?

Well, it depends on how you think that life survives after the flood. Just as a quick example, you have male and female being created at the same time, in great numbers, and being told to multiply, spread out and civilize the earth; they're basically described as hunters and gatherers. Now in the Edenic account, Adam is created in a singular way, at some point later, we don't know how long, Eve is created from his rib; he had the spirit of God breathed into him. They are agrarians and they are growing crops and orchards, and of course the Tree of Life and the Tree of the Knowledge of Good and Evil are all growing fruits within the garden, which is another word for "orchard." Once you understand that different order of creation, you carry that forward to the flood, you have another conundrum: how did the four races survive across the flood if only Noah's family, who are descendants of the Sethian line, are on the ark? Well the only way that that's going to happen is if the wives are of those different races. We're not told the names of the wives, or where they come from but the numbers add up; if there's four races, or even three races, created on day six, most polytheist accounts account claim that there are four that are created in the beginning when you had the separation of the waters, that's the only way they are going to show up after the flood. So, do day six people show up after the flood? I would say through marrying the sons of Noah. However, *The Epic of Gilgamesh* tells a story of a survival, or ark story, of giants, which coincides with these other stories all around the world of people surviving the flood with the aid of the gods, and that would lead to the recreation of giants after the flood. So you either have survival on the ark or second incursion, my preferred position is second incursion, but because we're not told exactly how that happens in the Bible, I'm open to all interpretations. I would say that how we have the day six people showing up after the flood is either they were on other arks helped by fallen angels and/or wives on Noah's Ark.

One of the things that I started to do while writing the book was I began homing in on these three figures: Hiram,

Melchizedek and Enoch. They exist at the margins of the texts and I call them "murky." Regarding Hiram, it's kind of confusing because there's a Hiram who was a king and another Hiram who was the builder of Solomon's temple and as a name that goes on to play this role in Freemasonry. And then there's a duality to Enoch because there's one Enoch who is holy and walked with God, and the other one is Cain's descendant, and he may or may not be Hermes, and this Enochian tradition continues into the story of John Dee and modern occultism. Finally, with Melchizedek he appears in the Bible, then later in Gnosticism and occultism, but after reading Jacques Vallée, we see his name reoccurring in modern UFO stuff. Those three characters are really interesting to me because they're not central figures, they're side-characters that never really get a good textual explication, yet they pop up at all these other points in history. You helped me a lot by clarifying the Enoch thing, but I want to ask you about Melchizedek, because I was under the impression that, unlike with Hiram and Enoch who there were other people with the same name, with Melchizedek it seems like there was just one guy and he was basically a holy person. But in your book you kind of make it out like he was not, like he was bad.

Not quite. Those are terrific murky figures, so to speak, and they become more murky because they are not well-known, and there are two different versions of each, or similar characters of each, related in the narrative but somehow different and often conflated. That's what really makes them confusing as you come down through history. So, with King Hiram of Tyre, who provides the building knowledge through his Dionysian knowledge, which was used in the building of the great temples and buildings of the ancient world after the flood. Then, lo and behold, he sends his master builder, Hiram Abif, who shows up in Freemasonry, who's going to help Solomon while also teaching the Israelites this knowledge of building. You don't get Hiram Abif showing up much more than in those two accounts, but the Temple comes down in history. For secret societies that's a very important turning point of history for them. Then you have Melchizedek, who has no genealogy, no mother, no father, and he comes out of nowhere and is honored by Abraham. Actually I think that this Melchizedek and the Melchizedek Order that Jesus will be part of is a pre-Jesus, who is the Word of God, manifesting himself to Abraham. It is an important meeting and honoring of Abraham to the future Messiah.

I had talked to this guy, Don Clasen, he's a more politically-charged fundamentalist Christian, and he speculated that the Melchizedek, who visited Abraham, might have been Jesus himself just appearing at that point in Biblical history. What are your thoughts on that?

That's what I was getting at, that I think he's a "pre-Jesus," he's the Word who came down from heaven and made himself known to Abraham and then later became flesh in the form of Jesus. So, I would agree with what that individual is saying, because there are no genealogies recorded in the Old Testament for this Melchizedek, and the Book of Hebrews says there isn't one. But remember that Melchizedek is also looked upon in Freemasonry as being Shem, one of the sons of Noah after the flood and they have a lot of history on that, but I think there's no genealogy there, and genealogy is the key. Returning to the third figure that you mentioned: Enoch. There were, as we've gone over, two Enochs. There was Enoch, the son of Seth, who is taken away to heaven in a rapture kind of event when he was 365 years old and is considered a saintly individual because he walked with God. Then you have all these other things conflated with Enoch son of Cain, who developed the sciences that Adam learned from God in Eden that was taught to Cain, and he develops that knowledge into the seven sacred sciences, developed sun-worshipping, mysticism and the mystery schools. These figures and other figures that come down through history that also seemingly play a role in the futurc and with things like the alien mythos. So, with that Melchizedek Order, you have the Canaanite, or Gnostic line of that order, as opposed to the Melchizedek Order, which is the one that David is entering into, that Jesus will become the priest for in the future-time. Then as you move forward, you're going to have that Melchizedek Order play out in prophecy, where you have Jesus coming back to be the head of the order as the Word of God and the Lamb of God, as he fulfills his position. And you're going to have an Antichrist figure, who's going to claim the Canaanite title and will conflate the two in the endtimes. Also, Enoch is associated with knowledge, who comes up all the time in regards to AI and quantum mechanics, in the form of the name "Metatron." So, these names keep coming up, and I think we need to pay attention to them until something more concrete comes out. Making sense of these figures might be part of what's happening today or what's going to happen, but again, we don't have that concrete evidence.

I'm starting to understand the tone with which you wrote your chapter on Melchizedek, it seems like you're cautioning people from getting drawn into this order that signifies itself as being official. Do you think that that is representative of the danger in our modern society: is that things take on the representations of older, more established things, and they then lose authenticity?

I think there are two parts to that, which are important. First, these things get watered down, they get changed, they get manipulated, they're designed to line the pockets of the people running it and they take from people who usually can't afford to be taken from and it gets used over and over and cheapens the whole concept. But then there's the other side, if that whole thing is real in it's original sense, then we need to understand that if there is a reality to that in the past, for both belief systems: monotheism and polytheism a sense of future reckoning, then we need to take that seriously. From a monotheist perspective, everything that the polytheists are doing is counterfeiting what God did. And that's why you have polytheists saying that the Sethian line is a counterfeit of the Cainite line. From the monotheist perspective this has been going on since the rebellion, this includes things like the Antichrist, who is a counterfeit messiah. We're going to have a counterfeit Armageddon, we're going to have a counterfeit "new Eden" presented to us; everything that is going to happen is a counterfeit of what God is planning.

To push you on one particular point: you classify the polytheist as being the antithesis of the monotheist and you also classify them as being dualistic. But then, you are replicating their own dualism in your own thinking by positing this dichotomy. You know what I'm saying? There's a kind of dualism that gets repeated in your ideology.

There is, but there's a significant couple of distinctions. The dualism that is in polytheism, is this perpetual, forever, one will never win out, good versus evil. In monotheism there's a time for that, because of the rebellion, but it comes to an end. In polytheistic dualism, the powers of evil are equal to the powers of good and that's why they're in continuous battle. In monotheism you don't have that because God is above the angels, in polytheism God is just an angel.

So for you, someone like Kant, who basically said that you treat everyone as an end in themselves and not a means to an end. And he was sort of bad for religion because he speculated that we don't need a divine mandate to treat other people as we ourselves would want to be treated, we should do it because they possess reason and they are an end in themselves. It's more of a secular humanist perspective. That would be something that contradicts your moral sense of goodness, right?

I would argue that he is propounding polytheist doctrine, in particular, the Gnostic doctrine. But that shouldn't be surprising once you understand that liberal arts, which are based on the seven sacred sciences are working in tandem with polytheist religion –they're guided by it. It's basically arguing for reason over faith. That's Gnosticism, and here's why, Gnosticism goes back to the word "Gnosis" which is wisdom, and it's occult knowledge. I don't think knowledge is either good or evil –it's how it's applied. But they also trace that idea of knowledge back to Eden, and the knowledge of good and evil that they would call the "tree of gnosis," which much of their knowledge comes from. So they need that reason over faith idea, as a development of their belief system, which involves becoming God, which they're all trying to do; whether it's through immortality or through attaining the knowledge possessed by God.

I think that today people subscribe to the idea of science as being this thing that fits into their political schema.

Well, they're raising it to the level of a religion but it's not true science because they don't allow all sides of the debate to be stated.

Now, going back to the three murky figures who have taken a central place in my book. Knight and Lomas add their own twist to the Hiram Abif story where they identify him as Seqenenre Tao, and in *Uriel's Machine* they identify the Sethian line with the line descended from Cain, essentially claiming that there was only one Enoch, one ...

That goes back to what I said earlier: that they would claim that the Sethian line is a counterfeit line.

Aren't they saying that there is just one line and that there isn't a dualism about it, that it's just one thing and that people have forced it into a dualistic schema?

That's what they're saying. I think that part of their writing is disinformation. Knight and Lomas are master-masons and they are very learned. For a while they were on the lecture circuit, going to Masonic lodges and educating their people on the history –so they know the history. But when they're writing for the public, they're putting out information that they want and they're putting out disinformation to go along with it. So, you have to be very careful and compare what they're saying and how it matches up with what other Masonic stories have said. That's why I write in the book that they're trying to conflate those individuals to confuse people. If you take Albert Mackey, who was one of the patriarchs of Masonic history, he's drawing on the oral traditions of Freemasonry, which is condensed in the *Polychronicon*, and in that they recognize that there were two different lines. I think that all they're doing is sell disinformation for a time, and ultimately it is done to undermine Christianity.

In *The Hiram Key* they're really excited about the revelation of Seqenenre Tao as Hiram Abif. Their agenda seems to be to push this scientistic, secular humanist thing into Freemasonry. Do you think that they really believe that Seqenenre Tao was Hiram Abif or is that part of their disinformation?

Well, those rituals involving Hiram Abif are at the lower levels, not at the adept levels. So, now you have this split in terms of what the lower level knows and what the higher levels know. Until they are third degree York Rite of thirty-third degree Scottish Rite, they're pedaled part of the information, but not the true meaning. In Gnosticism, the superficial narrative does not contain the true meaning, it's what is hidden in the narrative, and you need to be an adept to understand the true meaning.

You know that book *Proofs of a Conspiracy* by John Robison? So he was basically a Freemason and he's like: "Freemasonry

is this finc and upstanding thing and then all these Illuminati people came in and ruined it." And you claim that it was a perfect marriage between the two –that Freemasonry welcomed this corrupting Illuminati/Scottish Rite stuff with open arms. Do you think there's any validity to the people who claim that Freemasonry was this legit thing that God-fearing people could be a part of, then in the seventeen hundreds it got corrupted?

It sounds like a plausible story until you dig into it a little more. An "Illuminati" is somebody who's already enlightened -they're already an adept. There's a hierarchy, and above the adept Freemasons are the Illuminati, above the Illuminati are the Rosicrucians, and above the Rosicrucians you have the Committee of 300, and above that you have the council of 33 and then the thirteen families. Then you have all of these other organizations reporting to these groups, you might have the Bohemian Grove reporting in to the Illuminati, or the Bildeberg Group reporting in to the committee of 300, etc.

Speaking of the Bilderberg Group, did Allen and Abraham's book, *None Dare Call it a Conspiracy* influence your work?

I can't say that I'm familiar with that book.

How about *Bloodlines of the Illuminati*?

I haven't read that one either.

Neither did I. How about Michael Hoffman II?

I've heard the name, but I haven't read his work.

He's interesting. The vibe I get is that he's some sort of Catholic, he makes a lot of points that are similar to you. One difference that I noticed between you guys is that you ascribe a certain efficacy or usefulness to the occultism and mysticism that's entwined with the "spurious sciences" as you call them. Whereas, it seems like he sees them as a scam that is not only being run on the populace, but on the people who are propagating them as well.

I think that's a legitimate perception for people on the outside – like I am. What I look for, as a researcher, is to look for consistencies that arise over time. I take them at their word, when they talk about the powers that they think they are developing and are utilizing, and have utilized for over a millennia, there is something there that they have; and I take them on their word, but if they're kidding themselves they're kidding themselves. There's a very loyal following to these beliefs at the highest elite levels, like the Royal Family, so I don't think they would continue to do it if they weren't getting the benefits out of it.

Ok, I just have a few quick questions to finish up. You talk about the "Snake Brotherhoods," has anyone ever asked you about the serpent-handling Christian churches, and if there's a connection there?

Could you define what the serpent-handling churches are?

You've never heard of the snake-handlers?

Nope.

They're a sect of Christians who take this obscure passage from the Bible about taking up serpents and they actually pick up snakes and speak in tongues during their ceremonies. It's mostly in the south and I think it's been going on since the late 1800s.

That would be what I call a cult. If they speak in tongues, but there aren't any translators around then what's the point of speaking in tongues? It could be evil spirits speaking through them. Any organization that is working like that isn't really Christianity. Christianity has a lot of, I would say infiltrators, people who are setting up churches that aren't really teaching the true gospel or the whole gospel. I don't really know anything about these snake-handler people, but I would say they're a cult, and there's probably some brainwashing involved.

It's a very rural thing, it doesn't seem like there's a really well thought out brainwashing scheme. It's like being at a really intense Pentecostal service and then suddenly there's these snakes and they're passing them around.

Why would you tempt God like that?

I think it has to do with proving your faith, and when they get bitten they can't go see a doctor.

That's legalism, that's not part of Christianity. The New Testament doesn't teach a legalistic theory of religious law.

So now the penultimate question: your deal is kind of severe, you come off as a pretty strict guy in the book. Does it totally carry over into your day-to-day life or are you able to like, listen to the Rolling Stones and enjoy yourself, or is it button-up all the time?

I don't think entertainment is necessarily good or evil, like I don't think knowledge is good or evil –it's how it's applied. I'm aware of messages and things like that, but I love listening to music and I love watching Star Trek and things like that. I'm not a "no fun" ascetic kind of person. I think that if there's words in a song that you find objectionable, don't listen to it. If there are shows that you find objectionable, you don't watch them.

I really appreciate this interview Gary; it's touched on all the bases I wanted to cover. This is the last question, and you don't have to answer if you don't want to. What are your thoughts on the Corona virus?

Well we don't know yet whether it's natural or contrived, however, it's got all the earmarks of something that's not natural because of the way it's able to target so many different parts of the body. We'll have to see if that sort of thing is contrived or natural. We're going to see more of these pandemics, I think more of them will be contrived than natural, but there will be some natural ones as well. Corona virus is here, we'll have to see if it has the ability to mutate, if it doesn't mutate then that would suggest that it's not natural. I would not be surprised if it was a created virus but it certainly isn't the mark of the beast and there are more pandemics that will be coming and I think they will be utilized towards bringing about the new world order in terms of globalism and transcending borders. They've tested out a number of things that they can and cannot do in terms of lockdowns. I think it is sort of leading into a direction where it's going to change things as we know it. And of course, the power-hungry people who impose all these views are basically saying: "this is the new normal, we're never going back." The translation that I read of that is that they're not going to let it go back unless they're forced to.

PART THREE: Aftcrword

Early in 2020, while I was thoroughly enmeshed in assembling this book, the Coronavirus (Covid-19) pandemic engulfed the world. Like the other phenomena we have discussed, this outbreak has prompted countless conspiracy theories and doom-ridden predictions. Some of the more outlandish ones tie the virus to 5G technology, with claims that the government unleashed the virus to keep the population in their homes while they installed the 5G towers, or that 5G itself causes the Coronavirus.

For the purposes of this work, the pandemic is a sort of homecoming for Baudrillard's estimation that "the Gulf War did not take place." It is within this analysis that the war on the logical principle of the excluded middle by way of hyperreality is (once again) realized. Hospitals were both overwhelmed with the sick and staffed by bored nurses performing dance routines on Tik Tok. The simultaneity of the two contradictory phenomena boggled the rational mind. However, it also makes more apparent that our reality is not merely orchestrated by the media, but that we are given the option of selecting the media items we hope will confirm, if not our biases, at least our predictions. It is hard to say if we even "believe" these things are happening anymore, in the conventional sense of that word.

The thing about hyperreality that is central to this book is how it resonates at a very deep level with the issue of meta consciousness. This moment of hyperreality, and its apparent victory over the excluded middle of philosophy, happens to coincide with the return of myth, as Magee states:

> Myth, in other words, does not attempt to pin down its subject matter by definitively predicating one or more qualities of it. It does not say "God is just X" or "Nature is just Y." Instead, it "talks around" its object, describing it in many, sometimes conflicting ways, each of which indicates something true about it [...] The Egyptians, for instance, devised a number

of different and mutually contradictory cosmologies, all of which they seemed to regard as equally true.[1000]

After writing, editing, and rewriting this book, I realized that my central thesis could be encapsulated in the contrast between narratives and theories: my argument is essentially that, when conspiracy theories were interesting, they were narratively rich. They told us how things happened and what would happen, but more than that, they served as narratives: they told us a story. The conspiracy theories that I presented as being interesting were essentially exercises in world-building; and they told us fantastic stories in lieu of the space-age that was promised but never realized. The theories that took their place lost this narrative sense and set about aping scientific theories. So, essentially, at the heart of this book is the subtle distinction between narratives and theories. And in this distinction is a sense of uncertainty on the part of the theorist: the awareness that what he is putting forward is merely conjecture and does not have a firm stake on authenticating the source of the phenomena in question.

We have whittled down and molded three principal concepts throughout the preceding chapters; the first two, myth and conspiracy theory, have been addressed from a variety of angles, some theoretical and others factual. At the conclusion of this process, it is safe to say that conspiracy theories are not the same thing as myths, but that any power they hold over us is by virtue of qualities retained from their mythic antecedents. These qualities can either be in the delivery or the details.

The third concept, significance, is something I tried to explicate in the Introduction, therefore it is fitting to address it one final time. One of the Structuralist critiques of Phenomenology was that a pure unmediated interaction with the

---

[1000] Magee, Glenn Alexander (2001) *Hegel and the Hermetic Tradition.* Cornell University Press. P. 94

world, "a point where signification does not intervene,"[1001] is impossible. It is at the etymological convergence between "signification" and "significance" that our honing of the concept of Significance must conclude. Significance is not merely something towards which we address our *care*, that resists the leveling down of history, or warrants repetition. It is also a duplication of that basic semantic property, or structure of our consciousness, that separates us from the "real."

It should be noted by the attentive reader that as we have moved from the prehistoric and ancient to our present stage of modernity, the texts I have cited have transitioned from physical books to primarily online resources. This is a facet of how we consume *all* information in our postmodern lives, be it Zoom classes or articles that can only be accessed online. Conspiracy theorization has adapted to this predicament as well. Conspiracy theorists today are not merely being manipulated within the bounds of hyperreality, following the narrative set out by *The Matrix* films, but are able to extricate and isolate the hyperreal from our day-to-day information consumption and theorize about how nefarious conspiracies operate through it. In a more explicit sense, the paranoia attendant to conspiracy theorization has been displaced and projected onto the means of simulation in an entirely new and novel way. This is not to say that the animosity towards the groups perceived to be manipulating the simulation (the Russians, the Chinese Communist Party, Reptilians, etc.) has decreased. Instead, the battle has been moved into a realm of counter-simulation, and in this sense has engendered an even greater detachment from real-world political activity. No one is immune to manipulation, for it now seems that being prone to manipulation is an integral aspect of the human condition.

[1001] Boyne, Roy (1990) *Foucault and Derrida: The Other Side of Reason*. Routledge. P. 92

Bibliography

Alcock, Leslie (2001) *Arthur's Britain*. Classic Penguin. London, England

Allen, Gary & Abraham, Larry (1971) *None Dare Call it Conspiracy*. Dauphin Publications

Allison, Henry (2015) *Kant's Transcendental Deduction*. Oxford University Press. United Kingdom

Auerbach, Erich (2003) *Mimesis: The Representation of Reality in Western Literature*. Princeton University Press. Princeton, New Jersey

Baigent, Michael; Leigh, Richard; Lincoln, Henry (2006) *The Holy Blood and the Holy Grail*. Arrow Books. The Random House Group. London, United Kingdom

Baudrillard, Jean (1994) *Simulacra and Simulation*. The University of Michigan. Ann Arbor, Michigan

Baudrillard, Jean (2003) *The Spirit of Terrorism* translated by Chris Turner. Verso. London, New York

Baudrillard, Jean (2007) *Symbolic Exchange and Death*. Sage Publications Ltd. Los Angeles, London, New Delhi, Singapore, Washington D. C. & Melbourne

Baudrillard, Jean (2010) *The Agony of Power*. Semiotext(e). Pasadena, California

Baudrillard, Jean (2001) "Our Theatre of Cruelty" published in *Hatred of Capitalism: A Semiotext(e) Reader*. Los Angeles, California

Bell, Art & Steiger, Brad (1999) *The Source: Journey Through the Unexplained*. Paper Chase Press. New Orleans, Louisiana

Belzer, Richard (1999) *UFOs, JFK, and Elvis: Conspiracies You Don't Have to be Crazy to Believe*. The Ballantine Publishing Group. New York

Belzer, Richard & Wayne, David (2012) *Dead Wrong: Straight Facts on the Country's Most Controversial Cover-ups*. Skyhorse Publishing. New York, New York

Berman, Morris (2006) *Dark Ages America: The Final Phase of Empire*. W.W. Norton & Company. New York, New York

Borges, Jorge Luis (1999) *Collected Fictions*. Translated by Andrew Hurley. Penguin Books. New York, New York

Borges, Jorge Luis (1999) *Selected Non-Fictions*. Translated by Esther Allen, Suzanne Jill Levine, and Eliot Weinberger. Penguin Books. New York, New York

Boyne, Roy (1990) *Foucault and Derrida: The Other Side of Reason*. Routledge. London and New York

Brandom, Robert (2019) *A Spirit of Trust: A Reading of Hegel's Phenomenology*. Belknap Press of Harvard University Press. Cambridge, Massachusetts & London, England

Breitman, Richard; Goda, Norman; Naftali, Timothy; Wolfe, Robert (2005) *U.S. Intelligence and the Nazis*. Cambridge University Press. New York, New York

Burroughs, William (1993) *The Letters of William Burroughs*. Penguin Books

Burroughs, William (1987) *The Western Lands*. Penguin Books. New York, New York

Campbell, Joseph (2015) *Romance of the Grail: The Magic and Mystery of Arthurian Myth*. New World Library. Canada

Carroll, Peter (2008) *The Apophenion: A Chaos Magic Paradigm*. Mandrake. The United Kingdom

Cavendish, Richard (1967) *The Black Arts*. Perigee Books, The Putnam Publishing Group. New York, New York

Chalmers, David (2006) "Perception and the Fall from Eden" published in *Perceptual Experience*. Oxford University Press. United Kingdom

Chrétian de Troyes (1999) *Perceval: The Story of the Grail*. Translated by Burton Raffel. Yale University Press. New Haven and London

Collins, Jeff (2011) *Introducing Derrida*. Icon Books. London, UK

Conway, Jay (2010) *Gilles Deleuze: Affirmation in Philosophy*. Palgrave Macmillan. New York, NY

Crowley, Aleister (1979) *The Confessions of Aleister Crowley*. Arkana, Penguin Books. London, England

Crowley, Aleister (1988) *The Holy Books of Thelema*. Samuel Weiser, INC. York Beach, Maine

Crowley, Aleister (1994) *Magick Liber Aba Book Four Parts I – IV*. Samuel Weiser, INC. York Beach, Maine

Crowley, Aleister (1998) *The Book of Lies*. Samuel Weiser, INC. York Beach, Maine

Crowley, Aleister (1995) *The Book of Thoth*. Samuel Weiser, INC. York Beach, Maine

Crowley, Aleister (1991) *Little Essays Toward Truth*. New Falcon Publications. Tempe, Arizona

Crowley, Aleister (1997) *The Heart of the Master*. New Falcon Publications. Tempe, Arizona

Daraul, Arkon (1961) *A History of Secret Societies*. Citadel Press. Secaucus, N.J.

Davis, Erik (2019) *High Weirdness: Drugs, Esoterica, and Visionary Experience in the Seventies*. Strange Attractor Press & the MIT Press. London, England

Decker, Ronald; Depaulis, Thierry and Dummett, Michael (2002) *A Wicked Pack of Cards: The Origins of the Occult Tarot*. Duckworth Publishers. London, England

Decker, Ronald and Dummett, Michael (2019) *A History of the Occult Tarot*. Duckworth Publishing. United Kingdom

Deleuze, Gilles (1994) *Difference and Repetition*. Translated by Paul Patton. Columbia University Press. New York

Deleuze, Gilles (2000) *Proust and Signs*. Translated by Richard Howard. University of Minnesota Press. Minneapolis, Minnesota

Delillo, Don (1997) *Underworld*. Simon and Schuster. New York, New York

Derrida, Jacques (2011) *Voice and Phenomenon*. Northwestern University Studies in Phenomenology and Existentialism.

Derrida, Jacques (1991) *A Derrida Reader* edited by Peggy Kamuf. Columbia University Press. New York City, New York

Derrida, Jacques (1981) *Dissemination*. The University of Chicago Press. Chicago, IL

Dick, Philip (2011) *Valis*. First Mariner Books. New York, New York.

Dobbs, J.R. "Bob" (1994) *Revelation X* translated by The SubGenius Foundation, Inc. Fireside. New York, New York.

Donnelly, Ignatius (1976) *Atlantis: The Antediluvian World*. Dover Publications, Inc. New York.

Eliade, Mircea (1991) *The Myth of the Eternal Return*. Princeton University Press. Princeton, New Jersey.

Eliade, Mircea (1998) *Myth and Reality*. Waveland Press. Prospect Heights, New York.

Eliade, Mircea (1984) *A History of Religious Ideas 2*. Translated by Willard R. Trask. The University of Chicago Press. Chicago, Illinois.

Ellul, Jacques (1964) *The Technological Society*. Vintage Books, A Division of Random House. New York

The Book of Enoch the Prophet (2012) Translated by R. H. Charles. Red Wheel/Weiser, LLC. San Francisco, California

Evola, Julius (1997) *The Mystery of the Grail*. Inner Traditions International. Rochester, Vermont

Evola, Julius (1995) *The Hermetic Tradition*. Inner Traditions International. Rochester, Vermont

Fcycrabend, Paul (1993) *Against Method.* Verso. London and New York

Frank, Manfred (1989) *What is Neostructuralism?* The University of Minnesota

Freud, Sigmund (2001) *The Standard Edition of the Complete Psychological Works of Sigmund Freud Volume XXIII.* Vintage, Random House, London.

Gadamer, Hans-Georg (2008) *Philosophical Hermeneutics.* Translated and Edited by David E. Linge. University of California Press. Berkeley and Los Angeles, California

Gaddis, William (2012) *The Recognitions.* Dalkey Archive Press. Champaign/Dublin/London

Ginzberg, Louis (1992) *Legends of the Bible.* The Jewish Publication Society. Philadelphia, Jerusalem

Ginzberg, Louis (2008) *The Legends of the Jews, Volumes I & II.* Forgotten Books

Gorightly, Adam (2014) *Historia Discordia: The Origins of the Discordian Society.* RVP Publishers. New York, New York

Grant, Kenneth (1973) *The Magical Revival.* Weiser. New York

Grant, Kenneth (1980) *Outside the Circles of Time.* Billing and Sons Limited. Great Britain

Griffin, David Ray (2005) *The 9/11 Commission Report: Omissions and Distortions.* Olive Branch Press. Northampton, Massachusetts

Guyénot, Laurent (2018) *From Yahweh to Zion.* Sifting and Winnowing Books. Wisconsin

Haack, Susan (editor) (2006) *Pragmatism, Old & New.* Prometheus Books. Amherst, New York

Hawkes, Terence (1977) *Structuralism and Semiotics.* University of California Press. Berkeley and Los Angeles, California

Heidegger, Martin (1996) *Being and Time* translated by Joan Stambaugh, State University Press of New York. Albany, New York

Heidegger, Martin (2009) *Logic as the Question Concerning the Essence of Language.* Published by State University of New York Press, Albany

Heidegger, Martin (1975) *Poetry, Language, Thought.* Harper & Row Publishers Inc. New York, New York

Heidegger, Martin (1991) *Nietzsche: Volumes One and Two* translated by David Farrell Krell. Harper San Francisco, a Division of Harper Collins Publishers

Heidegger, Martin (2013) *The Question Concerning Technology and Other Essays.* Harper Perennial Modern Thought. New York, New York

Heidegger, Martin (2014) *Ponderings II – VI, The Black Notebooks 1931 – 1938.* Indiana University Press. Bloomington and Indianapolis

Herre, Benjamin Groff (1878) *Hyperborea: Or the Pilgrims of the Pole.* The New Era Steam Book and Job Print. Lancaster, PA

Hersh, Seymour (1997) *The Dark Side of Camelot.* Little, Brown and Company. Boston, New York, Toronto and London

Hoffman II, Michael A. (2009) *Secret Societies and Psychological Warfare* (Sixth Printing) Independent History and Research. Coeur d'Alene, Idaho

The Holy Bible (Authorized King James Version). Thomas Nelson & Sons. New York

Horton, Scott (2015) *Lords of Secrecy*. Nation Books. New York, New York

Howells, William (1962) *The Heathens: Primitive Man and His Religions*. Anchor Books. Doubleday & Company Inc. Garden City, New York

Huxley, Aldous (2004) *Brave New World and Brave New World Revisited*. HarperCollins Inc. New York, New York

Huysmans, Joris-Karl (2015) *The Durtal Trilogy*. Ex Fontibus Company

Jackson, Steve (1995) *The INWO Book*. Steve Jackson Games

Jacobsen, Annie (2011) *Area 51: An Uncensored History of America's Top Secret Military Base*. Back Bay Books. New York, NY

Jensen, Derrick (2006) *Endgame Volume I*. Seven Stories Press. New York. London. Melbourne. Toronto

Joseph, Frank (2006) *The Lost Civilization of Lemuria*. Bear & Company, a division of Inner Traditions International. Rochester, Vermont

Jullian, Philippe (1974) *Dreamers of Decadence*. Praeger Publishers, Inc. New York, New York

Jung, Emma & Franz, Marie-Louise (1986) *The Grail Legend*. Sigo Press. Boston, Massachusetts

Kaczynski, Richard (2010) *Perdurabo: The Life of Aleister Crowley*. North Atlantic Books. Berkeley, California

Kinzer, Stephen (2019) *Poisoner in Chief: Sidney Gottlieb and the CIA Search for Mind Control*. Henry Holt and Company. New York, New York

Klossowski, Pierre (2005) *Nietzsche and the Vicious Circle*. Continuum. London

Knight, Christopher & Lomas, Robert (2001) *The Hiram Key*. Fair Winds Press. Gloucester, MA

Knight, Christopher & Lomas, Robert (2001) *Uriel's Machine*. Fair Winds Press. Gloucester, MA

Kroker, Arthur and Cook, David (1991) *The Postmodern Scene: Excremental Culture and Hyper-Aesthetics*. St. Martin's Press. New York

Lacan, Jacques (2006) *Ecrits*. Norton and Company. New York, New York

Larrington, Carolyne (2017) *The Land of the Green Man*. I.B. Tauris & Co. Ltd. London, New York.

Laurence, Theodor (1972) *How the Tarot Speaks to Modern Man*. Stackpole Books. Harrisburg, PA

Lennon, Michael (2013) *Norman Mailer: A Double Life*. Simon & Schuster. New York, London, Toronto, Sydney, New Delhi

Lovecraft, Howard Phillips (1996) *The Road to Madness*. A Del Rey Book, Ballantine Books, New York.

Mackey, Albert (1996) *The History of Freemasonry*. Published by Gramercy Books, a Division of Random House Value Publishing Inc. Avenal, New Jersey

Magee, Glenn Alexander (2001) *Hegel and the Hermetic Tradition*. Cornell University Press. Ithaca and London

Malaclypse the Younger (2014) *Principia Discordia*. Lunatic Pope Press.

Matthews, John (2007) *The Grail Tarot: A Templar Vision*. St. Martin's Press. New York

Maximus the Confessor (2003) *On the Cosmic Mystery of Jesus Christ* (translated by Paul M. Blowers and Robert Louis Wilken). St. Vladimer's Seminary Press. Crestwood, New York

Maxwell, Jordan (2000) *Matrix of Power: Secrets of World Control*. The Book Tree. San Diego, California

McDonald, Hugh (1975) *Appointment in Dallas: The Final Solution to the Assassination of JFK*. The Hugh McDonald Publishing Corp. New York, New York

Melley, Timothy (2000) *Empire of Conspiracy: The Culture of Paranoia in Postwar America*. Cornell University Press. Ithaca and London

Michell, John (1972) *The View Over Atlantis*. Ballantine Books. New York

Michels, Robert (1962) *Political Parties: A Study of the Oligarchical Tendencies of Modern Democracy*. The Free Press. New York

Millar, Angel (2005) *Freemasonry: A History*. Thunder Bay Press. San Diego, California

Moench, Doug (1995) *The Big Book of Conspiracies*. Paradox Press. New York

Moench, Doug (1997) *The Big Book of the Unexplained*. Paradox Press. New York

Moon, Peter (2003) *The Black Sun: Montauk's Nazi-Tibetan Connection*. Sky Books. Westbury, New York

More, Thomas (2003) *Utopia*. Penguin Books. London, England

Mulhall, Stephen (2005) *Philosophical Myths of the Fall*. Princeton University Press. Princeton, New Jersey

Mystic Places: By the Editors of Time-Life Books (1987) Time Life-Books, U.S.A.

Nietzsche, Friedrich (1954) *The Portable Nietzsche*. Edited and translated by Walter Kaufmann. Viking Penguin Inc. New York

Ognjanović, Dejan (2017) *Rue Morgue Magazine's The Weird World of H. P. Lovecraft*. Rue Morgue. Toronto, Ontario

Orwell, George (2003) *Nineteen Eighty-Four*. Berkeley, an Imprint of Penguin Random House LLC. New York, New York

Pagels, Elaine (1989) *The Gnostic Gospels*. Vintage Books, A Division of Random House Inc. New York

Pefanis, Julian (1992) *Heterology and the Postmodern*. Duke University Press. Durham and London

Pope Leo XIII (1978) *Humanum Genus, Encyclical Letter of His Holiness Pope Leo XIII on Freemasonry. April 20, 1884*. Tan Books and Publishers, INC. Rockford, Il.

Project Blue Book (2019). Edited by Brad Steiger. MUFON Books an imprint of Red Wheel/Weiser, LLC. Newburyport, MA

Pynchon, Thomas (2006) *Gravity's Rainbow*. Penguin Classics. New York, New York

Redfern, Nick (2015) *Bloodline of the Gods*. The Career Press, Inc. Wayne, New Jersey

Riessman, Catherine Kohler (1993) *Narrative Analysis*. Sage Publications. Newbury Park, California

Robinson, James (1990) *The Nag Hammadi Library*. Harper San Francisco. California

Robison, John (2014) *Proofs of a Conspiracy Against All the Religions and Governments of Europe, Carried on in the Secret Meetings of Freemasons, Illuminati, and Reading Societies*. CreateSpace Independent Publishing Platform

Rapid Eye (1995). Edited by Simon Dwyer. Creation Books. London, UK

Russell, Bertrand (1998) *The Philosophy of Logical Atomism*. Open Court Classics. Chicago and La Salle, Illinois

Schopenhauer, Arthur (1969) *The World As Will and Representation* translated by E.F.J. Payne. Dover Publications. New York, New York.

Schrödter, Willy (1992) *A Rosicrucian Notebook*. Samuel Weiser, INC. York Beach, Maine

Silverberg, Robert (1996) *The Realm of Prester John*. Ohio University Press. Athens, Ohio

Skeptic Magazine (Vol. 25 No. 1, 2020) Altadena, California

Smith, Ken (1995) *Ken's Guide to the Bible*. Blast Books. New York, New York

Spengler, Oswald (2006) *The Decline of the West: An Abridged Edition*. Translated by Charles Francis Atkinson and prepared by Arthur Helps. Vintage Books, A Division of Random House, INC. New York

Stearn, Jess (1967) *Edgar Cayce –The Sleeping Prophet*. Bantam Books. Toronto, New York, London, Sydney

Stewart, Louis (1980) *Life Forces: A Contemporary Guide to the Cult and Occult*. Andrews and McMeel, Inc. Kansas City, New York, Washington

Talbot, David (2007) *Brothers: The Hidden History of the Kennedy Years*. Free Press. New York, New York

Talbot, David (2015) *The Devil's Chessboard*. Harper. New York, New York

Temple, Robert (1998) *The Sirius Mystery*. Destiny Books. Rochester, Vermont

Twyman, Tracy (2005) *The Arcadian Mystique: The Best of Dagobert's Revenge Magazine*. Dragon Key Press. Portland, Oregon

Vallée, Jacques (2014) *Passport to Magonia*. Daily Grail Publishing. Brisbane, Australia

Vallée, Jacques (2008) *Messengers of Deception: UFO Contacts and Cults*. Daily Grail Publishing. Brisbane, Australia

Waite, Arthur Edward (1970) *A New Encyclopaedia of Freemasonry (Combined Edition)*. Weathervane Books. New York

Walker, Jesse (2014) *The United States of Paranoia: A Conspiracy Theory*. Harper Perennial. New York, New York

Wayne, Gary (2014) *The Genesis 6 Conspiracy*. Trusted Books, A Division of Deep River Books

Webb, Gary (2014) *Dark Alliance: The CIA, the Contras, and the Crack Cocaine Explosion*. Seven Stories Press, New York

Weeks, Andrew (1993) *German Mysticism: From Hildegard of Bingen to Ludwig Wittgenstein*. State University of New York Press, Albany.

Wilson, Robert Anton (2016) *Cosmic Trigger I: Final Secret of the Illuminati* (Second Edition). Hilaritas Press, LLC. Grand Junction, Colorado

Wilson, Robert Anton (1998) *Everything is Under Control: Conspiracies, Cults and Cover-ups*. Harper Perennial. New York, NY

Wittgenstein, Ludwig (1965) *The Blue and Brown Books*. Harper Colophon Books

Žižek, Slavoj (2009) *First as Tragedy, Then as Farce*. Verso. London and New York

Žižek, Slavoj (1989) *The Sublime Object of Ideology*. Verso. London and New York

Žižek, Slavoj (2006) *The Parallax View*. Massachusetts Institute of Technology. Cambridge, Massachusetts

Made in the USA
Middletown, DE
23 December 2021

56936756R00409